Editorials	2
In Memoriam: Ray Harryhausen	3
Articles	
The Witch Lives Again!	10
The Odd and Unique Cinema of Larry Cohen	19
Rizal Mantovani's Kuntilanak Trilogy	22
The Search for Weng Weng: Shooting Diary	24
The Mick Travis Trilogy	35
The Devil Does Nollywood	39
The Stupendous Cinema of SyFy	42
Joe D'Amato: The Last Centurion of Eurotrash	46
The Legacy of Sonny Chiba	60
Top 10 Weirdest Improvised Weapons	65
Interviews	
Tim Doyle	69
Ryan Nicholson	83
Lubega Vicent	85
Columns & Regular Features	
Geek Roundtable: HOUSE BY THE CEMETERY	88
Box Set Beatdown	99
Beatdown/Heads-up	108
Stephen Bissette's Spiderbaby Sinema	110
Steve's Video Store Volume 2: DON'T	118
Mexican Monsters on Parade, Part Dos	121
Pimping Godfrey Ho	125
The Ferocious Aspect: Indian Fantastic Cinema Part 5	126
Cult Cinema Under The Gun	156
Reviews	163
The Bookshelf	190
The KrisWord Puzzle	215
Our Contributors & Final Thought	216

Front Cover: Jolyon Yates
Contents Page Art: Salvatore Tarantola

Brian Harris, Editor & Publisher • Timothy Paxton, Editor & Design
Tony Strauss, Editor & Proofing

WENG'S CHOP is published quarterly. © 2013 Wildside Publishing / Kronos Productions. All rights reserved. No part of this publication may be reproduced, distributed, or transmitted in any form or by any means, including photocopying, recording, or other electronic or mechanical methods, without the prior written permission of the publisher, except in the case of brief quotations embodied in critical reviews and certain other noncommercial uses permitted by copyright law. For permission requests, write to the publisher, addressed "Attention: Permissions Coordinator," at the address below.
4301 Sioux Lane #1, McHenry, IL 60050, United States • wengschop@comcast.net

Volume #1 / Issue #4 / September 2013 / 1st Printing, Cover A

A WORD FROM THE EDITORS...

THE BOOGER SUGAR BOOGIE: ELECTRIC SHOOGALOO

Welcome to the release of our 5th freakin' issue of *Weng's Chop* Magazine! Between issue three and this issue you hold in your hands, Tim and I have signed on the dotted line for a major motion picture to be produced about our rise to magazine stardom. Dennis Hopper is already growing facial hair to fill the role of Tim and producers secured Edward Furlong to play the role of yours truly! Apparently they paid him in Dunkin Donuts and cocaine—which is pretty much what they agreed to pay me, should the film do well at the box office. Our signing bonus has allowed us to do a few things we've always wanted to do, so the next issue (#5) of the mag will no longer feature cinema but will focus instead on cocaine and donuts. Tim doesn't know yet…but it will.

Anyhow, our success is all thanks to you. In honor of me being better than you, here's a list of things I'll be able to purchase with my remaining signing bonus money: 4 apple fritters, a few eight-balls of cocaine, 7 copies of *Home Run Derby* for the Wii, 2 bottles of warm water, a half-eaten Triple Cheeseburger from Wendy's, foam earplugs to block out the sound of chirping birds, dollar store sunglasses to block out the crack of dawn, a pair of latex gloves that I'll use to pull the remaining cocaine from my butt, 33 copies of **THIS IS NOT BLADE RUNNER XXX** on VHS and 5 midgets skilled in the art of group prostate massage. SEE YOU NEXT ISSUE, PEONS!!

~ Brian Harris, co-editor

EGGS, BASKETS, FOOD, & FILM.

Diversity in your diet is essential if you are going to live a long life. Consuming large quantities of one single genre will severely limit your appreciation of what is available. *Weng's Chop* has become the antithesis of that bit of sage advice. Brian, Tony and I share the love of diverse cinema. WC isn't just for geeks anymore, as we gather together, dissect, ingest, digest, and excrete assorted genre. Sure, the odd and bizarre is heavily hunted for its rare flavor, but we also like to include some hardcore roughage and malasa spice.

In past issues *Weng's Chop* has offered up delicious plates of Mexican, Indian, Chinese, Polish, Thai, Italian, Indonesian, and other tasty world treats, as well as the good old gut fill made in the U.S. of A. We plan on a continual menu of ever-changing and informative articles, interviews, and reviews of a wide variety of media.

I have never completely understood the compulsion to limits one's coverage to any particular country, genre, decade or studio, although I was guilty of it with my 'zines *Monster!*, *Monster! International* and *Highball* (it is a great way to focus your sales and your obsessions). Yes, there are always niche markets to fill, and many a magazine has covered sub-genres (Richard Klemensen's *Little Shop of Horrors* magazine comes to mind with its exhaustive coverage of Hammer Studios and other such British material). In the early days of 'zinedom, before the advent of high-speed Internet and the avalanche of blogs, there may have been a need to fill a genre void. Back then (the '80s and '90s) trading VHS tapes was an expensive process and no doubt that led to a certain tunnel-vision.

Recently there has been a rise in nostalgia publications, which isn't such a bad thing. I have little need of reading the umpteenth article on Bela Lugosi, Christopher Lee, Boris Karloff, Universal Studios, etc. I don't begrudge their existence—I just don't have any interest in them. This is why you won't find too much of that kind of writing in *Weng's Chop*. There are some reviews that border on repetition, but they usually offer up new insights or information not previously available.

So it doesn't hurt mixing in an article on Fulci's 1982 horror film **THE HOUSE BY THE CEMETERY** with an overview of the bombastic films shown on The SyFy Channel. Or an interview with Tim Doyle alongside an exhaustive analysis of Joe D'Amato's porn films, a Norwegian witch film from the 1950s versus The Mick Travis Trilogy. Add a ton of film reviews, and sprinkle in some book, comic and magazine reviews for that "*The Monster Times*" feel.

And then there're those films from the subcontinent. I've been called narrow-minded when it comes to the films I cover. I must admit that I do currently have a fascination with Indian cinema. However, for those of you who have been reading my magazines for the past thirty plus years know, I go through these obsessions. The problem with Indian films is that there are so freaking many of them!

That's what Brian, Tony and I want to deliver to your door every time an issue of the magazine is produced. An extra-large veggie, meat-lovers, extra-cheesy pizza with a six-pack of some obscure microbrew.

Something extra tasty and sure to clog your arteries with cinematic goodness.

~ Tim Paxton, co-editor

IT USED TO BE ABOUT THE LOVE, MAN.

No, not that self-deluded, hygiene-be-damned, mooch-off-yer-parents-type of hippie love you've heard so much about—I'm talkin' about the *real* love, the unending love, the kind of love that *really* matters in this universe: the love of cinema.

Used to be that reading about cinema almost exclusively involved reading the observations of authors whose love of the medium shined out from their writings like a beacon, often infecting the reader with the same love, even when reading about a film one normally wouldn't even consider watching. Reading about cinema used to inspire people to seek out new films in order to share in the love expressed by the writers they read. It was all about sharing one's love with others who held room in their hearts for the same kind of love.

That's what it *used* to be about.

Then, in the mid-'90s came this amazing new thing called the Internet, which afforded anyone with a keyboard and an opinion the ability to share their own thoughts and observations about cinema with everyone who cared to read them. No longer were film discussions and reviews relegated to the pages of specialty books and magazines; everyone who had a love for cinema could directly convey their thoughts and feelings without having to become a "published" author.

Well, it *seemed* like a good idea at the time.

And it *was* a good idea…in principle. Lovers of cinema now had the freedom to express their opinions and thoughts on the medium they loved, and share them with like-minded others. But along with this freedom of opinions exchange quickly came the birth of a new kind of film review: The Douche Review. This new kind of review is best described as the insecure ramblings of socially-challenged filmwatchers with severe inferiority/anger issues who'd rather place themselves on a holier-than-thou level regarding the medium they supposedly love than attempt to offer any honest insights or humility-based observations on the offerings of said medium. So, fast-forwarding 1.5 decades into the future, the world of film criticism (especially genre criticism) has largely evolved into a realm where ripping on movies—rather than discussing them honestly and civilly—has become the norm.

Well, fuck *that*.

We at *Weng's Chop* remember what it *used* to be about…and we miss it dearly. That's why you won't find any examples of The Douche Review within our pages. What you *will* find is criticism and reviews by people whose love for cinema shines out from their writings like the aforementioned beacon. Sure, we may write about obscure, "lesser" movies that aren't up to the production quality or distribution scope of your more popular films—but we won't be writing about those films from any other emotion than *love*. Because we know you're sick of that other bullshit. *Weng's Chop* is bringin' the love back. And we're shoving it deep inside you…without the assistance of either lube or condom. And we won't crawl out the window with your jewelry while you're sleeping.

Because it's all about the *love*, man.

~ Tony Strauss, co-editor

in memoriam

Ray Harryhausen on set with The Kraken from **CLASH OF THE TITANS** (1980)

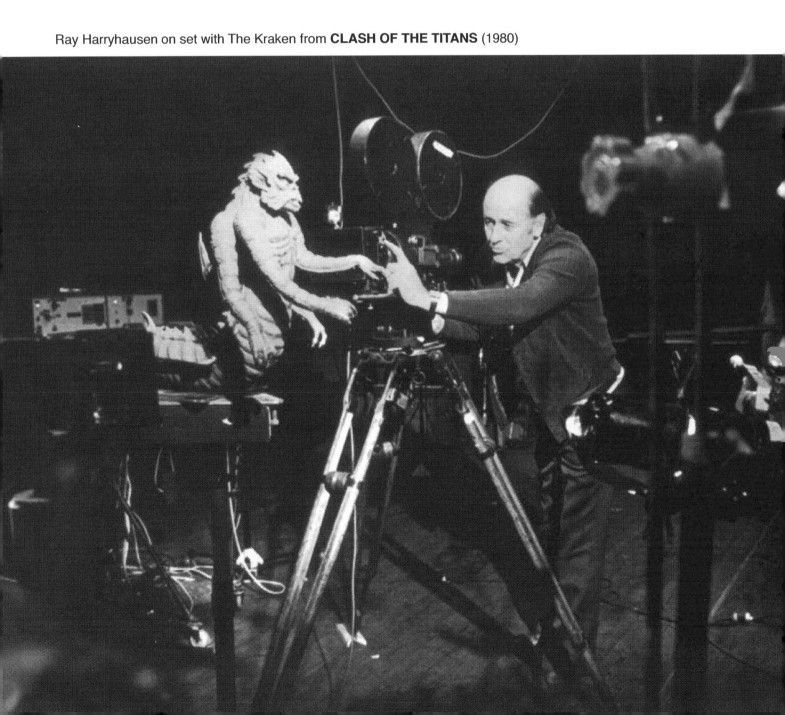

FAREWELL, RAY

I had a triad that made up some of my fondest childhood memories. Three guys that, while not always in my sites as a kid, nevertheless scored big when it comes to my very subversive cognitive development. I often write about my love of Karloff, Godzilla, Blaisdell, Quatermass, and other masters and monsters of the visual media I absorbed as a youth. With the passing of Forrest J.Ackerman, then Ray Bradbury, and finally Ray Harryhasuen, one of the final interlocking pieces of my lexicon of reality can be placed in the gestalt shrine I hold within. These three men, these American originals who grew up together and were the best of friends, formed a trinity which became a very solid foundation in my core.

And now Mr. Harryhausen has died.

His films weren't always my favourite. I loved a lot of them, but as with any artist you must be true to yourself when you say that some of "his" films stunk. I had issues with **IT CAME FROM BENEATH THE SEA, THE THREE WORLDS OF GULLIVER, SINBAD AND THE EYE OF THE TIGER**, and **CLASH OF THE TITANS**. They were dreadfully dull. But, and this is the important part, I know it wasn't *his* fault. Most of the films involved just had insipid direction. *Not his effects, though.* Most of the time the actors just seemed to be uninspired or enjoyed chewing the scenery. *Not his effects, though.* Harryhasuen created an alternate universe of the weird and the wonderful. And that's what I always look for in any fantastic film. That's what *he and his effects* brought to these films.

If I could choose a monster that I could hold close to my heart, and every time it would let out a peep I would think of Ray, then it would be his Ymir from **TWENTY MILLION MILES TO EARTH**. Man, did I want one of those little Venusian critters for my very own. So darn cute! As with Jack Arnold's **CREATURE FROM THE BLACK LAGOON** and Ishiro Honda's **GODZILLA**, this scaly monster nestled deep into my young psyche; claws dug in and its pitiful little eyes beseeching me to save it from the evil ways of mankind. And then the army blew it off the Colosseum in Rome. Fuckers.

I will miss you for that one very fact, Mr. Harryhausen.

I'd love a Ymir plushy right now.

– *Tim Paxton*

My favorite of all of Harryhausen's films was and still is **JASON AND THE ARGONAUTS**. In spite of many imaginative and magical scenes throughout this masterpiece as well all of his other seminal works, the best of the best will always be the battle with the skeletons. He raised the bar for stop-motion animation that was unparalleled until the introduction of digital effects. He defined an entire style and process as well as inspiring generations of burgeoning future filmmakers. RIP, Ray. You will be sorely missed...

– *Kevin Tenney*
(Director of **NIGHT OF THE DEMONS** and **WITCHBOARD**)

As a child, like many, fantasy films were just as important to me as horror was. I'd thrill to the amazing effects in films such as **JASON AND THE ARGONAUTS, CLASH OF THE TITANS, THE 7th VOYAGE OF SINBAD, THE GOLDEN VOYAGE OF SINBAD** and **SINBAD AND THE EYE OF THE TIGER**. Hell, I even shed tears watching **MIGHTY JOE YOUNG**. Losing Ray Harryhausen was like losing a family member; an irreplaceable pioneer and a living legend while he was with us. The industry, as well as my childhood, was shaped by his imagination. Thank you so much, Ray. R.I.P.

– *Brian Harris*

Two highlights of my life. Meeting Ray Harryhausen and Ray Bradbury on the same day. Almost twenty years to the day. R.I.P., Mr. H., the world lost some of its sense of wonder with you.

- *Arlene Domkowski*

I can't remember a time in my childhood that I didn't effectively worship Ray Harryhausen. I watched his films endlessly, made comic books about his monsters, sculpted them in clay, pretended to be them when playing with my friends, and just basically obsessed about them on a constant basis. When I was 8 years old, I begged and begged for Jeff Rovin's book, *From the Land Beyond Beyond*, for Xmas, and was elated when I actually got it. Carried it with me everywhere, and fixated on it and the films it focused on for years and years. I still have that now-battered and taped-up copy over 30 years later, and still visit it regularly. Harryhausen was responsible for my love of creatures, before I ever discovered the Universal monsters. Few artists have affected my life as profoundly as he did. R.I.P., Ray...and thanks for everything.

– *Tony Strauss*

I met Ray Bradbury at a cocktail party years ago. We spent a great deal of time talking about his friend Ray Harryhausen. What was interesting was the childlike enthusiasm he had for RH's movies. Like me, he was a huge fan of his friend's work, especially **THE BEAST FROM 20,000 FATHOMS**...naturally.

– *Steve Mitchell*

One step forward, two steps back. The more vocal members of an audience can never be pleased. With the triumphs of Ray Harryhausen, the unsatisfied complained that it looked to choppy, like a cartoon. So puppets and full body suits were developed to compensate. But of course the audience still could not be satisfied; they complained that it was just a man in a suit or a puppet. These techniques were a visceral triumph. Rick Baker's King Kong and I.L.M s' Yoda were satisfying in a way not dreamed possible. But, of course, that outspoken element of the audience was not satisfied. Now with C.G.I., all attempts at a yeti or a mummy and everything in between, look no better than an actual cartoon. Granted, it does not look like a man in a suit or a puppet, but these efforts are completely unsatisfying on the level of verisimilitude. Now for some reason, these "modern" vocal audience members could not be happier with the results...there is no satisfaction left in fantasy effects. So I say with a loud *yop*: ONE STEP FORWARD, TWO STEPS BACK.

- *Andrew Weinstein*

Dear Ray: Thank you for **JASON AND THE ARGONAUTS** and **THE 7TH VOYAGE OF SINBAD**. If it wasn't for your genius, I may not have my love of fantasy and horror today.

– *Sharon Walsh*

Interior. Day. A mid-1970s California movie theatre: A young boy sits wide-eyed in a darkened movie palace, eyes fixed on the screen, on the magical, the mystical; the battle of skeleton and prince, of Cyclops and dragon, of Minotaur and pirate. This boy's dreams, and the dreams of many others, have been made silver-screen reality by a boy turned man, a man turned artist, an artist turned magician. A man named Ray.

– *David Draper*

I remember going to see **SINBAD AND THE EYE OF THE TIGER** when it came out. Between Caroline Munro and The awesome gold Minotaur and the giant saber-toothed tiger, I was awestruck. The funny part was that we were at The Plaza 2 Theater in Portage and when I got out of the theater my dad and brothers and sister were coming out of a movie about some guy as a mountain man running from the authorities. I think it was Anthony Quinn. I came out of my theater with my shirt half unbuttoned and was warm. They were buttoned up and had their jackets on even though were in the same temperatures! Ah, good times!

– *Douglas Waltz*

Ray Harryhausen didn't just *have* an imagination...Ray Harryhausen *was* imagination. And he inspired countless others to follow theirs. A greater, and prouder, legacy can never be left than that.

– *Ryan Carey*

Animation was my foray into filmmaking when I was about 7 years old, and my folks bought me Harryhausen's biography around that time (my father having seen much of his work in theaters growing up). The book helped teach me the ins and outs of stop-motion and got my imagination churning with what I could pull off within the medium. Years later, I'm still a filmmaker with a deep appreciation for practical effects, and Harryhausen's influence was indispensable to me as a storyteller, and a daydreamer. Thanks, Ray.

– *Torin Langen*

Ray Harryhausen raised me. I grew up on his wonderful films. I would have to credit his work with making me not only a fanatic of monster movies, but of all cinema. Thanks Mr. Harryhausen, I will miss you.

– *Jeff Granstrom*

Farewell to the maker of magic, the creator of dreams. May your creations always be loved.

– *Steven Ronquillo*

Harryhausen's effects were what kick-started my interest in special effects and influenced my love for movie monsters. For this, I am eternally grateful to him. R.I.P., Mr. Harryhausen. Thank you so much for everything.

– *Seb Godin*

As a kid when I saw **CLASH OF THE TITANS**, I feel in love with this man's work. That was at age five, and now at almost 24, I will always owe him part for me wanting to get into film making. The man was and is a true legend, it is sad to now know he is gone. His work will live on in all of us and new people discover him every day. Being as timeless as ever I am happy to hold his box sets in my collection and will always cherish my childhood memories of watching his many works with dropped jaw and utterly speechless. R.I.P., Mr. Harryhausen. You will be missed.

– *Andrew Christensen*

Ray Harryhausen is who I wanted to be and stop-motion animation is what I wanted to do in grade school. I never outgrew it.

– *Jeff Goodhartz*

R.I.P., Mr. Harryhausen. Farewell to a genuine icon of cinema. I still watch **THE BEAST FROM 20,000 FATHOMS, IT CAME FROM BENEATH THE SEA, 20 MILLION MILES TO EARTH,** and many others. You were truly a creative genius and inspiration. Thank you.

– *Christopher Alan Broadstone*

My first experience with Mr. Harryhausen's work was **THE BEAST FROM 20,000 FATHOMS**. It was on television one weekend. As a child I was obsessed with dinosaurs...had every single dinosaur model Aurora made. This movie stunned and amazed me to no end. Then I saw the dinosaur sequence in **ANIMAL WORLD**. I also had stills in the old View Master. My grandmother had taken me to see a *Sinbad* double feature, **THE GOLDEN VOYAGE OF SINBAD** and **SINBAD AND THE EYE OF THE TIGER**, back in '77 or '78. Both those films rocked as did the original **CLASH OF THE TITANS**. I would like to thank him for shaping my memories of a great childhood and my continued interest in stop-motion animation which seems to be lost today by CGI. I have a huge DVD and Blu-ray collection which includes most of Mr. Harryhausen's work. Thank you for your contribution to film and a life time of entertainment for myself, my children and my grandchildren. Words could never describe the joy you bring to so many of us. Thank you.

- *Charles McVey*
(Owner of The Horror Congress)

I have virtually no memories of my childhood...except for one. I will never forget sitting with my Nan and granddad watching **CLASH OF THE TITANS**; in that moment I was enthralled by the effects put into the film, how it had been achieved. It's the one memory I cling to strongly; add to this Ray, you were a lot of the inspiration in me beginning to write stories I never dreamed possible. Wherever you are, I hope you are at peace, and your talent is greatly missed.

– *Samhain Bloodworth*

His effects for stop-motion are way ahead of their time. No one takes the unique craft seriously—as an added gem, to the ever-evolving science and magic it takes to create movies. He still will be felt for years to come. I salute you, Mr. Harryhausen.

– *David "DB3" Barnes*

Man, he was my hero as a child. His Sinbad films and **CLASH OF THE TITANS** are amongst some of my favorites. He was a guy who you would think was going to live forever. I just hope that a younger audience will learn and respect his amazing contributions to the film and effects industry.

- *Craig Klaviaturist Rosenthal*

When I was a kid the *Sinbad* movies would play on TV every now and again. It was one of the highlights of my childhood. I didn't know how the amazing creatures were made. I began to love the *Sinbad* stories without realizing that what I really loved were the special effects. When **CLASH OF THE TITANS** was released my family went to see it in the theatre. It was a movie that stayed with me. One of the scariest moments was the part with Medusa. I was thrilled. My love of movies and what was possible to create was definitely encouraged by Ray Harryhausen. When I think of him I feel a fond nostalgia and a sense of gratitude. Thank you, Mr. Harryhausen, for sparking my imagination as an adult and giving me a sense of awe as a child.

– *Tonjia Atomic*

He was my first exposure to Greek Mythology. Pure Genius who should be remembered as an *icon*. Before CGI, there was Ray Harryhausen.

– *Kevin "Kex" Hayes*

CLASH OF THE TITANS and **THE GOLDEN VOYAGE OF SINBAD** are two of the most memorable, fantastic movies of my youth. I was so amazed with the creatures and special effects, I thought it was all real, haha! I still love those movies and the other *Sinbad* movies, as well. Curse the gods for having taken you, Sir Ray Harryhausen! Perhaps we shall meet in the house of Hades and share some ambrosia, for your talents deserve to be immortalized. I shall cry "Release the Kraken!" and remember your name forevermore. Rest in Peace, Sir Ray Harryhausen.

– *Sonia Balderrama*

Art by Jolyon Yates

HARRYHAUSEN AND BRADBURY: THE DYNAMIC DUO THAT CHANGED MY LIFE

by Vicki Love

It's that time of year again...time to teach Fahrenheit 451, *my all-time favorite novel by Ray Bradbury. Last year, spring of 2012, we read so many books in my 10th grade GATE classes that we almost couldn't fit it in. We started it in late May and finished right before finals. We were smack dab in the middle of it, at the beginning of* The Sand and the Sieve, *when early on June 5th, I opened my Yahoo account and found out that Bradbury had passed away. I sat at my desk in front of my students and cried. I will never forget that moment for it was as if my own grandfather had passed again, because for me, the two men had both helped me through a childhood fraught with misery and abuse. They were my heroes and both were now gone from me.*

Today that same sadness confounds my soul as I again say goodbye to a man who, for me, made my life better and gave me something to look to and strive toward. That dang monster, **THE BEAST FROM 20,000 FATHOMS** (1953), has been a part of my waking dreams since I was five years old and watched the movie for the first time on the Saturday afternoon Creature Feature. A short story by Ray Bradbury come to life with the magic of Ray Harryhausen special effects. My imagination exploded. I was a changed person.

As Bradbury had a way with his characters, making them vulnerable and noble, and more like the guy next door than a superhero, Harryhausen had a way with his creations to make them more than just clay look-a-likes, but believable creatures. He gave them character and somehow infused a spark of depth in them that should not have been there, and yet, was unmistakably present.

Think of **MIGHTY JOE YOUNG** (1949), the younger version of the fabled **KING KONG** (1933), and how you couldn't help but fall in love with him and cry monster tears sitting on the edge of your seat as he risked his life to save the little girl in the burning mansion. Harryhausen, although billed as a technician on the set, worked his creature magic and Joe became even more popular and lovable than his larger cousin, and Harryhausen's career took off.

Who hasn't seen **THE VALLEY OF GWANGI** (1969) and not dreamed of roping an Allosaurus? That is Harryhausen magic. Who hasn't watched **THE 7TH VOYAGE OF SINBAD** (1958) or **JASON AND THE ARGONAUTS** (1963) and not wanted to pick up a sword and fight skeletons? Who hasn't seen Medusa in the original **CLASH OF THE TITANS** (1981) and thought, "Um, you'd never catch me stealing a glimpse of that nightmare creature!" Scorpions? Harryhausen had a thing for these nasty arachnids and featured them more than twice in his films.

Keep to your Horror slasher movies if that's what rocks your scary boat, because it's the monsters of Harryhausen that lived in my closet and under my bed or just around the dark, bush-covered corner on a moonless night. Nightmares of dino jaws tearing at my little girl body or fantasies of Pegasus whisking me through an azure sky. These are the movies of my childhood. These are the films that fanned the flames of my imagination and brought me to the place I am today, with *Star Wars* and *Star Trek* posters plastered all over my office walls. With dragons and wizards perched on shelves, swords and daggers standing in sheathed splendor near corners and upon veneered racks, models of the original *Alien* alongside the original Lunar Lander, with Yoda looking down upon them all...my office inspired by those geniuses of story and monster, effects and imagination, Bradbury and Harryhausen...the likes of which may never come again.

Thanks for the inspiration. That little girl turned out-of-her-mind Science Fiction fan, dinosaur-loving woman would not be the brave, imaginative soul she is this very day without the food of imagination that Ray and Ray, the Dynamic Duo, freely and forthrightly, spread throughout the film, book, and entertainment world. God bless them for their courage and the little boy in each that refused to grow old. May you find creative endeavors in the afterlife as much fun and as rewarding as in this.

articles

Ralph Richardson and Lindsay Anderson on the set of **O LUCKY MAN!** (1973).

MIKA WALTARI'S

"THE WITCH"

Campaign Plan!

A STORY OF SEX AND PASSION
recommended for
ADULTS ONLY!

Distributed by
SONNEY AMUSEMENT ENTERPRISES INC. and GEORGE M. FRIEDLAND
1656 Cordova Street
Los Angeles 7, Calif.

"THE **WITCH**" offers the broom to sweep NEW CUSTOMERS into YOUR BOX OFFICE!

THE WITCH LIVES AGAIN!

by Jared Auner and Timo Raita

*There have been relatively few Finnish horror or fantasy films. Contemporary cult hits like **RARE EXPORTS** (2010) or **IRON SKY** (2012) are a much more recent development. The* fantastique *is something the Finns never really seem to have embraced in either cinema or literature. In spite of this, in 1952[1] two horror films were made that have come to be considered classics of their type in the far Nordic country, though they are little-known elsewhere. The better-known of the two, Erik Blomberg's* **THE WHITE REINDEER (Valkoinen peura**), *has started to gather a cult around it thanks to an English-subtitled French DVD release. The other is more obscure, but just as worthy of attention. Its Finnish title is* **NOITA PALAA ELÄMÄÄN**, *which translates literally as "The witch returns to life" or, perhaps more idiomatically,* **THE WITCH LIVES AGAIN!** *But if it is known at all in the US, it's known under the generic title it received when it played in American theaters,* **THE WITCH**.

THE WITCH is a strange and erotic Fantasy/Comedy that literalizes the "return of the repressed", unleashing atavistic, pagan sexual powers onto a modern world trying to forget its wicked past. Certain scenes have an uncanny ambiance that wouldn't be out of place in later bizarre Euro horrors like **REINCARNATION OF ISABEL** (Italy, 1973) or **THE DEVIL'S NIGHTMARE** (Belgium, 1971). Other times it seems more like an early '50s Swedish sex dramedy. It's trying to have it both ways, and the odd balance struck between can hit you a little weird. Is this an old-fashioned Victorian morality tale? A modernist cautionary parable? Or a vibrant example of exploito fantastique? All of these, and none. It's a ghost itself, a spirit of a forgotten time, an ambiguous creature which eludes an easy grasp, a cinematic will o' the wisp. It sports wonderfully archaic special effects and has a crude-yet-stately non-style that is sometimes clumsy and overly theatrical. But the cinematography in the fantasy scenes is pretty far out, and occasionally beautiful. If there are too many drawing-room conversation scenes that are framed as though taken straight from a stage play (in fact, they were), nearly as many others veer off into oddball fantasy territory.

THE WITCH is a rare example of a subgenre of gothic in which an archeologist (or some kind of scientist or academic) is haunted by a female corpse he has uncovered during a dig. It's sort of a *Mummy*-styled variation on the old "Bride of Corinth"[2] mythos. There are only a handful of examples, oddities like Curt Siodmak's "The Girl in the Glacier" episode of the TV series *13 Demon St.* (Sweden, 1959-1960), Larry Buchanan's **THE NAKED WITCH** (USA, 1961; a semi-remake of **WITCH**, about which more later), Fatin Abdel Wahab's **BRIDE OF THE NILE** (Egypt, 1961), Kim Ki-Young's **WOMAN CHASING A KILLER BUTTERFLY** (South Korea, 1978), and even to a certain extent Andrzej Zulawski's **SZAMANKA** (Poland, 1996). The central protagonist is seduced by a phantom woman, who eventually breaks down the man's rational understanding of the universe. This trope is used for mostly comedic effect in something like **BRIDE OF THE NILE**, but for a more horrific, even existential effect in **WOMAN CHASING A KILLER BUTTERFLY** or **SZAMANKA**. THE WITCH straddles this line; it has comedic intents but also very serious undercurrents and themes, and overall it comes off much lighter than either the Kim or Zulawski films.

As an early example of European erotic horror, it isn't very surprising that THE WITCH made its way to the US in 1955, where it travelled in both the adult-film and art-house circuits. Again, the film is straddling lines, never re-

solving itself completely within the tenants of genre or distribution. But the unusual nature of its relation to genre made it rather ahead of its time, and it made few waves. This article looks to unearth the film for a wider audience and place it within its larger cultural and cinematic context. As the film is currently unavailable in any English translation, a full story synopsis will be necessary to understand this obscure work of commercial art. But beware! Spoilers loom…

---

[1] This was the year Finland hosted the Olympic Games. In general, this event marked Finland's re-emergence on the world scene after recovering from the destruction of WWII. That this year also produced two of the only horror films made in Finland illustrates the new openness of the country during this time. Also making their debut this same year in Finland: Coca-Cola and chewing gum.

[2] A famous 18th century poem by Johann Wolfgang von Goethe, wherein a young man falls in love with the ghost. Very influential in the development of vampire and gothic literature.

Top: Waltari checks Mirja Mane's leg; Helge Herala also sitting in the front. On the back from left to right: Sakari Jurkka, Hillevi Lagerstam and Toivo Mäkelä.

Above: Roland af Hällström, Mirja Mane and Mika Waltari

Page 13: Unknown lady and Waltari's wife at the table on the left, Hillevi Lagerstam (behind Waltari) Mika Waltari, Mirja Mane, director Roland af Hällström and DP Esko Töyri

The film opens eerily, with mists sweeping through a bleak and boggy landscape. While sloppily excavating an archeological site on the estate of the Baron Hallberg, two weather-beaten old men come across something interesting. Although the men are reluctant, even fearful, they bring the find to the attention of the Archeologist, Hannu (Toivo Mäkelä), and his wife/assistant, Greta (Hillevi Lagerstam). It's the body of a woman, but with a stake driven into her chest. The diggers are seriously spooked, but Hannu and Greta are intrigued and excited. Through the exposition of Hannu's research and the nervous whispers of the servants and local peasantry, we learn that this is the body of a girl murdered some 300 years previously. She had spurned the advances of a prior Baron Hallberg, one notorious for working his way through the local female population. Humiliated, he had her accused of witchcraft, and then killed, staked, and buried. But now she's been uncovered, and the superstitious locals are convinced that she will take her vengeance on the Baron's descendants.

The current Baron (Aku Korhonen) is himself a bit of cad, especially in his younger days. His philandering ways were such that his handsome son Veikko (Sakari Jurkka) will not date any local women, for fear of unknowingly committing incest with one of his father's bastard daughters. Neither of these well-educated men has any time for old wives tales of a witch's revenge. They are rational denizens of the 20th century and so the discovery of the girl's body is cause for celebration, not paranoia. They even laugh about it, with the Baron making the rather inappropriate comment "I've played around with a lot of girls, but I've never impaled anyone in the swamp." Har-har. Along with Hannu and Greta, the Baron has also invited an artist to stay in his villa, Kauko (Helge Herala), who paints odd and unflattering portraits of his benefactor, much to the old aristocrat's chagrin. It's clear when all of these characters are put in a room that there are some sexual tensions between Greta and Kauko, as well as resentments between the Baron and his son. It's a bit of a powder keg, and something is about to set it off.

Several days later, as a particularly hairy storm rolls in, a beautiful girl (Mirja Mane) is found in the pit at the excavation site, comatose and naked. Hannu, Veikko, and Kauko bring her in, drape her as best they can, and gape at her otherworldly beauty. When she awakes she has no recollection of how she ended up nude or in the pit. She does remember her name—Birgit, the same name as the girl murdered three centuries previously. The men joke that she is the witch resurrected, but the locals are decidedly not amused. They *know* she is the witch resurrected, and they don't like it one bit.

Veikko is immediately smitten, and the girl is invited to stay in the villa. In fact, all the men are infatuated with her. She is flirtatious and coy with all of them. It all seems to be innocent fun, but odd things begin to happen around her, suggesting something unnatural. In one scene, as Birgit is playfully running from the amorous Veikko, she is startled by one of the servants leading a horse. The horse panics and rears up, seemingly startled at the mere sight of her, and then collapses to the ground, breaking its leg. Birgit continues to rave and flutter around like madwoman. She comes upon a frightened old woman milking a cow. She shoves the old bitty aside and yanks on the cow's utters herself with an impish grin, revealing her insidious intent. Drops of blood splatter into the milk. The old woman completely loses her shit. In another scene Birgit handles a snake with no fear, and in general seems to have a close and peculiar relationship with nature.

Birgit generally gets everyone in a tizzy. She seduces the men and plays one against the others. Her mere presence terrifies the villagers, who are constantly popping up out of nowhere to threaten her with scythes and pitchforks. Even Hannu begins to suspect something is off about her, though he soon finds himself as much in her thrall as Veikko is. Eventually, this tension erupts into full-bore fantasy, and Birgit's occult nature is revealed. She comes to Hannu late one night to seduce him; she disrobes and then playfully runs away. She passes through the door without opening it. Hannu pursues her out into the fog-enshrouded landscape where he finds her leaping around and dancing wildly, like a pagan priestess of old. All three of the young men are drawn out, as well as the timid locals. She astounds them all with acts of seemingly real magic, all the while laughing maniacally. She makes horses disappear, turns fallen branches into serpents, causes bridges to collapse and even dissolve her flesh until she is a bleach-white skeleton.

Her amorous attentions vacillate between Hannu and Veikko, while Greta and Kakuo get caught up in their own love madness, making out furiously in front of Hannu. But he doesn't much seem to care anymore, as he is by now completely consumed by his desire for Birgit. At the peak of mania, the young witch persuades Veikko to set his ancestral manor aflame. While it burns, Birgit dances feverishly amidst the smoke as Hannu looks on, jealous of her passions for Veikko. He takes the stake which he had once removed from the corpse and uses it to drive her back into the pit. With sorrow and a touch of madness in his eyes, Hannu plunges the stake into her chest while the villa is engulfed in flame, finally bringing an end to the witch's supernatural fury.

And then Hannu wakes up. He is confused and frightened. There has been a fire in his bedroom. But he, the house, and everyone in it are just fine…including Birgit. Yes, it was all just a dream. At least, all the supernatural manifestations that have crowded the last 20 minutes of the film were a dream. The girl had been swimming in a local lake, gotten lost as the storm came on, and fell into the pit. In reflection, all the seemingly magickal incidents can be understood to have rational explanations; for example, the blood in the milk. Just before yanking on the poor beast's utters, Birgit had touched a stick used to mix paint. It coated her hand with a dark red. The other incidents are all misunderstanding, coincidence, or dream.

While this ending is perhaps a bit underwhelming (we'd prefer it if she really were a witch), there are perfectly good cultural reasons for this finale. After he awakens, Hannu says: "I have learned a hard lesson. How easily we start hunting witches all around us, when there is evil inside every man. All of us are all-too-easily willing to impale another in order to save ourselves. We need more understanding. Or the witch will return to life." The "witch" in the story represents the primal sexual impulses which threaten to rip the illusion of civilization away, and strip away all reason until man in nothing more than an animal. This film—and the play it's based on—were written in the aftermath of WWII, a time when civilization truly did seem to be endangered. The fear that man and all his works could be rendered obsolete by the atavistic forces of all-out war mirrors the film's concern with what Freud called "the black tide of the mud of occultism" and its association with powerful female sexuality.

THE WITCH began life as a stage play, which explains some of its stodgier, more dialogue-heavy scenes. It was written by Mika Waltari, perhaps the most famous Finnish author of the 20th century. The play opened in 1946 in Helsinki and was quite the *success de scandal*. The stage version was (originally, at least) quite a bit stronger than the eventual film, with hints of lesbianism and vampirism that were cut out by the time it made it onto screens. Although the part of Birgit required a certain amount of nudity, the first actress cast in the role, Ritva Arvelo, refused to do the scenes undraped and so played the part in flesh-colored underwear with the naughty bits drawn on! Later she was replaced by Ella Eronen, who played the part fully nude, likely the first actress to do so in the history of Finnish theater.

One controversial aspect of the play was cut out even before the piece was staged. In Waltari's original version, the story ends with Birgit revealing herself to be a real and true witch. It had no twist "it's all a dream" undercut. But the powers that be at the theater where the play made its debut balked at this supposedly backward and superstitious content, and Waltari was persuaded to re-write, something Waltari later came to regret. The son of a priest and a theological student himself in his youth, Waltari seems to have been haunted by religion and the supernatural. He wrestled with it his entire life, torn between conservative religious observation and a fascination with mysticism and the occult—in particular, as they relate to the erotic. These struggles inform **THE WITCH** as well as much of his other work. In 1949 he wrote a semi-fictional "diary" called *Neljä päivänlaskua* (or "Four Sundowns"). In it he describes an experience taking the hallucinogenic herb Fly Agaric and having visions of talking animals and naked phantom girls. If he's not fibbing, one can easily see how this trip could greatly influence the events depicted in **THE WITCH**. Or at the very least illustrates Waltari's continuing interest in these themes and images.

In 1950 Hannu Leminen, director of the campy '40s sex hygiene picture **SYNNIN JÄLJET** ("Ways of Sin", 1946), optioned the play for a film version, seeing the obviously exploitable content of the story. But he ran into a major hurdle when an appropriate actress could not be found to fill the demanding role of Birgit—one might speculate he had a difficult time finding an actress willing to bear all. Eventually, an actress was found by producer Mauno Mäkelä and director Roland af Hällström, who had taken over the project after Leminen abandoned it. They cast the stunning and wild-eyed Mirja Mane for the part, and it's hard to imagine how anyone else could be more perfect. Mane throws herself into the role with a feverish gusto, bewilderingly cute one moment; a tumultuous force of nature the next. Sadly, it seems Mane only made a handful of films during the early-to-mid-'50s. She married actor and director Toivo Hämeranta in 1953, and it would appear that she abandoned acting for a life of wedded bliss soon after. There are some indications that Mane received contract offers from American companies, but nothing seems to have come from it.[3] Alas, she died young, only 44, in 1969. It's a great shame she wasn't in more films, as it's her presence and performance which bestows the film with much of its power.

The director, Roland af Hällström, also died relatively young, at the age of 51, in 1956. Hällström worked consistently through the '40s and '50s. In 1944, he worked as an assistant to the eccentric Teuvo Tulio, and seems to have inherited some of the methods and themes of his mentor, exploring the

---

[3] In a handful of 1955 Finnish newspaper articles about Mirja Man, it was reported that the actress was offered a 5-year contract by a US entity called the Indo-American International Films Company. However, we can find no other information about this company, or if it even exists.

THE WHITE REINDEER is a folklore-inspired Gothic possessed with a wild, pagan spirit. A young woman is transformed into a vampire-like creature that sometimes takes the shape of a huge, pale reindeer.

archetype of the "fallen woman" through several melodramas. He was also no stranger to censorship; his 1946 film **HOUKUTUSLINTU** featured a steamy sauna scene with two naked women. It was too hot for the times, and 20 sexy seconds were left on the cutting room floor. The film was banned throughout most of Europe, but played uncut in France, Belgium, and Greece. It would not be the last time his work was provoked strong reactions from government bureaucrats.

When **THE WITCH** was released in 1952, like the stage version, it met with a certain amount of controversy. The Finnish censors trimmed a few minutes out of the film before they would allow it to be released for general consumption. Oddly, it wasn't the nudity which bothered them, but rather certain bits of steamy dialogue. Stuff along the lines of "I want to embrace your young, hot body...naked, in the heat of the fire, in the heat of the blood," or, "I felt how your hand touched my bare breast".[4] These salacious lines of dialogue were finally re-instated into the film when it was released on DVD in Finland in 2005. Nudity doesn't seem to have been a problem in and of itself; it's the prurient context provided by the dialogue which made the film obscene. Like their neighbors the Swedes, Finland has always had a somewhat nonchalant attitude towards exposure of the human body. This is, after all, the culture where the sauna has been a regular part of social life for centuries. And of course, casual nudity is an accepted part of the sauna tradition. Nudity has been cropping up in Finnish cinema here and there nearly since the beginning, with relatively little hubbub attending it. Glimpses of bare flesh can be seen in many productions from the late '40s on, mostly in saunas or in skinny-dipping scenes (see, for example, the gonzo melodramas of Teuvo Tulio), and they are mostly presented as being no big deal and are rarely the main focus of the image or the narrative.

In the early '50s, Swedish movies like **ONE SUMMER OF HAPPINESS** (Arne Mattsson, 1951) and **SUMMER WITH MONIKA** (Ingmar Berman, 1953) were among the earliest to feature frank female nudity and play widely around the world. Their themes of youthful and fleeting summer romance provided a healthy context for the light erotic images, while still giving the thrill-seekers just enough of the exposed flesh they were putting down hard-earned money for. These movies were very influential in Finland, which produced a series of its own variations, like Toivo Särkkä's **THE MILKMAID** (1953) or Matti Kassila's **THE SCARLET WEEK** (1954). The casual nudity in each guaranteed both domestic and overseas sales, as was the case with **THE WITCH**. As the '60s dawned and sexual content was on the rise in cinemas all over the world, Finland produced a few notable softcore productions like Mikko Niskanen's **UNDER YOUR SKIN** (1966) and Teuvo Tulio's completely insane **SENSUELA** (released in '72, but filmed in '67-'68), but as the '70s rolled around, rougher and more explicit fare from Sweden, Denmark and the US swamped the market. Similar to the end of the "nudie-cutie" craze in the US, soon enough the innocent sauna scenes that had permeated Finnish cinemas lost their power to titillate.

While nudity was relatively common in this era of Finnish cinema, horror and fantasy certainly were not. **THE WITCH** is one of the few examples. In 1905, the government laid out stringent restrictions targeting the depiction of violence and crime in films. This had the effect of essentially curtailing the development of any sort of action, noir, or horror cinema in Finland. And while these restrictions lessened over time, a cultural prejudice seems to have evolved which put as much of a damper on fantastic film as any government bureaucrat. These movies simply were not made, or at least not many of them. But there are a handful of examples besides **THE WITCH**.

Going back to the silent era we have **NOIDAN KIROT** (1927), perhaps the first out-and-out Finnish horror film. Set among the Sami people in Lapland, the northernmost part of Finland, the film features a shaman's curse, paranoid newlyweds, madness, rape, and even a wonderfully weird-looking hairy demon. It shares many elements and themes with a later film, Erik Blomberg's **VALKOINEN PEURA** (a.k.a. **THE WHITE REINDEER**).

Like **THE WITCH**, **THE WHITE REINDEER** is a folklore-inspired Gothic possessed with a wild, pagan spirit. It concerns an insecure wife who consults with a shaman to insure that her husband stays true. Everything goes wrong, of course, and instead of fixing her marriage she is transformed into a vampire-like creature that sometimes takes the shape of a huge, pale reindeer. The movie alternates moody and poetic passages with scenes that rattle with a crude and amateurish vitality, at times reminding me of some Turkish films from the 1950s and '60s. There are many haunting and bizarre moments, perhaps the most memorable being the scene of our were-deer, back in lady form, licking blood from her wounded shoulder. The animal look in her glassy, vacant eyes is truly uncanny. The movie is an almost-masterpiece, and is considered a stone-cold classic in its home country. **THE WITCH** shares some of the otherworldly power as **THE WHITE REINDEER**, but doesn't quite climb to the same heights.

Other than these two rare examples, Finnish film *fantastique* is a rather paltry affair, with most other early entries being Horror-Comedies where, like in **THE WITCH**, supernatural elements are exposed to have rational, mundane causes. You have to wait until 1988's **KUUTAMOSONAATTI** for a full-blooded horror outing. But even then, the film, though inspired by feral US productions like **TEXAS CHAINSAW MASSACRE** (1974) and **THE HILLS HAVE EYES** (1977), is really as much a spoof as it is a scare-fest.

If **THE WITCH** had been more successful, it might have inspired a wave of horror pictures. Alas, it bombed at the box office, but it did win two Jussi Awards in 1953, for cinematography and production design.[5] Indeed these are two of the stronger aspects of the picture, especially in the more overtly occult

---

[4] If these lines sound rather overheated, remember this is a comedy!

[5] The Finnish equivalent of the Academy Awards.

scenes. But the movie does not seem to have had much of an impact beyond that in Finland itself. Today, it's barely considered a cult classic in its country of origin, more often it's just thought of as an old B-movie oddity.

The film's bold nudity made it a potentially desirable property on the world cinema market. It was sold to Germany where it was released as **GEFAHRLICH SIND DIE NACHTE** (or "The Bright Nights are Dangerous", a reference to the "midnight sun" of the Far North). It was also released in the US in 1955. The film was imported—along with a handful of other Finnish films—by the infamous Raymond Rohauer. Rohauer was a film collector, exhibitor, and distributor. He has also been called a "pirate" and a "freebooter" for his often unsavory methods in obtaining quasi-legal ownership of films, both foreign and domestic. Having obtained film prints through private collectors, or duped foreign distributors, Rohauer would then alter the subtitles just enough that he could make a reasonable claim to having offered a unique version of the film, which he then claimed a copyright ownership of.

The person who provided Rohauer with the basis of his ownership claim of **THE WITCH** was Robert Wade Chatterton, who is credited with the "American Adaptation and Subtitles". Not much has been written about him, but he seems to have been very active on the outer fringe of Hollywood and the mid-century American counterculture. He had a small, uncredited role in the Danny Kaye vehicle **THE KID FROM BROOKLYN** (USA, 1946) and ran his own film society in LA around the time Rohauer was doing the same thing. He wrote a very rare, private press book called *What is a Beatnik?* and, in 1962, directed an experimental short film called *Passion in a Seaside Slum*. Though missing in action for several decades, in recent years, *Passion* has been shown in festivals and retrospectives as a pioneering work of Queer Cinema. One can assume that Chatterton and Rohauer knew each other through underground film circles in LA, but how exactly they came to work together is unclear.

In 1950, Rohauer took over the operations of a small Hollywood theater called The Coronet. There he exhibited silent films, several cutting-edge experimental works by filmmakers like Kenneth Anger or Maya Deren, and, most relevantly for this article, foreign films—more precisely, foreign films that had at least a modicum of sexual content. Rival collector and film historian William K. Everson called The Coronet "a bizarre combination of art house, film society, and exploitation cinema".[6] Although it's unclear *how* Rohauer obtained copies of the Finnish films he distributed, including **THE WITCH**, it's very clear *why*: nudity. Like most distributors of such fare, the ads often promised more than they could deliver, but European films at least offered something their American counterparts decidedly could not at the time: a veneer of prestige, of true artistic merit.

It was a time when independent producers and distributors were doing well circumventing the Hollywood system and its Hays Code restrictions by operating an entirely alternate American cinematic marketplace. Cheap and sordid domestic films filled out the low-rent drive-ins and hard-tops, but these films inevitably made promises they couldn't keep. The "sizzle" without the "steak", as it has often been put. But these failures were as much of an aesthetic nature as they were a moral one. They were cheaply and quickly made, and keen-eyed audiences, even ones looking for sleaze, would probably have seen right through most of them. But with the more daring European fare, distributors had something which provided cheap thrills with a definite touch of class. A template was set by roadshow impresario Kroger Babb and his release of Bergman's **SUMMER WITH MONIKA** as **MONIKA: A GIRL IN TROUBLE** in 1955. The film was well-written, well-acted and well-made. It also had a beautiful girl taking off her clothes. You could get it all: the sizzle, the steak, and a beautifully-embroidered napkin to wipe it all up with.

But while **MONIKA** was butchered by Babb, who took out nearly 40 minutes of Bergman artistry and slathered it with a careless jazz score, **THE WITCH** seems to have circulated relatively unscathed. Rohauer distributed the film himself for a time via his own Coronet Film Distributors, but distribution for this film and others like **THE SCARLET WEEK** and Aarne Tarkas' 1954 film **OLEMME KAIKKI SYYLLISIÄ** (a.k.a. **ASSAULT!**) was eventually taken up by the likes of Sonney Amusement Enterprises, Inc, a long-lived exploitation film company whose roots extended back into the '30s with true crime films, sex hygiene flicks and Dwain Esper exploito freakouts like **MANIAC** (1934).[7] Obviously interested in exploiting the film's nudity, and impressed by the success of films like **MONIKA** or the Italian import **BITTER RICE** (1949), distribution of **THE WITCH** in the

---

[6] Quote taken from an article Everson wrote about Rohauer in an obscure literary journal, the title of which is unknown to me. The article is on the web here: https://docs.google.com/file/d/0B61NVGCA4NISMmEzNGVjNTltYjFjOC00NTgxLThlYWUtM2UyMGYyZDQxMjBI/edit?pli=1

[7] In the US pressbook, the distributors of the film are given as "Sonney Amusement Enterprises, Inc., and George M. Friedland". Who Friedland is and how exactly he was involved in this film is rather mysterious, as we can find no definitive information about him. One possibility is that he is one and the same as Georges Friedland, a Russian-born filmmaker who worked in Finland, among other places, under the names George Freedland or Gregory Freed. He directed the Finnish/German co-production **MOONWOLF** (1959), a love story with just a hint of Sci-Fi throw in. Later, he made a film for Eurocine called **A VIRGIN FOR ST. TROPEZ** (1975) which, according to actor Paul Muller, was mostly filmed by Jess Franco! But we cannot corroborate that this is the same 'Friedland' which co-distributed **THE WITCH** alongside Sonney Amusements.

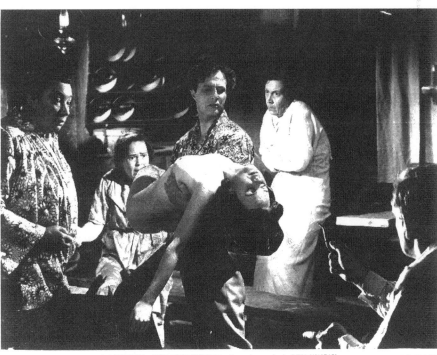

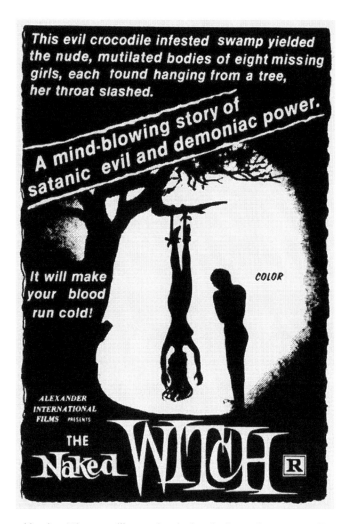

mid-to-late-'50s seems like a real no-brainer for just such a company. But what's more surprising is that the film was distributed seemingly as much as an art film as an exploito-grinder.

In the US pressbook the film is given the legend "Mika Waltari's **THE WITCH**". This is interesting, as you wouldn't think an exploitation film company would even bother advertising to its audience the literary pedigree of the film they're pitching. If the audience is just looking for quick glimpse of naked ladies, what do they care who the auteur of the piece is? But the crediting of Waltari and the pressbook's stressing of the film's Finnish origins points to a marketing strategy that sold prestige as much as it did sensation. Waltari was a best-selling author, after all; his classic historical novel *The Egyptian* had topped the charts in 1949 and Michael Curtiz made it into an expensive Technicolor Widescreen Epic in 1954. Seeking a crossover audience to bridge those interested in Waltari and those interested in unsheathed boobies seems almost at cross-purposes.

But foreign films were a hip and mostly socially-acceptable product in the mid-'50s, much more so than the grindhouse and roadshow flicks that people like Babb or Sonney had been churning out. One might suspect that some of these producers, ghettoized in the exploitation market, might have sought to release films like this almost as a point of pride—something they could talk about at parties, instead of being mostly embarrassed by the junk they had previously been hurling at audiences. Indeed, in further illustration of this point, in late 1959 Dan Sonney purchased the Fox La Brea, an abandoned movie theater in suburban LA, and re-dubbed it the Art La Brea Theater, opening with a screening of Bergman's **BRINK OF LIFE** (Sweden, 1958). For most of the decade this art-house theater had great success showing the latest sexy foreign fare. Given these developments, it's not far off to speculate that **THE WITCH** was imported as much for its possible prestige as a film as for its more libidinous aspects. But even this artsy veneer is just another kind of scam; another sort of exploitation. For all its social acceptance, most audiences went to foreign "art" movies for the same reason they went to nudist colony flicks: to catch glimpses of naked flesh.

And certainly the distributors of **THE WITCH** weren't shy about playing up the titillation factor. The pressbook screams "A Daring Frank Story of Sex and Passion!" and stresses that the film was held up for "6 months" by US customs officials. Interestingly, very similar language is used to describe the censorship hassles of another film imported from Finland by Rohauer and distributed by Sonney Amusements: **ASSAULT**. References to this sexploitation melodrama are few and far between but they always mention a "4-month" hold-up in customs before its release. At first, these similarities in language lead me to believe this might have been pure ballyhoo. By 1955 the Hays Code, always hard to enforce in the more independent areas of US film production, had begun to be dismantled by the landmark Supreme Court decision *Joseph Burstyn, Inc. v. Wilson*, which protected films as free speech.

But, parallel to this, during the 1950s the importation of films from foreign countries fell under the watchful, paranoid eye of the McCarran Act, a Cold War-era legislation that sought to prevent the importation of materials that might've contained a "threat to the American way of life." You might expect that a film coming from a country (even a friendly country) so close to the USSR would be placed under special scrutiny, aside from its potentially salacious content. The mention of the "6 months" it took to clear customs makes it sound like the film was endlessly debated because it was such hot stuff. But I suspect that it was probably just a victim of simple bureaucratic red tape. With so many foreign movies being imported into the US at this time, it makes sense that it might take several months to get through them all. So, in a way, it's all still ballyhoo. Nonetheless, when the film did play, black dots and smears were added to mask the more brazen nudity.

THE WITCH made little impact in the US, despite being perhaps the first Finnish film to play in the States. But it did inspire another film that, while no classic, is rather better-known than its source. Larry Buchanan's **THE NAKED WITCH** was made in 1961, some six years after Hällström's film made its stateside debut, but released in 1964. Although Buchanan always claimed that **THE NAKED WITCH** was based on a German silent film, this is almost certainly not true. In the commentary for the film on the Something Weird DVD, Buchanan names the film—although, for the life of me, I cannot make out precisely what he is saying. Certainly, my German is poor-to-nonexistent, but a simple Google translation of "naked witch" into German shows that what he says doesn't come close to the correct translation. And as far as we can tell, no such German silent sexy witch movie even exists… though if it does, we'd love to see it.

But Buchanan states this assertion with confidence, and one gets the impression that he's been telling that story for years. So, either he was lying to cover up the origins of the film, or his memory is really bad. He may have started lying about it in order to not upset the litigious Rohauer, who, despite the dubious legality of his own actions, was prone to suing anyone he perceived as treading on his copyrights. Or perhaps more likely, Buchanan was just an old man with a faulty recall. I suspect that if this is the case, it probably also has something to do with Rohauer. Buchanan may have been mashing up a memory of seeing Rohauer's print of **THE WITCH** with any number of silent films the collector/rogue exhibited and distributed during his heyday. Was Buchanan a regular attendee of Rohauer's film society in the 1950s? He did spend some time in Hollywood around then, so it's possible.

Whatever the case, **THE NAKED WITCH** is more or less a remake of the Finnish film, although spiced up with more traditional horror elements. The story revolves around a graduate student travelling to rural West Texas to study the superstitions of the German settlers there. Although treated coldly by the small-town inhabitants, he eventually learns the story of the "Luckenbach Witch". He visits her grave, digs it up, and of course, removes the stake from the rotting corpse. This brings the witch back to life and she begins to take revenge on the townsfolk for executing her a century before. The student seeks out the Witch in the caves on the outskirts of town and spies her swimming and dancing around in the nude. He falls under her spell, but when the witch threatens the pretty, innocent girl he has a crush on, our hero dutifully returns the stake to where it belongs: square in the witch's chest.

Many elements are taken straight from **THE WITCH**. The academic, who does not believe any of the superstitious nonsense that the villagers take so seriously, removes the stake from the body, assuming nothing will happen, bringing it back to life. The origins of the witch are remarkably similar, with a wronged woman accused of witchcraft by a pillar of the community for spurning his sexual advances. There is a long scene of the witch dancing in a diaphanous gown while the hero stares transfixed, completely under her spell. The witch has a special, unnatural relationship with animals, particularly birds and snakes. And it's the shaken intellectual who comes to his senses and sends the witch back from whence she came.

These are all plot points found in the original movie, though they're depicted rather differently. For example, the witch's origin is seen in flashback in **THE NAKED WITCH** while it's revealed through exposition in **THE WITCH**. Buchanan's film also gives the plot a much more conventional gothic twist. The resurrected witch seeks to take bloody revenge on the ancestors of those who condemned her, leading to a handful of scenes of poorly-staged supernatural murder. There is nothing like this in the Hällström picture. Indeed, **THE NAKED WITCH** is much more a straight-up all-around exploitation film. In an interview with producer/screenwriter Claude Alexander (also on the SWV disc), he claims that he had to liven up Buchanan's original script, make it more commercial. One might speculate that Buchanan stayed truer to the original movie, and Alexander, seeing this would not play all that well in Texas drive-ins, added the more conventional thriller aspects. But in any manner, **THE WITCH** is very rarely given credit as the inspiration for **THE NAKED WITCH**, an omission this article hopes to correct.

However, this origin for Buchanan's film is somewhat complicated by the rumor of a sexier edit of the Finnish flick which may have played briefly in US theaters. In a talk given in 1998 in Finland, legendary exploitation producer Dave Friedman revealed that he had been involved in making a 2nd version of **THE WITCH** with more risqué nude inserts added to spice up the film for the burgeoning early-'60s nudie-cutie/pussycat theater market. And it was called…**THE NAKED WITCH**! He claimed that *this* was the inspiration for the Buchanan movie. But this is only anecdotal evidence and we can find no corroboration that this version ever existed. Until a print or ad materials for this version comes to light, we must assume that Friedman was mistaken or confused, though it may also be that Friedman was just being Friedman, a showman all the way, and was "spicing up" the story for his audience.

THE WITCH pretty much drops off the scene for several decades after that. It received a few tantalizing mentions in the literature on international horror cinema. In the *Overlook Film Encyclopedia: Horror*, the film is damned as "rather timid", which, by the standards of later decades, it may be, but for the time it was anything but. The author of that entry also takes issue with Hällström's direction, describing it as "routine" and that he "fails to breathe any real life into the story". To a certain extent, I may agree, but at its best the film does have some real otherworldly power. Especially in its final scenes.

This part of the film—the last 15 minutes or so—is fairly extraordinary. With its supernatural sexpot dancing in a diaphanous gown through a mist-haunted landscape, these scenes bring to mind the work of French sex-horror surrealist Jean Rollin. Birgit in her most witchy aspects is a distant cousin to Rollin's more melancholy vampire girls, for example, Annie Belle in **LIPS OF BLOOD** (France, 1975), whose seductions lead the hero beyond reason and into the realm of memory and myth.[8] These ghostly vixens are all avatars of an ancient divine feminine ideal, an archetype which connects man back to nature in all its mystery and horror. This connection is broken by modern life, which seeks to deny this primal affinity at any cost. But Birgit and her unearthly kin emerge from the mists, beautiful and alluring, and beckon us to remember…

But in the end, **THE WITCH** recoils at this, pulls back from the precipice of this "mud of occultism" and nullifies its potential power. If it had been made a few years later, one wonders if it would have taken the same track. By the early '60s, gothic horror films with unambiguous supernatural elements were all the rage again. It's interesting to imagine what the film may have been like had it been more faithful to its original text, with its implied lesbianism and vampirism and full-on *fantastique* conclusion. One may reckon that it would have been an uncanny precursor to Rollin's work, a decade-and-a-half before the odd Frenchman began sharing his dream with us.

THE WITCH remains a peculiar and somewhat contradictory anomaly in this period of Nordic cinema. It's a movie that slips between cracks, both in

---

[8] Oddly, the character of Birgit has a real-world French inspiration. While visiting megaliths in Carnac in 1928, Mika Waltari became enchanted with a dark-haired local girl who eventually broke his heart. Wild and playful, she was the model for the witchy title character in Waltari's 1939 novella *Fine van Brooklyn*, as well as the later Birgit.

terms of genre and distribution—and for several decades, it nearly seems to have vanished. **THE WITCH** finally did return to life when an uncut DVD of the film was released in Finland in 2005. Though it lacks any English language options, at least the film is out there for new generations to investigate. The US version is currently languishing in the archives of the Cohen Media Group, who bought up the Rohauer estate in 2011. They have, as of this writing, not seen fit to give the film a release, either theatrical or digital. This is a shame, as **THE WITCH** is an entertaining and occasionally bewitching (bad pun fully intended) experience. But if looking at this film has taught me anything, it's that a powerful entity such as this never stays buried for long. **THE WITCH** will live again!

"THE WITCH"
First Film Shown from Finland

Most American movie-goers have been unaware that the country of Finland has been producing exceptional photoplays, but this situation is being remedied with "The Witch," the highly publicized and controversial picture which opens at the .... Theatre on .... The film has been acclaimed as an experience in the supernatural and presents nudity in an artistic and tastefully executed manner. Its star too, Mirja Mane, has been acclaimed as a second Hedy LaMarr by those who saw the film at its initial press showings.

101

PUBLICITY:
FOR BEST RESULTS MAKE USE OF THIS MATERIAL!

Cast — Credits

THE WITCH	Mirja Mane
THE ARCHAEOLOGIST	Toivo Makela
HIS WIFE	Hillevi Lagerstam
THE COUNT	Aku Korhonen
HIS SON	Sakari Jurkka
THE ARTIST	Helge Herala

THE WITCH	Produced in Finland
DIRECTED BY	Roland Hallstrom
SCREENPLAY BY	Mika Waltari (from his stage play)
AMERICAN ADAPTATION AND SUB-TITLES	Robert Wade Chatterton
PHOTOGRAPHED BY	Esko Toyri
SETTINGS BY	Lauri Ela
RUNNING TIME	70 minutes

Distributed by SONNEY AMUSEMENT ENTERPRISES, INC., and GEORGE M. FRIEDLAND
1656 Cordova Street, Los Angeles 7, California

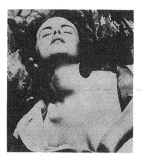

Mirja Mane, the sensuously beautiful European star of "The Witch" which opens at the .... Theatre on ...., has already received countless offers from almost every major studio in Hollywood.

1A

Synopsis

This highly controversial film, the first feature-length Finnish film to be released in this country, was held up by U. S. Customs for fully 6 months due to the large number of nude scenes in the picture. For a time it appeared that it would not be permitted to enter the country at all. It was screened again and again. The moot point seemed to be "Is nudity in itself necessarily immoral or indecent." Finally the picture was cleared, with some minor changes. Fortunately in this instance the censorship was intelligent: while there is some masking and veiling, the power and sweep of the story are in no way impaired. It is "all there."

The film itself is a fantasy, beautiful at times, stark at others — eerie, with touches of the supernatural.

An archaeologist and his wife are examining the contents of some old graves when they come upon the remains of a woman, buried some 300 years before with a stake driven through her heart. Against the protests of the superstitious villagers, who claim that the woman was buried as a "witch," the stake is removed. A few hours later, during a storm, the ancient remains are found to have disappeared, while in their place is the nude form of a girl — young, beautiful, seductive, and seemingly alive — as indeed, she is.

The story goes on from there, with the "witch" attempting to place several of the men in the group under her evil influence, with increasing manifestations of the supernatural, and with the townspeople, convinced now that they were right, bent on the girl's re-destruction.

Essentially a dramatization of Freudian theories of sex frustration and repressed love, the film is replete with tempestuous love scenes.

Design and photography are superb.

Taivo Makela, Mirja Mane and Helge Herala in a tense dramatic scene from Mika Waltari's "The Witch"

2-A

"THE WITCH"
Experience in Supernatural

Buried for over three hundred years with a stake through her heart as a witch, a girl returns to seek her vengeance on the living descendants of the man responsible for her death in "The Witch" which opens at the .... Theatre on .... She is promptly amorously pursued by the youngest descendant of this man who does not believe her to be a witch, or as a matter of fact anything but a voluptuously beautiful object of romance.

This is the basic plot idea of one of the raciest, spiciest and daring motion pictures to reach these shores, culminating in a nude dance which has been tastefully and artfully executed by the lovely and curvaceous star, Mirja Mane.

PROVOCATIVE AND BEWITCHING!

Old hat is the ancient conception of a witch as an ugly woman with black stringy hair, the cackle of a hyena, and wearing a tall cone-shaped black hat . . . for in "The Witch" Mirja Mane plays the title role and is a sensual dark haired beauty with a laugh as sexy as her face and form. It is the story of an archaeologist who stumbles upon the remains of a witch buried three hundred years before with a stake through her heart. Against the advice of superstitious villagers he removes the stake, and the witch returns to life as a seductive young girl.

THE UNIQUE CINEMA OF LARRY COHEN

by Karl Kaefer

Christmas in 1968 was the best! I was given a Mr. Wizard Chemistry set; soon I found myself unsupervised in the kitchen and I attempted my first experiment. After the explosion, my mother came running in to see me and the whole kitchen covered in purple goo. I was grinning ear to ear, so proud of the mess I'd made. Mr. Wizard's chemistry set was promptly thrown into the garbage, never to be retrieved. I didn't realize until much later that this event was my version of a Larry Cohen film: sloppy, messy, but oh-so-much fun.

Larry Cohen's films are odd. What seems to start off as a generic horror film becomes something else entirely. It is those small touches in the script, the acting, and the unusual sense of humor that mark Cohen's films as unique.

Larry Cohen began his career in the late 50's as a writer/creator for TV. He wrote scripts for *The Defenders*, and created the TV series *Branded*, *The Invaders*, *Blue Light* and *Coronet Blue*. He has written over 90 TV/movies scripts for such diverse projects as the *Maniac Cop* film series, *NYPD Blue*, and several *Columbo* episodes. I was hooked on both *The Invaders* and *Coronet Blue* when I was younger…to this day I can spot his scripts a mile away. He has such a satirical voice, and he is eminently quotable as a writer.

Any good writer will use a genre such as Horror or Science Fiction as a platform for social commentary. Alongside George Romero, Larry Cohen stands as one of the masters of this type of writing. But unlike Romero, Cohen tends to be much more subversive. His attacks on racism (**BONE**, 1972), parenting (the *It's Alive* trilogy, 1974-1987), the FDA (**THE STUFF**, 1985), government (**THE PRIVATE LIVES OF J. EDGAR HOOVER**, 1977), and religious extremism (**GOD TOLD ME TO**, 1976) aren't just single-minded attacks on the status quo.

If you take a look at Cohen's protagonists in most of his films, they are not innocent victims. In fact, Cohen will choose the most unlikely heroes for his films. From a small time petty crook who asks for a Nixon-like pardon for information regarding the whereabouts of a monster (Jimmy Quinn in **Q**, 1982), to an industrial spy (**THE STUFF**) to a father who wants to commit filicide (murder of his own child, in **IT'S ALIVE**, 1974), Cohen's protagonists are neither heroic or ethical. They're out for themselves, for their best interest.

The best example of this type of subversiveness is in Cohen's satirical horror comedy **THE STUFF**. This movie is a wonderfully over the top soufflé of satirical barbs aimed at the FDA, television advertising, right-wing conservative militias, and rampant consumerism. The heroes of this film include the aforementioned industrial spy (Michael Moriarity), a TV commercial director (Andrea Marcovici) and a right wing pinko-hating militia commander (Paul Sorvino).

This trait is inherent in most of Cohen's films, from his Blaxploitation gem, **BLACK CAESAR** (1973), to his biographical film, **THE PRIVATE LIVES OF J. EDGAR HOOVER**, to his directorial debut, **BONE**—where Yaphet Kotto plays a black thug who kidnaps a rich white woman in Beverly Hills—these are his heroes, the people who will bring down the status quo and expose all the hidden blackness of our sordid little lives.

We, the audience, are the targets for Cohen's ire. His message is simple: How dare we accept what is fed to us by the media? I can't verify this, but in my mind, the great late comic Bill Hicks saw **THE STUFF** and innately understood Cohen's message—as reiterated in his monologue, "If you're in advertising…kill yourself". The venom that Cohen packs into that film is truly incredible. And he doesn't stop there. In **THE STUFF**, after Cohen attacks the FDA, the military complex, and the postal service, he ends his film with an outrageous statement on drug addiction.

Cohen's *It's Alive* trilogy is equally subversive, but in a totally different way. These films are much more serious in their intention. Here the monster is created by pharmaceutical companies (much like the Thalidomide scare of the '50s). The monster comes from within the family. In the initial film, when the killer baby escapes, the police track down the culprit and draw their guns…only to have the camera pull back and show a normal baby just playing in the yard.

Much like in the black comedy **A DAY IN THE DEATH OF JOE EGG** (1972, adapted by Peter Nichols from his own play), we have a father who cannot abide that his child is deformed. Frank's (John Ryan) transformation from this fanatical father who wants to kill his child, to the character he becomes in the second film—an advocate for these killer babies being born all around the U.S.—is slow and painful. His ultimate realization that the child is *not* the fault of their own nature is Cohen's point. This is a film that should be shown to all parents of handicapped children.

Whether it be Cohen's hubris of grafting black-empowerment messages onto a classic gangster film (**BLACK CAESAR**) or his use of actual gang members as extras and assistants in his film **ORIGINAL GANGSTAS** (1996).

Here we have an example of Cohen being the true underhanded activist. During the filming of this movie in Gary, Indiana, gang-related incidents fell to an all-time low. Here's a case in point where Larry Cohen became an actual activist in real life, rather than just on the movie screen.

Lest you think that Cohen's films just pummel you with social messages (which they do, of course), Larry uses two other skills to balance the sledgehammer effect of his social commentary.

All of Larry Cohen's screenplays are witty, pithy and humorous, and are eminently quotable. Here are just a few examples:

"Hunting and killing babies doesn't seem to be my specialty".
- **IT'S ALIVE**

"What is your greatest influence?"
"Abraham Zapruder."
"Who?"
"Honest Abe never lies."
"How do you spell that?"
"J-F-K."
- **SPECIAL EFFECTS** (1984)

"I will permit this colored man to speak. But speak one word of the Commie party, or one word in code, and I will blow his head off!"
- **THE STUFF**

In addition to Cohen's sparkling dialog, he has a great knack for casting his roles with actors who understand and inhabit his characters with the sufficient gusto they deserve. Long before Quentin Tarantino, Cohen was casting older, forgotten actors in his films, including Sylvia Sidney, Guy Stockwell, Michael Ansara, Sandy Dennis, Robert Drivas, Broderick Crawford, Dan Dailey, Michael Parks (long before he became a stalwart in Tarantino's films), Jose Ferrer, Howard Da Silva, John Marley...the list goes on and on.

Then there are the casting choices that no one in their right mind would think of...How about Ed McMahon (in the film **FULL MOON HIGH**, 1981) as a gun-totin' NRA advocate whose son (Adam Arkin) is a werewolf? Or my favorite, James Earl Jones as a detective who is perpetually chewing gum, even while he dying from a car accident in **THE AMBULANCE** (1990)? And let's just be charitable here—Jones (and nearly all of Cohen's actors) is devouring the scenery, the cameras, and anything else he can get his hands on. And Cohen's go-to actor, Michael Moriarity overacts with such relish that no other condiment is needed.

The final element that adds to the appreciation of Cohen's films is the out-of-left-field scenes he adds into the films for no reason at all. At first glance, Cohen's pacing and editing seem off, but his directorial choices included quickly-added elements to the films. I can think of no other writer/director who could come up with such gems as a scene of undercover policemen posing as street mimes—or a battalion of militiamen hailing taxis *en masse*—or stopping the film's flow altogether so your lead actor could sing a unintelligible jazz piano piece with scat lyrics...and yet, Cohen has done all these things in his films.

I also have to single out two films that are arguably Cohen's best films to date:

GOD TOLD ME TO begins as a police procedural as an unknown gunman shoots down several innocent bystanders. When confronted by the police detective (Tony Lo Bianco) as to why he did it, the assailant states, "God told me to." But what starts out as a seemingly simplistic plot becomes something else entirely. Add Catholic guilt, alien abductions, and political conspiracy theories, and you get one of the most obtuse and strange films ever committed to celluloid. Interestingly, this is the most sedate of his films...none of the overacting and craziness is noticeable. And this is the film where, at the end, you feel for the characters and their plight.

The acting is top-notch, including great turns by genre stalwarts Richard Lynch, Sandy Dennis, Mike Kellin and Robert Drivas, but I must single out Sylvia Sidney, who has an incredible cameo as an alien abduction victim. She gives her all in this very emotional part, and her appearance elevates the film to a whole new level.

And for an added bonus, viewers are honored with the acting debut of cult comic Andy Kaufman as a NYC police officer who is the victim of God—or the alien—or the political conspiracy. It's actually a little strange to see Kaufman in the film, but that's what Cohen does just to keep his audience off-balance.

Another one of Cohen's gems is **Q** (a.k.a. **Q: THE WINGED SERPENT**). Michael Moriarity adds another quirky persona to his resume, as small-time hood Jimmy Quinn, who, by chance, happens upon the lair of the titular winged serpent on top of the Chrysler Building in NYC. He then attempts to embezzle one million dollars from the NYC Mayor, plus a pardon for any future crimes!

Along with Moriarity, the film is brim-filled with great genre acting talent: Richard Roundtree & David Carradine as detectives on the case and Candy Clark as Moriarity's girlfriend. As usual, the dialog is witty and acerbic, and the stop-motion model work by David Allan is incredible, even though it's just a bit underused in my opinion.

Cohen has written many film scripts for other directors, including **PHONE BOOTH** (2002, originally supposed to have been directed by Alfred Hitchcock), **CELLULAR** (2004), the *Maniac Cop* series (1988-1993), **UNCLE SAM** (1996), and my two personal favorites: **BODY SNATCHERS** (1993) and his best spec script to date, **BEST SELLER** (1987). But no matter the quality, crispness and orderliness of any of these films, none of them are as batshit-entertaining as his own films—a.k.a. "Larco Productions".

So if you're looking for a masterpiece of cinema, rent a Kubrick film. Plain and simple. *But*, if you want a good time with some thought-provoking (and possibly mind-numbing) ideas, crazy overacting, and just pure unmitigated insanity, you can do no better than watching a Larry Cohen film. At the end of it, you'll be smiling and covered with purple goo.

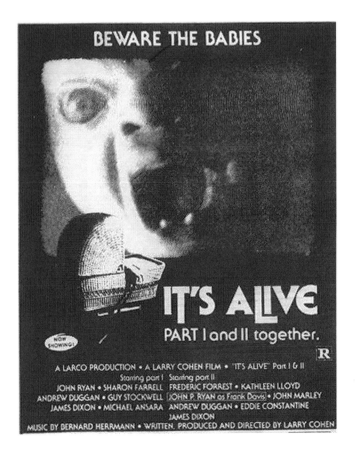

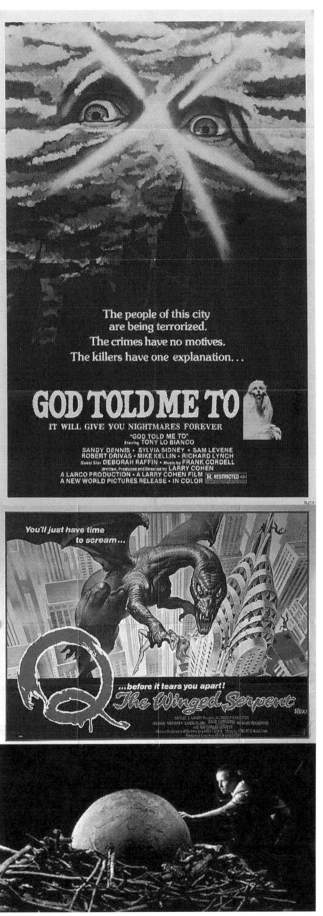

Michael Moriarty discover's the creature's nest in **Q THE WINGED SERPENT**.

THE CHANTING:
RIZAL MANTOVANI'S KUNTILANAK TRILOGY

by Larry Conti

I've always been a huge fan of cinema steeped in haunted lore, mythical creatures, and urban legends. High on my list are the especially wondrous frightfests of Indonesia. There's been quite the horror boom down there in the past decade, and most of the titles are luckily available on DVD with rather good English subtitles. While there's quite a lot of bottom-feeding drivel to be found in recent years (need I mention the 2012 turdtastic **MR. BEAN KESURUPAN DEPE***? Yes, a pocong [hopping corpse] flick involving a Mr. Bean wannabe), the trash pile is balanced by a few clever creature features that have made their way to the surface.*

With such a vast variety of creepy capers to choose from, I think it's quite safe to say that the top of the heap belongs to Rizal Mantovani's **KUNTILANAK** *trilogy. The English title given to it is* **THE CHANTING**, *and while not by any means a direct translation, it is quite fitting for this fantastic series.*

What the heck is a kuntilanak *anyway? Let's start with a basic definition. I also found a handy reference tome, aptly titled,* The Malaysian Book of the Undead, *by Danny Lim. (Quite a helpful resource, with many detailed illustrations to boot!)*

Kuntilanak: *A vampiric ghost in Malay and Indonesian mythology, also known as the* Pontianak *in some parts. They are said to be the spirits of women who died while pregnant, or during childbirth. The word* pontianak *is reportedly a corruption of the Malay* perempuan mati beranak, *or "woman who died in childbirth". Another theory is that the word is a combination of* puan *(woman) +* mati *(die) +* anak *(child). The term* matianak *means "death of a child". The creature usually announces its presence through shrill cries. If the cry is soft, it means that the she is close, and if loud, then it must be far in the distance. A* kuntilanak *kills its victims by digging into the victim's stomach with its sharp fingernails, and voraciously devouring the internal organs.*

KUNTILANAK: THE CHANTING (2006)
"Her laugh may be the last thing you will hear!"

After the sudden death of her mother, Samantha (Julie Estelle) is haunted nightly by mysterious dreams she cannot fully understand. She distances herself from her abusive stepfather by moving into a large boarding house farther from the big city, presumably Northern Jakarta. Upon finding the place, she marvels at the ancient tree in the yard, fenced in with ornately-decorated mosaic tiles, oddly familiar to her.

Landlord Yanti explains the house was once the Mangkoedjiwo Batik factory, mysteriously burned decades ago, killing many of the laborers. The owner now rents rooms to promising college students. With amazingly affordable rates, there has to be a catch. Well, there is one rule: Never, never ever, enter second floor for any reason. Sounds easy enough, right?

A creepy ornate mirror hangs over the vanity in her new room, with a fierce creature sculpted at its top. Sam mentions the ancient tree, and Yanti chalks it up to silly superstition. She explains that a female banshee, the *kuntilanak*, resides in the tree, and can only be summoned by a chant, and only by a person that has a special connection to the spiritual world. Turns out Sam is just that special girl, and things are about to get interesting.

The tenants are a mixed bunch, mostly throwaway stereotypes: pretty rich bitch, humble poor lass, hunky horndog jerkface, lovelorn nerd, etc. So, it's no surprise that they start dying in horrific ways, seemingly caused by accidents. There's the interesting decapitation by ceiling fan, some possessed furniture, and necks twisted round like Twizzlers.

Sam has inadvertently been summoning the *kuntialank* for revenge. Her inner power is strengthened when she's emotionally charged. After a fight with another girl, she enters a trancelike state and begins humming eerily and chanting, the girl's nose starts to bleed, and after a few minutes of panic, she's as good as dead. Afterwards, Sam vomits a handful of maggots and creepy crawlies…rinse and repeat throughout the flick.

The *kuntilanak* itself is quite the amazing creature. The makeup effects are quite spectacular. A lithe female phantom, draped in a white shroud, long web-like tresses float around her like wisps of smoke, razor sharp talons adorning her bony limbs, and sporting a pair of highly un-manicured cloven hooves. Cackling wildly and grimacing for the camera, she's quite the dastardly diva. The ornate mirror in Sam's room acts as a portal for her to move throughout the mansion, and also trap her in the otherworldly dimension.

Sam's boyfriend, Agung, seems a bit worried with his girl surrounded by these bizarre deaths—and her recurring dreams—and wants to help. They've been apart for some time, but he truly loves her and wants to see what he can do to protect her. He begins researching the local legends and finds that the Mangkoedjiwo family was actually a powerful black magic sect. Disapproved by the locals, they burned it to the ground, and the cultists disappeared.

The Mangkoedjiwo legacy has kept the *kuntilanak* under control for years, and it is now Sam's turn to take her seat as a member of the cult, and use the *kuntilanak* for their scheming evil purposes. She can either choose to follow her dark destiny with them, or rebel and face the wrath of the cult, and the creature itself. I'll leave the thrilling ending under wraps. I then prayed for something that rarely ever happens in Indonesian horror cinema…a sequel. My prayers were swiftly answered a few months later.

KUNTILANAK 2: THE ENCHANTMENT (2007)
"Everyone has a dark side."

Sam has since moved from the mansion, and is apparently on the run from the cult members. Agung is desperately trying to find her before they do, and before the dark power claims her forever. From the credits onward, this is definitely a darker film, which picks up almost exactly where we last left off. Its haunting atmosphere immediately pulls you in, and we hope for Sam's return to the light.

She rents a room from a distant family member, and tries to start life anew. Despite trying to surround herself with the new family she's made for herself, she cannot fully control her rage and continues to summon the *kunti-*

lanak to wreak vengeance on all those that wrong her, no matter how small the grudge. Assaulted by a smarmy taxi driver, (cue chanting) he's swiftly decapitated by the vehicle's possessed window, his noggin plummets to the rain-soaked street as rodents fight over his squishy eyeballs. Another girl meets an untimely demise just for urging Agung to help bring Sam back into the light. She's lost herself completely, and might not be the Sam we're hoping she is.

The Mangkoedjiwo are hot on her trail, and will stop at nothing to regain Sam. Without her, they are powerless and cannot use the *kuntilanak* for their evil schemes. They con unsuspecting clients out of their fortunes, and our monstress slays them mercilessly on command, as soon as their funds are suckled dry. By increasing their wealth, the cult's power grows; these greedy denizens of the dark side plan on ruling the world—with Samantha's unique powers, of course. Without her, they cannot control the demoness, and it seems Sam's mother was the last one with that role. We delve deeper in the backstory here, but the real truth lies in the shadows for now.

Sam's battle for control of her own soul continues. With Agung's help she continues to carry on, letting the light shine. Her inner struggle really is the focus of this film, and her dark journey up from the depths of Hell. We are told that the answers will be found in the mysterious Ujung Sedo, the birthplace of the *kuntilanak*.

KUNTILANAK 3: FINALE (2008)
"Every story has an ending."

We follow a group of friends searching for a couple that has strayed during a jungle expedition. Along the way, they come across Sam, hiking all alone, up the mountains, on her own personal journey. She seeks the village of Ujung Sedo, where she's been told she'd find the answers to her destiny. It seems her grandmother is the powerful sorceress that originally bonded herself with the titular creature. But, things may not be as cut and dry as they seem. The group offers their help as they are also going the same direction, and an uneasy bond begins to form amongst them all. Sam doesn't reveal her true intentions to the group; it's something she keeps deep down, afraid to accidentally summon the demoness once again. She's learned how to control her urges, and is ready to finally rid herself of her dark destiny once and for all.

In this film, the *kuntilanak* and spirits are stronger and able to act on their own; being close to the mystic village of Ujung Sedo they've gained power. There are quite a few jump-out-of-your-seat scares, and some inventive death sequences on display. What's also great is that you learn more about the *kuntilanak* mythos, as well.

As they traverse the dense jungle, they come across a dense fog, and an overgrown area that leads them to a deep cavern. It's refreshing to see they've added the adventure bit to this flick—really keeps the viewer entertained. The creature quotient has been significantly amped up a few notches, as well, with many devious denizens coming out of the woodwork. It's always nice to see good old-fashioned monster makeup effects, as we rely heavily on CGI these days.

As they cross over into the unknown, they reach an abandoned village. During the night a baby's cries are heard, which freaks them out completely. Upon investigating, they find a large buffalo carcass in the center of the village. The cries are coming from within the stomach of the putrefying animal! After a few slices of a machete, a humanoid infant crawls quickly from the innards and into their arms. I'll leave the rest of that happy scene to your imagination.

Samantha knows that she must confront her grandmother in order to reverse the curse placed upon her. When finally reaching the village of Ujung Sedo, Sam comes face to face with a large statue of the deity sculpted on the original mansion's mirror. An eerie thatched hut rests on stilts not far behind, and a low cackling can be heard from within. Why has her grandmother been hidden here all this time? What are her ties to the Mangkoedjiwo cult? Can she actually end this dark destiny? I will not give you those answers here, but I assure you, you will be enthralled with the outcome…and perhaps a bit sad, as there won't be another addition to this wonderful series.

Julie Estelle is a great choice for the role of Samantha. Whether it's her natural onscreen talent, her exotic Eurasian beauty, or her beautiful chanting, I'll watch anything she's in. I've scoured the 'net to locate as many of her films I could find (mostly un-subtitled, unfortunately); she's a true joy to watch. Available easily stateside is **MACABRE** (2009), which was truly an endurance test—even for avid gore hounds—and I loved every sloppy supernatural second of it. It's got organ-smuggling, black magic rites, and some sickly inventive kills; it's completely depraved. She has also starred in the intense coming-of-age drama, **SELAMANYA** (*"Forever"*, 2007), tackling such real-world issues as depression, suicide, and drug abuse.

You'll be able to track these films down on import DVD with a little digging. All three of these come complete with a truckload of extra features, and subtitled in grammatically correct English, to boot. Indonesian and Malay DVDs seem to go out-of-print rather quickly, but I'm sure you'll do just fine if you're an avid video archaeologist like myself. Good luck!

2006-2008, INDONESIA. DIRECTOR: RIZAL MANTOVANI

COMPOSITION BOOK
The Search for Weng Weng: Shooting Diary

100 Sheets (200 Pages)
9¾" x 7½" Inch

T. S. Inc **Andrew Leavold**
Made in China

Eddie Romero's Wake

*In short: I started a documentary on Weng Weng, the two-foot-nine James Bond of the Philippines, on my first Manila trip in 2006. I sold the project to a Brisbane producer who then pitched it to Australian TV channel ABC, only to find myself demoted to Associate Producer while **NOT QUITE HOLLYWOOD**'s Mark Hartley retooled the idea into **MACHETE MAIDENS UNLEASHED**, a much broader history of Americans making B-films in the Philippines. Last December I was finally handed back the rights and set out to make **THE SEARCH FOR WENG WENG** the way I originally envisaged. One successful Kickstarter campaign later, my co-writer and co-producer Daniel Palisa and I arrived back in Manila with a two-hour rough cut of the old footage, a budget to reshoot crucial interviews and film new material in HD, and after seven years in the wilderness, a sense of things finally coming full circle.*

From all reports the red light district in Makati—essentially the business precinct of the 16-city Metro Manila sprawl—is an insipid imitation of neighboring Ermita's glory-hole days in the Seventies and Eighties. Still, to a dedicated student of human weirdness, P. Burgos Street is a playground—equal bursts of baffling, depressing, sordid, an assault on the senses but never, *never* uninteresting.

It takes less than three minutes to walk the gauntlet of its pimps, hustlers, transvestites, bird whistle and fake Viagra salesmen, clustered in and around the thirty-plus girlie bars, some themed (the post-apocalypse public toilet chic of The Bronx is a favorite), some with impossible-to-resist monikers like "Tickles", "Bottoms" and "Dimples". To the casual observer's surprise there are no strippers—nudity is prohibited in most parts of Metro Manila—and sex tourists instead pay a "bar fine" to the resident Mama-San to take the girls to their own rooms, or to one of the four-hour sex hotels. At one end of Burgos is Makati Avenue and The Wild West, site of Makati's original go-go bar opened in '77 by English expat, future Sultan of Sleaze and bad guy in **THE ONE-ARMED EXECUTIONER** (1983), Nigel Hogge; at the other end is foxy boxing and midget oil wrestling at Ringside, and comfortably nestled in a side street off Makati Avenue is our hotel, a quiet, disinfected oasis of sanity amidst the piss-smell, child beggars and miscellaneous squalor.

That many of our friends and regular drinking holes live within throwing distance is perhaps no coincidence, but it's comforting to know there's an escape hatch when needed, even if it's guarded by a pack of rats ten-deep that patrol Neptune Street after dark. We're safe in their tiny, ratty hands.

First twenty-four hours in Manila meant not one but two wakes in Quezon City, 30 to 60 minutes by cab from Makati. The great Eddie Romero and Dani's friend Dante Perez both passed away two days before we arrived; Saturday evening was the last night of the Philippines' mammoth three-day funeral affairs. As National Artist, Eddie Romero—the director of such ghoulish delights as **BEAST OF BLOOD** (1971) and **MAD DOCTOR OF BLOOD ISLAND** (1968)—was entitled to full "necrological services" at the CCP the next morning; the wake was at the Mount Carmel Catholic Church close to his home.

I was even quoted in the Daily Inquirer about my memories of Eddie:

Australian filmmaker Andrew Leavold interviewed Romero for a documentary on diminutive action star Weng Weng and Filipino B-movies in 2006 and 2008. Leavold remembered Romero's "dry humor, self-deprecating wit, generosity [and] fearless command of the cinematic language." They would talk for hours, he said. "He humored me about his 'trashy' B-movies, which he knew I adored. In his home, I had the best coffee, imported from South America." Cirio Santiago, Bobby Suarez and Romero were the three big names in Filipino B-movies, Leavold said. "Now, they're all gone. It's truly the end of an era."

It was with a heavy heart that I walked into the crowded chapel lined with scores of flower garlands and saw Eddie's face through the glass under the open coffin lid. I wasn't wrong about his passing representing the end of an era, and although I never became as close to him as Bobby Suarez, I would miss the old gentleman and his thick, black Columbian brew.

Dante Perez, on the other hand, was no National Artist. He was an artist, a punk kid in his fifties, musician, cartoonist, actor, production designer for Lav Diaz, provocateur. He was in a much more modest chapel filled with drunken poets and the indie film scene. One guy stood in front of the coffin drunkenly reciting a Tagalog ballad; the well-wishers egged him on to sing another. Talk about polar opposites. Man, I needed a drink.

One ritual etched in rock each Manila trip is an all-night rum and karaoke effort at filmmaker Richard Somes' house in Cubao. Like a caveman covered in tribal tatts, Somes cooks up a big batch o' meat and lays on a table of Tanduay rum bottles; Dani, I and whoever we can rope in show up with two shopping bags' full of $2 rum and mixer. We drink and swap war stories. Around 2 a.m. the karaoke machine gets fired up and Joe Cocker battles it out with Jon Bon Jovi. The neighbors are too scared of Somes and his sentry dog to complain.

Erik Matti had just returned from Cannes, riding on the successful overseas sales of **ON THE JOB**, his tale of convicted hitmen released from prison to ply their deadly trade. Arriving at 3am, you could tell he was chieftain (Somes still works for Erik as production designer, nurtured as a director under his guidance) and the younger filmmakers hung on his every word. Somes himself commands great respect from his crew, and has evolved into one of the Philippines' most savage talents. Directing since 2008's brilliant *aswang* (Filipino vampire-like creature) film **YANG-GAW**, last year saw Somes follow up a Filipino-American War epic **SUPREMO** (2012) with the supremely confident **MARIPOSA** (2012), a dark and blood-caked fairytale of a young girl looking for her sister's killers amidst Manila's back-alley surgeries and illegal animal parts restaurants. Also present were the more aggressively experimental Ato Bautista, fresh from the set of his latest digital feature; director Jim Libiran (**TRIBU**, 2007), in **MARIPOSA** as a perverted morgue attendant; and Somes' extended clan of family and production staff.

Fellow horror specialist Rico Ilarde is another regular at Somes' house, a 20-year-plus genre veteran whose latest, **PRIDYIDER** (a.k.a. **FRIDGE**, 2012)—a reimagining of an Ishmael Bernal segment from the original in the *Shake Rattle and Roll* franchise about a fridge possessed by a serial killer—was heading with Somes in late July to PiFan in South Korea, where they're dedicating the main program to the Philippines.

Something is definitely happening in genre circles. The Philippines, it seems, is waking from a twenty-year slumber while remembering its glory days of Cirio Santiago and Lino Brocka, and is lurching into a two-pronged attack on the international market via its "indie" films—the buzzword since the early 2000s for artsy and no-budget (and at one time a by-word for gay erotica)—and via its horror and hyper-violent actioners. Genre is no longer a dirty word, and guys like Somes, Matti and Ilarde, along with **THE ROAD**'s (2011) Yam Laranas and others, are ready to unleash their dangerous and unseen-'til-now visions on the rest of the world.

At 9 a.m. in our hotel's eatery on the first day of shooting, Dani and I assembled our crack film unit: Kristine "Kints" Kintana, production manager and line producer usually alternating between Khavn de la Cruz and elephantine six-hour Lav Diaz projects; DOP extraordinaire Jordan Arabejo, fizzing with excitement over the rented Canon C300, a magnificent beast of an HD camera, and an outstanding deal from post-production studio Outpost which included lapel mikes, tripod, and a caretaker doubling as camera assistant, all thrown in.

One of the most recognizable faces in Filipino B-films is Henry Strzalkowski. Stocky, swarthy, and usually with beard or moustache, born to a Polish father and Filipina mother, the American-sounding Henry was originally a stage actor who did extras duties on **APOCALYPSE NOW** (1979) and **THE BOYS IN COMPANY C** (1978), and was subsequently drafted into General Cirio Santiago's film platoon, and was also in the inner circle of weed-loving white goons known as the "Pigs in Space". Since the decline in film production in the Philippines he does occasional voice-overs and acting jobs—last year in **OPERATION ROGUE** (2013) for Roger Corman, and as the Nazi Admiral in a stage version of *The Sound Of Music*—and has managed Makati's H & J Bar on and off for the last ten years, until it moved around the corner a few months ago to its new location near P. Burgos.

Inside the new H & J we framed Henry against the pool table and bar, and between recollections from his days with Cirio and co, recorded his Weng Weng story, how he sauntered into a girlie bar in Ermita in the early Eighties and did a double take ("Who let in

Dani and Andrew at Hobbit House

the six year old?") at the diminutive figure smoking and drinking, and with a Guest Relations Officer under each arm. "Oh…that's the James Bond guy!"

We'd been optimistic about the weather despite bleak reports of a typhoon sitting south of Manila in the Bicol region, and had packed up the camera gear just in time to watch the heavens dump their bedpans for several hours onto Metro Manila. All we could muster was a dry spot opposite H & J at the faux-Mexican cantina, order beer and street tacos, and watch Facebook reports of endemic flooding in Quezon City drown our next two interviews like unwanted kittens. Typhoon season in the Philippines lasts for around eight months, and the remainder of our **SEARCH FOR WENG WENG** shoot seemed poised precariously in the lap of the Film Gods.

Luckily for us the torrential downpours were intermittent, and even Manila gridlock couldn't prevent us from reaching Blumentritt Extension, the main vein leading to Sampaloc in old Manila via the President's Malacanang Palace and through the neighboring Pandacan, where Weng Weng's producers once lived. The cab pulled up outside a house atop a karaoke bar which our interview subject rents out to his sister-in-law. Inside, various female relatives lounged around the bar as hostesses to the local drinkers honking Bon Jovi "tunes" into microphones. Someone once described the sound of Manila as chickens, car horns and off-key karaoke singing, and on Blumentritt, they were bang on the money.

Dante "Boy" Pangilinan—60, jockey height, polite—guided us past the plastic tables to a private karaoke dungeon in the back. Inside the concrete walls, painted red over pockmarks of decay, were lit by a harsh fluro strip, giving skin a garish body-under-the-ice-blue tinge. I turned to Jordan, mindful of the morose *thump-thump* of Beyonce from the karaoke machine in the main bar. "Should we head upstairs?" "No way, man," Jordan foamed as he fired up the C300. "This is going to be some of my best work ever!"

I met Dante last year via the Film Academy. The old goons of the FAP were having brandies and goat soup around the corner, and Dante happened to see Weng's face on my business card. "I was Weng Weng's first director," he announced gravely.

"**CHOP SUEY MET BIG TIME PAPA**? Dante 'Boy' Pangilinan?" We embraced like lost brothers.

One of the major issues we faced when piecing together **THE SEARCH FOR WENG WENG** is the absence of Cora Caballes, Weng Weng's producer for Liliw Films and, along with her late ex-husband Peter, adoptive parent figures. I spoke to her twice on the phone before; for reasons known only to her, she stopped answering my messages.

Details on the Caballes have been sketchy to non-existent. Incredibly, Cora is Dante's godmother, following his director/screenwriter father Johnny Pangilinan's long association with the Caballes all the way back to their first film company, Jo-Ann Productions, in the late '60s. Via his father's relentless schedule, Dante grew up on film sets, either as a child actor (he starred opposite Mickey Rooney in 1966's **AMBUSH BAY**!) or as Assistant Director.

Dante's first film as director was **SILA…SA BAWA'T BANGKETA (THEY…ON EVERY SIDEWALK**, 1976) featuring a fourth-billed Weng Weng as a jeepney barker collecting fares for driver Rez Cortez. The pair runs afoul of the crime syndicate boss, played by Ramon "Boy" Bagatsing Jr, who also has eyes for Rez's rich-girl sweetheart (Ingrid

Somes House Party

Salas). Weng ends up a police informer posing as one of the syndicate's child drug couriers. Unseen since its brief theatrical run, even Dante has trouble remembering the plot, but it made money, and its two-foot nine star was noticed.

The same applies to **CHOP SUEY MET BIG TIME PAPA** (1978), Weng's first lead as secret agent "Big Time Papa", roping in hapless martial arts instructor Ramon Zamora (reprising his role from the 1975 Bobby Suarez-produced **THEY CALL HIM CHOP SUEY**) to bring down an American crime lord (Mike Cohen, a.k.a. Professor Von Kohler in 1981's **FOR YOUR HEIGHT ONLY**) and his syndicate. Along with **SILA...**, the film is currently MIA.

What Dante did reveal in the hour-long interview are the missing pieces in the Peter and Cora Caballes saga: how they entered movies, their relationship with Weng Weng, their connections at the Palace, and how Weng Weng became a real-life secret agent. "I can feel Weng Weng is extraordinary people," he told me. "Why? Because he has touches of luck—lucky guy. Like in my part, when I directed him, the luck comes through, force to me. God's will. I'm a Catholic, but still believe that if you believe in God, I feel Weng Weng is special child or guy that comes to me and gave me a bigger plate, a bigger luck, and even [made me] a bigger person."

There were rumors of an even earlier Weng Weng film, which Dante made great pains to dispel. "The first film participated by Weng Weng is **SILA...** That's when they met Weng Weng...and that begins their adoption to the kid Weng Weng. And then they made Weng Weng as an actor during that day, in my film. That's the first time Weng Weng appeared in a film." So he never appeared as an extra before in any films? "No, not yet."

Three days in the newspaper archives proved Dante wrong. A newspaper ad from March 1976 proves his first *credited* role is an even earlier Liliw production via Prima Productions, **SILANG MATATAPANG (THEY THE BRAVE ONES)**, an action film starring George Estregan, Dante Varona (also in the original Agent 00) and Sila's Ramon "Boy" Bagatsing Jr released a full nine months before **SILA...** It also confirms Weng Weng's uncredited presence in **SILAKBO**, a Prima production from October 1975.

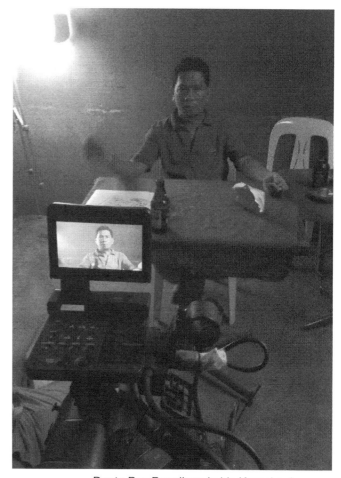
Dante Boy Pangiinan in his Karaoke dungeon

Eddie and Family watching **FOR YOUR HEIGHT ONLY**

For a serious Wengologist, **SILANG MATATAPANG** represents film number thirteen, with possibly more yet to discover.

One major stumbling block during the entire seven-year project has been access to materials. Most TV shows before 1986 went up in flames—literally!—as the tanks rumbled through the pro- and anti-government stations during the EDSA Revolution. In the media library of Imelda's grand Cultural Center of the Philippines (CCP), however, I struck gold: a 1982 magazine interview with Weng Weng, Peter and Cora Caballes, published just after their phenomenal success with **FOR YOUR HEIGHT ONLY** at the Manila International Film Festival. Those details unknown to Dante were all there in black and white, including some profound revelations about Weng's birth and religious beliefs (was he in fact the Child Christ, Santo Nino, as everyone believed, including Weng? Wait for the final cut for these beauties!) and life at the Caballes' mansion.

Six years ago I did the hours-long drive to **FOR YOUR HEIGHT ONLY** director Eddie Nicart's house in Taytay, the Western part of Rizal province bordering Metro Manila. "When you get to Taytay, just ask for me," were his instructions. "Everyone knows who I am."

And they know him for a good reason. As Barangay Captain for ten years, Eddie held an exalted position akin to Village Chieftain in the smallest division of government. At the time of our 2007 visit Eddie had only just stood down as Captain, but was monitoring the upcoming Barangay elections. Across the road from his home in his bamboo recreation room, the walls were lined with Barangay paraphernalia, not to mention countless trophies for basketball, movie props, Betamax tapes, framed photos with co-stars Fernando Poe Jr. and former President Joseph Estrada, and what was obviously an object of immense pride: a FAMAS Stuntman of the Year award for 1988.

Eddie started as a stuntman in the early '60s, as part of the celebrated SOS Daredevils. By the late 'Sixties he was a character actor making a name for himself in films such as **IMPASSE** (1969). After Burt Reynolds chases him from a cockfight to a cathouse, Eddie makes a spectacular leap from a first-floor window onto a moving jeepney. Burt subsequently declared Filipino stuntmen the greatest he'd ever seen. Throughout the 'Seventies Eddie worked on hundreds of action films, as stuntman, actor, fight instructor, assistant director (including Weng Weng's first lead, **CHOP SUEY MET BIG TIME PAPA**), or cowboy superstar Lito Lapid's personal trainer. Via Boy Pangilinan, Eddie was given the director's chair for the first time on Weng Weng's next feature, **AGENT OO** (1981), then Weng's four final films **FOR YOUR HEIGHT ONLY** (1981), **D'WILD WILD WENG, THE IMPOSSIBLE KID** and **THE CUTE THE SEXY AND THE TINY** (all 1982). As the man who trained Weng Weng to become a stuntman, and who helmed the most successful of Weng's films, Eddie is as close as you can get to Weng's forgotten tale.

This trip, the first person we asked past his Barangay's sign pointed to the next left turn. At the end of the street was the house and recreation hut, a little worse off than six years ago—a typhoon had ripped through the second floor, and his few remaining souvenirs from fifty years of film sets line the downstairs' walls. I walked in, gave his wife Eda a huge hug, and then heard, "Andrew!" I turned to see Eddie seated under a sheet getting his hair cut. Greyer, more gaunt (we later heard he'd just left hospital) but in high spirits, Eddie happily sat down for Interview Number Two, this time in Tagalog, giving his faltering English a rest as he recounted his life with FPJ, Lito Lapid, the SOS Daredevils, and a two-foot-nine karate-kicking dynamo named Weng Weng.

We then cranked up the laptop and watched **FOR YOUR HEIGHT ONLY** from start to finish while I took notes ("Eddie, this bit is pure *genius*!"). Deconstructing your favorite film with its director is a surreal experience, particularly with his family gathered around, clearly proud and entertained by their paterfamilias' work. His eldest son would interrupt every so often: "See when Weng takes off wearing his jetpack? I was standing behind the camera at that moment, aged two!" Eddie shared stories on the how, where and with whom his five-person crew completed a manic fifteen-day shoot, how he stage-managed Weng Weng's incredible stunts, and how a camera-hogging Peter Caballes ended up as one of Agent X-44's island task force. I've lost track of how many times I've seen the movie (seventy? eighty?) and I can honestly say I watched with fresh eyes.

For our most important interview we were forced to hire a driver; taxis refuse to take passengers anywhere inside Pasay City, as "Pasay" is often outsiders' code for "meth", and along any of its backstreets, drivers have been shot in the head for their meager bankrolls.

Malibay is one of the many barangays of Pasay, perched on the Eastern edge of the EDSA superhighway. The streets become narrower until you're on C. Jose Street, shoehorning jeepney and tricycles between its one- and two-

Hobbit House group shot

story dwellings, with barely room for two rows of traffic to pass each other. Looking for familiar landmarks, I'd forgotten the de la Cruz residence nests under a two-story building containing a video store and funeral parlor. Weng Weng's only surviving sibling, Cecilio (or Celing) dela Cruz, and his family live in a simple single-story cinderblock structure—one cooking and sleeping area, one small lounge next to the steps, and one narrow ablutions room.

When I first met Weng's remaining family six years ago, Celing drove a jeepney for a living, and his wife Editha operated a sari-sari store from the streetfront of their tiny yard. Nowadays Celing can no longer drive due to complications from diabetes, and lack of funds closed the store years ago. Thanks to the Kickstarter funds I was able to give the family the peso equivalent of $500 US for use of Weng Weng's image (they are the Estate of Ernesto de la Cruz after all) and promised them another $500; the amount was spent immediately on Celing's medicines and school books for their grandkids.

For our first interview I had few details of Weng's life with which to frame my questions, so I felt like I was flailing around in the dark. This time I knew exactly which facts I needed to nail once and for all, and so Kints and I were relentless in our pursuit of the minutiae of Weng Weng's short life. What was the palm-leaf roofed house like? What was his life like as a child? When did Weng Weng start karate? How did he meet his "adoptive parents", Peter and Cora? What happened when he stopped making films, and how did he react?

Celing's account of Weng Weng's final days between the first stroke which paralyzed half his body and the second stroke which killed him are devastating, to say the least.

Celing and Editha then dug out family photos in a recently-discovered album, long thought destroyed in typhoons, along with the rest of their mementos: of Rita de la Cruz, Celing and Weng Weng's mother, in the Baclaran neighborhood; a teenaged Weng Weng the same size as his infant nephews; and a haunting photo from the post-film wilderness years of a fatter and balder Weng sitting in his kitchen wearing oversized eyeglasses. It could be the last ever photo of Ernesto de la Cruz, a.k.a. "Estong of Baclaran", a.k.a. Weng Weng.

And with that, we walked the $50,000 camera through the crowded C. Jose Street and into a passing jeepney.

I've just finished editing the translated text of the interview, along with Eddie's, Boy Pangilinan's, and the rest of the footage from this and past Manila shoots. I'm proud to say our little film team has done Weng's story justice—equal parts bizarre, informative and heartbreaking. Ladies and gentlemen: we finally have a movie.

Dwarves and midgets are not just a staple of Filipino B-films. There's something otherworldly recognized in them, extending far beyond their God-given

Jordan captures Weng childhood photos

ability to mix a lethal Weng Weng cocktail at Hobbit House, a Tolkien-themed bar and live venue. Opened in the midst of Ermita's red light district in 1973 by former Peace Corps volunteer Jim Turner, Hobbit House has been a staple tourist destination offering folk music, decent food, and the world's smallest waiters.

They're not just waiters: the Hobbits have also starred in Cirio Santiago's post-apocalypse flicks, TV commercials, soap operas, and as Christmas elves every festive season. Even their former bouncer Goliath is the recognizable face of Mr. Giant in **FOR YOUR HEIGHT ONLY**. Forty years on, Hobbit House endures as a magical place outside of time, an oasis in a desert of Political Correctness, as well as a one-stop shop for all your Little Guy needs.

Pidoy has worked at Hobbit House since the 'Seventies and now manages the place, and he agreed to us filming shots of the Little Guys serving on the quiet Sunday night. Checking the HD footage, there is a fantastic continuous tracking shot of Dani and I surrounded by welcoming Hobbit waiters before walking into the bar and taking a seat near the stage. A mirror shot is of the waiters waving goodbye as the camera wanders backwards onto the street; on the right you'll see the Lord of the Shire, Jim Turner himself, quietly drinking alone at a table.

The National Shrine of Our Mother of Perpetual Help, a Redemptorist Church on Manila Bay in the Pasay City district of Baclaran, is only ten minutes' drive from the airport, and within walking distance to Weng Weng's family home. It was here in the late 'Fifties, as the present building was being constructed around her, that Weng's mother Rita would crave the Shrine's image of Mary and baby Jesus. So Baclaran myth goes, those children would not survive, as they were destined to join Mama Mary in Heaven. From age seven onwards, Weng Weng was dressed as the dark-skinned child Jesus—Santo Nino, or "Little Saint"—in the Baclaran Church's religious plays and yearly festivals.

Above: Henry Strzalkowski at H and J
Below: Celing and Editha

Dani and Andrew with Cecille Baun

The Church is an imposing structure at the end of the long walkway from Roxas Boulevard. A smaller building to its right is filled with metal frames for holding lit candles, religious statues, and a tiled version of Our Mother's image. The Church remains open 24 hours every day as a sanctuary for Pasay City's poorest of the poor.

Even on a morning Friday the church was teeming with parishioners, and plain clothes security guards could be seen everywhere whispering into their radios. Nevertheless, Jordan decided to steal a few shots of the devout lighting candles in front of a brightly-painted crucifix. From the other side of the candles I watched helplessly as a Church Goon the size of a Samoan bouncer in a floral shirt tapped Jordan on shoulder. "Shit!" I muttered under my breath. "There goes the footage…"

Church Goon simply asked, "Why don't you ask permission to shoot in the office over there?"

After a fifteen-minute wait a kindly old Church Mouse gave us the thumbs up.

Me: "We have ten minutes."

Jordan: "To pack up and get the hell out?"

Me: "No, to film!"

In all seriousness, I've never seen a DOP work in such a manic whirl. We filmed the shrine, the lighting of candles, the devout laying hands on statues and on the glass cover over the Santo Nino, all within the Church Mouse's allotted timeframe. And the footage will look fantastic in the finished cut—the sense of time and place is overwhelming; the very same temporal point where Weng Weng's mother prayed, no doubt for a miracle to befall her family and her unborn son.

Always planned as the final sequence was a scene bringing together as many of the actors, filmmakers and friends I'd collected over the seven years of Manila trips, and filming them watching a rough cut of **THE SEARCH FOR WENG WENG**. It's a mirror image of my 2006 appearance at Cinemanila Film Festival appearance where I screened clips of **FOR YOUR HEIGHT ONLY**, and shot the crowd chanting "We love Weng Weng!"

Upstairs at H & J was a perfect makeshift cinema: a data projector aimed at a screen in the corner, and seating for around sixty. H & J was also Henry's bar and our watering hole, and so has infinitely more meaning than a soulless cineplex.

At 7 our guests began to arrive: the One Armed Executioner himself, Franco Guerrero, and his nemesis in the film, Nigel Hogge; Henry, his cohort Don Gordon Bell, photographer John Silao, Rico Ilarde and Richard Somes, actress Althea Vega and filmmaker NP Picadizo, singer/poet Lourd de Veyra, Aussie embassy insider Sam Chittick; plus the family members of good friends no longer with us—Bobby Suarez's son Richard, Nick Nicholson's daughter Wanda, and Jo Mari Avellana's wife, daughters and granddaughters.

We had also organized for Nacy, our Pasay driver, to pick up Celing, Editha and their grandkids. They hardly ever go out, Editha told me as they tucked into fried chicken and ice cream.

At 8 p.m. I introduced the two-hour "**ROUGH AS WENG'S GUTS**" cut, pieced together for this screening of mostly 2006-08 footage. Dani and I estimate well over an hour of this version are destined for the Recycle Bin, and the old and new stuff combined will make a comfortable ninety-minute Final Cut. Still, even in its primitive rough-sketch form, the humanity of Weng Weng came through the mawkishness; Jordan filmed those in the film in the reflected light from H & J's screen, paying close attention to Celing's reactions as he watched his brother's legacy unfold.

My voiceover on the **ROUGH AS WENG'S GUTS** cut sums up the film's approach and philosophy: "So how do you come to really know someone separated by time, geography, language, culture, and the veil between this world and the next? You can't, but you can immerse yourself in others' memories, and make an educated guess. My guess is that Weng Weng was a remarkable little man who led an extraordinary life. Surviving not only his medical condition but his poor upbringing as well, he managed to become a cultural supernova in his own country, if only for a brief moment, and an international cult sensation. His heartbreaking slide back into illness, abject poverty and obscurity is overshadowed by his astounding moment in the sun; from the slums of Manila to the President's Palace and beaches of Cannes, then back to the slums. In a country of over eighty million people, holding your head above the crowd would seem an impossible task, and yet two-foot-nine Weng Weng's stage was the world. In spite of the absurd image of a karate-kicking James Bond, his humanity shone through, exuding an innocence which evidently touched everyone in contact with him, and a humility which humbled your narrator, at the very least, to seek out his truth against seemingly impossible odds. Even if no-one asked before or had willfully chosen to forget, his story, along with everyone else's in the film, can finally be told, hopefully never to be forgotten, and with his dignity restored. A kind of redemption, or maybe vindication." I'm glad I was able to convey those sentiments to Weng Weng's family in person. And so the seven-year cycle nears its logical end.

Afterwards I addressed Celing and Editha: "Tonight's screening is dedicated to you guys—you are the heart and soul of this documentary, and in fact, without you there would be no documentary." Celing was reportedly still smiling the next day.

Imelda Marcos portrait at Marikina Shoe Museum

THE SEARCH FOR WENG WENG
premieres November, 2013.

Exteriors at Eddie Nicart's house

Revolution is the Opium of the Intellectual
The Mick Travis Trilogy

by Karl Kaefer

Sometimes, I have to step back and ponder the great existential questions of life. Why are we here? Is there a God? Why did the chicken cross the road? And of course, what is the greatest trilogy in all of filmdom? And why do I get such blank stares from people when I answer that question?

*The Mick Travis trilogy consists of three films: **IF…** (1968), **O LUCKY MAN!** (1973) and **BRITANNIA HOSPITAL** (1981). All were directed by Lindsay Anderson and written by David Sherwin. And each film stars Malcolm McDowell as Mick Travis.*

Most trilogies have an arc which develops the main character through three specific plot lines. Look at the original Star Wars *trilogy, or the recently completed* Iron Man *trilogy. Audiences prefer this linear structure, and I certainly understand that. But the Mick Travis trilogy has none of that comfortable, easy accessibility in its nature, and so the films seem to have fallen by the wayside. Hopefully, by the end of this article, you will want to experience them in all their satirical glory.*

Of course, the question has to be asked: What is satire, anyway? Particularly in the context of these three films. When the word "satire" is used to describe a film, more often than not, the word actually means parody. Parody is taking a particular genre and applying pressure to its constructs to point out the inherent humor (and/or stupidity) in the original. **AIRPLANE!** (1980), **YOUNG FRANKENSTEIN** (1974), and **CABIN IN THE WOODS** (2011) are all great examples of parody.

But *true* satire is something completely different…or at least the satire in these specific three films. Here we have a director and screenwriter focusing on the political and social ills of Britain. But instead of using a sledgehammer to drive home their point, the artists involved use a type of magic realism. As you watch these three films, you are aware that you are watching a presentation…a carefully devised construct to highlight their displeasures of living in the plane of existence.

True satire has a philosophy, an overriding viewpoint that the artists want to impose on their audience. And true satire is vicious in its intent, wanting and needing to tip over as many sacrificial lambs as it can find.

The greatest acclaimed satirist in film history is Luis Buñuel (**VIRIDIANA**, 1961; **SIMON OF THE DESERT**, 1965; **BELLE DE JOUR**, 1967; **TRISTANA**, 1970). His attacks on Christianity and Catholicism in particular are unrivalled in their savagery, as are his attacks on the rich. But whereas Buñuel limited himself to a few targets, Lindsay Anderson and David Sherwin attack *everything* in the Mick Travis trilogy. You don't believe me, do you? Well, here's a short list, for starters:

- The upper, middle *and* lower classes
- British Colonialism
- Business
- Religion
- Politics, government and the law
- Idealism
- Medicine and Science
- Good and Evil

I saw **O LUCKY MAN** when I was 16. I was astonished and exhilarated by the experience. Never in my life had I seen a film so fragmented, and yet so concise in its critique of mankind. I then sought out **IF…**, and then waited another six years to finish the trilogy with **BRITANNIA HOSPITAL**. These films are impossible to define, so forgive me for the lack of plot summaries. All I can hope to do is explain my feelings and thoughts of the films from my memory. I will do my best to give reasons why all the films deserve adula-

tion, and how all three films fit into a specific world view.

O cinematic Gods….forgive me my faults, as I attempt the impossible task that is at hand.

Lindsay Anderson and Malcom McDowell on the set of **IF...** (Photos: Jane Bown).

IF...
(1968)

The iconic image of this film is Malcolm McDowell, armed with a machine gun pointed at the audience, and a title card flashes with the word "If..." And I now always connect that image to the tragedies of Columbine and Sandy Hook. Coincidence? Not by a long shot.

Anderson begins his tale an a very realistic manner—Mick Travis (Malcolm McDowell) returns with his two friends at the start of the new semester. He and his crew are tormented by the "Whips", a group of upperclassmen given authority by the headmaster to bully and persecute them. (If you think this sounds a bit like Robert Cormier's novel, *The Chocolate War*, you'd be right—Cormier has acknowledged **IF...**'s influence on his novel).

Another film/graphic novel that was influenced by **IF...** was *V for Vendetta*, with its Guy Fawkes imagery. One of the first lines spoken in reference to Mick Travis is, "It's Guy Fawkes again". This line is not without consequence, as the film aligns itself with the Fawkesian myth, much like *V for Vendetta*.

IF... soon veers off into surrealism. The film switches from color to black and white. Anderson has been quoted as saying this was for budgetary reasons, but I think there's something more subtle about this fluctuation. It simply puts the viewer on guard—we have been made aware we are watching a film. The patina of realism continues to fade as the various characters show their true monstrosity.

Teachers abuse their students in class. A matron wanders naked through the boys shower as she fondles herself and the soap that the boys have used. A headmaster frames Mick Travis and his friends, and canes them in front of the class. And Mick has to thank the headmaster for this punishment, because it's tradition.

Anderson's disdain of these institutional traditions is quite evident. And when the boys find a cache of guns and ammunition, they plan to use them on Founders Day, when their parents are due to visit. It is in these last scenes of planning that the connection to Columbine and Sandy Hook become relevant. The tragedy is inevitable. And it is that inevitability of tragedy—the sense that nothing can stop it—that makes me cringe.

If we as a society do not understand the need for change, and also cling to our sense of tradition, then we will feel the wrath of change when it occurs. If we as a society do not understand the individual and their needs, and cling to normalcy, then that individual will surely rebel.

You would think that Anderson as a filmmaker supports this rebellion, but he does not. Mick Travis is not portrayed as merely a victim. He becomes an angel of vengeance. The look on Travis' face at the final freeze frame is one of insolent anger—not just against his oppressors, but against anyone who gets in his way...even his friends. I suspect that Lindsay Anderson is cackling in his grave, laughing at all of us, saying, "I told you so!"

There is no comfort, no solace to be found...only a sad irony that one must live with.

O LUCKY MAN!
(1973)

O LUCKY MAN begins as a silent film, where we are introduced to a coffee plantation farmer (played by McDowell with an obvious fake moustache) who steals some beans for his family. He is caught and sentenced to have his hands chopped off. A subtitle proclaims, "He Was Unlucky". We then immediately segue to an empty soundstage where a rock group (Alan Price & the Set) begin the title song, whilst Lindsay Anderson is shown scurrying around the stage giving notes to the actors milling about. The lyrics set the tone of the film:

If you have a friend on whom you think you can rely—you are a lucky man.
If you've found the reason to live on and not to die—you are a lucky man.

From the outset of the film, Anderson sets the stage for a modern (circa 1970s) presentation of *A Pilgrim's Promise/Gulliver's Travels*. Like Swift, he and screenwriter David Sherwin take this episodic structure to truly satirize the politics and social mores of the era. And also like Swift, **O LUCKY MAN** is merciless.

Malcolm McDowell absolutely shines in this film as protagonist Mick Travis, and yet, he is not the same Mick Travis as in **IF...** Here, Mick Travis is an optimist, wearing a sincere smile and always wanting approval. This is much different than Mick Travis in the previous film. He wants the capitalist dream of succeeding, and we meet Mick as a novice coffee salesman who is seduced by the female head of the company, and sent off to Northern England to replace a salesman who's gone missing.

From one misadventure to another, we follow Mick as he rises and falls, from strip shows to medical experiments, from prison to true idealism... always smiling...until the end.

O LUCKY MAN is Anderson's magnum opus. The film has an incredible cast (Sir Ralph Richardson, Helen Mirren, Rachel Roberts, Arthur Lowe, Graham Crowden and Mona Washbourne) in multiple roles. By doing this, Anderson accentuates the fact that the film is not realistic. Arthur Lowe actually has a role which is presented in blackface—as a scrupulous African dictator *a la* Idi Amin, and also appears as two other completely different characters. Only Helen Mirren as Patricia, the daughter of industrialist Sir James Burgess (played by Ralph Richardson), portrays one character throughout the film.

Well, that's not completely true—Alan Price is a musician who is touring England, and Mick hooks up with him and Patricia in one of the longer segments of the film—but it is Price's musical contributions, as a Greek chorus commenting on the action, that truly elevate **O LUCKY MAN**.

Price's contribution to the film cannot be understated. The songs are placed at appropriate spots in the film as vital commentary. Whether Price is commenting on the action itself ("Everybody's going through changes"), making attacks on capitalism ("Sell, sell, sell, everything you stand for") or governmental justice ("Next to health is wealth, and only wealth will buy you justice"), Price's lyrics reflect Anderson's politics and beliefs.

Again, if you think that Anderson and Sherwin are one-sided in their critique of British society, you are dead wrong. Once Mick Travis is released from prison after being framed by his upper class employers, he is a true idealist who wants to help the poor and indigent. He even has that smile he had at the beginning of the film. And are the poor grateful for Mick's help? No, they beat him to a pulp.

There might be an argument that Anderson and Sherwin are advocating a Marxist type of philosophy, but I think that's far from the truth. In fact, Anderson is anti-everything. This is not surprising, considering the fact that Lindsay Anderson is reported to say that the epitaph on his tombstone should read, "I'm surrounded by fucking idiots."

At the end of the film, Mick wanders down the street, barely alive, into a film audition for **O LUCKY MAN**. He is picked out of the crowd by the director (Lindsay Anderson, in a cameo) and asked to smile. Mick replies, "What's there to smile about anyway?" The director then slaps him, and after a moment, you see the smile return. But it is no longer innocent—Mick has learned to survive.

The final image of **O LUCKY MAN** is the cast dancing and cavorting on the sound stage to Alan Price's theme song to the film—Mick Travis is a lucky man, for he has found a reason to live on and not to die.

BRITANNIA HOSPITAL
(1982)

Considered by many critics to be the weakest link of the trilogy, **BRITANNIA HOSPITAL** certainly does not live up to the previous two films in the trilogy. But in its defense, it is still a vital film, and provides a very satisfying conclusion to the series.

Anderson and screenwriter Sherwin set their sights on the healthcare system of Britain in pre-Thatcherite England in the early 1980s. Leonard Rossiter plays Vincent Potter, a hospital administrator trying to tiptoe his way through various labor disputes and strikes as the hospital prepares for a visit by the Queen. Here is a decent man (probably the most likeable character in the whole trilogy) struggling against governmental and union interference to get his job done.

We are also reintroduced to Professor Millar (Graham Crowden), who first appeared in **O LUCKY MAN** as the head of a experimental medical facility where Mick Travis almost became a guinea pig. In **BRITANNIA HOSPITAL**, Millar is about to introduce the world to his new medical breakthrough, "Genesis".

Mick Travis reappears, though again in a slightly different form than in the previous two films. Here Mick is a television reporter, trying to find out what actually is going on at the Millar Institute for Scientific Research. Mark Hamill (*Luke Skywalker!*) co-stars as Travis' perpetually stoned technical support staff.

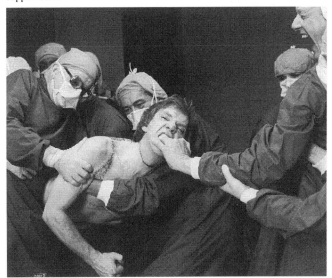

Social criticism with bite: **BRITANNIA HOSPITAL**.

Anderson's disdain of these institutional traditions is quite evident. And when the boys find a cache of guns and ammunition, they plan to use them on Founders Day, when their parents are due to visit.

So there's the set up for the film's plot. But **BRITANNIA HOSPITAL**, like the two previous films, defies plot synopsis because of its episodic nature. Again, I must grab at images that reverberate in my memory…

A dead-but-reanimated Mick Travis lurches about in a pastiche of *Swan Lake*, to the tuneful strains of Alan Price's musical parody of Tchaikovsky's theme. Mark Hamill tokes on a joint the size of New Hampshire. And there is the wonder of actor John Betts in complete drag as Lady Felicity Ramsden.

And of course, there's ample time for Anderson's rage to be shown. Whether it's the kitchen staff who can't cook, or the painters who can't paint, Anderson's view of unions is particularly nasty. But the hospital administrators and the Royal Court gets the same treatment. In fact, **BRITANNIA HOSPITAL** is the most satiric and brutal film in the trilogy. When shown at Cannes, the British delegation walked out in protest. British filmmaker Derek Jarman stated that **BRITANNIA HOSPITAL** would end Lindsay Anderson's career in Britain, and he was right.

Special mention has to be given to Graham Crowden, who portrays Professor Millar. Never have I seen such an unbalanced, mad doctor. Millar makes Victor Frankenstein seem downright sane, and it is Crowden's exuberance at being given such a part which shines throughout the whole subplot. "Genesis" turns out to be a computer powered by a human brain (which ends up to be Mick Travis'), and the final words that are spoken in a broken robotic voice echo through the hallway as several flabbergasted audience members just awkwardly gape at the spectacle before them…

"How like a God…how like a God….how like a God…"

In this repeated phrase, Anderson's contempt shines through—we are not like God; we destroy everything that is good in the world—humankind is a virus. Our government, our health system, and our selfishness are contemptible, and we are all guilty of crimes against humanity.

No wonder the British delegation walked out on **BRITANNIA HOSPITAL** when it was shown at Cannes. Upon returning to London after the harsh reception his film received at Cannes, Lindsay Anderson wrote a letter to Malcolm McDowell, which reads, in part:

"I've been in London about three or four weeks. I'm sure you'll understand when I say it's a dispiriting place to return to. The dark waters have closed over Britannia Hospital."

Conclusion

As I contemplate my thoughts on the Mick Travis trilogy, three specific points have to be made:

Lindsay Anderson and Malcom McDowell on the set of **O LUCKY MAN!**

Mick Travis is Malcolm McDowell's greatest triumph. In three films, he portrays the character in three different ways…and each one has the ring of emotional truth. In fact, in the whole trilogy, there isn't one false note by any of the actors. From the smallest of roles, to the featured players, everyone is exemplary.

Lindsay Anderson is one of the finest directors in film history. Anderson directed only three other feature films: **THIS SPORTING LIFE** (1963), **IN CELEBRATION** (1975) and **THE WHALES OF AUGUST** (1987). He also directed several documentaries and plays, but he only has six feature films, a few British television films, and a mini-series to his credit. And every one of them is worthwhile.

It needs to be mentioned briefly that Lindsay Anderson was celibate. Unlike several of his contemporaries, he was uncomfortable with his homosexuality. Tony Richardson nicknamed him the Virgin Queen. But I think it was that uncomfortableness that drove Lindsay Anderson to be such an angry, disaffected soul. It is those feelings that come through in every fiber of the Mick Travis trilogy, and it is what makes them so very special and dear to my heart.

Finally, as I was researching this article, I came upon a type of filmic haiku that surprised me, even though I have seen each of these films several times. If we take the last images of each film, and put them together…

"If….O lucky man…were but a god."

If we were like a God, what would this world be like? Would it be any different? Or would it be worse?

Certainly, from both Lindsay Anderson and David Sherwin's point of view, it would certainly not be any better than it is now. It would probably be a lot worse. Maybe that's disheartening, but I certainly believe it. In the 45 years since the release of **IF…**, we've had Columbine, Sandy Hook, and several other disasters. **O LUCKY MAN** foretells—at least in spirit—the housing crisis, the widening of the gap between the rich and poor and the governmental preference for the rich and powerful. The satiric plot of **BRITANNIA HOSPITAL** is a clear portent of our health care crisis.

And I can almost hear the wizened voice of Lindsay Anderson, speaking from the grave: "It's all shit. You can't fix it. And you know why? Because you're a bunch of fucking idiots."

As for me, I find that sentiment rather comforting. God bless Lindsay Anderson for giving us these films. They are a legacy to be cherished. Seek them out and be enlightened.

The author would like to acknowledge the following websites that proved invaluable in writing this article:
lindsayandersonfilms.comxa.com, imdb.com
guardian.co.uk/film/w008/sep/19/drama – "Sentenced to a Lifetime of Stress" by John Harris
efilmcritic.com/review.php?movie=2251 – **O LUCKY MAN** review by John Linton Roberson
dvdbeaver.com/film/articles/0_lucky_man.htm – **O LUCKY MAN** review by Peter Hoskin

Also, all lyrics ©1972 by Warner/Tamerlane Music – Written by Alan Price

THE DEVIL DOES NOLLYWOOD
The Helen Ukpabio Demonic Double Feature

by Brian Harris

*Nollywood. The name conjures up images of shapely, exotic women dancing seductively to raucous song and dance numbers and—wait…no…that's Bollywood. I know—it brings to mind great actors such as Laurence Olivier, Gary Cooper and the timeless grace of Katherine Hep—shit, strike that…I'm thinking Hollywood. So what in hell is Nollywood, exactly? Simple, it's one of the third largest film industries in the world and it just keeps growing, threatening to smother the world in shockingly bad cinema that is distinctly Nigerian. Intrigued? Here's the kicker: nearly 50% of Nigeria is living beneath the poverty line with the average Nigerian pulling in roughly $2,000 a year, yet Nollywood still rakes in $250 million a year! While that may not sound like much to Americans—**IRON MAN 3 (2013)** has already broken the $1 billion mark—keep in mind that hundreds of these homegrown films are released each month, most cost anywhere from $10,000-$15,000 to make, and nearly all sell for $2-3 each (VCDs). "Moving like hotcakes" would be the understatement of the century. More like cinematic crack.*

The Nigerian film industry as it is today is relatively young—unlike the cinema of Holly- and Bollywood—having only really come into its own in the early 1990s, so the quintessential Nollywood production really hasn't been made yet. Not for lack of trying on filmmakers' ends, though. With such small budgets, non-existent shooting schedules and incredibly tight release windows, taking time to craft a masterpiece isn't an option right now. As the industry continues to mature, that will no doubt change. Currently, **LIVING IN BONDAGE** (1992) is considered to be the first Nollywood production to kick in the industry's door and get the party started right.

Now that you've got the background, you're probably wondering what one might expect from a Nollywood film and my answer to that would be, "Anything goes." Most of the films deal with issues facing the Nigerian people, so outsiders may have a harder time grasping the cultural dilemmas depicted in these films, but, for the most part, we all share the same day-to-day issues which might include romance, religion, politics, employment and the possession of small children by Satan's vile minions from Hell. The closest thing we have here in the States to Nigerian cinema would be the "pre-*Madea* movie," gospel plays of Tyler Perry that used to tour the country's urban theater circuit (once derogatorily referred to as the "chitlin' circuit") in the '90s. If you're not familiar with Perry's stage work, then just know going into a Nigerian film that family and religion are two incredibly important components of these films, as are poor sound, terrible VHS quality, bottom-of-the-barrel acting, and laughably bad visual effects. Just kidding. Or am I? If you're capable of looking beyond the low quality, evangelizing and molasses-thick Nigerian accents (Americans can be a bit dense), you're definitely going to find a few films worth owning.

While it may sound like Nollywood is on the verge of something great—and at first glance it certainly appears to be—there is a force growing within the industry that seems to be aimed at watering down the content and forcing individuality out, leaving nothing but superstition, dogma and prejudice in its wake. Christianity. Now before you brace yourself for an anti-Christian rant, relax, this article isn't so much about religion itself but one particular person within it that seems intent upon insinuating her dangerous beliefs into films. Her name is Helen Ukpabio, billed as the "Lady Apostle" of Nigeria, and her teachings, writings and films may be directly responsible for hundreds of cases of child abuse, abandonment and possibly even death. There's far more to her brand of Pentecostal teachings than tongue-talkin' and running the isles; she not only claims to be a former witch—a claim hundreds of thousands of new converts the world 'round make in order to receive special attention—but also claims to be able to identify juvenile witches! Forget Salem…Nigeria has a child witch problem, and good old Helen Ukpabio is hot on their trail with Jesus riding sidecar! It doesn't take much imagination to figure out what this kind of volatile mixture of paranoid Christian beliefs and native superstition produces, I mean if prayer doesn't succeed in ridding a child of a demon or their witchcraft powers, there's only one thing left to do…make the child's body uninhabitable by way of torture and/or disfigurement. Chilling.

Somebody as dangerous as Ukpabio in the States would quickly be labeled a monster, chased from their ministry and quite probably introduced to the legal system at some point. In Nigeria, she has indeed been to court—only her visits were to sue the government for restricting…wait for it, now…*her right to identify and accuse child witches*. That's right, she sued the Nigerian government for an enormous sum, claiming they were infringing upon her religious rights, and demanded that she and her church be exempt from this rule. That stunning bit of arrogance is only compounded by things like her publically accusing Christian charity-based orphanage groups of being nothing more than frauds (419 scam) and even going so far as to send her followers to violently disrupt workshops on dispelling child witch fears and endorsing children's rights! She's everything Palin would love to be…without the whole being Black thing.

So, yeah…Helen Ukpabio dabbled in Nollywood for a few years until her films began attracting negative attention, and a well-deserved banning in

39

'04, from the National Film & Video Censors Board for pushing ideas that could cause major disruptions in Nigerian society between religious groups. These films not only slammed other religions but they constantly push the child witch doctrine, the evils of homosexuality (a lifestyle punishable by 15 years in prison), African superstitions concerning Albinos and even reinforce the outlandish belief that native religions endorse ritual killings. One of her most popular films, entitled **END OF THE WICKED** (1999), is considered by many to be a must-see film for those seeking to experience all that Nollywood has to offer. I disagree 100%, but if you are looking to check out some absurd, hate-filled fantasy/horror palmed off on the uneducated masses as "fact", without having to look at Alex Jones's bloated mug, you should seek out some of Ukpabio's stuff. Just be sure that you choose carefully how and where you see these films as I'd strongly advise against passing money along to Helen Ukpabio and her Liberty Gospel church, otherwise you'll be essentially funding more hatred and neglect. I'd never openly promote intellectual theft but…uh…*WINK*.

To find out more about child witch persecution, give HBO's documentary, **SAVING AFRICA'S WITCH CHILDREN** (2008) a look-see—just be prepared for cruelty on levels rarely seen here in the United States. I admit that I shed quite a few tears while watching. The fact that Helen Ukpabio denies this goes on in her own country is pretty telling.

END OF THE WICKED
1999, NIGERIA. DIRECTOR: TECO BENSON

I'd love to be able to give you a solid synopsis on this film but the truth is there's no real story here, just interconnected occurrences surrounding an old woman—who we know to be a witch—and the evil she visits upon her family. Some of the wicked deeds she performs include raping her daughter-in-law with a giant penis granted to her by Beelzebub, causing children to die, ruining car engines and a host of other screwed up shit. Why would she do all of this to her beloved son and his family? Simple, she's a witch and her only goal seems to be wickedness in the devil's name. But what does it all mean, Basil?

While watching **END OF THE WICKED**, a few things become abundantly clear. The first is that writer/producer Ukpabio sincerely believes that Satan worshippers are capable of transforming into animals—something adults capable of reason know is impossible. The second is that demon-possessed witch children will visit you while you sleep soundly and they will… *GULP…eat a meal of jollof rice on your back*. Yeah. And lastly the devil himself, the Lord of Liars and Prince of Darkness, is an Albino.

So children, what have we learned from Teco Benson's **END OF THE WICKED**? Well, we've learned that, while Christians claim their god is all-powerful, they're not capable of turning into animals, *ergo* their god is not stronger than the devil. Albinos are of the devil and only harbor diabolical intentions for you, your family and your wife's womb. And child witches seem to be hungrier at night. Wow, what a load of horseshit. If I wasn't so enthralled by the cult nature of this film, I probably would have been pretty damn pissed.

The acting was all pretty hit or miss; many Nollywood actors are amateurs and the films are shot in English, so if you don't have a problem with the accents (I didn't), you may find yourself taking issue with the dreary acting. Production design was almost non-existent outside of Beelzebub's "jungle court," so there's a bit lacking here, visually. What it lacks in acting and visuals, though, it more than makes up for with crudely-rendered-yet-oddly-fascinating special effects. Hell, just getting the opportunity to ponder how on earth a Christian production could think it was okay to show an old woman with an enormous penis perform a fairly graphic rape scene. One can only assume they were willing to show it because they honestly believe it's not only possible but happens all the time.

Sure, a big black dick and some post-Snoop Dogg "What's My Name?" animal transformations don't make for a huge amount of entertainment, but this is cult cinema—we watch far worse and love it! If you're lucky enough to locate this on VCD, cling to it for dear life, as the film seems to be pretty damned rare—the only other place it is available for purchase on DVD that I could find was directly through Helen Ukpabio and her ministry and for me that just wasn't an option. I won't go so far as to insist you should see this, but if you're interested in checking out the most celebrated examples of Nollywood horror/fantasy, you might want to view. If you'd prefer to avoid, I'd recommend the **666: BEWARE THE END IS AT HAND** film series instead. They're just as bad but there's more gore, demons, lesbians and man-rape to enjoy.

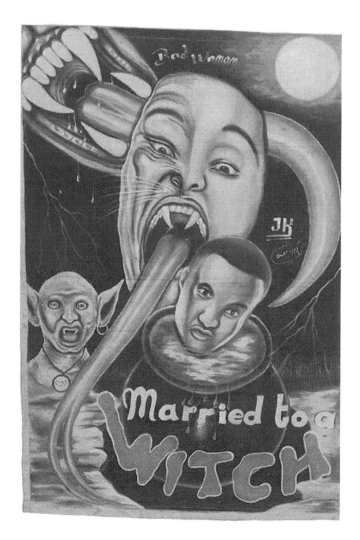

40

MARRIED TO A WITCH
2001, NIGERIA. DIRECTOR: FRED AMATA

When Michael's business dealings take a turn for the worse, a coven of witches decide to exploit his weakened spiritual state and enslave his soul. Before they can harvest his soul, though, they need to infiltrate every aspect of his life and alienate him from everybody he knows and loves. The best way to do this is to have him fall in love and marry one of the coven members—and boy, does he ever!

No sooner do they marry before his witch-wife begins driving a wedge between Michael and his household staff, best friends and family. She even stoops to barring his mother from their home and abusing the young orphaned niece in his custody, eventually sending her away to live with others. Despite all the evidence presented to him that his wife is evil, Michael refuses to listen, believing that it's jealousy that drives those he once trusted to speak ill of his beautiful, and dedicated, wife.

As evidence begins piling up, though, and it appears that his wife has started a vampire witch coven in his own home, Michael will seek out the help of the only person capable of breaking the bonds of the devil and bringing him into the light, his Born Again Aunt.

Witches cackle like they're shilling for a Halloween store, their outfits and makeup are awful, they jabber incoherently, pose in awkward positions and mug like they have brain damage. In other words, producer Helen Ukpabio wants you to know that witches are so thoroughly possessed by the devil that they can barely keep their rolling eyes in their heads. They're founts of uncontrollable evil that have turned them into soulless beasts. It's about as childish an outlook on witchcraft as one can get and it's pushed over and over, to the point where it almost becomes unbearable because it's so goddamn insulting. If Ukpabio believes witches can turn into animals, as she illustrated in **THE END OF THE WICKED**, and she also thinks they all cackle, slobber and trot around in unitards like in this film, there's apparently not much the woman won't believe so long as you slap Christ on top.

The acting on display in **MARRIED TO A WITCH** is actually decent; much of it is way over-the-top, but still pretty effective. The role of Michael, played by the late Kwame Owusu Ansah, was the real standout in this production and in my opinion, none of this would have worked half as well as it did without him. The same cannot be said for Ukpabio's presence. Production design once again just wasn't there. Not only am I convinced this film used the same sets from **END OF THE WICKED** but the quality of the special effects seems to have declined! So, better acting, a bit more story and worse effects—it's neither a step up or down, it's simply an Ukpabio production, and you really just accept it all for the wonderful badness it offers. Just as most Nollywood films, it feels like a glorified soap opera.

If anything, it's worth experiencing this whopping two-hour film just to catch the hilarious finale. I'll give you a hint: it involves consuming copious amounts of feces and I ain't talkin' about watchin' Fox News either. Need an alternate recommendation? Check out Ukpabio's **RAPTURE** films.

There you have it, Brian's two selections for the Demonic Double Feature, and what a pair of selections they are! Nothing, but nothing, beats the kind of Horror Cinema that reflects real-life horror because there is no better monster in the history of all that was, is, and is yet to come than mankind. The worst atrocities ever visited upon us have been devised and executed by us. What better way to understand ourselves than by witnessing man's limitless capacity for cruelty against others and identifying the ignorance and prejudice that fuels it? Exorcising it with education and acceptance is our only hope.

I won't judge people like Helen Ukpabio for believing in mermaid spirits (seriously) or for believing that innocent children are capable of being demonic witches; I judge people like Helen Ukpabio because they encourage others to believe it. In a world so damn screwed up as ours is, do we really need to sacrifice the safety and well-being of our children in order to prove

A wicked woman from **I MARRIED A WITCH**

to others that we embrace religious freedom? We see it all the time here in the States, when parents refuse medical treatment for their children or they expose ours to their often fatal anti-vaccination views. Must we accept and encourage ignorance in order to show others that we are not? Why do children have to suffer at the hands of mental egomaniacs like Helen Ukpabio before we ask ourselves just how much religion is too much religion?

END OF THE WICKED and **MARRIED TO A WITCH** can be used as blueprints to seek out and destroy innocence; they can also be looked upon as lessons used to illustrated ignorance and superstition. They can also mean I have exceptionally poor taste in cinema. To that I agree wholeheartedly. I really need to get a legit hobby…like bow-hunting Albinos. I hear their body parts go for a king's ransom in Nigeria. I'll finally be able to purchase a few Criterion Blu-rays. *Thank you, Christianity.*

For more information on how to help fight intolerance toward children, homosexuals and albinos in Nigeria please visit:
steppingstonesnigeria.org
ilga.org/ilga/en/countries/NIGERIA/
albinofoundation.org

THE STUPENDOUS CINEMA OF

Syfy

by Brian Harris

I know, some of you are probably shaking your heads right now and wondering out loud why in hell I would give the SyFy channel print when their films are so [EXPLETIVE HERE] bad, and I'll be the first to admit that most of their originals/premiers are trashola, but here's the thing: I love 'em. Seriously, in my opinion, it seems like today's generation has lost touch with horror and sci-fi cinema's most cherished form of entertainment: THE B-MOVIE. In contrast to all of the many ways you can see films today, the only way you could catch the newest films in the '70s and '80s was to go to the theater or wait months—sometimes years—for the Betamax and VHS to see release. There was also cable, but if you were broke and couldn't afford cable, forget about it—basic television was your only source for bloodshed and space invasion mayhem. You knew most of the stuff that played on the boob tube was cheap and cheesy but you didn't care; you loved it anyhow because it entertained, even when the blood looked like tomato soup and the monsters looked like dogs in bad wigs. That's what the B-movie was all about!

Things change, of course, and nearly everything these days—especially in Horror and Sci-Fi—can technically be considered "B-movies", and there are dozens of different ways to see them. Thankfully, cable TV has stepped up to the plate in recent years and brought the made-for-TV film and B-movie back from the dead. Now, depending on where your tastes lie, you can catch original B-movie productions on channels like Spike TV (men), SyFy (horror/sci-fi), Hallmark (family) and Lifetime (women). Most are filmed on the kind of budgets used to staff food services on mainstream productions, but you're guaranteed the same entertainment. Sure, you won't be seeing 'Brangelina' or any of the familiar faces from a Judd Apatow film, but you won't care because you'll be too busy watching Casper Van Dien fight ninjas, Richard Grieco plot against his brother Thor and Erick Estrada defend the Alamo against Latin American goat-suckers!

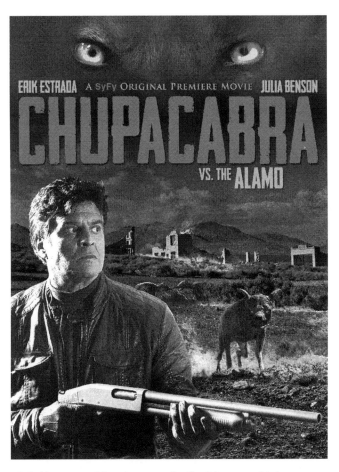

Three of my favorite places to get modern-day B-movie entertainment are The Asylum, Full Moon Pictures and the cable channel, SyFy. If you've never seen a SyFy Original film because somebody told you the CG sucked, the acting was terrible or the concept was unbelievable—like the recently-aired SyFy Original, produced by The Asylum, called **SHARKNADO** (next issue)—you're missing out on some quality cheese with only one goal: entertaining viewers. Nobody is expecting an Emmy nod or the verbal equivalent of a hand-job from some highbrow film critic; there's not an ounce of pretension to be found in these films. I mean, if you're planning to sit and view a film called **CHUPACABRA VS. THE ALAMO** (2013), by gum, you ain't looking for a rousing discussion on religious allegory in postmodernist cinema! At least…I hope not. I've heard them described as being mindless, pointless, and the lowest common denominator for the "bad" movie crowd, and that very well may be accurate. Lord knows I love me some mindless, pointless, lowest common denominator! Some of my favorite modern B-movie productions either originated from or premiered on SyFy at some point, including **BLOOD SURF** (2000), **FRANKENFISH** (2004), **MOSQUITO MAN** (2005), **BEHEMOTH** (2011), **GHOULS** (2008) and **SWAMP DEVIL** (2008). Every few weeks a new film livens up my Saturday night, and I genuinely look forward to them; hopefully I can bring that appreciation to some of you.

For this article I chose to focus on three recent SyFy Originals/Premiers, **BATTLEDOGS, RISE OF THE DINOSAURS** and **AXE GIANT: THE WRATH OF PAUL BUNYAN** (all 2013 releases). I figure what better time to start focusing on SyFy than in the here and now, right?

The first film I was able to settle in to watch was Alexander Yellen's **BATTLEDOGS**, a moderately entertaining horror actioner starring Craig Sheffer (**NIGHTBREED**), Dennis Haysbert (*24*), Ernie Hudson (**GHOSTBUSTERS**), Kate Vernon (*Battlestar Galactica*), Wes Studi (**DANCES WITH WOLVES**) and Ariana Richards (**JURASSIC PARK**). Sheffer plays Major Brian Hoffman; a military physician assigned to oversee a deadly outbreak of an unknown virus. Unlike the usual run-of-the-mill virus scares that normally threaten the population, this particular virus turns its hosts into snarling, bloodthirsty werewolf creatures! Just when it appears as though Hoffman has located "patient zero" and contained the spread of the virus, Lt. General Christopher Monning (Haysbert) steps in and takes control of the project—instead of eradication, the government is interested in unstoppable soldiers of the wolfy kind!

BATTLEDOGS was fun, no doubt about it, but I don't plan to see it again, nor do I have any intention of purchasing this on disc. While the acting was admirable—most of the primary cast is all solid actors—this is a creature feature, and everything hinges on how good or bad the practical/CG creature effects look. The good news is the CG werewolves in this production looked far better than four-legged atrocities in Waller's **AN AMERICAN WEREWOLF IN PARIS**. Granted, the latter was made in '97 when CG was still a bit iffy and one would certainly expect CG to have improved in 16 years but **AN AMERICAN WEREWOLF IN PARIS** is a masterpiece of crap to which all other bad werewolf films are compared. **BATTLEDOGS** is by far a better film but the CG is still terrible; the wolves look more like killer shrews, their movement (especially running) is awkward and they occasionally go from looking really cool to poorly-animated. My guess is they put a bit more work into the wolves we'd be seeing in close-ups and less into the "pack."

The story isn't anything new; the "government using *blah blah blah* as a weapon" has been done to death, and when you throw in the so-so animation and average acting, you get a mediocre affair that, while entertaining, just doesn't warrant further viewings.

Seasoned SyFy Channel junkies expect throw-away films like **BATTLEDOGS**; you get in, get out and move along. These aren't the kinds of

43

films you watch when you're looking for the next **VIDEODROME** (1983), **THE SHINING** (1980) or **NIGHT OF THE LIVING DEAD** (1968). No, these are the kind of films you set your DVR to record and you don't actually sit down to watch them for a month or so—or longer (2 months), in the case of Anthony Fankhauser's **RISE OF THE DINOSAURS** (previously titled **JURASSIC ATTACK**). Why in hell did it take me so damn long to sit down for 83 minutes and watch one measly little movie? Good question, the answer is...*dinosaur movies blow.* Blasphemy. Yeah dinosaur flicks may have been fun at one time but I'm not 6 years old; not only are dinosaurs not scary but they're really not even fun to watch any longer. Everything that came after **JURASSIC PARK** (1993) just pales in comparison, sort of like every shark film that followed **JAWS** (1975), you know? They make for great TV shows like *The Lost World* and *Primeval*, but everything that can be done with dinosaurs seems to have already been done. *Prove me wrong, Roger Corman!*

Once again, there's nothing new here; **RISE OF THE DINOSAURS** has been done a million times but it's all about the execution. In this case, it was made competently enough to sit through but I can hardly see anybody coming away from this film with a new favorite on their hands.

A covert military unit is parachuted into the jungle to rescue a scientist from a dangerous rebel but they get more than they'd bargained for when they run headlong into a jungle filled with prehistoric dinosaurs! Now they must maneuver through the dino packs and avoid T-Rex jaws just long enough to escape the jungle valley before the government orders a strike on the area, leaving nothing but scorched earth.

A race for time. Hot women. A nasty rebel leader. Dangerous dinosaurs. *YAWN.* Sure, it was a decent watch, but it nearly put me to sleep! They could have used a bit more skin, a bit less sexual tension and a wider variety of prehistoric beasties. I mean, we've got dinosaurs clomping around in broad daylight, what rule of logic states that we can't have big bugs and carnivorous plants too? It seemed to me that so long as the unit avoided most of the dinosaurs they were safe—of course a ton of dudes were still eaten; good thing a dozen soldiers seemed to have popped up out of nowhere in order to create a buffer between the main cast of characters and the dinos. Yeah, that's sarcasm. Seriously, the team parachutes down and all of a sudden there's a shitload of guys getting munched on and all I could think was, "Who the hell is that? This is the first time I'm seeing him." Ah, well. I think the thing I found really odd was the fact that the members of this presumably U.S. military unit were almost all British. Until I looked the film up on IMDb, I was thoroughly convinced this film was shot in the UK. Poor casting.

Anyhow, believe it or not, the dinosaurs looked good; I was expecting something sketchy but that wasn't the case. The only thing that marred an otherwise a decent visual experience was some seriously ugly CG blood; I don't know what the visual effects guys behind this were thinking but it couldn't have been quality. No matter though, the entire affair was easy to watch and easy to jump right back into if you need to take a piss break. It primarily consists of shooting, walking, dinosaur, shooting, walking, dinosaur. The only highlight for me was the back and forth cliché between a government spook played by Vernon Wells (**COMMANDO**) and a military officer played by Corin Nemec (*Stephen King's The Stand*). You know: "Give my men just 10 more minutes, you bastard! They'll make it!" "You've got your 10 minutes, Colonel. But if they're not out of there in exactly 10, I'll rain hellfire on top of their heads from the bowels of Hades itself." That's not from the film but you get it. It's right up there with, "You're a renegade cop and you don't play by the rules!" and "I'm only two days away from my retirement from the force. And my daughter is getting married!" Yeah, it's like that.

RISE OF THE DINOSAURS was mediocre; nothing too pleasant and nothing too offensive—it just sits there teetering on the entertainment fence, threatening to bore the shit out of you by not doing much of anything. Did I like it? Yeah, I did, but I wouldn't recommend a second viewing to anybody that has already seen it. That would just be cruel. If you haven't seen it, going out of your way to check it out will probably sour you, as the pay-off isn't equal to the effort it would take to seek it out.

The clear winner of the recent SyFy Channel original films I was able to catch though was Gary Jones's **AXE GIANT: THE WRATH OF PAUL BUNYAN**, a modern spin on the Northeastern folklore of the early 20th Century. Once again, we get another story that's fairly familiar to cinema

Two ferocious animal monsters; both puppets, both furry, and both with very, very large canines. What separates these two critters other than their need to tear apart their human prey? They exist fifty years apart in their conception and execution, but Ray Kellogg's 1959 classic **THE KILLER SHREWS** (bottom) is a hell of lot more terrifying that **BATTLEDOGS** (above).

geeks—a diverse group of kids head out into the wilderness thanks to some unlikely juvenile offender program designed to build character and turn their lives around. While plodding about in the woods, one of the kids happens upon a pile of bone and decides to take what appears to be a cattle horn as a souvenir. Bad move. Turns out that's not just any cow's horn, it came from Babe, the beloved Blue Ox that once belonged to Paul Bunyan! Noticing the bones have been disturbed, the reclusive giant grabs his axe and sets out on a mission to avenge the corpse desecration.

Cheesy visual effects—including CG kills—abound, but **AXE GIANT: THE WRATH OF PAUL BUNYAN** hits the spot with a story and an antagonist so absurd that there's nothing left to do but turn it off or enjoy yourself. I chose the latter because I am not an elitist…and I'm better than you. Gary Jones is no stranger to B-movies; he's directed such goodies as **MOSQUITO** (1995), **SPIDERS** (2000) and **CROCODILE 2: DEATH SWAMP** (2002). What he was able to accomplish on a low budget with this film is admirable; I thought Paul looked pretty damn cool stomping after a truck and reaching through a roof. He sort of reminded me of one of the inbred cannibals from the **WRONG TURN** series. There were a few times that his scale seemed to be off but he was imposing nonetheless. Just getting to see Dan Haggerty (*The Life and Times of Grizzly Adams*) and Joe Estevez (**SOULTAKER**) get their asses handed to them should be enough to warrant one viewing for crap fans, but there's also some adequate acting and a stellar score composed by soundtrack wizards Midnight Syndicate, as well. There are just enough little things to keep things fun and entertaining. I mean, it's about a giant killing teens—if you get anything less than that you've got every right to bitch and complain. Hell, I fully admit I'll be picking this up once it hits the $5 bin at Wal-Mart, and anybody that takes that to mean this was only worth $5 must not understand the true power of the bin. For us cult cinema fans, it's like digging in a pile of gold quarters for that one platinum coin.

The next SyFy article I'll be writing for the mag will feature my takes on their next original installments, **INDEPENDENCE DAYSASTER**, **SHARKNADO** and **BLAST VEGAS** (also all 2013 releases). Tell me those don't sound like a good way to waste some time and turn off the old dome skillet!

Remember, folks: not every film can be a classic, not every filmmaker a genius, there's more than enough room in cinema for all kinds of films and fans. Imagine Sci-Fi and Horror without the B-movie, without absurd concepts like shark/octopus hybrids and alien wooly mammoths. It would be a dreary genre indeed. Without fail I watch each and every original film to hit the SyFy Channel because I'm determined to keep the B-movie from dying and the only way to do that is to tune in and, when the price is right, purchase. I'm sending the message that I want more, and obviously the gods of low budget cinema are getting that message loud and clear.

If you'd like to find out more about SyFy original films, drop by their website at: syfy.com/movies/all

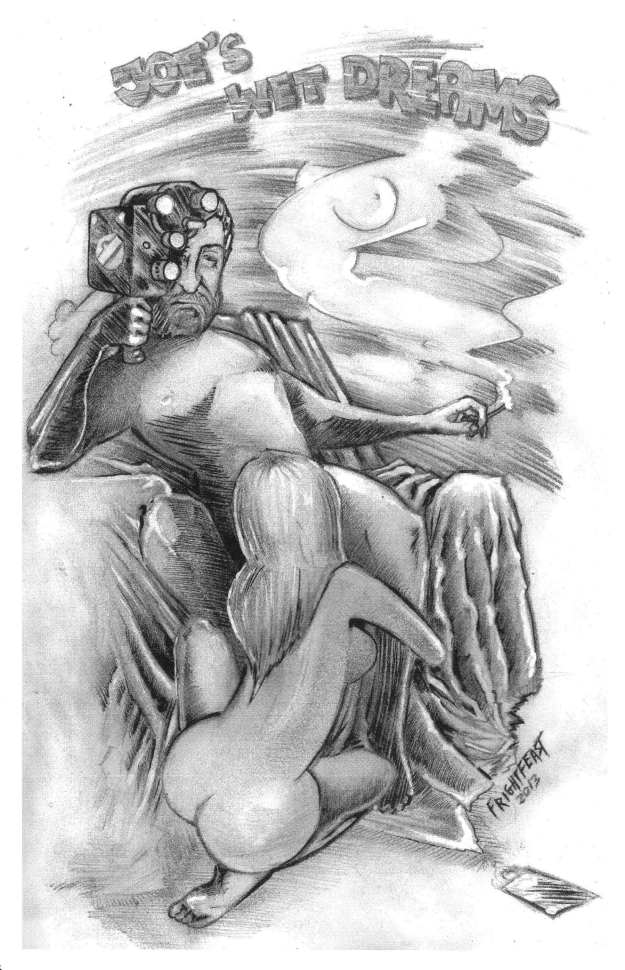

Art by Mark K. Allen

THE LAST CENTURION OF EUROTRASH CINEMA

Joe D'Amato in the 1990s... saving the genre cinema with sex!

by David Zuzelo

*Aristide Massaccesi—better known to fans of global trash cinema as Joe D'Amato (amidst a virtual legion of other names)—certainly doesn't need an introduction to readers of WENG'S CHOP. If there is one man that personifies the term coined by Craig Ledbetter—European Trash Cinema—it would be D'Amato without any doubt. A prolific producer, director, photographer and all-around titan of genre cinema, I would be hard-pressed to think of a genre that he didn't touch on over the span of his career. From cutting out letters by hand to create title sequences to contributing such iconic films to the cinema such as **EMMANUELLE AND THE LAST CANNIBALS** (1977), **ANTHROPOPHAGUS** (1980), **BEYOND THE DARKNESS** (1979) and the **11 DAYS, 11 NIGHTS** series (could you have had cable and not found these?)...D'Amato did it all! Sadly, he passed away at the young age of 62 and was working right up until the end of his time behind a camera. As we look at his work from start to finish it seems there are almost two completely different legacies in the 200 titles that the IMDb lists, and they aren't even completely accurate! A deeper appraisal is in order.*

A pioneer of genre-crossing and what is now termed "Mockbusting", D'Amato had a craftsman's skillset and the drive of a dozen men to take his gifts and make as much money as possible with the tools at hand. A true exploitation producer with the balls to produce material outside the usual single-genre fare, who could also handle the technical aspects of actually making the films which would generate the income to keep going onto the next production! And the next film. And the next. Until one day his production company, Filmirage, would close up shop. Perhaps the shuttering of that infamous house of weird wonder was the end of that first legacy. What came next would be just as interesting—just as much a craftsman's work in some ways, and certainly just as much a tale about an exploitation cinema mogul looking to keep on doing exactly what he did best...

Shoot films. Make money. Travel the world. Become a legend.

The porn genre was nothing new to D'Amato, he had been using sex films of both the hard- and soft-core variety to great effect. Upon hijacking the *Emmanuelle* series of films into his own bizarro universe, he began twisting the popular markets together, merging Sexploitation and Horror for the masses. Heading to the Dominican Republic, D'Amato made his infamous "island" films that stirred up elements of black magic and zombies, both traditional and popular '80s walking dead flavors, mixed with hard (and softcore variant) sex acts to create a sludgy stew that has his fans still seeking the next difficult-to-find film! And, who could forget his tossing in unique scenes such as crotch champagne openers in his zombie opus **EROTIC NIGHTS OF THE LIVING DEAD** (1980)? Not me. And if you forgot it, you need to get right back and watch it again!

But the times were changing as both cable TV and a global VHS culture that spawned a larger international audience was more important than getting a movie into both a porn cinema circuit or a "grindhouse" run. What was done was done, and there were distribution deals to be had on all these films. D'Amato and Filmirage were moving forward, satisfying markets for late-night cable fare with an outrageous zeal. Personally, I would set my VCR to record overnights on any cable channel I had that featured Skinemaxxing thrills in hopes that the "Filmirage Presents" title would pop up—and they did so on a frequent basis. Taking the title of the hit film **9 ½ WEEKS** (1986) and creating the **11 DAYS, 11 NIGHTS** series of films (most of which stand on their own and are retitled to create a franchise), the sexploitation thrills of D'Amato chugged alongside his jumping on any trend that the genres could present. They had **CONAN THE BARBARIAN** (1982)? He had

Left to right: Malisa Longo, D'Amato, and crew for the Rocco Siffridi film **TORERO**, shot in the scenic Spanish village of Chinchon.

ATOR, THE FIGHTING EAGLE (1982)! You loved **THE ROAD WARRIOR** (1981)? Have some **2020 TEXAS GLADIATORS** (1982)! **THE RUNNING MAN** (1987) tickle your fancy? Play D'Amato's **ENDGAME** (1983) too! And if you thought **CALIGULA** (1979) was crazy, check out **CALIGULA: THE UNTOLD STORY** (1982)! But the sex films seemed to be the cable favorites and these titles rarely collected dust on video shop shelves. But right next to the end of the "Mature" section lay black books with folded down big boxes...and the films within were making money. Big money. Though I've never seen it mentioned exactly why Filmirage closed down—outside of a mention in the interesting **JOE D'AMATO TOTALLY UNCUT** (1999, which you can find on several Media Blasters DVD releases)—it left D'Amato with a lot of skill and equipment, and he would charge headlong into a new phase of his career. Straight up, no filler, but all-holes-filled pornographic productions.

But he couldn't make it that simple, could he? In the **UNCUT** interview, he mentions that he—and those others like him making porn films—are in the business of, "Butt Holes...what comes in them and comes out of them." While that is surely true, what is left behind for those of us that love to unearth the odd and intriguing detritus of trash cinema is a mountain of fleshy mayhem that plays very differently from the sad "director pushed to porn" story we've heard before.

Joe D'Amato made *movies* instead of succumbing to what may have been the easier road of tossing a few lovely women on screen to get their orifices filled by robotic stunt-cock-wielders. Fulfilling the skin-and-fluids quotient was easy enough, but when you really look harder at these (and for most men I know, they will certainly prompt some hardness in the right places), you'll find out that D'Amato was using all the tricks his experience of decades of cinematic production to make entertainments that don't stray from his earlier work at all. Just as **PORNO HOLOCAUST** (1981) or **EMMANUELLE AND THE LAST CANNIBALS** mixed together the seemingly disparate markets, you can watch **TARZAN-X: SHAME OF JANE** (1994) or **LADY IN THE IRON MASK** (1998) and gape in erect wonder as elements of cinema collide in the best Eurotrash style—on 35MM film and forged with care! The Joe D'Amato School Of '90s Porn Power was open, and if you think that **ANTHROPHAGUS** played well around the world, then get ready to try and find all the releases of his '90s porn films. In America alone there were major companies distributing work from Capital Films, Butterfly Motion Pictures and other ventures he was involved in, including films that he worked on in several functions with Luca Damiano for varying credits. Damiano is another very familiar name to video seekers and can many times be relied on for the same level of entertainment as the D'Amato films. Video stores

were more likely to stock items from VCA, Sin City, In X-Cess Productions and so on in their black books or adult rooms than Private Screenings films, usually buying multiple copies to keep up with demand. And hey, that doesn't even count the versions of various Rocco-starring films I've found with *Russian narration over sex scenes*. It's an educational pursuit learning how to say "Unnnnnnnggghhhhh" with a bored Russian accent in my house after all of this!

While D'Amato would occasionally work in softcore and drama again with oddball films like **CHINA AND SEX** (1994) and **THE HYENA** (1997), his porn output would be a landslide of genre films made in a world where Italian genre films would be fewer and further between. He would take Caligulasploitation on again with **NERO: ORGY OF FIRE** (1997). He would tackle the Peplum headlong with **HERCULES: A SEX ADVENTURE**, **SAMSON IN THE AMAZON'S LAND** and **OLYMPUS: REFUGE OF GODS** (all 1997 releases). Adventure, your name is now **ROBIN HOOD: THIEF OF WIVES** (1996). Or is it **SELEN: QUEEN OF ELEPHANTS** (1998)? Or **OTHELLO 2000** (1997), featuring porn legend Sean Michaels? Westerns. Jungle Girls. Boxing Dramas. Ghosts. If you can think of a genre, it's represented in these films. Interestingly, the elements of horror are few and far between. There isn't a lot of nasty behavior on show (though some of the international versions of the Rocco Siffredi entries may push that).

One of the most interesting names to pop across the screen that isn't a D'Amato pseudonym is Luca Damiano, whose real name is Franco Lo Cascio and has some cool credentials of his own. Massaccesi worked with him on several films that really set the tone for the D'Amato films for the next year or two, most especially the two-part **X HAMLET** (1995) series. Lo Cascio had worked on several small genre films, mainly with Patrizia Gori, during the '70s before crossing paths with D'Amato's career in the '80s at M.A.D. Films, making several of the bizarre porn hybrids they were shoveling, teaming up with Marina Hedman several times in titles like **TRANSEX** (1988) and **MARINA UNA MOGLIE COSÌ PERBENE** (1988). Many of the films produced at M.A.D were undoubtedly made for very small markets, some of which are still hard to find. For the adventurous viewer (and aren't we all at this point of the article?) I would definitely suggest the Mario Siciliano film **ORGASMO ESOTICO** (1982), an exorcism porn that is so bizarre I had to watch it multiple times to be sure it existed. It even shares a score with **ABSURD** (a.k.a. **MONSTER HUNTER**, 1981)! After a few years off, Luca Damiano returned in full swing, and worked with D'Amato soon after as he pushed into the fairy tale and historical porn films that include **THE EROTIC ADVENTURES OF ALADDIN X** (1994), which is a lot of fun, by the way; it has an utterly insane premise that brings a working stiff into the magic carpet rides and four-ways of his dreams. D'Amato would shoot and even appear in the **X HAMLET** series, and there is not just a techno video featuring porn starlet Sarah Young that comes from The Bard's Boudoir (so to speak), but there are even behind-the-scenes segments shot with Damiano and D'Amato, only found on the German VHS of **SEX GYM** (1994)! The two careers split after a few years, but it is interesting to find "Kathleen Stratton" listed as an editor on a seemingly unrelated to D'Amato film such as **GAMIANI** in 1997.

While the costume epics would be popular, D'Amato retained some of his exploitation filmmaker edge on several productions, most notably as the seedier side of Italian Exploitation rears its head. 1995's **FUHRER'S DOLLS** (a.k.a. **OPERATION: SEX**) is the less-than-charming tale of Nazis using women prisoners as prostitutes to gain "a golden opportunity to gain remission of their sentences." Well, it's not exactly a new theme, and with minimal plot and lots of cheap set design to create the Nazisploitation vibe, the movie runs about 100 minutes of hardcore action with the occasional dialog sequence where officers talk about their Führer and all the expected nonsense. That said, D'Amato surely doesn't make its Nazi leads anything less than stupid and utterly uncaring about their cause above the idea of getting some action from the hookers around them. It does have a rather odd ending where the women seem almost let down as they wander away upon the villainous taskmasters taking their own lives after a radio conveys news of Hitler's demise. Outside of the setting, it's probably hard to generate too much outrage about the movie. When the villain dishes out goofy pervy Snidely Whiplash lines such as, "Say... your brownie has got the trembles... you want a colossal cock in there, don't you? Well, there is little comfort in here!" you can ascertain the tone of this mini-epic. However, there is another version in English that chops down a half hour and inserts a Mondo-style narration about the plight of prostitutes during World War II, entitled **THE JOY CLUB**. It's a stranger bit of cinema to contemplate, but to a filmmaker like D'Amato, it probably felt like second nature to exploit what he had already created. In the 1990s I doubt that the film found any additional success outside of adding titles for a different releasing company. D'Amato did dip into the Women-in-Prison scenarios again with **MIDNIGHT OBSESSION** (*Fuga di mezzanotte*, 1995) and **SEX PENITENTIARY** (1996), but barring some hardly-resisted cavity searching and briefly naughty Lesbian Prisoner frolics, these have no sharp edges. As a matter of fact, most of his other porn films have humor, titillation and in some cases a very Filmirage return to sex drama as their subjects.

One film would generate some notoriety—stemming from an estate in Tarzana, California taking umbrage upon seeing Rocco Siffredi swing his massive flesh vine in the face of his wife Rosa Caracciolo while letting out a certain Victory Cry. Yes, it would take something the Edgar Rice Burroughs Estate would see as **JUNGLE HEAT**, on CD-ROM no less, to bring **TARZAN-X: SHAME OF JANE** (or as the French might say, **DARD'ZAN**) a lawsuit naming not only D'Amato but distributors of the film Excalibur Entertainment and others as well. The film itself *is* a Tarzan rip off, as Siffredi goes about his business as "Ape Man" and lets out his triumphant "Ooowoa-heeoooo" on occasion, especially during the finale. Yep, he has his Jane. He has a monkey pal. And yes…he does get quite the Greystoke treatment as he tries to become civilized. But here is the kicker: it's a fun movie! Ape Man's loincloth does get the expected workout, and Siffredi does his best with the role and manages to look the part and bring an expected Jungle Vigor to the whole thing. Caracciolo is a stunning Jane, and of course there are other women that lure poor Ape Man down the road to civilized anal sex. While the ERB estate called it "nothing more than a lewd, vulgar and highly offensive film", I say it's one of the better porn films of Joe D'Amato's '90s era! Great sets, an actual story and hot sex scenes abound. And yep, it's even got a few laughs with a monkey! There have been worse jungle movies made. And if you are feeling particularly curious, seek out the extended soft core variant, **AVVENTURE EROTICHE NELLA GIUNGLA**, which features *more* story to replace the hardcore sequences! Flashbacks and more ERB mayhem await you!

It's a world of wonder, and for porn fans, excitement, as we jump on board with Joe D'Amato as he takes a parade of beautiful women from around the globe on a bizarre ride through 40 years of Italian genre film tropes! It's hard to take this massive body of work as a career footnote, because D'Amato was a worldwide success once again with these films, earning a tribute at the Hot D'Or in Cannes after his passing. I sometimes wonder how many people in the porn industry were even aware of just how many films the man born Aristide Massaccesi had made *before* rising to prominence in the final decade of his life. The man worked on hundreds of productions during these late years and even acted in some of them! These are non-sex roles of course, but having spotted his face in his early Spaghetti Western films, I was equally amused to see him in **X HAMLET** as Polonious. Really.

For both fans of D'Amato, and those of us with the trash cinema librarian bug, there is a joy in seeing a few of the greatest pseudonyms from D'Amato's past scrolling down the screen. You have Kathleen Stratton on editing! Fediriko Slonisko as DP! And on and on! I must cop to having a complete fascination with the credits here, look for lots of repeated names, my favorite of which is Teddy Chuck, which may or may not have actually been Filipino legend Teddy Page (?) at one point with a carryover of the pseudonym carrying on for him.

So cum on the ride with top porn stars such as Jill Kelly, Rocco Siffredi, Kelly Trump, Hakan, Selen, Erika Bella, Eva Henger, Sean Micheals, Anita Blond, Rosa Caracciolo and many, many more along with some incredibly hot D'Amato repertory porn players! From the castles for rent in the hills of Hungary and that country's extraordinarily beautiful women, many repped by Anita Rinaldi's Touch Me Agency, to the countryside in Rome and on the mean showgirl-strewn streets of Las Vegas, D'Amato and crew wander the world in search of more sleazy thrills! It's no-holes-barred territory for the trash fan. For me, these films flooding in on a monthly basis in big-box VHS at a local shop in the mid-'90s was a secondary ignition into trash cinema collection and enjoyment. With some of them still available from major retailers and many others floating about the Internet in various forms and fashions, this is a legacy that definitely should open up (wide) for some conversation and another outlet for us to enjoy all that D'Amato achieved. Regardless of budget, format or location, he always strives to meet the goals of his films, and with these epics of skin cinema he rarely falls short.

Let's take a face-first dive into the muff of the matter! What lies ahead is a guide to the films I've tracked down, which, while hardly complete, is a fairly sizeable collection of pop shots and Peplumatic pounding! If anything it is a deep starter's guide to an entirely unique course to the Masters class on the great D'Amato. There are so many global releases of these films that I'm relying on English-language versions for plot translations where available and will also try to list the titles in English, if available. Each film speaks the universal language of hard cocks and soft breasts in case you get lost in the minor details. So go and hydrate, get your favorite lubricant and put your Eurotrash Scholar Cap on, and take a few minutes to relax and enjoy the most unlikely tour of Italy's cinema of schlock with Joltin' Joe D'Amato!

A FIELD GUIDE TO THE WILD WORLD OF JOE D'AMATO
and the SEXY SKIN FLICKS OF THE 1990s – PART 1

ANTHONY AND CLEOPATRA
(1996, Butterfly Motion Pictures Corp.)
Olivia Del Rio is Cleopatra! When she finds herself endangered, she is lucky enough to have Caesar around to loan out his favorite *witch doctor* (I kid you not) to protect her, as he needs to return to Rome. We know what is coming for poor JC, but that won't stop Cleopatra from getting her groove on! Enter Hakan, D'Amato's favorite Turkish Hercules, and bear witness to his prowess and ability to handle multiple tasks (anal, oral and vaginal) at once! Cleopatra keeps herself busy, engaging in the steamy trials of Sapphic tongue-twisting with her handmaidens. Once Caesar meets his fate it is revealed that he is involved with Egyptians and witch doctors, and Mark Anthony is on the case. This guy doesn't bring a magnifying glass when he solves a mystery, though. The two titular lovers meet and Hakan delivers a classic line, "Power is like a pretty woman…you have to earn it." And earn it he does, but not without romantic entanglements and sorrowful music and so much butt stabbing that you'll scream, "Et tu, Brute?"

This is the first in a Neo-Peplum/Penthouse Caligulatronic series that includes movies featuring Caligula, Nero and Messalina! D'Amato is obviously familiar with the genre, where he dominated years before with the awesome **CALIGULA: THE UNTOLD STORY** and **UNA VERGINE PER L'IMPERO ROMANO** (1983, one of his "Robert Hall" porn films).

It's very well-made, and features some genuine (stock footage) battle sequences mixed over shots of the cast to relay the saga of how Mark Anthony loses everything in a drunken haze of liquor and pussy and pussy-licking to the armies of Octavius. Hakan is serious, but has a hard time selling the gravitas of the situation as he is more an action-hero-type in **HERCULES: A SEX ADVENTURE**, but you will probably be distracted by either his large

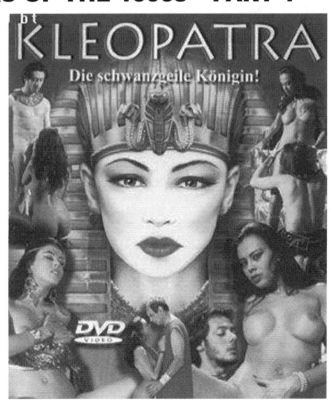

Selen
**SELEN ON TREASURE ISLAND
QUEEN OF THE ELEPHANTS**

Kelly Trump
**HERCULES: A SEX ADVENTURE
SAMSON IN THE AMAZON'S LAND**

Erika Bella
MIDNIGHT OBSESSION

Eva Henger
Hell's Angels series

penis or his most unmanly mandals to notice. D'Amato is having a good time and this is certainly a great revisiting of the themes that made Italian Exploitation Cinema great, just as it should be!

BARONE VON MASOCH
(1995, Luca Damiano Productions)

Leopold von Sacher-Masoch certainly makes for an easy historical figure to plop in a castle, surround with beautiful women and put through the sadomasochistic paces for an hour, and this Luca Damiano production does just that. The film looks great, shot on 35MM during the high-class days of Damiano/D'Amato, and it will certainly satisfy anyone looking for costume porn with a slightly darker vibe. With dirty castle walls and a little very-light bondage (stockades, ropes) the focus is on the Baron trying his hand, feet and penis in all kinds of pleasure-seeking ventures. It's actually lighter in tone than many of D'Amato's earlier porn films, though on the edgier side of the '90s releases, and even includes a gabbling midget who loves to watch blowjobs. Always a fun addition at any orgy! Loads of costumed group sex is on show with shockingly little, if any, dialog outside of a wraparound where the Baron talks briefly with his wife, Wanda. A little kink blended with costumed sex that may not be for all audiences. Roberto Malone definitely does not phone in his intensity as the Baron, which works to the film's favor, and he carries the proceedings along nicely. Malone is a great presence in these films, and he shows off a much more serious side here, giving a performance worthy of the drab and eerie lighting "Frederiko Slonisko" puts forth. For such a brief and nasty little film, it's an effective one.

CALAMITY JANE 1 & 2
(1998, Capital Film)

When a beautiful woman says, "But judge…I won!" and his eager response is, "Yuh, ya won the right to get naked in front of me!" you know you are in the wicked wild west of Joe D'Amato! It's time for saloon sex and damsels that are only in distress from facials and not getting the first shot off. The sex in these is top-shelf and after several years of grinding and bumping out porn, D'Amato seems to have hit his stride. Part 1's pairing of rebel outlaws in Maria Bellucci and Eva Falk provides some outstanding girl-on-girl scenes and one funny group outing that includes Rocco Siffredi dubbed with a "Virginian" accent that had me laughing every time he would speak. Calamity Jane says, "Thinking about, I was lucky…I like spreading my legs too much. And if it's for fun, so much the better. My life, in the end, is what it is!" That sums up the film!

And speaking of ends, Part 2 is interesting as the focus of the film shifts and more group sex and double penetration is the focus after Calamity decides that the town is boring her now. The sheriff needs things to do, so she provides a big batch of "trouble"! The *Calamity Jane* series feels like a lot of material was shot for a film, and providing two different markets with product—the first containing more solo and traditional sex, while the second contains lots of group sex, double penetrations and a bit where D'Amato throws a horseshoe at your head in the final scene. Missy and Roberto Malone partake in a three-way that also features popular gay porn actor Mickey G, who gets pounded in the rump with Missy's six shooter as she oralizes Malone. It's pretty striking and jarring at the same time, even to these porn-soaked eyeballs.

Rough at times, ready at others, there is a lot of poking going on in this Wild West! Calamity wistfully retires from the wild life at the end of Part 2 and she will ride into infamy for me, one ass crack penetration that shan't be forgotten.

CARMEN THE SPANISH WHORE
(1996, Capital Film)

The sexy Maria De Sanchez stars as Carmen in this continuation of **FLAMENCO ECSTASY** (also 1996). Set in the beautiful villa of Chinchon, Spain, it uses a local bullfighting ring as a centerpiece to set the stage. The movie hops out of the bullpen as Hakan (who plays a bunch of different roles in this cycle of shoots) gets down on it right away. It's interesting as the first two sequences don't involve the main cast, just two hot-in-the-pants hotel workers scoring dudes as they arrive for their stay. Monica Orsini delivers an amazing pick-up line in a bathroom as she just walks in and tells a guy she gets turned on watching men piss. Quite a line to get to giving a blowjob! Alright, it ain't classy, but the film does have "whore" in the title and I bet none of us reading this have been picked up in a bathroom in Spain with that line! Carmen finds herself in some intrigue involving money and animated army men (again, I kid you not) with Mike Foster appearing as a goofball bad guy. The film basically stops there as Carmen enters the scenes and is basically hold-over bits from **FLAMENCO ECSTASY**. Not much to dig into, the group scenes with Orsini, Foster, Eros Cristaldi, Ursula Moore and John Walton (!) fill up most of the required holes and happy pops anyway. Maria de Sanchez is very striking to say the least, and she does have a traditional dance sequence that is perfectly Filmirage tacky and sort of sexy to boot.

"The *Calamity Jane* series feels like a lot of material was shot for a film, and providing two different markets with product—the first containing more solo and traditional sex, while the second contains lots of group sex, double penetrations and a bit where D'Amato throws a horseshoe at your head in the final scene."

COP SUCKER 1 & 2
(1996, Joe D'Amato, Butterfly Motion Pictures Corp.)

"They call me Steinbeck around here, because I read so much. Maybe I should take that name literally and write down some of the crazy shit that happens around here." And so begins the epic 2-part saga of a tale of tail-chasing worthy of a title like **COP SUCKER!** A series of sexcapades set around police uniforms and what appears to be the storage closet of any warehouse, these three

hours creep along from cell to bedroom. The entire production feels cheaper than many of the other films in this list, and the L.A. exteriors would suggest it was shot in the US entirely. Porn workhorses like Vince Voyeur and Dave Hardman appear and the women aren't quite as attractive as the more European regulars in D'Amato's stable. If anything stands out it's that there is a genuine shot of an L.A. Police Station (Devonshire) and that the two films seem to break it up by showing police life (cops fucking) in Part 1 and more interaction with willing prisoners in the second installment. There is, of course, shared transition footage and this is certainly one long feature sliced in half, as D'Amato did several times. Not essential unless you happen to live in L.A. and want to know what's up in Devonshire County!

ELIXER
(1998, Butterfly Motion Pictures Corp.)
An old man and a young woman in period costumes take turns breathing in the magical "Elixer Bucal", and WHAM, the man becomes a hunk and of course, they get it on right away. Ah, love. Another scene in the same time period features spooky crypt walls and burning torches as Bruno SX is treated to an odd duck in the pornographic world, an oral internal popshot! Go Joe! But when the same old man offers the Elixer to the same woman years later, she is BAMFed into our present day to experience some sex on a desk and anal beneath a discarded satellite dish and *even more* athletic oral action with some upright 69'n! The old man reappears and even more three-way banging ensues. Annnd...The End. A meditation on the timelessness of sex, or a film cobbled together from different shoots and having no real distinct cast outside of Bruno SX appearing in two scenes? Who knows? It's certainly entertaining, though, especially the Judith Bella blowjob, and frequent cocksman Mike Foster makes an appearance in the endgame! I wonder if Gaetano Donizetti ever imagined his Opera would look like this?

EXPERIENCES 1 & 2
(1998 and 1999, Butterfly Motion Picture Corp.)
AT LAST!!! It's the adult film that shows off Eva Henger's poor typing skills! Why do I know this? Because **EXPERIENCES** is a D'Amato clip film with a wraparound that features an old-looking (by '90s standards, even) computer screen showing off boxy lettering saying EVA, as the actresses settles in for one unique masturbation scene as she watches clips from various skin flicks. Nothing really exciting, but there is definitely a positive to be taken. If you want a quick look over the styles and settings of the D'Amato porn canon of the 1990s then this is the way to do it. Sean Micheals appears in Gangster mode from **GANGLAND BANGERS** (1995), there are several Peplum Porn shots (yep, there is Frank Gun), some women in prison and it's all over in about 90 minutes. Only Part 1 is available for review, but I'm assuming that Part 2 is more of the same, given its release date of 1999 and the stars being from the earlier films, and almost identical to Part 1. It's the short way around the long and hard road around Castle de PornJoe!

FANTASMI AL CASTELLO
(a.k.a. **AMAZING SEX**, 1994, Luca Damiano Productions)
"Hey gang, let's all go to a castle for a little random vacationing and hardcore fucking!" That is a good enough log line, don't you think? A batch of fairly hot lads n' lasses pair up into the usual couple and girl/girl scenarios you'd expect. But wait...entering now in a cloud of dry ice are some costumed *fantasmi* (ghosts)! Roberto Malone walking into a room in a turban and loudly presenting his ghost dong got a huge laugh out of me. Sure, the dialog is in Italian but it didn't much matter. After a few scenes go by, we see a mischievous dude spraying dry ice around to fool the tourists! The slim running time is filled out by a massive orgy at the finish that climaxes with a pop shot on a little piece of toast for one of the ladies to enjoy. Ah, yeah...it's just kind of weird random sex scenes with a little more edge than usual. D'Amato films are usually heavy on the backdoor boudoir behavior, but this one takes it to a *hole* new level with some man-bottom getting attention as well. And hey, it ends with a nice shot of the castle!

Well-shot, this is a short film that seems more in-line with the oddities both producer Luca Damiano and D'Amato did at M.A.D. Films. Minus Marina Hedman. And tranny angles. The only major players and familiar faces are Malone (again, that guy is just plain funny), Christopher Clark and Mike Foster, though you'll recognize some of the ladies from smaller roles in the bigger productions, so it's an interesting footnote to the Damiano and D'Amato films, and if you become an enthusiast, I bet you'll enjoy it as much as I did.

FLAMENCO ECSTASY
(1996, Capital Film)
"Oh, it worked out all right, that actor knew what he was doing, but he didn't have that something added guaranteed to give me ecstasy." Don't you just have to feel for Spanish beauty Maria de Sanchez as Carmen? Trust me, everyone else is feeling her! After leaving her husband (referred to hilariously as "whatshisface") and going on vacation with her friend to find men to give her ecstasy. Well, her friend takes a few thousand licks at her crotch to prep her properly for this big adventure! There are some well-shot vignettes ranging from Chinchon Bullfighting to walking what appears to be in Cannes.

FLAMENCO ECSTASY is really Sanchez' show and she gets to disco dance, put on a bullfighting costume (I wonder if it was the same one Rocco wore in 1996's **TORERO**?) and shares three really different scenes with the always heroic and cocksure Hakan. There is some dancing as the title suggests, but it's set to tacky awesome disco and men telling Carmen that they feel like their "balls are about to burst" from watching her! Fans of porn will like this a lot, and trash fans will revel in Eros Cristaldi performing a hilarious "audition" of poetry that only D'Amato would plop into a porn flick! Totally out-of-place and absolutely excellent, you will hear Federico Garcia Lorca's "Lament for Ignacio Sanchez Mejias" read by one very confused dubber in a weird Southern American accent result in bathroom sex! Nothing like a lengthy mourning for a fallen writer and bullfighter to set the mood.

The distribution of this title by Adam & Eve in the US makes sense—this is couples porn for the most part—and D'Amato does it right. For more of the same cast, locations and costumes, tune in for **CARMEN, THE SPANISH WHORE** as well; it is lighter on the Sanchez, but after this you'll take anything she is in and say *thank you, Joe!*

HELLS ANGEL SERIES
(1997-8, Edizioni Effedue S.r.l.)
Okay, sensitive viewer, hear my plight! This is a series that will give a trash cinema librarian fits! I was unable to lay eyes on **HELL'S ANGEL** (1997) sadly, but **HELL'S ANGEL 2 - IL VISIO DEL PECCATO** (1997) and **HELL'S ANGEL 3 – CAPRICCI ANALI** (1998) run almost four hours between them and provide a definite feel for this trilogy of lust presented by a devil-costume-clad Eva Henger and a pair of sexy demon gals, which certainly satisfied my every interest in the deadly sinning they present. There is no plot to speak of, only some atmospheric wraparound sequences as Eva introduces the bits we are about to witness as awesome Filmirage-style music plays beneath them. Both 2 and 3 share some footage, and the films jump around in time periods and use scenes from previous D'Amato films. These include some bits that I haven't unearthed before, but given the massive girth and epic length of the canon of JoeNography I feel comfortable assuming these are retreads. Few of the "stars" appear, outside of Eva herself, but that is alright. Familiar faces like Bruno SX, Mike Foster and Frank Gun all work over the star with great aplomb, and when she needs a break, Anita Blond scenes abound! Certainly a lesser effort, this repackaging gets lots of style points—it even spawned a softcore variant. Given the immense amount of footage used, that couldn't have been too hard (and may lack the evident hardness of schlong on show as well). But wait—there is *more Hell's Angel* out there! **EVA & SELEN IL DUELO** is a compilation film that even includes Eva in D'Amato's **SHOWGIRL** (1998) on the cover. It's a clip film featuring some D'Amato and other greatest hits n' tits from both women, and includes a hardcore scene shot on the narrative set with Eva in full devil delight! Now, this could be from the original **HELL'S ANGEL** film, but it is a great bonus to have if you can't track down that initial entry. It may be the only original scene using the set, though I'm finding it hard to believe there isn't a three-girl devil knot out there...somewhere. The search continues. You'll get D'Amato porn of all stripes in any installment of this series, and they are worth finding!

HERCULES: A SEX ADVENTURE
(*Le fatiche erotiche di Ercole*, 1997, Butterfly Motion Pictures Corp.)
Playing off the title of the Peplum classic **LE FATICHE DI ERCOLE** (1958), Joe D'Amato brings us the young Turk, Hakan, in the title role with **LE FATICHE EROTICHE DI ERCOLE**! Yep, *The Erotic Labors of Hercules*, where the boulders he slings here are between his legs and aren't made of foam. Hercules is a character which lends itself well to porn, doing good and spreading merry cheer while adventuring about a land of beautiful

women, mysterious fog-enshrouded goddesses and mysterious gods that demand their daughters lie with the strongest men to continue "the lineage of the Gods!" Megara (played by Kelly Trump) is on the case, but needs some heroic wooing to really lubricate the situation since she is under a terrible spell. Hercules and his Peplum required little buddy companion/DP partner seek The Golden Apple under orders from Clitzia The Seer and must face the "rage and treason of the Queen of Gods", Hera. In fine Sword-and-Sandal tradition there are some sword battles (though Steve Reeves had certainly not staged those *inside* a maiden on camera) and adventuring that includes lots of slow motion running and random oral sex scenes shot with women in jungle girl costumes. This all works for Hercules, and it works for me! Someone should tell Megara that you don't get babies from having sex in that other portal to an inner world though…

Hakan isn't exactly the greatest actor D'Amato worked with (see him in 1997's **THE LAST FIGHT** for proof, as he is outdone by Rocco Siffredi saying "*The fuck you say*," over and over), but he manages to play the stoic hero with the at-first frigid Megara and then lifts the loincloth to drop the thunderbolts with great precision when time comes. Kelly Trump would do a number of productions during this time and she is really beautiful and benefits from having a veteran photographer like D'Amato behind the cameras.

One of the easiest-to-find of the films in this article, it's a surprisingly straight-faced film that doesn't really feel so much like a parody as a play on the Muscleman subgenre. While period porn was nothing new, it might be the first time the labors of Hercules included delivering a massive facial to save the lineage of the Gods! Big points for that!

IL MONACO
(1996, Joe D'Amato, Capital Film)
The Hungarian Castle Sex Tour continues! Spooky music sets the scene as an old man sets up a stand and hangs a mysterious sign in a language I can't read. The joke will be on me, but let's roll. A monk wanders through the stony halls…and a beautiful woman follows him to a silk-draped bedroll on the floor of a spooky antechamber. Well, it's spooky because the music is straight-up horror film synth drone. The monk is "seduced" by the woman. Are they ghosts? Well…a group of tourists arrive (thankfully, they are mostly hot women) and end up counting all kinds of pearly beads from various monks that appear throughout the castle. The trick? At the end of the film the old man's sign reads, in four languages, RENT A MONK-DRESS. The local men sure have it easy around here! Hot women that love ghosts just appear every day! One of our enterprising male leads turns in his uniform with tired hands, and you know he'll be back tomorrow for more. Rest up, heroic one! This film is wall-to-wall sex and is full of *stunning* women and a heavy leaning on interracial and anal blessings from the Monks. The opening scene with Vicca and Sean Micheals is D'Amato porn at its best, and with the weird musical choices, it has a unique vibe that buzzes all the right spots! I'm just happy I got the joke at the end. Thanks for the multilingual sign, Joe! The Gold Films presentation is in Italian with Russian voiceover during the typical "turn around and suck it" dialog, no less! If you want to skip plot and focus on castle action, this one is perfect stroke-per-sequence value for your buck. The sexy Ursula Moore does triple duty and D'Amato makes sure to probe every inch of her!

LADY IN THE IRON MASK
(1998, Joe D'Amato, Butterfly Motion Pictures Corp.)
It's time to go balls-deep into the world of Alexandre Dumas and The Man…urr…*Lady* in the infamous Iron Mask! Featuring the beautiful Anita Blond in the role of a King's *twin* daughters, Madeline and Jacqueline. One is very nice, of course, but the other just can't keep any man or woman at her fingertips out of her mouth and other orifices! The king locks up the wanton lass, but it only takes her a few minutes of Sapphic seductions on her guardian to make an escape and try to fuck her way all over the court—and they end up all over her for good measure! The good sister of course ends up trapped in the Iron Mask and even finds true love along the way. And of course a metal facial occurs—it had to happen, right? This film has a full softcore variant, but as hardcore goes, it's quite good, with D'Amato using outdoor locations to great effect. Watching this it is amazing how many of the Butterfly/Capital porn films look better than the last batch of Filmirage productions! Anita Blond certainly doesn't hold back and brings vigorous gyrations to both her characters. There is a lot of slow motion used in the hard version so I can assume this was to keep it long enough to reach the 90 minute mark as there is most likely deleted exposition from the softer cut. Highly recommended, this is class porn with great photography and costuming and even a cool facial chastity belt! I bet the dubbers had an interesting day with this, the dialog is mostly straightforward, but you can look for one of the castle maidens sporting a nifty shoulder tattoo to lighten the mood!

LOVE & PSYCHE
(*Amore & Psiche*, 1998, Tripolis Finances)
Neo-Peplum stylings abound in this late release from Tripolis. While he is a second stringer, favorite face Frank Gun takes center stage with three scenes, all featuring the super-hot Maria Papp, while the usual group sex sequences take up a big part of the running time. Shot on the familiar stone floor, outdoor field and with the same costumes as all the other Peplum porns, the only print I've seen is in Italian, but it certainly is a variation on Cupid and Psyche, as Joe was wont to do,

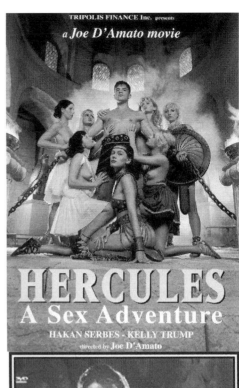

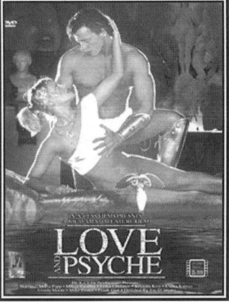

bouncing closely off classic tales. Gun endures (well...if he has to) many trials to get to his lady love, usually wielding his sensual sword to conquer all. As well-made as any of the entries, this is definitely a treat for fans of Gun and Papp. There is a scene inside Vulcan's workshop that will amuse long-time Peplum fanatics as well, shot with lots of style and jumping out from the rest of the movie. D'Amato seemed particularly engaged in using the environments for this film; there is a stunning night sequences that starts with Papp soloing on a set of stone stairs that looks just as great in stills as it does in motion. While it is listed as 1998 in the copyright, the material is probably a few years older. If you are going deep on these, it's a fun entry with familiar surroundings and some of the lesser-name players moving to the front of the action! Very similar to **ULYSSES** (1998), it's an interesting quickie.

MARCO POLO
(1995, Golden Hawk)

This one would have been titled *MARCO POLO'S ANAL EXPEDITIONS OF THE ORIENT* if I had my way! It is also one of the best-shot films in this entire list. Marco Polo features great performances from Rocco Siffredi, Simona Valli and Tabatha Cash as well as lush sets and intricate costumes that really make this one feel like a complete effort from co-directors Luca Damiano and D'Amato. The duo indeed worked very well, and this film is shot in the Phillipines in what appears to be the same places as the D'Amato soft core **CHINA AND SEX** (recently released to DVD in the US) and **ALADDIN X**. Marco arrives at the palace of the Sultan Rangoon and soon finds himself between the legs and behind the rump of the sexy Princess Lila. Bedroom hijinks abound as Marco finds himself facing sexual tests that involve an entire harem of Asian beauties ready to test the strengths, lengths (and girth) of Rocco! Can the princess find lust—and maybe even love—with the great explorer?

MARCO POLO won't go winning awards for narrative innovation, but this is a very well built piece of porn that shows off the best of both directors skill set, and I highly recommend it to anyone interested in the European Trash and Porn intersection of the cinematic world. Tabatha Cash is stunning enough, and D'Amato fans will love how much she is made to look as if the princess stepped right out of an old Laura Gemser sexploitation film and into the deepest and wettest adventure yet. When you see Golden Hawk on the title card, you are in for some quality! Top notch cinematography, a fun sense of humor, beautiful women and men and even a dude with a giant sword!

MIDNIGHT OBSESSION
(1995, Capital Film)

Using some of the same sets and as **SEX PENITENTIARY**, this is the evil twin to that film. Where **SP** was standard porn, this film is something else entirely. **MIDNIGHT OBSESSION** stars the Hungarian beauty Anita Rinaldi in a much harder-edged film that carries all the look and feel of a rugged early-'80s example of violent sexploitation. While it is straight-up pornography, D'Amato and crew were definitely making something that was a wild throwback to the early 1980s! Rinaldi goes *Midnight Express*, and after some establishing shots of her walking and getting involved in the drug trade our beautifully misguided woman ends up in a Hungarian prison where cavity searches involve anal gaping and forced lesbian sex!

Violent and shot with equal quality to most WIP Euroclassics, this film bridges the gap between some of the traditionally trashy films of D'Amato and the '90s porn era with style, though this is most likely not for all audiences. Perhaps it is much less extreme than what goes down in the porn of the current era, but given the high quality of the production, it's still a shock to the system. Very few of these sex films feel like you could add "-ploitation" at the end. Midnight Obsession definitely does that, taking the rough side of the Women-in-Prison genre and exploiting it up the shaft and down the ass. D'Amato shot the surprisingly soft core adventure **PREDATORS OF THE ANTILLES** (1999) not long after this and featured Rinaldi in a solid non-sex role, and I'm thinking there was definitely some payback going on. You can see that she is definitely great at the athletic assplay aspects of porn in **MIDNIGHT OBSESSION**, but it is also obvious that she aspires to more and is as good as many of the actresses from a decade gone by in this solid genre outing. I didn't find it terribly erotic, but I certainly found a lot to admire in this film.

NERO: ORGY OF FIRE
(1997, Butterfly Motion Pictures Corp.)

It's time to get Caligulatronic again! This time Hakan is Nero, who spends a lot of time playing the harp and banging multiple prostitutes, usually overcoming (or cumming over) their superior numbers. But Octavia the Horny (played by Nicolette Orsini) ain't having it! While he is busy spraying his seed all over the Empire's trollops she wants his baby...after she walks in on him finishing on a few ladies she grabs his cock and declares, "I'll put a bone in that filet!" She gets it, but Nero tells her off with some hysterical less-than-Romance Language. There isn't much more to it, this lower-ended film in the Neo-Caligula cycle is heavy on second string players, all of which dig into their roles with the expected gusto. Nicolette Orsini has a lot of scenes this time, and this Ukranian dynamo is a D'Amato regular with good reason! The VHS tape from Sweden features the hardcore edition and an amazingly funny English dub not by the usual team that is overflowing with great lines that include, "Fuck off, you aren't the leader around here, you are my wife...fuck off...fuck OFF!" delivered while Hakan's spent penis wags all over the screen. As an educational bonus, those of us that haven't mastered the language learn good Swedish sex words. Not essential, but if you find yourself a fan of Orsini or just want to see D'Amato billed as Raf De Palma on screen, this is your film! And yes, Nicolette Orsini is in the memorable **BUTTMAN IN BUDAPEST** (1998)! A D'Amato starlet on the rise!

OLYMPUS: REFUGE OF GODS
(1998, Tripolis Finances)
Apollo and a pal are sitting atop Mount Olympus, chilling out and drinking some "truly divine" nectar before engaging in some group sex with their goddesses that enter the scene. But wait, things change quickly as Kelly Trump shows up in the modern day castle location D'Amato porn fans will easily recognize. Her pink-shorts-wearing boyfriend decides to go nude but for his socks and sneakers while engaging in athletic anal sex with her doing a complete split on a stone ledge, then takes a post-anal-coitus walk, wandering about the castle when out of the blue—*POOF!*—up comes a harlot from Olympus for him to apply penile pressure most mighty upon. And—*POOF!* again—he vanishes, and narration kicks in…"And so it came to pass as if by magic," the two worlds collide and it is a full-bore Battle of Marathon Pop Shots! This one is a definite pass for anyone but the hardest hardcore fan of Kelly Trump, who, to be fair, looks great and pulls off a split sequence on a stone wall that had me doing a double take. If you want D'Amato gods and gals, you can dump this to the bottom of the triple-feature with **HERCULES: A SEX ADVENTURE** and **SAMSON IN THE AMAZON'S LAND**.

ROCCO E I MERCENARI
(1998, Capital Film)
An outstanding opening montage of Wanted posters that includes the "Magnifici 7", which includes Rocco Siffredi, Roberto Malone, Philippe Dean and Bruno SX kicks off another entry shot on the sets used for the **CALAMITY JANE** series and it is basically the same style with a slightly different cast. To be fair, Rocco looks great in his duster and there is even a sequence where he saves a fellow schlongslinger from being strung up in traditional Oater style, but this is a completely straightforward porn entry. Made in 1998, it features some of the rougher aspects of **CALAMITY JANE 2**, most notably Rocco being more true-to-form than in **TORERO** (for example) as he spanks and plays Five Card Draw by going in the backdoor of one of his co-stars with his entire hand! The US edition of this is entitled **OUTLAWS** and I'm very curious to see if it has toned-down sex (as is sometimes the case in Euro-to-US releases) and more story. For fans of Maria de Sanchez (**FLAMENCO ECSTASY**), this will be one that will definitely work the six shooter and is a must! Rocco is popular for several reasons, and he puts them all on show here. Let's leave this one as an open project and find out more in the US edition in the upcoming Part 2.

ROCCO'S GHOST
(1997, Joe D'Amato, No production company on print)
I MISTERI DELL' EROS sounds much better than the drab voiceover on the English dub that simply says **ROCCO GHOST** over the titles. Pure porn simplicity as D'Amato tells the tale of a leather-clad Rocco and his lady friend driving up to a "kind of gloomy" castle. The pair enters and splits up right away (?) and both begin fucking their way through period-costumed ghosts. These ectoplasmic horndogs are an energetic batch, and loads of group fucking ensues. They all stop, drop and roll when Rocco stops by, however. If my house gets haunted, I hope I'm as lucky as Rocco as it is explained gently, "We are as real as can be, observe how she sucks my cock!" Well, we observed, and it didn't take long for one of Europe's most famous studs to service 'em all. I guess when you are with a beautiful lady from the otherworld it doesn't bother them to double up on the double penetration! Rocco is fairly restrained, all things considered, and manages to actually give facials to every ghost in the film at the climax! No story, lots of women and the common castle scenario take the class out of the flick, but it leaves plenty of ass to admire.

SAHARA, QUEEN OF THE DESERT
(1998, In-X-Cess International)
Almost always billed on Internet sources as **QUEEN OF THE ELEPHANTS 2**, which isn't right at all. Where **QUEEN** is a fun jungle girl movie, **SAHARA** is more a boardroom, bedroom and occasional outdoor backdoor-drilling flick. Selen does appear, but not to the same extent. She does wander out of the desert in the opening sequence, but that hardly seems the same as being Sheena—urrr…*like* Sheena. Selen has three scenes, and two of them appear to be one scene cut in half, shot outdoors with fading light! That isn't to say that the porn isn't good, however. Sporting a cast anchored by the German Zenza Raggi as he goes from high profile role with Selen to large group sex scenes *a la* D'Amato with ease. I can't give more plot since the review copy was in Italian, but there is definitely some intrigue going on in what appears to be the same hotel rooms in Spain that were used for **FLAMENCO ECSTASY**! Good for the libido; not so much for the exploitation cinema fans. This is basically solid couples' porn. One lesson I took away was that a three-way in a full tub will get water on the floor and leave everyone feeling a little pruny, but D'Amato pulls it off with style.

SAMSON IN THE AMAZON'S LAND
(1998, Butterfly Motion Pictures Corp.)
The Italian title, **LE PORNO GLADIATRICI**, could be my favorite porn title in years. With the familiar setting of Peplum Porn from the legend of Hercules (**THE SEX ADVENTURES** version, of course), adventure and excitement carries on the saga! Shot on the same sets and with the same cast, there is plentiful re-use of "dramatic" footage from the earlier film as Hakan and friends now find themselves facing a tribe of sex-crazed Amazons (yes!) and one weirdly-made-up sorceress (YES!) to save the day. As plot goes, it's thinner than **HERCULES**, but basically looks and sounds exactly the same, and that is a good thing. Undoubtedly a quickie used to most likely cut down the first film's

length, many of the sex scenes are intercut for dramatic tension (well...) and slow motion shots abound. The new plot footage is very entertaining as the jungle girl costume reappears, as well as a few shields and swords. I couldn't help but be reminded of the Ed Fury film **COLOSSUS AND THE AMAZON QUEEN** (1960) at times—the plot is really similar! If only Al Brescia had done a porn version of **AMAZONS AND SUPERMEN** (1974), it could have looked like this. With more boinking sound effects though, just try and picture that. If **HERCULES: A SEX ADVENTURE** left you hungry for more, then follow the fleshy spear of destiny for more Hakan Heavy Lifting!

SCANDAL IN THE SUN
(a.k.a. **SHAMELESS**, 1995, Captial Film)
This film's credits are more intriguing than the film! The opening lists it as a Joe D'Amato film and then continues along and credits direction to Luca Damiano on the Italian version? The two were definitely working together and all other credits are D'Amatotized, such as Federiko Slonisko and Kathleen Stratton; this looks to be a game of pick-up ball dribbling during other shoots, as there is nothing to the show at all. Shot outdoors, it follows a couple visiting a swingers retreat. Luckily, for the most part, everyone is really attractive and fucks like it is their last day on earth! Lots of athletic assplay and men lined up for logside blowjobs. It is fun to watch something less stage-bound from D'Amato and Damiano, if not aesthetically appealing, and everyone appears to be having fun. It's like grabbing all your secondary players for a day at the beach with some "work" thrown in. The crew most likely had more issues getting all the equipment to the beach! You'll recognize our troupe, most notably the prolific Roxanne Hall, as they bounce various body bits and work on their tans! And I could just watch the Hungarian Cindy Scorsese all day. It's an after-dinner mint of a movie for sure, and you'll be in awe as the dialog consists of moaning for 20-minute stretches and the soundtrack just keep changing songs! When the soft romantic tune pops up over some anal close ups, though...odd. Even the cover art alternates around the world (and this got a lot of releases) between D'Amato and Damiano, proving that both men are top brand names in the Euro Skin Game!

SELEN ON TREASURE ISLAND
(*Selen nell'isola del tesoro*, 1998, Joe D'Amato, Butterfly Motion Pictures Corp.)
I love a good European Pirate movie! While this doesn't live up to Steve Reeves adventures or **LADY STILLETO**, Selen stars and grinds away as the granddaughter of an old pirate who was a close associate with the infamous Ahab which nets her...yep, a treasure map. After realizing that men just wanted her for the cartographic treasures she was holding instead of the pornographic nature of her inheritance, she gets into adventures that span both the seaways and the bedrooms of a mysterious land. Selen gets intimate with pirates of both sexes and even engages in a battle or two along the way. The pace is fast and the sex is shot in classic D'Amato fashion, mixing up costumed performers in lush bedrooms with spartan prison cells, one after the other. Selen actually shows some real acting range at times in her work with D'Amato, and she is especially good as she goes from tied-down beauty girl to full-on unbuckler of swashing! The Hungarian performer Karli Sweet has an excellent scene, as well; she would become a staple of many adult rooms around the globe in the various *Euro Angels* and *Buttman Goes to Budapest* films. I recognized her all these years later! This film is similar to the softcore **PREDATORS OF THE ANTILLES/SEXY PIRATES**, only without nearly as much talking—with good reason. Same sets, same stock battles...and if you want to see what one of the costume porn films would be like as a straight-ahead adventure, look that film up. It is available on DVD as **SEXY PIRATES** in the United States! Anita Rinaldi (as Anita Skulteti) appears as the lead in the softcore production, though not in the XXX film shot at the same time. Interesting, especially since Rinaldi had done some very hardcore work for D'Amato in the past and was also in charge of one of the major talent agencies for the adult market. A nice bit of helping each other out between the two!

QUEEN OF ELEPHANTS
(*La regina degli elefanti*, 1998, Joe D'Amato, In-X-Cess International)
If you loved **TARZAN-X**, you'll want to explore with Selen as Jenny Malory, "a beautiful female creature who dwells peacefully surrounded by the African savannah's most wild animals..." She doesn't know that she was a young noble girl whose family was killed in a boating accident while cruising the Sierra Leone. Many years pass (like...uh, *way* past puberty) and she becomes not just sexy and wild, but graduates into a full-on Jungle Girl! After word gets back to her family that a mysterious blonde girl is wandering the wild, a small band of intrepid explorers (who love fucking, by the way) seek her out and bring her back to civilization. Jenny learns about sex (of course) and intrigue (of course) as they try to *literally* screw her out of the family fortune. It's a sex-swapped *Tarzan*! Selen, as always, puts forth an excellent performance, following in Rocco Siffredi's schlongsteps by effectively bringing the savage girl's civilized and uncivilized behaviors together. After seeing sex for the first time, she certainly catches on quickly, mastering positions and techniques her totally perverse family demonstrates at every turn. D'Amato does make an interesting use of his settings; during the early part of the film there is a lot of outdoor sex that seems more organic—though you may take notice of one bit involving a rifle that jumps out of nowhere—and more passionate. Once everyone hits the mansion and the plots get messy, the action gets more "perverse" and focuses more on anal sex and follow-up facials. Character dimension or meeting the minimal requirements? I can't be 100 percent sure, but I think it's good scripting from a guy that used sex as plot devices for a long time. Definitely a winner for fans that enjoy Eurotrash Jungle films of the '60s and porn of the '90s.

Selen was very popular during her relatively short porn career, and while she rode some pretty big stuff while building her resume, this may have been the only time she rode a real elephant!

SEX PENITENTIARY
(1996, Capital Film)

And now it is time for a little Emmanuelle throwback with Joe D'Amato as he brings us Sara, an intrepid newspaper reporter that isn't afraid to take one (or two, or three) cocks for the team as she seeks out a story! After a police bust interrupts her "trying to get an interview with the boss" from some thugs, she finds that nobody believes her journalistic credentials in the **SEX PENITENTIARY**! Emmanuelle never had cavity searches this deep, but they do abound as teeth are counted and asses get probed. A ponytailed prick is in charge of moving the ladies around as they are stripped and deeply vaccinated in every possible orifice. The prisoners have their own problems and are a grim lot that push *gigantic* mops (seriously, these are the Rocco Siffredi style cleaning utilities!) and complain about how they don't get to joke in the **SEX PENITENTIARY**, but they all do have fun. Yes, I like typing sex and penitentiary in tandem, it's just a great exploitation title.

Simona Valli is beautiful, and while she can't hold the (admittedly tiny) bra of Laura Gemser, she makes the best of all her circumstances, even coming up with an escape plan and passing it along in real **GREAT ESCAPE** fashion. One guess as to this masterful plot folks…think on it…yes, it involves oral persuasion! Roberto Malone is the warden and his acceptance of said favors is just priceless. "Hmm, you are reasonable…uhhh…uhhh." Whatever works! But why escape when the Governor bursts in and wants to "hush shit up" and just releases everyone? **SEX PENITENTIARY** is cheap-looking and reuses the same examining room for several sequences, but the Italian women in the cast are stunning and the tone is soft enough that there are no unpleasant surprises or forced sex scenarios. Oddly, this is a WIP film with *no* lesbian sequence. That shocked me more than anything else!

SHOWGIRL
(1998, Butterfly Motion Pictures Corp.)

Joe D'Amato's final film; he passed away just a few days after returning home from shooting **SHOWGIRL** in Las Vegas. It's an interesting film that feels like much of the luster of the movies made just a few years ago in Budapest are long behind the crews of Butterfly Motion Pictures, as Eva Henger plays a girl sharing her joy and pain as she heads to the bright streets and shadowy clubs to find fame and fortune. Eva is ready for action and even some acting as she finds the road to being a featured dancer (aim high!) is one of sore knees and competitive environments just to get time on the not-so-brightly-lit stages just off the strip. Vegas, and the way it is shot, reminds one of another D'Amato hardcore film from many years before, **PLEASURE SHOP ON 7th AVE** (1979), which is a must for any D'amato-phile. It's grim, and while the city bustles and blinks, the characters' lives are shallow and get swallowed up by the realization that dreams and reality are nowhere close in these damn towns. Really, **SHOWGIRL** is just: a girl and boy show up, split up, bang a bunch of people, feel heartbreak and get out of town, but the dramatic bits are often enough for this to be vintage Filmirage sexploitation while not skimping at all on its given mission as a porn flick. It is a nice change from the earlier films that used beautiful locations, or in cases of films like **COP SUCKER**, very staged environments. The strip club promising shows by Kelly O'Dell and Ashlyn Gere add to the reality of Eva's plight for porn fans; they are marquee names and watching this character try to get on the same floor as them is really interesting. Maybe Joe was just in Vegas? Maybe he was feeling run down with the porn, and to be fair he must have been because on occasion he would slip in a softcore film or work on re-editing these into softer variants. The English language edition is interesting as the "dubbed" version is still in Italian with English narration to keep things simple. It's an odd way to watch a movie, like having a second writer explain a story to you as you watch the images, but let's not over think it. A solid porn outing that features some insane waterspout one-legged sex that still has me scratching my head. D'Amato trades storybook for fractured fairytale and brings us along for the ride. Worth seeking out for any fan of porn, Eva Henger or Joe D'Amato.

SODOMA AND GOMORRA
(2000, Tripolis Finances)

The familiar heroic synthotrax are back! The same sets as **HERCULES: A SEX ADVENTURE** and its related films are ready to Styrofoam rock you and roll you into the lands of times lost beneath furious wrath of…whatever! An outstanding opening sex scene is set into motion as the ground rumbles because of a volcano. Best answer to that? Anal. Thank you, Joe D'Amato. The awesome amazons of **SAMSON IN THE AMAZON'S LAND** return as the Queen of Gomorra (Kelly Trump, of course) summons the well-equipped men for a mission. "A strong man to a woman in Gomorra is nothing but a wimp!" Some oral trials get underway, climaxing in Kelly Trump opening all the gates for a DP to get her lads feeling way beyond missionary for their…mission. Meanwhile, crazy men are wandering about prophesying doom over stock footage of crumbling cities and cocksucking. Well, that sums it up. The Queen of Gomorra humps and bumps until they are all deep-throated by volcanic fire! Much better than expected, Kelly Trump really steals the show and puts in one of her hottest performances in a D'Amato film. The costumes from **HERCULES** make an appearance, but not for long, as they are flung off faster than Maciste hurling a band of thugs holding him down. Alley-oop!

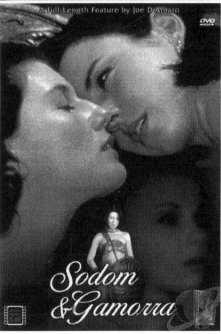

"Really, **SHOWGIRL** is just: a girl and boy show up, split up, bang a bunch of people, feel heartbreak and get out of town, but the dramatic bits are often enough for this to be vintage Filmirage sexploitation while not skimping at all on its given mission as a porn flick."

TARZAN-X: SHAME OF JANE
(1994, Capital Film / Butterly Motion Pictures Corp.)

TARZAN-X is, in my opinion, the best place to start watching the '90s porn films of Joe D'Amato! Everything about this is entertaining to the right audience as it sports a great jungle adventure score that doesn't skimp on the porno funk, a beautiful cast of women that are all-natural Europorn personified and a surprisingly earnest performance from Rocco Siffredi as "Ape Man" (urr...Tarzan). After a group of explorers seek out the mysterious man, it is revealed that he is John, the heir to a huge fortune. Of course, this gets discovered after Jane (real-life wife of Siffredi, Rosa Caracciolo) almost stumbles on some of her cohorts enjoying some outdoor backdoor action and knocks herself out cold. Whoops! Ape Man finds her and brings her to the relative safety of his home by the river (with pet monkey, of course). The King of the Jungle Boogie strips her down and is curious, having never seen a woman. He notes her lack of penis as well...unleashing the *Rocco Cock*, much to Jane's shock. She explains their body parts aren't the same by giving him a fantastic blowjob. Now, let's all think about this. Ape Man is very lucky and very confused by all this "civilized" behavior and has to explore it on his own. After he is brought back to the world of the wealthy and well-to-do, our well-hung hero struggles to find his way back to happiness and to his beloved Jane. Several ladies get in the way, but our hero swings his mighty vine over, around and almost *through* them. It's not heavy lifting in the plot department, but D'Amato and all involved in the production put forth a great effort with top-notch cinematography, and when Tarzan finally lets out his ultimate war cry at the big finish, you'll cheer.

The Edgar Rice Burroughs Estate was *not* cheering, as you could well imagine. They filed legal action, though it hardly seemed to have slowed the global distribution of the film, since I'm still writing about it. I have not seen the softcore variant edition, **AVVENTURE EROTICHE NELLA GIUNGLA**, which does feature more adventure in place of the lengthy erotic bits, including flashbacks of Jane being captured and tied up. The sex scenes are very strong and while Siffredi is never in doubt as a performer, the sequences with Caracciolo are intense and well done. It's porn without being terribly tacky, and it may represent the most serious attempt at erotica in this period of the mighty Massaccesi! A must-have!

THE BOXER 1 & 2
(1996/1997, Pico Motion Pictures)

Rocco Siffredi is *Rocky* (!) Mancini, a small-time boxer with a big-time cock! His girl wants him to give up the fight game, but when some scurrilous promoters try to get him to throw a fight to a world champion that needs to fulfill a contract, he trains for the fight of his life. How he manages to win after constant dehydration from fucking both his lady and a newfound boxing groupie sent there to sap his strength (his trainer warned him!) is a miracle, as big as any found in sports cinema. Sleazy sports cinema, that is! **THE BOXER** features Rocco doing his best with quite a lot of dialog in English

TARZAN X! The Burroughs wanted it banned, but this saga of Jane swinging from the Ape Man's massive jungle vine has become one of D'Amato's most popular and widely seen films! OooOHOEEEOOOOO!

and he actually does well in the surprisingly long boxing brawl sequences! He also, of course, does anal on a groupie in a boxing ring, but that's Rocco for you. The man has priorities. His best gal is played by real-life wife Rosa Caracciolo (Jane of **TARZAN-X**) and Sean Micheals is one of the bad guys that delivers a crazy DP to the most awesome pseudonym of the year, "Crayola Bleu" (better known as Precious Silver). There are only a few sex scenes, matched in number by training and battling. The matches themselves are rather funny, using *ancient* stock footage of New York and Madison Square Garden, some crowd shots and El Santo-style empty sound stage pugilism. Overall, **THE BOXER** is a lot of talk and some sex that is way less restrained than the couples-styled story would suggest. I can only review Part 1, since no version of Part 2 was available, which leads us to the next entry…

THE LAST FIGHT
(1997, Pico Motion Pictures)

It's actually the raging conclusion to a trilogy of Rocco movies where he plays Rocky the Boxer, and there is flashback footage to drive that home harder than a Siffredi piledriver! This time our man takes on a protégé in Hakan (who actually has played Samson, Hercules and Nero for D'Amato!) and trains him to be a true warrior of the squared circle. Honestly, though, they spend more time in bed and on the mat with various women, including Sindee Coxx and an appearance by the always-welcome Rosa Caracciolo. However, the younger boxer gains so much fame that he is offered a fight with his mentor for *fifty million dollars*—and you will watch in awe as Rocco says "THE FUCK YOU TALKING ABOUT, 50 MILLION" a bunch of times at this news. The sleazy promoter goads the pair into a street fight at the end that is well-done and brings a close to the series. It's not nearly as well-made as many of the other films during this period, but has a feel much closer to other US-shot productions from Filmirage than most. Take out the "I'm here because I want to fuck you" plotlines and add in a car chase and *WHAM*, this one could be softcore in a heartbeat. The young Turkish actor Hakan has an accent that makes his tough-talk hard to take, but certainly doesn't lack in the size or stamina department to keep up with Rocco. And that says a lot! Eurotrash fans will get a kick out of the editing by "Kathleen Stratton" that features stock footage to change settings that appears 20 years older than the film! And…AND…fans of "Eye Of The Tiger" will dig the musical variation that plays us out during the battle bits. Survivor would be pissed!

ULYSSES
(1998, Tripolis Finances)

Cue the heralding synthoboop once more and storm the *ass-le* for another Pneumatic and Peplumatic moment in the Joe D'Amato Neo-Peplum Porn binge! Ulysses is our subject this time, and the role of lead muscle man is familiar face Frank Gun (who I like to call "His Hugeness of Hungary") this time around. A narrator lets us know that Ulysses has forgotten about Penelope as we open, and has spent years on the island of the nymphos. I guess fans of *The Odyssey* will figure that he should have put wax in his ears, eh? Well, when Calypso the nymph is played by Ursula Moore, I guess I can see the holdup on pursuing heroics for other ventures between the thighs of the maidens. However, it can't last forever, and Ulysses decides to leave the island, only to be shipwrecked and washed ashore on a new island adventure where much group sex occurs, and he shares tales of titanic wonder with new friends. This includes a bit that sees him captured by a monstrous woman in one of the strangest episodes in all of D'Amato sinema. Erika Bella shows up to dominate our hero, adorned in full facial hair and sporting a painted-on third eye! Kirk Morris never had days like these! **ULYSSES** is definitely a fun entry into the fleshy sword series and Gun really carries the entire film on his shoulders for once. There are several extended group scenes shot with the usual vigor to extend the running time, but you'll be entranced—or at least curious—to see how the plot resolves. An outstanding final reward for our hero awaits between the legs of Penelope, who, oddly enough, is testing out new lovers when Ulysses bursts in with a "*WARRRGH!*" and sends the men away. Rita Cardinale is pure Hungarian hotness, and it's one of the more memorable climaxes to another sword-swinging, dong-slinging adventure!

"The Monk", take one!

A POST POP-SHOT MESSAGE FROM YOUR DEHYDRATED REPORTER:
There are many more films to go, and we'll be back at your backside with more in the next issue of WENG'S CHOP! More cowgirls and reverse cowgirls await your gaze… more Sexual Centurions are ready to unload with mighty spears across your screen… and a lot more Joe D'Amato remains to be explored!

DIRECT HIT! HELL FIST!
THE LEGACY OF SONNY CHIBA

by C.T. McNeely

If Bruce Lee floats like a butterfly and stings like a bee then Sonny Chiba charges like a raging bull and bites like a rabid dog.

This is not an article about Bruce Lee. This is about Sonny Chiba. You won't find these movies on TV. Sonny Chiba isn't on posters and t-shirts you can buy at Wal-Mart. However, these movies are damned good. Some of them are the best of their type that you will ever see.

Sonny Chiba was born Sadaho Maeda, in the Fukuoka Prefecture of Japan. In his early life he was a passionate athlete and martial artist. He started his film career in the 1960s with Sci-Fi movies like **INVASION OF THE NEPTUNE MEN** (1961) and crime thrillers like **GANG VS. G-MEN** (1962), directed by Kinji Fukasaku, who always got the best performances out of Chiba.

However, by the time 1970 rolled around, Chiba formed the Japan Action Club when he discovered that the majority of Japanese actors were not physically fit enough to handle stunts. The JAC, now Japanese Action Enterprise, handles stunts in Japanese movies and television, and it is with the help of the JAC that Sonny Chiba really came into his own and left a legacy on Japanese Action cinema and the world that lives on today. With more actors handling their own stunt work thanks to the JAC, the camera is not restricted to behind the head of a "stuntman" in fear of revealing their face.

He is perhaps best known in the West for his violent martial arts films and for his inspiration to Quentin Tarantino. Still, any cult movie fan or fan of Japanese movies, TV, Anime or video games has felt the influence of Sonny Chiba at some point over the course of his long and illustrious career.

THE FIST AND THE FURY

In 1974, Shigehiro Ozawa directed **GEKITOTSU! SATSUJIN KEN** (*Sudden attack! The killing fist*), better known in the West as **THE STREET FIGHTER**. Chiba plays Terry (Takura in the Japanese original) Tsurugi. This is the role that he would be best-known for, thanks to Quentin Tarantino's well-known love for it. Tsurugi is a tough, no-holds-barred mercenary. He holds allegiance to no one and is always looking out for himself above everyone and everything else. **THE STREET FIGHTER** is a hyper-violent martial arts extravaganza. Chiba knocks teeth out, breaks bones, tears out throats, and removes a certain body part from a would-be rapist. If you are a martial arts movie fan, you owe it to yourself to watch **THE STREET FIGHTER**, because when people talk about violent grindhouse martial arts flicks from the '70s, this is the movie they mean. It spawned two sequels and a spin-off, which will be discussed later.

The success of **THE STREET FIGHTER** set Chiba down a path of starring in many similar violent martial arts movies, sometimes with a healthy dose of humor added in. Nearly a year later, Chiba paired with the master of Japanese exploitation cinema, Teuro Ishii, for **CHOKUGEKI! JIGOKU-KEN** (*Direct hit! Hellfist*), also known as **THE EXECUTIONER** (1974). On paper this film doesn't sound like it will amount to much: Toei hired Teuro Ishii to make a martial arts movie with Sonny Chiba to capitalize on his newfound fame. However, Ishii never really liked to listen to what the studios wanted and his fans always benefited from it. Sure, **THE EXECUTIONER** is technically a martial arts film and it does star Sonny Chiba but Ishii took this idea and did what Ishii does: he went insane.

The result is an over-the-top, stylish to the point of being gaudy, violent to the point of being absurd, sex-filled to the point of being almost sexist slap in the face to anyone who thought this might turn out to be "just another" martial arts movie, all done with a sly wink to the audience. Also, there's a scene where Sonny Chiba rips out a man's rib. Just thought you should know.

Unfortunately for Ishii, the film was a rousing success and a sequel was ordered. **CHOKUGEKI JIGOKU-KEN: DAI-GYAKUTEN** (a.k.a. **KARATE INFERNO**, 1974) delivers an equal amount of zaniness and insanity but Ishii traded in the ultra-violent, sex-filled inferno of the first for a zany screwball comedy caper. Ishii prevailed, and there was no third installment. Both, however, are well worth watching.

In 1976, Kazuhiko Yamaguchi directed **KARATE WARRIORS**. It is yet another adaptation of Dashiell Hammett's *Red Harvest*, which has been famously adapted for film as **A FISTFUL OF DOLLARS** (1964) and **YOJIMBO** (1961). This is a Chiba vehicle, however, so it is like those others, except that it includes manic martial arts action. There is an attempt at sensitizing Chiba's character by having him befriend a small boy, but this is not a plot-heavy film. It is a sex-and-violence-heavy film. A Chiba film.

Also in 1976 came **KARATE KIBA**, directed by Ryuichi Takamori. It is known in the West as **THE BODYGUARD**, and contains extra scenes in

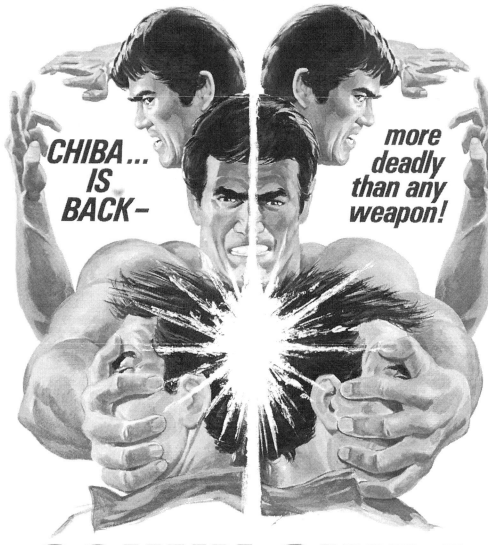

the U.S. print directed by Simon Nuchtern. By this time, Chiba had firmly established himself as a gritty, no-nonsense martial arts star and, as a result of this, his character in **THE BODYGUARD** is known simply as Chiba. At the beginning of the film, Chiba holds a press conference in Japan where he announces that he will be wiping out the country's drug problem. Then he does. Chiba's like that. He doesn't mess around. **THE BODYGUARD** is a cult film classic and the added scenes in the U.S. version are too good to spoil here.

In 1977, Chiba starred in the first in a trilogy of films that would round out his martial arts films. Called the *Mas Oyama Trilogy*, the first film was released in 1977 as **KARATE BEAR FIGHTER** (*Kyokuskin kenka karate burai ken*). Chiba plays Masutatsu Oyama, the real-life founder of Kyokushin Karate, and Chiba's own teacher. Since Chiba is playing his mentor and an important figure in the history of Japanese martial arts, you would expect this to be an understated and loving tribute. However, this film is called **KARATE BEAR FIGHTER**.

The first film, like its two sequels, is full-fledged gritty martial arts movie that owes more to fable than fact regarding its subject. The result is a movie in which Chiba is a drunk who fights bad guys, and I don't know anyone who watched this without wondering when the titular bear fight happens. It does happen—and the bear is a man in a costume because of animal rights laws, but that just makes the scene all the more insane.

The second film, **KARATE BULLFIGHTER** (*Kenka karate kyokushinken*), was also released in 1977. The titular animal karate action in this film is bloodier and more impressive. The rest of the film contains more of the great fights and stunts that you would expect.

The third and final entry in the trilogy, **KARATE FOR LIFE** (*Karate baka ichidai*, 1977), is the best of the bunch. The plot is very similar in ways to **ENTER THE DRAGON** (1973), but the direction from Yamaguchi is smoother and Chiba's action is rougher. He really is in top form here and the result is an incredibly entertaining film and an excellent place to end the discussion on Sonny Chiba The Martial Arts Star.

THE SWORD AND THE SHURIKEN

In 1978, the incomparable Kinji Fukasaku set to do for the *jidaigeki* (Japanese period dramas) what he had done for the yakuza film – turn it on its head and make a genre that was thought dead extremely popular once again. The result was **YAGYÛ ICHIZOKU NO INBÔ** (*The Yagyu clan conspiracy*) also known as **SHOGUN'S SAMURAI**. To star, he enlisted his good friend Sonny Chiba as Yagyu Jubei. It is a role that Chiba would consider his best ever, and this film he would consider his favorite. Outside of Chiba, the film boasts gorgeous cinematography, confident direction from Fukasaku, a great plot with inspiration from Japanese history, and an all-star cast that features virtually every important name in Japanese cinema imaginable: Kinnosuke Nakamura, Tetsuro Tanba, Mikio Narita, Toshiro Mifune, Isuzu Yamada, Chiba's protégé Hiroyuki Sanada, JAC member Etsuko Shiomi, plus many more. The film is incredible and one of my favorites of all time. There are many stunts and fights throughout, and the JAC really shines. The plot is a series of twists and turns leading inexorably to an unbelievable conclusion. Chiba is unforgettable as Yagyu Jubei, and the film was so successful that it spawned a television series which brought many of the stars back to their roles, including Chiba as Jubei. Fukasaku directed the pilot. Watch **SHOGUN'S SAMURAI**…ASAP!

In 1981, Fukasaku and Chiba both returned to Yagyu Jubei for **MAKAI TENSHO** (a.k.a. **SAMURAI REINCARNATION**). Rather than a *jidaigeki*, **SAMURAI REINCARNATION** is a horror fantasy which pits Jubei against Shiro Amakusa, a formerly Christian samurai who has sold his soul to the Devil to gain the ability to resurrect the dead after witnessing the slaughter of Christians 350 years ago. Amakusa plans to create an army of the undead to join him on a murderous rampage. It is up to Yagyu Jubei to stop him. It was based on a JAC stage play, which was itself based on a novel by Futaro Yamada. This film is *amazing*! Zombies, ninjas, samurai, and incredible old-school special effects abound. **SAMURAI REINCARNATION** is another display of what a master of his art Fukasaku was. There was nothing he couldn't do, and here the man does it all. Once again, a Chiba-Fukasaku collaboration could not come with a higher recommendation. Amazing work from folks who are amazing at what they do.

However, before Chiba put on the eye patch to return as Jubei for **MAKAI TENSHO**, he and Fukasaku tackled the famous 47 Ronin legend for **THE FALL OF AKO CASTLE** (*Akô-jô danzetsu*) in 1978. Running almost 3 hours long, Fukasaku takes the familiar story and does it the JAC way. Once the action starts, it doesn't let up. The last 45 minutes of this epic is a dizzying, fascinating, non-stop array of sword fights and death-defying stunts that you have to see to believe. The Fukasaku-Chiba samurai movies are the best of Chiba's career and where to go if you really want to see what Chiba is capable of. Unbelievable.

In 1980, Sonny Chiba would appear in another career-defining role in the TV series *Kage no Gundan* (or *Shadow Warriors*). Here Chiba plays ninja Hattori Hanzo. Hanzo is perfect as the ninja, and the series can now be obtained on DVD in the West under the *Shadow Warriors* title. It originally ran for four seasons and in each new series, Chiba played a new ninja, culminating in Hattori Hanzo XV. The series is full of great ninja action and more stunts from Chiba and other JAC members.

THE LEGACY

Sonny Chiba's legacy is deep. He took other members of the JAC—such as Hiroyuki Sanada and Etsuko Shiomi—under his wing. Shiomi starred in a spin-off of **THE STREET FIGHTER** called **SISTER STREET FIGHTER** (*Onna hissatsu ken*, 1974), as well as many of the other films mentioned here, such as **SHOGUN'S SAMURAI** and **SAMURAI REINCARNATION**.

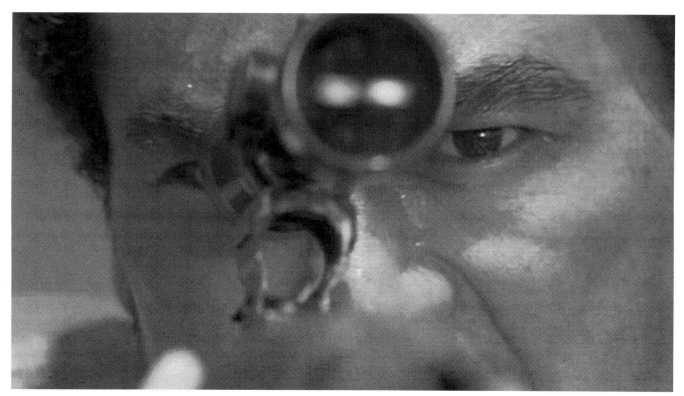

GOLGO 13 (1977)

Hiroyuki Sanada was Sonny Chiba's protégé. He rose to fame in the aforementioned **SHOGUN'S SAMURAI** where he delivers an amazing performance. He continued on to other vehicles featuring Chiba such as **SHOGUN'S NINJA** (*Ninja bugeicho momochi sandayu*, 1980), **SHOGUN'S SHADOW** (*Shôgun Iemitsu no ranshin - Gekitotsu*, 1989), and **SAMURAI REINCARNATION**. His stardom has lived on outside of martial arts and samurai action—he has been in the **RINGU** films, and starred in Yoji Yamada's unforgettable **THE TWILIGHT SAMURAI** (2002), among others.

Chiba's influence can be seen outside the world of cinema. The inclusion of Yagyu Jubei and Hattori Hanzo in the video game series *Samurai Shodown* is undoubtedly because of his portrayal of those characters. He even served as a stand-in for the titular character in the opening of *The Revenge of Shinobi*.

However, Chiba's real legacy is in what he contributed to the way Japan and the world thinks about action. Not content to work with stuntmen, Chiba started the JAC to train young actors to do their own stunts, adding a sense of realism to the films they appeared in. Whenever you think about a martial artist anti-hero with a "hell fist" or a rousing Japanese period film with complex plots and dazzling stunts, you think of Sonny Chiba. Even if you don't know that you are.

G.I. SAMURAI (1979)

THE TOP TEN WEIRDEST IMPROVISED WEAPONS IN FILM HISTORY

by Robin Bougie

T-BONE
In 2009's **LAW ABIDING CITIZEN**, Gerard Butler's imprisoned character makes a deal: information in exchange for a Porterhouse to munch on. The prison warden doesn't trust him, so instead of a steak knife, he gets a spork to cut his meat. Butler then finishes his meal, and then stabs his cellmate to death with the T-bone. The warden clearly made a mis-steak that time!

DILDO
There have been a number of movies—comedies, usually—that have shown a dildo used as a tool to bludgeon someone, but never has it been more unusual or noteworthy than to see stoic stone-faced actor Charles Bronson take rubber wang in hand and attack the butt of a helpless pervert. If you haven't seen **KINJITE: FORBIDDEN SECRETS** (1987) yet, what the heck are you waiting for? As a bonus, Bronson's character hates Asian people in this movie. Haha! He was never one for political correctness, god bless his crusty ol' ass.

CHOPSTICKS
In 1997's **FIREWORKS**, director and star Takashi Kitano's character is a former cop with a temper, and at one point he stabs a pair of chopsticks into a yakuza gang member's eye after the douchenozzle calls him a "bum". Brutal, but this scene always sort of cheers me up for some reason! Even crazier was when Anthony Wong went postal and crammed a handful of chopsticks into an innocent woman's cooze in the 1993 Hong Kong horror-classic, **THE UNTOLD STORY**.

CORN ON THE COB
In 1992's **SLEEPWALKERS**, a lady stabs a man in the back and kills him. Nothing unusual about that, right? Except that she does it with a rather blunt cob of corn. What the fuck, man? Who came up with this shit? And then she follows up the corny murder with a corny one liner: "No vegetables, no desert!" Mmmm! That's some hot-buttered violence, right there.

BASKETBALL
What is scary about someone coming at you with a basketball? Not a damn thing, unless that attacker is a super strong robot girl with the power to throw that ball so hard it literally knocks your fucking head clean off your shoulders resulting in a giant pulpy mess. Here's to you, 1986's **DEADLY FRIEND**! One of the greatest beheadings in film history. Take a headless bow.

LAWNMOWER
You've gotta love 1992's **DEAD ALIVE** (aka **BRAINDEAD**). It's one of, if not the single greatest horror-comedy of all time. Oh, there are many amazing highlights, but the movie's final showdown has the protagonist using a lawnmower to mow down an entire room of the undead. **NIGHT OF THE CREEPS** (1986) and **FRANKENHOOKER** (1990) may have done it first, but **DEAD ALIVE** did it best. Why cut the grass when you can chop some ass?

SNAPPING TURTLE
Harold Sakata (best known as "Odd Job" in **GOLDFINGER**) plays "The Pig" in Al Adamson's 1978 blaxploitation film **DEATH DIMENSION**, and like all nefarious bad guys, he threatens unarmed ladies with horrendous torture. Only this crazy sunnovabitch tries to take off nipples with a snapping turtle! Good thing Jim "The Dragon" Kelly (may he rest in peace) is around to protect innocent titties from shelled reptiles. The breast milk will curdle when it's threatened with a turtle!

TROMBONE
In **THE TOWN THAT DREADED SUNDOWN** (1976), the creepy masked killer ties a sobbing high school girl to a tree in the woods and then proceeds to murder her with her own trombone. That's right, a fucking slide trombone. Instead of just stabbing this chick like a normal person, he ties his knife to the instrument, and proceeds to play it—ventilating her in the process. Band practice was never like this! (Cue "sad trombone" sound effect.)

CDs
In 1990's **I COME IN PEACE**, the alien Dolph Lundgren goes up against a big alien guy who shoots frightened people with these silver discs that looked like compact discs, but they were actually just scary alien disc weapons. But you know what? Two years later in **HELLRAISER 3** (1992), a dude in a night club is messily killed by a whole stack of CDs being shot into his head from various angles! Damn! Clearly that place offers a selection of killer tunes. Honk.

HELLRAISER 3

CHILI PEPPERS
In Jackie Chan's 1987 terrific HK action film **PROJECT A PART 2**, Chan is chased by some bad guys up some scaffolding, where he takes his stand by cramming his mouth full of red chili peppers, chewing them frantically, and spitting the oily juice in his attackers faces. Yes, the peppers were real, and yes, he looked like he was in serious agony while doing this spicy stunt. Color him bright red, and color me impressed.

To read more from Robin Bougie as well as pick up a copy of his Cinema Sewer Magazine or book series, head on over to www.cinemasewer.com

DEADLY FRIEND

BACK ISSUES
WWW.WENGSCHOP.COM

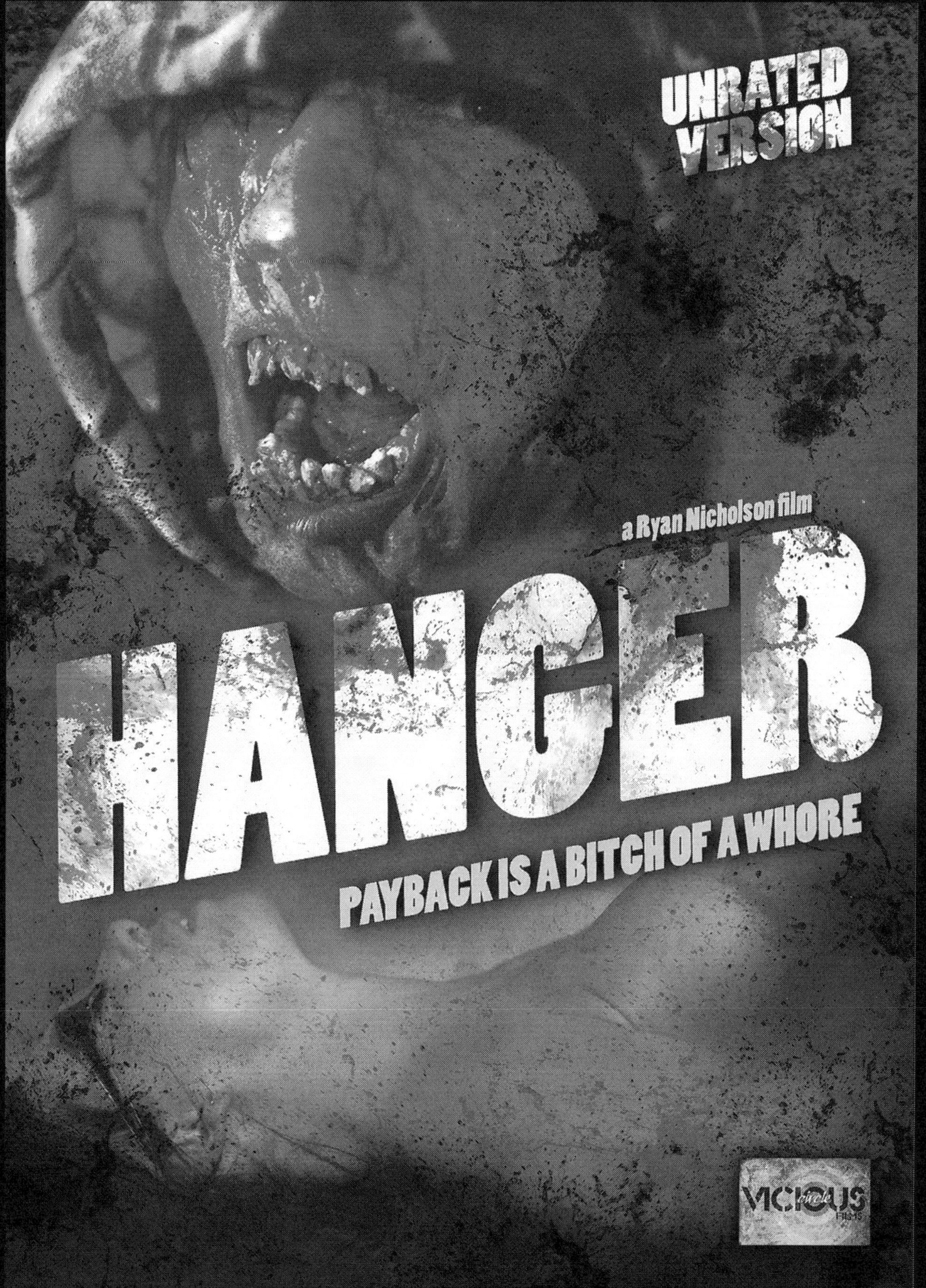

UNRATED VERSION

HANGER

a Ryan Nicholson film

PAYBACK IS A BITCH OF A WHORE

Vicious Films

interviews

TIM TALKS
INTERROGATING TIM DOYLE

Interview conducted by Tony Strauss

Chances are, if you're into cool poster art, you're familiar with Tim Doyle. Over the past few years, his work has graced many a one-sheet of the revival screenings of some of your favorite movies, and it's likely he's done a gig poster for one of your favorite bands. When you're doing some of your geekiest online image browsing, searching for awesome images inspired by your favorite nerdy obsession, you've seen his art. If you're a collector of limited edition posters, you probably own—or have at least bid on—some of his work. Tim Doyle is everywhere...in fact, he's behind you RIGHT NOW!

Mr. Doyle recently took time out of his are-you-fucking-kidding-me busy schedule to submit to a proper interrogation, WENG'S CHOP-style. Cleverly assuming the persona of a one-man Good Cop/Bad Cop with no pants and an unidentifiable tropical rash*, I quickly broke the poor lad's spirit, and he gave up the goods. Seriously...he spilled the beans on EVERYTHING—his Secret Origin, lackademia, the deceptive glamour of comics, the back hallway of the Alamo Drafthouse, defibrillating Mondo, proper video store management tactics, the secrets behind The Rise of the Mighty Nakatomi, starving artists, and world domination. Hopefully, with a few years of physical and psychological therapy, he'll recover nicely, and realize that it was all in the name of WENG'S CHOP getting what it wants—and therefore, totally worth the traumas he experienced.

* *Officer Kahuna McRash's Interrogation Techniques® instruction guides are available at your local library.*

Thank you for taking the time to chat, Tim! I'd like to start off by asking you about your Humble Beginnings, before you evolved into the Graphic Superstar that you are today. You're originally from the Dallas part of the world, correct? Did you have any formal art training there in your youthful days, or are you more of the self-taught variety of artist?

Thank you for doing this interview! I'd hardly call myself a "Graphic Superstar", but I'll take the compliment. I prefer "guy who pays his bills by drawing silly stuff," which I guess is pretty rare, all things considered.

I was born in Claymont, Delaware back in '77, but we moved to Plano, Texas in '79. Back then it was a smallish suburb of Dallas, and now the damn place is a giant, weird, town—full of shopping malls and aimless teenagers with more money than sense. Instead of getting into sports, or cars, or sports-cars, or black-tar heroin like the other kids I grew up with, I fell hard into comic books and cartoons—not *too* weird now, but this was the '80s—back when you could get called "faggot" for wearing a Batman t-shirt...you know—back when it was actually hard to be a nerd. And while I'm

Two of Tim's contributions to SpokeArt's "Quentin v. Coens" art show - *Mr. Orange Dying in a 1972 Pontiac Lemans Coupe Convertible* (left) and *Marcellus Wallace Becomes Acquainted with a 1980 Honda Civic Hatchback* (right)

at it—*YOU KIDS GET OFF MY LAWN*! Christ, I'm getting grouchy in my mid-30s. (I'm holding hard to the "mid" part of that sentence, there.)

My parents, while I wouldn't describe them as "artsy", I would describe as very supportive of my brother and I, and of our artistic or musical pursuits. My mother spent a lot of time drawing with me as a child, and between that and the comic books, drawing just became a thing I couldn't stop doing. Somewhere in there, my dad bought me a copy of *How to Draw Comics the Marvel Way*, and then it was all over from that point.

I took Choir in middle school for some damn reason, and switched to Art in high school. As an aside, the Choir kids I had been friends with for three years were really weird with me for "dropping out". One of the guys actually pulled me aside one day and said, "Why are you giving up on singing, Tim? You could have a real future in that!" Sure, man, sure. I just checked on Facebook—that guy is now a Choir Director at a middle school in the Dallas area. I literally just found that out now as I'm writing this. The irony… does…not…escape. Shoot for the stars there, buddy. Not knocking teaching by any means; I just find it scary when schools train people with a skill-set that can only get them jobs teaching the skills they just learned. It's a snake eating its own tail—when you think about how many people graduate art-school with their only prospects being teaching art-school, you start to see the pyramid-scheme that is a liberal arts education. There only so many positions out there, guys.

With that said—it comes as no surprise when I say I didn't go to an arts college or get a 4-year degree. I spent three years dicking around at Colin County Community College, finished their arts program there and just hung around taking life drawing and watercolor classes. I took watercolor *because Alex Ross*. I really did like the art classes, because they gave me time to paint and draw, but I don't think the staff knew what to do with me. I wanted to paint *Star Wars* book-covers, and they wanted to do abstract expressionism. Once I realized that I really couldn't learn what I wanted to do from the teachers there, I just kind of gave up. I was smart enough to know I didn't want student loan debt, but not smart enough to know where to go next. *So*, I went to Austin in '99—four years after High School—and that's where I am now.

Before we move on, I want to say my two best friends in high school and through community college were these identical twins—James and Jason Adcox—they were just amazing realist acrylic painters, and comic-book guys, as well. Being friends with those guys really kept me working at my craft through high school. I wanted to be better because they were so much better than me. It's important to not be the smartest guy in the room, the best artist you know—all that stuff. You can stop growing at that point.

It seems that so many artistic dreams get abandoned simply due to having no outside support or nurturing. Every aspiring artist should be lucky enough to have parental support and a pair of painterly identical twins to inspire them.

The point you make about art academia's self-devouring nature is interesting (and a bit sad), because that's the sort of complaint that used to be primarily reserved for degrees in things like Poetry, Philosophy, and Gaelic Literature, yet there is so much demand for art and illustration in the world—in practically every industry there is. So, if I took out, say, this gun right here, and put it to your head—like so—and forced you to become an art professor RIGHT NOW, what would you change in the world of art-school academia to make it a more valid degree, and less of a tail-eating snake? I'm giving you total dictatorial control here, so long as you don't get hair gel on my gun barrel.

I'm surprised and saddened that this came to firearms so quickly. Normally that comes later in most my interviews. Well, it had to happen sooner or later.

The one thing they can't teach—which is why most of these people become teachers—is *how to get a job as an artist*. You need to have real social networking skills; you need to know how to romance a client (in a strictly platonic way…obviously); you need to know how to manage your finances, how to negotiate a price, how to stick up for yourself when it comes to contract negotiations; you need to know how to walk away from a bad deal. These schools can fill your head up with theory and self-doubt and crippling self-examination. And don't even get me started on artist statements. I'd just chuck that shit out the window Day One. Sure, you can self-analyze and tear apart what your inner machinery is to find out why you make art—but it can be like pulling a grandfather clock apart: you'll never get all the gears back in the right place. It doesn't matter *why* you make art; it just matters that you *do* make art.

Here's my main reason why I'm so down on going to a college for art: debt. There is nothing you can learn in school that you can't learn yourself on your own now. Tutorials on YouTube, a few good books, a couple of like-minded friends, and the *will* to draw is all it takes. But if you're swimming in debt from school, you're going to have to get a day-job to service that debt. With that debt, you're going to have to make decisions you wouldn't otherwise because of it. All this is time spent *not drawing*. Because let me tell you: if you go to sit down with, say, an editor at Marvel Comics and get a portfolio review, all they're going to give a shit about is if you can draw Wolverine *real good*. If it comes down to you and a guy who got a degree, the degree is irrelevant to who actually gets the job. And if you spent time practicing your craft while the other guy had to worry about passing math and science and history classes—while also working a job to pay off his student loans—*you* are going to be the guy with the skill. End of story. Now, those classes are great and all, and will make you a well-rounded human being. But that's not what you want to do—you don't want to be a well-rounded human being—you want to fucking draw Batman for a living, so you're already a weirdo; why try to hide that? I'm using comic books as an example, but this applies to any art field—no one gives a shit what your degree is in, they just want to know if you can deliver. "But I need school to help me produce—I need someone giving me assignments or I'd just never get work done!" Well awesome, perhaps you should have majored in XBOX or whatever your passion

Lost in Your Eyes

is because it certainly isn't drawing stuff. If you're not making stuff on your own and need someone behind you pushing in an academic setting…that's cute, and all—just make sure you take my order down correctly, I said I wanted a *Diet* Coke. Yes, I'll pull ahead to the next window.

Wow, an art professor AND a life coach! You really deliver the value when wantonly threatened with violence! But it's damned solid advice—when it comes to a career in art, it's far less about credentials than it is about ability and drive, especially in the comics medium (or any illustration-for-publication arena), where the ability to meet a deadline is so much more vital than accumulating a haughty list of past accomplishments.

So, after realizing that the academic path wasn't the path for you, you set sail for the much-more-culturally-enriched land of Austin. Did you have a "lost and wayward" period there before you started getting the kind of jobs that could pay your bills, or did you hit the ground running and start getting yourself work fairly quickly? I guess I'm looking for what led you to the job or time that you feel represents your "breakout moment"—when you genuinely started feeling like a "professional illustrator" rather than a "struggling artist".

Oh, man…so this is kind of a long and meandering story.

Back in Plano I had worked off-and-on in a baseball card and comic book shop, I managed a Kay-Bee Toys, and managed at a Suncoast Video. Kind of just nerd-adjacent jobs. When I moved to Austin, I just sat on my ass for a few months and blew through my savings. I was 22 and was living away from home for the first time. My parents had given me precious little to rebel against, so I never had the urge to rush out the door as soon as I could. However, a bad break-up finally got me to leave town. After running dangerously low on funds, I got a job at a Hollywood Video in probably the worst part of town that had a video store at the time, and it was everything you'd expect it to be. Massive customer and employee theft—no one gave a shit at any point—as long as some money made it into the safe and no one was shot that day, it was a good day. We did rent a surprising amount of *Leprechaun* and *Chucky* movies, though. The lesson? Poor people like killer midgets. They tried to make me a manager there and I took one look around and just quit that day. No way in hell was I going to be responsible for that mess.

I went down to Asel Art supply by the UT campus and got a job there, and I really started experimenting more with different mediums, and began doing more canvas paintings. Talking to all the artists coming in the store, combined with a healthy employee discount helped me get a handle on the art scene here. After doing that for a while I started showing art in coffee houses and restaurants here in town, and surprisingly, the work started selling. From there I began showing in some local galleries like the late, great Gallery Lombardi. It was never enough to pay bills, but it was certainly nice. I was dating a girl who was also an artist, Jen Frost Smith, and it was a pretty cool set-up for a while. I eventually moved from there to waiting tables, and then to working at the comic book store on campus, Funny Papers. In August of 2001, I started a diary 'zine called *Amazing Adult Fantasy*, where I'd do a daily 3-panel strip about what happened that day, and I would print them monthly and distribute them around town for free. That was inspired by both my friend Jeff Lewis' (sorry…Rough Trade Recording artist *Jeffery Lewis*!) diary comics, and local legend Ben Snakepit's diary 'zine, *Snakepit*. The 'zine was excellent PR and became a promotional tool for my art shows and raised general awareness. This was all before social media was really a "thing" yet, and I daresay it was more effective on a local level than those outlets can be now. *Amazing Adult Fantasy* ran for two years and 25 issues.

I was painting and drawing this whole time—while at Asel I begun work on my 3-issue comic, *Sally Suckerpunch*, which was a lot of fun—all my com-

Two covers from Tim's diary 'zine, *Amazing Adult Fantasy*

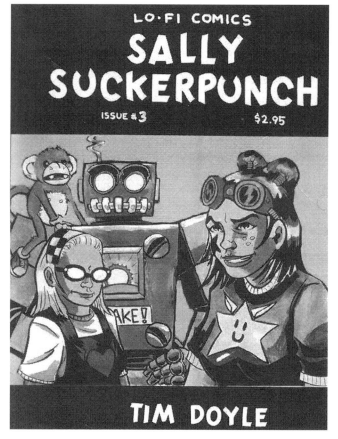

ics work at this time was done totally without the benefit of computers, too. (I really could have used a digital pre-press and Photoshop classes, come to think of it…)

About mid-2002, Funny Papers was in danger of closing down, and the owner sold it to a high-roller customer with the caveat that I would run the place. Within a few months, we had cleaned the joint up, and doubled monthly sales. Then he acquired another shop, called Thor's Hammer—mostly a table-top gaming/RPG store—and a few months later he purchased another "distressed property" called First Federal Comics. And I worked my magic by cleaning up and standardizing the shops—just applying the basic tenets of retail that I had learned from my previous management experience. And sales at all the stores shot up double or more each time. See, most comic shops are started by comic book fans who think their love of the medium will carry them through—and while you *must* be a fan to jump in, if you think that at any point it's going to be easy or fun *all the time*, or you can somehow subvert the laws of retail, you are in for a rude awakening. It was eye-opening and very educational for me, learning every aspect of a retail business from all angles. But the problem was…the guy who owned these shops—that high-roller customer who purchased the businesses that I ran for him—was totally insane. As time went on, I spent more and more of my time just trying to keep him away from the shops, away from the employees, and away from the customers. He didn't actually read comics anymore, or even know what the customers were buying. He was just a guy with a decent amount of cash, and he thought—like a lot of people with money think—that they have money because they are smart. That's rarely the case. I had pretty much stopped drawing at this point—no longer painting or doing my diary comic—and I was miserable at my job; I started having panic attacks from the stress. The owner was calling me "faggot" more than I ever was called in middle school—he was blowing all the cash on things like a Porsche instead of product, and generally being a huge bastard. Oddly, in all seriousness, he gave me a sword one day, saying it was an ancient sword that I should hold on to and pass down through my family, and he had the matching sword and would do the same, so our families would always be linked. It took me about 30 minutes to figure out it was a **HIGHLANDER** prop replica sword. (I later found out he did the same thing to the next guy he hired to replace me…) So one day I just walked out, left my key on the table and jetted. Within three months, one of the stores closed down, one caught on fire

and *then* closed down, and the other changed hands a few times before being padlocked shut for back-rent payments. Again, he had money…but was not smart. Somewhere in there I started dating the woman who is now my wife—Angie Genesi. If it wasn't for her, I would've probably stuck around at that job, but something in her made me more confident and daring, so it wasn't as scary as it should have been.

From there I called up a friend—Henri Mazza—who was programming shows at the Alamo Drafthouse Cinema here in Austin, and I just took an entry level position as a food-runner/ticket-taker there, until they could find a management position for me. I was a cook and a waiter for a while, which was a lot of fun, actually. Being a line cook was intense. That eventually led me to being hired to run the floundering *Mondotees.com*, which was a bootleg t-shirt shop and website that the Alamo Drafthouse ran out of their hallway in their old downtown location. They had blown through something like three general managers in about six months. It was a concept they had thrown together as an afterthought, and never had anyone that could take the reins and see it bloom. Which was more their fault than anything—I was just thrown in there with the instructions of, "Make it work!" and just left to my own devices, mostly. At the hours I had to put in, and the pay I was receiving, any sane person would have just walked away—no, *should* have walked away. I ran that place for four years and took it from making barely $70K a year to over $500K by the time I left. When I came on, Mondo had a dog-eared stack of posters in the back closet from past cinema events that no one really seemed to know what to do with; I thought they were *pretty cool* and wanted to do more. Working with artist Rob Jones (who was an outside advisory kind-of-guy at this point), I turned it into a juggernaut of a print series. Rob had all the artist contacts and the print industry experience, and I had the list of upcoming events, ran the site, and cultivated the press contacts—and it worked beautifully.

But…I had done a few posters for the print series myself when we needed someone on short notice, and they did really well. Working 60 hours or so a week for $35K a year can start to grind on you, so I asked if I could get paid for the prints I was doing. Well…I was told "no", that I was on salary and I couldn't be paid anything extra. So I pretty much shut down at that point. I was on salary as a retail manager, but I was doing about 70% of the

t-shirt design, organizing releases, hosting a small amount of events, designing retail spaces—pretty much everything an owner of a small business would do—but I had no ownership, and my pay wasn't up to where it needed to be. So me and a friend I had at the time—Justin Ishmael, who also was working at the Alamo, and also was very tired of the treatment he was receiving—started laying ground work to start our own business, which eventually became *NakatomiInc.com*.

We launched the site in January of '09, and shortly after that were called into a meeting at the Alamo where they gave us an ultimatum of either giving them the company we had just launched, or we'd have to go. I left (as that was the plan—to not work there anymore), but I guess they pulled a big loyalty play on Justin, and he stayed. They gave him my old job of running Mondo, where he still is now, and I went off on my own.

It was never really my plan to become one of the main artists on Nakatomi… I mean, we had working relationships with some of the best artists out there at launch, but after a couple prints I did sold out immediately and went viral—mainly the *Change Into a Truck* design—it became evident that people liked what I was doing and it was a great way to pay the bills. Shortly after that, my wife and I decided to get married, and somewhere around March we found out we were pregnant for the first time with our son, Rocco. If I had known I was going to have a kid that year I never would have left my job—which, with the way things are going now, would have been a *huge* mistake. Nakatomi has blown up much larger than my expectations could ever have been, and my own art career is doing well. All that I would have missed out on if I stayed at Mondo.

So…that's my not-so-secret origin story. Really meandering, but I think it's important to see what decisions and random events led me to where I am now. Rolling with the punches, and all that.

But—to answer the main thrust of your question—when did I know I had "made it" as an Illustrator? I'll let you know when that happens. I still feel like I'm constantly hustling. I think when my first solo SpokeArt show in 2012 sold out within a few days I realized I had reached a new level in my career. The money was really nice, and we paid off my house that year. I guess that more than anything said I had "made it". No longer having a mortgage over my head means I can slow down a bit and focus on more long-term goals. That goes back to my earlier statement about debt—financial debt is your enemy if you want to be an artist. I launched my business without borrowing money, haven't used a credit card in about four years or more, and have no car payments. And I got there with a series of smallish advances in my career, a few bona fide "hits", but really it's just a constant grind.

Would you say it was your time and experiences working at Alamo Drafthouse and cultivating Mondotees that moved you more toward the medium of movie posters and fine art prints, rather than becoming a full-on comic book artist, or was poster/fine art more of the direction in which you ultimately wanted your career to go?

Oh, absolutely. Like I said, I had been painting and doing comics for a while in Austin, but neither one of those mediums was really paying off in a way that I could support myself doing it. Making a living at comics seemed like a

pipe dream from where I was at—I wasn't good enough to do it at a "Marvel/DC" level—and I didn't have the knowledge to produce my own at a professional level and deliver it to market through the distribution channels that were available at the time. Once I moved in to Mondo and saw the potential and reach of silkscreen prints, I was definitely hooked. The successes of my early prints while I was there really lit a fire under my ass and got the gears turning. I learned every step of the process while I was there, from commissioning artists, designing prints, overseeing production, art direction, marketing, selling, fulfillment, the aftermarket—everything you needed to make the art and sell it. Having Rob Jones on speed-dial 24/7 was very influential; his knowledge base and guidance was crucial in my development as a silkscreen artist. I guess in many ways, by putting one guy in charge of all that at Mondo, they gave me all the tools I needed to just leave and do it myself. And for that, I'm very grateful, but I'm sure they were kicking themselves over that in the weeks after I left. (They do seem to do okay now, though, so no loss on either end.) I had minimal experience with selling things online before, but once I got my hands on the back end of Mondo and understood all the moving parts, I realized not only was it super-easy to do, but the only thing that mattered was content—and I knew how the content got made. My

A few selections from Tim's 2012 SpokeArt show, *UnReal Estate: (from left to right) Damn Good, Night Falls on the SNPP, Rusty Shackleford, No Fuckin Ziti, 10 Cents Gets You Nuts*

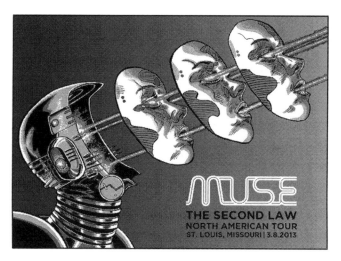

friend from the Dallas area, Nathan Beach, had done a lot of web design for me and other artists and musician friends (like my brother, Daniel Francis Doyle! *PLUG!*), so I tapped him to do the heavy lifting on the functionality of the site. God bless him—he did it all on faith with promise of pay on the back-end, and I'm eternally grateful for it. It paid off for both of us quite well. He still works with us today.

Oddly, as I've become more skilled and become friends with more and more comics professionals (and as some of my old friends have become comics professionals), I've received more and more offers for work—and the sad thing is that the shine is off that dream for me. I have a couple good friend who currently do work for Marvel and DC, and those guys…are…very…tired. It's a 12-plus-hour-a-day job with no time off to stay on that monthly grind. And the pay isn't what it was 20 years ago, so there's even less of a reason to do it now. I love comics, but at this point in my life, I think I'd rather be reading them. If I could afford to take the time off from what I'm doing now to make comics of my own, I could see myself doing it again, but right now everything is running really smoothly, so I'm a little afraid to step off this merry-go-round to do something more indulgent like comics.

I guess as far as the direction I wanted my career to go in—I never really gave it much more thought than this: can I get paid to draw what I want to draw? For right now, that answer is yes—so…mission accomplished?

Funny how quickly the glamour can dissipate when you get the insider's perspective on something, isn't it? Comics seem like a dream job to so many until they discover the labor-to-pay ratio in the industry. But still, t'would certainly be nice to attain the stability and freedom to do a comic for the sheer pleasure/inspiration of it, and not out of financial necessity… it sure would make all the labor required feel a lot less like "work".

I want to ask you a bit more about your movie-related work. You've earned quite a bit of popularity from creating original posters for some pretty iconic films' revival screenings. When it comes to taking work for movie posters, are you picky? Have you ever turned down an offer because you disliked the film, or maybe accepted a job you normally wouldn't have if you weren't a fan of the film?

Well, any freelance artist worth their salt can find an "in" to make just about any job interesting enough to do. There's a weird thing in the print-collecting community where collectors think that every print an artist does is done out of "love" for the band or film. But the truth is a lot of artists do gig posters or movie prints for stuff they pretty much couldn't care less about. I know a ton of artists who've done work for Phish, and almost to the man, they say they couldn't give a crap about Phish—or downright hate the band and their fans, but the prints sell like gangbusters, so they take the pay-day and move on. The nice thing about gig posters is that usually the band or management just wants a cool drawing with the band's name on it somewhere—so you can have an awful lot of creative freedom that way, and still get paid. I've done four prints for country musician Eric Church, and I've yet to make it through more than a couple songs. *But*…I did some research to make sure he wasn't an obvious racist or anything and found he's pretty progressive as far as I could find. *And*, most importantly, the design brief was great. It was pretty much (and I'm severely paraphrasing here), "Draw old rusty homeland middle-America stuff." That, more than anything is what hooked me. And, I think those four prints hang together in a consistent design sense, and I'm pretty proud of 'em, even if I have nothing in common with your average Eric Church fan.

Movie prints are a little more challenging, as the key visual moments and iconography are already built in to the property, so you have to find a way to remix them into your own design sense that is pleasing to you and the client. I've been pretty lucky in that just about every straight-up movie poster I've done—I was a fan in some way of the movie already. There are a couple exceptions—**FANBOYS** was difficult as the movie is just…so…blah. *But*, I was able to find a way in, because it's essentially about *Star Wars* fans vs. *Star Trek* fans, and so *that's* what I drew. I actually was contacted by the studio, as they wanted copies for their offices, and the guy who wrote the script is a local writer, and he was super-into it. So this film I really couldn't stand to watch again still spawned a final print that pleased me, the theater who commissioned it, and even the production team. (BTW, the credited writer of the film would agree with my assessment of the film as it was shot.)

As my career has progressed, though, I have been able to be more picky, and concentrate on just the stuff I want to draw, so that's a nice bit of freedom, there.

Now that Nakatomi, Inc. is up, running and proven successful, are there many things you would have done differently with the benefit of hindsight? Did you have preconceived notions going in that proved to be totally wrong, or did you pretty much work out the majority of your birth-of-an-art-dealer growing pains when you took over Mondo?

Well…not really. I mean, there's probably a few prints I might not have done, or done differently based on sales in hind-sight…or a couple people that I would have cut out at the very onset, instead of learning the hard way that some people were just unreliable. But really, it's been such a great ride that I don't think I'd change much, if anything. Although, I guess I would have started Nakatomi sooner. That would have been better.

I will say that everything we *thought* was going to be the "big hit" products at launch ended up being the wrong ideas entirely. Not that we lost money on them or anything, but the learning curve was steep and came at us quickly. I really thought t-shirts were going to be a bigger deal than they ended up being.

I try to learn from every experience—my next decision is based solidly on the results of my previous one. What some people might call a failure, I just see as a learning experience. I try to question the norms of every business model, find gaps to exploit, new markets to move product to…and I'm afraid that if I didn't have so many wrong guesses in the past to learn from, that I'd not be making the right ones now. And by "afraid", I mean only if I'm suddenly in possession of a time machine and could correct those mistakes. Not too likely. This week.

Yeah, but…if you acquired a time machine, who knows WHEN this week would be…OR WILL IT???

(Pauses for dramatic effect)

So anyway, if I were to force you back into the role of Art Professor/Advisor again (sorry I can't threaten you at the moment—using my gun barrel to stir coffee), what advice would you offer artists and entrepreneurs who aspire to get into the world of Fine Art Production that they never would've thought of in a million years? (If you feel I'm unfairly asking you to help out your future competition, feel free to unleash piles of bullshit advice that will steer them in all the wrong directions…just twirl your mustache menacingly whilst doing so, please.)

There's a mistake I see new galleries and websites and artists make time and time again—they see what other successful businesses do, and try to emulate that exactly. They make the same kind of products, use the same group of artists, and market to the exact same narrow customer base of print collectors. That will work…for a while. Until it doesn't. And if you've built your entire business on appealing to this small group, then the whole game will be up. These businesses aren't diversifying enough. I work really hard to get my work in front of new customers, while not ignoring the old ones. It's important to

I sell to who aren't active in the online poster community more than pick up the slack from any of those from the smaller group I alienate from time to time.

Finally, don't be a victim to middle men. There are some middle men who can do great things for you—Ken Harman at SpokeArt has worked his ass off to raise my profile, and it's been very beneficial to both of us. Other middle-men are just sponges. And when I say "middle men" I mean anyone that stands to profit by the interaction between you and the customer. Make them work for it. Too many artists just sit on their hands and wait for permission to come down from on high to do something. And that's where the middlemen can benefit and make a buck off your labors. You don't need them—just build your own thing, make it well, and the customers will find you. Contact a band or a movie theater directly to do a poster. Learn to print. Build your own site. You can no longer be "just an artist"—you have to be your own promotions machine, your own agent, and a businessman. It's hard work, but if you want the small measure of freedom I've carved out for myself, then *get the fuck to work*.

And *finally-finally*, price your work properly. Don't be afraid to shoot for the stars. If someone comes to you with a gig and a budget, that's great. But if they ask *you* what your rate is, ask for what it would take you to feel happy to do the job. And then throw some extra on top of that—because you're not going to be happy for the *entire* job.

I could go on and on, but really—so much of this you have to learn yourself, honestly…

One of the things you do that sets you apart from many other purveyors of Fine Art involves the occasional release of multiple editions of certain images—which REALLY seems to upset some of your customers and contemporaries. What do you have to say for yourself about that, Mister?

*Well…*this is the one thing that's caused me the most grief while also raising my profile and made me the most money. So mostly a win, there. It's something I feel very strongly about. That's not to say that someone might come at me with a very reasonable, logical opposing view one day—and I might change my mind then. But I've been defending myself against poorly-thought-out opposing views for so long now, that I may have become entrenched in my position.

Here's the skinny: I sell art. Usually, I print an edition of a piece in a quantity of as many I think I'm going to sell in about six months or so. That's the first edition, signed and numbered in a fixed quantity. (Like this: #45/300 total made.) Sometimes I print too many; sometimes I print too little, and a print sells out immediately. Now, if we were talking about books, or albums, or DVDs or hamburgers or *any* other form of consumable entertainment items, you would *just make more*. I don't want to make collectibles. I want to make and sell art. *But*, there's a financial-collectible aspect that some people want to put onto these items. And yeah, that aspect of the industry exists. A segment of the buying public wants to buy something and turn around and sell it immediately for profit. I have no loyalty to those people. They are an aberration of the marketplace. I have no problem with them buying my art and doing this—once they buy it, they can do whatever they want with it. Another portion wants to buy a limited item and be one of only a small handful of people to own something—this is how they feel special, and part of their identity is wrapped up in what they own. And, as a former action figure collector, I recognize that's a thing. But I also realize that defining who you are by what you buy—rather than what you do—is a problem with society. These groups of buyers want me to play by the rules that they established for their hobby—they want me to make *one* edition, and when it's gone, it's gone. They get to profit from their purchase or be a member of an exclusive club. And they scream to high heaven when I do a new edition of a print. My new editions are always differentiated in one way or another—by color, size, a Roman numeral by the edition size, and lately I've been just clearly putting a "2nd Edition" near the margin of the art to keep it simple.

But consider this: how many printings of *A Christmas Carol* are there? And yet…if you have a first edition, you're sitting on something both valuable and exclusive. No one is walking into Barnes & Noble (do they still exist?) and throwing a fit that there's shelves full of subsequent editions of a book.

keep branching out. There's a bit of elitism in the print collecting community where they want to believe they're collecting "real art" and other people are buying mass-produced crap. Well, when Mondo sells millions of dollars of posters a year, what exactly is a mass market again? The elitism is dumb and insular and will lead to a collapse. The smart people in the industry see it, and are making plans for it. People criticize the "house-mom" crowd of art-buyers, but I'd much, much rather sell prints to people (yes, even housemoms) who just want cool, cheap art on their walls than to a diminishing group of extreme hobbyists who think they're going to retire on their poster collection. If you believe that, I have a collection of Beanie Babies to sell you at a screaming deal.

On one hand, I shouldn't be giving this advice, because, yeah, competitors could benefit from it. But the way I see it, a rising tide raises all ships—the healthier this industry gets, the more it will benefit everyone involved. And I think I'm a decent enough artist to keep my head above water, no matter how deep and wide this pool gets. (To completely murder a metaphor, here.)

Also, listen to your customers, but don't let them dictate your business. If I listened to what the noisiest people online wanted, I'd be broke-ass poor—but that small group would be really happy. But the wide group of customers

No one is setting fire to their first pressings of Beatles albums because I can now buy 'em on CD. And yet, some of these "investment collectors" think my art is now devalued because more people can get it. It's just ridiculous.

Put yourself in my shoes—I do a drawing, and print it. It sells out, and I get a ton of emails from people who now want copies. I can say, "Nope," and I make less money, and those people are sad. *Or*…I can say yes—make more money and make people happy—but run the risk of alienating a small portion of the potential customer base. It's a no-brainer for me. In *any other* business, if you are leaving money on the table, you have done something wrong. The customers you lose by not having something in stock that they want to buy may *never* come back.

Some of those critics will read what I've written there and say, "*See*, I told you he was greedy!" And to that I say: I run a business. I pay my bills by doing that. I do not have a day-job to fall back on. I feed my children, pay my employees, and pay for health insurance for them *and* my family from that. You go into your workplace and argue that they should deliver less services, less products, pay their employees less, and make less money because… something something. See what happens then.

There's a website out there that tracks new print releases and their after-market value through a database of eBay sales. And it's an amazing tool. They also have a fairly active forum there. I was attacked there for doing what I do, and I used the site's own database to prove that nothing I was doing was lowering the "value" of a particular print—the sales were still trending up. Once I saw that my logic wasn't going to be listened to, I realized that the people doing the loudest complaining were just crazy people who wanted to yell at an artist online without fear of repercussion—hiding behind a username—and that there was no reason for me to engage in an online debate about it ever again. The people that buy my stuff buy it because they like it, and those that don't buy it aren't going to be my customer anyway, so there's no reason for me to keep them "on my side".

One thing I'm able to do with these further editions is really grow the hobby at large. I get emails time and time again from people who say things like, "My first print was a 3rd edition of *Change Into a Truck*, and now I'm a print junkie!" Or, "My boyfriend bought me the 4th Edition of *White Dragon*, and now I've purchased art from a bunch of other artists! I love it!" Which is just amazing. Would the world (or me) be served any better by getting emails like, "I saw a cool jpeg of a print on line, and I couldn't get it; I guess prints are dumb." Which are the kinds of emails and blog comments I see on other art businesses' sites. For every investment collector I might alienate by doing a 3rd edition of my squid print—that's 300 sold copies of my squid print that went out to people who might turn into print collectors one day, and really grow the hobby. That growth is key to the health of the industry.

I've seen first-hand what happens to niche hobbies that cater only to a diminishing collector customer base. Comics, baseball cards, etc. These hobbies move into selling collectibles and bank on the idea of "aftermarket value" to drive sales, and that creates hype—and you can make money at it for a while…sometimes a *lot* of money—but the thing about bubbles…is bubbles—*burst*. Baseball cards are never coming back. Comic Books are still a fraction of the sales they had *before* they were sold as collectibles, and a smaller fraction of what they were selling at their height of "collectability". The problem is that these businesses lost track of what they were selling—comics are stories and art—baseball cards are cardboard pictures of 'roided up millionaires. At no point should these items have been sold as "collectible". It's going to happen at the consumer level regardless, but to foster that attitude is some *baaad* mojo. It never lasts.

I'm in this for the long haul—I'm going to be doing this for decades to come—and I want a healthy industry to be here to support me. One full of a wide, diverse group of customers. And you're not going to get there by alienating the general public and appealing to a diminishing collector base of people that—let's be honest—are only are into it for the wrong reasons.

What really kills me (and forgive the ramble, but this is important) is when I see artists pushing back on this. All artists talk to each other in this scene. Whenever the subject comes up, I hear from a few that they "wish" they could do what I do, but they're afraid of what their customers would say. To which I always say: If you're afraid of your customers, then it's time to get new ones. These giants of the industry—these amazing talents who struck

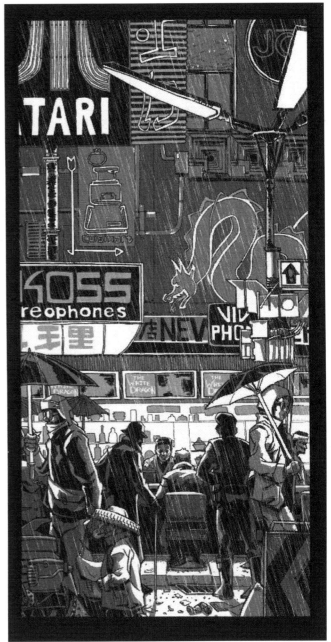

White Dragon

out on their own to work for themselves—are afraid of a couple loud-mouths online. And that's sad. Even more surprising is when lower-profile artists feel the same way. These are people who get a hit every once in a while, and maybe have day-jobs, but certainly aren't living large, and they're afraid to break the rules of a collector base that isn't even buying their product to begin with. They're living hand-to-mouth in the hopes of getting non-existent customers—while *real actual* customers are in line with cash in hand—but they have no "hot" product to sell. It's madness. Now…I'm a good artist. Not a *great* artist (at least in my estimation…gotta keep that ego in check), but I'm doing "better" financially than the majority of my contemporaries. And that's because of this. I live in a reasonable house in a lower-income neighborhood; my cars are all over six years old. *But*…they're paid for; I have health insurance, no debt (even the house is paid for) and a Self-Employed-Pension I pay into every year. That kind of security is priceless for a freelancer. I didn't get there by catering to the loudest, jerkiest segment of the online community. I didn't do this by following rules that people I never met decided to apply to this scene. You guys can do this, too.

There's a line of thinking out there that artists shouldn't be aware of money like this. Shouldn't think of business models. It's the myth of the "starving

Print from Tim's *The Sea Also Rises* series - *The Frog Prince Commands His Homunculus*.

He is the Zissou

artist". It's an entrenched idea that must be smashed. Trade out the word "artist" for *any other* profession and you'll see how crazy this is. "Starving plumber". "Starving IT professional". "Starving Realtor". In any other profession, making more money and being aware of how to maximize sales is considered a good thing. But as an artist, there's the idea that is supposed to be a bad thing. Smash that idea, burn the pieces and dump the ash into the sea, because that's harmful to everyone involved.

I have a large group of amazing, loyal customers, several galleries I deal with, about a dozen consignment shops who carry my work, and until my sales go down I'm going to assume that I'm proceeding properly. The business keeps going up every year so…yeah.

I couldn't agree with you more on the whole "starving artist" sentiment. It's a fairy-tale mystique that belies the whole concept of an artist who works hard and achieves success at their profession, as if success is something to be avoided in order to remain noble. What a crock.

I'd like to ask you a bit about your process as an artist. This may be a bit too in-depth-geeky for some, but it is something I always enjoy hearing artists talk about, so any disinterested readers can just skip this part. Once you have an idea for an art piece that you want to create, can you walk me through your usual process, from conception to finished piece? I know it depends on the project, but just in general. And be as meticulous in detail as you like, right down to pencil/brush/pen types and ink brands, and any other tools or weapons you might wish to reveal.

My process varies from print to print, but the majority of them go like this: Once I get a gig, I watch the movie or listen to the band, and just see what pops into my head. I usually know what I'm going to do before either is through. If it's a gig that needs photo-references, then I take screen grabs using VLC on my PC, and spend a lot of time on Google Image search. Also, if it strikes my fancy, I'll read up on a band or movie on Wikipedia or whatever,

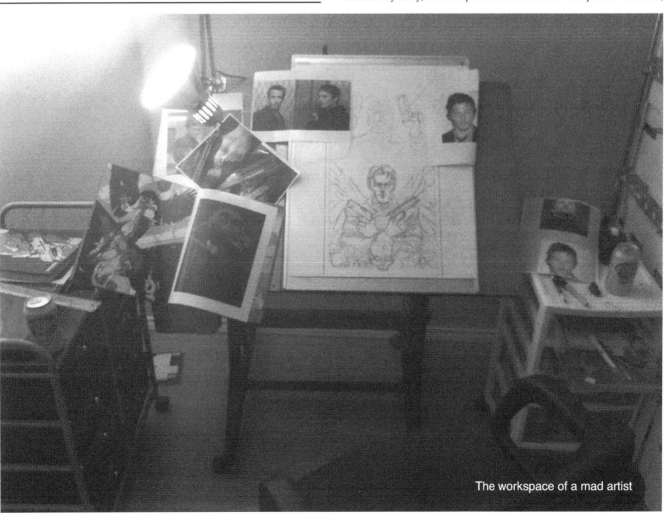
The workspace of a mad artist

Tim's magnificent **BLADE RUNNER** character prints

just to see if there's some nugget I could latch on to. So I sketch something out on whatever scrap I have laying around, then I do a full drawing on Bristol Board from there. If it's a likeness of an actor, I'll usually lightbox a face on my lightboard. I use pencil to lay it all in, and then I ink with a variety of pens or brushes, depending on the look I'm going for. For pens, I use PITT Brush-pens, or their liner-pens if it's more detailed. I actually just ordered a Gross of these Pentel ses15n brush-tip pens—they're a little more springy and tighter than the brush pens, but you don't get the broad lines you can with the PITT pens. It's a mixed bag, really. If I'm using an actual brush, I have a couple sable-hair watercolor brushes I really like, and have had for years now. Probably a decade at this point. For ink, I really like the deepness of the FW acrylic black ink.

There are a couple art supplies I have that belonged to my father, like a broken old ruler, an ellipse template—stuff like that. They're nothing special, but the history of them is what makes them important. And they work really, really well. Using them is comforting. I've had those for about 20 years or more now. Crazy.

Once I have a finished black and white drawing, I'll scan that in chunks on my 11x17 Mustek scanner (real cheap on eBay!) and composite the parts together in Photoshop, and start the coloring process. I work in layers, with each color on its own layer, so by the time I'm done with that, the separations are ready to go already. Some artists will spend weeks doing separations on a piece, but mine are already done as soon as the coloring is laid in.

Then I send the layers out for film, get the film back in the shop, and I hand those to my employees—and then magic happens. Step 3 is profit. No idea what step 2 is.

Suuuuure…just conveniently skip over your blood-sacrifice-related step in the process. You're not fooling anyone, you know. But we'll let that slide for now to avoid legal repercussions.

So, for pieces like your BLADE RUNNER character prints, were those client commissions, or more "because Tim just loves BLADE RUNNER"-inspired pieces? What is the approximate ratio of for-print work you produce from client commissions versus work you produce because you're just feeling inspired and think it will sell? And in the instance of the latter, how do you generally gauge your confidence/predictions on the piece's sales potential?

Well…I love the hell out of that movie. And the portrait/character series was something that I did to give away to customers as freebies. None were ever actually sold. The nice thing about having a print shop is I can afford to do stuff like that. I'm doing the same for Doctor Who right now, actually. One character…*so many faces*!

Honestly, it's been a while since something has come along completely on its own from my head—I've been so booked up with client and gallery work, I haven't done a straight-up "art print" that was completely of my own instigation. Even my last two *The Sea Also Rises* prints I did were for either a client or a gallery show. I was just able to bend the theme to something I wanted to draw, ultimately. I'm participating in a show this December in Chicago that is grouped under the loose theme of "evolution", which is great as you can pretty much do anything you want with that. Those pieces will be more "me" than anything I've done this year.

As far as making things because I "think they will sell"—sometimes I purposefully do shit that I don't think *anyone* is going to buy, and see if it can find an audience. And I've yet to be let down. Not that I'm making things that I think are bad—I'm just shooting for the narrow band of, "This is exactly what I want to draw—who knows if anyone wants this?" Audience of one—or, I should say—audience of me and my wife. I like drawing stuff I think she'd like to see as well. My *Goldie's Big Break* print was something just so incredibly personal for me (which is a weird thing to say if you've seen it) that I was surprised anyone wanted it. And while it wasn't an *instant sell out*, it's sold steadily and I'm down to like 3 copies now. So that weird little print found its audience, and I couldn't be happier.

Regarding confidence in how something will do…I always expect failure. I don't know if that's a self-defense mechanism or not, but I try not to set myself up for disappointment. And, if something does well, I'm over the moon. But—ask my wife—I'm usually a wreck before a release. Once I hit "sell" on a product, I usually run right to the gym or something to distract me for a while. The way I run my edition sizes is I try to print what I think I will sell in a few months. And I have so many sales channels now; I can spread around the "duds" to a bunch of outlets to where they'll eventually find an audience.

Through Nakatomi, you've now worked with some pretty prestigious and renowned talents—most recently, Bernie Wrightson and Geoff Darrow. Are there any "dream client" artists you'd like to land for Nakatomi? (Or maybe some that you've already lined up that you'd like to shamelessly name-drop?)

You know, the list of people I've been fortunate to work with though Nakatomi—either through publishing/selling their work on the site, or doing print jobs for them—is just amazing. Tyler Stout, Olly Moss, Jermaine Rogers, Todd Slater, Horkey, and many others on just the poster artist side of things. On the comics side, I've got Paul Pope, Shaky Kane, Wrightson, Darrow (more to come!) and on and on. It's an amazing line-up if I stop to think about it. I literally have more artists lining up to work with me than I can fit in the schedule, while also at the same time doing my own work. It's a great problem to have, that's for sure. I think it's because I offer one of the better deals out there for them now, and I try to make it as easy as possible to bring their work to market, while also exposing them to an audience they might not otherwise have. (Specifically the comic book guys on that one.)

Two of Tim's *Doctor Who* character prints

But as far as artists I'd like to work with in the future…man, I'm just mainly excited to do more work with the ones I have. Most of the people I work with today are actual friends—Russ Moore, Jon Smith, Jacob Borshard—and yes, it's scary to think that I'm reaching a spot where I'm pretty friendly with guys like Pope and Wrightson. Deep down, we're all just nerds here who want to make good work, and that's the binding element. I'm an artist, too, not just some middleman or a fanboy with a job selling art for someone else. And I think they appreciate that element. It's been quite the ride.

So, what should be causing the world to tremble in fear when it comes to your future world domination plans? What would you like to do in the future in a desired avenue that is, for you, yet un-tapped? (Bear in mind that we already know about your Death Ray, and it only mildly unnerves us.)

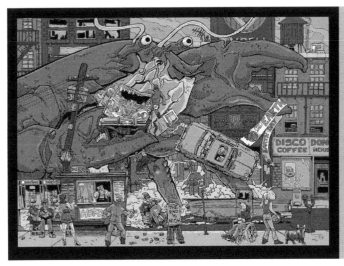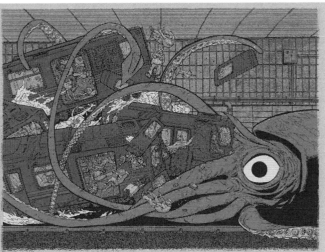

Two prints from Tim's *The Sea Also Rises* series - *Incident 6: The King of Crabs Claims His Throne* (left) and I*ncident 19: The 14th Street Station Squid* (right)

The Sea Also Rises – Goldie's Big Break

Look, that Death-Ray is only harmful for non-believers. As long as you're faithful to me, you've got nothing to worry about.

With that said…I'm not into world domination. I've worked for many people in the past who want to *crush* the competition. And that's just silly. People feel like they need to be *Number One* all the time—and it's not possible, and it's a fool's errand. You just do the best you can, and not worry about what the other person is doing. People are going to follow you or they're not. And sticking your finger in the other guy's eye isn't going to change that. Especially when it comes to art—no one is better than the other; just different. I think I have a better business model than most, but I realize I'm not the most detailed or inventive guy out there. But I know I can draw real well; I can network really well; I have a lot of talented friends. I have my fans and I have my haters. It might be the rum I'm drinking now, but I feel pretty Zen about it all.

I just want to draw the fun/dumb/stupid/silly/epic shit I always draw and sell it to people that want to buy it. The only thing that I need is more exposure to people who might enjoy cool affordable art. So show my stuff to your mom. Tell her I said "hi". She'll remember me.

My mother? Let me tell you about my mother…

(Removes gun from coffee)

<END OF RECORDING>

You can buy some pretty incredible art by Tim Doyle and other amazing artists at NakatomiInc.com, and you can browse for ages and ages through his galleries at MrDoyle.com.

The Sea Also Rises – The Exodus of Turtleton

THE SPIRIT OF EXPLOITATION

AN INTERVIEW WITH RYAN NICHOLSON
by Brian Harris

I admit I'm not incredibly fond of indie horror, but when I do find an indie filmmaker that delivers the goods, I'm a loyal fan that shows my support with my wallet. I came across Ryan Nicholson's work years ago, thanks to MTI's release of **LIVE FEED** *(2006), and I've never looked back. Join Ryan Nicholson, the owner of Plotdigger Films, and I as we talk about his career, his films and what we can look forward to from the Master of Gore-Sleaze.*

Weng's Chop Magazine: *Thanks so much for taking time out of your busy schedule to sit down with WENG'S CHOP, Ryan! I know you're busy as hell with your FX work in the industry and your film company. For those that aren't familiar with you and your films, let's talk about how you got your start in the industry in the early '90s and how that led to Plotdigger Films almost a decade later.*

Ryan Nicholson: I started a Makeup Effects company called "Flesh and Fantasy Inc." back in '98. This was a few years after working in shops. I had some big movies which led to television work. I wanted to make my own movies from the very beginning. *Torched* (2004) was really my first attempt at working towards a feature length project. Once we made it on time and on budget, we decided to go for something feature length, and **LIVE FEED** was soon made.

WCM: *Speaking of* **LIVE FEED**, *tell us about the CAT III release—that's such a fucking cool idea, by the way.*

RN: The CAT III release is a special package with hardcore inserts put into the film. A Chinese takeout box, chopsticks and a dicky roll all come with the disc. I have done hardcore releases of **GUTTERBALLS** (2008) and **HANGER** (2009), so it makes sense to finish off that early work with **LIVE FEED** and *Torched* Special Editions.

WCM: *By the way, is the upcoming film* **EVIL FEED** *connected any way to* **LIVE FEED**? *It feels like it has some thematic connections.*

RN: **EVIL FEED** is a standalone film I wrote in the vein of **LIVE FEED**. It is very action/horror-oriented. I came up with the story and wrote the first few drafts of the script. It was then tweaked by other writers. It looks cool and gory, action packed.

WCM: *When you started doing special effects makeup, did you always intend to eventually make your own films or did you have aspirations of being one of those lucky directors snatched up to do big-budget work for other people?*

RN: There's always the fantasy of doing bigger things but there's also the reality of the content I create being very underground and something that appeals to a small but very loyal audience. So it will remain a fantasy unless I change up my content. I don't see that happening. I need to keep growing my audience movie by movie and hopefully will have a "Tromaesque" empire at some point. I am perfectly fine with that. I also still do effects from time to time on movies I pick and choose. I like to work on fun projects with friends.

WCM: *You've done special effects on some damn cool Hollywood film productions and TV shows including The X-Files, Millennium, Stargate SG-1, Andromeda,* **THE CHRONICLES OF RIDDICK** *(2004) and* **BLADE: TRINITY** *(2004). It's obvious the industry is trending toward way more digital now than ever before. What's it like still doing hands-on practical effects in a field that many people (incorrectly) proclaim is all but dead?*

RN: It's very cool that producers still want practical effects on-set. It could have gone the other way with shops closing down but it hasn't…yet. Makeup FX will always be a mainstay in Hollywood but I don't see a movie like John Carpenter's **THE THING** (1982) ever being made in our lifetime again. So that's a bummer. But it's not dead. I hear people say that and they're wrong.

WCM: *How many of your own films have you directed up to this point and which one would you say is your favorite?*

RN: I have directed ten features and about five shorter length projects. Maybe more. I have lost count, actually. I would have to say that **LIVE FEED** is my favorite work. It's the one with the least amount of baggage, so to speak.

83

I look back fondly on that experience.

WCM: When you say baggage, in regards to your films, you mean distribution drama, right? Can you talk about some of the issues you've encountered in the industry? I'm shocked by how popular your films are and yet how fast, on and off, they go out-of-print.

RN: Basically, movies should be fun to make. But sometimes you can have a really shitty experience that creates bad memories. Most of my movies have been a blast but there's a couple I wish I could forget. Just too many cooks in the fucking kitchen. I only make movies now with my wife and close friends. I have no desire to work for anyone anymore in that genre of things. The releases are pretty small runs and the fans eat them up fast. I am very grateful to my fan base.

WCM: When you're making a film, do you ever ask yourself what you can incorporate in your work that you feel may be missing in horror cinema?

RN: I try to add a ton of humor. It actually just ends up being funny most of the time without any help from me. I think funny horror is far more entertaining than straight-up horror. You have a better chance of winning over an audience if you give them more to work with, more to enjoy.

*WCM: I'd have to say **HANGER** has to be your most offensive and outrageous film. I love it. I know you're working on a **GUTTERBALLS** sequel—have you considered one for **HANGER**, as well?*

RN: I have actually thought long and hard about a **HANGER** sequel. Hanger runs off with the girl. It's a perfect lead-in to a sequel and Nathan Dashwood is a great guy; I would love to do it and might. I need to get **GUTTERBALLS 2** finished before anything else though!

*WCM: Concerning the **GUTTERBALLS** sequel, what's it about and how close are you to finishing?*

RN: It's an ongoing process. The budget is very small and I shoot when I can with a very dedicated cast. I have only done very preliminary stuff, but the big stuff with Miholo Terzic (Sarah) is coming up pretty quick. It will be intense, man! Very, very brutal stuff!

WC: Outside of making your own films and doing effects for others, what's currently on your agenda?

RN: I watch a ton of movies, read and write odds and ends. Spend time with my family. I am trying to get my own makeup FX off the ground. It's a ton of red tape, but hopefully will be well worth it.

WCM: Why choose to do genre cinema? So many others seem to think working in horror/exploitation is a ghetto—what is it about horror cinema you love doing?

RN: I am a product of the genre...lived my whole life paying respect to horror. That's not to say that I won't make different kinds of movies that interest me but until that time, I am staying sleazy!

WCM: Ever consider doing a box set (a la Mill Creek or Echo Bridge) with a bunch of your films?

RN: I would love to do a box set. Currently there's a box set of four of my films in Germany. It would be great to have a complete collection in North America sooner than later!

Weng's Chop Magazine would like to once again say thank you to Ryan Nicholson for such a great interview. For more information on Ryan and his films, check him out at plotdigger.com.

Africa Addio

Interview with Ugandan filmmaker Lubega Vicent

by Graham Rae

You have to be careful what you wish for, or you can curse yourself horribly. Many a Faustian pact has been forged and then gone awry this way. This is the case for Ntale (Kasule David), who inherits a magical stick from his grandfather, with the express direction that he not shake hands with anybody from that moment on.

Of course, he forgets this admonition, or there wouldn't be much of a story, and sets female devil Nankya (Nabukalu Flavia) upon himself. He has to try and save his family heirloom and maintain his sexual composure and propriety, and by the looks of things he may have a pretty damned hard time ahead of him doing so...

Thus runs the storyline for **THE WORST MISTAKE** *(2012), the first film from new director Lubega Vicent, being billed as Uganda's first horror film. Uganda seems to be undergoing an unprecedented mushrooming of (no pun intended) native film talent lately, and YouTube is awash with new productions from that hitherto-unheard-from African country. We caught up with Vicent to see if he could give us an insight into what was going on round his home turf.*

Please tell us a little about yourself.

My name is Lubega Vicent. I am a 25-year old Ugandan from the Muganda tribe, and live alone in the Ndeeba-Rubaga Kampala District.

What made you want to get into filmmaking, and what made you make Uganda's first horror film? Why choose horror as a topic? Is it big in Uganda?

I was inspired by the movie called **ALIEN DEAD** directed, produced and written by Fred Olen Ray, which was released in the 1980s. After watching it I was inspired to want to try something myself.

What sort of camera did you use to shoot?

A Canon XL, though it was rented. Towards the end of the shooting we used a small Canon due to insufficient funds. The use of two cameras accounts for the picture variations in the film. We are planning to get our own camera, because hiring has cost us too much.

Why are there two different production companies listed on the DVD box?

Initially we started with SCEJ Productions responsible for photography, disco hires, video coverage, tent hires, etc.; the year after we started, we included production training. The primary function of SCEJ was to raise money for our projects (films) and training/educating actors. This was the role it played in the movie. By the end of 2009 we started BVN Productions with the intention of making movies, particularly horror, action, romantic, TV series and documentaries, with attendant related activities like educating in the region. Besides funding and training, BVN did the rest of the work on the film.

How did you raise the money for **THE WORST MISTAKE** *and how much did it cost?*

We used money from SCEJ Productions. The film cost 6,836,945.30 Ugandan shillings, which is roughly the equivalent to $2,650 US currency.

How did you get into filmmaking? Do you have training?

I studied online in 2008-2010 at Lights Film School, and I also use online tutorials and advice.

Are you inspired by the growing success of Isaac Nabwana and the attention he is getting with the **WAKALIWOOD** *(2012) documentary? Do you know him? Ever worked with him?*

Yes, I am inspired. But I know nothing about a Wakaliwood documentary. I know him, but have never worked with him.

Why has there been such a surge in Ugandan movies all of a sudden?

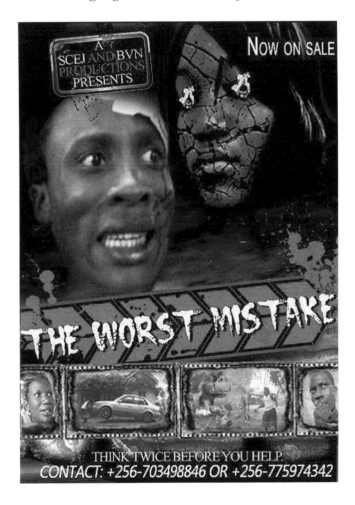

Uganda is a developing country with a growth rate of about 5.3%. Unfortunately, most Ugandans feel that there are no potential filmmakers, especially for films with special effects, so whenever a movie is out, they run to it to be proven right. Oddly, this contributes to market availability for movies, which encourages more filmmakers to join the industry, though we still lack skills.

Where do you find your actors?

There is no public organization [through which] we can find them. We have to find them privately, but are trying to locate at least one in the region.

Ugandan filmmaker Lubega Vicent

The movie is a morality tale against infidelity. Is censorship big in Uganda— is there any censorship in Uganda—and would the public not have accepted a movie that did not have a moral to the tale? Is Uganda a country big on religion? Can you have nudity in Ugandan movies?

Censorship is under construction by UCC [*the Uganda Communications Commission, which regulates Uganda's communications industry -Graham*] and the Uganda Federation of Movie Industry [*a copyright management organization/royalties collections agency -Graham*], but so far it's inactive.

Yes nudity is allowed. As long, that is, as you're in line with the law which states that you have to clearly relate the film's contents to the viewing public. You have to add "Potentially damaging to the human psyche or morality" to the advertising materials for movies with violence, brutality, pornography, or similar contents. The film must clearly be marked with the letters "L" for bad language, "S" for sex, and "V" for violence.

Any government interference in your work at all?

Not yet.

How long did the movie take you to shoot?

It took a week.

How has it been selling? Have you sold it internationally at all?

It's moving, and we have been able to sell 24,000 copies so far. As it's our first movie a lot of the framework for moviemaking is still not in place. We still haven't sold it internationally, though we wish to do so with our next movie.

Are you working on another movie or movies? If so, what genre are they? Horror? Different things?

One is horror, and another one is an action-romance film.

How would you like your career as a filmmaker to progress? Do you like horror films? Would you like to continue making them, or do you have other projects you would like to do as well?

I want to start the first filmmaking school in the region like that of Algeria.

I want to put in place an actor's gallery so that every filmmaker in the region (East Africa) rushes to BVN for actors and other requirements.

I hope to commence BVNWOOD, a place where almost every location needed for movie shooting is available, as it is in other moviemaking countries.

I want to be the number one producer on the continent of the following genres: horror, action, romance, TV series, and documentary. Perhaps those are my dreams in the industry, and once I get support for sure they will come true. Horror is my favorite genre, and I want to continue making horror movies.

How has the movie been received in Uganda?

Since our production is new on the market and we have insufficient advertising funds, the journey is not that smooth.

Got any favorite movies or directors or actors, Ugandan or otherwise?

ZOMBIELAND, LET ME IN, LEGEND, DEADHEADS, SIX DAYS, SEVEN NIGHTS, BROKEBACK MOUNTAIN, GIRL WITH THE PEARL EARRING, A KNIGHT'S TALE, MASK OF ZORRO, MISS CONGENIALITY, MY BEST FRIEND'S WEDDING, SENSE AND SENSIBILITY, NOTTING HILL, ICE MAN, etc.

What did you think of **THE LAST KING OF SCOTLAND** *(2006)?*

It lacked depth, and was not the real story of the late president Idi Amin.

Are there a lot of cinemas in Uganda that screen films from other countries? If so, which films do they screen? Are there films from a particular country that are favored in Uganda?

There are a few cinemas that screen international cinema, but not many. Uganda likes movies from all over the world, as long as they are action and romance.

Why are action and romance films received best in Uganda?

This is due to the composition of our population. We have almost 35% youth, 45% young and the rest adults. The youth in our country are the main consumers of films.

Is there one specific area of Uganda, one city perhaps, where people make films? Or does filmmaking happen all over Uganda?

The central region is the main area of film production.

How did you end up using a children's home/orphanage for a large part of the movie? What did you tell them to allow you to use the place to film?

Some of the actors we used work in children's home, so we decided to use it reduce expenditure.

Where do you see the Ugandan film industry going in the future?

By 2015, I hope we will be able to produce a movie with at least 30% 3D. And I hope by 2020 Uganda will be the number one movie producing country on the continent, because a lot of people have joined the industry in a very short period of time, and every genre of film is being made.

Who does your subtitle translation?

Ssemwanga Patrick, a student of literature, though he lacks experience. We used Adobe Premiere Pro to subtitle the movie. But we have now mastered Adobe Encore Professional and are using that software for subtitling.

How do you plan to avoid piracy?

The rate of piracy so far has not been high, but in the future we plan to use software to protect DVD duplicating.

Any last thoughts on making **THE LAST MISTAKE***?*

It was a learning experience.

And what did you learn?

We have learned that people are not interested in the horror genre.

THE END OF THE BEGINNING.

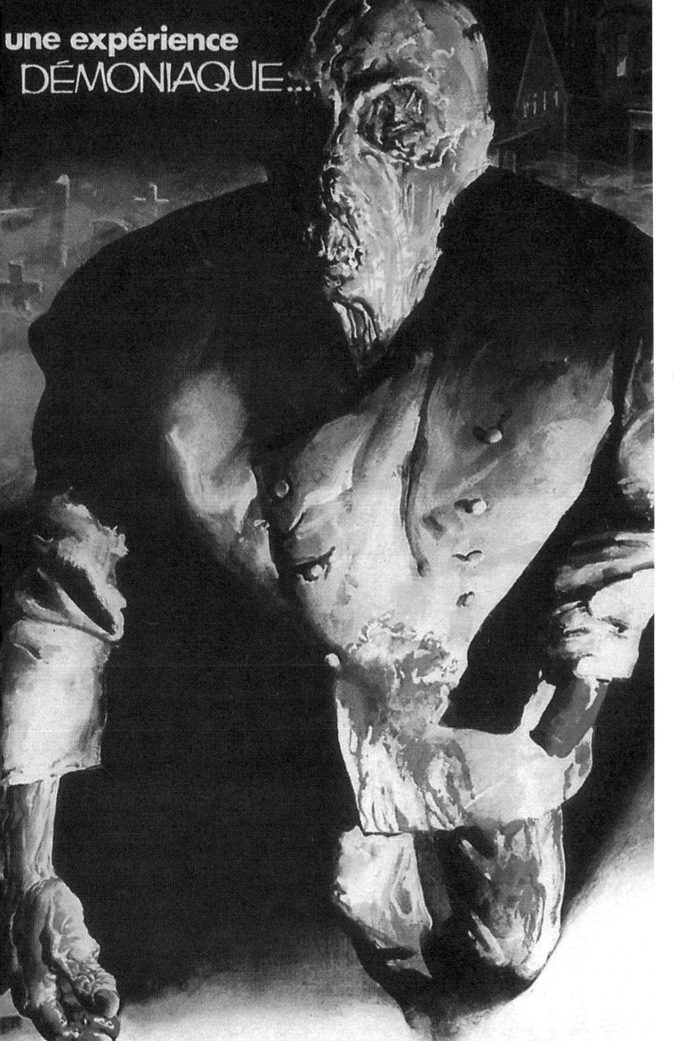

columns & regular features

Geek Roundtable

*Pretty much everyone with a hankering for horror has at least heard of Lucio "Il Maestro" Fulci—while not strictly a horror director, he is responsible for some of the genre's most famous offerings of '70s and '80s Italian Horror Cinema. Among genrephiles, he is perhaps best-known for his run of immensely influential horror films from 1979 to 1982, which consisted of **ZOMBIE** (a.k.a. **ZOMBI 2**, 1979), **CITY OF THE LIVING DEAD** (Paura nella città dei morti viventi, a.k.a. **THE GATES OF HELL**, 1980), **THE BLACK CAT** (Gato nero, 1981), **THE BEYOND** (...E tu vivrai nel terrore! L'aldilà, a.k.a. **SEVEN DOORS OF DEATH**, 1981), **THE HOUSE BY THE CEMETERY** (Quella villa accanto al cimitero, a.k.a. **ZOMBIE HELL HOUSE**, 1981), and **THE NEW YORK RIPPER** (Lo squartatore di New York, 1982). The oft-overlooked Action-Adventure **CONTRABAND** (Luca il contrabbandiere, 1980) was the lone non-Horror duck in this four-year hot streak for Fulci.*

*While all of the aforementioned Horrors are highly-lauded, endlessly-cited classics in their own right, probably the most controversial and divisive film among them is the atmospherically oddball, convoluted celluloid nightmare, **THE HOUSE BY THE CEMETERY**. Playing like a fever dream, it tells the story of Dr. Norman Boyle (Paolo Malco), his wife Lucy (Catriona MacColl) and their son Bob (Giovanni Frezza), who relocate from New York to Boston so Dr. Boyle can assume the work of his colleague, Dr. Petersen, who recently committed suicide after murdering his own mistress. Young Bob has received psychic warnings from a young girl named Mae (Silvia Collatina), who urges him to keep his family away, but of course his parents think it's all stuff and nonsense, and the Boyles move into the suicide house, where Norman discovers that Dr. Petersen was independently researching the home's original owner, the malicious Dr. Freudstein, whose evil influence seems to reach from beyond the grave to anyone who enters the creepy old house.*

Since this is one of the most argued-about films in Fulci's filmography, we at Weng's Chop decided, in the interest of starting shit and creating hostility, to ask our staffers to write up their own thoughts on this little gem, to be presented in a semi-roundtable-style review. Here's what our nest of nutbags had to say, in favor, opposition, and indifference. Viva la difference...failing that, divide and conquer, Freudstein style!

FREUDSTEIN'S FOLLIES!
A GALLIMAUFRY OF GANDERS AT FULCI'S
THE HOUSE BY THE CEMETERY

by Tony Strauss and others

[*Readers should note that those who have not seen* **THE HOUSE BY THE CEMETERY** *are hereby entering major spoiler territory, and are also seriously missing out on an insanely unique horror film.*]

BRIAN HARRIS:

Ladies and gentlemen, Lucio Fulci's films are often a tough nut to crack. (That's right, I said it: tough nut to crack.) They're not quite what I'd call "accessible"; it takes a real appreciation for the man's work, and sometimes a bit of patience. Some people refer to his horror as confusing, nonsensical and gratuitous, whereas I tend to see it as non-linear, dream—or nightmare, if you prefer—logic laced with multiple gore and violence set-pieces. I won't go so far as to say his work is high art, but whether people like to admit it or not, it is indeed art. No other Italian director delivered on strange and gory in quite the same manner; his workmanlike approach to violence combined with his eye for style over substance was second to none. His films were not meant to be followed like their American counterparts; it was the overall effect he was looking for.

When I first saw **THE HOUSE BY THE CEMETERY**— late '90s, I believe—my reaction went a little something like this: "What the hell? What the fuck just happened and what kind of an ending is that?!!" There seemed to be no rhyme or reason for anything we see. It starts with a **HELL NIGHT** (1981) Slasher film vibe and slowly develops into a **LET'S SCARE JESSICA TO DEATH** (1971) scenario where you're convinced Norman Boyle has brought his emotionally fragile wife (Lucy) to the house in order to drive her mad and make way for his lover, babysitter Ann (Ania Pieroni). It's not all that simple, though, as Norman's son Bob is having conversations with an "imaginary friend" named Mae. Is Mae real, an imaginary friend or something more? It doesn't take long before **THE HOUSE BY THE CEMETERY** lunges headlong into the supernatural, dispelling all suspicions about Norman, Ann and Mae.

Though this film is considered part of Fulci's loose *Gates of Hell* trilogy, comparing this film to **THE BEYOND** and **CITY OF THE LIVING DEAD** isn't really fair in my opinion. It's a different beast, in that the antagonist in this film isn't a zombie *per se*; Freudstein is a living being, an amalgamation of Frankenstein and his monster, a Saint-Germain able to extend his life using the flesh of his victims. The Boyle family is pretty damned one-dimensional, but rightly so; they're nothing more than flies in the spider's web. We don't need to know them anyhow because it's not about them; it's about the bigger picture. There's an ageless evil preying on the living and the Boyles won't be the last. Freudstein will continue on.

It took me years—no joke, years—before I was really able to appreciate this unique film and the sheer oddity it offers. It's fair to say it grew on me, and I'm not one of those slobbering fans that deify any old piece of cinematic shit (you know who you are, Freddy, Jason and Michael fans), but **THE HOUSE BY THE CEMETERY** deserves a second look and a little more consideration from its detractors. Fulci paints the film with broad strokes; it's not about the individual sequences or how they're strung together, it's about the overall effect the film has on the viewer and that effect is undeniably bleak and nihilistic.

Would I call this a masterpiece? Not by a long shot, but there's definitely more—or less, depending on what you're looking for—to it than what the average zombie film fan might expect, and that's the beauty of it—it's different; there's no ham-handed Romero to be found here. With almost no nudity,

of Lovecraftian terror, **THE HOUSE BY THE CEMETERY** may be a narrative Nazi's nightmare but it's pure gold for the cult cinema geek looking for a film that defies expectations and entertains. Do I count it as one of my personal favorites? Shit yeah I do—I'm eyeballin' that bad ass Arrow Video Blu-ray release to add to my collection as I type this review! From cut to uncut, Vipco to Blue Underground, **THE HOUSE BY THE CEMETERY** has weathered the test of time and continues growing in popularity. Fulci must have done something right.

TIM PAXTON:

THE HOUSE BY THE CEMETERY was not what was expected when I originally saw this film in the mid-'80s. By that time in my life I knew that the name Fulci usually meant gore and possibly some zombie action. Heck, I scoured the Friday entertainment section of the local newspapers looking for *any* horror or science fiction film with an Italian-sounding name as director. The poster art for the film had more of a mad Slasher bent, which almost threw me off my game (I have always been more of a straight supernatural horror fan rather than a Giallo buff). **THE HOUSE BY THE CEMETERY** was at a Columbus, Ohio drive-in, the second or third feature at a quadruple dusk-to-dawn show. To be honest, I don't recollect what it may have been paired with other than maybe **ALIEN CONTAMINATION** (1980) or 1978's **THE TOOLBOX MURDERS** (both of which seemed to be on some sort of unending drive-in circulation in Ohio). When the tale began to unfold in a sinister, dreamlike, alternate-Lovecraftian *Weird Tales* universe, I knew I was in for something special.

There is a dark house on the edge of Boston with its own cemetery plot; old and rotten to the core and exerting some evil influence over the surrounding town, smothering everything as if it were a wet woolen blanket of weirdness. Enter a young boy named Bob who has a connection with the "old Freudstein" estate that goes deeper than your run-of-the-mill *deja vu*. There is something horrendous and inhuman existing in the cellar of the old house, and his mother and father have rented it out for the summer. This creature is a shambling mass of body parts that exists in a quasi-"alive" form due to its harvesting of the local population. Could it be that the boy is what the monstrous Dr. Freudstein needs to escape his cycle of murder and harvesting?

At least that's what I read into the film when I first watched what I now consider to be Fulci's masterpiece (the fantasy film **CONQUEST**, made two years later, is almost as dreamlike in its execution). As far as the film making any sense, I wasn't concerned about that at all. This *was* a Fulci film, by the way, and he was never known to be a master at intricate plot development (no matter what genre he has involved in, from Comedies to Westerns to Crime to Giallo to Horror to whathaveyou).

Fulci's work, always detached (sometimes clinically so) was always very voyeuristic with an uncomfortable lingering on the gore in his films. He would zoom in, keeping a static camera lens glued far too long as chunks of over-red flesh filler would tumble out or an unhealthy amount of blood would bubble and gurgle from a wound accompanied by his usual flair for really gross and unusual sound effects. This has been his style of presenting gore since his Westerns (which included **MASSACRE TIME**, 1966 and **FOUR OF THE APOCALYPSE**, 1975) and his thrillers (**DON'T TORTURE A DUCKLING**, 1972, comes to mind). In **HOUSE BY THE CEMETERY** we have some of that, but, curiously, less than in the film he is better known for: **ZOMBIE**. Freudstein's domain is more of a slaughterhouse, with the (oddly fresh) remains of his victims piled up on tables and strewn about on the floor. If he was ever a doctor in his past life in the mid-1800s, this creature of horror has long since stopped existing as a human, his rotten brain fuzzy with the logic of organ replacement and lacking any sense of cleanliness.

Bob has a psychic contact with the mysterious Mae, a young girl who tries in vain to keep the boy away from the house. We learn that she is Freudstein's long-dead daughter. When Mae is unable to keep Bob from the house—and the boy witnesses the death of his parents—she fully envelopes him into her reality in order to shield him from the horror in the cellar. Freudstein is still in the house, and presumably killing and absorbing luckless humans into his being, but he will never get his claws on Bob.

Production-wise, this comes towards the end of Fulci's best creative period. The film is steeped in atmosphere with some chilling cinematography and very gooey gore effects. Freudstein looks every bit the slimy decaying creature, moreso than the zombies that appeared in other films from around this time. If you've ever seen a corpse up close (and nose closed) you would really appreciate how accomplished Giannetto De Rossi was with his Freudstein creation. Walter Rizzati's soundtrack, while not as an annoying ear-worm as the zombie-thump march of the Giorgio Cascio/Fabio Frizzi score for **ZOMBIE**, is very good although its use in the film is rather haphazardly placed at times.

One line from the film sums it up best, "I can't believe this is happening". Yep. It's mindless, unspeakable horror done right…for once!

TONY STRAUSS:

When we first started tossing the idea around of possibly doing a "Many Reviewers, One Film" article on **THE HOUSE BY THE CEMETERY**, I was painfully reminded of my status as a Fulci Novice. Up to that point, the only Fulci films I'd ever seen were **ZOMBIE**, **THE BEYOND** and **CITY OF THE LIVING DEAD**… and the only one of those I'd revisited since I first saw them (over 20 years ago) was **ZOMBIE**, when Blue Underground released their amazing Special Edition Blu-ray. So, despite the fact that I felt in danger of having my Geek Card revoked, I was interested in seeing for the first time a film that most of my peers knew like the back of their own severed hands.

So, I picked up a copy of Blue Underground's Blu-ray release of the film, and sat back to watch it with the intention of being forgiving (I have a tendency to be put off by many of the kitschier elements of "Italian Horror Classics", a fact that makes me somewhat unpopular at many Horror Fan Circle Jerk parties), due to my reflexive tendency to slap substandard storytelling upside the head, and my inability to be entertained for any significant duration by mere elaborate gore set-pieces.

I settled in during the opening credits. Enjoying the eerie synth theme by Walter Rizzati, I permitted myself a modicum of hope for at least an atmospheric experience—though I didn't dare hope for anything on-par with the atmosphere Fulci achieved in **ZOMBIE**…that would just be setting myself up for disappointment.

I needn't have been so trepidatious.

From the opening shot that pans up from the young girl (Daniela Doria) getting dressed to reveal the syrup-thick foreboding atmosphere of the Freudstein house, the downright stunning cinematography of Sergio Salvati pulled me into a dream world like no other I'd experienced on film before. It wasn't until the movie was completely over—and I'd successfully "come out" of the dream in which the film had so effortlessly ensconced me—that I realized how simplistic the story itself had been. In this film, the story services the experience, instead of the other way around. Sure, the story is important, but it is merely a small part of the window through which we view this otherworldly, Lovecraftian gothic horror.

I think that what we just might have here is the perfect cinematic depiction of a nightmare. Bob's nightmare. For this is Bob's story—all the other characters (except Mae, Bob's protector/spirit guide) are secondary; existing as little more than set-dressing in the dream Bob is forced to inhabit.

Everything about this film services that premise, from the often disjointed segues from scene-to-scene to the final moment, where we realize that Bob has both been saved from harm and seemingly imprisoned forever. Characters aren't so much introduced as they are allowed to fade into existence from blurred masses, their echoed voices becoming more distinct as they materialize into focus. Nobody in the film really seems to make any actual decisions; they tend to merely react to the things they encounter as they are moved by some unseen hand (perhaps the evil Dr. Freudstein's?) through a tableau of nightmarish horror. Like a dream, events and behaviors that would normally elicit strong reactions from the characters are passed by unnoticed. In almost any other horror film, Bob's creepy warnings from a mysterious little girl (and subsequent acquisition of a creepy old doll) would at least draw some attention from the other principals, but here they are merely pawns being pushed through the events leading to their inescapable fates.

It is the feeling of total immersion in a dream that, for me, allowed Fulci's trademark violent set-pieces to work better here than they have in any other of his films that I've seen so far. These types of drawn-out and overemphasized murder and gore work so much better when the tone of the film matches them as well as it does here. Even the endless and often-ridiculed "bat attack" scene—once the viewer gets past the limitations of the goofy-looking special effects—really works well within this context. In a real-life situation of this nature, anyone with an angry bat attached to their hands would be able to free themselves easily with one good whip-of-the-hand or smack against a wall, with minimal skin loss. But in our nightmares, even the simplest of threats can become endless and horrific, requiring us to endure myriad illogical steps—compounding nightmare upon nightmare—before ridding ourselves of such a danger.

The atmosphere of the film is like a more involving (and hence, more successful) version of Werner Herzog's **HEART OF GLASS** (1976), in which all the actors were allegedly required to perform their roles in a state of hypnosis in order to better depict the lost and aimless feeling that Herzog desired. However, whereas Herzog's film effectively distanced the viewer to a state of detached voyeurism by presenting characters behaving in a manner that is unrelatable for the viewer, Fulci's characters here are more-or-less "normal", yet unwittingly exist in a *world* that is unrelatable, allowing the viewer to sympathize with the characters more closely, while nonetheless still serving as voyeurs into another world.

And while Fulci is brilliant at delivering this dream-world feeling with confident, broad strokes, he is also very adept at dropping in smaller details to support it all. For example, the extreme close-ups on actors' eyes—such as those between Norman and the mysterious new babysitter, Ann—would normally be employed to convey either lust or adversarial intent, but they are here used to show a deeper connection; they subconsciously imply that Norman and Ann have both fallen under the influence of the evil that resides in the house, and share an understanding of their entwined fates that Lucy has yet to discover. Another good example is the seemingly throwaway dialogue between Mr. Wheatley (Carlo De Mejo) and Norman at the archives, where Wheatley is so sure that Norman has visited before, with a daughter that he doesn't have. On the surface, it's just a scene of a mistaken memory, but within the context of the film's mood, it serves to imply a deeper, not-quite-definable fate that these characters are bound to.

All of this works so well because the film takes a point-of-view from within Bob's nightmare. Whether Bob is in a scene or not, all scenes are in a sense depicted from his trapped-in-a-dream viewpoint, and *that* is the real genius of this film. We, as the viewers, are slow to realize that we have been trapped alongside Bob the entire time, and are forced to share his inevitable fate. Arriving at the film's conclusion, we realize that, like Bob, we were trapped within Freudstein's dark machinations before we even began. In the end, we are safe with Bob and Mae, but we have come to understand that we were never operating under our own wills, and we are never free to leave.

And now, this particular Fulci Novice not only has a new favorite film from *Il Maestro*, but has become ensnared by a newfound fascination, and is now on a mission to become a proper Fulciphile.

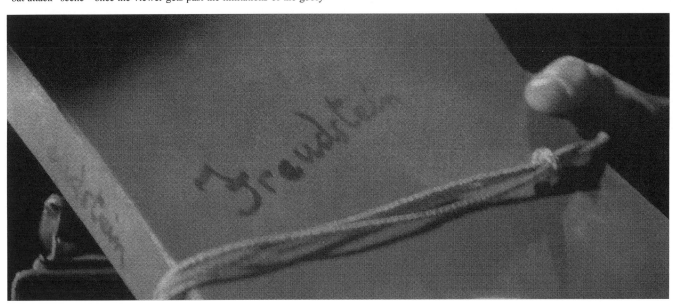

STEVEN RONQUILLO:

I first ran into Fulci's **THE HOUSE BY THE CEMETERY** on a late-night UHF station in the late '80s, I think. It was about 3 a.m., and I was shocked that it was on. They had cut the whole opening scene, and any trace of blood was edited out, but I liked it enough to want to see it uncut. After that, I didn't run into it again until '02 or '03 when high-speed 'net was the new kid on the block—and this new thing called "torrents" showed up—and it was one of the first movies I got to see.

Well, it didn't start out well, since at first I got annoyed as hell hearing my name about 20 times…"STEVE! STEEEVVE!" I was yelling at the screen by the time it was over. But then we get one of Fulci's most classic kills, then we get into the story, which is a creepy Lovecraftian tale with the smell of eldritch all over it. But the English version has been ridiculed over the years because of one of the worst damned dub jobs in the history of Bad Dub Jobs. But having gotten to see the Italian dub, it sounded 200% better. But Blue Underground screwed that up by putting in subtitles that were for the deaf and hard-of-hearing—rather than just translations of the spoken dialogue. So the way Blue Underground did the disc was just batshit crazy.

But that isn't as batshit insane as the illegal **THE HOUSE BY THE CEMETERY, REVISITED** Christian re-edit (see sidebar review) with all the gore cut out and a bible quote cut in every 20 minutes. It is a bizarre and hard-to-find edit—due to the fact it is a fooking illegal usage of Fulci's movie!

To sum up, it really is the stop-gap film from his great early-'80s classics to his misfires like **MANHATTAN BABY** (1982) and his '90s TV films. I liked it, but I would rank it as middle-ground Fulci.

JARED AUNER:

When I first heard about this project, I didn't give it much mind. **THE HOUSE BY THE CEMETERY**? Is there anything left to say about this film that hasn't already been said? Don't get me wrong—it's great and all—but if we're gonna talk Fulci I think I could find a lot more to say about **BEATRICE CENCI** (1967), **FOUR OF THE APOCALYPSE** (1976) or **THE DEVIL'S HONEY** (1986). Hell, I could go on for hours extolling the many virtues of such bottom-of-the-barrel fare as **CONQUEST** (1983), **MURDER ROCK** (1986) or even **DEMONIA** (1990). That's right! **DEMONIA**! But alas, **THE HOUSE BY THE CEMETERY** it is.

It was the last of Fulci's four major gore-gothics that I saw, and always my least favorite among them. But I've always enjoyed the film, particularly the alarming and totally bonkers final 15-or-so minutes. It has some of Lucio's most nerve-wracking work in horror, in addition to just being bleak as hell. Fulci was never afraid to dive head-first into the deepest, darkest waters of existential despair, and the climax of this film threatens to drown the viewer in this dreadful abyss. Once all the characters go down into that basement, you just know none of them are gonna make it out alive. And they don't.

I've always seen Fulci as the darkest and most nihilistic of the great Italian horror directors. Bava was cynical, but one gets the impression that he always found some great cosmic joke in all the terror he depicted. Argento is a fatalist, but still seeks to lead the audience out of the labyrinth of the inevitable using sheer bloody spectacle. Deodato just wanted to rub your nose in horror, like a bully. But Fulci wanted to take you *into* the dark, wanted you to *see* it, *feel* it. He wanted you to know that you're never going to get out of Freudstein's basement in one piece. Lucio's best work beckons us to gaze into the abyss and he never gave a fuck that it was gazing right back at us. And we don't either; we revel in it, wallow in it like pigs in the mud. And **THE HOUSE BY THE CEMETERY** is a deep, dark mud.

So I guess I'm wrong; there's still plenty to say about this film…just as there is still *plenty* to say about Lucio Fulci and his incredible body of work in general.

DANAE DUNNING:

After Dr. Peterson kills his mistress and commits suicide, his colleague, New York professor Dr. Norman Boyle, along with wife Lucy and young son Bob, move into Peterson's home to continue his research of the mysterious Dr. Jacob Tess Freudstein (Giovanni de Nava). Strange things happen almost immediately with Lucy hearing noises, the babysitter Ann (Ania Pieroni) behaving bizarrely, and Bob befriending a little girl named Mae and her mother, Mary (Teresa Rosa Pesante), whom only he can see. With the help of incredibly informative librarian Daniel Douglas (Gianpaolo Saccarola), Dr. Boyle and Lucy try to get to the bottom of things (instead of, I don't know, moving…but then we wouldn't have a movie would we?). Little Bob discovers that Dr. Freudstein is in the basement, still alive (more or less), and will do any dastardly deed he can to stay that way.

I amaze myself at times. I really do. I was able to stay awake during this mess, though how I struggled! I attempted to watch it once when I discovered it on VHS, but shut if off after 15 minutes. Then when I was doing my stint on Creep Show Radio's *Ghastly Reviews* a couple years ago, well guess what we had assigned? Yep. I didn't have the option of turning it off this time. The plot actually sounds interesting, but sometimes things that sound good on paper just don't translate well to film. I can't really comment on the acting, since I was only able to obtain a dubbed version for rental, but the dubbing was atrocious, as most dubbing usually is, particularly that of Bob. And, about Bob: This is a child—the one character I'm supposed to be identifying with and rooting for—but he was so annoying, I just couldn't. And then there is the character of Freudstein. Who exactly is he? What was he researching? Why is he a zombie? Folks, I'm not the kind of viewer who has to have every little detail explained to me, but I hate being teased. We have little snippets of information, diary entries and research notes that could barely be read, but no real answers. And then there's that stupid ending. The film just abruptly stops like they ran out of money or something.

My first Fulci film was his excellent undead masterpiece, **ZOMBIE**. This was my second. Oh, Lucio, how you've let me down.

DAVID ZUZELO:
THE HOUSE BY THE CEMETERY is one of my favorite films of all time. Yes, I mean that. When I hear the often-flung-about phrase "EuroHorror", I put it at the top of the stack right away. I don't need to tell you it's an astonishing film, but I'll tell you why it's my favorite. It's my favorite Fulci film, and that says a lot. But while I would love to just think of it that way, I see this film as the culmination of the Horror Golden Age of Italy, coming together with some of the best and brightest talent, all working together to make one unique entity that doesn't knock anything off, but instead creates a surreal and strange film that is the ultimate "Monster Lurking In The Basement" movie.

Producer Fabrizio De Angelis (Larry Ludman to his fans) brought together amazing talents to create **ZOMBIE, GATES OF HELL, THE BEYOND** and **THE NEW YORK RIPPER**, with each of them having truly stood the test of time. These films created the look, feel, pace and sound of '80s Italian Horror. The titans of terror behind the scenes include longtime cohorts of Fulci and craftsman in their own roles, such as editor Vincenzo Tomassi, cinematographer Sergio Salvati, soundtrack master Walter Rizzati, production designer Massimo Lentini, along with FX overlords of gore Giannetto De Rossi and Maurizio Trani! And how could you overlook the actors? Catriona MacColl, Paolo Malco, Dagmar Lassander, Daniela Doria, and Carlo De Mejo all bring their best to the strange goings-on in the weird sideways world of Fulci! And the immortal and iconic presence of "Bob" himself, Giovanni Frezza, can't be forgotten. It could be the bizarre dubbing or just the fact that he has a unique look (and reacts to what really appears like actual danger in some sequences)…but you can't forget him.

And perhaps most importantly is the story and screenplay from Elisa Briganti, Fulci, Giorgio Mariuzzo and the immortal Dardano Sacchetti. **THE BEYOND** is a film that creates a weird otherworld hinging on moments that defy logic, but **HOUSE** does not. On every viewing I appreciate the fact that this film is *not* clogged up with incoherence (unless you saw the video release shown with wrong-way reels, of course); the characters are interacting on different planes of reality and that is clear right from the start. When they happen to intersect it usually means something awful is about to happen. And make no mistake—this is full-bore gore splatter mayhem! Of all the credits I've come across in decades of Italian genre cinema, I always smile when I see Sacchetti, a true hero and creative wiz that never lets an idea go to waste and can bring in any idea that a producer could ever want.

And then there is New Whitby, Boston's (!) greatest citizen. Jacob Allan Freudstein[1], take a bow. A truly monstrous monster, his motivations and story—as well as the otherworldly existence of his family, doomed to bear his name as he clutches to life with stolen limbs—are just totally unique. A real horror in appearance, and bringing the grim certainty of death to all who dare enter…**THE HOUSE BY THE CEMETERY**.

Maybe it's like Dr. Petersen left behind in his recorded notes when he said, "I've lost all critical perspective." There is no film like **THE HOUSE BY THE CEMETERY** for me…long may Freudstein reign over the Italian Horror Legacy!

DAN TAYLOR:
It's early on a Wednesday afternoon in the late 1980s as I walk from the West Philly campus of Drexel University down to the strip of low-rent theaters that dot Center City's bustling Chestnut Street. Though my pals and I frequent all of these dying multi-screens on a regular basis (I love the way Eric's Place—site of 1985's Easter Sunday wilding after a screening of **THE LAST DRAGON**—smells like the nearby Roy Rogers), since I set foot on Drexel's orange-brick campus the Budco Midtown has become my favorite.

While The Midtown no longer screens the triple-Xploits of blonde sex goddess Seka and friends (damn!), it does offer up a continuous stream of exploitation fare and Wednesdays are a bargain-lover's delight—two flicks for the low, low price of $1.50, leaving me with enough dough to grab a Double R Bar Burger from Roy's and some Meister Brau on the way back to campus.

---

1 Editor's note: This is a weird glitch in the film, as the good doctor is first named as "Jacob Allen Freudstein," however on his tombstone it reads "Jacob Tess Freudstein". Oops!

Art: Amber Skowronski

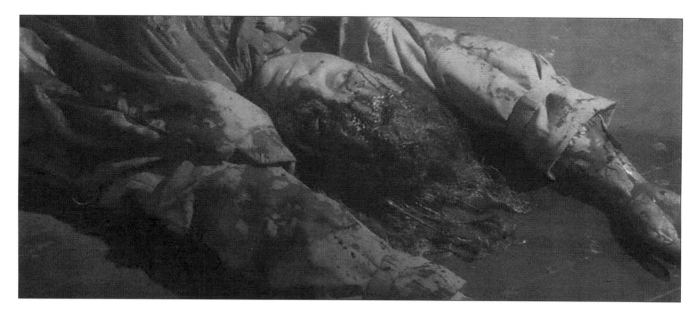

And though I will never get to experience Times Square in all its grindhouse glory, I imagine that this is as close as I'm going to get. The doors lead to a sharply-pitched auditorium complete with an inhumanly sticky floor and more than a handful of unusable seats haphazardly covered in dark green garbage bags. Judging from the look and smell of some of my fellow Wednesday matinee "regulars", what lurks under those bags is probably more horrible than what's about to unspool on-screen. Luckily, there is little or no evidence of the legendary "cat rat" that allegedly lurks behind the curtains of the Eric Pennsauken, another of our haunts on the opposite side of the Delaware River.

But for a trash film lover and neophyte 'zine publisher, these weekly outings to The Midtown (and its neighbors) are no less than a crash course in Exploitation 101. Unfortunately, I doubt that my professor—whose class I'm skipping on a weekly basis—will give me credit for these "extracurricular outings" to experience **THE PERILS OF GWENDOLINE** (1984), **SEVEN DOORS OF DEATH**, **WITCHBOARD** (1986), **THE GATES OF HELL** or today's screening of Lucio Fulci's **THE HOUSE BY THE CEMETERY**.

This is my first experience with **HOUSE**, which anchors the middle portion of Fulci's legendary run that began with **ZOMBIE** and ends with 1984's **MURDER ROCK**. And though I'll watch it countless times over the years to come, I'll never forget this initial screening in that smelly, sticky theater on Chestnut Street.

I don't recall what set off my fellow theatergoer that afternoon. All I know is that the exploits of Dr. Fruedstein, Bob, Ann, Norman and Lucy set him off. And set him off *bad*. As on-screen tensions rose and the audience shifted nervously in their non-garbage-bag-clad seats, one patron jumped to his feet and let loose an entire, jumbo-sized container of sweet, sticky soda as he shouted "Get the fuck OUT!"

I don't know if his command was aimed at the actors and actresses, Fulci, his fellow Midtowners or some unnamed personal demon, but the giant soda landed with a splattery bullseye that sent sticky rivulets slowly oozing down the screen.

And as quickly as it happened it was over. The rest of us shifted nervously in our seats, anticipating houselights and the end of the day's festivities. In true Midtown fashion, though, such reprimand never arrived and the rest of the flick finished without incident. The second feature rolled and once the day was complete we staggered out into the daylight, squinting in hopes of blocking out the reality that awaited us either on the streets or 30 blocks away at school.

A week or two later I ventured back down to The Midtown, plunked down my $1.50 and headed past the snack bar, fully expecting the Coke-splattered screen to have been cleaned up since my last visit. As I pushed through the doors and my eyes adjusted to the lighting I chuckled when I noticed that it was right where it had been: smack dab in the middle of the screen. Months went by and the stain elicited chuckles each and every time we walked into that auditorium, right until the sad day The Midtown shut its doors for good. Years later I returned to the theater, now given a major makeover and a new, highbrow name (The Prince Music Theater). Ostensibly the same place where I'd led a group of winos, junkies and hobos to demand our money back after a screening of **WITCHBOARD**, this just wasn't "my Midtown" any more. Sure, the pitched seating and neck-fracturing bathroom stairwell remained, but I was sad to see that when the lights came up there was no giant soda stain to remind me of those great days when an afternoon with Fulci was just a buck-fifty away.

TONY LEE:

Lucio Fulci's cult classic **THE HOUSE BY THE CEMETERY** was part of the new batch in a *Masters of Giallo* collection released by Arrow Video in the UK in 2012. This uncut and dubbed version has luminous photography and stunning audio quality, especially if compared to those VHS copies that I watched previously. A maniacal killer lurks in the basement of a mansion. When the Boyle family move in, Lucy (Catriona MacColl, star of Fulci's **CITY OF THE LIVING DEAD** and **THE BEYOND**) and Dr. Norman (Paolo Malco, Fulci's infamous **NEW YORK RIPPER** from 1982) struggle against some cheap-yet-proficient frights (bats ruffling hair, knife attacks, hanging corpses) that startle amidst the blander "haunted house" motifs—like noisy woodwork, mysteriously stuck doors, and screaming kids.

A lot of throat-slashing is depicted in lovely close-ups to inspire admiration from genre fans addicted to blood splatter fantasias. The hulking fiend, Dr Freudstein, is the silent perpetrator of excessive violence, and his presence here, against a background wave of shocking villainy that helped to launch the modern era of horror cinema, also heralded the fashion of slow-motion extreme gore effects which provided some of the "Video Nasty" ammunition to British censors, highly critical of such disreputable developments during the 1980s. Despite the controversies surrounding his work, Fulci remains a genuinely fascinating filmmaker, but I don't think that **THE HOUSE BY THE CEMETERY** is his finest picture.

The Italian schlock maestro's unique brand of crazily grotesque surrealism could be squished to unwatchability by the heavy burden of his trademark zooms, frequent overuse of wide-eyed close-ups, and intrusively ominous music that mars full appreciation of earlier offerings **ZOMBIE FLESH EATERS** (1979) and **CITY OF THE LIVING DEAD**. For me, **THE BEYOND** is the director's best movie. Its superior spaghetti splatter begins in 1927, with a sepia prologue showing how a French artist is accused of witchcraft, chain-whipped and crucified, doused in quicklime, then left to rot behind a wall in his own Louisiana bayou hotel.

Jumping forward to 1981, we see New Yorker Liza (MacColl) inheriting the rundown hotel. With restoration underway, a frightened house painter falls off scaffolding, and a plumber is attacked in flooded cellars, so poor Liza is really too busy to notice that most of the locals—including servants Arthur and Martha (yes, Fulci didn't care about the Anglo names!)—are all ghosts. "I've been looking for you," says blind pianist Emily, who's mysterious and creepy with it. Liza meets sympathetic Dr. McCabe (David Warbeck) but he "won't accept irrational explanations"—especially preposterous claims that the hotel building stands over a gateway to hell. Despite a few neat gothic frissons, subtlety is only a seething hindrance to outrageous events in this low-budget picture, where surreal atmosphere is abundant and oppressive but understated menace is roughly kicked aside by variable special effects work for splashy gore set-pieces. A woman in the mortuary has her whole face melted by acid. A scene with large spiders (only a couple of which are real tarantulas) eating a man alive is purest black comedy in its audacity. Corpse-occupied Room 36 is home to the first of some groaning, shambling zombies. A phone rings somewhat forlornly in the hotel's empty lobby, but who is calling? Perhaps this is symbolic of scientific rationality being totally ignored. Storm winds and bloody rains lash at McCabe and Liza while they are cowering indoors, and in the chaos that follows, the disfigured undead stampede—albeit at only a trundling pace—through the hospital's derelict corridors. Eventually, space/time itself is collapsing into a one-way maze of apocalyptic descent so that our pursued and beleaguered heroes somehow end up "inside" a grey painting of graveyard ashes that we saw right at the beginning of the movie.

The generally hysterical tone—and some laughably awful performances by a coterie of mediocre supporting players—really ought to be irksome. But, as if by Movie Magic, these potential faults all simply contribute yet more weirdness to the amateurish delirium of this scenario where a character's disbelief can banish evil forces, at least temporarily. We enter the realm where good taste, logic, common sense, and reason, do not exist, or have, at least, lost any influence over narrative structure or focused judgment. This is not slick horror filmmaking with a high standard of technical ability, but Fulci had a vividly macabre imagination like few other horror auteurs. **THE BEYOND** is superior to **THE HOUSE BY THE CEMETERY** because it conjures up a highly-stylized exploration of a proverbial "haunted house," and cursed reality as the antagonist, instead of a more clichéd force of evil centered on a named—and somewhat ridiculous looking—killer.

JOHN GRACE:

People get Lucio Fulci wrong. It is a tragedy that he is best known for his gore. His gore scenes are often laughable. The camera lingers far too long on what should be a quick shot. The eyes analyze an obvious mannequin, spurt tube, sheep intestines, darkly-colored syrup and other tools used to create the illusion. You see the faux eye of Olga Karlatos in **ZOMBIE** and your inner cynic shouts "Man, she ain't blinking!" I never came away from **ZOMBIE**, **THE BEYOND** or **GATES OF HELL** believing I'd seen some advanced technique In depicting cinematic evisceration.

Fulci's skill was atmosphere. And he was one of the best. When it comes to the grafting of music and visuals to convey a sense eeriness, distrust and fear, Lucio was hard to top. **THE HOUSE BY THE CEMETERY** is no exception. While a filmmaker like Argento will seem out of place using American locations, Fulci had no such problem. He depicts the forestry of small town New England and the tendentiously-loved urban blight of New York City with equal weight of Lovecraftian dread.

Speaking of H.P. Lovecraft, like the work of John Carpenter, I find movies like **THE HOUSE BY THE CEMETERY** evoke H.P.'s Weird Tales vibe more than anything Stuart Gordon directed. As enjoyable as Gordon's films are, Lovecraft isn't black humor, comedic gore or a naked Barbara Crampton; it's the dread and fear of the unknown. Fulci understood this and his horror films are more Charles Dexter Ward than **BLOOD FEAST** (1963).

Since I first saw the notorious Media VHS tape (or was it Lightning?) with the switched reels, **THE HOUSE BY THE CEMETERY** holds up every time I watch it. Giovanni Frezza's Bob may keep the cherubic smile on his face no matter what onscreen terror is depicted, but no character behaves logically and a lot of running time is spent watching characters look for each other ("Bob? Bob? Bob? Ann? Ann? Ann?"). Walter Rizzati's score is audio eeriness at its best, superior to 1000 tracks of Hans Zimmer bombast.

The usage of Boston locations brings back memories of lunch breaks near Downtown Crossing. There is a personal weight to an Italian horror film filmed where you walked to work every day. The location work in Concord conjures similar nostalgia for the Sunday afternoon trips away from the city. Yet it never feels foreign or manipulative with locations like Scorsese's **THE DEPARTED** (2006).

The revelation of Freudstein is the ultimate bogeyman in the basement moment in cinema. Never topped and no one even wants to try. The surrealistic ending with the imposturous Henry James quote just seals the deal. Sure, there are still questions that may never be answered. What was the backstory with babysitter Ann? Was she having an affair with Norman? Is that an erroneous deduction from Fulci's editing and zooms? Doesn't really matter overall, as the next viewing of this masterpiece will be enjoyed in another three years with enthusiasm and macabre relish.

JOHN SZPUNAR:

I first became aware of Lucio Fulci at some point in the early '80s. One of my earliest childhood memories is of paging through the Friday edition of *The Detroit News*—the entertainment section, to be exact (which was called "Lively Arts"), and pouring over the ad mats. I'd cut the things out if the movies looked good enough, and I was always on the hunt for anything with Martians or monsters. On one of those dream-filled Fridays, I opened the paper to have a look. I'll never forget the face that looked back at me.

A twisted, rotten skull with worms for eyes shot me an evil grin and the copy proclaimed, "We Are Going to Eat You!" A part of me wanted to see the film,

THE HOUSE BY THE CEMETERY - REVISITED (THE CHRISTIAN VERSION) — JOACHIM ANDERSSON

"The world's first Christian monster/horror film. How does a man of God face a monster? Get this DVD and find out, and you won't believe the surprise ending. This film is not intended for children.

"Watch as Dr. Froydstien comes with a demonic mission to steel peoples cells in an attempt to live forever!

"This film, originally directed by Lucio Fulci, is the old 80s Italian shocker made Christian, and re-edited by producer Jeff Teck."

So, some guy on the Internet has taken it upon himself to edit his own version of Lucio Fulcis gory classic **THE HOUSE BY THE CEMETERY** (1981), and has been selling it on Amazon. Just from looking at the guy's website, this promised to be something beyond belief. Who the hell would buy such a thing? Well, that would be me. I had to.

It starts with a new title screen: *Teckfilms.com and The MentalChurch.com Present a film by Jeff Teck. House by the Cemetary Revisited, The Christian Version.* Yes, the asshole actually states that he made the film. While watching this little cheap video animation we are treated to a MIDI-version of some Psalm or something, still hearing the pianos of the movie's original soundtrack until the film starts with the scene where Bob sees the little girl in the painting of the house. Yes, no sign of the scenes with Daniela Doria and her lover. Was it the boobies perhaps? Boobies are bad and make you go to Hell. Bob tells his mom that the girl told him not to come to the house, and when the camera zooms in on the painting we get an animated scene with flames "skillfully" edited into the picture along with a scary cheap synthesizer effect and a text that says:
"Someone may die, pray they don't go to Hell"
Oh yes, this is going to be awesome.

The movie then gets going, getting that obnoxious little kid and his parents to the Freudstein house, and I'm desperately waiting for more fun stuff. Sure enough, when they arrive at the real estate agency and Bob is talking to the little dead girl, that screen with the flames and the evil sound pops up again, this time with the following little tidbit: "Hell is not for children, they don't know their (*sic*) right from left hand" Along with editing, spelling is not Jeff Teck's greatest talent.

They arrive at the house, bicker a bit about Catriona MacColl's nerve pills and all of a sudden (through the magic of bad editing) it is night and the flames pop up again: "What's next, it's anybodies (*sic*) guess."

Yes, by now I am convinced that God is watching over all of us. Especially when the next scene comes, when Catriona is sleeping and Paolo Malco finds the empty Freudstein folder, with added voiceover from Jeff Teck: "Lord Jesus I come to you because you are good. There's just something about this house, something I don't get. The more I read about you the more I believe. Yet sometimes I feel our lives are in danger. I don't know. I wish I had the answers. The noises, the whining. Something about this house is just different. I hear the sounds that I have to go explore what the sounds are. Oh Lord, help me and my family escape the day of judgment when all will come down upon us. And I know whatever we face down in this house, we can handle it. That's what you are best at, Lord. Bringing things to a good end. I don't know what's through that door, I don't know what's under this house but it could be an evil for this is a sinful planet. Then who could explain it? Lord I just want to thank you in the name of Jesus that you are in control and I just want to thank you for all you do. No matter how spooky this place gets I know I got you! Thank you Lord. Amen."

The original scene is a pretty atmospheric one, showing that old Fulci had some pretty decent movie-making skills, greatly helped by Sergio Salvati's excellent photography. This version? Uhm, yeah. When the monologue is finished, Malco hears something behind the cellar door and goes to investigate. Too scary for Jeff Teck, who scissors the proceedings like he is blind, and all of a sudden we cut into a scene the next day, in the middle of a sentence. Later on, when Malco is reading his predecessors diary, Teck edits in a short scene where a frantic McColl tries to open the cellar door, and goes back to the diary scene like nothing happened. Why? Only Jeff Teck knows. All of a sudden we come to that classic scene where McColl finds the babysitter wiping the blood off the floor. You know—the "I made coffee" scene. This means that Teck also cut out the scene where the real estate agent meets her maker. This goes for the babysitter scene, as well. Surprised? And then we come to the climax that goes all Takashi Miike on us. The movie turns black and white (you know, the tenth-generation VHS dub black and white) when Paolo Malco attacks Dr Freudstein, an overdubbed voice says "Lord Jesus help me", the screen is bathed in fog and lightning comes down from above. Then the Earth explodes. The End, the end titles tell us as Catriona MacColl, Paolo Malco and Giovanni Frezza stare.

Okay, this is by far the poorest excuse for a "movie" I have ever seen. The editing is pitiful and seems to be done at random. The last half of the movie is full of skips, graphical errors and loud bursts of static, with the occasional repeating of a scene. Unfortunately, the Christian propaganda is kept to the first half, so I guess he got tired of it and just went haywire. It has to be seen to be believed.

THE HOUSE BY THE CEMETERY is a fine little gore flick, but the script is not exactly logical and rather fragmented; when a Christian hack starts messing about with it, cutting out all the gore, deleting random scenes (the whole thing is just 53 minutes; go figure) and adding animations that a five-year-old could have done better it turns into something totally incomprehensible. This is just fucked up. I wish there was a commentary track by Jeff Teck, but I would probably be too afraid to listen to it.

Thank you, Lord, for this little movie and the pleasure it has given me. All the spelling mistakes are taken straight from the movie. Amen.

[Editor's Note – How is it this guy hasn't had his ass kicked yet? MADNESS!]

1981/2008(?), ITALY/USA. DIRECTOR: LUCIO FULCI
RE-EDITED & BASTARDIZED BY JEFF TECK

This review originally appeared in Weng's Chop Special Issue Zero.

but another part (the wide-eyed 7-year-old in me) reasoned that it was probably nasty business. I put my scissors down and turned the page.

A few years later (again, while looking through the paper), I happened upon another ad. This one was for something called **THE GATES OF HELL**. I cut that one out, and asked my parents if they'd take me to see it. It must have been something like when John Waters asked his mother to take him to the junkyard. My mother's face was a cross between, "Why me?" and "Where did I ever go wrong?" My dad frowned and told me that the movie was too "violent". Violent? I'd read that word before in Mad, but I only had a vague idea of what it meant. I made it a point to look it up in the dictionary.

I didn't know it at the time, but most of the ad mats that caught my attention were from films made in Italy. There was **BURIAL GROUND** (1981, which I first mistook for a re-release the elusive **THE GATES OF HELL**), **DR. BUTCHER M.D.** (a.k.a. **ZOMBIE HOLOCAUST**, 1980), and something called **THE HOUSE BY THE CEMETERY**.

By the time my family finally got a VCR, all bets were off. I'd already been watching splatter movies at my friends' houses, but they always went for the standard fare. I had to endure countless viewings of **FRIDAY THE 13TH** (1980) before I was able to walk to the corner video store in my neighborhood. It was a place called Video Den, and the guy who owned it seemed cool. I tested the waters a few times with **FRIDAY THE 13TH, PART 2** (1981). Then, one day, I went to the shelf, picked up **ZOMBIE**, and made my way to the counter. All the while, I was thinking, "Will this guy actually let me rent it?" Turns out that Video Den would let kids rent *anything*…

As I got older and started reading fanzines, I realized that I was not alone in my love for **ZOMBIE**. Everyone seemed to be writing about the movie and about its director. So began my love affair with Lucio Fulci. I rented and loved **THE GATES OF HELL** and tracked down an uncut copy of **THE BEYOND**. When it came time to rent **THE HOUSE BY THE CEMETERY**, I had a pretty good idea of what to expect.

Or did I? It was immediately apparent that **THE HOUSE BY THE CEMETERY** was going to be different. The usual display of gore, blood, and guts erupted from the screen at a moment's notice, but this time, things were a bit more ominous. **ZOMBIE** had been an unbridled exercise in splatter, and **THE GATES OF HELL** wasn't too far behind. **THE BEYOND** took the surrealistic undertones of **THE GATES OF HELL** a few (ah, hell…a few million) steps further, but the doom, dread, and general uneasiness of **THE HOUSE BY THE CEMETERY** really got under my skin.

It's time for a confession. While I had enjoyed what I had seen of Fulci's cannon, I never really considered **ZOMBIE**, **THE GATES OF HELL**, or **THE BEYOND** the classics that they could have been. **ZOMBIE** was way too uneven; it started out as an all-out assault, but then the talking heads took over. And yeah, the worm-eye zombie was creepy as fuck, but the poor guy never really lived up to the expectations that scared the shit out of me as a kid. **THE GATES OF HELL** quickened the pace, but quickly lost sight of

itself in its attempt at all-out weirdness. And **THE BEYOND** just went too far. I love the fact that Fulci had the audacity to do what he did, but let's face it—the film is a complete mess. To this day, it remains my least favorite of Fulci's splattery salad days. **THE HOUSE BY THE CEMETERY**, however, is another story. That one was just right.

The film throttles out of the gate with a supercharged burst of mayhem, but the gears soon shift down with a smooth double clutch. Walter Razzati's beautiful score kicks in, the credits crawl, and the film effortlessly drifts in

and out of reality. Fulci had tried this trick many times before, but this time it actually worked. So what if every inch of plot and logic goes straight to hell before you can say "Freudstein"? The film is perfectly paced, and the madness and gore sing together in perfect harmony. A lucid dream *cum* cinema. Nothing makes sense, but it somehow does.

Fulci's most interesting work has always been about atmosphere, but he always seemed to lose his way in the madness of his own creations. With **THE HOUSE BY THE CEMETERY**, his dreams finally found their footing, and the result is the most satisfying film of his career.

POSTSCRIPT: I should probably point out that my childhood home was directly across the street from a cemetery. It was an old one with ancient trees and ancient graves. Every once in a while, I'd walk through it during the daytime, usually on my way to the park. I found it peaceful there, and I'd often try to find the oldest date that was etched on the tombstones.

Nighttime was another story. I'd read something in a book about "soul lights", and I spent many a sleepless night scanning the place from my bedroom window on the lookout for trouble. At times, I'd have terrible nightmares about a little girl that was buried there. Her name was Rebecca. I can't remember if I actually saw that name on a grave, or if it was one of my imagination's creation. Regardless, I was terrified that she would visit me as I slept. At times, she did.

I was also afraid of my basement. My grandfather once told me that something called The Rat Lady lived down there. Some sort of a twisted hag with a moldy robe and moldy skin. It was years before I would go downstairs without the company of my brother. Make of that what you will…

©2006, 2013 Stephen R. Bissette, all rights reserved, published with permission.

ITALY, 1981. DIRECTOR: LUCIO FULCI
AVAILABLE FROM BLUE UNDERGROUND AND ARROW VIDEO

BOX SET BEATDOWN
...ADVENTURES IN BIN DIVING!

by Brian Harris

We've all struggled with the same question when it comes to box sets: "Is this worth the money?" Well, I started the Box Set Beatdown *blog (defunct) and now this review section with the intention of answering that very question as only a broke (and lifelong) cult cinema fan can! Let* Box Set Beatdown *be your guide to the good, bad and ugly of the budget box world. Whether you're looking for genre film gold or you just love trash,* Box Set Beatdown *promises to be an adventure in bin diving.*

Each and every issue I will select films from the box sets below and offer up fun and insightful reviews. Once I've exhausted all of the films in each box set, I'll select new sets to tackle. This issue I've selected films from the GRINDHOUSE EXPERIENCE VOL.1 & 2, GRINDHOUSE EXPERIENCE – EYE ON HORROR, GRINDHOUSE EXPERIENCE – MERCS, RED NINJA COLLECTION, SCI-FI INVASION *and* SCREAM THEATER. *Welcome!*

GRINDHOUSE EXPERIENCE VOL.1
WOMEN'S CAMP 119
(*KZ9 - LAGER DI STERMINIO*, 1977)

You know, most generally don't think "entertainment" when sitting down to watch Nazisploitation, and yet that's exactly what exploitation fans—like me—often find. No, it's not socially acceptable, but many things that shouldn't be socially acceptable are, like Sarah Jessica Parker's nose, Justin Long's celebrity status and thongs for children. Don't get me wrong—I know why people find Nazisploitation reprehensible—but this is exploitation, by gum, and if it weren't twisted, perverse and offensive…well…it would be something my wife would watch, and that's not acceptable to me! I won't try to justify my passion for it, you'll either think me scum or you won't.

If you can find no other reason to cough up the money to purchase this *GRINDHOUSE EXPERIENCE VOLUME 1* set, how about this: it includes the rare Mattei-helmed Nazisploitation stunner, **WOMEN'S CAMP 119**! That's right, not only are you getting the sheer scuzzy pleasure of naughty Nazi mayhem but it's also directed by *legendary* sleaze-peddler Bruno Mattei, best known for directing pretty much everything that gives you a boner! If one more bit of goodness can be heaped on this production, it is this: it's rare—ultra-rare for us Statesiders, as there's been no official release of this film. Unless you count this box set and the Desert Island bootleg currently selling thru Amazon, which most don't.

Horror of horrors! When a fresh batch of concentration camp inmates are brought in to the medical experimentation camp Rosenhausen, a female prisoner with a degree in medicine is forced to aid the evil camp Commander (Ivano Staccioli) in his atrocities. Many of the supposed experiments are nothing more than butchery and the doctor soon finds herself considering suicide, if there's no other escape from the madness.

When the opportunity does present itself, to escape the camp, the doctor and three fellow prisoners make a break for it but the Commander isn't about to let anybody escape his grasp. If he is forced to retreat from the camp by the Allies, he'll make sure not one single person survives Rosenhausen—not even his own people!

Bleak, depressing and offensive, Mattei's **WOMEN'S CAMP 119**, unlike so many other Nazisploitation offerings (wink-wink), really isn't a very feel-good production. There's no happy ending, no light at the end of the tunnel. As if rape, medical atrocity, brutal beatings and necrophilia aren't enough, Mattei adds a few layers of filth by making prisoners complicit in the horrors of war, and no hero or heroine is safe from the Third Reich's pursuit of racial purity. Seriously, this was a dark, dark film, and one of the better entries into this exploitation sub-genre. Now there's not a ton of originality to the production—we've seen the same scenario before—but Mattei is still able to trump the rest by upping the ante in two shocking finales that are guaranteed to disturb even seasoned aficionados.

This particular "official" release was sourced from a Dutch VHS (hardcoded Dutch subs) and to say it looked like shit would be an understatement; you can't make out any significant details and there are mad tracking problems. So not only is it rare, it's also a tad bit hard to watch. That shouldn't stop the dedicated, though. I could easily see myself paying $10 or more for this film alone, so, believe it or not, it is this film that makes this box set worth every single penny. The rest of the films can just be considered a win. Grab it.

1997, ITALY. DIRECTOR: BRUNO MATTEI
AVAILABLE FROM FIRST LOOK PICTURES/FORTUNE 5 DVD (VIDEOASIA)

box set in a cut 89-minute incarnation. I haven't seen the 94-minute cut, and, unless you have, you probably won't be missing much either. The transfer is rough, like 1st- or 2nd-generation VHS quality rough, but perfectly watchable, and the sound is surprisingly clear. VideoAsia have definitely done cult cinema fans a favor by throwing this film into the collection as it seems to be a relatively rare title to find.

1975, ITALY. DIRECTORS: ANTONIO CLIMATI & MARIO MORRA
AVAILABLE FROM FIRST LOOK PICTURES/FORTUNE 5 DVD
(VIDEOASIA)

GRINDHOUSE EXPERIENCE VOL.1
RAW FORCE (1982)

All aboard for Warrior Island! A karate class looking to get in touch with their martial arts roots decide to vacation on a little rundown ship bound for a remote island rumored to be the final resting place of disgraced martial arts masters. According to local superstitions, and their tourist brochure, the island is also home to a group of isolated monks who supposedly possess the ability to raise the dishonorable dead! Where in the hell did they get that brochure?!!

As if bloodthirsty black magic monks, Karate cadavers and evil Kung Fu corpses weren't enough, a Nazi criminal who runs a kidnapping ring and his hired gang of thugs are looking to kill anybody that attempts to go to the island in order to hide the whereabouts of the missing girls and protect a secret jade mine run by the malicious monks.

Drop anchor and line up single-file, please, as **RAW FORCE** kicks ass, takes names, politely hands you back your ass and asks you to come again!

RAW FORCE may sound trashy—and truly it is—but it was so goddamn entertaining, so over-the-top, so absolutely gonzo that you won't be able to resist purchasing this for your own collection! I mean, how in the hell can a film go wrong when it delivers the lowest common denominator over and over again with such gusto? It had a sequence ripped straight from Dante's **PIRANHA** (1978), nefarious Nazis, malefic monks, cannibalism, kidnapping, sexy strippers, nude tramps, butt-slapping bondage, a Bruce Lee look-alike, genuine comedy and assloads of face-mashing martial arts mayhem!

When director Murphy isn't dazzling us with poorly-choreographed fight sequences, he's throwing nudity at us. When we aren't being treated to stiffy-inducing T&A, we get cackling Templar-esque monks and rampaging ninja, samurai and Shaolin zombies! If it's not one thing, it's another and another and another…

I kid you not, the entertainment value of this fantastic gem of golden garbage *alone* made up for the cost of the entire box set. I know many of the cult cinema elitists out there hate VideoAsia, but the large majority of the films being sold in their box sets won't ever see the light of day, and if (and when) they do, chances are they'll simply be released on another bootleg by another "shady" company. I applaud them, bootleg or not. The transfer for this film was on par with a 2nd generation VHS copy (maybe 3rd), which is what I expected, and it didn't faze me one bit, I love my trash to look like trash. It takes nothing away from a nice pair of tits or a perfectly executed roundhouse kick.

Whether **RAW FORCE** was good or not is really up to the beholder, and whether they're capable of being honest, it wasn't a particularly competent production in the technical sense but I still had fun watching it. Save your "so bad it's good" apologetic bullshit for the MST3K forums, in my house if I enjoy a film…it's good. I can see myself watching this quite a few more times, hopefully you'll feel the same way.

1982, USA & PHILIPPINES. DIRECTOR: EDWARD D. MURPHY
AVAILABLE FROM FIRST LOOK PICTURES/FORTUNE 5 DVD
(VIDEOASIA)

GRINDHOUSE EXPERIENCE VOL.1
SAVAGE MAN SAVAGE BEAST
(*ULTIME GRIDA DALLA SAVANNA*, 1975)

Those of you unfamiliar with Mondo may want to take note that it is most certainly not going to be everybody's cup o' tea as it is typically filled with bizarre rituals, nudity, sex and graphic, bloody violence from around the world. Often overflowing with gruesome sequences depicting mutilated animals and the human casualties of war, execution and accidents, watching a Mondo film is like settling in for a night of National Geographic edited by sadistic perverts. It cannot be stressed enough that while many Mondo films feature facts of zoological and anthropological interest, they're still exploitation films and should never be mistaken for anything remotely educational. You'd think most would know that but some folks might be tempted to see this thinking they'll learn something of worth. Trust me, you'll not learn anything from an anaconda choking the life from a writhing monkey.

The first of a documentary trilogy by filmmaking duo Antonio Climati (**THE GREEN INFERNO**) and Mario Morra, **SAVAGE MAN SAVAGE BEAST** delivers up the usual grotty hippy nudity, hokey reenactments and nature-on-nature violence as well as a few jaw-dropping rituals including African tribesmen digging holes in the ground for a copulation ceremony with Mother Earth and masturbating into leather sheathes topped with animal skulls. If it all sounds rather icky and disturbing, wait until you actually see some of it with your own eyes. I wouldn't say this is one of the more outrageous Mondo films out there—it's actually quite tame—but it does pack a punch without resorting to the mean-spirited exploitation of its successors. Currently unavailable as an official release (there's supposedly an uncut 94-minute Thai DVD floating around out there), you can still check this Italian exploitation film out on the *GRINDHOUSE EXPERIENCE* 20-film

GRINDHOUSE EXPERIENCE VOL.2
THE SHARK HUNTER
(IL CACCIATORE DI SQUALI, 1979)

DJANGO MEETS JAWS! Well, not quite. Enzo G. Castellari's **THE SHARK HUNTER** was obviously meant to cash in on some of the toothy goodness of Spielberg's **JAWS** (1975), made four years prior, but actually ends up sharing very little in common with the man-eating classic. Instead of a bloody beach and three men on a boat, this film stars *DJANGO* leading man Franco Nero as Mike Di Donato, a burned-out beach bum who hunts dangerous sharks for a living. Content to remain low-key with his native girlfriend, Mike is up to more than just fishing in his little neck of the woods, and as soon as he's able to connect with a trustworthy diver, we discover just what that is. See, there's $100 million sitting in the wreckage of a plane, buried beneath the waves, and only he knows where it is and how to get it!

The only problem with treasure is...everybody wants it. In this case, "everybody" would be a shifty police chief, his murderous henchmen and some mysterious criminal-types from Mike's shady past, sent by "The Organization" to retrieve the loot. Is Mike really willing to brave the shark-infested waters just for money he may or not be able to keep? You'd better believe your ass he is!

THE SHARK HUNTER was a nice double-feature with the German production **DEADLY JAWS** (1974), though Castellari's film was just a bit better, due only to the presence of the mighty Django...outside of that, it was a pretty tame affair. I wanted it to be a bit more about killer sharks, but the silent-but-deadly "mobster in self-exile" angle was cool, too. Throw in a score by Guido & Maurizio De Angelis and you've got yourself time well-wasted but nothing at all worth "hunting" down. I was glad to get it on this *GRINDHOUSE EXPERIENCE VOL.2* box set because there's no way in hell I'd seek this out for my personal collection as a single-disc release. I love me a Castellari/Nero sammich, but this had a made-for-TV vibe that left a funky flavor in the back of my throat...it tastes like...hmmm...it tastes like a *just okay* one-time viewing.

Concerning the quality of the transfer, well, check out the screenshots for yourself and keep in mind that this is a rather rare film. If you really want it, the transfer won't bother you a bit (didn't bother me), and the box set will be well worth the cash. Happy fishing!

1979, MEXICO, SPAIN & ITALY. DIRECTOR: ENZO G. CASTELLARI
AVAILABLE FROM FIRST LOOK PICTURES/FORTUNE 5 DVD
(VIDEOASIA)

GRINDHOUSE EXPERIENCE VOL.2
DEADLY JAWS
(EIN TOTER TAUCHER NIMMT KEIN GOLD, 1974)

A trio of treasure seekers is onto a huge score, but to get to the sunken Spanish treasure they'll need the help of a shady diver and a mysterious woman. Loyalties will be tested, pirates will come a-snoopin', nature gets scary and the group will be forced to defend themselves and their huge haul of priceless treasure before their expedition is over.

I'd like to be able to offer you a bit more about **DEADLY JAWS** (a.k.a. **DEAD DIVERS TAKE NO GOLD**), but the truth is there just isn't any. Despite the misleading re-title, this isn't the **JAWS** rip-off some of you will be hoping for. Actually it's a mildly interesting thriller, set on the high seas, pitting treasure seekers against their nefarious captain and both the former and latter against even more nefarious pirates looking to jump claim. And... that's about it! Forget the "Man vs. Nature" angle, as there were a merely few silly underwater encounters with an octopus, some sharks and a deadly little fish. Nothing that'll have the "Nature Run Amok" aficionados doing backflips of joy.

Here's what you *can* expect from **DEADLY JAWS**: tension. Believe it or not, this film actually generates a healthy amount of tension as, with each passing moment, you creep further and further to the edge of your seat, eagerly anticipating the axe to drop on the treasure seekers. Actor Marius Weyers does an excellent job of being a conniving murderer and the women were certainly pleasing on the eyes, but this almost comes across as a made-for-TV film as there's no graphic violence, nudity, sex or even cursing. Big on tension, lacking in the untamed beaver bush department. Ah well.

There aren't any official releases of this film floating about out there and the quality of this transfer was about as good as one can expect from an Asian VHS rip, but it's still better than nothing. Or is it? In any case, I liked it though I have no intention of seeing it again. I love the *GRINDHOUSE EXPERIENCE VOL.2* box set and while I probably wouldn't go out of my way to purchase this particular film as a single release, it fits nicely in the box alongside Castellari's **THE SHARK HUNTER**.

1974, WEST GERMANY. DIRECTOR: HARALD REINL
AVAILABLE FROM FIRST LOOK PICTURES/VIDEOASIA

GRINDHOUSE EXPERIENCE: EYE ON HORROR
JUNGLE VIRGIN FORCE
(PERAWAN RIMBA, 1988)

A young girl named Jelita (Lydia Kandou), lost in the jungle on an uncharted island for years as a child, is chosen by a tribe to be their queen but a wicked shaman and his forces oppose the abomination of making an outsider their leader, thus kicking off a violent confrontation between the men and women of the tribe. Meanwhile, a small band of university students heads to the island for some research, but they're not alone—they've been followed by a group of thieving murderers seeking a legendary treasure trove supposedly hidden on the island, protected by the natives.

Now all parties collide in an epic battle for survival, supremacy, untold riches and the meaning of life and love.

Natives. Fight. Students. Fight. Natives. Fight again. Fight, fight, fight. There's absolutely nothing here of value. We're not at all sure what these students are interested in researching—outside of finding treasure—and we have no real idea what the history behind the rift between the tribes is all about. It all just...*IS*. No nudity, no major violence, no characters worth liking outside of Kandou's Jelita. If the countless battles don't wear you down, the never-ending "Oo-oo ah-ee!" primate calls from the tribesmen will make you want to turn **JUNGLE VIRGIN FORCE** off and call it a day.

I watched it. It had a few fun, trashy sequences here and there but I won't watch this again. Chances are you won't either. Another dud, but still better than watching shot-on-digital indie horror.

1988, INDONESIA. DIRECTOR: DANU UMBARA
AVAILABLE FROM FIRST LOOK PICTURES/VIDEOASIA

GRINDHOUSE EXPERIENCE: EYE ON HORROR
HELL HOLE (1983)

Man, it seems like I watched this just a bit ago and I've already forgotten what the fuck it was about! Is that because it had no nudity? Could be. Maybe it was because there was no rape? Quite possibly. Did it have anything to do with the fact that it had no damn plot? Maybe all of the above.

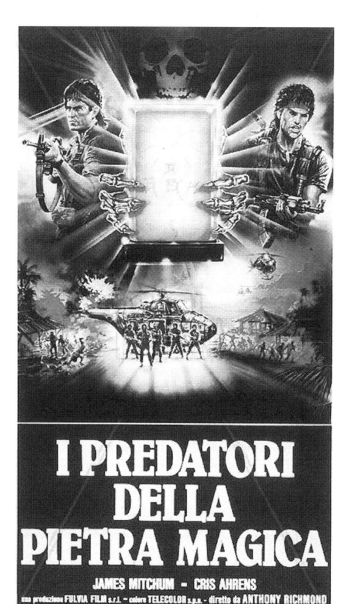

A young country girl (Guphy Sintara) is lured to the Big City Life by her worldly cousin (Eva Widowaty), but it's nothing more than a ruse to bring her to a nefarious pimp named MG (Dicky Zulkarnaen), a vile rapscallion with nothing more on his mind than tasting the fleshly pleasures of all the virgins that come through his doors. Once they've been used up, he discards them to a prison housing unit behind bars where groups of girls pretty much do nothing at all. They're supposed to be sex slaves but...there ain't much o' that. Some get beaten, others whipped; mainly they're hung up by their wrists.

Instead of caving in to MG's demands, the young country girl finds strength in her upbringing and refuses to allow MG to take her virginity or break her spirit. The stronger she remains, the more encouraged the other prisoners become and soon a revolt is a-brewin' and MG's time is limited. Now the prisoners want payback and the police are closing in...what the hell is a pimp to do?!!

Maman Firmansyah's **ESCAPE FROM HELLHOLE** (listed on the box as **HELL HOLE**) is quite possibly the lamest W.I.P. film I've seen in years. It's all so tedious, one girl after another is brutalized but never really raped, they're stripped but never naked, there's slight hints of lesbianism but, alas, none to be found. This is an Indonesian production and I'm not at all familiar with their obscenity guidelines when it comes to cinema, but my thoughts are that they were probably a bit strict. It even bordered on feeling...religious. Shades of Islam, perhaps?

Picture quality was passable. Dubbing was decent. What little action there was ended up being mildly entertaining. Not worth purchasing this box set for, but there's still nine other flicks to choose from, so don't give up hope just yet!

1983, INDONESIA & PHILIPPINES. DIRECTOR: MAMAN FIRMANSYAH
AVAILABLE FROM FIRST LOOK PICTURES/VIDEOASIA

GRINDHOUSE EXPERIENCE: MERCS FIREBACK (1983)

My cheesy trek through box set dreck continues with a *GRINDHOUSE EXPERIENCE: MERCS* box set film, **FIREBACK**. If you've never heard of or seen **FIREBACK**, you're missing out on what may be the most mindlessly-entertaining 90 minutes you'll ever experience while watching a Z-movie from the Philippines. No deep thinking required. Nearly all of the action in **FIREBACK** is comprised of failed attempt after failed attempt on the life of Richard Harrison's character, Jack Kaplan. Let me break down the synopsis for you:

We're first introduced to military officer Jack Kaplan (Richard Harrison) during a covert weapons demonstration in the jungles of Vietnam. During the demo, a detachment of Khmer Rouge soldiers ambush the camp, catching the Americans with their pants down, landing Kaplan in a Communist P.O.W. camp to rot.

Back in the States, Jack's wife Diane (Ann Milhench), still distraught over her husband's MIA status, is forced to defend herself against the sexual advances of big-time crime boss Duffy Collins (Bruce Baron), who's taken a shine to the beautiful young woman. Used to getting what he wants, Collins hires some thugs to snatch Diane from her home. Talk about your bad timing though, because around the same time she's being kidnapped, Kaplan is being rescued by a Special Forces unit!

Now that Jack Kaplan is home, he has only one thing on his mind, and that's his wife. When Diane is nowhere to be found, he hits the streets with a vengeance, looking to shake some trees and crack a few coconuts to discover her location. He'll stop at nothing to find her.

Word is, Harrison wrote **FIREBACK** in a few hours and I wouldn't be in the slightest bit surprised if that turned out to be the truth. I kid you not—this film was a kung fu cinema rip-off if there ever was one! Hell, there's even a character with a golden hand that's referred to as Man With The Golden Hand online but in the actual film he's dubbed...hold for it now...DENNIS (Ruel Vernal). Menacing, no? What's not to love about a film that pits Harrison against a man with a golden hand, a sword-cane-wielding assassin, a ninja named Shadow, a bomber, a stripper and a dude with an eye patch! Seriously, **FIREBACK** is one gonzo piece of work by Pinoy filmmaker Teddy Chiu and its all the more entertaining as Harrison, looking like a drug cartel enforcer, clomps around town, defeating what seems like a never-ending supply of assassins!

If films were scratch 'n' sniff, **FIREBACK** would smell like wet dog, Hai Karate, yeast, Sen Sen and cut-rate Pinoy cigarettes. It's that sleazy of a production. Don't let my description lead you to believe this will be filled with exploitative nudity and explicit violence, because that's simply not true. It is, however, filled with almost-nudity and loads of sorta-convincing violence. As for exploitative, well the minute you see Kaplan head for the jungle, make a little guerrilla warfare on local police and hole up in a cave to treat a wound in an unconventional manner, you'll know right away that Harrison was thinking kung fu and **FIRST BLOOD** (1982) when he wrote this up.

The acting was bad, but I've come across far worse in productions with bigger budgets so I really wasn't too put off. The film's score reminded of something one might hear in an old Universal serial; really thrilling and bombastic. In other words, it didn't quite match the film's actual action sequences. Though it's credited to Patrick Wales, apparently a Chiu regular, I wouldn't be surprised at all to find it was Chiu himself and he lifted it from some black and white film. Hey, it's a Z-movie, right? You get what you get!

FIREBACK is no action classic but it was effective nonetheless! The quality of the transfer is rough—very rough—but it's watchable and enjoyable so this is definitely a winner in VideoAsia's *GRINDHOUSE EXPERIENCE: MERCS* box set. I'll no doubt be revisiting this film at some point in the future. If you enjoy Richard Harrison's low budget work from overseas, you'll dig this film.

1983, PHILIPPINES. DIRECTOR: TEDDY PAGE
AVAILABLE FROM FIRST LOOK PICTURES/VIDEOASIA

GRINDHOUSE EXPERIENCE: MERCS -RAIDERS OF THE MAGIC IVORY
(*I PREDATORI DELLA PIETRA MAGICA*, 1988)

The next entry into the *GRINDHOUSE EXPERIENCE: MERCS* box set is a little slice of Tonino Ricci "Hutsploitation" cheese (thanks David Z.!) entitled **PREDATORS OF THE MAGIC STONE**, or **RAIDERS OF THE MAGIC IVORY**, and what a completely uneventful slice it is! Mmmm... uneventful cheeeeeeese...

Mercs Sugar (James Mitchum) and Mark (Christopher Ahrens) are hired to enter a dangerous jungle in an unnamed Asian country—an area named "The Hell From Which No One Returns"—and retrieve an ancient stone relic being held by a hostile religious sect. The two accept the job, but something about the gig just isn't sitting right, and their client may be withholding information vital to the mission and their survival. Money talks, though, and instead of walking away with their lives, they head straight into the heart of hell itself in order to secure the stone and the small fortune that goes with it.

I'd love to be able to tell you all that **RAIDERS OF THE MAGIC IVORY** was packed with action, but that just wouldn't be true. The only real action to behold in this film is seemingly endless sequences of walking—thankfully in beautiful locations—but walking nonetheless. When our heroes-for-hire aren't walking, they're jabbering, and when they aren't doing that, they just might be fighting off one of the many unsuccessful ambushes they happen upon. This was an incredibly tame Italian-made *Indiana Jones* cash-in that offers none of the perks one would normally expect to see (namely nudity or gore) from such a cheap concept. It's not at all hard to understand why this particular writing accomplishment from famed Italian genre film screenwriter Dardano Sacchetti is so rarely praised by cult cinema fans. That's not to say it was entirely devoid of entertainment value, but it's not something I'd recommend going out of your way to see.

For me, the one and only thing (outside of the aforementioned locations) that was truly enjoyable about this production was the presence of James Mitchum, son of legendary Hollywood actor Robert Mitchum, as Sugar. He has this soft-spoken he-man way about him that made his character likable and worth rooting for and it definitely worked well when played off against the mouthier character of Mark. I'm not sure he was the right choice for leading man, but that's neither here nor there considering the film didn't really deliver much excitement anyhow.

RAIDERS OF THE MAGIC IVORY wasn't a terrible film by any means. However the decision to throw Halloween masks on the religious sect was terrible and it really cheapened things. I suppose this was one of those, "We only have twelve extras and we already used them twice. How can we use them again?" moments and, in my opinion, it just didn't work. It was reminiscent of Franco's day-glo paint and comb-over natives in **CANNIBALS** (a.k.a. **WHITE CANNIBAL QUEEN**, 1980). Some may also find the casting of Franklin Dominguez as a Chinese man to be in poor taste as well; to them I say, "QUE PASA? AT REAST HE SPEAK ENGRISH, VATO!" Now *that shit* I said right there was offensive!

Bottom line: the film was watchable though very dark and it was subbed in Japanese so people that cannot watch anything less than the very best will want to avoid. Though I highly doubt there'll be a replay from me, I wasn't too put off as the final credits scrolled. Especially when two super-fine asses

appeared (see picture)! Was it worth the price of the box set? Not at all, but there's still nine other films to go through so there's always a chance, right? Enjoy!

1988, ITALY. DIRECTOR: TONINO RICCI
AVAILABLE FROM FIRST LOOK PICTURES/VIDEOASIA

RED NINJA COLLECTION
Ninjascope: The Magic World of Ninjas (*Kamen no ninja Aka-Kage*, 1967)

...But...but...it's not official! Knock the sand from your vagina, Sally! We all know VideoAsia is a bootleg company with legit distro so I'm not going to condemn or justify anything they've released except to say that without VideoAsia, many collectors and cult cinema fans would be left in the cold. We've all purchased boots before so let's drop the elitism and talk...NINJA! No, not Ninja Dixon...RED NINJA! Aka-Kage, The Red Shadow, that is!

Enter Japan's first live-action (color) Ninja television series, *Kamen no ninja Aka-Kage*, produced by Toei from 1967 to 1968. The show starred a dashing Yûzaburô Sakaguchi as Red Shadow, Fuyukichi Maki as the rough-around-the-edges White Shadow, and Yoshinobu Kaneko as the group's teen sidekick and comedic relief, Blue Shadow. Together, Red, White and Blue (huh?) fight the good fight to save Japan from a heinous religious sect that's forcing farmers and villagers to serve the Golden Eye God. Sent by Lord Oda himself to find out what happened to two royal spies, the three ninja run afoul of the leader of the Golden Eye God sect and his crew of bizarre, magically endowed henchmen. While the toadies with magic may not be any match for the ninjas three, a massive toad created by magic may be the very thing to defeat Red Shadow and his fellow heroes for once and for all!

Did I watch all 52 freakin' episodes of this wild, campfest? No, seems a portion of the early part of the series was edited into *Ninjascope: The Magic World of Ninjas*, while some of the later stuff was edited into the *WATARI* films, focusing more on the child-friendly Blue Shadow. *Ninjascope* is hard to follow, a tad bit confusing and tedious—in other words, this wasn't edited with pace or narrative in mind. What you get is a constant barrage of heroes-versus-villains segments, outlandish characters introduced with little to no warning and a finale that takes the word "cliffhanger" to new heights.

Do Daikaiju & Tokusatsu put a smile on your face? If so, this is a sweet little purchase, selling for about $5 for a 3-film set. If you're familiar with the *Red Shadow* anime, and/or the big budget **RED SHADOW** film from 2001, you're going to want to grab a copy of this and find out how it all started. This is some weird, wacky ascot-wearin' action that harkens back to the swashbuckling serials of America's cinema of yesteryear.

1967, JAPAN. DIRECTOR: MITSUTERU YOKOYAMA
AVAILABLE FROM FIRST LOOK PICTURES/VIDEOASIA

SCI-FI INVASION
ROBO VAMPIRE (1988)

Normally I'd start shit out with a synopsis, but you simply could not make one up that would even come close to doing the actual film justice. It defies a synopsis.

What can I say about **ROBO VAMPIRE** that hasn't been said already? It's bad, epically bad. Absolutely bonkers and completely nonsensical. Yeah, those are pretty accurate. It's a cut-n-paste Frankenstein of a film, that's for sure, but as a whole it has this magical charm, the kind of mojo only the most seasoned trash fan can grow to love. We may never know who the enigmatic director "Joe Livingstone" is/was (wink-wink) but we do know that **ROBO VAMPIRE** is…is…wait, what was I talking about again? Seriously, finding **ROBO VAMPIRE** in a box set isn't the score of the century, but it's shitty gems like this that make those box sets so much fun to purchase and wade into.

If you've never seen this film, do yourself a favor and catch up on your sleep first, then prepare yourself for a **ROBOCOP** rip-off involving trained Chinese vampires, a heartbroken ghost with exposed nipples, a little bit o' Thai action cinema, a lot o' Hong Kong insanity, and a genuine robot warrior in a poorly-stitched silver lamé outfit! He looked like a Central Park mime. If that sounds like good, clean fun to you…you're a fucking clown-show. I suppose I'm one of you, though, because I can't get enough of this film. If I can successfully stay awake through the entire runtime on a lazy day, I consider that to be a true accomplishment.

I won't bore you with blather on aspect ratio or any of that other shit because the simple fact that this film exists is a goddamn miracle of cinema! Asking for fancy widescreen and all that other tech-wiener mumbo-jumbo is just being anal. You can't get it your way, hipster douchebags, this isn't Burger King…it's Mill Creek! Personally, I think the inclusion of this golden turd only makes this box set worth checking out all the more. Yeah, there are much, much better films contained on it, but how many films can you say you've seen that contain a gorilla-masked vampire battling a lumbering silver train-wreck of a robot in the middle of a busy HK street?

NONE! Be gone!

1988, USA & HONG KONG. DIRECTOR: JOE LIVINGSTONE
AVAILABLE FROM MILL CREEK ENTERTAINMENT

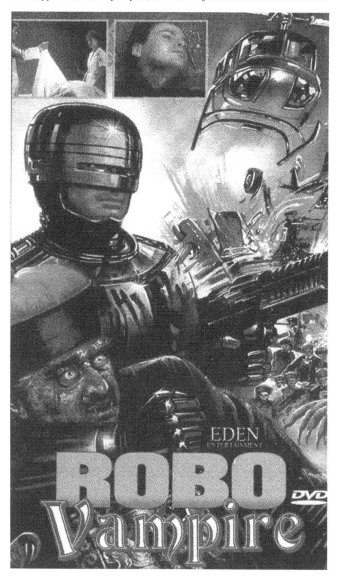

SCI-FI INVASION -
THE RAIDERS OF ATLANTIS
(*I PREDATORI DI ATLANTIDE*, 1983)

A secret government project designed to raise a sunken Russian nuclear submarine goes awry, setting off a catastrophic chain of events leading to the

»PLJAČKAŠI ATLANTIDE«
distribucija »KINEMATOGRAFI« Zagreb

resurrection of Atlantis! The domed island of myth may have, at one time, been run by a benevolent civilization, but their descendants are far from that. Calling themselves "Interceptors," these terrifying tribal punks pillage and murder in a violent attempt to reclaim the world in the name of Atlantis!

Can mercenary Mike Ross (Christopher Connelly) and his partner Washington ("My name is MOHAMMED!"…played by Tony King)—with the help of scientists—reach the island and stop the onslaught before the world is forced to bend its knee to Atlantis's Interceptors?

Directed by Ruggero Deodato (**CANNIBAL HOLOCAUST**), this nutty pre-nuke, Italian sci-fi action-adventure may make little sense but you get the gist when the bullets begin a-flyin', swords a-swingin' and explosions… explodin'(?)! In this is Italian action baby, for every bit of nonsensical plot, a hundred bullets are spent leveling dozens of stuntmen. Iffy dubbing? Check. Groovy score by the De Angelis brothers? Check. An all-star Italian cast including Connelly, Ivan Rassimov, George Hilton and Michele Soavi? Triple-check. This is what it is all about—great action, recognizable actors and tons of futuristic laser sound effects.

The true stars of **THE RAIDERS OF ATLANTIS**, though, are the post-nuke-esque tribal punks and the surprisingly high-quality of the transfer contained on this Mill Creek box set. Led by a visually-striking villain sporting a translucent skull mask, the Interceptors themselves are painted, leathered, armed-to-the-teeth and vicious as hell. If you're a fan of post-nuke punkers in BDSM outfits riding on outlandishly modified scooters and junkyard specials, **THE RAIDERS OF ATLANTIS** has all of that and more. Speaking of the outfits…you know, I always wondered why people in the future—living in a presumably arid future-world—would wander around in leather outfits. I mean, I understand polyester wouldn't be in great supply but what's with them all looking like Village People?

Good or bad? Forget it; that shit is subjective. **THE RAIDERS OF ATLANTIS** (a.k.a. **ATLANTIS INTERCEPTORS**) is a wild ride and well worth the cost of this box set. The source was clean, widescreen and very watchable. Would I recommend you purchase this box set based on just one film? Well, yeah, in this case I would. Grab it and you'll score more than just this film, you'll also be getting films like **HANDS OF STEEL** (1986) and **FUTURE HUNTERS** (1986)! Nice.

1983, ITALY & PHILIPPINES. DIRECTOR: RUGGERO DEODATO
AVAILABLE FROM MILL CREEK ENTERTAINMENT

SCI-FI INVASION - STAR KNIGHT (*EL CABALLERO DEL DRAGÓN*, 1985)

The peons of a wealthy count's kingdom quake with fear when the horrifying form of a dragon casts its foreboding shadow over the land. Now the people refuse to pay their taxes until the count's forces dispose of the dragon before it ruins their crops and murders their virgins and cattle.

Ignoring the murmurs of the people and concern of the court, the count's daughter (Maria Lamor) sneaks out of the castle and heads for the hills for a quick skinny-dip. Instead of a refreshing swim, though, she's dragged beneath the waves of the lake and into the clutches of the dragon! Determined to retrieve his daughter and slay the dragon, the count (José Vivó) and his soldiers head for the lake to do battle with the beast. Instead of confronting the dragon, they come face-to-face with a spacecraft emerging from the waters! Turmoil threatens to tear the kingdom apart when the "dragon" still has not been slain and none of the count's best men seem capable of stopping it. Thankfully, the count's sorrow is short-lived when his lovely princess is found wandering in the forest in a daze. Unable to relay her terrifying ordeal, the royal alchemist journeys to a desolate part of the kingdom to confront the dragon and discover its secret of eternal life. The alchemist has competition, though: a love-struck captain and an overzealous priest will stop at nothing to destroy him and break his hold over the count.

What evil lies within the reptilian armor of the monster? Who is the mysterious knight in black armor, and has the alchemist truly found the elixir of eternal youth?

What a steamer! I have to admit that I was seriously gung-ho for this flick because it sounded intriguing and I figured at the very least it would be a quality film with Keitel and Kinski involved. Silly me. **STAR KNIGHT** (a.k.a. **THE KNIGHT OF THE DRAGON**) comes off like a cheesy mash-up of **STARMAN** (1984), **DUNE** (1984) and the Martin Lawrence vehicle, **BLACK KNIGHT** (2001); it combines elegant, unearthly production design with ineffective, bumbling comedy and unlikable characters. The alien, his "suit of armor" and his ship were gorgeous; they deserved a film worthy of their design, not this goofy meandering crap.

I wanted to like Kinski, his ice-cold blue eyes and dazzling smile, but the vibe his character gives off is decidedly sinister and therefore hard to connect with. Keitel's "brave knight" is idiotic and it only gets worse when the Brooklyn accent spills forth during his poorly delivered Olde English dialogue. Honestly, this was a real forehead-slapper. I suppose the alien "Ix" (Miguel Bosé) was okay, but he doesn't get lines and his acting consisted of wide eyes and head nods.

STAR KNIGHT was about as basic as they come: "Alien comes to Earth to study our world and he falls in love." Big whoop, right? Well as simple as it is it really could have succeeded (in its own way) had the characters worked better and the film was played straight. They didn't and it wasn't, though, and in the end, instead of finding myself mildly entertained with a cool time-waster, I was bored to tears by "just plain bad." I wish I could say that it got better at some point but it didn't.

If you're all about dumb-as-rocks Sci-Fi comedies like **THE ADVENTURES OF PLUTO NASH** (2002) and **GALAXY QUEST** (1999) then you may find this only a little disappointing. Everybody else, though, should steer clear unless you're a glutton for cinematic punishment, like me.

1985, SPAIN. DIRECTOR: FERNANDO COLOMO
AVAILABLE FROM MILL CREEK ENTERTAINMENT

SCREAM THEATER
THE TWILIGHT PEOPLE (1973)

While out on an undersea excursion, well-known diver Matt Farrell (John Ashley) is kidnapped by unknown assailants and brought to a remote island run by the brilliant geneticist Dr. Gordon (Charles Macaulay). His intention is simple: he plans to use Farrell in an experiment that would change him from a man…into a manimal!

Turns out ol' Doc Gordon believes the only hope for mankind's future survival is to actually leave its humanity behind and become more animalistic. None of this is mere theory though; Farrell soon discovers that Gordon is keeping all kinds of half-man/half-animal creations locked up in a dungeon below his villa. Naturally, Farrell isn't exactly game, but escape looks to be hopeless, especially with the dangerous hunter Steinman working as head of security.

His only hope for escape is the beautiful Neva (Pat Woodell), Gordon's daughter, who appears to disagree with Farrell's forced participation and the treatment of the manimals below.

Whether you're a fan of Pinoy genre cinema—Eddie Romero, specifically—or you just purchased this box set blindly, the presence of **THE TWILIGHT PEOPLE** on this box set alone warrants the money spent. The film looks fantastic, the acting was quite good, locations were beautiful and Pat Woodell's body was outstanding! It's not at all perfect—don't get me wrong, some of the FX/Makeup was sketchy and the film is an uneven adaptation of H.G. Wells' *Island of Dr. Moreau*—but it all works in a brilliantly cheesy B-movie way.

Considering the fact that this was a box set flick, which is rarely looked upon as a good thing, I was taken aback by the wonderful quality of the transfer. I'm not sure how VCI's previous Y2K DVD standalone release of **THE TWILIGHT PEOPLE** looked, but one rarely sees transfers so clean on box sets as most films are ripped from dodgy VHS sources. Not so here.

Cult cinema fans will want to check this out, and at a little over $10 for the 12-film set, breaking down to roughly $1 per film, you simply cannot go wrong.

1972, PHILIPPINES & USA. DIRECTOR: EDDIE ROMERO
AVAILABLE FROM VCI ENTERTAINMENT

SCREAM THEATER
HANNAH, QUEEN OF THE VAMPIRES
(*LA TUMBA DE LA ISLA MALDITA*, 1973)

While chasing an unknown culprit through some ruins, Professor Bolton (Mariano García Rey) plummets down a hole and into the hidden crypt of the vampire queen Hannah (Teresa Gimpera). Before the realization of his archaeological discovery sets in, however, he's strangled from behind and his body is stuffed beneath the massive marble sarcophagus and crushed.

Bolton's son Chris (Andrew Prine) is summoned to the island to make arrangements, and he's adamant that the sarcophagus be lifted and his father's remains be removed for a proper burial. Naturally, the villagers are none too happy about this as they're convinced that by disturbing Hannah's undead slumber they will also awaken her insatiable blood lust. Refusing to believe in local superstitions, Chris pushes on with the help of some of his father's acquaintances.

During the removal process, Hannah's corpse is indeed freed from its sealed tomb and, much to the horror of onlookers, she's far from dust! When bodies begin piling up and no clear culprit, Chris is forced to believe in the impossible, but is it already too late?

It's no secret that this version of **LA TUMBA DE LA ISLA MALDITA** (or **HANNAH, QUEEN OF THE VAMPIRES**) is actually the hacked-up Ray Danton version, so don't go into this expecting a complete, cohesive flick. I mean, when a film clumsily reveals the killer in the prologue, effectively destroying the possibility of any real tension being built, you know you're in for some disappointment. Just how much, though, is completely up to your bad cinema tolerance levels. It may still hold some appeal for Euro Horror fans by including the presence of Andrew Prine, a decent amount of atmosphere and a few choice gore gags, but I can't see the average viewer finding anything worthwhile here.

The quality of the transfer itself was…well…viewable. Intermittent fading was evident, grain was highly visible, definition was hazy and the colors were oversaturated and blurry; it appeared to me as though the film might have received a "remastering" on a consumer-level video editing program by somebody unfamiliar with balancing colors. Skin tones resembled severe sunburn at times and an ocean sequence almost burned out my retinas with blinding blue. Seriously though, it was viewable, but nobody will care as it was all so ho-hum.

1973, USA & SPAIN.
DIRECTOR: RAY DANTON & JULIO SALVADOR
AVAILABLE FROM VCI ENTERTAINMENT

BEATDOWN/HEADS-UP

by Brian Harris

*Remember when Mill Creek Entertainment used to release those fun box sets—some of which were in my article—before focusing on licensed stuff for Blu-ray? Those were the days. Well good news! It seems Mill Creek Entertainment is once again in the business of releasing sweet little themed box sets filled with all kinds of cheese, crap, trash and hidden gold. As a matter of fact, they've already released two new kung Fu sets entitled, **KICKIN' IT SHAOLIN STYLE** and **FLYING FISTS OF KUNG FU**.*

Upon seeing these two sets announced, I immediately pre-ordered. Now they've got six new themed box sets on the way this August, so get yer spastic plastic ready! Here's the art and lineup for each set:

AMERICAN HORROR STORIES (12 films)

Sure, some of these films are out there on a million different formats but this is an amazing little starter set for somebody that doesn't own some of these films. The great thing is, there's more good than bad in this collection.

BLOODY PIT OF HORROR (1965) / **A BUCKET OF BLOOD** (1959) / **DON'T ANSWER THE PHONE!** (1980) / **DON'T LOOK IN THE BASEMENT** (1973) / **THE DRILLER KILLER** (1979) / **DRIVE-IN MASSACRE** (1977) / **HORROR EXPRESS** (1972) / **HOUSE ON HAUNTED HILL** (1959) / **THE LITTLE SHOP OF HORRORS** (1960) / **NIGHTMARE CASTLE** (1965) / **POINT OF TERROR** (1973) / **SILENT NIGHT, BLOODY NIGHT** (1972)

DAWN OF THE IMMORTALS (12 films)

Peplum fans are going to want to check this out. These kinds of boxes always have some flicks that have been previously released on another Mill Creek set, but most of the original sets they appeared in have gone out of print. There are some awesome Sword and Sandal epics here worth checking out.

ATLAS IN THE LAND OF THE CYCLOPS (1961) / **COLOSSUS AND THE AMAZON QUEEN** (1960) / **THE CONQUEROR OF THE ORIENT** (1960) / **DAMON AND PYTHIAS** (1962) / **DUEL OF CHAMPIONS** (1961) / **FIRE MONSTERS AGAINST THE SON OF HERCULES** (1962) / **FURY OF HERCULES** (1962) / **THE LAST OF THE VIKINGS** (1961) / **QUEEN OF THE AMAZONS** (1947) / **TRIUMPH OF THE SON OF HERCULES** (1961) / **VENGEANCE OF URSUS** (1961) / **THE WHITE WARRIOR** (1959)

FREAKSHOW CINEMA (12 films)

I may sound like a total ass-clown saying this, but I plan to pass on this box set because it's filled with indie horror and that's just not my bag, baby. I can't get down with poorly-made shit like this. Yeah, that's right, an elitist trash fan. Go figure.

TALES OF THE DEAD: GRIM STORIES OF CURSES, HORROR AND GORE (2010) / **ZOMBIE GENOCIDE: LEGION OF THE DAMNED** (2012) / **THE CURSE OF BLANCHARD HILL** (2006) / **IDOL OF EVIL: HELL IS FOREVER** (2009) / **BELOW GROUND: DEMON HOLOCAUST** (2012) / **ORDER OF ONE: KUNG FU KILLING SPREE** (2011) / **COLD CREEPY FEELING: PARANORMAL EXORCISM** (2011) / **INDEMNITY: RAGE OF A JEALOUS VAMPIRE** (2011) / **GLITTER GODDESS: QUEEN OF THE SUNSET STRIP** (1991) / **DARK MEASURES: GANG WARFARE** (2012) / **BY THE DEVILS HANDS: THE 666 KILLER** (2011) / **TUCK BUSHMAN AND THE LEGEND OF PIDDLEDOWN DALE** (2009)

TABOO TALES (12 films)

Exploitation gold! Some of this was previously released on Mill Creek's **CULT CLASSICS** 20-film collection, so if you already own that set, you may want to compare the lineup before purchasing this. If you haven't seen any of these films, *you need to*. This is the stuff that made the sleaze we see today possible.

CHAINED FOR LIFE (1952) / **COCAINE FIENDS** (1935) / **DELINQUENT DAUGHTERS** (1944) / **GAMBLING WITH SOULS** (1936) / **MAD YOUTH** (1940) / **THE MARIJUANA MENACE** (1937) / **REEFER MADNESS** (1936) / **SEX MADNESS** (1938) / **SHE SHOULDA' SAID "NO"!** (1949) / **THE TERROR OF TINY TOWN** (1938) / **TEST TUBE BABIES** (1948) / **THE WILD AND WICKED** (1956)

THE BEST OF THE WORST (12 films)

Oh look, another "so bad it's good" cash-in. *SIGH*. Seriously, yes, the films on this box are bad. Some very bad. Very, very bad. Still, they've all got their own charm and it should be a fun box to pop in on a rainy Sunday afternoon. I'll be grabbing this when the price drops to $5.

THE AMAZING TRANSPARENT MAN (1960) / **THE APE MAN** (1943) / **THE ATOMIC BRAIN** (1963) / **THE BEAST OF YUCCA FLATS** (1961) / **DEMENTIA 13** (1963) / **EEGAH** (1962) / **THE INCREDIBLE PETRIFIED WORLD** (1957) / **MANOS: THE HANDS OF FATE** (1966) / **MESA OF LOST WOMEN** (1953) / **THE TERROR** (1963) / **TRACK OF THE MOON BEAST** (1976) / **UNKNOWN WORLD** (1951)

ZOMBIES UN-BRAINED (12 films)

Wow, here's a nice selection of classic horror and mind-blowing duds. Yeah, this is a keeper if you don't own any of these films. I'm stoked to see **OASIS OF THE ZOMBIES** on this set, as it gets absolutely no love. Perhaps rightly so, but to each his or her own.

CARNIVAL OF SOULS (1962) / **DEAD MEN WALK** (1943) / **HORROR OF THE ZOMBIES** (1974) / **HOUSE OF THE LIVING DEAD** (1974) / **KING OF THE ZOMBIES** (1941) / **THE LAST MAN ON EARTH** (1964) / **MUTANT** (1984) / **NIGHT OF THE LIVING DEAD** (1968) / **OASIS OF THE ZOMBIES** (1981) / **SNAKE PEOPLE** (1971) / **TEENAGE ZOMBIES** (1959) / **WHITE ZOMBIE** (1932)

There you have it folks! Keep those eyes open because these sets will be dropping the end of August, just around the time many of you will be reading this mag. Hopefully you dig them. I'll be back next issue with a whole new installment of Box Set Beatdown so, until then, have a great few months!

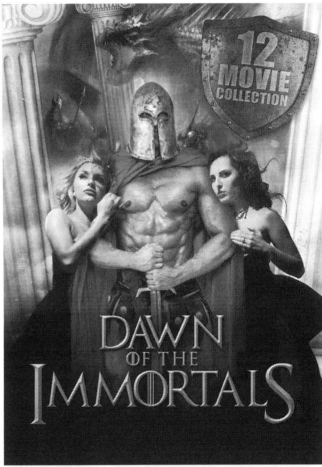
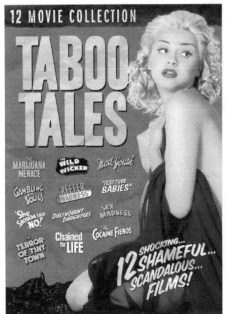

LE STREGHE

SPIDER BABY SINEMA

by Stephen R. Bissette

Kasso Kino: Where Evil Dwells

Peter Filardi's **RICKY 6** (2000, unreleased) starred Vincent Kartheiser (*Madmen*) in top stoner/sleazer/suburban Satanist mode, based on the same true-life drugs/Satanism/murder case Jim Van Bebber (appearing in the Kartheiser role, both surrogates for Richard "Ricky" Kasso) forged into **MY SWEET SATAN** (1994) with far more urgency and impact in a fraction of the running time. Kasso murdered a fellow teen in Northport, Long Island, New York in the spring of 1984; both Van Bebber and Filardi's films capture some of the crystalline intensity of David St. Clair's lengthy account, *Say You Love Satan* (1987, Dell), while offering their own takes on 1980s teen tedium and madness culminating in death. Nothing in **RICKY 6** burned into my brain like some of Van Bebber's indelibly savage imagery or St. Clair's book, but it's superior to **BLACK CIRCLE BOYS** (1997) and the doc **SATAN IN THE SUBURBS** (2000), the only two other film versions I've seen (there are more). Kartheiser did this after **ANOTHER DAY IN PARADISE** (1988, D: Larry Clark) and **CRIME + PUNISHMENT IN SUBURBIA** (2000) had pulled him out of family-friendly **INDIAN IN THE CUPBOARD** and **ALASKA** mode (1995 and '96, respectively), and he's the black heart of **RICKY 6**, appropriately enough!

I only persisted in seeking **RICKY 6** due to clips from the film being used as "dramatic reenactments" for the doc **SATAN IN THE SUBURBS**. The Ricky Kasso case also inspired **WHERE EVIL DWELLS** (1985), which is damn near impossible to see. More folks have seen or read photos/interviews with filmmakers David Wojnarowicz and Tommy Turner than have actually seen this 28-minute underground 1980s polemic. There's also **UNDER SURVEILLANCE** (2006), referenced in some venues as another feature derived in part from the Kasso case, and in fact shot in Northport, a block from the Kasso "crime scene"; we'll see about that one someday, I hope.

WHERE EVIL DWELLS is interesting, in the context of the inchoate Cinema of Transgression (CoT) from which it came. Genre staples (horror host—a possessed ventriloquist dummy, itself another archetype—ersatz satanic mass, with baby sacrifice, etc.) are clumsily-but-gleefully grafted onto the sketchiest conceivable distillation of the Kasso case, with crude-but-vivid gore (including the case's horrific fireside murder) and much enthusiasm, but to little effect. The only fretting this prompted was "are they really going to toss that dummy onto expressway traffic?" at one point (whew—they didn't; the usual poseur Cinema of Transgression flirtation with staged disaster). This definitely leaves Van Bebber's **MY SWEET SATAN** as the most compelling, substantial, and memorable of all the Kasso-crime-inspired films to date.

Joe Coleman fans, take note: Coleman is in **WHERE EVIL DWELLS**, in full-blown (pun intended) mid-1980s self-detonation mode! Joe was in his geek/demolition phase here (see the RE/Search "Pranks! issue); he later appeared in Jeri Cain Rossi's **BLACK HEARTS BLEED RED** (1992, from Flannery O'Connor's terrific "A Good Man Is Hard To Find") and Asia Argento's **SCARLET DIVA** (2003), but if I ever revisit **WHERE EVIL DWELLS**, it'll be to see Joe in his stage-crazy prime. I'd love to ask Joe if he was channeling (in his head) Walter Huston's Scratch from **ALL THAT**

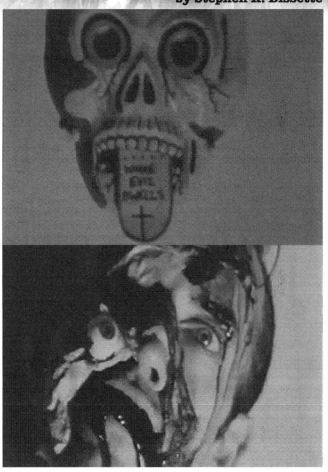

MONEY CAN BUY (a.k.a. **THE DEVIL AND DANIEL WEBSTER**, 1941); he sure looks like he is!

Seen without some knowledge of the Kasso case, **WHERE EVIL DWELLS** would make no sense whatsoever; still, it is what it is, and it's pretty much a mish-mash. For all the transgressive posturing going on, it recalls for me Warhol's **VINYL** (1965) in many ways (including the real agony being inflicted on background "players" in the sadomasochistic staged warehouse "black mass"), and is just as underwhelming *as* cinema. As with most CoT, there's just no entry point to anyone onscreen as a character, or even surrogate emotional place-holder, which was, after all, part of the point. Still, overjoyed to have seen it at last.

1985, USA. DIRECTORS: TOMMY TURNER & DAVID WOJNAROWICZ

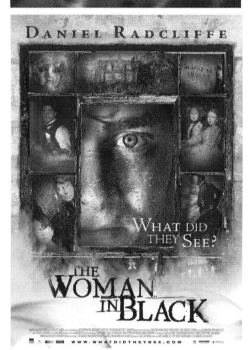

FEARDOTCOM

I've never quite understood why nobody liked WIlliam Malone/Josephine Coyle's **FEARDOTCOM** (2002); any movie that opens immediately with Udo Kier in fear and the spectral lass from Mario Bava's **KILL BABY, KILL** (*Operazione paura*, 1966) has my attention from the get-go.

Stephen Dorff, Natascha McElhone and Stephen Rea starred in this curious fusion of **VIDEODROME** (1983), **RINGU** (a.k.a. **THE RING**, 1998), and **KAIRO** (a.k.a. **PULSE**, 2001) that hit the same year as the Gore Verbinski **THE RING** remake for American theaters, and as such is a bridge between Bava, Cronenberg, Fincher (**SE7EN** dank lighting dominates), and J-horror motifs that also anticipated the whole **THE PASSION OF THE CHRIST** (2004)/**SAW** (2004)/**HOSTEL** (2005) torture cycle (and did so with more taste and restraint than any of what followed). Adolescent Dorff opened **THE GATE** (1987); here, adult Dorff stumbles upon a string of mysterious Ebola-like deaths linked by a portal to Feardotcom.com (don't click the link!!), which, via an inexplicable cross-wiring of uncanny Internet technology and genuine supernatural haunt kills its "subscribers" in 48 hours if they click to play. McElhone is the anchor and at one point takes an Argento/**INFERNO**-esque plunge into an abandoned steel mill "well" that also evokes Kôji Suzuki's many watery ghosts/graves, borrowing yet another **RINGU** motif that reverberates right up to the new 2012 Hammer **THE WOMAN IN BLACK** feature (*reviewed below*—which also lifted countless Bava motifs, so **FEARDOTCOM** is a precursor there, too).

I like Malone's films, and this is a fun one, whatever anybody says.

PS: See Malone's latest, **PARASOMNIA** (2008). As for Malone's other films, I haven't missed a one—been with his work since seeing **SCARED TO DEATH** (1980) in a NJ theater!

2002, USA. DIRECTOR: WILLIAM MALONE
AVAILABLE FROM WARNER HOME VIDEO

THE WOMAN IN BLACK

Though it was made for British TV (Granada), cinematically, Nigel Kneale's adaptation of Susan Hill's **THE WOMAN IN BLACK** (Dec. 24, 1989) is the missing link between post-Shirley Jackson **THE HAUNTING OF HILL HOUSE** (a.k.a. **THE HAUNTING**, 1963) ghost movies and the "haunting as contagion" horrors of Takashi Shimizu's (likewise originally made-for-TV) 呪怨/**JUON/JU-ON/THE GRUDGE** (2000 and on) series. Director Herbert Wise perfectly realized Kneale's script, working with great locations and a stellar cast (Adrian Rawlins, Bernard Hepton, David Daker and Pauline Moran as you-know-who); this is easily one of my all-time favorite ghost tales and films; as a lifelong rabid Kneale fanatic, I snapped up copies of the fleetingly-available VHS and DVD releases (at cost, since I worked/co-managed a video store then) over a decade ago. In the new context of the theatrical film version (it will be tough to beat Kneale's sly adaptation), trivia abounds: Daniel Radcliffe stars in the new version, and coincidentally, the role he plays—solicitor Arthur Kidd—was played in the original version by Adrian Rawlins of the Harry Potter films—*and* Adrian was born on the same day as James Potter, the character he plays in the Harry Potter films!

I quite enjoyed the James Watkins/Jane Goldman/Hammer Films adaptation of **THE WOMAN IN BLACK** (2012), too. Goldman's adaptation deviates from the get-go from Hill's novel, forging its own path while maintaining fidelity to the core narrative and premise. Daniel Radcliffe and vet Ciarán Hinds (though I suppose Radcliffe is a vet, too, now) carry the film, as does the entire production/art direction/set design team (Kave Quinn, Paul Ghirardani, and Niamh Coulter); Eel Marsh and the village are evocative, superb locales, in and out. As with all adaptations, some of the changes assert effective new elements (here, solicitor Kipps is a haunted man from the first shot of the film, and the Spiritualism movement that was sweeping the globe is given some emphasis), others diminish the tapestry's impact (I won't itemize them, as I don't want to tip any hands)—pull one thread, and the whole design changes, and not always for the better. I'll forever prefer the Nigel Kneale version, in part because I savor its place in the whole of Kneale's canon, but this is an effective chiller in its own right, and a happy manifestation of the new Hammer. FYI, the old Hammer never did any ghost films, per se; that was left to other British studios and filmmakers, like Vernon Sewell, though Hammer did populate its Jimmy Sangster cycle of **LES DIABOLIQUE/PSYCHO** 1960s thrillers with bogus "haunts," and offered **MAN IN BLACK** (1949) and **THE BLACK WIDOW** (1951), similar in name only. The strongest whiff of the old Hammer in **THE WOMAN IN BLACK**, for me personally, was fleeting but tactile, via the sequence involving spinning car wheels and mire; my first-ever Hammer Film experience was **X: THE UNKNOWN** (1956), in which spinning tires and muck (sentient, atomic muck, mind you) figured in that climax.

Given reports of Hill's upset over Nigel Kneale/Herbert Wise's excellent 1989 ITV adaptation, this new one must have her ready to haunt somebody. All in all, though I've never had the good fortune to see the stage play (nor heard the British radio adaptations), I've heard it's excellent, so I'd say she has little to complain about: three solid variations on a 1983 novel is a pretty good track record! Goldman and Watkins reinstate some of Hill's novel elements Kneale/Wise didn't incorporate; Kneale's changes included Kidd (Kipps in the novel and new film, restoring the reference to H.G.

Night terrors:
THE WOMAN IN BLACK (1989)

Wells' famous novel that Kneale eschewed, for his own ethical reasons) having a family from the get-go; adding the sequence involving the gypsy child and accident in the village; changing the dog Spider's gender (Spider is in the new film, but Hinds only says his name once, softly, and he's never named again; easily missed by viewers); and other changes I don't want to cite as they'll give away key elements of the new adaptation. No spoilers from me! I love adaptations; the changes, twists, and turns endlessly engage me, so none of this put or puts me off.

1989, UK, DIRECTOR: HERBERT WISE, OOP
2012, UK/CANADA/SWEDEN. DIRECTOR: JAMES WATKINS
AVAILABLE FROM CBS FILMS

THE SOUTHERN STAR

Sidney Hayers's **THE SOUTHERN STAR** (1969) is among the underrated and forgotten adventure movies of the 1960s, a G-rated last hurrah of the decade's distinctive African opuses and the 1950s-1960s Jules Verne cycle, adapted from *L'Étoile du Sud* (published in English as *The Vanished Diamond*) by Verne. Hayers helmed two of my all-time favorite 1960s horrors (**CIRCUS OF HORRORS**, 1960, and **NIGHT OF THE EAGLE/ BURN WITCH BURN**, 1962), and he brought a deft touch to this outing that anticipated **ROMANCING THE STONE** (1984) and its kind—though Hayers and his editor make far, far better use of impressive locations and wildlife footage than any filmmaker of the 1960s since Cornel Wilde's **THE NAKED PREY** (1966).

Ursula Andress is crack-shot adventuress Erica Kramer; George Segal is her opportunistic but likable fiancé Dan. Erica's diamond-mine-owner father (Harry Andrews, in top form) loathes Dan, preferring Chief Inspector Karl (Ian Hendry, also in top form)—who still wants Erica as his own, using the apparent theft of the largest diamond in the world, the Southern Star, to stalk Dan and his sidekick Matakit (Johnny Sekka) with intent to kill Dan and claim Erica in the bargain. Positioning himself to claim both the Star and revenge against Karl is discredited former Chief Inspector Plankett (Orson Welles, mesmerizing even when sleep-walking through a role). Welles reportedly directed the opening scene of the film, according to Welles biographer Charles Higham; Hayers appears in the sequence as the mine overseer, stepping into the part when the scheduled performer failed to show due to illness.

I've always enjoyed this movie; it's still comfortably adult in tone (unusual for almost all 1960s Verne film adaptations) without resorting to sadism at any point, lending a taken-for-granted naturalism (including Andress going for a swim) and considerable gravitas (particularly in Karl's menace) to the proceedings without ever deep-sixing the fun quotient. Plankett's brand of checkers—played with shots of whiskey as all the in-play pieces, which must be savored as each piece is taken—was the most memorable bit, and still a delightful touch, along with the ostrich's key role. Nothing's overblown here—the heroics, the villainy, the scope of the adventure—it's all executed at an always-convincing human scale unusual for its genre, which made this linger in my memory since seeing it at the Capital Theater (Montpelier, VT) as a teen, and rewarded my recent long-overdue return visit in unexpected ways. What a jewel.

Here's a long-forgotten '60s adventure gem, happily restored to its widescreen glory by Columbia's DVD-R release, now available via Warner Archives. Highly recommended, if you're an adventure/Andress/Verne buff.

1969, USA. DIRECTOR: SIDNEY HAYERS
AVAILABLE FROM SPHE (DVD-R)

THE CAREY TREATMENT

A botched terminal abortion performed on a 15-year-old girl makes Blake Edwards's **THE CAREY TREATMENT** (1972, one year before Roe v Wade) curiously timely seen today (via Warner DVD-R). This Boston-set-and-shot James Coburn vehicle (essentially a hospital mystery) trickled out of MGM during head honcho James Aubrey's austerity tenure, with critics claiming it had suffered cuts before release. If so, it doesn't suffer for it, though it has an odd initial rhythm (or lack of same). It's also among the few

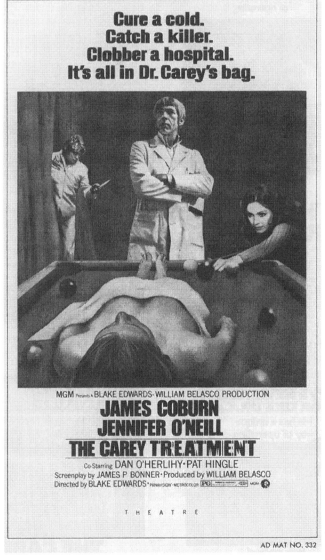

Michael Crichton films M.I.A. (adapted from Crichton's novel *A Case of Need*, published under his "Jeffrey Hudson" nom de plume).

THE CAREY TREATMENT is very much of its sexist, swingin' '70s vintage, with Coburn and Edwards on comfy cruise control with a nifty cast (Jennifer O'Neill, James Hong, Daniel O'Herlihy, Pat Hingle, etc.) and late actor/author Michael Blodgett (he was Lance Rocke in **BEYOND THE VALLEY OF THE DOLLS** [1970] and was in **THE VELVET VAMPIRE**

[1971], and later authored the novels *Captain Blood* and *Hero and the Terror*) in a key role late in the game. Coburn's crisp sass even maintains equilibrium during a laughable sequence where he torments a teen girl into spilling the beans by driving like a fucking lunatic, including a leap over an opening span bridge—even for 1972, that's some stupid-ass shit, which considerably spiced the entertainment value for me.

Enjoyable blast-from-the-past, much like other '72 MGM unpretentious star vehicles I caught at the drive-ins (**SKYJACKED, THEY ONLY KILL THEIR MASTERS, KANSAS CITY BOMBER**, etc.). This is an efficient, no-nonsense programmer of a type that ceased to exist only a short time later.

1972, USA. DIRECTOR: BLAKE EDWARDS
AVAILABLE FROM WARNER ARCHIVE (DVD-R)

LE STREGHE
(a.k.a. **THE WITCHES**)

Thanks to MGM's DVD-R releases, I've finally caught up with a movie I've wanted to see since it was pictured in the *John Willis Screen World Film Annual* for 1967/68, the Dino DeLaurentiis production of **LE STREGHE/THE WITCHES** (1967), starring Silvana Mangano (**BITTER RICE** [1949], **ULYSSES** [1954], **BARABBAS** [1961], **TEOREMA** [1968], **LUDWIG** [1972], **DUNE** [1984], etc.). The allure of the title and cast alone never faded…

The "witches" are all played by Mangano, but they're metaphoric "witches", you see; this is not a horror film, nor was that my interest (even when I was a kid). It's among the most peculiar of all European portmanteau films I've seen, comprised of five anecdotes (I hesitate to call them "stories") directed by Luchino Visconti ("La Strega Bruciata Viva"; longest, most coherent, and best of the lot), Mauro Bolognini (the cynically comedic "Senso Civico"), Pier Paolo Pasolini (the grotesque "La Terra Vista Dalla Luna," co-starring Totò in a misbegotten pastiche of Chaplin, *fumetti*—all the costuming and much of the set design is in flat, bright primary colors—and fables), Franco Rossi ("La Siciliana"; a brief, bitter snapshot of rural superstition, female lust, and jealousy-fueled revenge killings), and Vittorio De Sica (the flat "Una Serata Come le Altre").

The latter is the reason I've long ached to see this, as it co-stars Clint Eastwood, shot while he was still making films in Italy; he plays a bored, sleepy American husband disappointing an affection-starved Mangano, whose fantasies find Eastwood in particularly uncomfortable mode, giving it a game try overplaying unfunny comedic flashes of her musings, broodings, and sexual fantasies. The funniest bit has Eastwood dead-panning absolutely zero interest in a night out to the movies, wherein (in the English version only, generously included on MGM's DVD as a bonus) **A FISTFUL OF DOLLARS** (1964) is the third title he drones through. At the 13-minute mark, Mangano clears up their (unseen) kids' fumetti stash while tidying up the front room, Eastwood flips through a stack topped by the fumetti neri *Diabolik* and *Kriminal*; Mangano's subsequent fantasy features all the fumetti heroes glimpsed attacking Eastwood (including Diabolik, Mandrake the Magician, a red-costumed Phantom, Flash Gordon, Batman, etc.) with *Batman* TV-stylized "Pow! Paff!" sound effects superimposed. Also note: In De Sica's segment, there is a fleeting shot of a black-clad Eastwood gunfighter, shooting down an army of lovers mobbing Mangano. It's a curious—if brief—bridge between Yul Brynner in **THE MAGNIFICENT SEVEN** (1960), Dirk Bogarde in **THE SINGER NOT THE SONG** (1961), Jodorowsky in **EL TOPO** (1970), and Brynner in **WESTWORLD** (1973)!

A neat artifact, and I'll likely include that short clip in my CCS classroom lectures about the fumetti industry, but it's a pretty vapid entry in a decidedly lackluster feature, redeemed only by Visconti's first chapter. *Not* recommended, but glad to have my curiosity satisfied at last.

1967, ITALY. DIRECTORS: MAURO BOLOGNINI, VITTORIO DE SICA, PIER PAOLO PASOLINI, FRANCO ROSSI, LUCHINO VISCONTI
AVAILABLE FROM MGM (DVD-R)

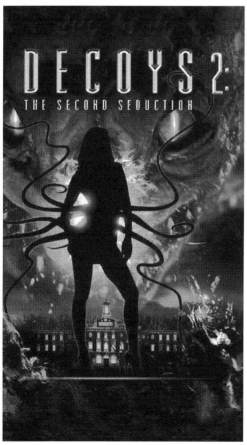

DECOYS and DECOYS 2: ALIEN SEDUCTION

Finding my diet sorely lacking in Canadian tax-shelter direct-to-vid exploitation movies, I recently dove into a home double-bill viewing of two Columbia/TriStar $3 wonders purchased long ago from Big Lots bins: Matthew Hastings/Tom Berry's **DECOYS** (2004) with Corey Sevier, Stefanie von Pfetten, and Kim Poirier; and Jeffery Scott Lando/Tom Berry/Miguel Tejada-Flores's **DECOYS 2: ALIEN SEDUCTION** (2007), with Sevier and Poirier returning in their original roles.

With over 60 movie/TV credits, Sevier is sort of Canada's C. Thomas Howell, and just as dead-earnest whatever the script inanities, but it's the blonde babes, led by Poirier, who dominate screen-time in this chilly northern clime **SPECIES** (1995)-spin that proved dumber (lots of sexist frat-boy "comedy" in both) but far more entertaining than the **SPECIES** franchise to me. Tobin Bell (**SAW**) adds some spice as a biology prof in **DECOYS 2**, but it's Scottish Meghan Ory who kept me watching the first entry (as the "female-friend-of-numb-hero-who-can't-see-she-loves-him" archetypal "pal"). As in **SPECIES**, these are femaliens ravaging the male population in search of breeding fodder (their sexual organs require the *de rigueur*-since-**ALIEN** (1979) surrogate-fellatio/male body as womb); unlike **SPECIES**, they stake out college campus populations, cherry-picking the date-rapers and frat brats. Oh, and this is Canada: the femaliens require *cold* temperatures for their, uh, sperm (?) to "take". Got that? That's not a recommendation, but hey, I did have fun.

DECOYS: 2004, USA. DIRECTOR: MATTHEW HASTINGS
DECOYS 2: 2007, USA. DIRECTOR: JEFFREY SCOTT LANDO
AVAILABLE FROM SONY PICTURES HOME ENTERTAINMENT

POISON PEN

Flora Robson, Robert Newton (the Long John Silver of my youth!), Reginald Tate (as the Reverend), and Ann Todd were among the fine cast of Paul L. Stein's rarely-screened **POISON PEN** (1939), a tight 66-minute British programmer that fascinates as much for its portrayal of small village life as it does for its unspoken brink-of-war premise. Austrian Stein brought an edge to telling the tale of an anonymous "poison-pen" letter plague turning villagers into gossip-mongers, home-wreckers, and terrified rabbits, depending on the twist of the nib.

This modest melodrama takes some surprising turns for a British period film, including a subversive jab at religion and what it can breed; in this, it's as much a precursor to Peter Walker's **HOUSE OF MORTAL SIN** (a.k.a. **THE CONFESSIONAL**, 1976) as it is to its much-more-famous successor, Henri-Georges Clouzot's **LE CORBEAU** (a.k.a. **THE RAVEN**, 1943), for which **POISON PEN** is long overdue credit as Clouzot's blueprint. Clouzot, by nature, took all his films further in the 1950s—and certainly further than any British film would have been permitted to go in 1939. That said, the pleasures of Flora Robson's performance, and especially seeing the original Quatermass (Reginald Tate was the first of the BBC/Nigel Kneale Quatermasses, in **THE QUATERMASS XPERIMENT** [1955] and **QUATERMASS II** [1957]) as her brother and the village moral center are cinematic virtues worth extolling.

Whereas Clouzot's 1943 film gets the Criterion treatment, **POISON PEN** is only available via Sinister Cinema, but Sinister's print is crisp, clean, and the transfer is terrific. Alas, its UK DVD release is long out-of-print, making the Sinister Cinema DVD the best option for curious UK viewers, too. Recommended!

1939, USA. DIRECTOR: PAUL L. STEIN
AVAILABLE FROM SINISTER CINEMA

1960s Psychos:
THE COUCH and BERSERK

I've avoided snoozing on Robert Bloch/Owen Crump's **THE COUCH** (1962), which I never much cared for from my teenage late-night TV viewings, but gave another shot (via Warner Archive DVD). Grant Williams (**THE INCREDIBLE SHRINKING MAN**, 1957) gave his all as Bloch's lead psycho here, with a major crush on a rather ethereal Shirley Knight (soon in *The Outer Limits* gem "The Man Who Was Never Born," and later the ravenous Lula in the UK film version of LeRoi Jones's harrowing **DUTCHMAN** [1967], my favorite of all her performances). Crump stages some nifty Los Angeles nighttime stealth stalk/stab sequences (the weapons of choice being a procession of ice picks, 22 years after Trotsky's assassination and 30 years before 1992's **BASIC INSTINCT**), and the film's dedication to its psycho is earnest, but it's a lackluster, dreary affair.

It begins and ends with *The Andy Griffith Show* character players (Hal Smith and Hope Summers) who ground it in its decade snugly. I must confess, though—*SIGH*—I was rarely a fan of Bloch's screenplays. This is as

mannered, schematic, and plodding as any he ever crafted (his teleplays were almost always sharper), and Hope Summers's final line is Bloch's lamest ever. Like the same year's Bloch-scripted **CABINET OF DR. CALIGARI**

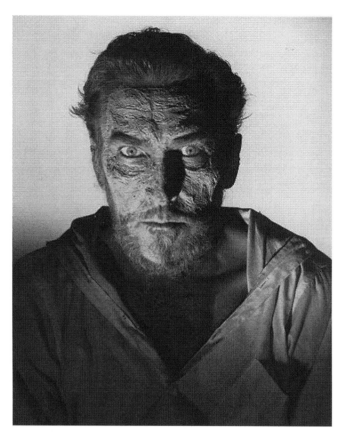

THE THING THAT COULDN'T DIE

remake (which at least boasted some startling delusions, like the "baby baking" imagery), for all its atmospheric meandering, **THE COUCH** never really goes anywhere that isn't obvious from the get-go. That was how it hit me in 1967, when I first saw this on TV (at age 12), and nothing in this revisit convinced me otherwise; it's on a par with Bert Topper's thudding **THE STRANGLER** (1964), which also sported a great lead performance (Victor Buono) but little else. Mind you, Tim Lucas liked it far, far more than I did (read Tim's initial notes at *http://vwpro.blogspot.com/2012/01/10-couch-1962.html*, with Tim's full review published in February 2012 in *Sight & Sound*), and Tim knows his stuff. I almost wrote "knows his shit," but didn't want to imply **THE COUCH** was worse than it is—it just, well, *is*. Too bad. Grant Williams deserved better; and where did it get him? Al Adamson's **BRAIN OF BLOOD** (1972) was his final screen role. Quick, Henry, the pick! Even Bloch's **THE PSYCHOPATH** (1966) remains livelier viewing, if only for its demented finale and some neat Freddie Francis flourishes; I far prefer Bloch's novels and short fiction to his movie scripts, for the most part.

Another lesser 1960s psycho-on-the-loose opus I recently revisited was Herman Cohen/Aben Kandel/Jim O'Connolly's **BERSERK** (1967), starring Joan Crawford, who vainly dominates the proceedings with stern professionalism. Give me **TROG** (1970)! There are some great circus horror pix, from Tod Browning's silent era wonders to **SANTA SANGRE** (1989), and some fun bad circus horror pix—but this sure isn't one of 'em. Like almost all 1960s circus pix, the mayhem is spread mighty thin and it's far too fleeting when it does erupt; the circus acts seem interminable (though shot with infinitely more energy than the static stage-acts of **THE INCREDIBLY STRANGE CREATURES WHO STOPPED LIVING AND BECAME MIXED-UP ZOMBIES!!?**, 1964). Dreadful Cohen/Kandel drudge of a script was turgid in its day, despite the presence of Diana Dors, George Claydon, and (too briefly) Michael Gough, the fact that cheapskate Cohen actually built the film around real circus acts (A *lot* of elephants! *Five* lions! A pack of poodles!), and so many sterling dialogue highlights ("And now, ladies and gentlemen—presenting Phyllis Allen, and her intelligent poodles!"). Zzzzzzzzzzzzz... The Scotland Yard procedural is tiresome as can be; Crawford's daughter (Judy Geeson) finally wanders in at the 54-minute mark, and she picks things up a bit, but only a bit. O'Connolly went on to helm **THE VALLEY OF GWANGI** (1969); this is efficiently-done stuff, but it's lazy mystery/horror by any standard, and don't seek it out expecting

shocks or gore. It's a cheat. The murders that pumped the Warner Bros. ballyhoo were and are few, far apart, timidly staged, and insipid; when in high school, brother/sister Diane and Tom Georgi told me to see this because it was so hilarious (they found the tent-peg-through-the-skull the risible highlight: the peg shown is visibly too short to do what it does!). It damn near put me to sleep then, and damn near did again. There's some fun to be had, though: Hammer character actor Milton Reid has a role; Crawford's costumes (and the odd, shadowy lighting of some of her favored shots) are a pip; and the damned bizarre "It Might Be Me" musical number is one of the oddest in the genre, and that's saying something. If the film had an ounce of what Judy Geeson gives her line at the 94 minute mark—admittedly, a little late for a movie just over 96 minutes—it would have been a *lot* more fun.

THE COUCH: 1962, USA. DIRECTOR: OWEN CRUNCH
AVAILABLE FROM WARNER ARCHIVE (DVD-R)

BERSERK: 1967, USA. DIRECTOR: JIM O'CONNOLLY
AVAILABLE FROM SPHE (DVD-R)

THE THING THAT COULDN'T DIE

As I'm currently amid a hefty research arc concerning anything remotely related to **THE BRAIN THAT WOULDN'T DIE** (1959/1962), it was inevitable that I would crash-course with one particular immediate precursor. On a particularly scorching spring afternoon, I turned on the A/C and chilled with the Universal-International chestnut **THE THING THAT COULDN'T DIE** (1958) from Scottish-born producer/director musical specialist Will Cowan and vet Sci-Fi novelist (*Occam's Razor*, 1957) and screenwriter (**THE BLACK SCORPION** [1957], **MONSTER ON THE CAMPUS** [1958], **THE LEECH WOMAN** [1960], **THE TIME MACHINE** [1960], **FANTASTIC VOYAGE** [1966], etc. and lots of non-genre work) David Duncan.

It's a real curio, and somehow eluded me all my life 'til now, though I recall when I was a kid my cousins telling me about it and how it absolutely traumatized them. I imagine most folks of the current generation caught this on *MST3K*, which I've deliberately avoided until I could see the actual movie, sans the robots. Now I'd love to see their riff on it.

This is the "living head in the hatbox" movie that scarred many a youth's late-night TV viewing in the 1960s. It's also the only genre film I know that begins with dowsing being tagged as ominous and potentially evil (original working title and story was "Water Witch"); on a (then-) modern California ranch, the need for water inadvertently leads to the excavation of a 400-year-old chest. Greedy/sleazebag handyman James Anderson (vet of over 130 films and a contract U-I player, best remembered as the wicked incestuous father of 1962's **TO KILL A MOCKINGBIRD**) conspires to open the chest, unleashing a still-living warlock's head that asserts its will over any in sight in hopes of finding and being reunited with its body.

Though derivative of countless stories (including Washington Irving's "The Legend of Sleepy Hollow", natch), this U-I programmer (it's a fleeting 69 minutes) ended up being incredibly influential, spawning a trickle of "living head" movies (including the already-cited **THE BRAIN THAT WOULDN'T DIE**) that even spilled into Mexico (Chano Urueta's **LA CABEZA VIVIENTE** [a.k.a. **THE LIVING HEAD**, 1963/1968]; Alfredo Salazar's **EL CHARRO DE LAS CALAVERAS** [*The Rider of the Skulls*, 1965—*reviewed below*], etc.) and beyond (is it too much to note Paul Naschy and Carlos Aured's **EL ESPANTO SURGE DE LA TUMBA** [a.k.a. **HORROR RISES FROM THE TOMB**, 1973] as an imitation?)—though maybe it was the Reynold Brown ad art that really prompted all the imitations, really. Yes, it was that memorable!

Sure, Charles Saunders and W. Lee Wilder's **THE MAN WITHOUT A BODY** (1957, with the living-head-of-Nostradamus) was out beforehand, but much of what followed copped this film's resurrected warlock shtick (Nostradamus had the gift of prophecy, but a warlock he wasn't). The flashback to the conviction and beheading of the wicked Gideon Drew (vet character actor Robin Hughes, who makes being a whispering severed head encrusted in Bud Westmore makeup memorably creepy) also resonates, and along with a similar scene in Roger Corman's **THE UNDEAD** (1957), codified similar flashbacks in countless movies afterwards (including **HORROR**

HOTEL [a.k.a. CITY OF THE DEAD, 1960, BLACK SUNDAY [1960], EL BARÓN DEL TERROR [a.k.a. BRAINIAC, 1962], etc.). That's a lot of mileage from a slight, it's-over-before-it's-begun creaker like this!

Cowan has over 120 director credits and 180 (!) producer credits, but this was his last, and his *only* genre effort, best as I can tell—all short films!—with the same year's ersatz rock 'n' roll THE BIG BEAT (1953) with the same co-stars (William Reynolds, Andra Martin, and Jeffrey Stone) his only other feature. What happened? Cowan lived until 1994, but this and THE BIG BEAT (1958) were his final films. Maybe Tom Weaver knows...

1958, USA. DIRECTOR: WILL COWAN

EL CHARRO DE LAS CALAVERAS
(*The Rider of the Skulls*)

Alfredo Salazar's **EL CHARRO DE LAS CALAVERAS** (*The Rider of the Skulls*, 1965) played theatrically in Mexico, where Salazar was a mad movie-machine in the 1950s and '60s, but it *feels* like three episodes (26 minutes each) of a TV series strung together, including "camera drifts up to sky" capping shots to each of the trio. It *plays* like three TV installments, too, playfully mashing genuine "B" Westerns and serial tropes (the title directly recalls the American *3 Mesquiteers* programmer **THE RIDERS OF THE WHISTLING SKULL**, 1937) with the venerable Johnston McCulley *Zorro* archetype and an unholy trinity of boogeymen: one lycanthrope, one vampire, and three damned earthbound souls led by the headless horseman, the Jackal.

The horrors are calculated to be not really scary, so it's fun for all ages, as long as your idea of fun includes checker-shirted werewolves and a vampire with a face like a rotting melon.

Salazar was a seasoned genre vet by 1965, having scripted a ton of my generation's favorite Mexi-monster opuses (including Rafael Portillo's *La Momia Azteca* series), and much, much more, and having directed a handful of films. There's nothing striking or exceptional about Salazar's direction, visually or kinetically—with precious few exceptions, all three episodes unreel with straightforward, pragmatic efficiency—other than the usual Mexi-monster delights we so love.

Herein, those charms include a slag-faced talkative corpse resurrected by a hag-witch—both of whom appear solely to provide exposition on the werewolf—a curious take on shape-shifting (clothed man dissolves to bared skeleton dissolves to clothed werewolf and vice-versa, repeatedly), the flitting phony bat transformations into the big-eared, smear-mugged bat-man, the hooded skull-visaged undead bandits, the black-clad headless horseman (with prominent veined neck-stump protruding) astride a black stallion wielding a mean machete, and best of all, the asymmetrically-pop-eyed pasty-faced mop-topped flabby rubber mask passing as the Jackal's century-old "head in a box."

When the Jackal speaks, the chills are closer to the weird mobile lips of *Clutch Cargo* than anything in **LA CABEZA VIVIENTE** (1963, starring **THE BRAINIAC** himself, Alfredo's brother Abel, the man who all Mexi-

monster devotees know and love)—those pursed rubber lips gasping out cryptic lines had me in stitches.

The black-masked (well, sort of a black doily mask thingie) Rider of the Skulls (Dagoberto Rodríguez) is an astonishingly useless "hero", inexplicably leaving vulnerable characters alone to be attacked and even die, shooting at supernatural beings clearly unfazed by lead, and at one point even fondling straw listlessly long enough to be choked into unconsciousness by a bone-faced predator tip-toeing up behind him.

His stooge sidekick Cléofas (the not-as-funny-as-he's-supposed-to-be Pascual García Peña) is just as useless, but after all, he's *supposed* to be.

In glorious black-and-white, with numerous day-for-night-that-look-not-a-bit-like-night shots throughout. The head in the box made the whole movie for me, amigos!

1965, MEXICO. DIRECTOR: ALFREDO SALAZAR
AVAILABLE FROM LIONS GATE

All reviews and artwork © 2013 Stephen R. Bissette

STEVE'S VIDEO STORE VOL.2 - DON'T!

by Steven Ronquillo

Before we start this installment you may be asking, "Why 'Steve's Video Store' when you are a member of the anti-VHS brigade?" Well, VHS I could give a damn for, but the mom and pop video stores were my safe zone in the '80s—a haven full of cheap movies and even cheaper-made S-O-V titles. To me, as a kid and a teen working in a place where all your workday consists of is watching movies, recommending movies and all the free video store posters, you could take home is pure paradise!

So in the spirit of my old dreams of owning and running a video store, I started this column and I am grateful the powers that be at WENGS CHOP decided it was good enough for their magazine. So imagine you're in one of those old dusty and dingy video stores with the sun-bleached VHS cases as you read this, and hearing crappy rock music through an old radio as you walk the aisles looking for the latest obscure find—that's Steves Video Store, and I hope you enjoy your time here.

Ok the first film I'm going to discuss is the one that started the "Don't" craze: 1973's **DON'T LOOK IN THE BASEMENT** (a.k.a. **THE FORGOTTEN**), directed by S.F. Brownrigg. This was a major drive-in hit all through the '70s—big enough that for a while a lot of exploitation films took the *Don't* moniker and ran with it like a quarterback with the football.

You have to remember that a movie had a hell of a lot longer screen life than the instant, see-it-now-or-it-will-be-gone shelf life of most movies nowadays. Back then you had the first-run market, then the second-run markets, then you had double-features or package deals. So a good movie could have a lot of legs in the end. But I digress…let's get to talking about the movie.

Ok, this is about a nursing home out in the middle of the Florida backwoods where a doctor at the start is conducting hit-a-big-ol'-chunk-o'-wood-with-an-axe therapy when a nurse asks him a question and the crazy man chopping wood hits him on the neck. Personally, in my 42-odd years of experience at this thing we call life, I am assured that *we never give the crazy person a golldurn axe*! After all that mess is settled, we meet the new nurse who is arriving for the job, and we are introduced to the cast of people there who have more of a realistic tinge than you would think for a B-movie—because Brownrigg had an aunt who ran a nursing home like this, and all the crazies in this movie were based on actual patients of his aunt he ran into during his childhood years. As the plot goes along, things start to get screwy and a few of the patients start to get killed as we wonder what the hell is going on there.

This is a very creepy little movie, and worthy of all the praise it gets because of the creepy authenticity of the performances from all the actors and actresses in it. This is on a stunning amount of PD sets so if you have at least one cheap PD DVD set, there's a good chance you have it!

Next up is 1974's **DON'T OPEN THE DOOR!**, Brownriggs' follow-up to **DON'T LOOK IN THE BASEMENT**. This was a boring **PSYCHO** rip-off about a woman who gets word that her grandma is in trouble and goes home, where horror hijinks ensue. I wish I had more to say about this one, but that's about it. Boring, forgettable and just plain "meh", this one is for S.F. Brownrigg completists only.

Ok and now onto 1975's **DON'T OPEN THE WINDOW**, the US titling of Jorge Grau's **LET SLEEPING CORPSES LIE** (a.k.a **THE LIVING DEAD AT THE MANCHESTER MORGUE**, a.k.a **BREAKFAST AT THE MANCHESTER MORGUE**). I don't know why in the blue hell they could take **LET SLEEPING CORPSES LIE** and get **DON'T OPEN THE WINDOW** out of it…but they did, so I am talking about it. This is a very unique zombie film that is pre-**DAWN OF THE DEAD** (1978)—which is the movie that cemented the zombie rules—so this one has some wild and unique twists, like the one zombie not appearing on camera or the anointing of blood from the zombies on eyelids as a reason they rise from the dead.

The story follows a man from the city who is taking a motorcycle trip when he runs into a woman who gets him involved with the zombie attack, and an asshole fascist cop who keeps hounding him throughout the movie, which leads to a very interesting finale in which to avenge himself against the cop he must become one of the walking dead. This is a very creepy and slow-paced movie, and not your standard post dawn zombie epic, which is probably why I love it so much. If you haven't seen it I highly recommend you do.

Next is the 1980 sleaze pic **DON'T ANSWER THE PHONE!** (a.k.a. **THE HILLSIDE STRANGLER**), which is a disturbing and sleazy slice of early-80s exploitation when Nicholas Worth is on screen, but when he's not…ugh. We get a couple who are supposed to meet cute and have romantic sparks but instead have soul-crushing hate for each other, plus a smartass coroner that you will want dead within ten minutes of his ass being onscreen. And the silly scene with the two cops at the brothel that ends with them killing the only freaking lead to the killer is very pointless and absurd

But what is it that made Heath Ledger and Michael Rooker watch this in preparation for their respective roles in **THE DARK KNIGHT** (2008) and **HENRY: POITRAIT OF A SERIAL KILLER** (1986)? Nicholas Worth's amazing performance as Kirk Smith—a.k.a. the killer, a.k.a. the strangler, depending on if you trust the movie or the beginning and end credits. Yes he is so bad-ass the credits give him two different names! But about 90% of this was improvised by Worth, and he has said in interviews that the part was bland on paper but when he kicked so much ass on set with the opening scene they shot with him, they expanded his part quite a lot.

And to be honest, the movie stops when he isn't onscreen, but when he is, he is just amazing. From his two weightlifting scenes to the scene where he asks his dad if he is proud of him as he walks around ranting about how he kicked a black pimp's ass are some of the best in sleaze history. For Worth's performance this is a grade-A classic and a must-see for any student of sleaze.

Next is a sick gem called **DON'T GO IN THE HOUSE** (1979, released 1980). Donny Kholer is a man-child who, as the movie opens, is seen at work as an accident happens while he just stands there watching. Later, he goes home and finds his mother dead. Then voices in his head tell him he is free now and can do anything he wants, so he does the same thing Macaulay does in **HOME ALONE** (1990), and plays his music loud and dances on the furniture. And in short order he builds an elaborate room to burn the girls alive. This movie is so sleazy even the house he lives in is a sleazy dilapidated dump. This came out in the '80s but it's a pure '70s mood piece from the get-go, as we get to know the killer more than we would once the '80s style took over, so if you're expecting a real sleazy **SAW**-style gorefest, it ain't that kind of party, and you need to move along now, please. But if you like that slow-burn type of movie then I can highly recommend it, from the opening to the ending which is very similar to another film about a **MANIAC** that came out the same year. Their release window was so close that it was probably a fluke they had the exact same ending, but who knows.

Next is 1979's **DON'T GO NEAR THE PARK** with Crackers Phinn (real name: Robert Gribbin)…I love saying and writing that name—*Crackers Phinn*! Crackers Phinn is to bad actor names what our beloved Editor-in-Chief Brian Harris is to midget hookers. But I digress, as usual. The movie is about a brother and sister who are cursed to die forever—but not die—and then they find out they have to wait 'til the 80s to screw Linnea Quigley and make a child with a stupid-ass name. So it cuts to 16 years before the 80s so Crackers can eat the guts of a little boy 'til the boy turns old and Crackers turns young and his sis says it's time to go diddle Linnea, so he meets her at a crappy parade and walks into her house while she is showering, and since he looks like a deranged rapist she rents him a room.

Then we see his sister help a young lady out of a bear trap by eating her guts and then she becomes a young, Christina-Lindberg-in-**THEY CALL HER ONE EYE**-lookalike. We then see a paper that was written by assholes, it seems—not by me, a self-admitted asshole, but some real stupid assholes—it reads CHILD STILL MISSING. So I assume there is only one child? I bring this up because Crackers has a briefcase in his room, and all it contains is a machete and the paper—so he's sort of keeping track, I think?

They get married and have a baby, which they name Bondi. Why, I don't know, because he gives a big stupid speech on why it is, but all it does is make his wife jealous. So from there we go to 16 years later and the wife is a bitter bitch because Crackers gives his daughter a medallion and then the movie gets random as hell…like talking to someone suffering from ADD while they are snorting coke.

She grows up to be a teen, so he gives her a pendant so we can hear his wife bitch about how she never got any cheap shitty-looking jewelry from him, then she runs away…because a movie about three cute runaways is so damn random we don't give a damn if it doesn't have anything to do with the main plot. This goes on for a while before we have to get to the ending, which is Crackers forgetting his daughter is a virgin sacrifice and tries to rape her to kill time before the zombies show up for no reason…then the shocking twist ending we totally expected happens.

Yes this movie is stupid, ignorant and goofy but I think it's fun and watchable, unlike the next—and thankfully, last—disaster in this article.

You see, **DON'T GO NEAR THE PARK** was competently shot, had good audio and some semi-decent acting which are nowhere to be found in **DON'T GO IN THE WOODS** (1981), a film that may be the worst Slasher of the '80s—and yes, I've seen **THE MUTILATOR** (1985).

Dear god, I knew this movie was going to be bad, but nothing I've seen before prepared me for the pure shittiness of this film. This is about some reject from **THE HILLS HAVE EYES** wandering around the woods killing folks for no other reason than the movie needed a killer. This is the most ineptly-dubbed movie I've ever had the pain to see. But on the good side, I didn't give a damn if anyone got killed because I hated them all—so that's a good thing, I guess—and we got to see a baby playing with a hatchet, so that rocks in a my-god-that-is-unsafe kind of way. But the end song…good god, it makes Chester Novell Turner's soundtracks sound awesome! I can say from the bottom of my heart that this is what you get when you give a mentally disabled child a Casio and tell him to write an end theme song.

So to sum up, this was a bizarre run of movies in a short span of time that have been grouped together as the *Don't* films, which were lovingly paid tribute to by the **SHAUN OF THE DEAD/HOT FUZZ** crew in the misfire of a movie that was called **GRINDHOUSE** (2007). My gripes about that movie will be talked about in a future article, but for now it's time to say goodbye 'til the next time, and I will leave you with the Steve's Video Store mantra:

Always keep looking. There are always new titles to find.
Be nice to the new fans. Because you were once a wet-behind-the-ears fan yourself.
Embrace the past. But don't drown it in nostalgia.

…And always remember: it's our love that keeps these movies alive more than anything else, so keep scanning the shelves!

DON'T MISS IT!

The Weng's Chop Halloween Special Issue #4.5 100% FREE of annoying tributes to hoary ol' Universal or Hammer monsters... well, with the exception of our special Bela Lugosi cover art by Heather Paxton.

Issue 4.5 goes on sale October 31st, 2013!

GET YOUR CHOP ON WITH YOUR VERY OWN WENGS CHOP T-SHIRT FROM...

EL MUNDO DE LOS VAMPIROS (1961)

MEXICAN MONSTERS ON PARADE
PART DOS
by Douglas Waltz

This time around I got to watch one of the creepiest Mexican monster movies ever and a series that I didn't know was a series...at first. It's time, once again, to head south of the border for some authentic Mexican! (Monsters, that is.)

THE WORLD OF THE VAMPIRES
(1961)
(*El Mundo de los Vampiros*)

I went into this thinking, "Oh, another travesty from K. Gordon Murray." Murray was famous for taking Mexican Cinema and, with some terrible dubbing, turning it into Saturday Matinee fare for the kiddies. If I was a kid in 1961 and saw this at the movies, I would still bear the scars.

Directed by Alfonso Corona Blake, this film is filled with creepy shadows that seem to have a life of their own. Blake would go on to direct two of the better Santo films: **SANTO VERSUS THE VAMPIRE WOMEN** (*Santo vs. las Mujeras Vampiro*, 1962) and **SANTO IN THE WAX MUSEUM** (*Santo en el Museo de Cera*, 1963). While both excellent films that embrace the wrestling/horror genre of Mexico, this is where Blake brought his A game.

The basic premise is that Count Subotai (Guillermo Murray) brought the powers of darkness together to wipe out mankind. Julius Coleman learned of this plot and used his sorcerous powers to stop the plans of Count Subotai and drove a stake through his black heart. The Subotai family retaliated by destroying the Coleman clan. All except for one (José Baviera) who escaped to America. Now, he travels to the New World to grow a vampire army that will destroy the last of the family that killed their leader.

Mexican lobby card for **EL MUNDO DE LOS VAMPIROS**

The atmosphere of this film manages to destroy anything K. Gordon Murray could have done to it. The vampires are creepy as hell. The leader of the vampire clan exudes *nasty*. He has this huge organ made of skulls and bones that he plays to bring the vampires from their grave to hunt humans. There is no mercy for anyone in this flick.

Luckily, there is a man in America, Rudolph Sommers (Mauricio Garcés), a friend to the Colemans of America that has done experimentation with music to show that it can affect mood. It can also tick off vampires. And remember that huge skull and bone organ I mentioned? Yeah, bad idea to use the one thing that can destroy you as a way to summon your minions. Probably seemed like a really cool idea at the time. How was he to know he'd come head to head with a music major?

This movie has it all. There are femme fatale vampires, vampires with huge bat heads, and a hunchbacked assistant. They even mention a Lovecraftian-type creature that they worship named Kaydor. The whole movie exudes a level of creepiness that is mind boggling.

I would like to mention that there is this huge, spiked pit into which Subotai throws his victims and minions that fail in their missions. For years I was haunted by a huge black and white picture of some guy impaled multiple times in a spiked pit. It was in an issue of *Famous Monsters of Filmland* and I can still see it as clear as the day I first read the magazine, some forty years ago.

Yeah, it came from this movie. When it happened in the movie my little boy psyche slammed into present day so fast my head twitched. If you forced me to pick a shining example of what was being done in the world of Mexican Horror Cinema, this would be my choice.

THE HEADLESS RIDER
(1957)
(*El Jinete sin Cabeza*)

I thought I was going into a "Headless Horseman" situation...and I was... sort of. I had no idea it was a series. The movie starts off pretty creepy with a group of men in robes and skull masks who pass judgment on a man by cutting off his hands. There is a disembodied hand at the proceedings that roams throughout the rest of the picture. Then along comes a well-dressed man who flirts with the new female sheriff and sings her love songs. I didn't think anything of this and thought it was just some weird subplot.

Later a mummified body is found in the walls of a home in the village. Only this body is not dead. It seems that there are some weird goings-on with

Above: Mexican lobby card from **LA CABEZA DE PANCHO VILLA**.
Right: Mexican poster and exciting scenes from **EL JINETE SIN CABEZA**.

this robed cult that holds the town in a grip of fear…then the Headless Rider (Luis Aguilar) appears!

Before we move along, I would like to mention that Luis Aguilar was one of those actors who could do it all: sing, dance, act, ride, and shoot. There was nothing he couldn't do and with his nickname of El Gallo Giro (The Wild Rooster) he had a bit of a reputation, as well. Add his performances in over 173 films and he was one of the main actors from the golden age of Mexican cinema.

Watch him when he is flirting with the sheriff. You see this little grin like there is some inside joke he keeps telling himself throughout the picture. Add that excellent singing voice and this is a man's man.

He's a lawman who wears a special piece of cloth on his head that makes it appear invisible! It serves a twofold purpose: One, it keeps his identity a secret, and Two, it sometimes appears that he has no head. That has to be unnerving to some people. For a no-budget effect this works quite well in more scenes than where it failed miserably. I'm amazed that this basic premise never went beyond the three films covered here. Westerns were flourishing. The Headless Rider could have been an agent that travelled from town to town, having adventures. One season would have been epic.

Director Chano Ureta gave us *Blue Demon* movies where Blake gave us *Santo* films. Apparently, if you direct in Mexico you are bound to make some masked wrestler films. His were **BLUE DEMON VS. THE SATANIC POWER** (*Blue Demon vs. el Poder Satánico*, 1966) and **BLUE DEMON VERSUS THE INFERNAL BRAINS** (*Blue Demon Contra Cerebros Infernales*, 1968).

I liked this because it gave you a Western with elements of horror and a few musical numbers thrown in for good measure. It made me excited to see…

THE HEAD OF PANCHO VILLA
(1957)
(La Cabeza de Pancho Villa)
This little sequel to the exciting first one starts off with three men violating the grave of Pancho Villa. Years later, an old man gives his six friends a black box. Soon, outlaws are after them killing them off one-by-one. The Headless Rider enters the fray, kicking butt and taking names. Until…well, that would be cheating, wouldn't it?

The second in the series seems a little less supernatural than the first. Aguilar reprises his role as the secret agent who wears a mask that makes him appear to be headless. Well, some of the time, anyway. There is a lot of the same cast in this film. Apparently it was intended to

An extremely poor reproduction of a very rare lobby card for Chano Urueta 1957 chiller-diller **LA MARCA DE SATANAS**.

WORLD OF THE VAMPIRE, US TV press-sheet.

be a serial and, for whatever reason, was turned into a trilogy of films instead.

You can get the feel of a Hollywood serial, Mexican-style in the proceedings. Knowing that this is the middle of a serial explains why it feels the flattest of the bunch. Serials tend to bog down in the middle. It's just the nature of the beast.

I did find it fascinating that they inserted such a famous, near-mythical character like Pancho Villa into the proceedings, even if it was just his head.

THE MARK OF SATAN
(1957)
(*La Marca de Satanas*)

This one goes berserk in getting us to the end of this wild ride. Everyone from the first two films is called to a village where they try to figure out a strange ax, the Mark of Satan, and the death of Maria's sister. Filled with amazing things like a wild-looking zombie, an axe floating of its own accord and, of course, lots and lots of singing. Throw in our Headless Rider from the first two pictures and you know that you are in for a fun-filled ride.

Director Ureta pulls out every trick in the book with this final installment. Remembering that it is set up originally to be a serial, it makes perfect sense that this would be the most exciting of the three. While the first one was suitably eerie, the gruesome zombie in this one more than makes up for the lackluster second film.

I was amazed by the amount of grue in this film compared to the others. Mummies and heads in a box are nothing when compared to a gooey zombie.

The Headless Rider pictures are pretty ambitious in that they were all made by a single director. If you look at the majority of Hollywood-released films around the same time period, they almost always utilized two directors. Chano Ureta needed no help to give a *Zorro*-like spin to the legend of The Headless Horseman. The monsters were never hammed up. They were always treated as a real threat throughout the pictures. It was interesting to see a Mexican movie with a Bollywood feel to it with the musical numbers. No dance numbers, but lots of magnificent singing.

While this column is dedicated to Mexican Monsters and The Headless Rider doesn't really count as one because it's just a costume and he's the good guy, there are still plenty of thrills and chills throughout the entire trilogy. It really deserves a release on DVD or even Netflix for people to discover again.

PIMPING GODFREY HO:
NINJA IN THE KILLING FIELDS

by Jeff Goodhartz

Here's the first in what is hoped to be a regular column in Weng's Chop, centering on the ubiquitous Godfrey Ho. The Omnipresent One's output would seem to fall somewhere between that of Edward D. Wood, Jr. (bewildering, jaw-dropping awfulness) and Jess Franco (sheer ballsy quantity). His specialty is his patented cut-and-paste technique. Ho will often shoot thirty-odd minutes of cheapo-yet-outrageously-hilarious footage (usually involving ninjas) and edit it (seemingly randomly) into another, older (and usually unidentified) film, often leading to schizophrenic results. Most will either love his work or hate it for this very reason. There is no middle ground here. For me, I find that at their best, these can be wonderfully weird anomalies and great fun. Since I almost always seem to really enjoy Ho's goofy inserts, my recommendation (or not) of these films would rest on the hour or so of older footage used. If that footage (the bulk of each film) is entertaining, then we have a winner. Which brings us to **NINJA IN THE KILLING FIELDS** (1984), because (as I channel my inner Lewis Black) when I think of **THE KILLING FIELDS** (or any serious war film), oh yeah, I think of ninjas!

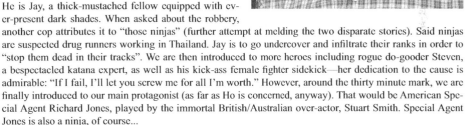

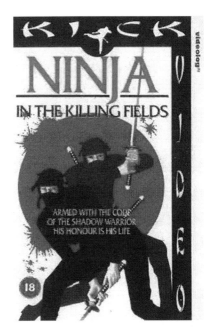

As the film starts, we are introduced to a villainous ninja gang and their red-uniformed leader. On a small TV they watch a botched robbery (cleverly introducing the older footage; an unnamed Thai film which Ho would often plunder). Disgusted with what he's viewing, the red leader angrily switches it off. We are then introduced to our plain clothes detective hero in the Thai footage. He is Jay, a thick-mustached fellow equipped with ever-present dark shades. When asked about the robbery, another cop attributes it to "those ninjas" (further attempt at melding the two disparate stories). Said ninjas are suspected drug runners working in Thailand. Jay is to go undercover and infiltrate their ranks in order to "stop them dead in their tracks". We are then introduced to more heroes including rogue do-gooder Steven, a bespectacled katana expert, as well as his kick-ass female fighter sidekick—her dedication to the cause is admirable: "If I fail, I'll let you screw me for all I'm worth." However, around the thirty minute mark, we are finally introduced to our main protagonist (as far as Ho is concerned, anyway). That would be American Special Agent Richard Jones, played by the immortal British/Australian over-actor, Stuart Smith. Special Agent Jones is also a ninja, of course...

For the most part, the two stories merged surprisingly well—this being one of Ho's earliest, he seemed to still actually give two craps about continuity here. It helps that the Thai footage also featured ninjas, which certainly made it easier for the new footage to blend—though re-watching this, it's possible that two separate Thai films were used in addition to the inserts. It also helps that said original footage is mostly entertaining with a fair amount of decent '70s-style action scenes. The film does begin to falter in the final third as the Thai film opts for intrigue over action, a risky and ill-advised proposition. Fortunately, just as the proceedings threaten to grind to a halt, the second finale kicks in, and it's Gonzo Godfrey Time! Here is where the film truly lives up to its title as we are whisked away to the Thai jungle (I think), where the evil, drug-dealing ninja gang has a final confrontation with the army. Watching ninja getting blown away via machine guns, grenades, bazookas and tanks is a giddiness-inducing experience. And for the *coup de grace*, Special Agent Jones dramatically (far too dramatically) transforms into his yellow ninja alter ego and stealthily takes out the rest of the gang one by one ("Hey, we're missing a ninja!") before his final one-on-one showdown with his red-garbed nemesis. These final ten minutes are easily some of Ho's best ever. It all concludes with one of the most head-scratchingly bizarre final images I've ever seen in a movie (frogs???).

All in all, a brain-cell-killing good time, and the perfect intro for this column.

1984, HONG KONG. DIRECTOR: GODFREY HO
AVAILABLE FROM BCI/NAVARRE

THE FEROCIOUS ASPECT
Shocking Shakti of Fantastic Indian Cinema (Part Five)

by Tim Paxton with Cara Romano

Like many in the Abrahamic world, I grew up with the concept of God as a being of good (as opposed to evil)...and male (as opposed to female) and single (as opposed to plural). This is not to say that I was never aware of the other gods, as my family was fairly liberal-minded and hippies in theory, if not, at times, in practice. We had a wooden Jesus crucified on the wall in our front hall, a wooden Guanyin (a type of Buddha) on the mantelpiece over our fireplace, and kachina dolls inhabiting various bookshelves. I am still at a loss as to why I never developed any taste for a "personal god" and grew up lacking a want for the concept. There never was and still does not exist such a desire. The house of my childhood may have been full of deities, but none could match the sheer volume of gods, goddesses, and demons that populate Hindu beliefs. I am still trying to wrap my head around that concept.

As you may have noted from the subtitle of this article, this is the fifth installment in what is has been my continuing column for Weng's Chop. With each chapter my love and appreciation of Indian cinema grows, as does my comprehension of Hinduism and its complex array of beliefs, sub-beliefs, and hundreds of gods, demigods and demons. This time 'round the focus will be on devotional films. I could call them fantasy films, but that would be degrading. Maybe fantastic devotional or maybe devotional realism horror...this genre, unlike the Cobra Lady films I covered in last issue, really was a tough one to tackle.

20th century Indian cinema approaches these gods in a very kathenotheistic manner. That is, despite the popularity of Shiva, Vishnu and Durga in modern film, each god is supreme. The German philosopher Max Müller created the term kathenotheism to help explain the baffling concept of worshipping so many gods[1]. This gestalt-worship really confused me at first until I began to dig deeper into the how and why of the gods and their existence in Indian society and culture. The idea that someone could worship all gods as one and at the same time with equal reverence is fascinating. A devotee treats each individual holiness as one would look at the facet of a fine cut jewel: each facet is gorgeous and worth the same appreciative study as they are all just one aspect of the same stone, as are collective deities as a whole.

However fascinating and ultimately cool I find the Hindu gods (and believe me I could rattle on for pages without even touching film at all), this is a movie magazine, so I'd better concentrate on the subject at hand: the ferocious aspect of the Divine Mother.

Religious or devotional movies are, to most of us in the West, rather dry and dusty. Even during the 1950s, the heyday of Hollywood's fascination with the epics, and on through the Italian take on the genre throughout the 1960s, there was, for me, never a stand-out film. Maybe that was because I found most of the source material a bit dull. Outside of the Book of Job, Moses, and other various Old Testament entries, there was little in the way of truly spectacular storytelling. If you want a thrilling tale of supernatural devotion, stay away from the New Testament, which may have inspired a lot of films that were, sadly, not very inspired filmmaking. A few devotional tales were packaged neatly into Hollywood's epics, including William Wyler's **BEN HUR** (1959), Cecil B. DeMille's **THE TEN COMMANDMENTS** (1956), Robert Aldrich's **SODOM AND GOMORRAH** (1962), Edward Small's production of **SOLOMON AND SHEBA** (D: King Vidor, 1959) and assorted other films produced by smaller film companies. But the thrills were few and too-far in-between for me as a kid.

But then again, it's all how you as the viewer are connected to the film. Mel Gibson's **THE PASSION OF THE CHRIST** (2004) is probably one of the best examples of a New Testament devotional film that can be compared to **AMMORU** (1995). Had I been a pious child I may have sat through every second of **THE TEN COMMANDMENTS**, gazing in religious wonder at the parting of the Red Sea instead of wondering how the effect was pulled off. This religious disconnection is no doubt the reason why I find the tales of the Hindu mythologies so utterly fascinating. I never grew up with the deities as part of my life, hence their devotees. That disconnection is what

Lobby cards for the Tamil film **THAYE BHUVANESWARI**

makes writing about Devotional Goddess films so engaging. With these films there is a fine line between what can be seen as devoutly cool and mockingly inane. Not unlike the Nagin film, this subgenre of Indian fantasy is hard to really pigeonhole. What can start off as a wholly devotional film full of pious wonder can quickly, and for no apparent reason other than its playing true to its core subject, turn into a psychedelic freak-out full of multi-armed goddesses and a bloodbath. Never have any of these films ended on a downer—I mean, why would they? These *are* devotional productions. Happy endings are essential to their very existence.

Almost all of the films covered involve devotees of the Goddess Durga. The devotees are almost always women, although men also make up a large part of the contingency. And, for the most part, these films are made *for* women. At least that's what I have come to understand after talking to a few people I know who grew up in India. There have been hundreds of devotionals made since they became popular in the mid-1970s, and their major draw has been The Goddess and her love for her devotees.

But that wasn't always the case.

Prior to 1975 the mythologicals that were once popular with many of the movie audience since the early 1900s "had virtually disappeared by the 1950s ... a fact that would make the success of **JAI SANTOSHI MAA** more striking."[2] By the 1970s Indian cinema was being overrun by the brutal macho-driven antics of **SHOLAY** (Ramesh Sippy's deliriously fun 1975 bandit film), politico-dramas, and other such male-friendly film fare. Then along came a small mythological movie called **JAI SANTOSHI MAA** (1975) which instilled the virtue of The Goddess and how she looks out for those who worship her. How did this no-budget, papier mâché production about an obscure goddess become one of the biggest films of the 1970s? And how did it kick-start the Devi-devotional genre? More about that later.

But first, time to lay down some facts about The Goddess and her sisters.

---

[1] "Coined by Friedrich Max Müller (December 6, 1823 – October 28, 1900), generally known as Max Müller, was a German-born philologist and Orientalist, who lived and studied in Britain for most of his life. He was one of the founders of the western academic field of Indian studies and the discipline of comparative religion." n.wikipedia.org/wiki/Max_Müller

[2] Philip Lutgendorf, "Who Wants to be a Goddess? Jai Santoshi Maa Revisited"; Columbia University Online Library.

Shakti Appendix 1
Know Your Goddess

ABOVE: An outdoor idol from the Tamil film **MARIYATHAA** (2009?), featuring a fairly accurate statue of the Goddess Mariyathaa (a.k.a. Mariamman) which is a variant of Kali. Now when I say variant, I mean that The Goddess is probably as old as Kali and shares some of her characteristics without actually being Kali. There over 160 goddesses, and this is one of the most popular for Tamil and Telugu cinema. Whenever someone falls ill with the pox you need to pray to Mariamman or any of her cinematic cousins like **AMMORU, ANGALA PARAMESWARI** (2002), etc. The Goddess is both the cause and the cure of the pox, so no matter what you do she is always in your life. You may notice that the idols are dressed in clothing and often adorned with flower wreaths. These are living gods, that is, you must wake them up in the morning, get them dressed, feed them, worship them, and then put them to bed at night.

Almost all of the goddesses in this article are related in one form or another to the one primordial mother goddess, the ancient form of nature worship that was around prior to the introduction of the Vedic gods like Shiva and Vishnu to the subcontinent. The Shakti or Devi or Mahadevi[1] has always been the most powerful deity in many cultures, and despite a constant attempt to dominate this feminine force for over the past 3,000 years, she is still dominant in the minds and lives of many Indians.

In some South Indian traditions, Vishnu, the most important male god of the Hindu pantheon, may threaten Lakshmi, his "wife", but he is actually ineffectual because she is far older, wiser *and* more powerful than he. If he even so much as raises a weapon against Lakshmi she will take away his powers. Shiva's "wife" Parvati is related to the ferocious Goddess Durga, who figures into almost all of the "Angry Goddess" sub-genre of devotional film. Durga, a.k.a. "she who can't be approached" or "the invincible one"—depending on your translation of the original Sanskrit—is who you pray to when you have demons on your tail.

A goddess can manifest herself in a variety colors: green, red, blue, yellow, brown and black. She has up to ten arms, each typically holding a weapon of some sort. Durga and Kali's weapons of choice are the trident, the sword, and the bow and arrow. She is sometimes seen atop a lion or a tiger as her steed. As with many Hindu deities she has both a light and a dark aspect to her being. That said, she will grant a boon to anyone who follows the proper channels of worshipping her. You could be a devout woman who loves everyone and prays for only good things from Parvati, or you could be someone who is into increasing his power of evil through the dark arts through Kali. But remember one thing: you gotta follow the rules and never, *ever* piss off The Goddess.

[1] http://en.wikipedia.org/wiki/Devi, "Many texts, myths and rituals concerning goddesses subsume them all under one great female being, named generally as Mahadevi or Devi."

LEFT: There are a few facts that you need to know if you want your goddess to answer your plea for help...especially if an evil *tantrik* is out to get you. First, always have a pocketful of lemons. The yellow fruit is offered to Durga, Kali, or, in the case of the film **DEVI**, a form of Manasa, the snake goddess. The lemon is placed at the idol's feet or impaled on the holy *trishul* (trident) inside the temple to ward off evil. Second, you must prostrate yourself on the ground in front of the statue and roll around as you enter the temple. These scenes have often confused Western audiences; it is a form of greeting your deity if you are a devout follower of The Goddess. This form of worship is commonly seen in *filmi* (the musical portion) sequences in movies, and it is performed along with women and girls dancing with and shaking grass "pom-poms". With all of those steps out of the way you can now beseech a boon from your goddess, which usually entails a lot of pleading, bullying, and sometimes belittling your goddess into taking action and helping you.

LEFT: Drama is an essential in devotional films—and what is more dramatic than the histrionics that accompany a devotee's passionate plea for divine assistance, as seen here in Bharati Kannan's **RAJA RAJESWARI** (2001)? A devotee flings herself about the temple, sometimes bashing herself up in the process, all in hopes that the godddess, in this case, Pidari Amman (a variant of Kali), will take notice and come to her devotee's rescue.

BELOW: The popular foil in any Goddess Devotional is the evil *tantrik*. Not necessarily bad, these men (and rarely, women) dabble in the black arts in hopes of achieving some sort of magical treasure, or power over an individual or god. They are devotees of the ferocious aspects of deities and demons. Images of Kali, Bhavani, or any of the numerous powerful regional goddesses are typically found in their lair. Skulls, demonic paintings and flashing lights are not uncommon decor. From **SRI RENUKA DEVI** (2003).

ABOVE: Not all idols and statues in goddess temples are human in shape. The shapeless rock idol of the Durga variant **AMMORU** is very common in rural and village temples and shrines. This is an aniconic as opposed to an iconic representation.

ABOVE: The classic Northern Indian temple statue of Kali from the Hindi film **JAI DAKSHINESHWAR KAALI MAA** (1996). This is your typical dramatic statue, and one of the more popular forms of Kali that you will encounter outside of film.

THE MYTHOLOGICAL GODDESS

Hinduism, even after months of research, remains to this day one of the most confounding religions I have ever had the pleasure to explore. It is ancient and does not contain any core doctrine or single system of behavioral norms unlike the Abrahamic religion I grew up in. There are many forms of Hinduism with the Hindus, the Brahmans, the Shaktas, the Vaishnavas and the Shaivites all quarreling with each other as to which is the true form of worship. For this article I'll stick with the Shaktis, which is a loose confederation of goddess traditions primarily from southern part of the subcontinent.

The mythological treatment of the Shakti, or Devi, the primordial feminine energy (that seems to be the basis of every culture I know of—that is, until the male gods made their mark) in Indian cinema is a fairly recent development for the industry. The Goddess may have been in the subcontinent for eons, but her active appearance in Indian cinema is relatively new, and may been connected to the recent popularity of films from the south. Not always the case, mind you, but compare Soni's standard Bollywood mythological affair **JAI MAA VAISHNAV DEVI** (1994) with Tamil director K. Shankar's 1987 film **MUPPERUM DEVIYAR**. There is a huge difference in approaching the same basic mythological tale. You could take into account a director's individual taste, but I would also toss in regional tastes. Another example would be to go on a different route with films about Hanuman, the monkey god; compare the 1976 Hindi classic **BAJRANGBALI** (D: Chandrakant) with its stagy papier mâché sets to the ruggedly exciting 1981 classic **SRI ANJANEYA CHARITRA** (D: Ganga) with its on-location shooting in and around Andhra Pradesh. You may say that it's all apples and oranges; what's the big deal how a devotional film is created as long and the message is conveyed? For me it's all in the presentation. I love gaudy, organic, free-wheeling tales of the Hindu pantheon and their assorted epic battles and bickering gods. South Indian films, those that are Tamil, Telugu, Kannada, and Malayalam, reflect this more than their northern Hindi-speaking cousins in Mumbai (which is technicality not really the Northern part of India, but is where Bollywood got its start back in early 20th Century and after the influx of talent from the more Northern city of Lahore in the 1920s and '30s).

This then brings us to the Mythological as a genre. Since cinema was introduced in India in the early 1900s, the tales of the gods have always been very popular. There was little need to have elaborate sets or realistic representation of the deities as they were immediately recognized by almost everyone in the audience for what they were (in some cases early audience members would prostrate themselves before cinematic images of their gods, not unlike European and American cinema goers who would dodge out of the way from on-screen trains and so forth). The reign of the Mythologicals ran throughout the 1920s and on up to the 1950s where their popularity waned due to the influx of socio-dramas and later in the 1960s and '70s with action-packed Dakku (bandit) cinema. Oh, they were still produced, as the want of devotional films would never die out, but their sheer abundance was nowhere to be seen.

In 1975 the Goddess Gevotional **JAI SARITOSHI MAA** helped to usher in a new era of religious cinema. That, in turn, infused some new life into the genre. But the myths of just Hindu gods and goddesses and their respective tales alone never regained their blockbuster footing from decades previous. There have been some smash hits on occasion, however, most of those were regional blockbusters. The following films are only a smidgeon of what is available on VCD or DVD or even on YouTube. And considering how long India has been in the movie-making business and the sheer annual volume of films produced, I'm sure that the 100+ Mythologicals I have in my personal collection are just the tip of the proverbial iceberg.

Goddesses have always been a part of the modern Hindu pantheon; few Goddess films have ever approached their true "mother earth" roots. Of the Mythologicals I've seen, there seems to have been great care taken for them to be made with a note of caution not to offend the dominant Shiva and Vishnu-based branches of the religion. In cutting a broad swath in the colorful sari that is Goddess Cinema, what follows is a short list of some of the more interesting finds. These are very brief capsule reviews, and are by no means something you can pick up and watch and expect to know what the hell is going on even if they have subtitles (which most don't). When I watch them I usually have to pause the film every so often and consult one of my encyclopedias or source books on Hinduism.

MATA MAHAKALI
1968, D: Dhirubhi Desai, Hindi, DVD, no subtitles
MATA MAHAKALI is a Hindi mythological melodrama only recommended here for the first five minutes of the film, wherein an angry Durga and blood-thirsty Kali dispatch demons left and right in a massive battle. Heads, arms, legs, and torsos are sent flying, and loads of blood gushes from severed limbs as the goddesses wade through demons and men bent on annihilating the world. Kali is presented as a husky she-hulk of a goddess, wild-eyed and frantic to drink as much blood as possible. The world would have been destroyed if Shiva didn't calm her bloodlust by lying prostrate underneath her. The remainder of the film is rather dull with only a few dance numbers to spice up the plot.
Cast: Ashish Kumar, Jayshree Gadkar, Nalini Chonker, Niranjan Sharma, and Shahu Moda ; music: Avinash Vyas

JAI JAGAT JANANI
1976, D: K.S. Gopalakrishna, Hindi, DVD
A Hindi remake of the 1971 Tamil film **ADHIPARASAKHTI**. Low-budget but entertaining '70s version of the tale of the creation of Durga and her battle with an assorted cast of demons. One of the many Mythological/Devotionals that were rushed into production after the 1975 mega-popular hit **JAI SARITOSHI MAA**. Features other goddesses and some delightfully trippy dance numbers.
Cast: Gemini Gansen, Padmini, Vanisri, Jayalalitha J, S.V. Ranga Rao, and Ragini; music: S.N. Tripathi

SRI SRINIVASA KALYANA
1974, D: Vijay, Kannada, YouTube, subtitles
Director Vijay's **SRI SRINIVASA KALYANA** is a playful, intelligent and very, very fun mythological film that allows various popular South Indian actors to flex their thespian skills portraying very humanistic deities. There is one scene in particular that struck my fancy and fits neatly within this article. The god Vishnu is arguing with his wife Lakshmi over his annoying tendency to brag. They get into a verbal tussle wherein Lakshmi informs her husband, possibly the ultimate male god in Hinduism, that he is nothing without her. He threatens to kill her with his mace which she pops like a balloon. He then hurls his *Sudarshana Chakra* (a sort of super throwing star) at his wife. She transforms into Durga and easily snags the spinning weapon on her forefinger, casually informing him by threatening her he will lose his power. The Devi is the ultimate force in the Universe, and don't you forget it!
Cast : Rajkumar, B Saroja Devi, Raja Sankar, Manjula, Srinath, Vajramuni; music: Sri Vadiraja Theertharu

MAA CHHINNAMASTA
1978 D: N. A. Ansari, Bengali, VCD
The only film I have ever found that has to do with the Goddess Chhinnamasta. This obscure variant of the Devi is infamously misunderstood by Westerners. Her temples are scarce and her imagery is very strange even for Asian religions (although she is popular in Tibetan Buddhism): The Goddess is presented nude with a necklace of skulls (not unlike Kali), dancing on a copulating couple. She holds her own severed head which was just cut off with a large curved sword. Three streams of blood gush from her severed stump of a neck and into the mouths of her decapitated head and those of each of her attendants. I lucked upon a VCD of **MAA CHHINNAMASTA** a few years ago. The film is a beautifully-shot strict devotional tale with few supernatural elements other than the appearance of two deities and some floating sprites. I was thrilled to see that there was a very brief scene of The Goddess lopping off her own head. If you blink you'll miss this early example of Indian gore…albeit, not as some exploitational horror film.
Cast: Ashim Kumar, Mihir Bhattacharya, Sabita Bose, Gyanesh Mukherjee, Gita Dey, Shekhar Chatterjee; music: Rathin Ghosh

MUPPERUM DEVIYAR
1987, D: K. Shankar, Tamil, DVD, no subtitles
A lush South Indian classic full of sexy goddesses, jealous gods; an assortment of dharmatic drama with a cast of devotees, holy men and mischievous demons. The climax is a wildly garish dance featuring Parvati, Durga and Kali as they battle a demon. A wildly entertaining Mythological that, sadly, lacks subtitles. Director K. Shankar was a well-respected craftsman whose output of 80-plus films included some of the industry's some most colorful mythological, devotional and fantasy films including **BHOOKAILAS** (1958), **BALANAGAMMA** (1981), and **JAI GANESH DEVA** (2001).
Cast: Prabhu, K R Vijaya, M N Nambiyar, Delhi Ganesh, Sangili Murugan, Senthil, Lakshmi Sujatha; music: M S Viswanathan

JAI MAA VAISHNAV DEVI
1994, D: Shantilal Soni, Hindi, DVD, no subtitles
One of Soni's better Mythologicals, as it features a wide array of bickering and battling gods and goddesses involved in the usual drama full of beseeching devotees, scheming *tantriks*, and an annoying demon. About two hours in, we are treated to a fun wrestling match between an ascetic who insists on bothering a meditating goddess, and Hanuman, who is there to guard her. Which results in a pissed-off Durga decapitating the holy man.
Cast: Aparajita, Kiran Juneja, Arun Govil, Rakesh Bedi; music: Amar Utpal

SHR ADHA SHAKTI JAY AMBEY MAA
2000, D: R. Om Shakti Jagdishan, Kannada, VCD, no subtitles
Devotional composite film which features bickering holy men accompanied by action sequences lifted from an assortment of much older (and far superior) Durga/Goddess Mythologicals. Director Jagdishan has made other devotionals and even a Naag film, although he never seemed to have much of a budget to work with. Some of the scenes look as if they could have been from the cutting room floor. In a sequence of Durga cutting the head off of a demon, the actor playing the decapitated head of the demon is clearly wrapped up to his neck in a blue screen blanket with no special effect, well, in effect.
Cast: Sunil Bhumkar, Nishi Verma, Ritvika De, Master Kumar, Sanjay Wankhede, Shreeniwas Chitte, Kirti Shah, Ajay Sinha, and Sahukar Bhumkar, music: K V Mahadeva

Kali in a frenzy of bloodlust from **MATA MAHAKALI**

MAA CHHINNAMASTA

Mythologicals have always been popular on Indian TV. Here's an ad for one of the newer ones.

SATI BEHULA
2010, D: Manoj Kumar, Bengali, VCD, no subtitles
SATI BEHULA is a loose remake of the 1954 Sunil Ganguly-directed Bengali classic of the same name, which itself was based on the series of popular medieval epics called "The Manasamangals". These are tales about a devout woman named Behula, and her tussle with Manasa, Shiva's bitchy daughter and southern goddess of snakes (played to the sassy hilt by actress Bhagyashree Patwardhan). Hema Malini shows up halfway through the film as a blue-skinned Durga that annihilates a pesky wizard. **SATI BEHULA** features many Gods and Goddesses, and there is even a fun scene where Manasa and Durga square off in deciding the fate of the young woman's dead husband (whose bones she carries around with her).
Cast: Hema Malini, Bhagyashree, Sidharth, and Ashok Kumar; music: Uday Singh

THE TRIMURTI

Shakti Appendix 2

THREE MALE DEVOTEES OF SHAKTI CINEMA

As with the US film industry, very few women are directors in India, and there haven't been any that I know of that have made any of the "Angry Goddess" films I have covered. What makes India unique in this cinematic fraternity is that their religion, Hinduism, has powerful goddesses as part of its structure. However female-centric this genre seems to be, that is by no means to say that the men who make these films do so on a lark. As a fact, Durga and Kali are very popular deities among men as well as women, especially in the southern part of the subcontinent. These are devotional films, by the way, and as far as I know they are created as such...with some additional thrills to spice things up a bit. For this article, I chose the directors that I felt sincerely covered the genre...Kodi Ramakrishna, Rama Narayanan, and Bharati Kannan are, in my opinion, The Trimurti of Devi Cinema.

The term Trimurti is in reference to the three major male gods of Hinduism—Shiva, Braham, and Vishnu—who were powerless to defeat a demon that was indestructible. The demon tricked Brahma into making him impervious to

The Trimurti in Hinduism: the male gods Brahma, Vishnu and Shiva praise the great Goddess Durga.

any male god or demon, so his takeover of heaven was assured. The Trimurti was powerless against the demon, so they had to call forth the primal force of The Femenin in the form of Durga. Being female, Durga easily defeated the demon by running him though with her spear and cutting off his head, a scene often represented in the genre of Angry Goddess films.

AMMORU
1995, D: Kodi Ramakrishna, Telugu, DVD, subtitles

1975 was a fateful year for Goddess films when **JAI SARITOSHI MAA** became a blockbuster and helped jump-start round one of positive women-oriented Devotionals. Twenty years later, **AMMORU** hit the screens with similar results, albeit a lot crazier and a heck of a lot more bloody.

I didn't like **JAI SARITOSHI MAA**, so, for me, at least, **AMMORU** is the most important film for this sub-genre of devotional entertainment. The tale is not a new one, as can be seen from some of the earlier films (similar plot development, characters, etc.), but the manner in which director Ramakrishna rolls out his movie is altogether something new. The old elements include the usual pot-boiler family drama, which in this case is a troubled devotee who is also the unwanted daughter-in-law. Ramakrishna borrows folk elements seen in earlier devotional films such as **BETTADA THAYI** (1984, D: Perala), wherein a holy child arrives on the scene to assist the young woman, and eventually the local village goddess lends a hand. The big difference is the way Ramakrishna infuses a sense of terror and horror into the project, making **AMMORU** a sensational, kick-ass movie.

But let's start from the beginning.

The film opens in a rural Indian village wherein the desperate populace is in need of divine intervention. A plague has arrived, and there are prayers being offered to the local deities. Devout women gather and burn food offerings in hopes that one of the gods will bless and save them from the sickness. Unbeknownst to the women offering *pooja*, a wandering goddess witnesses the ceremony and visits the chanting women of the village. The goddess, Ammoru, disguised as an old beggar woman, slips into ceremony to observe the mortals. She goes to each woman and asks each in turn for a bite of the food that they are offering to the deities. She is turned down by all of the devotees, although one old woman gives The Goddess some nourishment at her home. In turn The Goddess informs the woman she can help the town and proceeds to make a magical concoction of plants that will protect each and every villager. Once this magical salve has been placed at the houses in the village the old woman must return to Ammoru and The Goddess can leave and all will be well. The old woman does what she is told, but realizes that the stranger is The Goddess and kills herself rather than allowing the deity leave to leave. True to her word, and since the woman never returned to her home alive, Ammoru stays put and eventually becomes the village protectorate.

Years later we are introduced to Bhanaia, who is a low-caste orphan, and a devotee of the Goddess Ammoru and assistant priestess to the local temple. All would be well in her world, but she falls in love with local town doctor, Surya. Apparently, Leelamma, the local bigwig in the village, wanted to marry her daughter off to the doctor and she isn't happy. If that doesn't cause enough problems for Bhanaia, she also witnesses Leelamma's son, an evil wizard by the name of Gorakh, burying a young virgin alive during a black magic ritual. The dark wizard, a devotee of the evil demon/monster Chanda (some demons and monsters are worshipped as much as gods and goddesses in parts of India), and is caught and placed in jail. In the meantime, Bhanaia marries the man of her dreams and moves in with his extended family, that of his cousin Leelamma (to be honest, I am still confused on some of India's family structure works).

Life gets even tougher when Gorakh is let out of prison early for "good behavior" and Bhanaia learns that he's actually part of her new family. The wizard sets his sights on torturing his accuser with black magic, and gets a lot of assistance from his relatives who detest the young woman. Bhanaia's pleas to The

Goddess are answered when a creepy little girl appears to her. The girl, a reincarnation of The Goddess, is able to protect Bhanaia for the most part, but she is turned out of the house after the family begins to complain of her anti-social behavior (hurting Gorakh, for example). Things get worse when her husband leaves for the USA—she is pregnant and expecting their first child—as her in-laws turn up the level of psychological and sociological torture from painful to deadly.

Eventually, even as her husband returns from his trip abroad, and as her world crumbles around her, the wizard kills her infant daughter and takes possession of Surya soul. The classic confrontation between good and evil is about to explode into action.

Bhanaia and her ailing husband are chased into the village temple by a gloating and hateful Gorakh. Trapped in the temple she pleads to The Goddess to do something—*anything*—to save her family. She pleads, begs, and eventually accuses The Goddess of standing around doing nothing as she, her most devoted servant, has her life threatened by an evil man. The wizard mocks Bhanaia and attacks her, and insults her goddess as he casually splashes blood on the temple idol. This is too much for The Goddess, and the stone eyes on the altar's idol spring to life. Ammoru manifests herself into her ferocious blue-skinned form and attacks the wizard. First she zaps him with divine lightening that throws him to the ground. Then, as did Durga in the classic Hindu epic of the Buffalo Demon, The Goddess spears the wizard with her trident, lops off his head, and holds a coconut bowl underneath to capture all the blood and gore. That accomplished, The Goddess transforms into the little girl, restores her devotee's family—husband and baby—before disappearing back into the idol.

The film would have become yet another dull devotional melodrama if it wasn't for the burst of wonderful fantasy elements: a giant divine hand rises out of the swirling water of a pond holding the holy child, a flying trident destroys a man and his cart, and the final gripping confrontation between good and evil. All of these scenes were presented in a newly-exploited tool of special effects: the computer. Prior to **AMMORU** most of the special effects in Indian cinema were primarily of the "in-camera" variety: crude stop-motion animation, wire work, bad miniatures, split-screen, double exposure, or some (very rare) post-production traveling matte sequences. The effects in Ramakrishna's film were digital effects and post-production work primarily created outside of the country in the United Kingdom (see Appendix 3 and the interview with Christopher Holmes, the man responsible for the look of **AMMORU**'s effects). To say that these effects were an important milestone in Indian film is an understatement. The sad fact is, very few films after **AMMORU** exploited this form of digital art to any impressive advantage.

Apparently, Ramakrishna was brought into the production only after its original director and a few of its principle stars left the project. The result was to catapult the film's "trinity" of Soundarya, Ramya Krishnan, and Rami Reddy into stardom. Soundarya was the most successful of the trio. She starred in many important films and was fast becoming a superstar until her death in 2004 at the age of 32. Her fragile-yet-powerful role of Bhanaia earned her a Nandi Award for Best Actress as well as the Filmfare Award for Best Actress (Telugu). Ramya Krishnan would go on to star in many devotional films, typically as a goddess of one form or another. To date she has appeared in over 200 films in five different languages. Rami Reddy, who died in 2011 from liver failure, would get typecast as the brooding bad man for many a low-budget horror and action film. His occasional big-budget appearance would be the result of his association his long-time friend Kodi Ramakrishna.

AMMORU had another plus going for it: the unusual soundtrack. Ramakrishna shied away from the typically over-produced slickness of a series of rocking, bopping pop musical numbers. Instead he concentrated on more folky compositions, which gave the film an edge of legitimacy over past and future devotional films. Chakravarthy and Chakravarthy's soundtrack is still the best ever produced, and not unlike the scores for the essential cobra lady films **NAGIN** (1976, D: Rajkumar Kohli) and **NAGINA** (1986, D: Harmesh Malhotra), this soundtrack was to forever influence the genre.
Cast: Soundaraya, Suresh, Rami Reddy, Ramya Krishnan, Baby Sunayana, and Babu Mohan; music: K. Chakravarthy and K. Srinivasa Chakravarthy

KANNATHAL
1998, D: Bharathi Kannan, Tamil, YouTube, no subtitles
KANNATHAL is first Angry Goddess film from director Bharathi Kannan (a.k.a. Bhaarathy Kannan, a.k.a. S. Bharathkikannan), and it is one heck of an introduction. Or maybe I should rephrase that to read "the first film that I know of", as there is very little information on Kannan anywhere. In the first five minutes a young woman is having the life force of her unborn child drained from her body by an evil *trantrik*. A group of Kali worshipers storm his encampment, and in a pitched war of magical words and devotional chants the wizard is struck by divine fire and falls into a river. After that explosive introduction, we are treated to a wonderful credits sequence featuring traditional Goddess ceremonies (actual footage, something Kannan will always weave into his films). Just what that has to do with the rest of the film is beyond me.

Kantata, a young devout woman, comes under the spell of a womanizing jerk (actor Karan), who drinks, curses, smokes, and abuses her. When he forces her to be his common-law wife, her father, a poor temple musician, dies of a broken heart. Her extended family of twin sister and younger siblings moves in with her boyfriend's equally abusive family. After suffering under their daily beatings, the sister poisons herself and the young children. The jerk decides that he wants to get married, but not to Kantata, who he finds is pregnant. She gives birth to a daughter which he doesn't love, and in a bid to make his life more pleasant, he murders Kantata at a local village shrine dedicated to the demon Ravana. He buries her there and leaves to go live his life (it is unclear at this point just what happens to his and Kantata's daughter—subtitles would help).

Later that night during a rather a intense prayer session at a local temple to the Goddess Kali, The Goddess enters the body of the dead girl and she is reincarnated as the aspect of the living Goddess Kannathal. Meanwhile,

Very top: The Telugu DVD art
Above four: photos from **AMMORU**: The actors and the roles which are now archetypes: Baby Sunayana as the *Child Goddess*, Ramya Krishnan as the *Goddess*, Soundaraya as the *Devotee*, and Rami Reddy as the *Evil Tantrik*..

the jerk has moved on to someone else, not knowing that this new woman in his life is a friend of Kantata. The vengeful spirit begins to kill off his family one by one, and his new girlfriend suspects that it is her friend back from the dead. In the meantime, the jerk is back to his old game of raping women. In the end he is confronted by Kantata as The Holy Trinity of Hindu goddesses: Parvati, Durga, and Kali. In a riveting sequence she transforms from one goddess to the next as the horrified man looks on. He is hunted down, speared, and finally beheaded and in a sequence full of cut-aways to a nearby devotional procession, that of Durga's slaying of the buffalo demon Mahisasura.

Kannan has a wonderful cinematic eye, especially when capturing the startling scenery of festivals and temple folks. The digital graphics by The EFX Chennai Company are kept to a minimum, and whenever The Goddess appears she is not so much of a cartoon character as some other directors present her. The obvious comedic elements are agonizing to sit though, and I doubt that subtitles would have made me like them any more. For once I would really love to see a film of **KANNATHAL's** potential caliber not have the horrible comic relief that permeates almost every Indian film outside of a few arthouse productions. Just when the plot really knuckles down for the final half, we are treated to long boring segments of some babbling idiot. Kannan must find the comedian hilarious as he has a cameo with the guy about drinking whisky. Ugh. On a final note, the soundtrack and musical interludes are especially well done.
cast: Karan, Neena, Music: Deva

DEVI
1999, D: Kodi Ramakrshna, Telugu, DVD, subtitles
AMMORU may still be Ramakrishna's most accomplished work, but it was **DEVI** that first grabbed my attention. The plot is slightly less convoluted than usual, although it holds tight to the usual suspects and god-awful comedy bits often found within this genre. Like her sister film **AMMORU**, **DEVI** stands as one of the best examples of Shakti Cinema.

Devi, a lovely cobra goddess (the actress Prema), is left stranded in our realm when the colossal Shiva mothership that deposited her on Earth leaves without one of its crew. She befriends a young woman (Vanitha) who is tormented by family members who doubt her sincere devotion to the Goddess Kali. Together, they overcome the evil *tantrik* Dantra (Abu Salim), who has buddied up with a demon to destroy Devi. In the meantime, both fall in love with some handsome leading men, all the while dodging magical bullets aimed at them by the *tantrik*. The final explosive showdown is a metaphysically-infused special effects dance number featuring a stone idol that comes alive, a giant six-headed cobra, exploding planetoids and the return of the mothership. In the end Devi renounces her divinity so that she can stay with the humans and marry her man.

DEVI falls in the middle ground between a Naag and Goddess film with the main character straddling both territories (**DEVI** was also covered in Weng's Chop #3). The film was heavily promoted as a "Special Effects Movie", and unlike some of its cousins, it didn't disappoint me or the general audiences—**DEVI** was a massive regional hit. The crazy effects for this film are by Madhava Reddy, who later went on as a digital film technician (under the guise of "Rainmaker") for over 40 films primarily in the fantasy genre, including Hollywood productions **THE CORE** (2003) and **I, ROBOT** (2004). **DEVI** is the only film of this genre that has been officially released to a wide audience in the United States with English subtitles. **DEVI** was retitled **GODDESS** (natch) and it is currently available for streaming through Netflix. This film should not be confused, in any way shape or form, with the 1960 Bengali classic **DEVI** from famed arthouse director Satyajit Ray. Ray's film is a Devotional, but the plot is more of a social drama without all of the trappings of your typical fantastic Goddess production.
Cast: Prema, Vanitha, Abu Salim. Bhanuchander, and Babu Mohan; music: Devi Sri Prasad

Now we come to the third member of the Trimuti, and the one director that tries his damndest to be like his brothers but just can't seem to pull everything together.

PALAYATHU AMMAN
2000, D: Rama Narayanan, Tamil, DVD, no subtitles
PALAYATHU AMMAN opens as a yogi is announcing the birth of a virtuous child that will end evil in the world. In the meantime we see a pregnant young woman having an ultrasound exam at a nearby hospital. On the sonogram screen we see the usual image of a child holding a trident, the holy weapon typically associated with divine power. An evil *trantrik* gets wind of this and attempts to put the kibosh on the birth by first killing the yogi with a magic flower and then going after the expecting mother.

(At this point I have to point out that director Narayanan has to have the oddest sense of costume design of any devotional filmmaker. The bad guys in **PALAYATHU AMMAN** are perfect examples. First of all, our evil wizard has a gang of bumbling sidekicks (which are annoying to say the least), and second of all, they all wear bright orange parachute-style jumpsuits with white boots and opera gloves. You know who the head man is by the large chartreuse devil's head embroidered on the front and back of his outfit. This sort of clownish appearance certainly knocks this villain's credibility down quite a few pegs. Still, he is a ruthless killer and knows the black arts…he just has a horrible fashion sense.)

Top to bottom: The Goddess takes names and collects heads in Kannan's **KANNATHAL**, the US DVD art for Ramakrishna's **DEVI**, and poster art for Narayanan's **RAJA KALIAMMAN**.

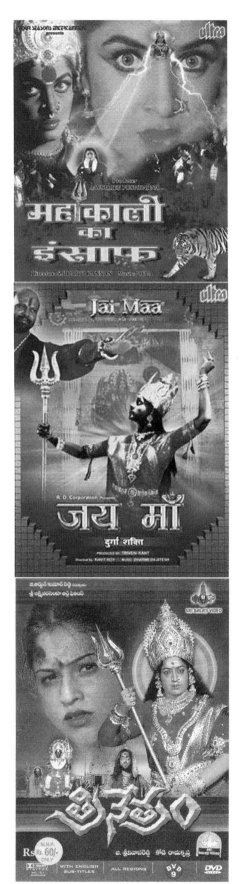

Top to bottom: DVD art for: Kannan's **SRI RAJA RAJESWARI**, Narayanan's **KOTTAI MARIAMMAN**, and Ramakrishna's **TRINETRAM**.

The young mother gives birth to a baby girl, and after some time visits the temple of the Goddess Palayathu. On one of her visits she is befriended by the deity herself in the guise of a fellow devotee. Over the course of the film the Goddess Palayathu (a Parvati variant played by Meena) looks after the woman, the woman's charming husband and their child, intercepting and sometimes confounding the wizard in his attempt to kill the family. She offers the wizard a chance to turn over a new leaf, but instead he laughs at her, kidnaps the child, and sends a titanic fire-breathing horned skeleton (whose roars sound suspiciously like Godzilla's) after the little girl's father. The wizard throws the child to the ground preparing to kill her…this proves too much for The Goddess. In a rage, she invokes Durga and then Kali. The giant monster is demolished and, in a scene lifted from **AMMORU**, The Goddess storms out of a temple to kill the *tantrik*.

Narayanan's **PALAYATHU AMMAN** was released a year after **DEVI**, and it is his most blatant attempt to cash in on Ramakrishna's visuals. Narayanan is a competent director, and he has shot the musical *filmi* sequences for other movies, however it's his love of cheap post-production digital effects that does him in. Despite the horrible effects, **PALAYATHU AMMAN** was very popular as a devotional "woman's film", and was well-known for the comedic styling of actor Vivek (ugh, I find him just awful, but who am I to criticize another culture's Jerry Lewis?). **PALAYATHU AMMAN** is much easier to locate under its Hindi dub title of **DEVI MAA**.
Cast: Ramki, Meena, Vivek, Divya Unni, and Mayilsamy; SA RajKumar

AAJ KA DEVI PUTRA
2000, D: Kodi Ramakrishna, Telugu, YouTube
AAJ KA DEVI PUTRA is essentially Ramakrishna's take on **RAIDERS OF THE LOST ARK** (D: Steven Spielberg, 1981), and the film turns out to be one of the master's best works, almost on par with **AMMORU** and **DEVI**. More of an action adventure film than devotional, **AAJ KA DEVI PUTRA** is all about a race to find the ancient holy relic of Dwaraka, the village where Krishna is said to have grown up. The relic, a chest, was thought lost after a monstrous tidal wave sent the village to the bottom of the ocean—however, it has been located. In the box is a wealth beyond measure as it contains the essence of a goddess. The ghost of a little girl leads a trio of adventurers to the chest, but they are intercepted by a band of men out to possess its power. The climax of the film has The Goddess annihilating the thieves and returning the chest to the bottom of the sea.

AAJ KA DEVI PUTRA is a thoroughly entertaining film and, happily, Ramakrishna delivers a devotional fantasy that does not follow all the conventions of his previous movies. A.k.a. **DEVI PUTRUDU** (Hindi dub).
Cast: Venkatesh Daggubati, Anjala Zaveri, Soundarya, Bhupinder Singh, Baby Cherry, and Prema; music: Mani Sharma

SRI RAJA RAJESWARI
2001, D: Bharati Kannan, Tamil, VCD, no subtitles
Here we have the second film in what I consider director Bharati Kannan's Devi "quadrilogy", and it is darn good in my opinion. The story is reminiscent of the popular Nagin genre wherein revenge is the driving force for its supernatural entity. Come to think of it, it's a pretty decent remake of Rajkumar Kohli's **NAGIN** (1976).

Ramya Krishnan stars as a rural tribal woman who is murdered along with her lover the day before their wedding. The murderers are city men out for the thrill of raping a "savage" (actress Ramya Krishnan). They double their bad karma by running the woman through with a ceremonial trident stolen from an outdoor temple belonging to the popular rural goddess, Pidari Amman (a variant of Kali). She dies cursing them. On the same day she dies a young city couple have a child while visiting the temple of Raja Rajeswari (a deity related to Pidari Amman). Because of this there will be a fateful connection between the two.

The young child grows into adulthood (actress Bhanupriya), unaware that she is in any way connected to the death of the tribal woman decades earlier. That horrible realization occurs on a fateful day at the very same temple where she was born. She is stunned by violent visions triggered when she witnesses the ritual pouring of milk over the idol of The Goddess. The spirit of the vengeful nag possesses her and she sets out to destroy the lives of some very bad men. She is able to change into a cobra or just about any form she chooses to accomplish her goals, but there is one problem. The Goddess Piadari has a fondness for the children of the evil men, as they are very devout and worship her daily. She is not about to let the nag *devta* destroy their lives. The two entities cross paths more than once, and when the film reaches its climax we are treated to a very entertaining deity dance-off. Pidari forces her hand by invoking Kali, and the cobra deity is beaten but allowed to rejoin/reincarnate as the Goddess Raja Rajeswari.

Or so I am led to believe. There are over 100 different local South Indian goddesses, many that are indigenous to a single village (as is the goddess in **AMMORU**). *These deities are themselves different aspects of the Mahavidyas, which are Devi in origin. Each goddess can be identified by her special iconography, which is typically what she holds in her hands (weapons, plants, shells, tools, or even severed heads) or possibly what she may be seated upon (lion, tiger, peacock, mule, etc.) or even what kind of jewelry she wears (necklace of skulls, garland of flowers, and so forth). Identifying a goddess through the combination of these icons is rather tricky, especially if you are not familiar with the language (which I am not). I am bound to get some of the goddesses mixed up, but I'm sure I got this one right.*

SRI RAJA RAJESWARI is definitely one of the better Nagin/Goddess films and a showcase for Kannan's emerging talent as a director. He was lucky to get Ramya Krishnan before her career took a tumble. There is one disturbing sequence which has our possessed woman transforming into the likeness of a child. In this form she visits the home of one of her attackers and befriends the man's wife. The child stays the night but is discovered by the man to be a *nagin*. He summons a *tantrik*/snake-charmer who plays his horn to charm the demigoddess and then lures the little girl out of the house. She is led into a clearing in a forest and buried alive! Of course, the possessed creature returns anyway to complete her mission by killing the man.
A.k.a. **MAHAKALI KA INSAAF** (Hindi dub title).
Cast: Ramki, Ramya Krishnan, Bhanupriya; music: Deva

DEVULLU - *"Gods"*
2001, D: Kodi Ramakrishna, Telugu, no subtitles
DEVULLU is Ramakrshna's follow-up to his wildly successful film **AAJ KA DEVI PUTRA**. Maybe he wanted to tone his style down or follow a different path of a more child/family-oriented Devotional, but whatever the case, **DEVULLU** failed to keep me interested (although I managed to sit through its 150-minute running time, as I'm a true fan of the director). The film follows the devotional adventures of a boy and girl as they travel from one to temple to the next looking for what must be spiritual guidance. The only part of the film that I found in any way compelling was the appearance of Ramya Krishnan as the Goddess Kanakadurga. She appeared around halfway through the film…for all of about five minutes. **DEVULLU** is very popular with Indian film critics. It got rave reviews and a whole host of "thumbs up" from critics who may have grown tired of Ramakrishna's more action-based devotionals. I, on the other hand, had a hard time swallowing the horrible comedy, the sappy child actors, and the awful musical numbers.
Cast: Baby Nitya, Nandan, Prithvi, Ramya Krishnan, Raasi; music: Vandemataram Srinivas

KOTTAI MARIAMMAN
2001, D: Rama Narayanan, Tamil, YouTube, no subtitles
KOTTAI MARIAMMAN is freakishly entertaining Goddess insanity and Narayanan's most accomplished film in this genre. None of his films are *fantastic*—most are mediocre or just plain horrible—nevertheless, **KOTTAI MARIAMMAN** manages to deliver where his other works fail. Surprisingly, the plot is not all that convoluted, which is a good thing as most of his films get lost in family drama and foster logic loopholes you could ride an elephant through. Then we have his digital effects which are cartoony but integrated quite effectively into the film. The final confrontation between good and evil is exceptionally psychedelic…but we'll get to that in a minute.

The film opens with an arrogant *tantrik* (played by a brooding Rami Reddy, the Telugu heavy filling his post-**AMMORU** duties as the film antagonist), materializing in a temple dedicated to the Goddess Mari Amman. He's decked out in a Narayanan classic low-rent evil *tantrik* outfit consisting of a bright blood-red robe embroidered with images of skulls. His attempt to damage the main idol is met with divine lightning and he is zapped back to his lair. With his mission to defile The Goddess and her temple waylaid, he plots another route.

Lakshmi, a young woman, learns that her husband's vision is in danger of never returning, so she approaches a temple and becomes devoted to The Goddess in hopes of divine intervention. She plucks out the stone eyes of the oversized head of The Goddess and returns home with them. With the idol's eyes in her possession she now sees the truth: she was tricked into blinding the idol by her scheming husband who is aligned with a corrupt doctor and the *tranrik*. She gathers up her baby girl and flees her home, still possessing the eyes. Her husband gives chase, and Lakshmi is eventually shot by her spouse. She collapses to the ground dying, but not before she affixes the eyes to a nearby tree. The tree becomes animated and dances about full of The Goddess's goodness. The husband is blown to smithereens by a divine trident that emanates from the tree, and the *tantrik* is sent scurrying back to his lair once again. The child, Prya, is left alone in the forest to be raised (we assume) by The Goddess.

Prya grows into adulthood as the gorgeous temple priestess (the actress Roja) to The Goddess. This is where the film gets really weird…in a good way. There are numerous *filmi* numbers featuring Prya with the green-skinned goddess. They are best friends, with the young woman treating Mari Aamman as if she was her own mother—or better yet, a loving older sibling. There is a simply ridiculous scene featuring a multitude of goddesses marching around the temple. They are accompanied by a dancing trident which boogies about, bopping and jiving to the rocking dance number. As silly as this may sound, these sequences add to the film's sense of fantastic wonder rather than being a deterrent.

As is typical for these films, Prya is a single woman with no family connections, and as is a common practice, she is "adopted" by a cruel family who treats her badly. Luckily for her, The Goddess helps her deal with her horrid family in the form of a holy child. The child is very similar to the girl that appears in **AMMORU**, although she is far less creepy. The child runs interference between Prya and her family and rights wrongs with magic. The film bogs down for a bit as we are introduced to the comic relief and the criminal activities of her step-brother. The saving grace from here on in is a series of charming interludes of her interaction with The Goddess as they meet at the holy tree to discuss girly stuff.

Not that far away from the woman, we have the *tantrik* gaining strength and knowledge in the black arts from a horned demon. However, every time he attempts to do something dastardly The Goddess shows up to spoil his plans. She laughs at him for being so foolish. Far from discouraging the wizard, these interactions only steel his determination to take revenge against Prya and The Goddess.

The final confrontation between Prya, the wizard and The Goddess comes to a weird special effects head wherein the wizard transforms into giant scorpionoid monster to kill Prya. Just when things appear dire, a grinning Goddess blows the monster apart with one hearty laugh.

I was surprised that I liked this film as much as I did. There is an overwhelming positive interaction between Prya and The Goddess which was as refreshing as it was unusual for this genre. With other directors, the connection between devotee and divine is often one of unknowing friendship (as in Kannan's **SRI BANNARI AMMAN**, 2002, *reviewed below*) or worship from afar. Here it is very human, as if The Goddess represented is the woman's best friend, albeit green-skinned, decked out in regal garb and wielding a huge trident.

A.k.a. **JAI MAA DURGA SHAKTI** (Hindi dub; with misleading information on various VCDs and websites as directed by Ravit Roy).
Cast: Roja, Rami Reddy, Devayani, Vivek, Karan; music: Deva

TRINETRAM - *"The Third Eye"*
2002, D: Kodi Ramakrishna, Telugu, DVD, subtitles
Nine variants of the Shakti are represented in yet another colorful and special effects-filled epic from the hyperactive mind of Telugu filmmaker Kodi Ramakrishna. Other directors (Om Sai Prakash, for example) have attempted to deliver on the deal, but few have done it with Ramakrishna's style. While the film isn't one of Ramakrishna's best, it is still head and shoulders above anything that Narayanan could ever hope to achieve.

The film begins with the tale of a tidal wave threatening to wipe out an ancient city called Hayagreerapuram (not unlike in **AAJ KA DEVI PUTRA**). The divine feminine manifests herself as the Goddess Trinetram to save and protect the city. However, by doing so she is bound to that location, and when one of her devotees is in trouble in another city, the Goddess Trinetram is prohibited from leaving her city to help the young woman. So, she calls on the aid of eight other goddesses as well as Lord Narasimha to help out her devotee. Her young woman is being held captive by an abusive husband and his nasty *tantrik* buddy. It's up to the God Narasimha to work with The Goddesses to help free the woman (a nice change of pace for these estrogen-filled epics).

TRINETRAM is somewhat more subdued than most of Ramakrishna's work, although way too many comedic moments and dodgy effects work all but destroy a film that could be been stellar. The appearance of Lord Narasimha, the ferocious lion-head avatar of Vishnu, was a total surprise and well worth sitting through the film to see. Such an odd thing to have the most manly form of all of Vishnu's avatars show up and save the day in what is otherwise a goddess-oriented devotional film.
Cast: Sijju, Rasi, K.R. Vijaya, L.B. Sri Lam, and Shiva Reddy; music: Vandemataram

Billboard art for the Tamil film **THAYE BHUVANESWARI**

SRI BANNARI AMMAN
2002, D: S. Barathi Kannan , Tamil, YouTube, no subtitles
You know what is going to go down when within the first fifteen minutes a greedy man (played with mustache-twirling nastiness by famous Tamil actor Karan) destroys a statue to the Goddess Durga under instructions from a shifty demon-worshipping *tantrik* (played by the late badass actor Rajan P. Dev). Underneath the shattered idol the man finds the riches he is after, however The Goddess soon comes a-calling. A slick and entertaining Devotional with a wonderful soundtrack as well as some memorable musical numbers. In her travels to find the criminal and his wizard sidekick, The Goddess (played with warmth and style by the actress Suganya) visits an assortment of villages and aids women with troubled childbirth, ill children, and other such things that the goddess of health is right to do. Her only request for payment is a simple bowl of food. Along the way, The Goddess befriends a proud and devout woman (super-cute actress Laya) who previously identified our criminal as the killer in a series of murders of young girls and is in need of divine protection. The killer gets off on a technicality and sets about to ruin the life of the woman who fingered him. The Goddess saves her from an acid attack (something not uncommon in India) and saves her village from a plague of smallpox, among other abuses. In the meantime, the *tantrik* is having a hard time battling The Goddess, as he has to deal with both her ethereal and material versions thwarting his evil plans.

I found **SRI BANNARI AMMAN** to be utterly fascinating in that the young woman in the film didn't have to rely on some boyfriend or husband. She buddies up rather quickly with The Goddess and they hang out a lot in the film chatting, brushing each other's hair, dancing and other girly stuff. As much as most Goddess films are female-based in their structure and theory, very few of them are as fully feminist in delivering their message. That is until about half way into the film, when our heroine is blackmailed into marrying the criminal. It's all part of the *tantrik*'s master plan, bent on screwing with The Goddess and weakening her power so he can gather more celestial power for himself.

The men scheme to take control of the famous Bannari Amman temple. However, girl power stages a comeback for a rip-roaring finale wherein our heroine is divinely impregnated by Kali under instructions from a priestess of the Goddess Māri (an aspect of Durga), and all three goddess are invoked to put an end to the male plan of domination. In an effects-filled finale the *tantrik* is able to invoke a devilish bull-headed titan which is sent to destroy the woman, but faces off with Kali instead. Kali, known for her demon-killing abilities, makes short work of the monster then sets her sights on a boasting *tantrik*. She catches up with the *tantrik* and eviscerates him. As Kali is just about to stomp the husband into jelly his wife pleads for his life holding "their" newborn. Kali down-shifts back into a loving Durga who lets him go free, hopefully a changed man. The end.

As I have said previously, Kannan has a love for idiotic humor in his films. In the case of **SRI BANNARI AMMAN** there are seriously unfunny sequences involving dwarves smacking people with sticks, drunks doing ridiculous things, and loads of funny sound effects. Excise those elements and director Kannan would have had a nearly-perfect film as far as fantastic Goddess Devotionals go. The digital effects are kept to a minimum, and the *tantrik*'s dark and horrible temple surpasses the usual crappy sets with plastic skulls hanging from blinking Christmas lights that you usually see. Director Kannan has a cameo as a Durga priest who calms The Goddess after her statue is destroyed at the beginning of the film.
Cast: Karan, Vadivelu, Srikanth, Rajan P. Dev, Laya, Vijayashanthi, Suganya, and Nalini; music: Vijaya T. Rajendar

RAJA KALIAMMAN
2003, D: Rama Narayanan, Tamil (no subtitles)/Hindi (subtitles), YouTube/VCD/DVD
Director Rama Narayanan is known as the busiest man in Indian cinema, and he holds the world's record for directing the maximum number of films during his career (although, as a fan of the late Spanish director Jess Franco, I would consider disputing this fact). Narayanan has something in the order of 125 films under his belt and he dips into all sorts of genres. His Goddess-based Devotionals are plentiful but hard to track down. That may sound like a contradiction, but considering dodgy Indian distribution and film rights, not all of his productions in this genre are available. What you can get are his Ramakrishna-wannabe movies like **RAJA KALIAMMAN**, which looks to be his last Goddess film for a while, as the fervor for such plots has waned in favor of reincarnation films like Ramakrishna's **ARUNDHATI** (2009) and ghost/horror films by the likes of Ram Gopal Varma, Vikram Bhatt, and Puja Bedi.

Goddesses abound in this classic tale of an abused devotee of Kali who is in dire need of divine intervention. The film has the same basic plot as **KOTTAI MARIAMMAN** without the girl power bonding. **RAJA KALIAMMAN** flaunts its ample budget with decent sets, okay cinematography and the musical numbers are fine, but it is nowhere as good as some of his previous films. Ramya Krishnan, as usual, is stunning as the Goddesses Durga and Kali. Her devotee Meenakshi is played with a puzzled conviction by the super-cute Tamil model-turned-actress, Kausalya, and Nizhalgal Ravi is perfect as the mustache-twirling, goatee-stroking evil *tantrik*.

The effects are pretty standard for a Narayanan film, and one wonders why he keeps using the same material over and over. Surely there was room in the budget for better digital imagery. Goddesses blip in and out of the scenes, throw magical tridents and so forth, without any real pizzazz. Luckily for the viewer, the last fifteen minutes more than make up for the two previous lack-

luster hours as The Goddess destroys the *tantrik* and then blinds Meenakshi's jerk-of-a-husband (played with perfect nastiness by Indian cinema bad boy Karan). But just as The Goddess is going in for the kill, her devotee pleads for her husband's life and the deity, forever friends with her devotee, forgives his transgressions (and thus he is "born again").

Also known as **TU HI DURGA TU HI KALI**, which is the Hindi dubbed version more commonly found with English subtitles. Not the best example of the director's work, but he's made a lot worse.
Cast: Karan, Kausalya, and Ramya Krishnan; music: SA Rajkumar

THAYE BHUVANESWARI
2003, D: Bhaarathy Kannan, Tamil, DailyMotion, no subtitles
An excellent post-**AMMORU** film with some fine horror elements including possession of a little girl by an evil spirit, but that's not unexpected coming from director Bhaarathy Kannan.

Prema stars as the wife of a good man (popular Malayalam actor Sai Kumar) whose father is the temple priest for the Goddess Bhuvaneshwari (one of the ten aspects of the Kali/Mahavidya goddesses) who is played by Soundarya. They have a child called Devi who is your typical bratty six-year-old. The temple priest is very popular with the devotee of The Goddess as he is able to cure illnesses and help those bitten by cobras just by beseeching the deity. Unbeknownst to them, a villain has been released from prison, and with the help of his manservant and his insane mother, plans on enacting vengeance against the priest and his family. Why? Oh, that's where everything gets complicated. And what's an Indian film if it isn't twisting and confusing?

In a bizarre move, the villain's mother is killed during the holy ceremony of Vijayadashami (one of the alternate titles of this film which commemorates the victory of Goddess Durga over the demon Mahishasur) and her blood splashes on the temple's portable Bhuvaneshwari idol. The statue's desecration is really where the film begins to pick up steam. Devi is possessed by an angry spirit and proceeds to cause all sorts of mischief and eventually kills both her grandparents. In desperation, Devi's parents turn to a Kali priest who is able to exorcise her, but the terror doesn't stop there as the villain-cum-wizard transforms into a three-headed, six-armed demon for a showdown with The Goddess. The boasting wizard miscalculates as the Goddess Bhuvaneshwari invokes a really, *really* pissed off Kali who chases the man down and devours him in a single gulp.

The horror elements are fairly low-key digital effects; grainy images of gory weirdness and supernatural strangeness. As with his previous films, Kannan is able to effectively integrate them into his well-composed and well-shot set-pieces. He's no Kodi Ramakrishna, but Kannan is fairly close to getting there. Prema is excellent as usual and Soundarya, like other actresses in the role of The Goddess such as Meena and Ramya Krishnan, makes for a sexy deity.
Cast: Soundarya, Prema, Sai Kumar, and Anandraj; Music: Deva

KUTTY PISASU
2010, D: Kodi Ramakrishna, Telugu, DailyMotion, no subtitles
From what I can make out, **KUTTY PISASU** is Ramakrishna's take on what constitutes a kiddie flick with some silly Goddess involvement. An obnoxious little girl is possessed by dead female wizard when her guardian goddess (Ramya Krishnan) withdraws her protection. She goes on a rampage of destruction and assortment mischief until the deity returns to assist her. Not that fun of a film despite its obvious family-friendly plot and abundance of, ugh, child actors.

The film is loaded with the usual Ramakrishna digital effects, although most of these are of the Saturday morning cartoon variety: a Transformers-style robot, a dancing teddy bear, goofy elephants, etc. The soundtrack is even less thrilling.

I've only included this film because of Ramya Krishnan, who has little to do in this film other than look glamorous as The Goddess, *and* the film was produced by Rama Narayanan. No wonder **KUTTY PISASU** is so horrible.
Cast: Ramya Krishnan, Sangeetha, Kaveri, Keerthika Baby, Delhi Ganesh, and Ramji; music: Deva

JAI BHADRAKALI
2010, D: Kodi Ramakrishna, Telugu, *whereabouts unknown*
Produced late in the current cycle of Goddess films, **JAI BHADRAKALI** is

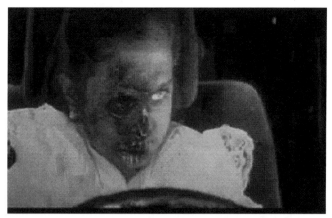
Demon-possessed brat from **THAYE BHUVANESWARI**

a mystery. It started production in 2008, but was stalled when Ramakrishan was hospitalized with a blood clot. This film was supposed to be his follow-up to his blockbuster reincarnation fantasy **ARUNDHATI**. There was an announcement in 2010 that the film was ready for release, but it is nowhere to be found on any form of visual media, VCD, DVD, YouTube, DailyMotion, or even torrents. A few of Srinivas' *filmi* compositions are available for download, but they are mediocre at best, which may be one reason for the film's mysterious demise.

JAI BHADRAKALI starred Prema, Ramya Krishna, and Rami Reddy—pretty much the classic lineup for any devotional production by Ramakrishna or anyone looking for a hit. It even stars Abu Salem in what looks like a reprise of his badass role from **DEVI**. A sexy Naag couple is also in the mix. So where is it? The plot is unknown and I can only find some very stagy production stills. Hell, even if the film was garbage I would still watch it.

Not to be confused with the 1967 A.C. Thiruluga Chander-directed Telugu thriller of the same name. Chander's film features symbolic rather than actual Goddess elements.
Cast: Prema, Rami Reddy, Ramya Krishnan, Saikumar, Abu Salem, Nagesh, Ramaprabha, Prasadbabu, AVS, Babumohan, MS Narayana, Rajitha & Radha Prashanti; music: Vandemataram Srinivas

AVATHARAM
2013, D: Kodi Ramakrishna, Telugu, *not yet released*
AVATHARAM looks like it could possibly be yet another very cool Ramakrishna devotional fantasy film. The film is currently in post-production as of the printing of this article. The plot sounds pretty cool. The time is 2013 and the Hindu gods are in need of saving by their devotees. In a recent interview Ramakrishna was reported as saying, "This film will cater to mass audience. We have given priority to graphics in this film." Which could be good thing…or not. Here's hoping that the director doesn't shelve this film like his last few projects.
Cast: Bhanu priya, Rishi, Radhika Pandit, music: Ghantadi Krishna

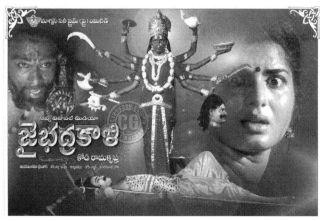
Promotional art for Kodi Ramakrishna's MIA film **JAI BHADRAKALI**

THE GODDESS ANNOYED

Although my love of these films is for the Angry Goddess, the really pissed-off deity that emerges from her temple to rain bloody vengeance down on whatever poor soul happens to be in her way, there is a slightly different variant. I have come to appreciate the lighter side of The Goddess. This calmer aspect is a side which is far more popular with the fairer sex than your usual Durga or Kali rampage, although I have been told that a good divine hammering of an evil tantrik elicits a murmur—if not a very vocal expression of appreciation—from the female audience. The following films are of a milder response, atypical to those found in the rest of this article. They will range in their divine intervention. The significance nod from a loving goddess can change the life of a miserable devotee (as in *JAI SARITOSHI MAA*). Then, as in *JAI KAALI*, The Goddess may possess her devotee in order to right some wrong. Or The Goddess can appear in a hospital and zap a dying man back to health because his family prays for her help. In these films The Goddess seems slightly annoyed, but will lift a hand to help those who worship her. Nothing too crazy (well, *JAI KAALI* is pretty intense)—just enough to keep the world in balance.

(It may be noted that in films such as *JAI SARITOSHI MAA* you will see a lot of ritual and devotional ceremonies. I am utterly fascinated by ritual and find even the most tedious film of this category to have some redeeming value when some obscure liturgy is observed. Call it anthropological interest.)

JAI SARITOSHI MAA
1975, D: Ahmed Siddiqui, Hindi, VCD/DVD

If I were to hand you a DVD and say, "Watch this film as it is without a doubt the most important production in Shakti cinema," it would be Siddiqui's **JAI SARITOSHI MAA**. The movie is in no way a thriller. Not much action in it, either. It is pure family drama that mixes in devotion and an assortment of gods and goddesses. **JAI SARITOSHI MAA** was a meager low-budget production that turned out to be one of the biggest hits in Indian cinema. The film's folksy plot about the Santoshi Maa, a.k.a. Goddess of Satisfaction (the god Gancha's daughter), made perfect sense to millions of Indian women. The Goddess Saritoshi Maa is easily accessible to the everyday woman through a simple ritual (which the film also demonstrates).[1]

---

[1] Das, Veena. 1980. "The Mythological Film and Its Framework of Meaning: An Analysis of Jai Santoshi Ma." India International Centre Quarterly 8:1, 43-56.

The plot: Satyavati, the daughter of a poor widower, falls in love with a young man and they are soon wed. Turns out she has married into a family of tyrants and she is abused both verbally and physically. In her woe, she turns to the Goddess Santoshi Maa for strength. She is also tormented by three *other* goddesses that are jealous of her devotion. In the end, Santoshi intervenes and happiness is again bestowed on Satyavati.

I don't particularly like this film, although because of its importance, I had to watch it. Many similar dull films followed suit in an attempt to cash in on this new fad, and there were also Shiva and Vishnu devotionals that tried their hand at generating a similar gut response from Indian audiences. Vijay Sharma's Shiva-devotional **MAHAPAVAN TEERTH YATRA** (1975), released shortly after **JAI SANTISHU MAA,** has all the hallmarks of a blockbuster if you count the calamities that befall the film's main character, a woman. But her pleas were to Shiva rather than Durga, Kali, or any of the 160 other goddesses. A good film—and a popular one—but nowhere near the quality one would expect from a Goddess film that is still one of the highest-grossing Indian films of all time.

Kanan Kaushal, the actress who played Satyavati, was no newcomer to the devotional scene, as she starred in a wonderful 1974 Hanuman epic **HANUMAN VIJAY**, and had appeared as a goddess in the film **SATI SULOCHANA** (1969), and later in **JAI DWARKADHEESH** (1977) and **108 TEERTHATRA** (1987). But none of her other roles ever touched the souls of Indian women like that of Satyavati.

JAI SANTOSHI MAA was remade in 2006, and although this "modern" take on the '70s film was successful, it was nowhere near as powerful on the Indian psyche as the original version was. (For those of you interested in just how influential the original was—and to some extent still is—there is a wide range of web-resources and papers written about the film and its cultural relevance). As for the hundreds of other Devotionals produced since the 1900s, most of them seem to have been lost or are languishing in film vaults or decaying on old VHSs or VCDs. As far as I know, after **JAI SANTOSHI MAA**, it was two decades before Kodi Ramakrishna's **AMMORU** took names and kicked ass, ushering in the second revival of Shakti cinema—the angry variant.
Cast: Bharat Bhushan, Ashish Kumar, Kanan Kaushal, and Anita Guha; music: C. Arjun

CHOTTANIKARAI AMMAN
1976, D: Dubai Mani, Malayalam, YouTube, no subtitles
The movie is based on the miracles of Bhagavathi, the name for a variety of popular local deities in Western India; typically a variant of Durga, Kannaki, Parvati, Saraswati, etc. The Goddess shows up in a wide variety of forms to help devotees. There are scenes of The Goddess appearing to women who pray in forest clearings, in devotional ceremonies, and, in one scene, to a woman who pounds her forehead against a nail in a temple until The Goddess acknowledges her. Not an amazing production, but one of many that tumbled out of various Indian film companies after the success of **JAI SANTISHU MAA**…not unlike the many **AMMORU** clones that followed that film's smashing success.
Cast: Sreevidya, Unnimeri, Meena, Ravi Menon, Vincent, Sreelatha, Adoor Bhasi, Balan K Nair, Cochin Haneefa, and Shobha; music: unknown

JAI MAA VANDEVI
1990, D: K S L Swamy, Hindi, DVD, no subtitles
Pretty lame supernatural family squabble devotional comedy film about a lecherous man who murders a woman and in the end trips and falls on a trident outside of a Durga temple chasing some divine tail. He is impaled on the weapon and dies, but not before confessing his sins to grieving family members. A clumsy but entertaining film with some funny bits wherein a false swami tries to swindle the good town folk out of some cash.
Cast: Kalyan Kumar, K R Vijaya; music: unknown

JAI DAKSHINESHWAR KAALI MAA
1986, D: Shantilaal Soni, Hindi, DVD, subtitled
A widowed man remarries but his daughter is never accepted into his new blended family. His daughter, Jyoti, is devoted to the Goddess Kali and worships and sings her praises daily. She even offers her plaster idol of Kali, her only real possession, sweetened milk which The Goddess drinks. Nevertheless, the child is beaten, starved, and spoken to harshly by all but her doting father (who is pretty much a kind-hearted-but-dense guy).

Jyoti is often visited by The Goddess as she grows older, and her devotion never wavers. Later, to spite their step-sister's beauty, the two horrible family members trick her into marrying a young man with brain damage. Miracles still happen and The Goddess gives her devotee a new wedding sari and gold jewelry on her nuptial day. The Goddess even heals her damaged husband, and you would think everything would be hunky-dory from there on out. Nope. Due to an unfortunate turn of events she is accused of cheating on her husband and is, again, treated very badly, this time by her new family. The abuse comes to a head when her mother and sister-in-laws consult a *tantrik* who worships Kali but dabbles in the black arts. He attempts to exorcise Jyoti utilizing his knowledge of bad magic, but Kali appears to set things right. Okay, so I was waiting patiently for Soni to pull out all the stops and have a showdown between the wizard and the goddess. You know, **AMMORU**-style. Well…no. Turns out everyone is stunned to see the stone statue of Kali turn into the green-skinned Shakti who then praises Jyoti for her pious ways and scolds the *tantrik* for using The Goddess's boons for evil. Everyone gushes and all is well. Wait…what?

Despite the film's non-action, Shantilaal Soni manages to keep the plot rolling with a darn good child actor (something I find rare in Indian films) playing the young daughter, and the dancing skills of the gorgeous Hema Malini as the adult Jyoti and as the Goddess Kali. The supernatural elements of the film are your usual floating idols, food changing into rocks, and so forth. So, when Kali finally materialized I was really expecting action, especially since Soni is no stranger when it comes to fantastic cinema, having made one of the first Indian SF films called **MR. X IN BOMBAY** (1964). The director also made other devotional productions as well as four Naag movies. His final film was **MAHIMA KAALI MAA KI** (2003), which, from what I can tell as I have yet to see the film, is more or less a remake of **JAI DAKSHINESHWAR KAALI MAA**.
Cast: Hema Malini, Ajinkya Dev, Mrinal Kulkarni, Alok Nath, Jayshree Gadkar and Vilas Raj; Music: Aditya Paudwal

JAI KAALI
1992, D: Nikhil Saini, Hindi, VCD, no subtitles
The film opens and we are introduced to the young woman Shikaali (Hema Malini) who is in prison for murder. It takes almost two hours of the film's running time for us to learn the reason why; she beheaded a villainous man

(Saeed Jaffrey). After being beaten and left for dead, a local Kali priest calls upon his goddess to possess the young woman. After a spectacular *filmi* number, Shikaali takes hold of the temple's ceremonial sword and tracks down her tormentor. After explaining everything in court she is, of course, found innocent by reason of divine intervention.

One of the better supernatural "nudge" films, the standout performance being famed actress Hema Malini's transformation into Kali. Hema Malini is a trained Bharatanatyam artist and devout Hindu. Although she hasn't been in a film in years (one of her first being **SHOLAY** in 1976), she still performs on stage as Kali, Durga, and an assortment of other goddesses to this day. Actor Rajesh Vivek has a small role as the scene-chewing Kali priest that assists in Shikaali's "reincarnation" of The Goddess. Vivek has appeared in a similar role numerous times, including famous stints in Shyam and Tulsi Ramsays' **VEERANA** (1989), Sibte Hassan Rizvi's **JOSHILAAY** (1988), Vinod Talwar's **HATYARIN** (1991), Shekhar Kapur's **BANDIT QUEEN** (1994), and any number of horror or drama movies that needed the actor to resurrect his holy man persona. I love that guy!
Cast: Saeed Jaffrey, Jeetendra, Hema Malini, Ranjeet, Paresh Rawal and Rajesh Vivek; music: Usha Khanna

JAI MATA VAIBHAV LAXMI
2003, D: V. Menon, Hindi, VCD, no subtitles
A brutally dull film full of family strife and a goddess that appears every so often to give sage advice to her devotee. The only highlight of this yawnfest is the appearance of a very tall and lanky Goddess. I was sucked in because the cover art for the VCD made it appear that **JAI MATA VAIBHAV LAXMI** could possibly turn out to be very cool. Nope. Another $1 wasted. On a note of interest, director V. Menon has had a very profitable but infrequent run of genre films. His 1990 **JUNGLE LOVE** was a very popular and very unofficial Tarzan film, and his Nagin epics **TU NAGIN MAIN SAPERA** (1989) and **NAAG MANI** (1991) weren't all that bad.
Cast: Shikha Swaroop, Sudha Chandran, Rajesh Sabharwal, and Priya Khanna; music: Murlidhar

SRI DURGA POOJA
2006, D: Om Sakthi Jagadeesan, Tamil, YouTube
Low-budget Devotional produced towards the end of the cycle, when interest in making such films along with their distant cousins, the Grade C horror films, was waning, although it isn't like director Jagadeesan even took notice. Just why the audiences for these films waned has me miffed, although I could hazard a guess it had something to do with this film.

Using devotional song and dance, a long-suffering Durga devotee (is there any other kind?) heals the sick and people stricken by cobra venom. During one such healing session, she collapses into a coma from which she will not recover. A holy child appears and, giggling, revives the woman before vanishing into a small Durga idol. The remainder of the film consists of an assortment of devotional tests for the young woman. She has her husband jailed on false charges, has a no-good swami and family member plot against her, and suffers various assaults on her womanhood. In an exciting conclusion, a holy cow saves the woman from being stabbed by a trident-welding male attacker. The man is then chased by the bovine into a nearby Durga temple. There he confesses his sins and comes clean to everyone involved including the little holy girl who appears just in time to bless everyone, giggle, and yet again disappear into the temple idol. A.k.a. **DURGA POOJA** (Hindi dub).
Cast: Laxmi, Shruti & Raghuveer; music: unknown

AYYAVAZHI
2008, D: Nanjil P.C. Anabazahahan, Tamil, VCD, no subtitles
Low-budget but ambitious period piece that deals with a greedy local Raj. The film has village conflict, cart loads of devotees, an evil wizard battling a good swami, and a lot of blue-skinned gods walking the earth. There are numerous scenes of devotional action that all lead up to a rather dull climax wherein Vishnu oversees a lackluster end of the world. No angry goddess as advertised in the film's opening credits, just a brief flash of a few female deities milling about, and the VCD's deceptive sleeve art. A.k.a. **JAI MAHA SHAKTI** (Hindi dubbed).
Cast: Raja, Suji Bala, City Babu, Pandu, Senthil, and Baby Lonia; music: Bagavathi Sivanesan

JAI MAA AMBA BHAVANI
2009, D: ?, Rajasthani, no subtitles, YouTube
Simply horrible. Dreadfully dull family drama about a young couple continuously hassled by the husband's ill-tempered mother. A low-grade devotional film with little or no action other than family arguments and a scene of the young wife emotionally praying to The Goddess for help with all the problems they are having. An off-camera car accident sends the husband to the hospital wherein The Goddess shows up in the last few minutes of the film to save his life by shooting him full of powerful *shakti* energy. I can't believe I sat through this hoping to see something...*anything* cool. Nope. Didn't happen. Nada. Even the soundtrack sucked.
Cast: unknown; music: unknown

JOY MAA DURGA
2009, D: Shantilal Soni, Bengali, VCD, no subtitles
A schizomanic production by old-timer Shantilal Soni, who went the practical effects route when he wanted something magical to happen. Maybe there was no budget for Rama Narayanan-style digital effects, or maybe Soni just enjoys crude stop-frame animation. The end result is fairly charming tale of a jungle boy (who rides an elephant, carries around a rabbit, and communes with nature) and his connection with the Goddess Durga. Most everything about the film is silly and carefree until the final twenty minutes when shit hits the fan and the young lad's happy adopted family comes under some hard times. The Goddess intervenes in a rather cheerful manner and all is restored.
Cast: Debasri Roy, Arun Govil, Avishek Chatterjee, Arun Banerjee, and Nimu Bhowmik; music: Usha Khanna

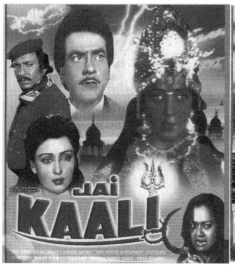
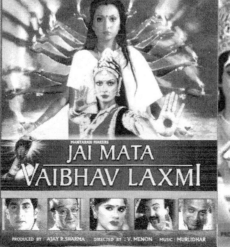

AMMORU THE GODDESS REALIZED

Shakti Appendix 3

Interview with Christopher Holmes on the SFX of AMMORU.

*Tim: I saw **AMMORU** about ten years ago, and after reviewing it again for an article on Hindu Goddess Cinema I am still awe struck as to how beautiful the effects work is for this film. How familiar were you with the subject matter of the film?*

Christopher Holmes: The producer, Shyam, narrated the story to me many times, and so I got to know the story very well. I was encouraged to make suggestions to help the devotional feel work for the VFX [video effects]. One of these which became particularly important was that the villain have supernatural powers to justify Divine intervention.

How where you approached to handle the effects work?

I was working in Chennai at a post-production facility where I met the producer Shyam.

What strikes me is how the director integrated his cinematography with the effects in the film. The final sequence of the Goddess Ammoru emerging from the idol and attacking Rami Reddy's character has never been topped. Even some of the newer Goddess films made years after this production have trouble duplicating the film's look. Did you storyboard with director Ramakrishna and cinematographer Vijaya Kumar?

Kodi Ramakrishna came on board to re-shoot the principal photography after we had wrapped the VFX shoot.

Based on conversations with the producer, I storyboarded the shots and directed the VFX 2nd unit. Storyboards were a novelty at the

time, but were essential for me to communicate the continuity of action and to get a budget together for the VFX post-production work in the UK. You might notice the villain is a different actor from the one in the final film [*page 120, top image*].

The producer, Shyam, pleased with the quality of the VFX shoot, became disappointed with the first unit footage shot by the original director during principal photography, and so decided to re-shoot the entire non-VFX part of the film. This was when Kodi Ramakrishna came on board. Kodi was to re-shoot the entire non-VFX part of the film but the decision was also made to re-cast the villain with Ram Reddys' character. I was already in the UK about to start the post-production for the VFX when I had to return to India to re-shoot the villain's parts to cover the new casting. So the film was effectively shot twice.

Where was the post-production work created?

In the UK, I did the 3D animation for the watery hand. Some of the spot effects were done in India and later transferred to film in the UK.

*Most South Indian film industries at that time relied on practical effects work. **AMMORU** broke new ground and I'm sure caused a stir. What were some of the techniques you used for the film?*

Mostly 2D compositing effects, The Goddess's multiple arms were all lined

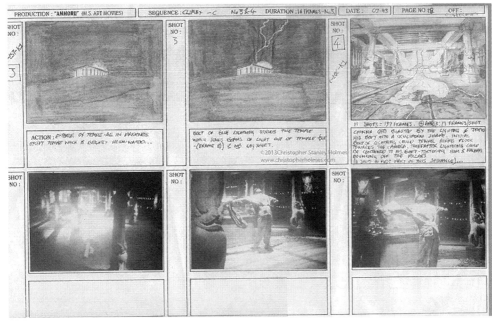

All storyboards ©2013 Christopher Stanley Holmes, used with kind permission.

2003 pre-production sketch of actress Ramya Krishnan as the Goddess Ammoru.

All production images from **AMMORU** are ©2013 Christopher Stanley Holmes, used with kind permission.

up in camera using a metal harness behind Ramya Krishnan which I made at a roadside metal worker's stall. This ensured that the plates all lined up in post. We used 2D drawn line animation for the **HIGHLANDER**-inspired lightning sequences, 3D Softimage for the watery hand and trident and some 2D morphing techniques for the Goddess transitions.

We shot on 35mm and digitised the footage at TV PAL resolution (that's 720 by 576 pixels). This was the main risk. If it was not for the excellent work by Mike Boudry and his team at CFC, this would not have been feasible. Without this [technique] however, we would have had no workable budget. Getting usable footage was the main challenge in a challenging environment and persuading the producer, actors and crew to be patient and stick with it. This meant a lot of art direction was required, close supervision of props, sets, costume, action and lighting.

Great performances from Rami Reddy, Ramya Krishnan as The Goddess (who was especially patient with me re-designing her costumes and make up!), Suresh, and of course the late, lamented Soundaraya as the heroine, are ultimately what made the film such a success, with a great crew, and of course the producer Shyam who had the idea in the first place.

Thank you, Mr. Holmes for your kind assistance in supplying my magazine with images and allowing for this interview. I do so love your work on the film!

Christopher Holmes began his career in digital effects with the film AMMORU after studying Fine Art at The Royal College of Art (U.K.). He would later work on Kodi Ramakrishna's 2004 film ANJI (DILER being the Hindi dub title) which is a bizarre effects-filled devotional action adventure film. He has worked on a wide assortment of British and Indian computer animated productions. Mr. Holmes occasionally tutors at the NFTS in The United Kingdom. A montage and sketchbook of his work can be viewed at christopherhomes.com.

THE ANGRY GODDESS

My fascination with the Goddess films is primarily their sexuality. That may sound oxymoronic, but the archetypal Mother Goddess—call her Devi, Maa, Shakti, etc.—is at the heart of the matter a powerful feminine force to be reckoned with. As the primal creator and preserver of life, she better be a darn good looker—and in the vast majority of these films, she sure is!

There is no denying that Indian art—both ancient and modern—is highly sexualized, even if the culture is fairly oppressive towards women. Whereas most images of Durga, Kali, and other forms of the Ancient Mother show the Goddess as a sexually-charged and non-subservient deity, outright displays of perceived feminine wiles seem to be offensive and threatening to most Indian males, whether they're rural or city dwellers. Recent much-publicized accounts of rape and murder of women in India only seem to support this notion, while popular images of Baby Krishna and his nurturing mother Yosoda are festooned on the walls of stores, shops, homes, and temples about the country. Is the powerful and wild Kali dancing on the prone figure of Shiva, her male consort, too psychically powerful an image for Indian men to bear? That may be a very broad, Western oversimplification of the problem, but to my thinking, this fear of female power may be one factor in these abuses.

Personally, I would rather that, as in **AMMORU** and other Devotionals, the Goddess utterly demolish the man. The Angry Goddess is what I want to see in these films.

In most Indian fantasy-based (read: devotional, mythological, etc.) films, you don't want to piss a goddess off. Most of the male gods are laid back and don't do much with humans nowadays. Even in a the few Shiva-based devotional films I've seen, where instead of a female devotee being harassed by some tantrik it is a Shaivite who is under attack, the god goes on a walkabout and nonchalantly assists his ailing devotee. If it was a follower of Durga or Kali that was having her faith tested, I guarantee you that some very annoyed goddess would have eventually manifested and taken the troublemaker out. That's the point of these films, especially in the ones where women are under constant attack. The divine intervention may take awhile, but when it happens, get out of the way!

The plots of these films are basically the same. Very few directors will approach them any differently, with probably the only exception being Kodi Ramakrishna (see Appendix 2). The drama unfolds thusly: a young devotee of a local goddess or major goddess gets married to/is adopted into/has a family who is horrible and mean to her. They mock her piety and make her life a living hell. Sometimes they just torment, starve or beat her. A good percentage of the time her death is planned so that her relatives can get some financial windfall or magical powers. Other times she is murdered outright because they don't want her around…and when that doesn't work (goddess intervention and reanimation is a good thing in this case) it's time to call in the evil tantrik. The proverbial shit hits the fan as it is a showdown between the dark arts and the love of the devoted follower…even if they are both devotees of the same goddess. This is where it gets tricky! Who will gain the boon of The Goddess? The evil man who worships the darker side of Kali, or the weeping woman who pleads to the nurturing and loving face of the same deity? It doesn't matter, even before you walk into the theatre you will know what the outcome will be: The Goddess, as fierce and scary as she may be at times, will always side with the fairer sex and stomp the bad old man into the ground.

The Ferocious Goddess has always been around in Indian cinema. In the mythological tale of "Devi Mahatmyam", when the demon Mahishasur was made impervious to all the male gods that attempt to destroy him, it was up to the divine Shakti, in this case Durga, to make her presence known. She took the demon down. The primal force of the Devi—the female Goddess—has always been around. Her presence in South Asian culture pre-dates the Aryan introduction of Shiva and the other male gods. Her roots run very deep, despite the current overtly masculine domination over women in Indian culture (a trend referred to as "Ramafication" by author William Dalrymple…the purposeful shutting down of the Shaktian and the Goddess worship, the very existence of popular strong female characters in films). This is also true in almost all film for the past three decades: strong female leads, usually a fierce warrior class, have become very popular. It's an empowering effect that is very popular in cultures that have been traditionally male-dominated (unless it's a country that has recently gone under fundamentalist change where it can be dangerous for a woman to cheer on or be seen watching a strong female presence).

In decades prior to Ramakrishna's **AMMORU** (1995), there were a few Angry Goddesses storming out of temples to kill bad men, but most confrontations lacked the wild intensity of **AMMORU**. Typically, there would be a very stagey appearance of Durga or Kali or whoever, performing a ritualized dance not unlike something that would have been seen at a rural "passion play". Most of these earlier films were of the mythological genre, and typically show the killing of actual demons and not tantriks or wizards, the exceptions being films like **YETU-YEDURETU** *(1981)* and **JAI KAALI** *(1990)*. *The abuse of women has always been a part of this sub-genre of devotional films. You need a reason to plead to a goddess to give you some relief. And what better feeling is seeing the idol you worship springing to life, chasing down that evil man who has been tormenting you and annihilating him, possibly by decapitation?*

Essentially, then, most of these films are all the same. And most of them have the same plot. The best of the lot are those that tell the same story but with a tantalizing amount of pizzazz to make them interesting. And of course it doesn't hurt that some of the sexiest ladies in the Indian film industry have portrayed the Angry Goddess, slathering their skin in red, green, black or blue grease paint and taken up the trident for these films.

YETU-YEDURETU
1981, D: Mani Murugan, Kannada, DVD
A Kannada film wherein a young man must choose between the forces of good and evil. In this case he has help from the monkey god Hanuman and, at the very end, a very annoyed Kali.

A misguided swami wants to revive the long-dead body of his yogi master. To do so, he must corrupt a devout man and his wife and use their young son in a magical ceremony to raise the corpse. He consorts with a demon and a plan is hatched after he also contacts the Goddess Kali. In a chilling climax set in a graveyard, the swami offers the child up for sacrifice to the baby's Kali-possessed mother. Just when it seems that the dark deed will succeed, the woman's husband arrives on the scene. He's a devout follower of Hanuman and with his god's help he convinces Kali to leave his wife and child alone and take out the evil ascetic.

YETU-YEDURETU is an exceptionally good-looking film with an engaging and original plot, a wonderful soundtrack by Satyan, and overall superior acting and effects. One particular sequence that is beautifully-shot is on location by the seaside where our hero is tempted by Lord Hanuman, the wily monkey god, who transforms himself into a gorgeous woman to test his devotee's morals. There are other fun scenes with The God, including his playing chess with a swami and causing all sorts of mischief typically associated with this playful deity. The best fantasy-devotional film (that I've seen) to ever to come out of the Kannda film industry. A real pity this was never subtitled.
Cast: Srinath, Lakshmi, Ashwath, Sundar Raj ; music: Satyam

KASAM DURGA KI
1982, D: Joginder, Hindi, VCD, no subtitles
A bandit flick with a devotional/supernatural twist; uses many scenes from other films, which is not uncommon when you consider other piecemeal productions by Joginder. For even more insanity, consider his 1975 film **RANGA KHUSH**. I have yet to see that film, but as in this one, a bandit calls for the powers of the Goddess Durga as well as those of Jesus and Muhammad.

Actor-director Joginder was an odd bird. His acting style is best described as frenzied lunacy and his characters are always worth the price of any film. In **KASAM DURGA KI** he is in fine form as a raving bandit (more or less a reprise of his role from **RANGA KHUSH** (1975), a film which made him a household name in the '70s). For the absolute extreme example of his directorial style, I suggest any one of his horror films. These no-frill features are always worth catching, if anything, for their incomprehensible plots, funky practical effects, and overacting by all involved.
Cast: Raza Murad, Rajni Sharma, Jayshree T, Joginder, Vijay Arora, Padma Khanna; music: Sonik Omi

BETTADA THAYI
1984, D: Perala, Kannada, VCD, no subtitles
Essentially a devotional love story with a supernatural child. Popular Kannada actress Aarathi plays a poor young woman who falls in love with a wonderful flute-playing young man who is equally as poor but very kind. They have a child together, a girl they name Chamundi, who is blessed by the local goddess, Devi Mata. Meanwhile, a local moneylender hopes to obtain the riches offered by a smarmy swami. As payment for the boon, the swami demands the sacrifice of an innocent child. The blessed child Chamundi seems like the perfect choice for the role. When poison and kidnapping don't work, the criminal finally manages to kill the girl by crushing her with a boulder. An angry Goddess reanimates her young devotee and possesses her body, turning the little brat into a really pissed-off mini-Durga who goes on to kill the evil swami and his money-loving toady of a sidekick.

The wide-eyed holy child is played by Baby Kokila in a manner that predates the creepiness of Baby Sunayana in Ramakrishna's **AMMORU** by a decade.

Never a good idea to hand a baby to a woman possessed by the ferocious Hindu goddess Kali. From the film **YETU-YEDURETU**.

Remade in 1987 by K. S. Reddy as **DURGA MAA** with the actress Baby Pooja in the role of "Little Durga". A.k.a. **DEVI MATA** (Hindi Dub).
Cast: Shreenath, Aarathi, Umashree, Vajramuni, Dinesh, and Baby Kokila; music: Sathyam

MAA BHAWANI
1986, D: Om Shakti Jagdishan, Tamil, YouTube, no subtitles
MAA BHAWANI is a drawn-out and rather dull tale of devotion to Maa Bhawani, a ferocious aspect of the Hindu Goddess Parvati. With ferocious in mind, you would expect some terrible retribution for the film's jerk of an antagonist. Nope. After abusing his devout wife for most of the last half of the plot, he finally gets his come-uppance when he trips on a stone in a Maa Bhawani temple and is impaled upon a trident.

Director Om Shakti Jagdishan (a.k.a. Om Sakthi Jagadeesan, a.k.a. Jahadish) made several additional Goddess-theme Devotionals including **SRI DURGA POOJA** (2003) and **MAA SHAKTI MAYEE** (2004), but his output for sheer entertaining films is very low indeed.
Cast: not available; music: Hemant Kumar

DURGAA MAA
1986, D: K S Rami Reddy, Telugu, DVD, no subtitles
Essentially the same tale told in the Kannada film **BETTADA THAYI** with a few minor character adjustments. A young couple has a holy child that is doted over by the Goddess Durga. The production has some great dance numbers, including a fantasy number that involves the God Krishna. Despite the banter between the evil swami and the money-lender, which is pretty fun at times, the film falls flat where it counts the most: when little Durga decides she's had enough and snuffs the evil duo. The finale lacks the bloody lion and trident double-whammy of death that gave the original film its edge.

Baby Pooja, the actress that portrayed the holy child, later went on to guest star in a few horror films, including the Certificate A/Grade C thrillers **KABRASTAN** (1988, D: Mohan Bhakri) and, a little later, Salim Hyder's **KHOONI RAAT** (1991).

Director K S Rami Reddy is, as far as I know, no relation to the late bad boy of Devi cinema, Rami Reddy.
Cast: Beena Banerjee, Shubha Khote, Raj Kiran, Pradeep Kumar, and Baby Pooja; Music: Ravindra Jain

SARVAM SAKTHI MAYAM
1986, D: P.R. Somasundar, Tamil, DVD/VCD, no subtitles

Two fine young adults fall in love and plan to have a family. Unbeknownst to them, there are family members plotting against their happiness. In a horrible sequence of events they poison the young woman, who has a miscarriage. Distraught and needing condolences, the couple wanders the countryside and finds an abandoned Kolakara Kaliamman Kovil temple. They decide to make it their own, cleaning it up and restoring it to its former glory. Little do they know that it is considered haunted and people have died there on previous occasions (hence it being abandoned). Their devotion to The Goddess is rewarded when they have a baby girl. The child, named Devi, is no ordinary little girl, as she is holy and doted on by The Goddess.

As per the devotional script, the evil family members try various ways to kill Devi. They send a cobra after her, but she tames the snake when it recognizes her divinity. The same thing happens when a leopard is set upon the child. An assassin is then hired to murder Devi, but instead, he is led to the Kolakara Kaliamman Kovil temple by the little girl, where an angry Goddess dispatches the fiend.

By the end, all the evil doers are killed off or converted to devout believers in Kali's love. At the end of the film little Devi is somehow bitten by a cobra and is dying. Her parents rush her to the temple and everything is set right when Devi transforms into a small version of Kali and then vanishes into the temple idol. Her mother and father seem a little confused, but they accept that Devi was an incarnation of Kali and their daughter's place is now among the gods.

Not the best devotional film I've had the pleasure to sit through, but it wasn't unbearable either. The highlight is the five-minute segment when the assassin meets The Goddess in her temple. Kali, played by the always-stunning Ramya Krishnan, does an elaborate and ritualized dance of death before finally impaling the man on the temple's statue. Turns out that all the murders that had taken place over the years in that temple were because of the assassin. The Goddess was a wee bit pissed-off about that, as well as his insistence on killing Devi. Ramya Krishnan, like Prema and Soundraya, appeared in many devotional films playing either a devotee or The Goddess herself.

The DVD and VCD editions lack English subtitles, but there is a multi-part subtitled version on YouTube. The VCD sleeve art wrongly credits Jagadhish (a.k.a. Om Sakthi Jadadeesan) as the director. This head-scratching information is made even more complicated by the fact that director Somasundar is also known as "V. Swaminathan". Apparently this is not uncommon and makes for tough credits verification. For those seeking this film out it has various titles: **DEVI MAHADEVI** (Hindi dub), and **MAA AMBA KI SHAKTI** (Kannada dub), are two.
Cast: Sudha Chandran, Rajesh Chandran, and Manorma; music: Ben Surender/Ramalingam-Lingappa

KAALI MAHAKAALI
1989, D: Om Shakthi Jagadeesan, Kannada, VCD, no subtitles

I have very little information on this film other than it is Kannada-made and is about Mahakali and her relationship to a family of devotees. Of course an evil *tantrik* is woven into the plot. In a bid to have Kali grant him some boon of power, the wizard calls forth The Goddess and proceeds to boast to her of his supernatural prowess. That is not something you do if you want to impress any deity. She laughs at him and leaves without bestowing anything on the now severely pissed-off *tantrik*. During the course of the rest of the picture, he proceeds to harass the devout family until Kalli has had enough. As with most of these devotional films, it's in the final two minutes that a very annoyed Goddess shows up to kick some butt—in this case she swallows the *tantrik* whole! The family rejoices and we have another successful ending to a devotional film.

The first five minutes of **KAALI MAHAKAALI** introduces us to four goddesses, including the Tamil variant of Kali called Mahakaali who shows up decked out in what looks like a European pirate hat (adorned with cobras) and a nice set of fangs/tusks. This version of Kali is also seen occasionally riding an elephant in the film. Old school practical effects rule in this film, made just a few years before **AMMORU** changed the game for everyone.

My favorite toothy variation of Kali; a brilliant character design from Om Shakthi Jagadeesan's **KAALI MAHAKAALI**

As for director Jagadeesan (a.k.a. Jaga Deesan, a.k.a. Jahadhish), he is credited for a few other devotional films, including **SHRI DURAGA PUJA** (2006-Tamil) and **MAHA SHAKTI MAAYE** (1994-Hindi).
Cast: K.R. Vijaya, Jai Shankar, Viji, and Rajvi; Music: Sawan Kumar Sawan

GOMATA - *"The Mother Cow"*
1990?, D: Ram Narayan, Kannada, VCD, no subtitles
Just when you think you've seen all the devotional Goddess films and think they're all the same, **GOMATA** comes along and blows your mind.

What can I say about this film? It's one of the most insane devotional films ever made. Produced on a shoestring budget from what looks like the late 1980s or early 1990s (date of production is not listed anywhere), **GOMATA** ("Mother Cow"; also a common medicinal beverage made from distilled cow urine) has a ghost, a sacred cow, an intelligent dog, and a crazy climax that includes loads of stock footage of lightning, shots of various goddess idols, a gang of motorcycle riding bad-ass bald monks, killer plastic toy robots (that duke it out with the monks), a dancing green-skinned cutie of a goddess, and the aforementioned cow that chases folks to their death. The end result of all this madness? An instance of reincarnation.

At first I had thought this to be an early film by the prolific director Ramanarayanan, who made **KOTTAI MARIAMMAN** (2001), **NAAG LOK** (2003), and **MAA DURGA DIVYA HAATHI** (2005). After some extensive research, I believe I may have mistakenly attributed some of Ram Narayan's nagin films to Ramanaryanan. They could easily be confused at first, seeing that all of Ramanarayanan's hallmarks are also in this film: his love of sacred animals, technology (well, in this case toy robots), cheap special effects, and really, really odd stories. But this is nowhere on his filmography. I could be getting him mixed up with Ram Narayan, as Ramanarayanan also goes by Rama Narayanan…which makes for some very perplexing research!
Cast: Ravo, Sitara, Indira, and Indrajeet; Music: Shankar Genesh

Poster art for the Hindi-language Possession-Devotional-Police Drama **KARISHMA KALI KAA**.

KARISHMA KALI KAA - *"The Miracles of Goddess Kali"*
1990, D: Ashok Pinjabi, Hindi, DVD, subtitles
KARISHMA KALI KAA is a fairly obscure Hindi-language Devotional/Horror/Police Drama (I do so enjoy a good Indian genre mash-up), and one that is a marked departure from the usual southern variety.

Parvati, a young devout woman, is divinely made the vessel for the Goddess Kali when a priest sets about to retrieve a treasure stolen from the temple. With trident in hand she visits each of the men responsible for stealing the temple's golden jewelry. Parvati arrives in a shaft of light and kills the men, usually by way of her trident, but she does use the Sudarshana Chakra (a spinning multi-blade weapon that resembles a super-duper throwing star) to chop off one criminal's head. The best sequence is towards the end of the film when she storms the plush hideout of the criminal gang. The Goddess-infused mortal shrugs off machine-gun fire to get at the men responsible for her vengeance. In the end Kali herself makes an appearance and we are surprised to learn that the temple priest was behind the theft all along and was using his goddess to mop up some lose ends. Kali is none-too-pleased at finding this fact out and pierces him with her holy sword, and he is immediately consumed by flames.

Music is provided by the multi-talented Bappi Lahiri, whose scores for Babbar Subhash's **DISCO DANCER** (1982), Babbar Subhash's **ADVENTURES OF TARZAN** (1983), and Ram Rano's **HAIWAN** (1977) rank as some of the oddest and most entertaining in all of Bollywood.
Cast: Shatrughan Sinha, Amrita Singh, Roopesh Kumar, Raza Murao, and Ranjeet; music: Bappi Lahiri

AMMAN KOVIL THIRUVIZHA
1990, D: PR Somasundhar, Tamil
Another unknown film that sounds and looks like it would be a wonderful addition to this article. No video sources have so far been located. Often confused with the 1986 action/drama **AMMAN KOVIL KIZHAKALE**. Well, unless of course I am the one confused!
Cast: Nizhalgal, Ravi, Senthil, and Kanaka; music: Ilaiyaraaja

DURGASHTAMI
1991, D: Geethapriya (a.k.a. Geetha Priya), Kannada, DVD, subtitles
DURGASHTAMI is yet another one of those nightmarishly popular kiddie/family devotional flicks which follow the exploits of a bumbling family's attempt to subjugate a young girl who is a Durga devotee. Luckily for the young girl she has a guardian goddess and an elephant for a buddy. There are many scenes of animal hijinks, until the last ten minutes of the film wherein a wizard hired by the family has a show down with Durga (a very popular plot element in these films). Not the best thing to do—piss off a goddess and all. The elephant and a cobra also show up to trash the wizard's shrine. After all of that, Durga tracks down and offs the family patriarch. Luckily for me there's a fun soundtrack by the Kannada duo Shankar-Ganesh.
Cast: Ashok, Mahalakshmi, Vajramuni, Lakshman, M.V.Vasudeva Rao; music: Shankar Ganesh

KARUNINCHINA KANAKADURGA - *"God's Blessing"*
1992, D: B. Vittalacharya, Telugu, VCD, no subtitles
A young couple is in a hurry to get to a doctor when their ox-driven cart careens down a steep hillside. The driver is injured and the husband is separated from his expecting wife. In one of the most insane on-camera

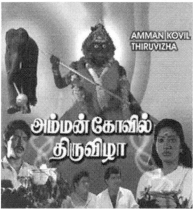

Mystery Tamil film
AMMAN KOVIL THIRUVIZHA

births ever, the young mother wanders dazed into a Durga temple where she *slips on a banana peel* (yes, you heard me) and falls onto a ceremonial trident. A splash of blood gushes forth, decorating the Goddess Parvati's face, and the baby is born. A group of passing Shaivas hears the cry of the newborn and discovers the child. The monks reunite the baby with a distraught father who takes the child home. The Goddess Durga visits the family in the form of a loving wet nurse to make sure that the child gets both physical and spiritual nourishment. In the meantime, a mad scientist and his bumbling assistants are deep in the study of some arcane knowledge that brings them face-to-face with a demon. The terrifying creature resembles a rubber-faced black-skinned demon in circus garb. Years pass, and with Parvati/Durga's loving care, the child soon grows to adulthood.

While B. Vittalacharya (a.k.a. B. Vittala Charya) was once called one of the most influential filmmakers in the Telugu industry, having made **MOSAGALAKU MOSAGAADU** (1971, the first Indian Western), as well as **ALIBABA 40 DONGALU** (1970). However, as times changed, his style of filmmaking fell out of favor, and he was left manufacturing sub-juvenile nonsense like **KARUNINCHINA KANAKADURGA**. The film is charming in the weird way that a '70s Saturday Morning live action kids' show once was in its final ten minutes of action. Similarly, in the last sequence of events in **KARUNINCHINA KANAKADURGA**, Durga gets pissed and annihilates the wizard and the fancy-pants demon by jabbing at them with her trident in a rather bloodless and random way.

As a fun footnote to this drab film, Ganehsa, the elephant-headed son of Shiva and Parvati, makes an appearance, and with the assistance of his giant rat sidekick, makes like hell for the wizard/scientist. A.k.a. **JAI JAI DURGA MAA** (Hindu dub).
Cast: K.R. Vijaya, Yamuna, Disco Shanti, and Kota Srinivasrao; music: unknown

DURGAI AMMAN - *"The Goddess Durga"*
1999, D: Om Sai Prakash, Tamil, DVD, no subtitles
Om Sai Prakash's best feature, and works on several levels as both a horror and devotional film.

Sivaranjani stars as a devout young woman who is troubled by dreams of a ghost stalking her. That doesn't stop her from hooking up with her life-long boy crush whom she plans on marrying (they even got matching tattoos on their forearms when they were teens). After forty minutes of family drama, comedic misadventures (involving a sleepwalker—the popular Telugu comedian Babu Mohan), and two very nice musical numbers, we finally get to the meat of the film. The young woman discovers that her family wants her to be married off to another man, and she tearfully begs the Goddess Durga (or some variation thereof) to help her or she'll kill herself. The Goddess hears her prayers, and just before she munches down on a plate of poison, her boyfriend arrives to knock the plate out of her hands. They get married and on their wedding night they hug and are about to kiss when the spirit of the female ghost storms out of her grave and zaps the both of them. Her boyfriend becomes possessed and for a moment appears in the visage of a blue-eyed, hairy, fanged demon. But that doesn't bother her enough to leave the love of her life, and after their local physician says he's okay, they get back to married life…

However, she suspects something is wrong when he's still changing into the blue-haired beast-man, and she turns to her parents for some sage advice. In the meantime, the ghost again visits the husband, and we get the full story as to why she is possessing him. Seems like she's the spirit of a young woman who knew him while he was away at college. She was infatuated with him, but he rejected her expression of affection, and in turn she burned herself to death. Now she has returned to take what she believes is rightfully hers. A powerful swami is called in to exorcise the ghost, but she's too powerful, and tougher measures have to be arranged.

Enter Rami Reddy as a master of the dark arts. His power source is Kali, and it turns out that he is behind the possession of the young man, as the ghost is that of his dead daughter…he was present when she burned herself to death. To make matters worse, he places a curse on the young woman, turning her into an old hag. The final battle of good versus evil is set and it's Rami Reddy's evil *tantrik* against the powers of the Vishnu Swami and the Durga devotees! In the end, The Goddess (actress Banupriya) steps up to the plate and emerges from the swami's forehead to take out the *tantrik* and the ghost of his daughter.

What I find both surprising and pleasing about Sai Prakash's film is the utter lack of digital effects. Wire work, post-process animation, and an abundance of split screen, double exposure, colored lights, and smoke from fog machines and monstrous fans abound. These practical effects are refreshing break from the CG onslaught to follow, which will include his 2001 film **ANGALA PARAMESWARI**. I suspect that Sai was a fan of the film **MANGALSUTRA**, a 1981 ghost-possession horror film starring Rekha. The plot is very similar, and even the possessed husband resembles the creature in this film. Also known as **JAI MAA DURGA SHAKTI** (Hindi dub, not to be confused with Rama Narayanan's **KOTTAI MARIAMMAN** which is also available as **JAI MAA DURGA SHAKTI**). Also made: **ANGALA PARAMESWARI, NAVASHAKTI VYBHAVA**.
Cast: Banupriya, Sivaranjani, Sasikumar, Rami Reddy, and Babu Mohan; music: Dharmesh

AATHA KANTHIRANTHA
1999, D: Suriya, Tamil, DVD/VCD, no subtitles
Cross-genre film that deals with spectral possession as well as magic and goddess worship. **AATHA KANTHIRANTHA**'s visual magic is supplied by the very busy EFX Chennai group that specialized in inexpensive digital effects as well as your usual wire-work. No actual goddess makes an appearance except for in the final showdown at an outdoor Kali temple, which is fairly entertaining. In that sequence, a Kali priest

AATHA KANTHIRANTHA & DURGAI AMMAN

Hindi dub **MAA DURGA SHAKTI** of **AATHA KATHIRANTHA**

Demonic creatures in Indian films come in all shapes and sizes. For the most part they look pretty cool. However, there are always exceptions to that rule. Take for example this very lame, overweight, opera-gloved, rubber mask-wearing embarrassment of a supernatural monster from director Vittalacharya's **KARUNINCHINA KANAKADURGA**.

KAN THIRANTHU PARAMMA

Top to bottom: Hindi dubbed versions of **DHARMA DEVATHE**, **PADAI VEETU AMMAN**, and **SRI KALIKAMBA**.

musters all his devotion to exorcise and finally destroy a ghost that has a hold over a young woman. The final battle has a wild dance number with grass pompom-pumping devotees of a ferocious Kali who appears swinging a huge scythe. Although The Goddess doesn't directly engage the ghost, her very presence is all that is needed for the priest to get the job done.

AATHA KANTHIRANTHA is an exceptionally good production with minimal use of CG for its divine/devilish effects. This film would benefit from some English subtitles. Also known as **DURGA SHAKTI** or **MAA DURGA SHAKTI** (hindi dubs).
Cast: Sruthi, Saarukasan; music: Ramesh Ramnath

KAN THIRANTHU PARAMMA
2000, D: L.C. Gnana Selva, Tamil, YouTube, no subtitles
Minor devotional film from director Selva, who is usually dishing up melodramas and remakes of other director's films for hungry Tamil audiences. What makes Selva's variant on the Goddess genre a bit better than its cousins is the film's use of digital effects. They abound in the film, of that that is no doubt, but rather than cartoonish representations of monsters and gods, we have a bevy of weird psychedelic imagery. One scene that stands out is the killing of a hateful mother-in-law by dozens of small tridents penetrating her eyes, and another is at the climax of the film, when our horrible wizard has cornered a young woman and her husband in the temple of the local goddess (not a good idea, fella). He torments the couple by threatening the life of their child, but The Goddess has had enough of his foolishness and sends him to hell. Literally. His fiery descent is one of the few excellent examples of low-budget CG done right.

KAN THIRANTHU PARAMMA is an early film from popular Tamil actress Sangeetha that isn't listed on any of her filmographies that I know. Also features actress Y. Vijaya, who apparently enjoys playing the part of a nasty mother-in-law, as she reprises her role as the evil matriarch from Om Sai Prakash's **DURGAI AMMAN** and a dozen other such films. Released in a Hindi dub as **DEVI TERE ROOP ANEK**.
Cast: Ranjith, Sangeetha, Babu Mohan, Alphonsa, Chapolin Balu, Y. Vijaya, Surya Kanth; music: S.P. Eswar

JAI MAA DURGA SHAKTI
2001, D: Ravit Roy, Telugu, VCD/DVD
This is one of the major frustrations that come from researching Indian films: there are eight sequences from **JAI MAA DURGA SHAKTI** on YouTube. The film mocks me with its tantalizing images of sorcery and gob-smacked low-tech computer animation effects, but I just can't seem to be able to track the entire film down. It has been out of reach as an OOP title on two Indian websites, and there is precious little production information on it other than a date and director—*and* it shares a similar cast and musical director as Om Sai Prakash's **DURGAI AMMAN**. Alternative Hindi dub title **JAI MAA**.
Cast: Roja, Anjan, Alisa, Simran, Rami Reddy; music: unknown

ANGALA PARAMESWARI
2001, D: Om Sai Prakash, Tamil, no subtitles, VCD
You know you're in for a visual treat when the VCD sleeve art's tagline is "A Special Effects Film"…even if they are crappy and cartoonish. The film opens with a wild dance number that features the Gods Shiva and Parvati, while various other deities show up to watch the show. Shiva requests that his consort, Parvati, reincarnate as the Goddess Angala Parameswari and descend to earth to help mankind. An orphaned baby of a devoted family has been left in a rural temple and is found suckling milk from the breasts of the stone idol of Angala Parameswari. She is raised under the protection of the temple priest and soon grows into a beautiful woman named Kaveri (devotional mega-star Prema).

Kaveri is a very devout follower of The Goddess who must face the cruel family of the man she is to marry, along with a *tantrik* wizard bent on sacrificing human beings in order to revive a mummified yogi. What follows is pretty much your standard family squabble, and various attempts on Kaveri's life. Matters are made worse when she marries and has a young son who grows into an annoying five-year-old, seemingly overnight (the passage of time, as in a lot of these films, is something irrelevant and taken for granted). In a pitched battle of good versus evil, a possessed Prema is about to decapitate her only son with a huge saber. Luckily, The Goddess has had enough with the arrogant wizard. She attacks the magician who tries to confuse her my multiplying his image (an old demon trick), but a helpful divine nudge from Shiva and Parvati exposes the real wizard and Angala Parameswari stomps him into the ground, thus freeing everyone from his evil grasp.

Director Om Sai Prakash is better known as an auteur of the "sentimental film" genre, but he does dabble in the supernatural from time to time. Unfortunately, in **ANGALA PARAMESWARI** he relies too heavily on cheap CG effects rather than the crude practical effects that I find work better in this genre. **AMMORU** is the exception as its sparse effects dazzle rather than bore the viewer. Om Sai Prakash lacks skill such as that of director Kodi Ramakrishna when it comes to handling his actors and developing an interesting supernatural tale. He compensates with springy electronic dance numbers and, of course, the participation of two very talented actresses; Prema as the devotee, and Meena who shows up as the rather pretty (pissed-off) Goddess (a variant of Karumariamman who is a variant of Mariamman who is a variant of Kali) wearing a huge gold crown of seven cobras.

Sai Prakash entered the fantasy world of devotional films with his 1994 **LOK PARLOK/YAMAGOLA** (1977)-inspired comedy **INDRANA GEDDA NARENDRA**. He made the very entertaining cobra goddess film **NAGADEVATHE** (a.k.a. **NAG SHAKTI**) with Prema and Soundarya in 2000, as well as **SRI NAGA SHAKTHI** (2003, released in 2011) and **NAVASHAKTHI VAIBHAVA** (2007), again starring Prema. Most of his films are sentimental and mushy. **ANGALA PARAMESWARI** has also been released on VCD and DVD in Hindi under the titles **MAA DEVI MAA** or **DEVI MAA**, and as **GRAMA DEVATHA** as a Kannada dub.
Cast: Saikumar, Meena, Prema, Roja, Ranganath, : music: unknown

ZAKHMI SHERNI - *"The Wounded Tigress"*
2001, D: Surinder Kapoor, Hindi, DVD/VCD, no subtitles

ZAKHMI SHERNI is most definitely the lowest movie on the Angry Goddess totem pole when it comes to production values. It has none. ZAKHMI SHERNI is a film which I have included just because it's so zany, *and* it just *barely* fits into the category. Truth be told, Surinder Kapoor's association with India's premier sleazeball producer-director, Mr. Kanti Shah, is a major plus. The late Kapoor (he died in 2011) had worked with Shah on numerous other films, and this entry into the genre features all the hallmarks of a Shah production. The direction is sub-standard with very little care given to character development, the cinematography is nonexistent, there are has-been actors milling about (Hemant Birje, Dharmendra, Kiran Kumar, etc.) and the music is dull and predictable.

That said, it's tale of a young woman (actress Sapna, wife of Kani Shah, and one hell of a thespian) who is wronged and raped and left with nothing in her life. She turns to The Goddess (Durga) and in a moment of piety she asks for a boon. The Goddess bestows upon her a magical trident which the woman then uses to kill all the men that made her life a living hell. She hunts down each man while dressed in traditional *daku* (bandit) garb and riding a white stallion. In the end she returns the trident to The Goddess, and is united with the local police inspector with whom she has always been secretly in love.

The Goddess makes no appearance in this film other than as a disembodied voice that instructs Sapna's character to kill her abusers. ZAKHMI SHERNI is a guilty pleasure, and I only included it because of that. The title ZAKHMI SHERNI is based in part from Harmesh Malhotra's 1988 film SHERNI, which stars the adorable Sridevi as a pissed off, leather-clad, rifle-toting bandit queen named, of all things, Durga. No supernatural elements in that film unless you count Sridevi's scene-chewing performance which Sapna so neatly channels for her character. SHERNI also stars the actor Birbal who also has a lead role in this film as a spectral father figure to Sapna's bandit queen.
Cast: Birbal, Hemant Birje, Chandrashekhar, Dharmendra, and Sapna; music: Abhiraaj

DHARMA DEVATHE
2002, D: Nagendra Magadi Pandu, Kannada, DVD, no subtitles

DHARMA DEVATHE is based on the story of Bhimambika Devi, a Kannada-based devotional myth involving a woman who is born of divine impregnation by the Goddess Minakshi, one of the (many) South Indian avatars of Parvati. Bhimambika is the holy woman's name, and she is tormented by an assortment of bad folks and ill fortune, although she is very devout to her goddess throughout the film. DHARMA DEVATHE is a slow-moving movie that takes its good old time to eventually get to the much-anticipated showdown between a grumpy (and very bitter) *tantrik* and The Goddess, who has been reincarnated as Bhimambika Devi. The *tantrik* has a connection to The Goddess, as he worships one of her more savage aspects (Kalaratri?) in a bid to gain some kind of power. However, his devotion doesn't stop The Goddess from literally stomping him into the ground when he makes the bold and foolhardy attempt to destroy Bhimambika, her vessel. The Hindi-dubbed version of this film is called MAA PARVATI, which, as usual, just adds confusion to any sort of research. Subtitles would help a great deal, as my Hindi is very rudimentary, and my understanding of Kannada is next to nonexistent other than recognizing a few root-words shared by most of the Indian languages.
Cast: Devraj, Shilpa, Raagasudha; music: Upendra Kumar

PADAI VEETU AMMAN
2002, D: Pugazhmani (aka Pugal Mani), Tamil, DVD, subtitles

CG-crazy film wherein we have tag-team goddess action with the gorgeous Tamil actress Meena playing dual roles of Goddess Padai Veettu Amman and the neighboring deity Māri (a variation of Mariamman). Meena, like Prema, Soundarya, Hema Malini and Ramya Krishnan, is another favorite of directors in the devotional genre.

The film follows your typical route of devotional horrors: nasty family members, an evil *tantrik*, doom and gloom, devotional song and dance, and way too many scenes of bad digital effects, before the final showdown of good versus evil. In this case, an intensely furious green-skinned Goddess sings and dances as her crew of drummers and grass pom-pom-pumping devotees rip into the climatic tune "Aayce Main Aayce" (note: the musical interludes were choreographed and shot by seasoned devotional director Rama Narayanan). This frenzied dance invokes the Goddess Kali who, with bow and arrow in hand, defeats a black magic *tantrik* who has transformed into a giant fire-breathing mongoose, intent on destroying her cobra shrine.

Not a classic by any stretch of the imagination, but you could do worse. A plus is that this film is easily found with English subtitles under its Hindi-dubbed title DEVI DURGA SHATKI. Digital effects by the EFX Chennai group.
Cast: Meena, Devayani, Senthil, Ramki, Rawali, and Baby Akshaya; music SA Rajkumar

SRI KALIKAMBA
2003, D: Ram Narayan, Kannada, VCD, no subtitles

Another oddball devotional flick with helpful animals and a sister act of two very hardcore devotees of the Goddess Kaaligaambaal/Kalikamba (an aspect of Kali/Durga, I would suppose). The film starts out as some kiddie adventure fodder as the two tweens and a silly elephant (who sports a huge floppy hat and sunglasses) help to free an injured nag goddess from a sacred cobra mound. Later on as the girls mature and are married off they both encounter harsh treatment from their respective in-laws. And if that isn't bad enough, wouldn't you know it, an evil *tantrik* is hired to get rid of the devout women. Just as he is about to sacrifice one of the women in hopes of obtaining additional black magic powers, Kaaligaambaal shows up very annoyed, does her dance, and runs the bastard through with her trident.

From director Ram Narayan (also spelled Ramnarayan) who really attempted to rock the digital effects with a gigantic bargain-basement winged psychedelic demon, and other oddball "magical" elements. I bought this film as a Hindi-

Top to bottom: Hindi dubbed versions of **SRI RENUKADEVI, DEBI, KAN THIRANTHU PARAMMA,** and **ANGALA PARAMESWARI**

Bengali VCD of **MANASHA AMAR MAA**

dubbed VCD under the title **MAA DURGA DIVYA HAATHI**, the Tamil dub is **SRI PARAMESHWARI MAHIMALU**, and the Telugu dub is **ANNAI KALIGAMBAL**.

Actress Ramya Krishnan also starred in Ramakrishna's **AMMORU**, and **DEVULLU** (2000), and Superstar Krishna's **MAANAVUDU DAANAVUDU** (1999), so one wonders how she got talked into appearing as a green-skinned goddess in this low-budget crappy CGI fest.
Cast: Ramya Krishnan, Anu Prabhakar, Livingston, Jayanthi and Vennira Aadai Moorthy; music: Devi

SRI RENUKADEVI
2004, D: Nagendra Magudi Pandu, Kannada, DVD
SRI RENUKADEVI is an effects-heavy film with a rocking score and is a fine example of post-**AMMORU** devotional cinema. In a role switcharoo, Prema plays Shanti, a devotee of the Goddess Devi Maa Renuka, played by Soundarya. Yet again the film is your usual nonsensical family drama where a young woman meets and falls in love with a promising writer, they get married, have twins, he turns into a drunk, she leaves, is harassed by family member who hire a wizard to torment her and her son, and life is shitty all around. However, she comes under the protection of the local Goddess Renuka (Soundarya) and it is then that the family steps up their wicked game. The wizard kidnaps the boys (whose resemblance to the mythological twins of Sita and Ram is made somewhat overt) and shit hits the fan. When The Goddess tries to reason with the wizard, he spitefully throws holy vermilion into her face. He realizes all-too-late that this probably wasn't the smartest thing to do and he attempts to flee the high-powered goddess-on-a-stomping-rage. After a colorful dance, divine cosmic rays emanate from The Goddess's eyes and blow the wizard away. The end.

Soundarya makes an extremely gorgeous Goddess! Seriously, someone has to make a "Best of" DVD wherein all there is are scenes where Durga, Kali, etc. do nothing but annihilate the baddies and dance around in celebration afterwards. Hindi dubbed title: **MAA KA CHAMATIKAR**.
Cast: Soundarya, Jaya Pradha, Prema, Charan Raj and Tej Sapru; music: Hamsalekha

Forget Ramya Krishnan (see top photo), the real star of Ram Narayan's epic **SRI KALIKAMBA** is this stylish pachyderm, pictured here with the director (far right).

MANASHA AMAR MAA
2004, D: Bijoy Bhoshkar, Bengali, VCD
I must admit I am confused with this find. In *Weng's Chop* #4, I wrote about what I believe was an Oriya-made Naag film by the same director (sometimes credited as Vijay Bhaskar) as this entry. That was **MANI NAGESWARI** (1995), and **MANASHA AMAR MAA** is pretty much is the same plot only with a larger budget and better direction and cinematography. Had the film not inserted crude digital effects lifted from Rama Nararayanan's 2003 film **NAAG LOK** then this would have been an exceptional devotional film. That said, **MANASHA AMAR MAA** is your typical tale of a young woman who has a special bond with the local goddess, this time around it is Manasa, the snake goddess often associated with Vasuki the Bengali Nag god. The young woman is smoking hot but very devout and married to a real shithead whose three sisters torment her daily. She is then murdered by the husband for her gold jewelry and buried in an unmarked grave. Too bad for him, as a nāgiṇī takes the form of the murdered woman and returns to torment him and his family. Eventually, a wizard is consulted and in a confrontation he is impaled by the trident-welding nāgiṇī. The Goddess Manasa appears to stop the nāgiṇī from killing the husband and in turn he pleads his love for the snake woman. Manasa hears him and the nāgiṇī out (she suddenly turns very loving) and resurrects his former wife so she can return to her now born-again spouse. The end.

MANASHA AMAR MAA is a darn good-looking film, and if it didn't have the aforementioned CG effects inserted for god knows what reason, it would have made my top ten devotional "horror" movie list.
Cast: Siddhanta, Mihir Das, Brajo, Lisa, Parvati, and Pradyunna Lenka; music: Akshay Mohanti, Rishav Supriyo

DEBI
2005, D: Swapan Saha, Bengali, VCD, no subtitles
An adequate Bengali remake of the most visually exciting and important Angry Goddess devotional film in Indian cinema. Of course, I'm talking about Ramakrishna's **AMMORU**. Director Swapan Saha blows it big time with way too many sequences of cheesy CG rather than the beautifully-crafted effects that appeared in the original film. The soundtrack is just awful. A.k.a. **DEVI** (Hindi dub).
Cast: Jishu Sengupta, Debashree Roy, Rachana Banerjee, Ramaprasad Banik, Kaushik Banerjee, Sunil Mukherjee, Sanghamitra Banerjee, Ashok Mukherjee, and Locket Chatterjee; music: Ashok Bhadra

NAVASHAKTHI VYBHAVA
2007, D: Om Sai Prakash, Kannada, DVD, no subtitles
A mediocre devotional film dealing with the ten aspects of The Shakti and their relationship with a family of honest devotees plagued by horrible family members. If that sounds familiar it's because that plot element is what drives a large portion of the Indian devotional cinema, and by 2007 Sai Prakash didn't want to upset the apple cart. A loving couple has been without children even though they are very devout and the wife prays daily to all her nine goddesses of choice. One day she is kind to a passing beggar who turns out to be one of the goddesses, and she grants fertility upon the couple. Very soon the wife becomes pregnant and twins are born, a boy and a girl. In this case, the two "lovable" (ugh) children are blessed by one of the nine goddesses and they become famous as devotional singers, winning awards and admiration the world over. Enter the mother's shithead relatives who attempt to murder the boy and girl, who are saved from a deadly poison by another goddess. They recover from the murderous attempt, but are not altogether healthy. The rest of the

Popular bronze statue of Kali. These and other figures of Hindu deities can be found in gift shops the world over.

film follows their exploits, and those of the goddesses that love them as they recover their talents and the baddies are put in their places.

The most interesting aspect of this film is that you, the viewer, get to watch ten of the most popular southern goddesses strut their stuff in the guise of ten popular actresses of the day: Kollur Mookambike (Dr Jayamala), Badami Banashankeri (Vijayalakshmi), Belgaum Yallamma (Dhamini), Horanadu Annapurneshwari (Anu Prabhakar), Katilu Durga (Radhika), Annamma Devi (Ruchitaprasad), Shringeri Sharadambe (Sudharani), Gokarna Parameshwari (Ruthika), and my current favorite Indian actress, Prema, as the Goddess Mysore Chamundeswari (the fierce form of the Shakti Durga). The actresses are in the film for their beauty, as their roles are very minimal, appearing one by one throughout the film to right wrongs and eventually uniting into one really pissed off Goddess (that of Koller Mookambike, a *jyotirlinga* deity that incorporates both Shiva (male) and Shakti (female) divine powers, and is keen on killing demons). Once united, the deity puts a stop to the annoying family members and their hired gun of a wizard by blowing them up with her holy trident.

I would imagine the overall lackluster of **NAVASHAKTI VYBHAVA** is primarily due to Sai Prakash's attempt to make a family-friendly film. The end result is bright and gay, full of positive elements, many dance numbers (each goddess has her own), and way-too-much ridiculous humor which, for me, destroys any sense of drama. The final *filmi* sequence with all ten of the goddesses taking turns singing their divine hearts out is rather amusing, but I wanted a better climax and some Hindu mythological Rockettes. Sai Prakash's zeal in representing all of the goddesses goes one step further. By filming all of his location shoots at various famous temples and festivals around the South West state of Karnataka, Sai Prakash lovingly exploits his goddesses, making **NAVASHAKTI VYBHAVA** more of a colorful travelogue than anything else.

Director Sai Prakash's most recent film, **SRI KSHETRA ADICHUNCHANAGIRI** (2012), is a devotional "biography" that incorporates gods and goddesses into the plot. I have yet to locate a copy of this film which looks like a comedy, but I'm happy to see that deities are still featured in Kannada cinema.
Cast: Dr. Jayamala, Shruthi, Ramkumar, Sudharani, Prema, Anu Prabhakar, and Vijayalakshmi Radhika: music: Hamsalekha

JAI MAA SHERAWALI
2008, D: Shashi-Samir, DVD, Hindi, subtitles
Another horrible Honey International Pictures release of a low-budget Rajasthani devotional family drama production. Despicable family members plan on eliminating their annoying daughter-in-law who is a devotee of Durga. The Goddess foils their plans a few times until they hire a wizard to dispatch the young woman. Unfortunately for them, Durga is more than annoyed by their antics and shows up in the final seven minutes to zap the baddies into goodies, and love is in the air once again. Ugh, why do I put myself through these things?

Above: DEVI (Hindi dub of **DEBI**).

Below: Lobby card art from Om Sai Prakash's Goddess smorgasbord **NAVASHAKTHI VYBHAVA**.

Not to be confused with Israr Ahmad's **JAI JAI MAA SHERAWALI** (2012) which, although I have to see it, has got to be better than this mindless dreck.
Cast: Aman Joi, Rakesh Kukreti, Neha Sahay, Reshma, Asha Shrama, Dev Malhorta, and Birbal ; music: Krishan Kumar

MARIYATHAA
2009?, D: P. Krishna, Tamil?, no subtitles

MARIYATHAA is a late addition to this article and I have very little information on the film other than it is pretty good for such a low budget. Director P. Krishna, whom I have no information on, borrows heavily from earlier devotional goddess films but managed to cobble together an entertaining product.

As the film opens, we witness a young pregnant woman being chased by a group of angry men (possibly due to her child being illegitimate?). She eludes her captors, and in distress she collapses in front of a rural temple begging for the Goddess Maritathaa to help her. The Goddess appears, and with the help of four of her sister deities, helps deliver a healthy baby girl before the mother expires. The goddesses deposit the orphaned baby in the temple where she is found by a priest who raises the child.

Years later the baby girl grows into a gorgeous woman (Devi Chitram) and the rest of the film is your usual amalgamation of an assortment of plots, characters, and musical numbers seen previously in many such films. The final confrontation between an evil *tantrik* and the multi-armed Goddess Maritathaa is pretty good. The Goddess chases down and corners the man in a clearing outside of her temple. He does the usual boasting before The Goddess (which never works out well). The Goddess grows to giant size, sprouting numerous arms and looking glorious, and then spits forth a glowing divine orb of death which strikes the *tantrik* and blows him apart.

MARIYATHAA is well worth tracking down on DVD or VCD of it exists in those formats. I found this on YouTube (it has since been taken down), and the source seems to have been a very worn VHS or Beta video tape (there are many drop-outs and mistracking abounds).
Cast: Devi Chitram; Music: unknown

PANCHAKSHARI
2010, D: V. Samudra, Telugu, DVD

Fresh from making a name for herself in Kodi Ramakrishna's phenomenally successful (and very good) **ARUNDHATI**, actress Anushka Shetty plays yet another dual role in V. Samudra's **PANCHAKSHARI**. She should have picked her follow-up film a bit more wisely. Samudra is no Ramakrishna, no matter how hard he pushes his meager budget and vision.

Anushka plays a dual role—one of the temple-born visionary Vaishnavi who, when possessed by the Goddess Devi Maa, is known as Panchakshari, and the other role being that of her half-sister, Honey. When Vaishnavi is killed in what appears to be a freak inferno at the temple, Honey is adopted into the family. Little does anyone know that the accident was an intentional killing by a psychopathic criminal bent on robbing the temple of its hidden treasure. Unfortunately for him, the temple grounds are guarded by the ghost of Vaishnavi who has buddied up with the Goddess Devi Maa Panchakshari. To counter the deity's power, the criminal hires an ascetic to nullify the ghost, but the power of love is too much for their plan to work and The Goddess is able to manifest herself and destroy the evil-doers.

I must say that the film looks good, especially whenever the special effects kick in, and Anushka Shetty, who is 6 feet to begin with, cuts a fine regal figure as the Goddess Devi Maa. But the script and plotting are mediocre at best, with too much emphasis on ridiculous comedy relief and some crappy musical numbers. On a happy note, Shetty is currently attached to a film project called **RUDRAMA DEVI**, which sounds like it could be a pretty fun period piece about India's few warrior queens from the 13th Century.
Cast: Anushka Shetty, Samrat Reddy, Nassar, Pradeep Rawat, Chandra Mohan, and M S Narayana; music: Chinna

Above: The regal Anushka Shetty in full divine headgear from **PANCHAKSHAR**. Most goddesses wear such adornment and the detail of these traditional crowns, sometimes called *Kirita Mukuta*, are incredible. Some gods have crowns as well, while Shiva, always the fashion rebel, sports a *Jatakas* which is his trademark ascetic -style conical-shaped dreadlocked mass of hair piled on the top of his head.

Want to buy Goddess films in bulk? Sure you do! The best way to do this is to purchase some infamous "3-in-1 DVD" compilations from the Internet. Of course, the quality will be bunk, but the films will still look better than if you bought them individually on VCD. They're pretty cheap, to boot. Ah, but there's a catch! Two, in fact. First, there will be no English subtitles. Second, the S&H for most of the webstores from India is pretty atrocious. My suggestion is to try eBay or watch even crummier-looking editions of the films you want on YouTube. Either way you'll find something worth your while...eventually

Shakti Appendix 4

Graven Images
Pimping the Angry Goddess for Fun & Profit

When you have a film industry that produces as much stock as does India, there is always the chance that someone will take advantage of the popularity of Shakti Cinema. Dust off old vaguely mythological or devotional films from the era of pre-AMMORU and slap on some annoyed blue-skinned and wide-eyed goddess and you will have someone buying that VCD. I know I fell for that enticement a good many times. Many of the VCD and DVDs I bought to review for this article failed to live up to what I assumed I was being sold. Two examples of this bait and switch are:

DEVI MAIYYA
2000, D: Renuka Sharma, Bhojpuri, VCD, no subtitles
Best on-screen Shiva dance ever. Often confused with Vijay Sharma's 1976 film of the same name. More of a Shiva devotional film, with some deceptive VCD artwork. Sure, a goddess shows up in this film—heck, about twenty deities make an appearance along with a cartload of saint and demons—so the cover promoting an snarling and very wide-eyed goddess is very misleading. A.k.a. **JAI MAHALAKSHMI MAA**, a.k.a. **MAHAA DEVI** (Hindi dubs).
Cast: Bhavya, Vinay, Prasad, and Shridhar; music: P. Madhadevan

FARISTA AUR BHAGVAN - (Hindi dubbed title)
1988, D: Ramnarayana, Tamil, VCD, no subtitles
Another nutty though very entertaining film by the director of **GOMATA**, and despite what appears on the cover of the VCD I purchased, there is no goddess in this film. The image is of some form of role-playing from "sexy scene" between a man and his wife. He gives her a costume and then waits for her to change into his own personal Lakshmi, and I assume he considers himself Vishnu as they have a bed board shaped like the Shesha Naga. Oh so kinky.

Bait-and-switch issues aside, the film is primarily about a small boy who tends to the local temple dedicated to the Tanil deity Murugan. The boy, who is also the leader of the temple's band, plays a mean Nadaswaram, which is like an oboe and loves to watch the ladies dance to his music. The first half of the film is very lightweight, but the second gets dark as a group of criminals decide to off the kid when he gets wind of their schemes. In the end, it's the young boy that transforms into Murugan and takes out the criminals with his ceremonial *vel* (divine spear). He completes his transformation and becomes an idol in one of the temple's shrines, much to the amazement of his mother and father.

It isn't all that surprising that the young boy in the film is friends with a cobra that also tends to the temple. Then again, this is a devotional film by Ram Narayana, so it's a given. A solid production with the director's usual choice of filming on location in and around an actual temple complex, and better-than-usual cinematography and choreography. The dance numbers by lead actress Bhanu Priya are exceptionally sexy and well worth the price I paid for this VCD…which was $2.
Cast: Bhanu Priya, Nazar; music: Shankar Ganesh

In Closing...

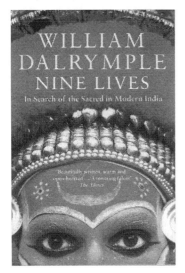

I have come a long way in appreciating Indian culture and their film, and I hope to make others aware of their fantastic cinema. I am sure that many of *Weng's Chop*'s readers may find my love of this peculiar cinema perplexing. As with any region of the world, there are both wonderful and horrible things within its borders. A great way to chop though the sensationalism of filmmaking and news reporting is to read some books. Good books. William Dalrymple's *Nine Lives: In Search of the Sacred in Modern India* is a great place to start. The passage below pretty much sums up a lot devotional films in India. This scene may not be wide-spread in that huge subcontinental country, but I am sure it is also not that uncommon.

"In villages across South Asia, hundreds of people would gather around a single [TV] set to watch the gods and demons play out their destinies. In the noisiest and most bustling cities, trains, buses and cars were suddenly stilled, and a strange hush would come over the bazaars. In Rajaasthan, audiences responded by offering *aarti* and burning incense sticks in front of their television sets, just as they did to the *bhopa's phad*, the portable temple of the *phad* giving way to the temporary shrine of the telly."

AFTERTHOUGHT

My research into Indian cinema has been a road to discovery with many, many detours into dead ends and unknown territories. I honestly don't see an end to my meanderings. In my travels I have uncovered crates of relatively unknown films. Unknown to me, but not to a country so large it's known as a subcontinent. So, that being said, I need to clarify some points that may have been made but could have been misconstrued. Firstly, I do believe that the Mother Goddess religion/belief in Indian culture was developed and being practiced eons before the arrival of the Aryan gods (which were predominately male). Over time, both sets of beliefs were blended and for the most part a consolidation of said religions formed what is now commonly referred to as Hinduism. The Shakti-Devi is the core foundation of today's form of Hinduism despite the cries of foul from many who are die-hard Vishnu or Shiva devotees. All the deities are one and the one deity are all the deities. That said, both men and women who are Hindus adore the goddesses and for the most part treat them with just as much reverence and respect as they do the three male gods Brahma, Vishnu, and Shiva and all their various aspects and avatars. It's all just a matter of degrees. And who has the power to say so.

As far as presenting an accurate and factual basis for these films, please do not take them at face value. Yes, there have been horrendous accounts of sadism, rape and murder of women whenever India is being reported on the news. Nevertheless, what is portrayed in their cinema isn't 100% true. Sounds like a simple thing to say, but you wouldn't believe how many people believe what they see on TV or in the movies.

Moving on to fact checking. Researching many of the genres and sub-genres of Indian film isn't an easy task. Unlike the fans and scholars of Western and Japanese cinema, there is very little in the way of a movie database for the Indian films. There have been books on the subject, but few cover those genres that I find the most interesting. Pete Tombs's *Mondo Macabro: Weird & Wonderful Cinema Around the World* (1998, St. Martin's Griffin) is an essential for anyone wanting to begin to explore Indian film. Online blogs like the film-based *diedangerdiediekill.blogspot.com* and the religion-based *freebsd.nfo.sk/hinduism/inebohyne.htm* and *hindudharmaforums.com* have been exceptionally helpful in exploring Indian cinema and culture. Nevertheless, there are precious few Indian blogs or websites that give any kind of data that can be correlated. Most sites tend to copy and paste information from *bollywoodhungama.com* or *induna.com* (a great source for obscure VCDs and DVDs). What I have to do is cross-reference data and try to get the facts on these films as accurate as possible. Sometimes I fail...and do so spectacularly.

Mononyms are another confusing mess when it comes to research. A mononym is the crunching together of a first and last name or going by just a single name; be it a first name, surname or some made up variation. Like a vanity plate you can purchase for your car. Apparently mononyms are quite common in the subcontinent as we have a few examples of this in our entertainment industry, which include Mondanna, Prince, Rhinna, etc. This has been very common with actors and actresses in Indian cinema for decades: Prema, Sridevi, Soundarya, Karan, Vinay, Sapna, Srikanth, etc. The "Romanizing" of the Sanskrit or Dravidian writing system (which in no way bares any resemblance to our Latin-based system) has been very useful for the most part of my research, but it has also muddied the matter of identification. I had a hell of a time keeping the directors straight, as one single name could be spelled three or four different ways depending on what was more common for a particular country's release of his films. A prime example of this is the Tamil director Ram Narayan. He is known as Ram Narayan or RNarayan, or Ramnarayan, or Raammarayaan. *AAAAARGH!*

When two or more individuals are responsible for composing the musical scores or the soundtrack of a film it is not an uncommon to combine their last names. This has led me in circles on more than one occasion. Some of the more famous of these musical couplings are: Shankar Ganesh, Laxmikant Pyarelal, Kalyanji Anandji, and Shankar Jaikishan.

The names of gods and goddesses are also Romanized differently depending on what region of India they originated. You will notice that Kali is spelt both as "Kali" and "Kaali". This "aa" phenomenon is often extended to other words including the names of actors, actresses, producers, directors, etc.

You may also notice that the sources for these films are pretty varied. Most I have purchased on VCD or DVD. A few I found on VHS while on a shopping trip to Toronto years ago before my fascination for Indian cinema really took off. The remainder I scored from YouTube, DailyMotion, and a few Chinese streaming sites. Whenever I fail to list director, cast or musical credit it is due to the fact that all I have to go on is the film itself which, if it happens not to be a Hindi dub, will rarely have their credits in English. As for the translation of the film titles, most are just the names of the goddesses featured in the film, so I didn't bother.

Disclaimer: *I do not claim to be a scholar or know the culture or languages of India by heart. I love the films and research and write about them, but don't expect scholarly text. Any misinformation will be corrected in the future when Brian, Tony and I get around to releasing* Weng's Chop: Fearbook Volume One *sometime in 2014. I will be updating and annotating my past articles in an attempt to correct as many past blunders as possible. There may also be a book in the works, but that project won't see fruition for quite some time. In the meantime: research, research, and still more research.*

Books that were helpful or sourced for this article:
Doniger O'Flaherty, Wendy. *The Origins of Evil in Hindu Mythology*, University of California Press, 1980.
Jones, Constance A., and Ryan, James D. *Encyclopedia of Hinduism*, Checkmark Books, 2008.
Doniger, Wendy. *Hindu Myths*, Penguin Books, 1975.
Johnson, W.J. *Dictionary of Hinduism*, Oxford University Press, 2009.
Jain, Kajri. *Gods in the Bazaar*, Duke University Press, 2007. Kajri Jain
Smart, Ninan, & Denny, Frederick, editors. *Atlas of the World's Religions*, 2nd Edition, 2007, Oxford University Press.
Chopra, Swati. *Sadhus and Shamans*, Luster Press/Roli Books, 2012.
Dalrymple, William. Nine *Live: In Search of the Sacred in Modern India*, Alfred A. Knopf, 2010.

Fans of the Chop
MONSTER BASH 2013
in Mars, PA, USA

Photos: Steven Ronquillo

by Danae Dunning

Cult Cinema Under The Gun
Reevaluating the Classics & More

BURIAL GROUND: THE NIGHTS OF TERROR
(Le notti del terrore)

Professor Ayres (Raimondo Barbieri) has just discovered how to bring the dead back to life. The reanimated corpses show their gratitude by having him for dinner. To make matters worse, he's expecting guests. When Janet (Karin Well), Mark (Gianluigi Chirizzi), James (Simone Mattoli) and Leslie (Antonella Antinori), as well as George (Robert Caperali), Evelyn (Mariangela Giordano) and their young son Michael (Peter Bark) show up, they express mild concern at their host's disappearance, but nonetheless settle in and start exploring the place. And making out in graveyards (a popular pastime in these flicks, apparently). Everything seems fine until the undead denizens decide that the Professor just wasn't filling enough and converge upon the group. Will they make it out in time, or will they become zombie chow?

What a wonderful, cheesetastic trip of a movie! As most of you know, I am sick of zombie films, but I love to revisit the "classics." A lot of them don't live up that classification, in my opinion, but **BURIAL GROUND: THE NIGHTS OF TERROR** (1981) does for both the right *and* the wrong reasons—I feel like it belongs in the Zombie Film Hall Of Fame (if such a thing exists).

First, the right reasons: The characters—with the exception of the creepy Michael, whom I'll get into later—are likable, not your typical zombie fodder. The atmosphere is thick with dread and suspense, and the attack scenes are appropriately brutal without going over-the-top—a scene where a woman is decapitated by a pane of broken glass while being dragged through a window conjures up memories of the infamous "splinter in the eye" scene in Fulci's **ZOMBIE** (1979). And the zombies are creepy as well.

And now, the wrong reasons: The over-acting, by both the Italian and English casts, is what gives this its cheese factor. And the making out in the graveyard scene, well, it's just a setup for another, "corpses rising from the grave" scenario that, while well-played in **ZOMBIE**, just looks ridiculous here. And this isn't cheesy, but just plain *wrong*. The character of Michael (played not by a child, but a proportional dwarf, for obvious reasons) is creepy. He likes to watch his mom and dad make love, prompting fits of jealousy. His mother encourages his fondling of her, and then will slap him. This leads to one of the most notorious (and painful-to-watch) scenes.

Is **BURIAL GROUND: THE NIGHTS OF TERROR** as good as **ZOMBIE**? No, but it is entertaining, and definitely in a class by itself.

1981, ITALY. DIRECTOR: ANDREA BIANCHI
AVAILABLE FROM MEDIA BLASTERS

PERFECT BLUE
(パーフェクトブルー / Pāfekuto Burū)

Mima Kirigoe (Junko Iwao) is a member of the successful clean-cut pop group Cham, but sagging album sales and boredom has her longing for a change. The opportunity arises when she is offered a part in a television police drama called Double Bind. The only drawback is that her character is graphically raped onscreen. After a little trepidation, she decides to take the role, over the objection of her horrified manager and best friend, Rumi (Rika Matsumoto). After that and a nude photo shoot, Mima starts receiving faxes calling her a whore and a traitor, and then begins having hallucinations of being taunted by herself. It gets progressively worse when people start dying around her. Is it Mr. Me-Mania, the creepy guy that's been following her around, or has the stress of her image change caused Mima's already fragile psyche to fracture?

Most people are aware of Anime featuring cute characters, demonic beasts and fantastical storylines, but Satoshi Kon has created instead a stylized and brutal psychological thriller. The gore is restrained and a little cartoonish, but that is a selling point. The beautiful animation (by too many talented artist to name), solid script by Sadayuko Murai (based on the novel by Yoshikazu Takeuchi) and tense stalk-and-attack scenes is what makes this little Anime film the beauty that it is. Not to mention that both the Japanese and English voice casts do exceptionally well. Bridget Hoffman, who does Mima's voice in the English version was also Echidna in *Hercules: The Legendary Journeys* (1995-1996), and has lent her vocal talents to the English dubs of many other Anime including **EL HAZARD** (1998), and **VANDRED** (2000).

156

If all you know of Anime is kid's stuff, then take a chance on this wonderful movie. It will pleasantly surprise you.

1997, JAPAN. DIRECTOR: SATOSHI KON
AVAILABLE FROM MANGA VIDEO

SECRETARY

Lee Holloway, played by Maggie Gyllenhaal (**HYSTERIA, SHERRY-BABY**) is a fragile young woman just released from a mental hospital. Her stifling home life with her over-protective mother Joan (Leslie Ann Warren), depressed father Burt (**PONTYPOOL**'s Stephen McHattie), and her lackluster relationship with fiancé Peter (Jeremy Davies) don›t do much to speed her recovery along, so she gives in to depression and takes to self-mutilation to temporarily relieve her frustrations.

Life begins looking up for Lee when she gets a job as a secretary, working for demanding lawyer E. Edward Grey (James Spader of **PRETTY IN PINK**)—whose first name is never mentioned. Noticing nicks in her stockings and the fact that she carries a small sewing kit, even though she doesn't sew, Grey puts two and two together and orders Lee to stop cutting herself. This simple command has a more profound effect on her than he'd expected, as she does indeed stop, a feat that years of therapy had not been able to accomplish.

When a critique over a poorly-typed letter leads to an enthusiastic spanking session delivered by Grey, Lee—who has never been excited about anything in her life—finds herself deliberately making mistakes so she can receive further "punishment." She even becomes more assertive with her mother. In the meantime, after discovering this unfamiliar side of himself, Grey becomes ashamed, not realizing that Lee not only finds it liberating, but she has also fallen in love with him!

I first heard about this in the IFC series *Indie Sex*. Here you have it folks: a sweet and gentle love story about…sadomasochism. That's right, sadomasochism. But that's not the only thing that distinguishes this from your average Rom-Com outing. Instead of the "Idiot Plot," as the late Roger Ebert called it—where characters do dumb things to move the plot along—screenwriter Erin Cressida Wilson (**STOKER, CHLOE**) has crafted intelligent, likable and non-stereotypical characters, and uses them in an engaging story that will keep you invested whether you're into the topic of BDSM or not.

2002, USA. DIRECTOR: STEVEN SCHAINBERG
AVAILABLE FROM LIONSGATE

RED WHITE & BLUE

Meet Erica (Amanda Fuller). Erica wanders from bar to bar having casual sex with one man after another, night after night. ("I don't stay the night, I don't fall in love, and I never fuck the same guy twice.") Things are pretty much routine for her until she catches the attention of boardinghouse neighbor Nate (Noah Taylor, *Game of Thrones*, **TOMB RAIDER: CRADLE OF LIFE**) who is not exactly normal. She resists all his attempts to establish a rapport until he gets her a job at the hardware store where he works. Things are actually progressing rather sweetly between the two until Franki (Marc Senter of **THE LOST**), one of Erica's one night stands, finds out he's HIV positive, and she might have been the one who infected him. To make matters worse, Franki's been regularly donating blood to his cancer-ridden mother. This sets in motion a shocking chain of events that wreaks havoc upon not only our three protagonists, but practically everyone in their paths.

Ok, I know…that little synopsis really didn't tell you much. But at least I didn't start out with "five annoying twentysomethings go into the woods to party and are killed off one-by-one," because (thank God!) it's not that kind of movie. For one thing, it's actually something I have not seen before: A slice

PERFECT BLUE

(no pun intended) of life horror film. This movie starts out slow—a little too slow for my tastes—but I bore with it because the time is filled with character development, not with endless scenes of people wandering around aimlessly and spouting stupid dialogue. These are not cannon fodder stereotypes, but flesh and blood people you start to care for even when you shouldn't.

And that was the best part. When the action started, my emotions were toyed with. I simultaneously felt sympathy and disgust for the same characters. Gorehounds will be highly disappointed. There is some blood, yes, but as I said, this is not a hack-and-slash, but a character-driven, psychological and emotional horror movie.

So if you're tired of the same old fare, I would highly recommend adding **RED WHITE & BLUE** to your menu.

2010, UK/USA. DIRECTOR: SIMON RUMLEY
AVAILABLE FROM MP1 HOME VIDEO

MANIAC

Frank Zito (Joe Spinell) looks like you average guy—okay, slightly creepy, but relatively harmless. Problem is, he's not. He spends his nights killing women who remind him of his late, abusive prostitute mother. Then he nails their scalps to mannequins dressed in their clothes. When Frank meets the lovely photographer Anna (Carolyn Munro) in the park after she snaps his picture, he thinks he just might have his "mommy" back.

I know this isn't really much of synopsis, especially about the infamous "video nasty" **MANIAC**. Yes, **MANIAC**: that piece of vile misogynistic offal; that morally reprehensible trash.

But I didn't feel that way at all about this movie. Yeah, there are women getting brutalized, but I don't think that's what really disturbed people. This is not a **FRIDAY THE 13TH** where the killer is unseen and the focus is on the victims trying to avoid getting bumped off. Nor is this a police procedural. No, folks, we as an audience spend day after day with Frank, getting inside his head. This is not a larger-than-life entity such as Jason Voorhees, or a smooth sociopath like Hannibal Lecter. This is a mentally ill human being who literally can't help himself. As repulsive as he is, we just can't help feeling sorry for him. Hell, I was even in tears during a scene in which Frank is reliving his abuse in his head—kudos to the late Joe Spinell for this very effective performance. Now, of course I have to give a shout out to Tom Savini's excellent special effects work—especially where he, as one of the first victims, has his own head blown off—but this is Joe's movie all the way.

So if you're not put off by the trailers, or by the naysayers, or if you just want to see what all the fuss is about, put aside any preconceived notions and watch this movie. You might find yourself pleasantly surprised.

1980, USA. DIRECTOR: WILLIAM LUSTIG
AVAILABLE FROM BLUE UNDERGROUND

Joe Spinell is a MANIAC

ELFEN LIED
(エルフェンリート / *Erufen rîto*)

On an island outside of the village of Kamakura, Japan, a vicious mutant named Lucy escapes from a mysterious scientific facility. Lucy is member of a species of mutant called the Dichlonus Dichlonii, which are distinguished by a pair of horns resembling elf or cat ears, but their power comes from a set of invisible arms, called vecters, that can pass through solid matter, deflect bullets, and rip people apart. After cutting a bloody path through the facility, a sniper is finally able to shoot Lucy in the head as she makes her way to the cliff. She falls into the water and disappears into waves.

When Lucy washes up on the beach, she is found by college students Kohta and Yuka, but she is different. Her personality is very child-like, almost infantile, and all she can say is "Nyu! Nyu!", so that's what she's called by the two. Lucy/Nyu is taken in by the cousins and the three form a family unit, later joined by a young runaway named Mayu and her puppy Hanta. Meanwhile, Chief Kurama has sent a Special Assault team, led by the sadistic Bando, to make sure Lucy is dead. He also sends out two other Dichlonii to track her: Nana, an innocent who refuses to kill even when provoked, and Mariko, who's been kept in isolation since birth and is eager to "come out and play." When all paths cross it won't be pretty.

The series has something for everyone. There are fully fleshed-out characters that you care about, and ones you love to hate. The Dichlonii are kept naked and subjected to cruel tortures to test their powers. The theory is that their sole mission is to wipe out the human race, but it is actually their treatment at the hands of humans that spark their violent tendencies. Not to mention the fact that the animation looks absolutely beautiful.

Now for the downside. Yuka is incredibly annoying. She is hopelessly in love with Kohta, even though he's her cousin (Eeew). She is extremely jealous when he pays attention to any female other than her, even going so far as striking him. And he puts up with it. Also, this is based on a manga that was ongoing at the time of production, so the ending isn't really clear and there are a lot of plot holes for those who haven't read the manga, which is still unavailable in English at this time. One glaringly obvious plot hole is the title itself. "Elfin Leid" (Elf Song) is a German folk song that a character in the manga—who is not in the anime—sings to Lucy. Lucy can relate to the alienation and loneliness felt by the little elf in the song. It would have been nice to have included that. And while the opening song, a beautiful Gregorian chant called "Lillium" is effective in capturing the mood of each episode, it ends with a cheesy pop song called "Be Your Girl," performed by Chieko Kawabe.

But, the pluses outweigh the minuses. If you're an Anime fan, you have to add this to your collection. If you're not, this is a good introduction.

2004, USA. DIRECTORS: MAMORU KANBE, SUMIO WATANABE,
AKIRA IWANAGA, KEISUKE ONISHI, TAKEYUKI SADOHARA
AVAILABLE FROM ADV FILMS

CAMP HELL

Young Tommy Leary (Will Denton of **FRIGHT NIGHT**, 2011) is not looking forward to going to Camp Hope this year. The repressive atmosphere is not only causing him to question his faith, but he begins to question his own sanity when he becomes plagued with demonic nightmares. Worse comes to worst when the monster from his dreams crosses over to the real world upon his arrival, and the camp director, Father Phineas MacAllister (legendary cult film actor Bruce Davison) may or may not have something to do with it.

I've read a lot of unfavorable reviews of this film by people who were disappointed because they assumed that, because of the summer camp setting, it was a Slasher film—although the trailer and plot synopsis make it quite obvious that it's not. I was expecting a cheesy, low budget time-killer, what I got instead was a well-acted, well-made story of what happens when repression and fear take the place of love, grace, and free will. The "based on true events" tagline is not a chain-yanker; this movie was inspired by writer/director George VanBuskirk's experiences growing up in the People of Praise charismatic movement. The People of Praise consist of loosely-connected groups who combine Catholicism with Fundamental Charismatic Protestantism. They form covenant communities in which the people become bound to one another and a council of leaders set "guidelines" for their standard of living. Mini-cults, if you will.

If you've seen ads for the film or the DVD box, you will be wondering why I didn't include Jesse Eisenberg's (**ZOMBIELAND, THE SOCIAL NETWORK**) role. Even though his name is above the title, and the trailer I saw was cut to make it look like he was featured prominently in the production, he's only in the first five minutes of **CAMP HELL** and a brief flashback towards the end. Andrew McCarthy (**PRETTY IN PINK**) does an excellent job as Tommy's stern Dad, as does Connor Paolo (**STAKE LAND**) as Jack, another disillusioned camp member, who Tommy ends up bonding with.

Check your prejudices, but not your brain, at the door and give this little gem a chance.

2010, USA. DIRECTOR: GEORGE BUSKIRK
AVAILABLE FROM GRINDSTONE ENTERTAINMENT GROUP

Alternate theatrical poster for **CAMP HELL**.

DANAE GETS RELIGION...AGAIN: CHRISTIAN HORROR DOUBLE FEATURE

By Danae Dunning

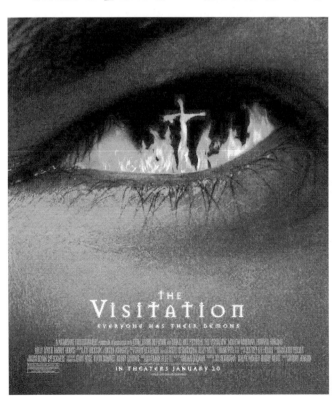

THE VISITATION

Antioch, Ohio, is a small, quiet, close-knit community where nothing exciting ever happens...that is, until drifter Brandon Nichols (**TERMINATOR 2**'s Edward Furlong) comes to town, preceded by three black-clad men who proclaim, "He is coming." Mass healings (including the resurrection of a dead dog) and tent revivals abound. Everyone seems to think that he's the second coming of Christ. Everyone except Travis (Martin Donovan), a former minister (Randy Travis) who's lost his faith, the replacement pastor at Travis' old church, and Morgan, the new town vet whose teenage son Michael (Noah Segan of **DEADGIRL**) is swept up in "Brandon fever." Is Brandon actually Jesus Christ returned, or something sinister?

I know, I know. Both Christian and non-Christians alike cringe when they hear the term "Christian-based horror," as they expect trite, sanitized storylines with heavy-handed preaching. **THE VISITATION**, based on a book by Christian author Frank Peretti, is far from trite, sanitized, or heavy-handed. It is a well-acted, well-written story that sucked me in immediately, making me care about the characters and concerned about their fates. Martin Donovan's tortured performance as the fallen man of God who turns to alcohol after the brutal murder of his wife is truly heartbreaking. And yes, it is scary. Not to mention that a cameo from Bill Moseley (**THE DEVIL'S REJECTS**) is always welcome.

So cast aside your prejudices and preconceptions and experience The Visitation.

2006, USA. DIRECTOR: ROBBY HENSON
AVAILABLE FROM 20th CENTURY FOX HOME ENT.

THE FAMILIAR

Gunsmith Sam (Bryan Massey) has fallen away from God and into alcoholism since the death of his beloved wife Katherine (Stephanie Young) five years ago. (You're sensing a pattern here, I know, but stay with me.) Desperately trying to keep him on the straight and narrow is Sheriff's deputy Charlie (Jeff West), Sam's best friend since childhood. His life gets more complicated when Katherine's estranged sister Laura (Laura Spencer) shows up at his door without warning. Laura keeps going on and on about someone named Rallo, whom she refers to as her "spirit guide." Pretty soon, Sam starts to see and hear a demonic being, along with what he thinks is the ghost of Katherine, and Laura is building a bizarre altar in the backyard while exhibiting other strange behavior. At first Charlie is skeptical, chalking it up to the booze, but when he starts seeing things too, he is reminded of an experience he had over at Sam's house when they were boys, an experience that Sam has blacked out of his memory. In desperation he turns to Sam's preacher/father Nathan (Ben Hall), with whom Sam had a falling out. Will Sam and Laura be saved, or will "Rallo" gain the upper hand?

I didn't know that this was a Christian movie when I first rented it, but I have to be honest, even if I weren't a believer, I don't think I would have felt "had." Just like **THE VISITATION**, the story and the message are woven together so well that one never feels like they're getting a sermon. The cast of unknowns give excellent performances and their characters feel like real people as opposed to stereotypes. The ending almost strays into **THE EXORCIST** rip-off histrionics, but pulls back before ruining the scene. And the demon—though rarely seen—is quite creepy. Definitely not a time waster.

2009, USA. DIRECTOR: MILES HANON
AVAILABLE FROM CELEBRITY VIDEO DISTRIBUTION

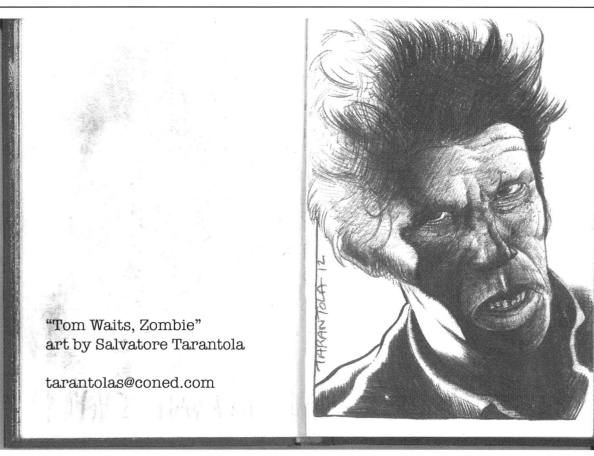

"Tom Waits, Zombie"
art by Salvatore Tarantola

tarantolas@coned.com

ZOMBIES ATE MY COMMON SENSE

A Lucio Fulci Triple Feature
by Danae Dunning

ZOMBIE
(a.k.a. **ZOMBI 2**, 1979)

A derelict boat drifts into a New York Harbor port containing several mangled bodies, one incredibly animated one starts chowing down on one of the investigating police officers. The owner of the boat is missing, and his daughter Anne (Tisa Farrow) along with reporter Peter West (Ian McCulloch) charter a boat to take them to the island of Matool, where the doctor was doing mysterious research with a Dr. David Menard. It seems that the good doctor is experimenting on how to extend life and he's using the natives as guinea pigs. They don't take to kindly to that, and neither does the doc's fed-up wife Paola (Olga Karlatos) When Anne, Peter and the tourists who own the boat arrive on the island, all hell breaks loose as, not only do the newly dead, but also a whole cemetery full of Spanish Conquistadores, rise to feast on the living.

This was my first exposure to "Il Maestro". And boy oh boy, was I impressed. The acting was amazing (in both dubbed and subtitled versions), the characters were likable instead of typical zombie fodder, and unlike other of Fulci's work I have been subsequently exposed to, the plot actually made sense. The special effects by Giannetto De Rossi are breathtaking and cringe-inducing, such as the "zombie vs. shark" scene (unlike in JAWS, I was rooting for the shark.) and the infamous "splinter in the eye" scene that I still can't make myself watch to this day. And when the conquistadores rise from their graves, it is quite creepy and atmospheric. I just knew that I would join the throngs of fawning Fulci acolytes until...

CITY OF THE LIVING DEAD
(*Paura nella città dei morti viventi*, 1980)

When Psychic Mary Woodhouse (Catriona MacColl) sees a vision of a priest committing suicide in the New England town of Dunwich (a Lovecraftian nod?), she is concerned because according to the book of Enoch (my favorite bedside reading), it signifies the opening of the gates of hell, which will spew forth the living dead. Not very good for tourist season. She teams up with skeptical reporter Peter Bell (Christopher George), psychiatrist Gerry (Carlo de Mejo) and his patient Sandra (Janet Angren) to stop the mini-apocalypse before it's too late.

Yeesh! What a mess. The dubbing is over the top, and the whole movie makes no sense whatsoever. Yes, we have some gore goodies such as poor, retarded Bob (Giovanni Radice, **CANNIBAL FEROX**) getting a drill press to the temple and one unfortunate young lady vomiting up her intestines, and while that alone might satisfy hardcore gorehounds, it's just not enough to keep my attention. And the movie just abruptly ends, leaving me scratching my head and saying, "huh??" Still I was not quite ready to give up on Il Maestro just yet...

THE BEYOND
(*...E tu vivrai nel terrore! L'aldilà,* 1981)

Fresh from New York, Liza Merril (Catriona MacColl, **CITY OF THE LIVING DEAD**) travels to Louisiana after inheriting a dilapidated hotel from a distant uncle. She meets a young blind woman named Emily (Cinzia Monreale) who warns her to leave the hotel immediately, because it's built over one of the seven doorways to hell. In 1927, a warlock named Schweick (Antoine St. John) attempted to open it using the Book Of Eibon (which is surprisingly similar to The Book Of Enoch in **CITY OF THE LIVING DEAD**), and was lynched by the townspeople for his efforts. (I'm sure the realtor purposely neglected to mention this.) Not swayed in the least by this story, she plows ahead with making renovations, but when nasty accidents start happening Liza starts hearing and seeing things, and is told that there is no Emily, and that no one has lived in Emily's home in 15 years! She starts to think she's losing her mind, until John McCabe, (David Warbeck, **TWINS OF EVIL**, **RAZOR BLADE SMILE**), a sympathetic doctor, starts experiencing the same phenomena. Schweick has returned to finish what he started and has brought an army of the undead with him.

THE BEYOND starts off well, but then begins to meander and drag a bit and situations start to become a tad implausible. The effects by Giannetto De Rossi were subpar at best, which is shocking because of his excellent work in **ZOMBIE** (1979), and Fulci really seems to have a fetish for eye violence, because there are three scenes of ocular trauma and one near miss, though nowhere near matching the "splinter in the eye" scene from **ZOMBIE**. There is a scene involving spiders that I thought was cheesy, but might give arachnophobics nightmares. Best line: "I'm a doctor, Liza, I only accept rational explanations. I'm consulting Harris. Then I'm calling the FBI." Good luck with that, doc.

While much better than **CITY OF THE LIVING DEAD** (1980) and **HOUSE BY THE CEMETERY** (1981), I won't be re-watching this anytime soon.

1979, 1980, AND 1981; ITALY. RESPECTIVELY. DIRECTOR: LUCIO FULCI
ALL THREE TITLES AVAILABLE FROM BLUE UNDERGROUND AND ARROW VIDEO

STEVE BISSETTE

is forever peddling all manner of his own comics (S.R. BISSETTE'S TYRANT®, SPIDERBABY COMIX, etc.), anthologies (TABOO), books (THE VERMONT MONSTER GUIDE, TEEN ANGELS & NEW MUTANTS, etc.), and new horror/monster prints (TYRANT® IN SLUMBERLAND, ALPHABET OF ZOMBIES, etc.) via his online shop. Visit his store at srbissette.com/store/

and happy horror hunting!

Back issues of WENG'S CHOP are available from Amazon.com or contact the fine folks at Kronos Productions for international sales:
kronoscope@oberlin.net

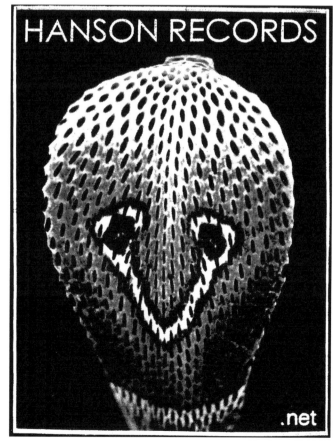

reviews

BAD MEAT (2011)

BAD MEAT

Reviewed by Dan Taylor

As I sat down to pound out this review, I looked at my notes and chuckled as I read the first thing I'd scribbled down: "Stylish opening—hope they don't blow it".

I'll save you the trouble of guessing: they blow it. And not by a little bit. They blow it in spectacular fashion.

No big deal, right? Plenty of flicks suck and leave us feeling defeated and deflated by the time we've wasted; the 90 minutes we could have spent reading, watching another flick, hanging with our loved ones or, hell, doing pretty much anything else.

Unfortunately, **BAD MEAT** (2011) is that rare, worst-case scenario in which the first 78 minutes of the movie don't just deliver but had me wondering how such a gross-but-fun twist on cannibals and campers had managed to elude me. I couldn't wait to sing its praises, as if finding this diamond-in-the-rough made sitting through all the other garbage worthwhile.

But I'm getting ahead of myself.

When a computer is wheeled into the room of the bloodied, bandaged form that "everyone's going on about", it becomes clear that something has gone horribly, horribly wrong at Camp Hardway, a remote delinquent camp run by the Hitler-loving Kendrew (*LOST*'s Mark Pellegrino) and his crew of panty-sniffing, ass-pounding, pot-growing, peeping tom "counselors".

With only a pair of terrified eyes visible, the form clubs at the keyboard, relating to the hospital staff how things went from awful to worse at what is clearly the world's lousiest teen rehabilitation camp.

Seems that a disgruntled cook, sick of the abusive treatment from the likes of Mr. Skullet (Andrew Berg), spikes the staff's dinner with tainted meat. But what starts as offensive gas turns into guffaw-inducing projectile vomiting and, eventually, full-blown psychosis and cannibalism as the staff turn on their charges and begin to hunt them down for food.

What ensues is a manic siege flick as the kids wonder what the hell is going on and how they're going to survive the clearly fucked-up counselors.

So, who is the bloodied, bandaged survivor? Is it the Sensitive-But-Claustrophobic Animal Rights Protestor? Misunderstood Goth? Hoodlum Wannabe? Hoochie Mama? Cutesie Pyro? Tattooed Christian with Lesbian Tendencies?

Alas, we'll never know. Despite a spectacularly solid and entertaining first 78 minutes, director Lulu Jarmen and writer Paul Gerstenberger completely and utterly drop the ball. In fact, the final, crushing six minutes is such a mess that I convinced myself I must have fallen asleep and missed the real ending. One rewind later confirmed that I had done no such thing and I was left staring at the screen in slack-jawed disbelief.

I'm willing to give Jarmen and Gerstenberger the benefit of the doubt and hope that they simply ran out of funding and couldn't complete what could have been a pretty slam-bang take on cannibal crazies making life miserable for stereotype teens.

In fact, **BAD MEAT**'s first 78 minutes is awash in enough blood, gore, underwear-clad cuties, bad taste, over-the-top sexual hijinks, black humor and violent mayhem that I'm almost willing to recommend it.

Almost.

But any ending that cheats the viewer that bad is sorta like the tainted meat served up by the cook. I just can't stomach it.

2011, USA. DIRECTOR: LULU JARMEN
AVAILABLE FROM MVD VISUAL

SEXCULA

Reviewed by Dan Taylor

Nothing sets the hearts of trash film geeks atwitter quite like the news of a "lost film" unearthed from some dank and musty vault. Just the idea of such talk takes me back to my tape-trading days of the 1980s when word of a long-forgotten Spaghetti Western or underground European splatter-fest would keep the US Postal Service and blank VHS suppliers in the black for weeks as tapes shot across the country and around the world for curious eyes to see.

So when Impulse Pictures announced that they were releasing **SEXCULA** (1974), an elusive slice of '70s North-of-the-Border Canuxploitation "transferred from the rare theatrical print stored in the basement of the Library and Archives of Canada", even my long-dormant sick flick radar started going haywire.

Unfortunately, one viewing was all it took to remind me that sometimes lost…is better. (Apologies to Stephen King.)

Playing like a dementoid, over-sexed Canuck version of **LADY FRANKENSTEIN** (1971), **SEXCULA** features Debbie Collins as a young woman who brings her boyfriend (screenwriter David Hurry) to the old family castle and promises to relate stories that will "curl your pubes". One naked picnic later, we're being treated to tales of Baroness Fellatingstein (Jamie Orlando), a curvy scientist with a problem. Seems as though her latest creation—John Alexander as "Frank"—is cursed with "sleeping sex cells" and isn't interested in pleasuring her.

Cue Countess Sexcula (Collins again), a tan (?!) vampiress who is more than happy to answer the call and help the Baroness. (And when I say "answer the call" I mean it literally. Even though we're told that **SEXCULA** takes place in 1869 the Countess has a mid-'70s phone in her boudoir, a full seven years before Alexander Graham Bell declared, "Mr. Watson, come here…I want to see you".)

Armed with a deep, abiding interest in erotic health and sexual healing, Countess Sexcula sets about diagnosing and attempting to cure Frank's dormant dong through a series of hardcore vignettes featuring everything from a burly lumberjack and a horny drunk to a porn film studio wedding that turns into an orgy.

Unfortunately, and perhaps predictably, it's the sex scenes that bring **SEXCULA** screeching to a halt (especially the endless wedding orgy). Your fast forward button is likely to get as much of a workout as some of the Canuck beaver on display throughout this bizzaro cinematic artifact.

Despite the Catskills lodge humor and stilted cue card readings from the female leads, the flick's non-sex scenes have a certain, undeniable charm. And when John Alexander is around, **SEXCULA**'s wasted potential is on full display. His take on the flaccid Frankenstein is the film's highlight, with the "monster" portrayed as a dopey, fey,

undersexed goofball who would rather have Sexcula make him a sandwich than suck his...well, you know. He's like a low-rent Dick Shawn and seems to be having a grand old time throughout even when his dick is flapping around as he chases Sexcula, Fellatingstein and another cutie through a field.

Not quite successful as a horror spoof and certainly not titillating enough for a porno, **SEXCULA** unfortunately comes up short on all counts. Too bad director John Holbrook (billed here as Bob Hollowich) didn't go all in on more of the flick's offbeat components like the bizarre stripper/ape bump and grind, the horny hunchback or the telepathic sex robot. Had he fully embraced the idea of **SEXCULA** as a horror spoof maybe it would be more deserving of the "lost cult classic" label.

1974, CANADA.
DIRECTOR: JOHN HOLBROOK
AVAILABLE FROM IMPULSE PICTURES/ SYNAPSE FILMS

THE DAY AFTER HALLOWEEN
(a.k.a. SNAPSHOT, 1979)

Reviewed by Greg Goodsell

Angela (Sigrid Thornton) is anxious to get on with her life. Living with her persnickety mom (Julia Blake) and spiteful younger sister, she yearns to flee her home life and drab job at the hair salon. Even worse, her far-older and creepy boyfriend Daryl (Vince Gil) has taken to stalking her in a white-and-pink ice cream truck. Wealthy client Madeline (Chantal Contouri) tells Angela she should take a stab at modeling. Introduced to quirky photographer Linsey (Hugh Khys-Byrne), Angela makes a big splash by posing topless for a cologne ad. Moving into a communal-like setting with other photographers and models, it soon becomes clear that she's traded in her original family for a far harsher one. Older gentlemen begin to ply her to pose for sessions where the camera may not contain any film. It soon becomes apparent that someone has begun to stalk her in earnest, her dresses shredded to ribbons along with vile surprises left hidden in her bed. Getting a too-good-to-be-true job overseas, Angela packs her bags and heads for the airport—but it's far from over, just yet.

Originally known as **SNAPSHOT**, this Australian film became notorious for trying to sell itself as a slasher picture in the wake of John Carpenter's **HALLOWEEN** (1978) with the titles **THE DAY AFTER HALLOWEEN** and **THE NIGHT AFTER HALLOWEEN**. Also sold as a soft-core sex film under the title **ONE MORE MINUTE**, anybody in the market for thrills and chills as well as skin and sin would not walk away disappointed. **SNAPSHOT** builds to an especially grim conclusion, involving two gory murders and the heroine hurtling to an even worse situation. The surprise ending, upon careful consideration, logically charts Angela's descent into yet another horrid domestic situation...

Entertaining and engaging, **SNAPSHOT** moves very briskly and benefits greatly with capable actors. Genre fans will remember Contouri from the techno-vampire film **THIRST** (1979), and both Khys-Byrne and Gil starred in the highly influential **MAD MAX** (1979) the same year with Mel Gibson. Director Wincer went on to bigger and better things with the international family film hit **FREE WILLY** in 1993. The year 1979 was a highly successful one for "Ozploitation", it appears.

The DVD from Scorpion Releasing offers an introduction from hostess Katarina Leigh Waters, which is part of the *Katarina's Nightmare Theater* series. There is also an audio commentary by Producer Anthony Ginnane, moderated by Waters, and includes both the US and International cuts of the film, with different opening credits. All in all, despite a highly misleading title (does anyone out there know if they celebrate Halloween in Australia?), this film is definitely worth a spin.

1979, AUSTRALIA.
DIRECTOR: SIMON WINCER
AVAILABLE FROM SCORPION ENTERTAINMENT

SINNER'S BLOOD

Reviewed by Greg Goodsell

Orphaned after their mother dies in a traffic accident, sisters Penelope (the slutty one, played by Nanci Sheldon) and Patricia (the naïve one, played by Cristy Beal) are shipped from Chicago to live with their uncle Clarence and his battleaxe wife Grace in small-town California. The girls take up residency with their cousins, semi-retarded Aubrey (John Talt) and older, Sapphic Edwina (Julie Conners), and quickly adapt to their low-budget Peyton Place surroundings. The unnamed burg they've landed themselves in is the kind Jeannie C. Riley sang about in "Harper Valley PTA"—everyone is peering out the windows to check on their neighbors while privately indulging in sin, sin, sin.

In time, the girls ingratiate themselves to the local male population. Zach, the preacher's son and his best friend Gentry introduce themselves to the gals. Penelope is freshly introduced to Gentry and they go riding off into the forest for some quick patty-cake action. Zach entertains ditzy Patricia on the front porch with promises of future bike rides.

Determined to spice things up, Gentry and Zach visit a local motorcycle gang and plan a rumble the same night as the local church social. Said gang rides around on cheap Japanese motorcycles and can't afford leather jackets. After two of the gang members have a good ol' fashioned fist fight in the hills, fellow gang member Shiv, a tall chap in menacing sunglasses and pockmarked face, trills, "Absolutely marvelous!" He then shoots Gentry a sideways glance and says, "See you later tonight..."

Uncle Clarence and Penelope indulge in some light uncle-niece incest. Patricia and cousin Edwina engage in some lesbianism. Aubrey—seven feet tall, no shirt, cut-offs, orange socks and black

tennis shoes—spies on everybody and is denounced as a "peep freak" by Gentry. After spying on Patricia and Edwina, Aubrey confronts Patricia and says, "You're taking Edwina away from me!" Aubrey tries to rape her but can't perform.

The night of the church social is rudely interrupted by the biker gang. One of the motorcyclists drives by and smacks the preacher's face with a chain. At an outright orgy in the woods by the gang later that night, deceitful Penelope spies Gentry and Shiv in some discrete *Brokeback Mountain* action! Dosing Gentry's soda with three hits of acid, Penelope joins him on an impromptu motorcycle ride (safety last). Overwhelmed with guilt, Gentry is taunted by hallucinations of people laughing and accusing him. Wiping out on his motorcycle, Penelope crawls away from the wreckage when Shiv appears. Unhappy that his secret lover has bit the dust, Shiv reaches into his tool box to cut away what Penelope has been rubbing in everyone's faces for her entire stay...

Phew! This writer would wax eloquent on **SINNER'S BLOOD** in Chas. Balun's *Deep Red* magazine back in the day. Shot in and around the

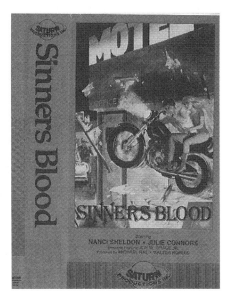

SEMEN DEMON

SINNER'S BLOOD (cont.)

Los Angeles area, the movie-making capital of the world, the film could have been shot in Wisconsin. Grimy, amateur and slipshod, **SINNER'S BLOOD** is as regional and raw as it gets. Seeing it again on DVD from the fine folks at Code Red, I was struck at just how all the characters spend an inordinate amount of time spying on each other. There's Aubrey, the "peep freak", but virtually everyone—in particular the adult characters—spend a lot of time peering out of windows. In this hellhole town, where everyone is into everyone else's business, there seems to be an unspoken pressure to perform deviant acts worth seeing. An ideal drinking game would be to take a shot every time one of the characters in this film engages in voyeurism.

Shot on crappy 16 mm film, **SINNER'S BLOOD** has the look and tenor of a classroom scare film. Night scenes, shot in the daytime relying on the old standby technique of setting the F-stop back a few, tingeing everything with an ugly blue. A casual look at other cast and crew members of **SINNER'S BLOOD** on the IMDb reveals that they did nothing else later on, with the notable exception of Walter Robles, still working today as a stuntman in movies.

For their DVD release, Code Red has dug up actor John Talt for a brief interview. Talt reveals what this writer has long suspected: that **SINNER'S BLOOD** had no real script, and the actors mostly ad-libbed everything. Leaving acting shortly after appearing in the film, Talt still looks good at 70 years of age. He doesn't recall ever getting paid for appearing in the film, although he remembers it netted him a girlfriend for about a year-and-a-half. Code Red includes a "grindhouse version" of the film, which is merely the old VHS version of a brighter print. There are also the expected trailers for other Code Red DVD releases.

1969, USA. DIRECTOR: NEIL DOUGLAS
AVAILABLE FROM CODE RED DVD

SEMEN DEMON
(*Hentai kazoku niiduma inran zeme*)

Reviewed by Travis Goheen

It's **JAPANESE WIFE NEXT DOOR** (2004) meets **THE EXORCIST** (1973)—actually, make that **THE ENTITY** (1982). Reiko Yamaguchi is *hot*—I mean, she plays Akiko, a newly-married, naive virgin completely unaware of the sexual deviancy in the world. (I'm not buying it either, folks.) Unfortunately for Akiko, she is going to be thrust into it ass-first, and oh, what an ass it is.

Akiko quickly develops a serious problem with her new husband in the bedroom, and it's not one that can be solved with a little blue pill. Apparently, Akiko's new husband is possessed by a Demonic Entity, and later on when asked by an exorcist how she knows this, Akiko answers, "He showed me his penis and asked me to suck it in bed." *Bwa-hahaha!* If that's not Paranormal Probability, I don't know what is. Unfortunately, things get much worse for poor little Akiko—not only is she tied up and turned into a human water balloon, but she's also forced to watch her beast of a husband rut on the local whore.

When she can't take it anymore and she seeks the help of her elderly father-in-law, she is raped by the old bastard, leading up to an ill-favored three-way, adding insult to injury. This leads Akiko to seek out an exorcist in order to find out whether or not her husband is actually possessed or just a panty-cutting pervert son of a bitch. With the help of the exorcist, Akiko learns that her husband and father-in-law are both possessed by the horny spirit of an ancestor. There are scenes where Akiko is meeting up with the exorcist that, while they are humorous, tend to sort of stand out at times amidst the outrageous nature of the film. The final sex scene tends to feel mundane because it's so normal it almost stands out of place with the rest of the movie.

While the film **THE JAPANESE WIFE NEXT DOOR** is immensely popular with movie fans around the world and perverts alike, the sequel wasn't received quite so lovingly by the fans. The perverts—um, I mean movie fans—were absolutely pissed that Reiko Yamaguchi wasn't the main character in the second installment, only appearing in not much more than a glorified cameo. While the first film is quite light, whimsical and fun—though somewhat perverted, it was quite tongue-in-cheek (and in a bumhole or two) throughout the entire film—the second film tends to be a little less light and not as silly. However, where **THE JAPANESE WIFE NEXT DOOR 2** (2004) lacks the quirkiness of the first film, it definitely surpasses the first film in kinkiness and perversion.

Which brings us up to **SEMEN DEMON** (2005). A lesser-known film in this trilogy of sorts, it was far better than the second installment but not as good as the first film. **SEMEN DEMON** could have, would have, *should have* been the sequel to **THE JAPANESE WIFE NEXT DOOR**.

2005, JAPAN. DIRECTOR: MINORU INAO
AVAILABLE FROM PINK EIGA

IT TAKES A THIEF

Reviewed by Jeff Goodhartz

Since this summer marks the 25th anniversary of my initial exposure (and subsequent lifelong fanhood) of that femme phenom that was/is Yukari Oshima, I figured this was the right moment to review one of her last films (and arguably her last good one): 1999's **IT TAKES A THIEF**.

Yukari plays Shum Ling, a Hong Kong Police Inspector. The film opens on an operation gone awry as one of her men, Ye Jin (Chin Siu Ho), is killed during a shootout. Worse, Ye was engaged to Shum's sister, Tong. Tension arises as Tong blames her sister for her fiancé's death. After an investigation that leads nowhere, Tong decides to take matters into her own hands and dresses as a costumed vigilante. All the while, it turns out that Ye has in fact faked his own death in order to infiltrate a powerful gang led by one Hong Bao.

A partial remake of 1990's **MIDNIGHT ANGEL** (also starring Yukari), **IT TAKES A THIEF** suffers from a dirt-cheap budget and appears to have been shot on video. But while this makes for an obviously less-than-ideal visual experience, it still manages to be a near-great return to '80s-style Hong Kong action. It is kinetically filmed by veteran action director Chan Cheun, whose career goes all the way back to the late '60s. After working extensively as an assistant throughout the '70s, Chan struck out on his own and lensed some lesser-but-curious pics like **KUNG FU VS. YOGA** (*Lao shu la gui*, 1979), **TWO FISTS AGAINST THE LAW** (*Shuang la*, 1980) and 1981's **THE EXECUTOR** (*Zhi fa zhe*, a.k.a. **KILLERS TWO**), which is notable for being the first teaming of Chow Yun Fat and Danny Lee. Here, he proves that he is able to rehash a well-worn storyline and keep the proceedings moving in a tight, workmanlike manner.

As for our star, it was a joy to see The Osh's return to form after languishing in so many mediocre productions. Okay, maybe she's not quite as fast or athletic as she was in her earliest Hong Kong and Taiwan productions, but for a woman in her late thirties, she can still punch and kick with the best of them. To this day, no screen-fighter male or female can match her unique and utterly hypnotic combination of real-life black belt karate skills and gravity-defying gymnastics. And, if anything, her natural screen presence has grown even stronger with age. When this lady enters a room, all eyes are automatically on her. It is true star power (even if stardom was something she apparently did not want—talk about irony). Fortunately for the sake of the film (and we diehard fans), she is given more screen time than usual and her character is allowed to develop a little, something which sadly was often not the case in previous productions. And her patented "stare" (a distinctly Japanese trait) is still capable of freezing and withering the average male in his tracks. Joining her in the pushing-forty crowd is Chin Siu Ho, a great fighter/actor in his own right who never quite achieved the stardom he was seemingly destined for. Chin also is given some great opportunities to cut loose, and proves he is up to the challenge. Watching Yukari and Chin do their stuff here is proof that ex-stars of the '80s still have it all over those who have come along since.

Despite its production woes and seemingly rushed shoot, **IT TAKES A THIEF** managed to represent a welcome last gasp from a bygone decade that ruled like no other. Even in 1999, '80s-style Hong Kong action leaves everything else in its wake, as does the ever-awesome Osh herself.

1999, HONG KONG. DIRECTOR: CHAN CHUEN

IZBAVITELJ

Reviewed by Timo Raita

Here we have a rare example of *cinema fantastique* from Croatian Yugoslavia. The film is set in small European town, probably sometime between the two World Wars. The entire continent is in turmoil; there's poverty, mass unemployment and hunger. We are introduced to a philosophy student, Ivan Gajski (Ivica Vidović), whose manuscript has just been rejected by a publisher. Adding insult to injury, he has also just been evicted from his apartment. Without money for rent or even food, he is forced into selling his worldly belongings. While trying to sell his books in the street, he meets and falls in love with the beautiful Sonja Boskovic (Mirjana Majurec). One night, while sleeping on a park bench, he is awakened by a kindly night watchman who suggests he might be better off sleeping in the abandoned Central Bank building. Inside the bank, Gajski blunders onto a grand orgy of sex and feasting, and notices that some people at the orgy look a lot like rats! Shocked, he spies on the rats' leader, Izbavitelj (which means "redeemer", played by Relja Bašić), and overhears his plans for world domination. The Police are incredulous when Gajski tells them about the orgy of rats and their evil plan. Only Sonja›s father, Professor Martin Boskovic (Fabijan Šovagović), believes Gajski, and in fact he seems quite knowledgeable about these rat-men. The professor gives Gajski an old German book called *Das Vermachtnis des Rattenzkönigs* ("The Legacy of the Rat-King"), which explains the nature of the shape-shifting pests. These strange rodents can take the form of any human being, and have infiltrated all levels of society. Gajski and the professor team up to create a poison gas called Indicator B, which they hope will solve the rat problem once and for all.

The film is a fascinating, though sometimes uneven, East European variation on the 'Capgras syndrome' films such as Don Siegel's 1956 thriller **INVASION OF THE BODY SNATCHERS**. While Siegel's classic can be read as an anti-communist film, **IZBAVITELJ** is clearly an anti-National Socialist film. The rat-men's long black leather coats and the half-swastika-shaped table in the orgy scene are the definitive clues. It's interesting that the film dehumanizes Nazis into rats, as rats were a popular metaphor for Jews in Nazi propaganda, such as the 1940 Fritz Hippler film, **THE ETERNAL JEW**. Also interesting, but even more morbid, is use of the Indicator B poison gas as a 'final solution' to the rat-man problem. The poison infamously used by the Nazis in the death camps was called Zyklon B. It was originally invented in the early 1920s as a pesticide. Clearly, director Krsto Papić and screenwriters Zoran Tadić and Ivo Brešan wanted to turn the tables and give the Nazis a taste of their own medicine. In this light, it is easy to see the fictional German book *Das Vermachtnis des Rattenzkönigs* as reference to the equally-fictional book *The Protocols of the Elders of Zion* or some other poisonous anti-Semitic text.

The film is based on the 1924 novel *Krysolov* by Russian writer Aleksandr Grin, probably best known for his book *Scarlet Sails*. Director Krsto Papić's early films were part of Yugoslav cinema's "black wave" which gave us interesting films like Dušan Makavejev's **WR: MYSTERIES OF THE ORGANISM** (1971). **IZBAVITELJ** is not considered part of the "black wave", but it's a fantastic film still loved in its native country. In fact, Krsto Papić filmed the Alexander Grin novel again in 2003 as **INFEKCIJA**.

1976, CROATIAN. DIRECTOR- KRSTO PAPIĆ

HARMAGEDON

Reviewed by Timo Raita

Jussi Parviainen is bit of an *enfant terrible* in Finnish theatre circles. He wrote and played the lead in three plays about his alter ego, Juska Paarma (emphasis on the word ego): *Diletantti* ("Dilettante", 1983), *Jumalan Rakastaja* ("God's Lover", 1984) and *Valtakunta* ("The Kingdom", 1985). *Valtakunta* was still playing when **HARMAGEDON** opened in 1986, and the film picks up right where the play left off. In the play, Paarma had killed his lover Tarja and is then killed himself. He says, "When I killed Tarja my world died", and, "When I killed, I thought I was God, as I didn't know how to be human". The film begins in hell. Or is it heaven? Anyway, it looks like an empty garage with two beds in it. God (or the Devil) gives Paarma a white shotgun and says, "Come back only after you run

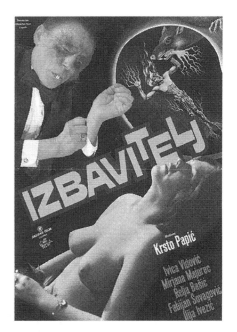

out of people." Next thing you know, we are back on the streets of Helsinki and Paarma kills a passing tramp. Not long after this, he kills a young man who has just tried to commit suicide. After a while Paarma tries to go home, but in the staircase of his apartment building a woman in her underwear informs him that someone else is now living in his flat. Paarma looks stoned, and the woman asks him if he would like to fuck. She starts to rubs herself against the railing as Paarma just stares. And then he kills her. This goes on and on. In his existential agony, Paarma runs into people from his past and murders them. Most of the women worship Paarma and want to fuck him, but according to his solipsistic worldview, everyone has to die now that he's dead himself. And for the gore-hounds out there: no, the killings are *not* gory. The film was done on a shoestring budget, so there wasn't much money for special effects. Paarma just shoots them with his white shotgun and they fall over dead. One by one, Paarma kills everyone from his past, including his alcoholic mother, his little brother and his reverent sister. I guess his father is already dead? If he wasn't, I'm sure he would have killed him, too.

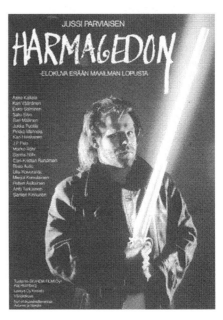

The film has some strange, animalistic charm even though the story is very straightforward. Everything feels like a dream—a bad dream. It's filmed beautifully by Slawomir Idziak, who is best known for his work with Krzysztof Kieslowski. According to Parviainen, "The film ends in total destruction; the end of one man's world. Because no one offered any resistance, no one took responsibility and no one had the moral courage to rebel." Even if this is the end (or total destruction) of Paarma's world, Parviainen continued his story in his 1994 play, *Moniminä*.

Juha Rosman is credited as director in the end credits, but at the beginning of the film it reads, "Harmagedon by Jussi Parviainen". The idea, script, editing, lead role and even set design and costumes are credited to Jussi Parviainen. When asked what exactly Juha Rosman did in the film, Parviainen said, "He was standing between the camera and the fire extinguisher," and after moment of silence added, "Maybe closer to the fire extinguisher."

There have been no TV screenings, no DVD, not even a VHS releases of **HARMAGEDON**, as Parviainen has refused to have it released. The only way he agrees to show the film is if he comes and talks to the audience. So for now, the only way to see it is at one of these special screenings. And there's only been handful of them. Part of the movie's cult status is due to this egocentric practice.

1986, FINLAND. DIRECTOR: JUSSI PARVIAINEN

BLOOD OF 1,000 VIRGINS

Reviewed by Brian Harris

Just when you thought the marketing frenzy surrounding the buzzword "grindhouse" had finally begun tapering off, along comes Charles Band with a sub-imprint, dubbed GrindhouseFlix. While some may automatically dismiss this as

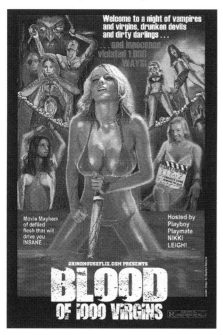

just another attempt by Band to cash in on current industry trends, the films he offers through this website (most of them anyhow) actually do qualify as actual grindhouse cinema. Go figure. Now, they're not remastered, so don't even think about HD. These releases look and pretty much sound as they did on VHS thirty years ago. If you're not anal about that kind of thing, they're just what the doctor ordered when it comes to good, clean sleaze. A bunch of the GrindhouseFlix releases have gone to DVD, while many have remained digital-only. Prices for disc/download purchases run about $7 and streaming is $1.99. Whether you admire Band's shrewd marketing prowess or despise what appears to be "money-grubbing," this endeavor has definitely caught the positive attention of cult cinema fans.

It was only a matter of time before Band and GrindhouseFlix began pulling in enough profit to start on some original productions, and that's just what happened. The three originals (trailer/clip compilations) announced were **BLOOD OF 1,000 VIRGINS** (Sexploitation), **NAZITHON: DECADENCE AND DESTRUCTION** (Nazisploitation) and **BADA$$ MOTHA F**KAS!** (Blaxploitation). Each compilation film was to be hosted by a celebrity (or pseudo-celebrity), just as Band's **FILMGORE** was hosted by Elvira back in '83. This particular production features Playboy Playmate Nikki Leigh handling hosting duties, and she looks simply stunning doing so. Admittedly, she barely made it through some of the tongue-twisting bits of monologue, but no worries, as it'll only be her non-verbal bits you'll find yourself concentrating on. She's there to look gorgeous, crack sexy puns, introduce the sexploitation trailers and leave you wanting more (trailers and skin). In my opinion, she succeeded wildly on all counts.

This 71-minute compilation is split up into five segments, each with its own theme and trailers. Here's what you get:

Segment One: *Female Virgins* - **THE CURIOUS FEMALE** (1970), The Shaw Bros. Kong rip-off **MIGHTY PEKING MAN** (1977), **A VIRGIN IN HOLLYWOOD** (1953), **RUN VIRGIN RUN** (*DIE JUNGFRAUEN VON BUMSHAUSEN*, 1970) and Ted Post's **THE HARRAD EXPERIMENT** (1973), starring James Whitmore, Tippi Hedren and a super young Don Johnson.

Segment Two: *Male Virgins* – Box set regular **THE TEACHER** (1974), **THE GIRLS WHO DO** (*LIEBESJAGD DURCH 7 BETTEN*, 1973), **CHARLIE AND THE HOOKER** (*LA PRIMERA EXPERIENCIA*, 1977), Doris Wishman's 1977 shockumentary **LET ME DIE A WOMAN** and Burt I. Gordon's **LET'S DO IT!** (1982).

Segment Three: *Reasons to Stay a Virgin* – The 1967 exploitation classic **TEENAGE MOTHER**, **THE DEVIL WITHIN HER** (a.k.a. **SHARON'S BABY**, 1975) starring Joan Collins, Donald Pleasence and Caroline Munro, **INVASION OF THE BEE GIRLS** (1973) starring Big Will Smith, Armando Crispino's 1972 giallo **THE DEAD ARE ALIVE** (*L'ETRUSCO UCCIDE ANCORA*), the "talking vagina" film **CHATTERBOX** (1977) and **MOTHER GOOSE A GO-GO** (a.k.a. **UNKISSED BRIDE**, 1966) starring comedy legend Henny Youngman.

Segment Four: *Who Hunts Virgins?* - **ANDY WARHOL'S DRACULA** (a.k.a. **BLOOD FOR DRACULA**, 1974), **THE VIRGIN SLAUGHTER** (a.k.a. **LISA, LISA**, 1974), classic Pinoy horror **BRIDES OF BLOOD** (1968) directed by Eddie Romero, **LUCIFER'S WOMEN** (a.k.a. **THE LUCIFERS**, 1971), Luigi Batzella's **THE DEVIL'S WEDDING NIGHT** (*IL PLENILUNIO DELLE VERGINI*, 1973), **VIRGIN WITCH** (1972), **THE DEPRAVED** (*EXPONERAD*, 1971) starring Swedish softcore goddess Christina Lindberg, and Jean Rollin's **CAGED VIRGINS** (*VIERGES ET VAMPIRES*, 1971).

Segment Five: *Revenge of the Virgin* - **THE BLOOD SPATTERED BRIDE** (*LA NOVIA ENSANGRENTADA*, 1972), Abel Ferrara's **MS .45** (1981), **SAVAGE STREETS** (1984) starring **THE EXORCIST**'s Linda Blair, **ACT OF VENGEANCE: THE STORY OF THE RAPE SQUAD** (1974), **THEY CALL HER ONE EYE** (*THRILLER - EN GRYM FILM*, 1973) more Lindberg, and the "you need to see it to believe it" **DEADLY WEAPONS** (1974) starring porn legends Chesty Morgan and Harry Reems. If you've never seen a film in which a woman's only weapons are her massive breasts, you should check this one out.

So there you have it. GrindhouseFlix's first original outing and it really wasn't bad at all! **BLOOD OF 1,000 VIRGINS** offers a nice selection of Sexploitation, from well-known classics to some oddball unknowns. I must admit I'd never seen the trailer for **CHATTERBOX**, so you can just imagine how elated I was to come across a film in which a woman's vagina sings the National Anthem! I'll be damned if I don't hunt that one down for my collection. That goes for **DEADLY WEAPONS** as well. Suffocation by breast is a terrifying concept that can only be appreciated by the lowest of the low (read: Brian).

Right now, the only place you can check **BLOOD OF 1,000 VIRGINS** out is on the GrindhouseFlix website, up for streaming. Whether Band intends to offer this on DVD as well is anybody's guess. Personally, I love trailer compilations, so when and if he releases it to disc, I will indeed be purchasing this. This is nowhere near as good as something like Synapse's **42nd STREET FOREVER: THE BLU-RAY EDITION** but it's a classy little production from the undisputed KING of modern low budget B-movies.

[*Editor's Note – This compilation will have been released on disc by the time this review goes to print! REJOICE!*]

2013, USA. DIRECTOR: CHARLES BAND
AVAILABLE FROM FULL MOON/GRINDHOUSEFLIX

MERMAIDS: THE NEW EVIDENCE

Reviewed by Brian Harris

Back in September of '12 (Issue #1) I wrote up a review of an Animal Planet mockumentary (or docufiction) entitled *Mermads: The Body Found*. It was entertaining, interesting, visually impressive and surprisingly creepy for a faux documentary on mythical creatures. Those behind the project did a damn good job crafting something that, by all appearances, was a serious exposé on a once-thought-impossible aquatic animal. I don't think it came as a surprise to anybody that Animal Planet immediately began work on a follow-up in an effort to recapture the interest of the 3.4 million viewers that tuned in to see the first installment. One year to the day later, *Mermaids: The New Evidence* is released, but instead of bringing those 3.4 million viewers back, they set a new record by reeling in 3.6 million! Now ain't that just the catch of the day!

Like the first, Animal Planet offers no disclaimer (up front) stating the subject matter you're about to see is fictional, so don't be surprised when a few unsuspecting dupes try to engage you in an earnest discussion about the possibility of mer-being existence. It's a shame television viewers have to be told that what they're watching is fake, but they should be told anyhow—not everybody is as cynical as you or I, right? Just look how many people are convinced reality shows are actually… well…real.

Unlike *Mermaids: The Body Found*, this follow-up fails to generate the sense of wonderment achieved in the first. Instead of beautifully-rendered CG cut-scenes of mermaid life beneath the waves, we're treated to a few talking heads sitting on a CNN-like set, chattering over shamefully obvious CG footage of "real" mermaids obtained from legit sources like…the Internet, Russians and teens with cell phones. Yeah, let's just say everything that made one ask, "I wonder if this could be real?" about the first film is replaced with, "Why would they show so much bad CG?" Leaving more to the imagination seems to have been their last priority. The one and only thing that unnerved me were "vintage" photos of a mermaid's body displayed in a circus sideshow.

I think what struck me about this installment—which was far less up-front-and-center in the last—was the overt anti-establishment agenda put forth in this. If you didn't know mermaids were real, it's because THE GOVERNMENT is confiscating all of the important evidence. If you didn't learn about the existence of mermaids in school, it's because SCIENCE is conspiring to hide the facts because it could force them to admit their "theory" of evolution is wrong. If you're wondering who else might benefit from trying to disprove mermaid existence, look no further than the CORPORATIONS and their ungodly lust for profit. See? It all makes sense; "they" don't want you to know about things, ergo those things must be real. In my opinion this production would have been better suited nestled between shows dealing with "Ancient Aliens" and "Bigfoot Hunters" because the overall tone seems to have been aimed at the conspiracy theory crowd moreso than the crypto crowd. I kept expecting Giorgio A. Tsoukalos to pop up and proclaim mermaids to be aquatic aliens.

On a positive note, the acting was all pretty damned good and some of the news clips looked convincing enough but, ultimately, *Mermaids: The New Evidence* fails miserably. If *Mermaids: The Body Found* was a feature film, *Mermaids: The New Evidence* would be one of the DVD featurettes.

Despite being a diehard skeptic, I occasionally enjoy kicking back and watching the slop aired on cable channels like History. I'm not sure why, but I just love watching shows and specials that present new (but usually old) theories on topics such as UFOs, Sasquatch, early Christianity and the Bible, and pseudo-history archaeology. As a child I obsessed over much of it, though as an adult I take most of it with less than a grain of salt. In other words, I know it's bullshit. When programs come along like this, I'm always ready to check them out but I do firmly believe disclaimers should be used to notify people that what they're about to watch is for entertainment purposes only (like Tsoukalos's hair). It may not seem that important, but it's easy to mislead people that are desperate to believe in something bigger than themselves. To be fair, there was a small disclaimer tacked on to the end of this production pointing out that all of it was fiction but claimed that the U.S. Navy conducting sonar tests that have been connected with several whale beaching incidents was fact. Interesting. Who in the hell waited around until after the credits though to read that? Me.

If you enjoyed *Mermaids: The Body Found* you may want to give *M:TNE* a try, just don't expect the same quality.

2013, USA. DIRECTOR: CHRISTINA BAVETTA

GO GOA GONE

Reviewed by Graham Rae

You're on holiday. You go to the beautiful tropical paradise of Goa in India, and on your first day there you meet a beautiful woman who invites you to an underground rave on a nearby mysterious island. You hit the tent it's being held in and the deep-vein bass is throbbing and the glowsticks are fireflying and the obscuring, squirting mist is thick and the strobes are spraying and the place is thumping and the bikini-top tits are bouncing and the water bottles are being drunk and the tight asses are shaking and your eyes are popping and the sweat is dripping and your core is vibrating with the sound and all celebratory hands are raised high to the darkening sky and the sunglasses are reflecting and the dancing is growing wilder and the whole ecstasy-vibrating tableau is climaxing…and somebody comes through the crowd and hands out expensive new glow-in-the-dark pills that kill everybody and turns them into flesh-chomping zombies! Then you and your friends have to fight your way off the island, with scant resources and maybe—just *maybe*—the help of a weird Russian mafia zombie-buster and his monosyllabic cohort when they suddenly and unexpectedly appear out of the jungle…

Let's face it, we've all had dazed holidays like that, eh?

GO GOA GONE is apparently India's first successful zombie movie, from what I have read on the 'net. Apparently FLESHEATING GANDHI'S REVENGE ("*He's tired of eating curries and being nonviolent!*") didn't do much box office. How much of an achievement you think this success is depends on what you think of the subgenre

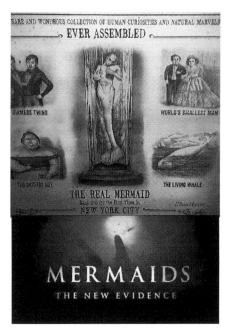

in general, and, more particularly, zombie comedies (or the risible truncation, "Zom-Coms"), which this is. I normally hate that sort of stuff, but have to say I enjoyed this film for what it is, which means basically a fawning riff on **SHAUN OF THE DEAD** (the irony of a zombie comedy film being influenced by a zombie comedy film influenced by a zombie film gets a bit too Escher-like for me) and, stylistically, the **DAWN OF THE DEAD** "reimagining."

I have absolutely no frame of reference *whatsoever* for any potential Indian horror scene, but will say that this movie is absolutely up-to-date, both in style and (non-) substance. There is extreme gore, fastchopshakegrindcut editing and camerawork, wry cynicism, somewhat tiresome self-reflexive Kevin Williamson-like dialogue, bemused musings on pop-cultural globalization…and no real depth at all. Pretty much par for the course, movie-wise, these days, so that's no problem. As eye candy the film makes good use of its vibrant neon-color locations, and you can practically feel

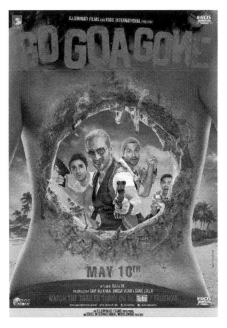

the beating heat and buzzing insects and smell the steaming jungle vegetation. Just a pity they were was no nudity from the gorgeous females in the running (around) time, but, well, *c'est la vie*.

GO GOA GONE (a title I would assume is a clumsy riff on the expression "going, going, gone") at points morphs into pretty much every other zombie movie ever made (with a side salad of Alex Garland and Danny Boyle's **THE BEACH**), but once again we (somewhat sadly) expect nothing more than endless past-pop culture references (endless years of unoriginality has trained the contemporary movie fan to just hope for a few good moments, and anything else beyond that is a bonus) and go with the blood flow. I confess I got excited during the climactic zombie attacks for the same reason I got excited during the **DAWN** remake—it brings back memories of the *real* **DAWN OF THE DEAD** from my youth, when I saw it in 1981 at age 11. So I know I am just getting a pale echo of that brain-wrecking epochal experience, but can deal with that, and this movie had some damned good FX, laughs, and fun ideas.

I confess what I found most interesting and culture-clashy about the film was its moralistic tone. Before it came on in the local AMC multiplex, they had one of the actors from the film come on and talk about how he had nearly had a heart attack at age 32 through smoking and, when the audience sees people in the film smoking (and there was a lot of pot consumed in it) that they shouldn't think it was cool. A somewhat mocking title card saying that smoking and drugs are bad came up. Then the expletives in the English-language subtitles were censored (looking like, for example, "f****r") and when somebody lit up a joint or cigarette onscreen, a wee note came up at the bottom right of the screen that informed you that "Cigarette smoking is injurious to your health." There was no nudity in the film, unfortunately, and no onscreen sex. Characters would cry out mocking God then repent of their atheistic screaming a scant few moments later when things started to go right again. It was like they were hedging their bets in the blasphemy stakes.

The cumulative effect of this oddly chaste extreme violence and drug-naysaying was like a contemporary version of **REEFER MADNESS** or something, with India showing its cultural lag behind the Western world (though not the American South, it has to be sadly said) in the depiction of violence and sex and chaos onscreen. I saw a couple Indian reviews saying it was worth watching because it was quite unlike anything the audience had ever seen, but that only counts for an Indian audience. Everybody else has seen this sort of thing a thousand times, and whether or not you want to see it again will be entirely up to you. I enjoyed it for what it was, and have had way worse experiences in a theater. Like the time when my younger brother threw up on the floor during a screening of the 1986 Eddie Murphy vehicle **THE GOLDEN CHILD**. But that's a whole different story altogether...

2013, INDIA. DIRECTOR: RAJ NIDIMORU & KRISHNA D.K.
AVAILABLE FROM EROS INTERNATIONAL

THE PEKING MAN
(Bei jing ren)

Reviewed by *Jeff Goodhartz*

I've been playing catch-up these last few years with Hong Kong's early "Bashers" (the pre-"Shapes" films made from 1970 to around 1975). Though repetitive (as most overloaded genres tend to become), seeing the best of these films (many of the rarer ones for the first time) has been a ferociously fun experience. It's a particular pleasure when I come across one that offers a little originality in its premise. A solid entry on the subject is this oddity from 1974.

The film takes place in 1929 (never mind that 1970s automobile that shows up early on). The discovery of the skull of the Peking Man frightens the Japanese people. Its existence would apparently challenge the myth that the Emperor had so carefully orchestrated, and threaten the very foundation of Japan itself (seems a tad extreme, but *okay*). Desperate to rid themselves of such an incriminating item, the Emperor sends agents to China to destroy said remains. Not ready to give up their prize discovery, the Chinese dispatch top agents, led by Fang Shi Chieh (Yeung C. Lee) to guard it. Complicating matters are Russian agents who also want to get their hands on the remains.

Director Cheung Mei Gwan keeps the convoluted story moving at an interesting pace. Much of the first half takes place on and around a train (the Peking Express of the alternate title). There's the expected intrigue (spying, double crosses, etc.) and a memorable battle atop the moving vehicle. The film does lag briefly in the middle as the agents converge and after getting the Russians out of the way (a good thing, as they are fairly lousy screen fighters) they plot on how to recover the coveted prize from the Japanese (why the Japanese didn't simply destroy it on the spot is a fair question to ask). However, things pick up considerably in the final third with what feels like an endless series of exciting duels. I'm not familiar with star Yeung C. Lee, but he seems to possess strong martial arts skills. The finale is a tense and exciting one.

THE PEKING MAN may not be among the very best early Bashers that I've seen, but it is a good one. Its unusual plot devices, odd structure and solid, hard-hitting action makes it a winner for those seeking something that's just a little off the beaten path.

1974, TAIWAN. DIRECTOR: CHEUNG MEI GWAN

JOURNEY AMONG WOMEN

Reviewed by *James Bickert*

Here's a piece of chocolate thunder from Down Under! This is the tale of nine unattractive female convicts who are constantly raped by even-less-desirable drunk soldiers and horny aristocrats in an unnamed Australian colony during the late 1700's. When noblewoman June (Elizabeth Harrington) pulls *coitus interruptus* with a musket

on a young inmate's attacker, the prisoners break loose and flee into the outback. After many hardships on their walkabout from hell, they are befriended by an aboriginal girl who teaches them how to forage and create their own Wiccan utopia free from ugly menfolk.

Not knowing the full story behind the soldier's death, Capt. McEwan (Martin Phelan) believes June to have been kidnapped by the women. He sets out to find ol' koala face and, lo and behold, is quite shocked to find his beloved playing naked native with a group of crazy whores and lesbians. With his mind seriously frazzle rocked, he grabs some soldiers and a cannon to blow this heathen settlement to Kingdom Come.

What opens as an artsy-fartsy period piece quickly sharks into full-blown exploitation with tons of screaming bush beaver ("Mappa Tassie", or "Map of Tasmania" in Australian) running around killing' folks and acting like werewolf women. Apparently, this 16mm mess was mostly improvisational and the actresses rebelled on-set over the film's ending. It's an ugly and rarely-interesting feminist "epic fail" that was successful at the box office due to the controversial lesbian themes, full frontal nudity and 13-year-old nude actress Rozanna Lilley. Yeah, all the wrong reasons.

The film is only available in Australia from Beyond Home Entertainment on a special two-disc DVD edition which includes a 20-page booklet, commentary, interviews, two featurettes, stills, four short films by director Tom Cowan and a trailer. The Australian Film Board seems to believe this weekend workshop is an important piece of cinema. This makes me believe that if someone filmed 90 minutes of dingo poo, they would give them a screening at the Sydney Opera House. The director would go on to be a cameraman for one episode of the reality TV show *Survivor: Australia*. I repeat: one episode. Poorly-lit, badly-edited, no script, ambiguous ending, child porn and enough nasty wombats to give ya the liquid laugh. Skip it. If you want some good Aussie entertainment, seek out the Brian Trechard-Smith films **STUNT ROCK** (1980), **DEATH CHEATERS** (1976) and **THE MAN FROM HONG KONG** (1975).

1977, AUSTRALIA. DIRECTOR: TOM COWAN
AVAILABLE FROM TELEVISTA

DESTROYER

Reviewed by James Bickert

Here's a mess of a Slasher mish-mash starring former NFL defensive end, Lyle Alzado, as the gameshow-obsessed con, Moeser. During his electrocution for the rape and murder of 23 men, women and children, the proud Moser cackles, "It was actually 24". The giant goon short-circuits the entire prison, resulting in a riot that leaves 13 guards and 37 inmates dead. Years later, the town folk don't talk too much about the event or the strange happenings at the abandoned prison. That is, until Robert Edwards (Anthony Perkins) shows up to direct his Women-in-Prison picture, *Death House Dolls*.

Before we can enjoy the obvious fun of a reanimated Lyle Alzado zombie running around killing the crew of a W.I.P. set, we are forced to spend half an hour with our bland leads, comprised of stunt girl Susan Malone (Deborah Foreman from **VALLEY GIRL**), and her screenwriter boyfriend, David Harris (Clayton Rohner). It's painful, but just as your mind wanders towards unpaid taxes, Moeser shows up with a giant jackhammer to save the bloody day.

The numerous in-jokes, rip-offs, groan-inducing stock characters and blatant use of dream sequences (very common around this time) to emulate the **A NIGHTMARE ON ELM STREET** series actually added more nostalgia than "seen it before" snobbery to my viewing experience.

Yeah it's predictable, poorly written, and badly directed, but **DESTROYER** throws in enough nudity, explosions, rats, and body parts to make for a decent six-packer. Anthony Perkins and the one-note Alzado put forth some effort; seeing the big lug simulate the tornado tongue using a pair of scissors must have caused some serious soda spit takes from theater patrons. Sadly, Lyle Alzado would die four years later at age 43 from brain cancer, blaming it on a 22-year addiction to anabolic steroids. The same year as **DESTROYER**, Renny Harlin directed an electric chair horror film called **PRISON** starring Viggo Mortensen, and Waldemar Korzeniowsky directed **THE CHAIR**, and 1989 would see two more hit the big screen with Sean S. Cunningham's **THE HORROR SHOW** and Wes Craven's **SHOCKER**. Only available on VHS and Laserdisc, **DESTROYER** will most likely be the one forgotten.

1988, USA. DIRECTOR: ROBERT KIRK

LETHAL FORCE

Reviewed by Jeff Goodhartz

I needed this movie. I needed this movie in the worst way.

I›ve endured enough of Hollywood-style action over the past decade—plus, I stopped going to the movies. From the advent of CGI that causes action and stuntwork to resemble little more than glorified cartoons to the eventual life-sucking that was done to Hong Kong legends like Jackie Chan, Chow Yun Fat, John Woo and Ringo Lam and even to the self-inflicted harm done to Hollywood›s own once-proud franchises (try sitting through the latest **DIE HARD** disaster for a good example), I just couldn't take it anymore and made a conscious decision to basically deal with periods and genres that appealed to me. Life's too short to torture one's self over somebody else's mega-budgeted mega-crap. Thank God then, that I came across Indie writer/director Alvin Ecarma and his wonderful, clever and often hilarious love letter to Grindhouse-style action films (and particularly to classic Hong Kong action), **LETHAL FORCE**.

Jack (Frank Prather) discovers his wife murdered and young son kidnapped by the ruthless wheelchair-bound baddie, Mal Locke (Andrew Hewitt). Jack learns that in order to get his son back, he must sell out his best friend and one-time partner-in-crime, Savitch (Cash Flagg Jr.—an obvious pseudonym as I highly doubt he›s Ray Dennis Steckler›s son). Seems Savitch had previously taken Mal down and left him for dead (which explains his new confides). However, as we discover through the course of the film, Savitch is a nearly-indestructible killing machine. Unfortunately for him, it also means he has made quite a few enemies, most notably the mysterious Rita (Patricia Williams, in the expected giant afro). Eventually through Jack›s double-crossing and with the aid of a sadistic lesbian (wearing the largest fez imaginable) and, most memorably, an army of faceless mask-wearing lackeys, Mal is able to capture Savitch and torture him mercilessly (and in *way* over-the-top fashion) with various saws and power tools. This only manages to draw Savitch's ire. Breaking free, he kills Mal, Rita, and everyone else before turning his attention toward his traitorous friend who only wishes to rescue his son.

LETHAL FORCE is nothing less than a micro budget miracle. Director Ecarma has achieved the seemingly impossible: to create a big-time action/satire epic for next to nothing without sacrificing the integrity of either. Doing a satire of the action genre is at best a risky proposition that few would dare attempt and even fewer would pull off successfully. In fact the only other one that I can think of is the Edgar Wright-directed, Simon Pegg-starring **HOT FUZZ** (2007), and even that, as good as it was, did not quite accomplish the level of ingenuity and verve of Ecarma's film. Ecarma's love for vintage Grindhouse action of the '70s and '80s is blissfully evident in every frame of its 70-minute running time. The homages come fast and furious—and every one of them, from **FASTER, PUSSYCAT! KILL! KILL!** (1965) to **A BETTER TOMORROW** (1986), are absolutely spot on—but even moreso, the homage, in fact, *is* the film. And it manages it in such a way as to be a celebration rather than plagiarism (something that Quentin Tarantino's films can be accused of to some degree). The film's sharp wit (there is no scene funnier than the wistful flashback segment which culminates in Jack and Savitch gunning down dozens of people in stock footage from some Vietnam war pic) is matched by its genuinely exciting martial arts battles which, though no match for its Hong Kong inspiration of the '80s, is still very much preferable to the crappola camera-enhanced non-fights that Hollywood insists on belching out. That it also contains a lucid storyline in which no true good guy is established (we want to root for both Jack and Savitch, yet both are alternately revealed to be unworthy in

Lyle Alzado

the truest antihero sense) only adds another layer of joy to the proceedings.

Complete with a memorable final showdown that is equal parts **THE GOOD, THE BAD AND THE UGLY** (1966) and *Lone Wolf and Cub* (think the manga's finale), **LETHAL FORCE** proves that exciting and creative genre filmmaking is still possible, though apparently you have to go the Indie route to find it.

2001, USA. DIRECTOR: ALVIN ECARMA
AVAILABLE FROM UNEARTHED FILMS

UNA MAGNUM SPECIAL PER TONY SAITTA

("*A Special Magnum for Tony Saitta*", a.k.a. **SHADOWS IN AN EMPTY ROOM**)

Reviewed by Steve Fenton

Export trade press catch-line: "A Cop With a Deadly Thirst for Justice."

Deriving its domestic handle from the Italian release title (i.e., **UNA 44 MAGNUM PER L'ISPETTORE CALLAGHAN**) for Ted Post's Eastwooder **MAGNUM FORCE** (1973), here we witness the urban Italocrime experience effortlessly transliterated across the Big Soup and up to the Great White North. Early export ads in the trade press had promised "A 100% American Action Picture." Although originally planned to be shot exclusively on locations in the USA (including New York), the production ultimately wound up in Canada in downtown Montréal, Québec (as did Maurizio Lucidi's **L'ULTIMA CHANCE** /a.k.a. **STATELINE MOTEL**, 1973), and even in the staid Canadian capital of Ottawa, Ontario, of all places. That said, it's amazing how Italian filmmakers succeeded in transforming our peaceful Canuck streets into some anarchic criminal no man's land right out of Roma, Napoli or Milano!

This is basically a whodunit plotline set to enough tough poliziesco action to fill five films! For its US theatrical release, AIP's ad campaign ("Enter at Your Own Risk…For There Is No Such Thing as a Truly Empty Room!") made it seem more like a Giallo mystery, which it is…partially. Director de Martino's razor-honed skills in that genre came in very handy here, but he was no slouch at making straight-ahead actioners, either—his **IL CONSIGLIORI** (a.k.a. **COUNSELOR AT CRIME**, 1973) is another stand-out—so he came with impeccable credentials to tackle this polished hybrid of the two styles.

Following a tasteless college party prank, the butt of which is prim-and-proper faculty member Dr. George Tracer (future Oscar-winner Martin Landau), one of his students, Louise (alluring French-Canadian art film diva Carole Laure; most notorious as the uninhibited heroine of Dusan Makavejev's **SWEET MOVIE**, 1974), dies suddenly. The dead girl's older brother, Ottawa Police Captain Tony Saitta (Stuart Whitman), suspects poisoning to be the cause of his sister's death, and Dr. Tracer—with whom Louise had been having an extramarital, extracurricular affair—quickly becomes the prime suspect. Prime—if blind—witness Julie Foster (Tisa Farrow, future heroine of Lucio Fulci's **ZOMBIE**, 1979) is soon bludgeoned to death with a lead pipe, and Captain Saitta must wade through a maze of false leads, red herrings, redder tape and vital clues—including a black pearl necklace stashed in a security locker—to solve the convoluted case and avenge his sister's murder. Also numbered on the long list of potential suspects/witnesses are (quote) "ravishing campus tramp" Margie Cohn (Gayle Hunnicutt) and a student named Fred (impassive pretty-boy Jean LeClerc).

Without ever even mussing his hair, Whitman launches unyielding rock-jawed machismo into the stratosphere of the sublime with his ultra-hip performance as the utterly inexorable, inexhaustible Captain Saitta, who walks softly but carries a big bang-stick, scorns such time-consuming formalities as search warrants and suspects' basic inalienable human rights, and is not above the occasional curt belly-jab to loosen witnesses' stubborn tongues if needs be (and they do). Culminating a frenetic foot-chase through the Metro subway, he kicks the *merde* (i.e., crap) out of a suspect in a washroom then half-drowns him in a sink. In a Montréal sex shop arrayed with blow-up rubber dolls and giant dildos, Saitta's poker face remains stoically rigid as he announces "I'm lookin' for a transvestite" (but then, isn't everybody nowadays?). While he subsequently interrogates a belligerent topless tranny named Sinderella in a Marilyn wig and silver tights ("I'll give ya a mouthful of information!"), proving that you should never judge a book by its cover "s/he" attacks Saitta with a straight razor and kung-fu kicks him through a glass patio door. Having almost taken an unscheduled high-dive off an apartment complex balcony, just to drive home his displeasure at being (wo)man-handled Saitta beats his antsy attacker to a pulp then inserts a red-hot curling iron up what's left. Elsewhere, another drag queen known as Jean Harlow is tossed into a rock crusher.

Whitman's cop colleague, Sgt. Matt Matthews, is played by Yank co-star John Saxon, who can shoulder in an apartment door with the best of 'em. The supporting cast also includes a bald dwarf bookmaker named Dutch who smokes a stogie that's almost as long as he is tall. In a later scene, a newborn baby is juxtaposed with an open switchblade (cringe). There is also a topless candlestick bludgeoning and, amid moody chiaroscuro lighting, a key character's murder by stiletto is expertly staged (both cinches for de Martino with his CV).

But even with all these other eye-catching details around to distract and hold your attention, it's the automotive action which really grips you and won't let go like the locked jaws of a dead pit-bull. In this prime case of vehicular manslaughter, it's the automobiles that get slaughtered (second-unit director/arranger of the exceptional car chase sequences was celebrated Gallic motomaster Rémy Julienne). First-degree autocide reaches truly balletic proportions with an airborne leap over the flatbed car of a coasting Canadian National freight train, and a synchronized two-sedan downhill fly-over which I truly believe equals – and dare I say at risk of offending purists possibly even surpasses – anything seen in BULLITT (1968). Indeed, de Martino was so proud of this stunt that it's instantly replayed precisely three more times from as many different camera angles. How's that for showmanship!). Decapitating fire hydrants and pulling 80 m.p.h. donuts on loose gravel, a smash-up derby along the Rue Barrée concludes by reducing a finely-tuned Pontiac and Mustang to doggy-do ("I'm sorry about the scratches," quips the star to the other driver as both cars lie flipped onto their roofs in the middle of the road). This entire sequence – totaling in more ways than one just about the greatest car-nage in all of Italocrime! – runs pedal ta da metal for eight consecutive minutes, and Julienne seldom slams on the anchors. Right when you think it's over, things just keep barreling right along, extra fuel injection provided by Armando Trovajoli's kinetic music (which here sounds a lot more like that to your typical '70s Italocrimer).

And you've gotta love all those neat little "Canadian" touches too; for instance, the wailing cruisers marked Ottawa Police that show up in response to the opening bank robbery, and later into the narrative when Whitman works in collaboration with the Toronto force (decades later to become renamed as the more euphemistically PC Toronto Police Service, which many of the power-tripping pigs in its employ likely considered a great disservice. After all, Force has a much more macho ring to it, right? But I digress). The film's only real detractor is a noticeable lack of any Italian supporting cast. We personally would perhaps have liked to have seen Luciano Rossi or Alan Collins getting their butt kicked by Saitta behind the scenes at a Canadiens or Alouettes game, for instance (but you can't have everything, right). Against the Italo norm, most scenes were shot with direct sound, and the principals all read in English (bona fide Canajun accents in a Euro crimeslime flick, eh!). Audiovisual components are all impeccably integrated—and, having begun with a more understated, melancholy main theme—Trovajoli's score also includes an excellent pummeling rhythm piece that drives through you like a nitro-burnin' runaway Mustang with its accelerator flat to the mat and brake cables snipped. Inspector Tony's title Magnum comes in just jim-dandy for the final showdown (still another vivid action highpoint). All this and another stinger of a revelation too!

This is definitely one of Italy's—and Canada's—Top Ten Most Wanted. (But wouldn't you know it, even though the career of M. Julienne is well

covered within, the present title doesn't even receive so much as a passing mention in Jesse Crosse's otherwise fine book *The Greatest Movie Car Chases of All Time* [Minnesota: Motorbooks, 2006]! Go figure.)

Screw CGI-enhanced, over-hyped Hollywood mega-shite like the *Fast and Furious* franchise: this here's the real deal, speed freaks. Vroom-vroom!

1976, ITALY.
DIRECTOR: ALBERTO DE MARTINO

LADIES OF THE BIG HOUSE

Reviewed by James Bickert

Poor little flower girl Kathleen Storm (Sylvia Sidney) has just married the man of her dreams, fancy-lad Standish McNeil (Gene Raymond). Before the couple can fly to Russia and start a new life that will most likely have him killed on the front lines, Kathleen's gangster ex-boyfriend, Kid Athens (Earle Foxe), shows up to rub em' out, see. Seems the old thug never got over this dame and vowed to kill anyone who took dem gams away. A copper shows up to get Kathleen as a witness in a case against Kid just as the thug is breaking into her apartment. He fills the flatfoot full o' lead, leaving the couple to take the rap. Hotshot Assistant Attorney, John Hartman (Purnell Pratt), who works for Kid Athens, manipulates the jury to a guilty verdict. Standish is sent to death row and Kathleen to tuna town. Thus begins the mucho melodrama of failed appeals, publicity stunts, undying love, stoolies, riots, bust-outs and the hangman's noose. Writer Ernest Booth was serving a life sentence in Folsom Penitentiary for bank robbery when he wrote this script with Louis Weitzenkorn. After his early parole due to health reasons in 1937, Booth would write the prison flicks **WOMEN WITHOUT NAMES** (1940) and **MEN OF SAN QUENTIN** (1942). His script steers clear of some overly-dramatic pitfalls common with these pictures. Unfortunately for Ernest Booth, he didn't steer clear of the law. In 1941 he was arrested and questioned in a case involving the death of wealthy socialite Florence Stricker. As a result of the arrest, he was jailed on a weapons violation charge. Several years later, Booth was found guilty of a string of armed robberies and sentenced to life in San Quentin where he died from tuberculosis. What can you say? Ernest wrote what he knew and lived by it.

Paramount really packs in the production values with some impressive action sequences and more extras than I have ever seen in a Women-in-Prison Film! Gloomy and fast paced, **LADIES OF THE BIG HOUSE** is solid pre-code trash that should be sought out by old-timey exploitation lovers.

1931, USA. DIRECTOR: MARION GERING

STEALING LAS VEGAS

Reviewed by Tony Strauss

Nick Davis (Ethan Landry) once had a promising baseball career, and was on his way to professional sports superstardom when he suffered a career-ending knee injury while attempting an ill-advised base steal. Now he works on a maintenance crew at the Olympus Casino in Las Vegas, and rents a room from single-mom coworker Maria (Krissy Terry) in a working-class Vegas neighborhood. He and his work friends exist in the Unseen Vegas—the part hidden behind the glamor, which consists of dim grey service tunnels and casino storage rooms—a world far from the flashing neon osten-

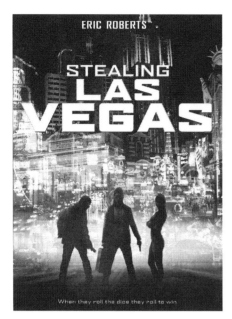

tatiousness for which Sin City is known.

The Olympus Casino is owned and run by charismatic sleazebag Alex Stratholme (Eric Roberts), who has just announced a big promotional incentive to boost business in the currently crippled economy: a $20 million jackpot, which will be awarded to one lucky gambler with one lucky pull of a slot handle. Just as this announcement is being made, Nick learns from his cocktail waitress ex-girlfriend Stacy (Anabella Casanova) that Stratholme is planning a mass layoff of casino employees, including herself as well as Nick and his work buddies.

Nick has just lent his friend Jorge (Eloy Méndez) five thousand dollars, who plans on doubling or tripling it on a "sure thing", hoping to use the money for knee surgery, and to pay back the money he "borrowed" from Maria's secret cash stash. Unfortunately, Jorge loses the money, leaving Nick not only broke, but owing both rent and personal funds stolen from his friend and landlord.

In an attempt to save the jobs of himself and his friends, Nick breaks the chain of command and approaches Stratholme with an idea to save the casino a great deal of money in unnecessary maintenance costs. All he asks for in return is job security. Stratholme hears Nick out, then humiliatingly shoots down the idea, and accuses Nick of theft—the news about the pending layoffs was confidential, therefore Nick has stolen information that didn't belong to him. To show how magnanimous he is, Stratholme doesn't fire Nick on the spot, rather demotes him to toilet cleaning duty for the short remainder of his employ at the casino, and sends the humiliated Nick on his way.

Broken, broke, and with unemployment looming around the corner, Nick reluctantly agrees to listen to Jorge's latest get-rich-quick scheme—a scheme that involves teaching that bastard Stratholme a lesson and setting them all up for life. All they have to do is rob the casino of the $20 million jackpot money…piece of cake, right? *Riiiiiiiiiight…*

What follows is a multi-layered and impressively-constructed heist plan, involving not only Nick, his ex-girlfriend (for whom he still carries a torch) and their work friends, but also an anonymous blackmailer who wants half of their take once the job is done. There are several twists and turns along the way involving all sorts of characters various and sundry, ranging from the denizens of the underground unlicensed MMA fight scene to the designer-suit-clad honchos on the casino floor.

The movie was Executive-Produced by the great Roger Corman, which I'll admit made me a bit hesitant at first. I have, through experience, formed preconceived notions of the Corman-produced films of the past decade or so. The majority of them tend to be barely watchable, poorly-written, -directed and -acted knockouts made for so little money that they're practically guaranteed to turn a profit no matter what. They tend to be fine for what they are—mindless entertainments aimed at the easy-to-please genre crowds—but normally just aren't my thing.

Imagine my surprise when I discovered this to be a damned entertaining and engaging Heist film with almost none of the standard handicaps we've come to expect from such low-budget genre quickies! I was totally expecting crappy dialogue delivered by crappy actors (aside from the one or two "tentpole" recognizable actors one finds in this sort of film—in this case the always-intense Eric Roberts and the hilarious Antonio "Huggy Bear" Fargas) acting out a poorly-constructed story that takes place on no more than four or five set locations. Not the case here. Though obviously still a very low-budget endeavor (it *is* a Corman Production, after all), the production value, acting, directing and editing are *leagues* above the quality one would expect from a film of this ilk. What's more, one does not get any sense that there were location restrictions in this film— I'm sure there were, but those limitations do not come across in the least while viewing the film. Knowing what we all now know about the Typical Corman Shoot, it is simply astonishing that the filmmakers managed to accomplish so many locations, camera setups and overall coverage within the allotted time (reportedly a mere 18 days)!

The impressively tight script, co-written by director/editor Francisco Menéndez with producer Warren D. Cobb and Nr Miller, keeps things moving at an engaging pace, while managing to avoid many of the clichés commonly associated with the subgenre. Sure, there are a handful of predictable moments and clichés (for instance, the heist money is not only needed for "an important surgery", but also to pay for an Autistic child's special schooling) here and there, but I challenge you to name a Heist film that has none; the very nature of the subgenre requires certain clichés in order to make the structure work, so quit your complaining.

I'm not trying to convince anyone that this is a Masterpiece of Modern Cinema, but when stacked against other genre films of similar ultra-low-budget origins, it sure seems like one. Regardless of such comparisons, on its own it easily stands as a fun low-budget Crime film that keeps the viewer entertained and the intelligence uninsulted…and isn't that all we really want from a Heist movie? To be entertained and uninsulted? I've certainly come away far less satisfied from far more extravagant productions, to be sure.

2012, USA. DIRECTOR: FRANCISCO MENÉNDEZ
AVAILABLE FROM ANCHOR BAY ENTERTAINMENT

THE GUY FROM HARLEM

Reviewed by Steven Ronquillo

There are so-called "so-bad-they're-good" classics like **THE ROOM** (2003), **BIRDEMIC: SHOCK AND TERROR** (2010), and **TROLL 2** (1990). But in my opinion those are liked by a set that likes those movies because they think themselves to be better than the movies. Me, I think if a movie gives you enjoyment for whatever reason, how in the name of Ed Wood Jr. can it be "so-bad-it's-good?"

I am admittedly a Bad Movie fan, and love cheesy movies. It's been my love since I was a kid, and this title I'm writing about seems to not be on the Bad Movie Lovers' radar, so in the name of Bad Movie Lovers everywhere, let me clue you in to this no-budget gem.

Al Connors (Loye Hawkins) is the titular "guy from Harlem", a private eye working down in Miami. The movie follows the series of adventures he has while taking down Big Daddy, a bad honky with weightlifter armbands. The first three minutes establishes the fact that Al is a Grade-A horn dog, but the ladies always trust him, and he always screws them no matter what.

The first story starts with a call from a man from the C.I.A. whom Al doesn't remember when his name is spoken—he doesn't remember the guy's names because either he is an idiot or he knows a lot of men with the same first and last name. Then he goes into his office and does his favorite thing to do when they need to fill time in the movie, and that is screw around with his files and call someone. Soon, the C.I.A. guy comes in and says he's with the C.I.A and makes damn sure to call Al "the guy from Harlem" *twice*…because we are too stupid to remember the movie's title.

He wants Al to shack up in a hotel with a foreign dignitary's wife from Africa (with a southern accent, no less) so she will be protected, because there's a supposed leak in the C.I.A. and he wants them to keep him informed as to where they are. So it's no surprise when (a) Al tries to screw her, and (b) the masseuse is so freaking stupid she makes the most overt signals to the villains in the history of overt signals. So he stops her and almost gets some but they need two New York strip steaks and a bottle of J&B scotch before any booty action can actually happen. But the New York strip steak smells like a .38 when it's carted into the room so he punches a woman so hard she turns into a man.

Then we get one of the worst fight scenes ever as a goofy fat Cuban who looks like he doesn't know what the hell he is doing and a goofy white guy fight with Al. Then they kick a white woman out of her apt and throw a $20 at her. I feel sorry for her because this happens to her *twice* in the movie. Then some witty banter that makes me want to gouge my ears out happens and they screw…end of first section.

The second section involves a jive-talking, Slappy-White-rip-off of a mobster who gets Al to free his daughter from the world's worst actors—I swear they read off of cue cards. His daughter is kidnapped by Big Daddy, the king of the underworld with cool-ass wristbands. He is to take some cash and coke to Big Daddy, so he goes to this low-rent gym and meets a greasy, fully-dressed man in a sauna (yes, you read that correctly). They decide on a meeting time and place and we go back to the cabin from the first scene, where Mr. I-Can't-Even-Read-Off-Cue-Cards-Worth-A-Crap is trying to seduce her by saying her hair looks like pubic hair. He asks her if she would like to be blown away, and has she been blown away before...*okayyyyy*. So, being a typical movie idiot, the greasy guy leads him to the cabin for more bad fight scenes and then she is rescued, but she doesn't want to go home, so he kicks the white girl out again and throws another $20 at her. Then the trauma of almost being raped and suffering multiple beatings makes her want to jump our main man's bones...thus, we end another part of it.

So, because he killed two guys, Al has destroyed Big Daddy's crime ring...what is a major drug lord and evil mother to do! Call him at his office and challenge him to a fight, of course—but not before his secretary can get hungry for some greens while talking to his mom and him asking the traumatized victim to be his girl.

Then he goes out to meet Big Daddy and it all comes together in another of the worst screen fights in history. Rudy Ray Moore would be embarrassed at the quality of the fighting in this movie. And the soundtrack is the main theme played over and over whenever the hell they need music.

My god, this was shot in some of the most low-rent sets the '70s could offer. I can promise you I've seen low budget two-reelers with better rooms and furniture. This movie is filled with every damn tacky home furnishing idea that came out of the '70s. And good god almighty, does Al like rearranging his files! Plus, the fashions in this movie are laughable even by '70's standards. "No, you will look good in a pink leisure suit, trust me!"

You may be shocked, but as badly as this movie was directed, Rene Martinez Jr. helmed two other movies after this: **ROAD OF DEATH** (1973) and **THE SIX THOUSAND DOLLAR NIGGER** (a.k.a. **SUPER SOUL BROTHER**, 1978). This movie is a feast for Bad Movie Lovers and those who like to swim in the low-rent waters. See this before the hipster crowd ruins the fun. I promise, you won't be disappointed. And there is a RiffTrax version of this—which is one of their best out there—for you MST3K fans.

1977, USA. DIRECTOR: RENE MARTINEZ JR. AVAILABLE FROM MILL CREEK ENTERTAINMENT

THE JAIL: THE WOMEN'S HELL
(Anime perse)

Reviewed by James Bickert

Bruno, Bruno, Bruno. A year before his death, 74-year-old Bruno Mattei returned to the W.I.P. genre for this shot-on-video craptasterpiece. Made in the Philippines with a cast resembling the islands' best pimps and hos, one has to imagine the script was written on a Tampax wrapper the night before principal videography began. The plot, if any, goes something like this: Three women are sent by steamboat to an undisclosed jungle prison called "The Home of Lost Souls". Here they experience the usual beatings, whippings, cat fights and humiliations. The butch warden has a deal on the side with a local pimp who forces them to dance bikini-clad at a nightclub and obviously sexually service the patrons. Tired of cages, rape, torture and rats, the girls kill the resident snitch and escape into the jungle. The pimp learns of the bust-out beforehand and arranges the ol' *MOST DANGEROUS GAME* (1932) bit for some of his clients. Complete with cannibal guides, they stalk the inmates and butcher them in what feels to be Bruno's attempt to top Umberto Lenzi's **CANNIBAL FEROX** (1981).

THE JAIL: WOMEN'S HELL is packed with both naked and ripped flesh, but also contains some of the worst acting and head-banging dialogue I have ever experienced. Seriously, this makes **THE EXPENDABLES** (2010) sound like eavesdropping on Helen Mirren and Judy Dench having tea. Screenwriter Antonio Tentori (**A CAT IN THE BRAIN**) must be a 12-year-old from Compton because he uses the word "bitches" more than the entire N.W.A. discography. Then there's the score. That goddamned score. It's a 90-second rip of EMPIRE's theme from **STAR WARS** (1977) on a loop through the entire running time. Drunk college kids could probably invent a drinking game with this gorefest, but I'm convinced this flick will cause cancer quicker than the gruel at Georgia Southern University's Landrum Hall. Originally screened at the Marché du Film in Cannes, **THE JAIL: WOMEN'S HELL** was never picked up for distribution and is only available on a Czech bootleg DVD. If you would like to buy the rights to this film for any territory on the planet, you can contact FilmExport Group s.r.l. You could change the dialogue, add a plot, put your band on the soundtrack or make an obscure reference to your alma mater. Anything would be an improvement. It pains me to give a film in which a woman's breast is hacked off and the fatty tissue within sucked out such a poor review but its one colossal aneurysm. No wonder Bruno died of a brain tumor. I feel one coming on.

2006, ITALY. DIRECTOR: BRUNO MATTEI

CAGED BEAUTIES
(Chau mui gwai)

Reviewed by James Bickert

More obscure than white dog poo, this Hong Kong flick starts as an exercise in Grand Guignol and spirals into kung fu madness. Despite their massive film output, there are not many Chinese W.I.P. films. The Japanese pretty much cornered the genre in the Far East so it's always nice to discover a gem from our dim sum brothers and sisters.

This hybrid begins with All-American homeboy Jeffrey Falcon (**SIX STRING SAMURAI**) attending the wedding of Sien to Wai, who is the son of the village leader. Before they can cut the cake, a revolutionary greaseball wearing soccer

mom pants shoots the guests and has the couple spending their honeymoon at a coed jungle slave camp where they apparently use riding crops to mine crucified hot chicks.

At this third world bed and breakfast—I mean, cave prison—we are introduced to muscle woman Tina, the sunglasses, tight camo pants and red beret-wearing butch warden in charge of anyone scantily-clad, and Commander (Sing Chen, the king of the snake cult from **BRUCE LEE IN NEW GUINEA**), a horny, overweight sadist in charge of the male inmates. Yes, it's a win-win situation for all involved. One recently-abused inmate informs us that women are used as hookers and men are used for target practice. Another barks at a sobbing new fish, "Stop your crying. Who here hasn't been raped?" Is there any hope for our protagonist Sien and Wai in this hellhole? Well, not really.

Commander, whose interior decorating skills involve wallpapering his bedroom with Juggs magazines, likes to get his kicks in all sorts of bizarre ways. We first see him cut the hair off a nude prisoner, mix it with a lard substance and shove it up her baby-maker, apparently causing great itching and discomfort. Bored with inflicting yeast infections, he ties up another sexy inmate, masturbates her with a whip, sticks an ice cube up her pinks and throws a foot-long centipede on her breasts! He enjoys a glass of cognac and cackles hysterically while using his ice tongs to determine the bug's route around the poor victim's fleshy hills. A sight to behold, I assure you.

Commander's attentions aren't just for the ladies. He takes great amusement in stringing up a male prisoner from the guard tower, shooting him down days later and filling his cries for thirst with some hot pee straight from the trouser tap. Once relieved, he places a bullet in the poor bastard's noodle. His piece de resistance is tying Sien to a gate with an M-16 pointed at her crotch. With a string attached from the trigger to Wai's big toe, Commander begins to brand the bottom of his feet just to see if Wai will accidentally shoot his wife. Good times.

Tina the bad-ass dyke doesn't care much for Commander's sexual depravity, but does enjoy making the ladies catfight while the men squat and jump around like frogs! Yep. You read correctly. The leader of the revolution eventually shows up and promises Sien that if she gives up her virgin clam he will set the couple free. She reluctantly complies and the douche bag kills Wai anyway during a long, drawn-out sequence of the two abused lovers crawling across gravel to cheesy undying love music. I must admit it's pretty banana-peel funny in an "I'm glad there's no God" kind of way. With nothing to lose, the women plan a bust-out that plays more like a slow motion wet t-shirt contest. Hey, I'm not complaining, I'm just informing.

Wow. Not only does **CAGED BEAUTIES** toss in the requisite W.I.P. clichés of showers, suicides, hot boxes, jungle traps and rape, we get castration, sodomy-by-hot-pistol-barrel, and worm geeking thrown in for bonus fun. Packed to the hilt with boobs and bush, there is even enough squib action to recommend this flick for the gorehounds. You get all kinds of stabbings, a bowie knife to the vagina, and a log to the back of a noggin even splatters the lens with plasma. Sure it's all ugly, but the women aren't. Nope. Usually in a W.I.P. film there are four good looking gals with the extras in the back looking like hobo bait. No throwaways in this group. **CAGED BEAUTIES** is silly enough not to get deep under your skin, sleazy enough to piss off critics and fast-paced enough to need a beer cooler beside your chair. The only place I've been able to find this film is DCS Video Screams Film Archival & Transfer. Their DVD-R appears to be transferred from a 2-disc English subtitled Laser Disc. Highly recommended.

1993, HONG KONG.
DIRECTOR: YUEN CHING LEE

WOMEN OF DEVIL'S ISLAND
(Le prigioniere dell'isola del diavolo)

Reviewed by James Bickert

Should one rip apart the historical inaccuracies within this Italian swashbuckler involving female felons sent to French Guiana to become crocodile food? Hell no! Not when the production throws in pirates, revolutionaries, double-crosses, cannons and tons of sweaty, heaving bosoms! Yes, it's the seedy cover of a men's pulp magazine come to life in glorious widescreen color. Aristocrat Martine Foucher (Michele Mercier) and a whole bunch of other hotties are transported across the blarney sea where the chained lassies must mine swamp gold and bend to the sexual whims of their captors just to achieve a moment's rest. With the arrival of dreamy Commander Henri Vallière (Guy Madison), looks like change is in the sultry air—but are things truly what they seem?

Veteran Peplum writer/director Domenico Paolella (**HERCULES AGAINST THE BARBARIANS, DANGER! DEATH RAY!**) knows how to shoot an epic and keeps the action moving—only slowing down to linger on some curves. Predating the book, but obviously inspired by the tall tales of Papillon authored by Henri Charrière, **WOMEN OF DEVIL'S ISLAND** should be sought out by all land lubbers of cleavage classics. The version available by Mill Creek Entertainment's "50 Drive-in Movie Classics" box set is a nasty, chewed-up, full-screen sepia tone print of the US release which cuts out an interracial romance. Luckily, the film is also available uncut on DVD in a beautiful widescreen Italian and French language DVD with only Spanish subtitles under the title **ATRAPADAS EN LA ISLA DEL DIABLO**. You might not understand the plot, but Italian and French sounds sexier than English anyway. I synced the English audio with the International print. I'm a nerd.

1962, ITALY & FRANCE.
DIRECTOR: DOMENICO PAOLELLA
AVAILABLE FROM SYNERGY ENTERTAINMENT

DEADLOCK

Reviewed by Nigel Maskell

Fans of Sergio Leone westerns will absolutely love this! Despite the fact that it has a more contemporary setting, with modern trains and cars, **DEADLOCK** is very much in the style of **THE GOOD, THE BAD AND THE UGLY** (1966). It is all about three men, two guns and one suitcase full of money. All three men are amoral, motivated by greed and play one off against the other. They double-cross and switch the contents of the case in a running Rock/Paper/Scissors-type exercise in trying to get the upper hand.

Stylistically, the film owes much to *The Man with No Name* trilogy, as Roland Klick and his **BÜBCHEN** (a.k.a. **LITTLE VAMPIRE**, 1968) cinematographer, Robert van Ackeren, get the best from an Israeli desert ghost town. Filmed around the time of The Six Day War, the location makes the perfect stand-in for a windswept and sun-kissed abandoned US mining town with its sandstorms, decrepit petrol station and obligatory squeaky sign. Close-ups of sweaty, sunburned faces complement the whole spaghetti western vibe. This is accompanied by an absolutely mind-blowing score from Can.

While there are excellent performances from Marquard Bohm as The Kid, *der junge Killer*, and Anthony Dawson as Sunshine, *der alte Killer*, it is Mario Adorf, two years before his role in the

WOMEN OF DEVIL'S ISLAND

majestic **CALIBER 9** (*Milano calibro 9*, 1972), who really makes this film. As Charles Dump, *die Ratte*, he is, as always, brilliant. Swiss-born Adorf seems to manage, successfully, to appear to be over-the-top and bordering on madness without in any way being hammy.

Of the supporting roles, the sexy **WORLD ON A WIRE** (1973) star Mascha Rabben is a stand-out. A scene in which she allows dust to blow symbolically from her hand, heralding the arrival of Sunshine, is one of the most iconic and memorable of the feature, while a scene in which Adorf attempts to ride a freight train and then being chased away by a guard with a spanner anticipates the Lee Marvin and Ernest Borgnine hobo-on-a-train feature, **EMPEROR OF THE NORTH POLE** (1973).

Sadly, unlike **THE GOOD, THE BAD AND THE UGLY**, there is no defining set-piece finale. Instead of utilizing the opportunity for a Mexican stand-off, it all ends far too abruptly and in a somewhat underwhelming fashion. This minor quibble aside, this is an absolute classic from Roland Klick and ranks alongside India's fantastic curry-western **SHOLAY** (1975) in the non-Italian and not-strictly-a-western Sergio Leone tribute stakes.

1970, WEST GERMANY.
DIRECTOR: ROLAND KLICK

LITTLE VAMPIRE
(*Bübchen*)

Reviewed by Nigel Maskell

Maverick German director Roland Klick is not really as well-known as some of the other directors aligned to Oberhausen Manifesto, such as Wim Wenders, Werner Herzog or Rainer Werner Fassbinder. He is without a doubt the outsider of German film.

Despite his name receiving little in the way of international recognition, Klick has allegedly worked on several features in America (though this was under an as-yet-undisclosed pseudonym). Klick directed **CALIBER 9** (*Milano calibro 9*, 1972) star Mario Adorf in the cult western **DEADLOCK** (1970), which featured the music of Krautrock pioneers, Can. He also worked with both David Hess and Dennis Hopper on **WHITE STAR** (1983). However, he turned down the chance to direct the acclaimed drug-themed biopic **CHRISTIANE F. - WE CHILDREN FROM BAHNHOF ZOO** (1981), which was ultimately helmed by Uli Edel.

Roland Klick made his feature film début in 1968 with **BÜBCHEN**. Despite being an assured first effort, the film initially met with poor reviews. It would, however, find some recognition the following year when re-released with the alternative title of **LITTLE VAMPIRE**. Sadly though, today the film is largely overlooked. Nevertheless, the young director—who dropped out of college in order to start work in the film industry—would go on to win six German Film Awards over the ensuing decade.

LITTLE VAMPIRE has an almost documentary feel to it—it uses natural lighting and there is no incidental music. There are only the ambient sounds that are recorded on location and for those who are used to moments of tension accompanied by dramatic music; this may seem a little unfamiliar. However, the murmur of nearby conversation, maybe a neighbor practicing a musical instrument or the faint sounds of a distant car is, in the context of the material, particularly effective.

In **LITTLE VAMPIRE**, no one, it seems, is prepared to accept that a young boy may be guilty of a child murder. However, in an especially bleak opening we learn that this is indeed what he has done. When Achim (Sascha Urchs) and his baby sister are left in the care of young woman named Monika (Renate Roland), the babysitter skips off with her partner, thus leaving the children without supervision. While Monika is with her boyfriend learning to drive, Achim suffocates his sister and disposes of her body at a nearby rubbish dump. Given that **LITTLE VAMPIRE** has an infanticide theme, there is little in the way of light relief.

In some respects **LITTLE VAMPIRE** has a vibe akin to the features that were being produced as part of the British New Wave around this period. Though in this instance all the smudges, rust and dirty fingerprints are captured in Eastmancolor rather than the more familiar black and white of **A TASTE OF HONEY** (1961) and its ilk.

Houses appear a little battered and lived-in with chipped paint, litter-strewn streets and unkempt lawns. Latchkey kids play amongst fly-tipped rubbish, abandoned cars and in disused or derelict buildings. They kick a football around on a muddy scrap of land. Everything in this film looks a little grubby and there is an apparent attempt to reject any conscious hint of glamour. Even scenes in a bar reveal the place to be sparse and not especially inviting. The place is full of slurring, wobbly losers and ruddy-faced drunks.

The cast of young newcomers are excellent in this film, and all are believable. Moreover, the older and more experienced actors such as Sieghardt Rupp are moved into the background. This allows newcomers Renate Roland, Sascha Urchs and a roll-call of assorted street urchins to shine—and shine they do.

Despite a title that suggests otherwise, there are no vampires in **LITTLE VAMPIRE**. It is not even a Horror film. It is a Thriller and Drama. It is, in a way, a film about seeing and accepting the evidence before the eyes. From the outset, the viewer is a witness to all events. The audience looks on as both police and family members are either unable or unwilling to accept what is before their eyes. This may well of course all be allegorical. This was, after all, a film from a period when the young began to challenge the older generation over their role in the Nazi era. Those who saw, those who participated and those who simply refused to see.

This is a very dry film with a serious tone. It is a compelling one nevertheless. It should appeal to fans of European exploitation films, as there is a police procedural aspect that is reminiscent of the Italian *poliziotteschi* wave or even Massimo Dallamano's *Schoolgirls in Peril* series.

1968, WEST GERMANY.
DIRECTOR: ROLAND KLICK

Sascha Urchs in **BÜBCHEN**

RELEASED BY FILMGALERIE 451
[R2, CURRENTLY OOP]

DEVIL DYNAMITE

Reviewed by Jeff Goodhartz

The VHS and DVD packages call it **DEVIL'S DYNAMITE** (1987), yet the film itself is minus the apostrophe. Regardless, this film represented my introduction to Godfrey Ho (here billed under the pseudonym Joe Livingstone!) as well as frequent partner-in-crime producer Thomas Tang, even though I wasn't aware of it until much later. I learned of this film back around 1990 or '91 while reading the latest copy of Damon Foster's *Immortal Oriental Cinema* 'zine (pre-*Draculina* years) and the brief description of it sounded just too oddball and cool for its own good. I bought it for cheap shortly thereafter in a video store dump bin (man, I miss those days) and wasn't disappointed.

Our story begins with a Taoist Priest aiding a gangster (I think) by summoning a group of hopping vampires (*jiangshi*) to do away with his rivals. This apparently includes a ninja gang (Ho can't let those ever-present ninja costumes go to waste) which is made short work of. In a unique twist, the ninja become hopping vampires themselves. Just when all hope is lost (or something), there suddenly appears a silver-clad (more like cellophane clad) "shadow warrior" named Alex (Suen Kwok Ming) who combats the now-transformed ninja vampires (as well as the original plain old everyday hopping ones). Integrated with this bit of confusion is a rare 1979 Taiwanese film called **THE GIANT OF CASINO** (as well as possibly its sequel, **THE STUNNING GAMBLING**, 1982, though I'm not 100% sure as I've never seen that one). Featuring a name cast, this redubbed footage reveals the real person in charge is a gangster's moll named Mary (Elsa Yeung). She is the one who has summoned the vampires (cough!). She and her no-good gang of backstabbers are angered to hear that one-time casino king Stephen Cox was freed from prison and headed their way for revenge. Mary figures that the best way to get him out of the way is to have the vampires kill him (never mind that they never actually meet at any point). Sounds reasonable…

DEVIL DYNAMITE turned out to be one of Ho's better hatchet jobs. While for the most part it's obvious which scenes are from the older pic versus which are the newly-shot ones, I have to admit there was one point early on where I was sure I was watching the Taiwan footage only to have a gang of hopping vampires enter the scene. Props for that, at least. It also helps that Ho shot more original footage this time—at least 40%, which is a good thing as it is, as usual, provides most of the entertainment. I'm not sure what the deal is with the silver-garbed superhero but since he is referred to as a shadow warrior, it's possible that he is a genetically-altered ninja. I'll go with that; it sounds cool. Being a big fan of the foreign superhero genre (*Ultraman, Kamen Rider,* **INFRAMAN**, the **THREE FANTASTIC SUPERMEN**, not to mention Mexico's Lucha Libre genre), I had a great time watching this chintzy-looking hero battle hopping vampires. It tickled me to no end. Of course, as with Ho's *Catman* films, I wish the entire movie was just this footage. As for **THE GIANT OF CASINO** (and maybe **THE STUNNING GAMBLING**) Taiwan footage, it's your typical gangster potboiler. It's not particularly good, but not terrible either. And it was fun to spot no less than the legend herself, Angela Mao Ying. Her mere presence gave the film an air of validity. Unfortunately, her character disappears around the halfway point after getting shot in the arm (figures!). Overall, not the most exciting pilfered footage Ho has utilized, but better than much of that found in the many Thailand films he later forced upon us (particularly, the aforementioned *Catman* films).

DEVIL DYNAMITE was paired with Ho's more notorious **ROBO VAMPIRE** (1988, thank you, BCI) for an unbeatable superhero-versus-vampire double-feature. A memorable experience if ever there was one.

1979/1987, HONG KONG/TAIWAN. DIRECTOR: GODFREY HO/CHAN JUN LEUNG
AVAILABLE FROM BCI VIDEO

ARABIAN ADVENTURE

Reviewed by Brian Harris

Imagine that: Christopher Lee—a white man—playing an ethnic character. Not that he's ever done *that* before! You've just gotta love how filmmakers in the past always eschewed authentic ethnic actors in favor of Caucasians in "minority face". One has to wonder whether casting director Allan Foenander was forced to hire a cast of whites to play Middle Easterners for this film or he honestly believed John Ratzenberger was perfect for the role of…*Achmed*. This kind of practice was nothing new back then ('79), of course, though it seems especially egregious now considering today's highly-politicized atmosphere and heightened sensitivity to matters of race. Then again, if Mickey Rooney jabbering away incoherently like a brain-damaged baby—because fantasy or not, that *must* be what Middle Easterners actually sound like—doesn't bother you in the slightest bit, you've thicker skin than I!

The vile Caliph Alquazar (Lee) is on a quest to become all-powerful, but to do that he'll need a magical rose—and there's a catch: only somebody pure of heart can pluck it. In other words, the Caliph is shit out of luck…or is he? When the brave, dashing Prince Hasan (Tobias) and his young sidekick Majeed (Sira) arrive in the city, Alquazar sees his opportunity to obtain the rose by promising Hasan the hand of his step-daughter, Princess Zuleira (Samms). Can Hasan reach the rose before the city falls to a rebellion, and will Majeed find his true destiny?

ARABIAN ADVENTURE is an interesting production and a surprisingly obscure Lee film considering his status; I actually hadn't even heard of it myself up until a few weeks ago! Limited availability probably has quite a bit to do with that as the only stateside release of this I could find is carried by the "infamous" bootlegging outfit, Televista (love 'em!). You'd think with an all-star cast featuring Christopher Lee, Peter Cushing, Emma Samms, and Mickey Rooney and a proven director like Kevin Connor (**THE LAND THAT TIME FORGET**, 1975; **MOTEL HELL**, 1980) that this Brit production would get some kind of press or word-of-mouth in cult cinema circles but, nope—zip. I'm tempted to chalk it up to being one of those cool neglected films that just slipped through the cracks but that would be giving it credit I really don't think it deserves. I'm hesitant to pump it up too much as it does have its issues and I don't want readers blowing a fistful of scratch on a film they'll probably find boring.

The production design…wow, the production design was gorgeous, everything from the Caliph's throne room to a miniature model of the city (used in overhead shots) and Rooney's steam-powered machines were impressive; it was plain to see that the budget was on the higher end of low. My disdain for inappropriate casting aside, Lee's presence certainly gave it an air of legitimacy. He's an actor's actor, the kind of man that takes his craft seriously no matter how sketchy the script. Great design values and solid acting, sounds like a successful combo, so what's my deal, right? Well, **ARABIAN ADVENTURE** has everything a good fantasy film should, except that whole excitement thing. The hero and his sidekicks go from one adventure to…pretty much the end. No joke. The one and only opportunity to really kick things up a notch—when they happen upon a genie and his lamp—and Connor lets things fizzle. Good thing there were monsters…*oh wait*—there weren't any monsters. An adventure-lite, monsterless affair filled with white guys pretending to be Arabs? Wow, how could this *not* dazzle the masses with sophistication?!!

You know what really kicked sand into my cooter,

though? It was the choreography; it was terrible, mind-bogglingly terrible. At first I thought, "One messy fight isn't a big deal," but it just continued spiraling. The worst culprit of all was actor Oliver Tobias as Prince Hasan. Occasionally the heroic lead can play a little fast and loose with battle to give the production an unscripted swashbuckling feel but Tobias just stumbled, fumbled and flopped about like an awkward eleven-year-old in a grade school production of Peter Pan. I suppose if I hadn't been privileged enough to experience films like **THE THIEF OF BAGHDAD** (1940) and the Harryhausen-produced *Sinbad* trilogy as a child, I might have enjoyed this more but... yeah...

After all that I'm betting you think I didn't like **ARABIAN ADVENTURE**, but that's really not the case; it's not a *bad* film, but it isn't all that good either. In other words, it's the perfect example of something a cult cinema fan would watch and own (like me). Sure we may be a nerdy lot but we're never at a loss for something to watch, that's for sure! Seeing how this has no real release I feel it's safe to say that you may be forced to download or stream this if you're interested in checking it out. I'd only recommend purchasing to the geekiest amongst us. With just a few monsters and better action/fight choreography, I think this film could have been a bit more "must-see/must-own." As it stands, it's a curiosity, at best.

One of the **ARABIAN ADVENTURE** posters I came across proclaims this to be **STAR WARS** with flying carpets but *I'll be damned* if that's not an outrageous crock of shit from the very pits of hell itself! Connor is no Lucas and Tobias's Hasan was definitely no Luke Skywalker. I'll be the first to admit that a few goddamn Ewoks might have actually helped this production considerably. On second thought, a film with both Mickey Rooney and Ewoks may have been too much for the world to handle. Perhaps it's all for the best.

1979, UK. DIRECTOR: KEVIN CONNOR
AVAILABLE FROM TELEVISTA

SASORI

Reviewed by James Bickert

I'm a huge fan of the original **FEMALE PRISONER #701** series. Such a nerd that in 2001, I tracked down a print of the second film in the series **JOSHUU SASORI: DAI-41 ZAKKYO-BÔ (FEMALE CONVICT PRISONER: JAILHOUSE 41**, 1972) and had it shown at Atlanta's Starlight Six Drive-in, causing misery to many inebriated subtitle-phobic rednecks. It would be unfair to judge this shot-on-video J-Vid re-imagining by the same criteria as the 38-year-old original. Other than using the Meiko Kaji theme song Urami Bushi, there are not many similarities, anyway.

In this version, housewife Sasori (Miki Mizuno) becomes the victim of some psychotic thugs hired by a wealthy bioengineer to assassinate her father in-law. These thrill-kill super villains like to get their kicks as well, so they force her to kill noodle-happy dad and the sister in-law while her cop hus-

band (Dylan Kuo) watches. By some inexplicable comic logic, she never explains who forced her to do it and the husband never saw the four fashion foes standing in their house!

Sasori is sent to prison where the inmates fight in caged death matches for booze and give the fat warden (Lam Suet) sucky-sucky. When her husband tries to kill her on visiting day, she loses all hope. After several humiliations, Sasori visually learns kung fu from watching fights and we watch montages. When she murders the Queen Bee's sister, this brings down the wrath of all the inmates. To restore order the warden has Sasori thrown into some outdoor suspended bondage where she dies and is resurrected by a martial arts guru called the Corpse Collector (Simon Yam). He turns her into a sword-wielding killing machine with a ten-second training montage.

Seeking vengeance, she reunites with her husband who turned into an alcoholic musician with an erased memory and has become an attraction for a local bar. Many sword fights follow. I have a sneaking suspicion that the end of this film was shot first then the production ran out of money. Other than the lighting, the first hour of **SASORI** looks like a 50-buck budget and contains so many annoying fading, zooming and dissolving jump cuts punctuated by loud sound effects it almost induces seizures. The prison sequence is so no-frills that the number designating Sasori as the infamous prisoner 701 appears to be written in Sharpie on a "Hello my name is" sticker! The last 30 minutes resembles a completely different film with a 150K budget and better crew. There are even plot revelations in the end that were never set up in the beginning, so they don't make any sense. What the hell?!

179

SASORI

Wacky plot and jaw-dropping logic aside, the biggest problem with **SASORI** is the lead, Miki Mizuno. She has good choreography and wire skills but she isn't the least bit attractive. Her face is very skeletal and her frame doesn't fill the sexy costumes. Not even wig changes create an illusion of beauty. There are some nice-looking women in this movie who run the gamut from butchy hot to lipstick femme fatale and each displays more on screen charisma and acting chops than Mizuno, who apparently is a TV star in Japan.

Let's be honest: with J-VID, it all comes down to the sex and violence quota. Sadly, **SASORI** misses the mark. There is only one wet t-shirt scene in the skin category and the gore is all over the map. Occasionally it enters **MACHINE GIRL** (2008) territory but the majority of kills are pathetic and never graphic. Director Joe Ma relies more on showing a bloody prop than performing an actual effect. There is one cheap-but-very-creative scene involving a vodka bottle, but it can't save the overall experience. This is for die-hard J-Vid fanboys only. Meiko Kaji fans and lovers of the original series should avoid at all cost. **SASORI** is currently only available with English subtitles so bad they should be called "Engrish" subs, on a PAL format Region 2 DVD from the UK. There is an unsubbed Thai and Japanese release with the same running time.

2008, JAPAN & HONG KONG.
DIRECTOR: JOE MA
AVAILABLE FROM MEDIA BLASTERS

NAZITHON: DECADENCE AND DESTRUCTION

Reviewed by Brian Harris

I know what you're thinking: a swing and a miss, right? That's what I thought too when I read Michelle "Bombshell" McGee was going to be hosting this trailer compilation. I mean, I get it, she's got a bangin' body and tattoo/fetish models have been "in" for a few years now but this just feels like Band was scraping the bottom of the *Surreal Life* barrel. While her neo-Nazi tattoos and flirtation with fascist fetish fashion officially may qualify her as white trash, it doesn't really make a ton of sense to have her presenting Nazisploitation trailers. If you didn't keep up on the freakish media circus surrounding motorcycle/automobile customizer Jesse James and actress Sandra Bullock, you'd have no idea who "Bombshell" was. Was Dyanne Thorne or Helmut Burger too busy or were they just asking too damn much? Thankfully the real star of this production—the super sleazy trailers—made up for this casting misfire.

Let's just hope the mystery host for Band's fourth GrindhouseFlix original production—dedicated to Women in Prison films this time—doesn't end up being Casey Anthony. Seriously.

So, just what should one expect to see in **NAZITHON: DECADENCE AND DESTRUCTION**'s 80 minutes of jiggling genocidal goodies and sleazy cinematic sin? Here's the trailer lineup:

Sector One: *Camps & Torture* – The legendary David F. Friedman-produced **LOVE CAMP 7** (1969); **SS CAMP 5 WOMEN'S HELL** (*SS LAGER 5: L'INFERNO DELLE DONNE*, 1977); **SS SPECIAL SECTION WOMEN** (*LE DEPORTATE DELLA SEZIONE SPECIALE SS*, 1976); Luigi Batzella's insane rapefest, **THE BEAST IN HEAT** (a.k.a. **SS HELL CAMP**, *LA BESTIA IN CALORE*, 1977); **SS EXPERIMENT LOVE CAMP** (*LAGER SSADIS KASTRAT KOMMANDANTUR*, 1976).

Sector Two: *Decadence & Destruction* – Sleazemaster General Bruno Mattei's **PRIVATE HOUSE OF THE SS** (a.k.a. **SS GIRLS**, *CASA PRIVATA PER LE SS*, 1977); Tinto Brass's classic **SALON KITTY** (1976), starring Helmut Berger; **THE DAMNED** (*LA CADUTA DEGLI DEI (GÖTTERDÄMMERUNG*, 1969), another starring Helmut Berger.

Sector Three: *Nazi Babes* – Don Edmond's **ILSA, SHE WOLF OF THE SS** (1975), starring the ravishing Dyanne Thorne and her massive breasts; **THE BEAST IN HEAT** (a.k.a. **SS HELL CAMP**, *LA BESTIA IN CALORE*, 1977); **FRAULEINS IN UNIFORM** (a.k.a. **SHE DEVILS OF THE SS**, *EINE ARMEE GRETCHEN*, 1973); **ILSA, HAREM KEEPER OF THE OIL SHEIKS** (1976), not really Nazisploitation, but Thorne and her jugs return; Jess Franco's **WANDA THE WICKED WARDEN** (*GRETA - HAUS OHNE MÄNNER*, 1977), more non-Nazisploitation starring Thorne, her juggs and Spanish sex starlet Lina Romay; **ELSA FRAÜLEIN SS** (1977); the third official sequel, which has nothing to do with Nazis, **ILSA, THE TIGRESS OF SIBERIA** (1977).

Sector Four: *Neo Nazis* - **THE BLACK GESTAPO** (1975); **THE TORMENTORS** (1971); the Spanish cult classic, **MAD FOXES** (*LOS VIOLADORES*, 1981); Al Adamson's **HELL'S BLOODY DEVILS** (1970).

Sector Five: *Supernatural Nazis* - **SHOCK WAVES** (1972), starring genre legends Peter Cushing and John Carradine; **SHE DEMONS** (1958); Jean Rollin's epic stinker **ZOMBIE LAKE** (*LE LAC DES MORTS VIVANTS*, 1981), starring Antonio Mayans; Jess Franco's **BLOODSUCKING NAZI ZOMBIES** (a.k.a. **OASIS OF THE ZOMBIES**, *LA TUMBA DE LOS MUERTOS VIVIENTES*, 1982); **NIGHT OF THE ZOMBIES** (1981), directed by Joel M. Reed; **DEATH SHIP** (1980), starring George Kennedy and Richard Crenna; **ZOMBIE LAKE** (again?).

That's a respectable selection of trailers, though I would have liked to of seen **RED NIGHTS OF THE GESTAPO** (1977), **GESTAPO'S LAST ORGY** (1977), **THE NIGHT PORTER** (1974) and **SALÒ, OR THE 120 DAYS OF SODOM** (1975) included in the lineup. You're bound to leave a few out here and there, though I do feel the latter two are what most exploitation fans would consider unforgettable classics. Oh well, right? I think, as a whole, this production does indeed work, despite McGee's shitty pacing, inability to project her voice, lack of emotion and bloated Botox lips—they looked like over-fed earthworms. I'm sure they were going for an on-screen presence that screamed Nazi dominatrix (ala Thorne's Ilsa), but McGee ended up coming across more like a washed-up blow-job queen in major need of her next Meth fix. Good thing Band brought in the intimidating Ian Roberts (**KILLJOY GOES TO HELL**, 2012) to play opposite McGee as an SS soldier and the trailers were overflowing with full frontal nudity, otherwise this might have ended up being a major bust.

This is the second original production—the first film, **BLOOD OF 1,000 VIRGINS** (2013) is reviewed in this issue, as well—from GrindhouseFlix, the third, **BADA$$ MOTHAF**KAS!**, will feature Blaxploitation trailers hosted by legendary ultra-badass Fred "The Hammer" Williamson and fourth is entitled **BREASTS BEHIND BARS**. It's a simple series, some could read that to mean cheap, and it's obviously meant to cash-in on the current trailer compilation trend; it's a good thing Band and company are giving theirs a bit o' class by producing original segments to insert between trailer blocks. Just don't expect remastered trailers or anything like that because this ain't Synapse; the quality of some of these is on par with shit you'd see on YouTube. Good thing the upcoming disc will probably retail at $12, any more than that and they risk losing a ton of trash collectors (like me).

If you enjoy watching trailers like I do, you'll want to check **NAZITHON: DECADENCE AND DESTRUCTION** out for yourself, but out of the two GrindhouseFlix releases, I preferred **BLOOD OF 1,000 VIRGINS**. Now grab yourself a copy when it drops, pop you some popcorn and brew, kick your feet up, give your cranks a few tugs and have yourself a good ol' time!

2013, USA. DIRECTOR: CHARLES BAND
AVAILABLE FROM FULL MOON/GRINDHOUSEFLIX

THE DARK DEALER

Reviewed by Dan Taylor

It seems you can't swing a re-animated cat these days without hitting some sort of horror anthology. **V/H/S** (2012) and its sequel, television's *Masters of Horror*, **THE ABCs OF DEATH** (2012, which has also been given the green light for a follow-up), **THE THEATER BIZARRE** (2011), the Chris Columbus-produced adaptation of Warren's *Creepy* and even Johnny Dickie's meta **SLAUGHTER TALES** (reviewed elsewhere in this issue) all came to mind when I went to the P.O. Box one afternoon and fished out the blackjack-themed anthology **THE DARK DEALER** (1995).

"But what's this?" I ask myself as I remove the wrapper and get ready for a night of viewing. The stills on the back of the box have a decidedly retro feel (torn denim, non-CGI monsters) and there's a 1995 date?

1995?! Now we're talking about my wheelhouse!

Turns out that instead of being some shot-on-video attempt to hop on the recently-hot anthology bandwagon, **THE DARK DEALER** is actually a nearly 20-year-old, Texas-lensed compilation that began as two short films by writers/directors Tom Alexander and Wynn Winberg. Add one titular wraparound tale and "voila!"—you've got an anthology flick that's more reminiscent of late-'80s syndicated horrors like *Monsters* and *Tales from the Darkside* than anything of recent vintage.

Opening in a deserted corporate office, **THE DARK DEALER** wastes no time—nor exposition—as Ray (Richard Hull) finds himself on the run from a destructive, crackling ball of energy that has already wasted one security guard and seems determined to do the same to Ray. Taking refuge in a darkened room, Ray gets sucked into a high stakes game of blackjack presided over by The Dark Dealer (a very Penn Jillette-esque Mark Fickert). The stakes? Their very souls (natch).

With the set-up complete, the flick plunges headlong into "Cellar Space", the first of the two original tales, which, like the wraparound, was written and directed by Alexander. After shaking down and killing a "business partner", petty thieves Pete (Rocky Patterson, who looks like the bastard love child of Joe Piscopo and Christopher McDonald) and Fred (Charles Carroll) take refuge in the basement apartment of Nickodemus (Gordon Fox), an "alchemist" who witnessed the murder and seems to be lying to the two at every step of the way.

"Blues in the Night"—written and directed by Wynn Winberg, who would go on to co-write the documentary series **THE FEARMAKERS COLLECTION** (2007) with author John McCarty—seems to end before it begins as Samson Burke (Vincent Gaskins) "busts" and dies in a seedy hotel room in a too-modern 1961. Doubling down in an attempt to save his soul, Burke returns in the form of a possessed demo tape discovered by entertainment lawyer and wannabe songwriter Phillip Barton (Kevin Walker)…and we all know how those possessed demo tapes work out for people.

Returning to our opening, "The Dark Dealer" shows us how Ray got to the deserted corporate office and why he's being chased by a killer ball of static electricity. Seems that his squeeze Denise (Kim Frazier) is a "recovering" junkie who owes eight-grand to a pipe-smoking drug dealer named Cracker (the excellent Jeff English) and Ray agrees to swipe his dad's pharmaceutical lab security card in exchange for wiping her debt clean.

You won't get any bonus points for connecting the dots and figuring out where each of these segments go or who survives the game. But Alexander, and, to a lesser extent, Winberg, keep the segments moving and rarely give the viewer time to dwell on such things as "why is that 1960s Mexican hooker dressed like it's the mid-'90s" or "how does that skinny lawyer hoist that footlocker brimming with LPs like it's packed with toilet paper".

Filled with practical effects, stop-motion monsters, demons, pentagrams, spooky TRS-80 style computer graphics and decent performances from its regional cast (most of whom have few, if any, additional credits to their name), **THE DARK DEALER** is never great but definitely succeeds at being disposably entertaining in the same way as the syndicated horrors whose memory it evokes.

1995, USA. DIRECTOR: WYNN WINBERG
AVAILABLE FROM MVD VISUAL

SNOW SHARK

Reviewed by Dan Taylor

"Every town has its legends…Bigfoot, Chupacabra, Loch Ness Monster. We have a Snow Shark."

When I was nine my brother and his buddy took me to a dollar theater for a screening of **JAWS** (1975)—they simply wanted to see my reaction to the head popping out of the boat hull—and since that day I've been a sucker for "nature run amok" cinema. Doesn't matter if it's land or sea, real or cryptozoological, I am all-in when man's hubris, ecological tampering or misplaced curios-

ity comes back to bite us in the ass.

Thanks to the unquenchable thirst of outlets like SyFy Channel, Redbox, Netflix and Amazon, "when nature attacks" cinema is back with a vengeance. Whether it's a deep psychological exploration of an urban legend (2011's **THE BARRENS** in which Canada poorly apes the Garden State), a boobified remake of a trash classic (I'm looking at you **PIRANHA 3D** franchise), or a high-concept "you had me at the title" schlockfest like this summer's **SHARKNADO** (2013, starring Ian Ziering and Tara Reid!), nothing catches my eye quite like a cover that suggests I'll be watching some washed-up '80s pop star get eaten by a creature with the body of a crab and the head of a social worker.

Sam Qualiana's **SNOW SHARK** (2012)—in which an earthquake unleashes the long-dormant titular creature from its icy tomb—barely attempts to disguise its ultra-high-concept ("JAWS In The Snow"). After a trio of university researchers disappear in 1999—presumably eaten by the computer-generated monster (courtesy of **THEY BITE** director Brett Piper)—we fast-forward to the present day when another snow shark has reared its ugly head. After the monster makes a late-night snack of the local sheriff's son, things get personal and it's up to the cops, a trio of experts, and a cadre of armed hicks led by Mike (writer/director/director of photography/star Qualiana) to destroy the creature.

I have to give **SNOW SHARK** points for playing the ridiculous material totally straight. While the sight of the creature's dorsal fin cutting through the snow is occasionally guffaw-inducing, the flick never succumbs to the desire to wallow in parody (like the wretched, almost-unwatchable **GUMS**, 1976, starring Brother Theodore) and never had me scrambling for the remote. And though he looks like he's late for his gig as a Teddy Roosevelt impersonator, C.J. Qualiana (the director's father) lends the proceedings a certain somber tone and gravitas as the widowed sheriff who has just lost his ne'er-do-well son to the creature.

Like **MACHETE** (2010) and other faux-grindhouse Coming Attractions-*cum*-features, **SNOW**

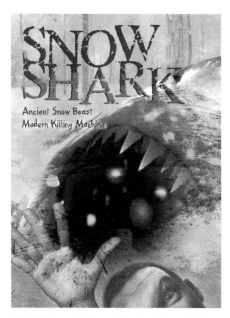

SHARK is probably an idea that plays better as a two-minute trailer or short than a fleshed-out feature. There's perhaps a couple lead characters too many and despite its 79-minute running time I found my interest starting to wander during both recent viewings. But, like a cheap fast food meal grabbed during a long road trip, **SNOW SHARK** knows what it is and never raises your expectations too high, and there's something to be said for that.

The 27-year-old Qualiana—who won the Filmmaker to Watch Award at the 2010 Buffalo Screams Horror Film Festival—is currently back in the writer/director/actor chair for the upcoming found footage monster flick THE LEGEND OF SIX FINGERS. Based on what he accomplished with **SNOW SHARK** I'll certainly give it a look.

2012, USA. DIRECTOR: MIKE QUALIANA
AVAILABLE FROM INDEPENDENT ENTERTAINMENT

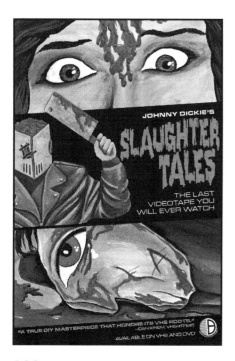

SLAUGHTER TALES

Reviewed by Dan Taylor

Reviewing **SLAUGHTER TALES** (2012)—Johnny Dickie's VHS-inspired, shot-on-video love letter to trashy low-budget horror cinema—is not an easy task.

Sure, I could slam it for looking cheap and amateurish. But guess what? It was made by a teenager for about $65 and looks only slightly worse than, say, **BOARDING HOUSE** (1982).

I could definitely complain that it's often confusing, frequently stupid and occasionally terrible. Then again, the flick's protagonist (played, naturally, by Dickie) refers to the film-within-a-film as "a pile of shit" and laments that "something tells me this is going to suck," while another character sports a t-shirt that reads "This Movie is Terrible".

In other words, **SLAUGHTER TALES** is largely review-proof, a fact that might annoy the hell out of me if I didn't get such a kick out of its frequently-successful attempts to meld such influences as Lucio Fulci, Andreas Schnaas and Sam Raimi.

The mayhem starts when a teen (Dickie) steals a tape titled SLAUGHTER TALES from a neighborhood garage sale. Despite warnings from a spectre who appears in his bathtub and informs him that the tape is cursed—as well as his own gut feeling that he's in for a rough 90 minutes—the kid pops in the VHS.

What follows is a horror anthology film-within-a-film interspersed with Dickie's own observations about what he/we have just witnessed, many of which are so harshly critical that I found myself defending the flick to the on-screen director! Like I said, it's pretty review-proof—Uwe Boll could learn a lesson or two from this kid.

Eventually, the tape's contents bleed from the reel world into Johnnie's as we're treated to corroding hands, hacked-off appendages, decapitations, **NIGHT OF THE CREEPS**-style slug creatures, eye violence, demonic possession and a nod to Schnaas' *Violent Shit* franchise.

Don't get me wrong. I'm not about to praise **SLAUGHTER TALES** as some must-see masterpiece. There are long rough stretches, it's occasionally hard to tell where the movie-within-a-movie ends, the reliance on "fuck" grows tiresome, and the whole thing probably could have been chopped down to a more user-friendly 75 to 80 minutes without losing any of its impact. (The jokey epilogue featuring notorious ham and Troma honcho Lloyd Kaufman feels especially expendable.)

That said, one can't help but marvel at what Dickie accomplished with a budget that goes well below "micro", a cast that seems to be made up mostly of the director, and a reliance on nothing but practical, old school effects (including at least one makeup gag gone wrong).

Already at work on his next feature, CITY OF THE DREAM DEMONS, Dickie is certainly somebody to keep an eye on. I can't help but be reminded of **THE DEAD NEXT DOOR**'s J.R. Bookwalter and his lengthy career as a writer, director and producer, though something tells me that Dickie is more likely to deliver ambitious, over-the-top horror a la Brian Paulin (**BONE SICKNESS**, 2004).

In an era when most kids his age have microscopic attention spans and a what-can-you-do-for-me sense of entitlement, Johnny Dickie gets a ton of respect for putting his $65 where his mouth is and delivering something more than a YouTube clip or viral video to share with friends.

Plus, I can't help but dig any movie with a line like "you're not my friend, you're just an unholy fucktard!"

2012, USA. DIRECTOR: JOHNNY DICKIE
AVAILABLE FROM BRIARWOOD ENT.

THE GREEN-EYED BLONDE

Reviewed by James Bickert

Here's a misleading title produced by Doris Day's sketchy third husband, Martin Melcher, for the popular JD market. It does contain a curvaceous teen named Greeneyes, a.k.a. Phyllis (Susan Oliver), but this sordid tale is really about ticked-off little Betsy (Linda Plowman), the new fish at The Martha Washington School for Girls. After a kooky credit sequence and theme song resembling a '50s sitcom, we learn that Betsy is being incarcerated for giving birth and not revealing who knocked her up!

Everyone but the audience is clueless to the fact that the father of her child is the boyfriend of Betsy's alcoholic mother. When these sauced guardians show up on visiting day to inform Betsy

they are taking the unwanted runt to an orphanage, suicidal inmate Cuckoo (Norma Jean Nilsson) snatches the baby from a wooden crate in the backseat of their car. It takes half a day and a few bars later before they realize the little bastard is gone. After a few seconds of inebriated thought, they return to the reformatory to inform Betsy they found a good home for her baby.

The inmates hide the toddler and form stronger bonds from the new responsibilities of motherhood and Betsy finally warms up to her kid, but the staff eventually becomes suspicious when the girls constantly break into loud group singing to cover the babies crying, and Renie (Beverly Long) is busted burying soiled diapers made from the disappearing linen. The baby is found in the possession of Greeneyes and taken to an orphanage resulting in a massive and quite impressive reform school riot.

THE GREEN-EYED BLONDE tries to cram as many moral arguments into the running time as possible. Most of its ideas center on the answer to juvenile delinquency and reformation being the need for a loving family environment. Surprising for the era, this isn't a segregated facility, and African-American Inmate Trixie (Tommie Moore) is the only character who is reformed when her father returns from overseas and gives her the love that her busy working aunts can't deliver. **THE GREEN-EYED BLONDE** puts forth some fairly progressive racial attitudes for a film that dishes up such heavy spoonfuls of traditional opinions on a woman's role in society. When the inmates name the child Buddy—because a baby is a girl's best friend—you really get a good serving of the backward ideas on display.

Oscar winner Dalton Trumbo's (**ROMAN HOLIDAY**, **JOHNNY GOT HIS GUN**) script even tosses in some Christian pro-life messages in the form of a new caring head matron who grew up in an orphanage and turned out just fine; the importance of having an infant around at Christmas like baby Jesus, and an outlandish moment when Cuckoo, to the horror of the sane inmates, kills a kitten because she felt it was better off dead since nobody wanted it. These are all presented with varying degrees of subtly and, for the most part, enhance the exploitation experience and stifle the intended message.

So what about Greeneyes? Well, her story feels like an added wraparound to cash in on the success of **UNTAMED YOUTH** with Mamie Van Doren from the same year. Susan Oliver does appear throughout the film, but often the camera will cut within a scene to her on a different set. After being the one caught with the baby and given a longer sentence, she breaks out and reunites with her paroled boyfriend. We later hear on a radio that the two died in a police shootout. Yeah, it's a half-assed attempt at the virtues of virginity, negated by the fact that they were running away to get married anyway?! Isn't this thing about the power of love and family? I guess family does win out, since Betsy never fingers the rapist and her mother doesn't do a stint for child abandonment. Maybe the message really is, "Don't be a snitch!" There is plenty of jailhouse code on display for one to make the case. Anyway, everything abruptly ends leaving many plots unresolved. If

GHOST MAN - Toho ad slick

you don't take this garbage seriously, it's a quick watch full of chuckles, head scratchers and the occasional jaw-dropper. Did I mention the riot? I must admit, I did enjoy watching a gaggle of gals do demo on a staircase, trash some windows and fling themselves at barb wire fences. It was livelier than most of these reform school yawns.

For you Trekkies out there, Susan Oliver went on to play Nina in the two-part *Star Trek* "Menagerie" episodes. Producer Martin Melcher would go on to squander Doris Day's money in bad investments, turn down the offer for old Doris to play Mrs. Robinson in 1967's **THE GRADUATE** (without her knowledge) and die right after signing his wife to a CBS TV series (without her consent). Obviously, Melcher liked to live up to the high moral codes of the pictures he produced.

1957, USA. DIRECTOR: BERNARD GIRARD

GHOST MAN
(Yurei Otoko)

Reviewed by Jolyon Yates

There are several points of interest to this curiosity which, like **RAINBOW MAN** (*Niji otoko*, 1949) is a mystery with a Horror tinge rather than a tale of the supernatural as the title might suggest. This is the earliest example I have seen of the "masked killer artfully knocking off models" plot with which Mario Bava would run wild the following decade. It is a Toho production directed by Motoyoshi Oda during the months he also helmed **INVISIBLE MAN** (*Tomei ningen*, 1954) and **GODZILLA RAIDS AGAIN** (*Gojira no gyakushu*, 1955). Those who follow Japanese detective films might also want to see this entry in the 1950s run of *Kindaichi Kosuke* movies based on the stories by Seishi Yokomizo, although the hero only turns up halfway through. Also: nudes, nudes, nudes.

A grotesque stranger (characters describe him as looking like a phantom) turns up at a "Model Club" where women can be hired to pose for artists. Although the women back away in fear, the male management is happy to take his cash, and off one poor model goes, alone, at night, to his studio. Her survival instincts in full effect, she knocks back the drink he offers, strips, and collapses in a chair. At this point, enter The Invisible Man, or at least someone in a coat, hat, shades and a bandage covering his head. The "artist" dives out the window, but alas, when the rest of the Model Club turn up, their colleague is dead in a bathtub soaking in her own blood. The following night's victim is laid out on a tiger rug, but before she dies she is photographed by the bandaged man, who calls himself Taro Yamada. The Model Club heads out to a resort hotel for further nude posing, but the killer strikes again. This time the unfortunate's legs are in a garden, and her top half posed in a pond, where Detective Kindaichi is taking her picture. Back in Tokyo, a body is found draped over a bed, then a stripper is murdered during a show involving a spider-web set which reminded me of a far more stylishly-shot nightclub scene in Jess Franco's **THE DIABOLICAL DR. Z** (1966). 'Taro' is shown seated beneath a staircase adding the latest picture to his photo album. However, soon afterwards, Kindaichi traps him and chases him over the rooftops. Although Kindaichi later produces a pistol, for most of the chase he seems to rely heavily on 'Taro' being a lousy shot, even at close range. Eventually the person Kindaichi calls "devilish" is cornered, catching the bandage on a wire so that his identity is revealed as he flees.

Although featuring excellent photography by Kazuo Yamada—especially the *ero-guro* tableaus—and a cast recognizable from many Fantasy, Yakuza and Samurai movies and films by Akira Kurosawa and Yasujiro Ozu—and despite the surprisingly high exploitation quotient—**GHOST MAN** manages to be less than thrilling. Should this be blamed on Oda? He was relegated to churning out up to seven programmers a year

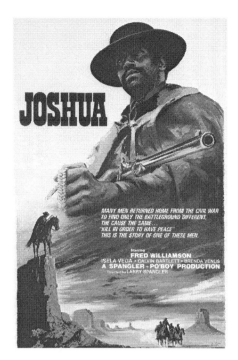

from the war through to the late '50s, so perhaps he never had time to develop as a director, unlike his stable-mates Kurosawa and Ishiro Honda. The editing is sometimes dull; even at 72 minutes **GHOST MAN** needs to lose a bit of flab. In the worst case, the Model Club is unnecessarily shown leaving their office, descending stairs, heading away from camera down an alley, packing into a car and exiting the shot. The basic structure is also awkward, introducing the hero so late when I was already struggling to track, or care for, over a dozen characters (although Yu Fujiki's reporter character has a few layers to him).

Kindaichi Kosuke is played by Seizaburo Kawazu (also the hero of **INVISIBLE MAN**) for the only time. The previous actor in the role for six films had been Chiezo Kataoka, who would return for one more, **THREE-HEAD TOWER** (*Mitsukubi to*) in 1956. Kindaichi has appeared in dozens of movies and television episodes over the years, including **THE INUGAMI CLAN** (1954, 1976, 1994, 2006) and **VILLAGE OF EIGHT GRAVESTONES** (1951, 1977, 1978, 1991, 1995), and directors have included those known in the West for their Horror titles such as Nobuhiko Obayashi and Nobuo Nakagawa.

1954, JAPAN. DIRECTOR: MOTOYOSHI ODA

JOSHUA
(aka: THE BLACK RIDER)

Reviewed by Steve Fenton

Lone Star Pictures' press-sheet ad-line: "Many men returned home from the Civil War to find only the battleground different, the cause the same…'Kill in order to have peace.' This is the story of one of those men."

Fred Williamson as the fatalistic Joshua, who ain't just joshin' ya: "Wanna keel me? Go 'head!"

Unidentified surly: "A stranger ain't welcome 'round these parts."

Co-produced by director Spangler and screenwriter/star Williamson's own Po' Boy Productions—a '70s movie made on a '30s-sized budget—this ultra-cheap if generally humbly (very humbly) effective revenge Western tells the tale of title Union veteran (Williamson) who returns to the old homestead after the Civil War only to learn that his beloved ma has been murdered, and sets out to avenge himself on the five degenerate honky saddle tramps responsible, led by Jeb (Calvin Bartlett). Along for the ride is a kidnapped young woman (Brenda Venus), who is subjected to periodic non-explicit sexual molestation by the outlaws. While much of the tone here recalls an American roughie Western, nudity is non-existent, leaving any prurience to be conveyed entirely by the dialogue ("I ain't had so much cunt since I raped my nine-year-old sister!" brags a shrill-voiced Gabby Hayes surrogate, aptly nicknamed Weasel).

Dressed all in black and constantly being mistaken for either an outlaw or a bounty-hunter ("That ain't no black lawman!"), Williamson as Joshua ("I can ride around ya, or through ya...") disposes of his enemies via rattlesnake, stake, pistol, noose, trip-wired Winchester and dynamite. When wounded, Williamson is nursed back to health by a sexy, lonely Mexican widow named María (Peckinpah alumnus Isela Vega; prime MILF material, for sure), whom he subsequently rescues from renegade gunfighters.

At times there is a sloppy, almost documentary-like urgency to the imagery. Action works best out in wide-open country (Utah?), where any obvious shortcomings in the props/sets departments are least evident. Shot following genuine winter snowfall—prompting fleeting, faint echoes of Sergio Corbucci's **IL GRANDE SILENZIO** (a.k.a. **THE GREAT SILENCE**, 1968)—Williamson hides in a snowdrift to bushwhack pursuers (i.e., extras dressed in off-the-rack urban cowboy casual wear).

An endless harmonica solo of "Oh, Susanna" is heard down at the spartanly-furnished saloon shack, where the star's lackadaisical knife-throwing levels a bar tough ("You gotta big mouth, Stranger, and I'm aimin' ta shut it!") Them's mighty big words, Mr. Soon-To-Be-Dead Guy. Even while sounding highly unspaghetti-like indeed, via simple repetition Mike Irwin's heavily-synthesized score somehow still succeeds in becoming strangely hypnotic. For the unconvincingly-staged conclusion in a mountain cave, Joshua ("I'm my mother's son...")—set to a suddenly spaghetti-style whistling theme—dons a black cape and snipes at a cluster of TNT sticks using his late Pa's Sharps rifle.

Co-starring C&W singer Stonewall Jackson and occasional Spaghetti Western player Neil Summers (seen in **MY NAME IS NOBODY**, 1973, among many others).

1976, USA. DIRECTOR: LARRY SPANGLER
AVAILABLE FROM REEL CLASSIC FILMS

STORIE DI VITA E MALAVITA
("*Stories of Life and Lowlife*", a.k.a.
THE TEENAGE PROSTITUTION RACKET)

Reviewed by Steve Fenton

World-worn hooker, regarding pimps: "You fill your slits, and he fills his pocket!"
Pimp, inspecting lineup of hirsute-boxed whores: "Some men like a little bit o' hair wid their meat!"
Mature hooker: "They call me 'The Electric Tongue'!"
Drag hustler: "Instead of a hole, I gotta pole!"
If those above potty-mouthed muck-nuggets of

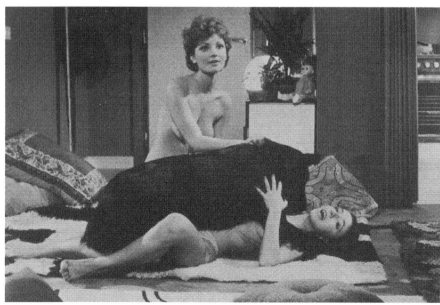

Move Over, Rover: Just one of the indignities heaped upon underage prostitutes in Carlo Lizzani's **STORIE DI VITA E MALAVITA**

smutspeak don't adequately prepare you for the grungey narrative to follow, boy did you ever misread the signposts up ahead.

This sexploitative social drama (allegedly "Based on Research by Marisa Rusconi"), was, fittingly enough, co-produced by Adelina Tattilo, editrix of the top Italian nudie magazine *Playmen*. Lizzani's cast is largely comprised of amateur Milanese actors, which enhances the generally scuzzy docudrama-like tone of this sinfully sordid story of prostitutes and procurers laid amid the gutter fauna of Milan. As a concerned nun explains, "Ninety percent of prostitutes come from broken homes." Direct and indirect causes such as poverty, incest, drug addiction, mental affliction, social injustice or sometimes just plain complacency compel teenage girls to go "on the game." Individual segments connected by a general linking theme expose several tales—and tails—of the vice ring's victims...who are jailbait in every sense of the term.

Girls are bought and sold like horseflesh on the white slavers' black market. Fresh off the boat from Sardegna ("Sardinia"), naïve country signorina Rosina (Cinzia Mambretti) finds piecework assembling bootleg audiocassettes for music pirates but quickly falls prey to the 'charms' of Salvatore, alias "Velvet" (Nicola del Buono), a smooth-talking pimp who first takes her virginity then brainwashes her into selling her body for his profit ("It's as easy as apple pie!"). After being coerced into a house of ill repute ("You're a hooker, Little Miss Muffet!"), Rosina narrowly escapes thanks to a conscientious social worker. Upon trying to flee back home to Sardinia, however, Rosina gets her face slashed by Velvet's switchblade as punishment and apathetically resigns herself to remaining a cut-price prostitute, already jaded and over-the-hill at only seventeen.

Parents' negligence in providing their children with adequate sex education is cited as another reason why some teenagers become ensnared in the procurers' nets; as in the case of Gisella (Cristina Moranzoni), a coddled bourgeois sweet sixteen who falls under the influence of Alberto (Sandro Pizzochero) and is entrapped into posing for nude photos at drunken call-girl orgies ("You're very photogenic in all the right places!"). Daniela (Anna Rita Grapputo) is a by-product of wealthy-but-emotionally-bankrupt, loveless parents who trade off genuinely demonstrative familial affection with empty material possessions. Her own father is himself a secret "customer" of the teenie racket into which the "frigid" Daniela becomes willingly initiated, then blackmails her alienated parents afterward to suppress the scandal.

After her own father knocks her up ("Nice, but it ain't easy ta sell!"), working class 15-year-old Antonietta Bani (Anna Curti) shacks-up with a muffdiving lesbo pimpette and the emotional trauma of giving up her highly illegitimate (i.e., incestuously-spawned) baby for adoption sees her committed to an asylum by her shrink (Enzo Fisichella, one of the relatively few pro actors in the cast). 18-year-old Albertina (Daniela Grassini) is an ex-novice nun who was raped by a petty bureaucrat and ever since can only enjoy sex in public places where there is a high risk of being caught in the act. Her 16-year-old girlfriend Laura (Lidia di Corato) despises the male gender so

much ("All men are disgusting. Just monsters!") that she much prefers the unconditional affections of her sleek black Alsatian, Argo, who is so much more than just a girl's best friend. After her dog is eviscerated by malicious pimps, Laura bloodily commits suicide, such is her grief.

The sleaze commences to flow right in the prologue: having been tempted by her elderly female "guardian" ("Just think, she's only thirteen! ...Come on, it's only 3000 lire!"), a truck driver pulls over for a furtive quickie with an underage hitchhooker who gives him a below-the-dashboard BJ then matter-of-factly rinses with mouthwash afterward. Moranzoni initially has her hymen inspected by a seedy gynecologist to verify her virginity and masquerades as a harem concubine named White Orchid to service a septuagenarian retired judge. Sickos torment puppyfat nymphets with whips and stilettos. While a slobbering dirty old man gropes Curti's pregnant belly, his mistress masturbates graphically using a buzzing vibrator. Grapputo (or her body double?) participates in intercourse, showing bona fide vaginal penetration. Other footage depicts a man receiving authentic oral sex at a party that also includes some badly-simulated dyke strap-on dildo action. Hardcore footage (intact on Astron's smutty, English-dubbed Greek pre-recorded videocassette released circa the '80s) seems to have been shot at the same time as the bulk of the film, is integrated very smoothly and does not appear to have been crudely "inserted" after the fact (a fairly commonplace practice with Euro sleazemakers hoping to boost a film's sexploitability). For the most stomach-churning scene, an infantilist pervert dunks a loaf of bread into a urine-filled toilet, then forces a distraught lolita to take a bite.

Complete with at least one misspoken phrase ("It's absolutely irrevelant!" [sic]), an almost gleefully pornographic tone is instilled by sweaty-palmed flirtations with pedophilia, queasy voyeurism and unabashedly grubby dialogue snatched right out of a penny dreadful pulp porn novel ("17 years old! She gives a blowjob that'll blow your brains right out of your ears!" – "There can't be any other 17-year-old girl in the world who can enjoy sex like you do: you cum like a rabbit!", etc.)

Morricone's slightly off-key compositions well convey the hectic inexorability of the dog-eat-dog metropolitan existence. Offering no solutions to a complex socio-sexual problem and merely confirming the infinite vicious circle of the world's oldest profession as plied by some of its youngest purveyors, the film ends much as it began. While it lacks many of the genre's traditional trappings such as pyrotechnics (or even a single visible firearm), **STORIE DI VITA E MALAVITA** literally drips with deviant criminality, pathological perversion, unsafe sex and unclassifiable social diseases...amounting to the crimeslimiest title in the entire Italo crimeslime cosmos. Which we suppose is some kind of a recommendation to the cinematically (and criminally) broad-minded.

An Italian version of this film which I downloaded from an online torrent site (naughty me!) does not contain any hardcore footage, which leads me to believe—though I could well be wrong about this—that on its home turf the film was released only in a softcore version. If anyone knows the facts behind this, please feel free to take me to

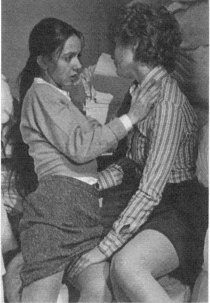

STORIE DI VITA E MALAVITA

task for my error, as it is your duty as a WENG'S CHOPper to do your bit in furthering the cause of world scum sinema.

[*NOTE*: Also shot on Milan's mean streets, Lizzani's thematically-related companion piece to this present title is **SAN BABILA ORE 20: UN DELITTO INUTILE** ("*San Babila, 8 p.m.: A Senseless Crime*", a.k.a. **KILL TO KILL**, 1975, which one scribe has described as "kind of **A CLOCKWORK ORANGE**, Italian style." Again, as here, that film utilized a cast largely consisting of non-pro actors.]

1975, ITALY. DIRECTORS: CARLO LIZZANI, MINO GIARDA
AVAILABLE FROM MINERVA PICTURES [REGION 2]

BADA$$ MOTHAF**KAS!

Reviewed by Brian Harris

Come on, jive turkeys! You just had to know I'd hook you up with this righteous little production from Full Moon / GrindhouseFlix the minute it came out. Their third original production in and by far, it is their best effort to date. Did this trailer com-

Segment One: *Badass Brothas* – **HELL UP IN HARLEM** (1973) was Larry Cohen's same-year follow-up to **BLACK CAESAR**, Melvin Van Peeble's **SWEET SWEETBACK'S BAADASSSSS SONG** (1971), **SHAFT** (1971) starring Richard Roundtree, **SLAUGHTER** (1972) starring a whacked-out Rip Torn, **SLAUGHTER'S BIG RIP-OFF** (1973) with legendary Carson sidekick Ed McMahon as "The Man," **THE HAMMER** (1972), **SUPER FLY** (1972), **BLACK GUNN** (1972) featuring Martin Landau as an Italian mob boss, **THE BLACK GODFATHER** (1974), **BLACK SHAMPOO** (1976), **TRUCK TURNER** (1974) features an all-star cast including Isaac Hayes, Yaphet Kotto, Nichelle Nichols, Scatman Crothers and Dick Miller, Cirio H. Santiago directed **SAVAGE!** (1973), **WILLIE DYNAMITE** (1974).

Segment Two: *Fine Foxy Ladies* – **TNT JACKSON** (1974) directed by Cirio H. Santiago, **CLEOPATRA JONES** (1973) starring Bernie Casey, Antonio Fargas, Esther Rolle, Don Cornelius and Shelley Winters (!) as a crazy drug kingpin, Jack Hill's **COFFY** (1973) starring Pam Grier's massive jugs, Allan Arbus (*M*A*S*H*) and Blaxploitation regular Sid Haig, **FOXY BROWN** (1974) more Hill, Grier, boobs and Haig, **SHEBA BABY** (1975) starring Grier and D'Urville Martin.

Segment Three: *Martial Arts Masters* – **DOLEMITE** (1975) directed by D'Urville Martin, Al Adamson's **BLACK SAMURAI** (1977), **THAT MAN BOLT** (1973), **THE HUMAN TORNADO** (1976) starring Ernie Hudson, **DISCO GODFATHER** (1979)

Segment Four: *Far Too Many Monsters* – **BLACULA** (1972), **BLACKENSTEIN** (1973), **DR. BLACK, MR. HYDE** (1976), **SCREAM BLACULA SCREAM** (1973) starring Pam Grier, **ABBY** (1974) starring William "Blacula" Marshall, **THE THING WITH TWO HEADS** (1972) starring Rosey Grier, **SUGAR HILL** (1974).

Before the fifth segment is introduced we get a side-splitting skit featuring The Hammer demanding the writer show himself or he'd kick his ass. A skinny, nerdy "cracker" comes out and The Hammer forces him to announce the next segment. His answer is, "Niggers on Horses." It's hard to contain yourself during Fred feigned disgust.

Segment Five: *Negroes (Niggas) On Horses* – **BOSS NIGGER** (1975) a Western with Fred Wiliamson, D'Urville Martin and Big Will Smith? Insanity!, **BLACK RODEO** (1972) featuring cameos by Muhammad Ali and Woody Strode, Antonion Margheriti's **TAKE A HARD RIDE** (1975) the big three Blaxploitation stars Fred "The Hammer" Williamson, Jim Brown and Jim Kelly face off with Lee Van Cleef, **SOUL SOLDIER** (*THE RED, WHITE AND BLACK* – 1970) starring Cesar Romero.

Segment Six: *Unity* – **THREE THE HARD WAY** (1974) the first time William, Brown and Kelly starred together, **THE MACK** (1973) starring legendary comedian Richard Pryor, **BLACK SAMSON** (1974) with Big Will Smith, **BUCKTOWN** (1975) Williamson, Grier and Carl Weathers, Ossie Davis's **COTTON COMES TO HARLEM** (1970) starring Calvin Lockhart and raunchy comedian Redd Foxx, **MONKEY HUSTLE** (1976), **THE SPOOK WHO SAT BY THE DOOR** (1973), Duccio Tessari's **THREE TOUGH GUYS** (1974) starring Isaac Hayes and Fred "The Hammer" Williamson, **ZEBRA FORCE** (1976).

What an insanely cool trailer compilation! It's well worth viewing and definitely worth owning if you like these kinds of productions. I found very little wrong with **BADA$$ MOTHAF**KAS!** outside of a few noticeably absent trailers. Now I know you can't always include everything but the *Badass Brothas* segment was noticeably missing **BLACK CAESAR**, *Fine Foxy Ladies* - **FRIDAY FOSTER**, *Far Too Many Monsters* - **JD's REVENGE**, *Negroes On Horses* – **THE LEGEND OF NIGGER CHARLIE & THE SOUL OF NIGGER CHARLIE** and finally the *Unity* segment might have used **BLACK GESTAPO**. The flicks I listed above may not be represented in this trailer compilation, but it's hardly noticeable and really more of a geeky nitpick on my part. The quality of the trailers were all relatively decent; there were a few that showed signs of pixelation and what-not but for the most part they all looked and sounded good.

BADA$$ MOTHAFKAS!** comes highly recommended to Blaxploitation fans.

2013, USA. DIRECTOR: CHARLES BAND
AVAILABLE FROM GRINDHOUSEFLIX

pilation have more money to work with than the previous two or was it the addition of talented jack-of-all-trades writer/editor Leroy Patterson to this ass-kicking production? Not at all sure about the former but I think I'm onto something with the latter. Patterson not only wrote and edited; he played a small role and animated a super cool, action-packed opening title sequence (á la JibJab). The fantastic production design—a decrepit alley set—combined with the animation, Fred "The Hammer" Williamson's intensity and the fun dialogue make **BADA$$ MOTHAF**KAS!** a slam dunk.

Having Fred "The Hammer" Williamson host this compilation not only kicked the geek factor up a few notches for cult cinema fans such as myself but it really lent some class and "street cred" (*WINK*) to the entire affair. It would be like getting one of the cast of the original *Star Trek* series to host a "Best of Trek" retrospective; having one of the originals sends viewers the message that a stamp of approval has been given and it's okay to settle in and enjoy. Knowing Williamson's storied history with "Black Action" (Blaxploitation) films, I would've liked to have seen a bit more from "The Hammer" himself but, hell, it's a trailer *compilation*—and hot damn, do we get those!

WENG'S CHOP ISSUE ZERO

The 'zine that started all this madness! Digest-size, 56 pages, color cover, reviews, articles, interviews! If you liked Weng's Chop #1 you'll go bonkers over SPECIAL ISSUE ZERO!
Available from amazon.com *-or-*
We have a *very* limited supply of our first printing for only $6 PPD USA & Canada or $12 PPD overseas. Paypal: orlof@oberlin.net.
Offer good while supplies last!

THE SUPER

Reviewed by Tony Strauss

George Rossi (Demetri Kallas) is a Vietnam vet who lives in Astoria Queens, and is the superintendent of an apartment building that has been in his family for over 40 years. It's a station he's proud of, and he treats his tenants with respect and warmth, trying to provide the best life possible for his wheelchair-bound wife, Maureen (Lynn Lowry), and their withdrawn daughter, Helen (Logan De Sisto). Oh, sure, some of the tenants take advantage of his kindness—as Maureen never hesitates to point out—and some of them are downright disrespectful, but George does his best to take these things in stride.

George's job carries a lot of pressure. Russian dominatrix Olga (Manoush, in a masterpiece of a performance) refuses to pay her rent while obviously making plenty of money, resident racist meat-head Tony Bava (Bill McLaughlin) constantly complains, threatens, and criticizes George's every move, new tenants Andre (Edgar Moye) and Karen (Ruby Larocca) are annoyingly stand-offish to George's friendliness, part-time helper/full-time junkie Frannie the Tranny (Brandon Slagle) has nowhere to stay for the holidays, and all the while Maureen harangues George for never spending time with his family.

On a much-needed night out drinking with his buddies, George gets into a verbal altercation with some lippy punks who start badmouthing soldiers who fought in 'Nam. Without warning, George opens up a family-size can of whoop-ass on them, and has to be pulled out of the bar by his friends. It's understandable that he might go ballistic on some much-deserving douchebags—especially after a couple rounds—but this event is just the first clue that George may not be handling things as well as he seems to be. You see, George not only has his own ways of dealing with stress and getting even with his transgressors, but he also has his own master set of keys. And, as he himself admits, he has a hard time letting things go…

As George's petty revenges accelerate, so does his fugue from sanity. When one act of self-defense turns into grisly murder, the flood gates are officially open, and soon the bodies are piling up at an alarming rate. George seems no longer able to control himself, and now a dirty cop (rapper Ron "Necro" Braunstein) has started snooping around, and seems to really have it in for George. Things quickly spiral out of control, culminating in a jaw-droppingly brutal, Grand Guignol of a finale that must be seen to be believed!

Remember back in the '70s when you and your friends would pile into cars and spend the weekend at the drive-in watching endless onslaughts of low-budget exploitation violence and mayhem? No? Well, fear not—writer/director team Brian Weaver and Evan Makrogiannis are here to remember it for you, and short of parking your car in your living room and pulling a filthy speaker in through the driver-side window, they deliver the complete experience! The filmmakers' attention to detail is astonishing—the use of zooms and handheld cinematography, the "dirty splices" in the film print, the use of the long-gone "single shot", the balance of brutal violence and twisted humor, the excellent period-style score, right down to the color of the blood—you'll be so convinced that you're watching an authentic piece of late-'70s New York Exploitation that you'll be half-expecting a Joe Spinell cameo!

But the thing that really sets **THE SUPER** apart from other modern exploitation homages is its skillful handling of story and character. This movie isn't just a collection of horrific events and weirdos; it's a story about *people*. The narrative gathers momentum at a perfect pace, with the characters fully-fleshed and realized by fearless and committed performers (Kallas, Lowry and Manoush deliver some truly career-defining work here, and Slagle is downright unforgettable as Franny), so as the movie slips into over-the-top madness, you have no other option but to go careening over the edge with it! All this, combined with the fact that repeat viewings deliver a wholly new experience from the first, make this a definite must-own—and it's highly recommended that you try to get your hands on the limited Red Scare Edition, which contains exclusive footage shot in Russia by **PHILOSOPHY OF A KNIFE** auteur Andrey Iskanov!

Exploitation fans who complain that they don't make 'em like they used to just haven't seen **THE SUPER** yet. I highly recommend remedying that situation immediately.

2010, USA. DIRECTORS: BRIAN WEAVER & EVAN MAKROGIANNIS
AVAILABLE AT *www.thesuper-movie.com*

MEGALODON: THE MONSTER SHARK LIVES

Reviewed by Brian Harris

On April 5, 2013, a chartered fishing vessel went down in a tragic accident off Cape Town, South Africa in Hout Bay, taking with it the lives of a group of tourists. During the investigation that followed it was determined that a breaching whale may have capsized the boat, that is until a digital camera was recovered from the wreckage. The footage clearly showed that the boat was not destroyed by a breaching whale but was struck from beneath by an unseen force. Once the footage's audio was cleaned up it was possible to hear one of the missing tourists shouting about a shark. Chilling.

Days after the incident, a Discovery Channel documentary crew led by marine biologist Collin Drake is on the scene and attempting to get to the bottom of the mystery. Just what kind of shark is capable of bringing down a large boat with such violence? As the documentary begins amassing more and more evidence, the answer becomes startlingly clear; only one species of shark known to man could have been capable of this—a creature thought extinct, that ruled the oceans of the

Cenozoic era unchallenged—the massive Megalodon. A killing and eating machine, so big, so hungry, that it fed on whales.

Are Drake and crew on to something on par with the discovery of the colossal squid or has cable television, once again, succeeded in fooling the gullible viewing public with a well-crafted mockumentary (or docu-fiction) in the same vein as Animal Planet's *Mermaids: The Body Found*? If the latter never crossed your mind, you just may be one of those gullible viewers. While nobody really made a stink about *Mermaids: The Body Found*—only idiots believe in mermaids, right?—the Internet is currently ablaze with indignation over this phony documentary. Genuinely pissed off over being had, many celebrities and media personalities are sounding off and demanding apologies from Discovery over this Shark Week misstep. In other words, quite a few out there have egg on their faces and are nursing bruised egos. As I mentioned above, only morons would believe in mermaids, but a prehistoric shark…

well…c'mon…*that's possible*. Right? Stranger things have turned up in nets, buuuut…

While channel surfing, I happened upon *Megalodon: The Monster Shark Lives* and immediately spotted the production for what it was. All the tell-tale signs were there, including great acting that seemed "too convincing," less-than-subtle digitally-doctored evidence and the kind of ambiguous finale seen on monster- and ghost-hunting shows on a weekly basis. Now, I'm not saying I'm smarter than everybody else; I'm just a dyed-in-the wool skeptic and a genre cinema fan well acquainted with mockumentaries. Just because it was obvious to me, though, doesn't mean it would automatically become obvious to others. Discovery Channel had a real responsibility to notify those viewers beforehand. Granted, a quick disclaimer had flashed on-screen for roughly three seconds around the final quarter of the program but, seriously, that was nowhere near long enough or prominent enough.

If this brings to mind the infamous Orson Welles/*War of the Worlds* radio incident of 1938, you may be onto something, as that immediately came to my own mind. It also brings to mind something P.T. Barnum once said.

Unlike, apparently, the entire goddamn universe, I do not clear my schedule for Shark Week. Hell, I couldn't even tell you the last time I sat down to watch anything on it. The only reason I did this time was because I happened to have some time to kill and I initially assumed it was a B-movie that I hadn't seen. If it had been titled *Seeking Ancient Sharks* or *The Cape Town Expedition*, you probably wouldn't be reading this review right now, so when you think about it, the hook did its job and they reeled in one hell of a geek. I ain't mad at 'em. *Megalodon: The Monster Shark Lives* was interesting and relatively riveting; I mean, I wouldn't run out to grab this should it ever go to disc but I've seen it twice, so there's that. The production values were high; you can't go wrong with the narration, acting, graphics and videography. Considering the overwhelming response by viewers to made-for-TV docu-fiction productions like *Megalodon: The Monster Shark Lives*, *Mermaids: The Body Found* and even *Mermaids: The New Evidence*, I expect to see many more of these in the future. And why the hell not? If people for the most part dig them and they're cheaper to produce than feature films, bring them on. I wouldn't mind seeing a few for NatGeo (National Geographic) or the Science Channel. But next time, let's be sure there are some clear disclaimers in place so people aren't forced to retract their Tweets and bring the social networking world to its knees.

Yeah, more sarcasm.

2013, USA. DIRECTOR: DOUGLAS GLOVER

THREE-WAY SPLIT

Reviewed by Steve Fenton

Adline: "Three 'Sex-O-Pathic' Killers Attempt the Most Daring Heist of Their Sordid Careers… Sharing the Danger…The Money…And the Women…In a…'Three-Way Split'!"

Here's one that even a lot of sleaze sinema experts seem to have overlooked: a highly obscure Yank "roughie" (originally made by one Green Dolphin Productions), put out on an ancient (ca. 1979) VHS pre-recorded videocassette struck from an exceedingly worn and scratchy transfer print. For much of the first reel, film and audio track ran wildly out of synchronization, and all its technical imperfections merely served to further enhance the basic scuzziness of the product.

In Nevada, sadistic slobs go for a desert joyride in a WW2-vintage Wehrmacht armored halftrack vehicle (still emblazoned with Nazi insignia). A car-smashing spree segues into a drunken living room orgy, replete with simulated sex and full-frontal female nudity galore. Next follows a sexless amorous tryst upon a hideous orange-and-green floral print bedspread, with a guy kissing a chesty brunette's bestockinged legs and pantied, acned ass. Three seasoned bank robbers, Joe, Dick and Mack (Peter Owen, G.L. Vitto and Alec Abram, respectively, just for the record, as if anybody cares) plot to relieve a Las Vegas mining company of its so-called "$2.8-million payroll".

Middle-aged "co-star" Vitto (with pock-marked complexion and wonky dental work) apparently got the role simply because he donated his personal two-man helicopter to the production. In one of the more amusing moments in what is generally a "straight" drama, Joe fits a telescopic sight (!) onto a German army-surplus Schmeisser sub-machinegun in order to snipe at a passing car from a mountain road (with a single bullet, yet!) Violence is plentiful and bloody—shot in gaudy, no-name "KetchupColor"—exemplified when one of the leering lowlifes chops off a dead man's hand so as to remove a money-filled briefcase which is cuffed to his wrist.

The crooks stash their loot underwater at a secluded lake, planning to reconvene later for a little innocent "fishing trip" in order to reclaim it once the fuss blows over and the heat dies down. In the meantime, an incidental party of scuba divers happens upon the sunken strongbox and salvage it for themselves (don't expect any underwater photography in a movie this technically limited [i.e., inept]). The chauvinistic divers are delayed when, in a fit of pique, one of their bitchy girlfriends—evidently suffering from PMS?—chucks the speedboat keys in the lake just to put a damper on their plans. After the robbers arrive to stake their claim, they murder the belligerent divers and kidnap their mamas as hostages. After punching one of the fleeing women out cold, Joe slices off her bra and panties with a switchblade and attempts to screw her unconscious body right on the beach. Next follows the misogynistic degradation of a blonde female captive: at knifepoint she is forced to remove her brassiere ("Strip, bay-bee! Strip!" leers Vitto, clearly relishing his part), then she is slapped around and raped. Post-coitus, she stabs the vile Vitto to death with his own stiletto, then is re-raped and murdered in turn by Abram. Back at their hideout, the two surviving girls, Nicole (Danou Franchetti) and Shirley (Shirley Mallar) are forcibly stripped and violated. This scene might well be disturbing if not for the alleged actresses' insistence on openly grinning at both one another and their "tormentors" (a common symptom of the genre, wherein retakes were generally a no-no due to the added expense incurred for wasted footage). Upon surmising that Nicole is of the Sapphic bent, Joe and Mack pour hot coffee on her then coerce her and Shirl—who wears kinky white vinyl go-go boots—into a lesbian lingual liaison.

When they somehow find themselves "surrounded" by a solitary highway patrolman, the fugitives threaten to blow up their hideout, chicks'n'all, but are permitted to make their getaway with hostages in tow. Chased out into the desert by wailing cruisers, Joe and Mack shoot it out with the fuzz ("Come an' get me, you miserable faggot!"), leaving the sand littered with gory corpses (judging by the choppiness of this footage, some gore seems to have been cut, or at least "shortened" by a few frames). The cast, like the plot, is uniformly unappealing, especially when undressed. Despite lousy acting and even worse direction, this is occasionally ambitious stuff for a no-budget drive-in crimeslime cheapie boasting a bona fide car crash, several explosions, motorboats, police car chases, plus the aforementioned chopper and lotsa noisy tommygun spray (and lest we forget, nipples the size of plunger heads too!).

THREE-WAY SPLIT is in the inimitable politically incorrect tradition of roughies like **SATAN'S BED** and **THE DEFILERS** (both 1965), notable solely for its obscurity value and some perky, photogenic breasts (shot with a macro lens for that "up close and personal" effect!). For its would-be stylish final moment, the herky-jerky camera pans onto a bullet-riddled road sign poignantly reading "END". The end is right!

Something Weird Video seems about the most likely place to turn up a copy of this thing nowadays, for those that might wish to inflict it on themselves. Students of American skid-row sinema may well take note. However, all others beware!

1970, USA. DIRECTOR: CHARLES NIZET

THE HEADHUNTERS
(*Nueva Vizcaya*)

Reviewed by Steve Fenton

The first official Filipino/American coproduction, Eddie Romero's **CAVALRY COMMAND** (1957), was fittingly enough a pseudoater (i.e., an imitation western). Odd though it might seem, the term "Filipino Western" is not such a geographical contradiction. In keeping with the common trend of naming cinematic genres after popular culinary dishes in their countries of origin, perhaps we might even refer to such films still more informally as "Adobo Westerns" (we might alternately call them "Karé-Karé Westerns," after another popular domestic dish). While certainly one of the first, **CAVALRY COMMAND** was by no means the only example of its kind, which also includes our present title.

Complete with English dialogue, **THE HEADHUNTERS** was formerly (circa the early-/mid-'90s) available for rental at many Pinoy (Filipino) video outlets across North America.

Though very much a mediocre exploitation programmer rather than a serious historical document, this film was evidently inspired by Ralph Nelson's **SOLDIER BLUE** (USA, 1970), but comes from the opposite side of the political fence. Set in 1930 amid the mountain region of Nueva Vizcaya, located on Luzon some 200 miles from Manila, capital city of the Philippine Islands, locales are dusty, sun-scorched partial desert. This is the dwelling place of the primitive Tarikan Indians, whom a narrator (in English) describes as "The most feared minority group called... **THE HEADHUNTERS**." Part of the Tarikan mating ritual requires a young warrior to present his betrothed with "the head of a Christian." This is accomplished in gory fashion by first removing said head via machete (a process depicted with crude panache on more than one occasion).

The Stars and Stripes banner hangs in the Filipino mayor's boardroom. Two decades before, the Tarikan had swept down and beheaded every last man, woman and child in a nearby village. Fearing another such raid, the mayor (later seen wearing a Stetson) calls in a troop of Cavalry, which rides under both Filipino and American flags (Yank-style Taps is sounded when both flags are raised simultaneously). The general plan is to exterminate the Tarikan tribe. **THE HEADHUNTERS** is equally as racist as any antiquated Hollywood 'Cavalry vs. Injuns' adventure before it. Captain Reyes, evidently following General Custer's lead, refers to the Tarikan as "those uncivilized cannibals" ("...there should be no mercy for those wild cannibals...the life of a Tarikan is worthless"; "...we are their masters, and they are nothing but animals!"; "...gutless cut-throats from the mountains!" etc.) The Tarikans, meanwhile, wage a territorial war with "all evil Christians!" Lieutenant De Mesa opposes his superior officer's genocidal policy, desiring to forge a lasting peace treaty.

When Tarikan war-chief Lupe's bride is murdered and his sister (played by Miss Philippines 1973, Eva Reyes) is made prisoner at the bamboo army stockade, he vows—you guessed it—revenge on them damn dirty Christians. To settle their differences "off the record", the two-fisted lieutenant and bigoted Sergeant Mercado stage a fistfight (Rod Taylor and Ernie Borgnine had played out a similar scene in the 1967 American wannabe Spaghetti Western **CHUKA**). When De Mesa goes hand-to-hand in a duel with Lupe and spares his life, the scene could almost have originated in a Teutonic *Winnetou* entry. Of course, a major taboo is violated when our Left-leaning lenient lieutenant falls in love with Lupe's virginal sister, Dewata. Wise old Tarikan chief quote much fortune cookie-league sage advice (e.g., "Any man who lives in darkness is afraid of the light of the truth!") A pre-climactic nocturnal sortie against the fort by the Indians (who emit war-whoops like stereotypical Hollywood Apaches) deploys flaming arrows. A renegade Tarikan who opposes signing of a truce gets hold of some army rifles to fight both his tribesmen and the Christians. Peace is at last cemented.

Made by Roda Film Productions, starring Zaldy Zshornaci, Vic Vargas, Eddie García, Paquito Diaz, Van de León, Scarlett Revilla, Rocco Montalban and Joaquín Fajardo, it was written by Armando de Guzman, with stunts performed by "TNT Stuntmen". Violence—often rendered in slow-motion—is bloody and plentiful, including poisoned arrows piercing through throats, spurting bullet wounds, spear impalements and machete mutilations. As with many Filipino films of the late '60s and early '70s, instead of native Tagalog, the film was recorded in stiff, would-be "Shakespearean" English and features dual gender (slo-mo) frontal nudity, an ingredient which virtually vanished from Filipino screens during the '80s and '90s. Tito Arevalo's music sounds much like that to a typical old-style Hollywood western. An interesting foreshadowing of the late-'70s Italo cannibal cycle, **THE HEADHUNTERS** is at least as good as (and probably even better than) milder Euro Cavalry-versus-Indians equivalents like Sidney Pink's **EL DEDO EN EL GATILLO** (a.k.a. **FINGER ON THE TRIGGER**, 1965), starring Rory Calhoun.

1973, PHILIPPINES.
DIRECTOR: PABLO SANTIAGO

Above: Cannibal ladies from **THE HEADHUNTERS**.

Above: Original Filipino admat
Below: **THE HEADHUNTERS** VCD sleeve art.

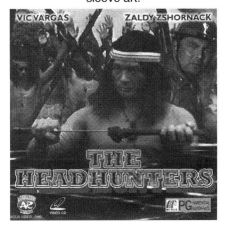

KEY TO TITLE FORMATTING:

MOVIE TITLES — all caps, bold
TV or Movie Series Titles — title case, italicized
(*Foreign release movie titles*) — sentence case, in parentheses, italicized
(*"Translations of Foreign Movie Titles"*) — title case, in parentheses and quotes, italicized
Book and Magazine Titles — title case, italicized

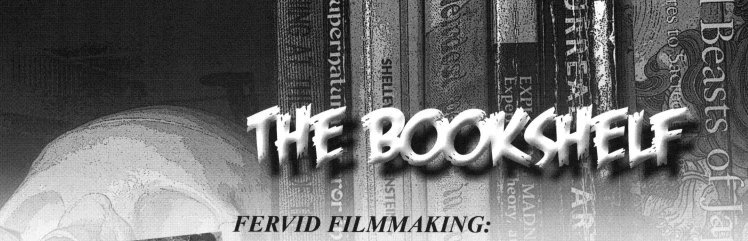

THE BOOKSHELF

FERVID FILMMAKING:
66 Cult Pictures of Vision, Verve and No Self-Restraint

By Mike Watt
McFarland & Company Inc. Publishers
List Price $39.95

I have known Mike Watt for a few years. He made one of my favorite movies, **THE RESURRECTION GAME** (2001). My favorite book of his is *The Incomplete Works of Mike Watt*. I'm pretty sure he would shoot me in the foot with one of his many guns for that last one. I can't help it. I thought it was good.

Now he is tackling the cult film. I have always been a fan of cult films. I am of the opinion that a cult film cannot be manufactured. People often try, and it fails miserably. Of course I'm one of the people who think that **SHOCK TREATMENT** (1981), the sequel to **THE ROCKY HORROR PICTURE SHOW** (1975), is a better film. Say that in your loud voice and people look at you like you took a dump in their shorts. While they were wearing them.

So, *Fervid Filmmaking* gives us 66 cult flicks that are unique, different and, in some cases, nearly impossible to find.

When I got mine from the author at the only convention worth bothering with in the United States—Cinema Wasteland—I immediately leafed through to see how many of the movies I had seen. Mr. Watt makes you work for that because *there's no freaking index of the films at the beginning*!

No, no, it's cool. Just give me a minute. There. I'm fine.

Actually, by eliminating the index it makes it a better book. It forces you to read from front to back and not cherry pick what you want to read. It is in alphabetical order which helps a little, but, by not knowing what is coming, you have the surprise at turning the next page. By the way, I had seen 36 of the movies in the book.

Some of the movies I was glad to see were things like **THE FINAL PROGRAMME** (1973), a movie I really like even though it bears little resemblance to the source material by Michael Moorcock and **THE RETURN OF CAPTAIN INVINCIBLE** (1983). I was always sure I had been the only one to see **THE BONEYARD** (1991) and admit it before reading this book. Good to see I'm not alone.

And while it was good to see micro-budget filmmakers like Chris Seaver and Eric Stanze get some recognition, I was a little disappointed in not seeing anything from Massachusetts filmmaker Michael Legge. Maybe he figured that the book I wrote was enough on the subject. Who knows?

I think that this would make an excellent text book for a bizarre college course. It is also good for taking with you everywhere and showing people who think they know movies that they don't know shit.

Bravo, Mr. Watt. I'll take a book that will be reduced to a dog eared shadow of itself over something that just sits on my bookshelf any day.

~ Review by Douglas Waltz

Cult Movie Magazine A-Z Guide
Richard Gladman, web editor
www.cyberschizoid.com

The Bookshelf is primarily for objects in the physical realm, those tomes made of paper or other such printable material that you can hold in your mitts and thumb through—sometimes relishing the faint scent of fresh ink. Nevertheless, I thought I should mention a website that fits rather well into this column. Richard Gladman's "Cult Movie Magazine A-Z Guide" features many of the currently-published film genre magazines from the world over. Some titles I knew about (and was glad to know they were still around) and some I have recently purchased. A few titles popped out as I had never heard of their existence and plan to buy an issue soon. Most of the recent publications have a vintage horror aspect to their coverage; although what caught my eye was *Creepy Images* (from Germany), *Latarnia Fantastique International* and *Paracinema* (both US).

You will find the guide as a 'blog-link from Gladman's *www.cyberschizoid.com*. The page is laid out neatly with links to publishers, and, thankfully, it seems that it is updated regularly (as it even includes *Weng's Chop* #3). A wonderful jumping off point for those who enjoy the archaic real-world of paper publications.

~ Review by Tim Paxton

Xerox Ferox
The Wild World Of The Horror Film Fanzine

by John Szpunar
Headpress 2013

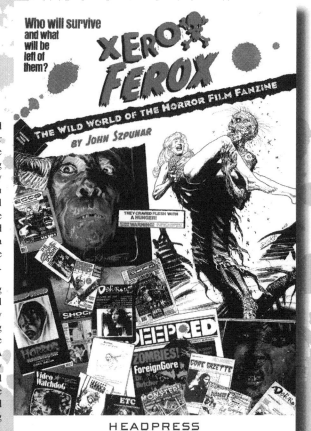

An 800-page book dedicated to Horror Fanzines! Never would have I imagined such a wonder would exist, but even with the anticipation (and basically a 3-hour drive to pick one up and meet the author at Fantacon 2013), never could I have imagined that it would be this damn entertaining. 'Zines of any stripe are something so personal to the creators and the audience that read them with the fervor that many of us had before the Internet shattered the communication and communicable film disease barriers that this book will probably elicit a lot of responses that are equal of the reader. From the first page to the last, the amazing cover from artist Steve Bissette to the deliriously designed interiors that replicate the feel of a 'zine created by Mark Critchell, *Xerox Ferox* is as much an experience as it was to tear open a new issue of *Gore Gazette* and end up chuckling for hours/years/decades about the caustic rendition of the **HOME ALONE** poster that Rev. Rick cocked up (literally).

The book consists of 43 (!) 'Zine editors being interviewed as well as some perspective from several figures whose reputations were made—by my accounting, at least—by these publications including Buddy G, Roy Frumkes and Jim Van Bebber. The account of Van Bebber's drunken kick-back Q&A alone had me laughing out loud. Each interview is fascinating in their own way as the subjects and interviewer manage to cover the topic at hand while also digging a bit deeper in to the motivations and community experience the 'zines were providing not just the readers, but the authors even more so. There are so many authors covered I can highlight just a few, but *all* bring something interesting to the story. Some favorites are Chas. Balun, Jimmy McDonough, Steve Bissette, Stefan Jaworzyn (when he calls out "The *Deep Red* dingleberry" I couldn't agree less but smiled more in that nostalgic 'zine-reading way), Tim Paxton, Uncle Bob Martin and a zillion others. I really enjoyed the Tim Lucas interview as well; both he and Chris Poggiali tackle the Internet topic in different ways. And like the best 'zines I may not agree with some of the comments but I was fascinated to gain some perspective on just how the 'zine boom was affected by the seemingly sudden influx of blogs, review sites and aggregate engines of search 'bots that changed the world of sharing passion for cinema of all kinds. *XF* bridges the gap that time and technological shifts have built with a deceptive brilliance as the reader rides along the high and low roads of being a horror film fanatic in a way that really doesn't exist anymore. With the creation of social media it is much easier to reach out and interact not just with writers, but the actual subjects.

I really enjoyed Ant Timpson's reflection on his time working with the legendary (and thematically important to *Xerox Ferox*, for sure) Bill Landis. The lessons learned for better or worse—both, in this case—hold true in the click/send/wait/receive era of instant communication. "It's a weird feeling to be taken advantage of by an idol. It's simultaneously humiliating and liberating." In a way, it's a bit how this tome works, in most cases the pages of typeface and hand-photocopied print ads that created the images I held of these mystical names fall away and you get a glimpse at the people behind them. Just as the 'zines once did, you get to form a unique bond with some, and smile at others and think about how bizarre a beer or four with them could be.

I miss the 'zines. *Xerox Ferox* proves this. However, we live in a great time for horror (and all) fandom when the right groups of people can collaborate or the one lone voice can shout loud enough to beat back the sometimes endless tide of "gay for pay" hucksterism for studios and Facebook friends that inspired many of the original pioneers in this book. You are reading one right now. *Weng's Chop* is a hybrid of writers that started in the '00s and beyond (fuck, some were probably *born* after the last issue of *Gore Gazette* was published) and pioneers that are hungry and fired up to go beyond the borders of what is already available in mass quantity to provide new journalism. New perspectives. And I'll be damned if *Xerox Ferox* won't stand as a defining text for anyone interested in getting their own views across to an audience about why they feel true passion for what they are writing about. A rallying point, if you will.

If you were there for the days of driving to the only place you could find a certain 'zine, you'll love *Xerox Ferox*. You'll get nostalgic. You'll remember *why* you made those drives.

If you weren't there, you won't get bogged down by any kind of loss; instead you'll enjoy seeing just how much work it took to be able to see the things we take for granted and hopefully be inspired to dig deeper and find your own passions.

Do something cool, and your work may just be forever (Deep) Red…Chas. would approve!

It's 800 pages.
It's inspiring. It's pure nostalgic bliss.
It's essential. Stop reading this and go buy it. Right now.

~ Review by David Zuzelo

Xerox Ferox cover design © 2013 Stephen R. Bissette;
blood (paint) splatter design: keepdesigning.com

GUN AND SWORD:
AN ENCYCLOPEDIA OF JAPANESE GANGSTER FILMS, 1955-1980

By Chris D.
Poison Fang Books
List Price $35.00

I've been waiting on this book for years! Author Chris D's previous tome, *Outlaw Masters of Japanese Film,* was a seminal influence on my dawning interest in the wider—and weirder—cinematic realms of Japan back when it was published in 2005. For me, it really solidified the fascination with obscure (to me, at the time) figures like Kinji Fukusaku and Teruo Ishii, with its in-depth interviews and whiplash descriptions of wild films like **GRAVEYARD OF HONOR** (1975) and **HORRORS OF MALFORMED MEN** (1969). It was a wonderful portal into a world which seemed as fresh and different as anything I had yet encountered in the annals of cult filmdom. Well, that book was just a set-up for this, Chris D's decades-in-the-making magnum opus.

Gun and Sword: An Encyclopedia of Japanese Gangster Films 1955-1980 is a ridiculously complete overview of the ever-fertile "Yakuza" genre, from its emergence in the post-war reconstruction of the Japanese film industry to the cusp of its restriction to the direct-to-video markets of the '80s and '90s. In fact, he endeavors to be as complete as possible, at the very least giving each entry an English-translated title and cast/crew info if he hasn't been able to track down a copy of the film itself. Those he has seen get a brief synopsis and a quick critical take. This method gives the work a marvelous breadth, though somewhat at the detriment of depth. There were several films I would have liked to learn more about, but the author seems content to hip his audience to these films, let them know which ones he finds worthwhile, and leave the rest up to the readers. My only quibble is that some reviews are rather synopsis-heavy, but that's more of a personal preference than a direct criticism. Somewhat oddly, the format of the reviews (their relative brevity and four-star rating system, for example) reminds me a little of Thomas Weisser's Asian film guide-books. But you can rest assured the similarity ends there. Unlike Weisser's dodgy assertions and reviews of films he had obviously never seen, Chris D's work is never less than authoritative and backed by decades of watching and researching.

Gun and Sword is helpfully divided into seven main sections (with two appendices, concerning period-set films and independent productions, respectively), each detailing the relevant films of a particular studio. Although the studio system was on its way to being broken down by the '60s and '70s, the old, large conglomerates were still responsible for the lion's share of films made in Japan during this period, with their own stars and styles to mark out each as unique. It proves an efficient method of categorization, if for no other reason than 800 pages of movie listings might be a little overwhelming if simply organized A-Z. Each section gives an introduction laying out the history of the respective studio, giving the individual film reviews a proper historical context. The book is also lavishly illustrated with wonderful, garish ad art for many of the films. It's a shame the entire volume is in black and white, however. A color section would have really livened up the book and sent it into orbit.

It might have had just such a section, if earlier plans for its publication had gone through. In his introduction to the book, D. tells us about the years of plans with various publishers that eventually fell through. The author had been working on this project since the early '90s and while many were interested in bringing this work to the bookstores, the size and scope of the book frankly scared several suitors away. Eventually, a small publisher who had put out a few of Chris D's fiction pieces stepped up to the plate and here we are. It may not be the massive color-illustrated doorstop it might have been, but what we have is still very, very impressive. Personally, I adore these sorts of encyclopedic movie-guides. I love idly leafing through them, discovering new films to search for each time I pick it up. This is exactly that kind of book. The kind that I'll be returning to again and again throughout the upcoming years. Definitely worth the wait!

~ Review by Jared Auner

MONSTERS AND GIRLS: *The Legend of Loup-Garou*
By Denis St. John
etsy.com/shop/denisstjohn
Cover Price $5.00

Denis St. John's new comic *Monsters and Girls: The Legend of Loup-Garou* is in my top ten favorite books of 2013, along with both issues of *Monster Pie* (issue one was reviewed in WC #3). Not only does it feature the two titular obsessions of mine, but the book is rendered in an exciting free-wheeling style that instantly reminded me of Vernon Grant's obscure classic book *A Monster is Loose in Tokyo* (Tuttle, 1972). St. John weaves a swampy tale of terror as two nubile young ladies decide to spend a night looking for an old voodoo queen's cabin and camping out in the backwaters of a Louisianan bayou. Their situation becomes dire when personal issues are mixed up in the mystical more of a monstrous swamp critter. Man, I love this book.

Scripted, paced and drawn with obvious love of the subject matter, St. John captures the look and smell of the bayou and its denizens. For those of you wondering what a "Loup-Garou" may be, I learned of it while watching an episode of *Lost in Space* in the 1960s. It's French for werewolf, but within the context of St. John's tale its existence is much more than that which most of you may have assumed. Its appearance is much closer to the classical (non-Hollywood) version I grew up reading about. In other words, this comic gets two hoary thumbs up from this ol' monster.

Word of warning: this comic has a limited run, so get it while you can. You can contact St. John at his 'blog to check for availability: *denisstjohn.blogspot.com*.   *~ Review by Tim Paxton*

ZOMBI MEXICANO
By Keith J. Rainville
From Parts Unknown Publications
List Price $20

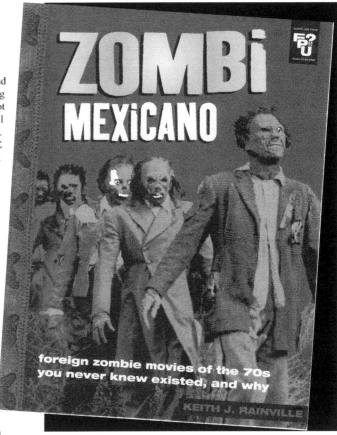

Zombies are everywhere. Seriously, between **WORLD WAR Z** (2013) and *The Walking Dead*, you can't take a piss these days without hitting something zombie related. While that's a great thing for the rabid zombie fanatic, it's not quite as good for those of us looking for "unique." Sure we can always fall back on our tried and true Italian undead—like Pupi Avati's **ZEDER** (a.k.a. **REVENGE OF THE DEAD**, 1983) or Michele Soavi's **DELLAMORTE DELLAMORE** (a.k.a. **CEMETERY MAN**, 1994)—but it's nice to mix things up, leave our comfort zones and dabble in the absurd and outrageous. There are times when you just don't care if the makeup is Savini-quality or the zombies do obviously "un-zombie" things like delivering an expert suplex or clothesline. Yeah, you read that right, *suplex*. You want entertainment and you want it any gotdang way you can get it. Well, Lucha guru, trash cinema fan, ninja aficionado, accomplished author/publisher, possible conqueror of all sentient beings and great guy Keith J. Rainville's newest print endeavor, *Zombi Mexicano*, aims to do just that!

Now, amongst the Illuminerdy, a heated battle continues to rage concerning what does and does not constitute a zombie. For example, vampires are undead but generally not considered zombies. The "infected" in **28 DAYS LATER...** (2002) are called zombies but the general consensus is that they are not zombies. Can zombies run? Can zombies use tools? Can they talk? So on and so forth; they take that shit pretty seriously. If true zombies are corpses reanimated by magic, then no undead creature fits the bill more so than the mummy. It is this very shambling monstrosity of death that Rainville focuses his attention on...and we get Luchadores, to boot!

Mummies and Lucha films go together hand-in-hand like slasher films and Crazy Ralphs. Well, mummies and midgets, but I digress. Rainville presents an interesting, entertaining overview of the most popular entries in the Luchador/Mummy sub-genre and he does so with the respect and admiration of a true fan, which it's plain to see he is. It's nice to see somebody write about a subject so open to ridicule without resorting to *MST3K*-style sarcasm. He's knowledgeable, honest and straight to the point, offering interesting tidbits and factoids when applicable, all the while treating readers to beautiful full-color stills, posters and lobby cards. This is one hell of a quality publication, containing 65 whopping pages covering over a dozen of the most popular—and probably most accessible—Lucha films involving mummies/zombies. A few pages are even dedicated to Lucha cartoons and comics! If you don't come away from *Zombi Mexicano* with a few films on your must-see list, you just may be a filthy, hatin'-ass Rudo.

Here's the kicker, *Zombi Mexicano* not only kicks trash fan ass, but it's incredibly limited, like 250 copies limited. It's not available to the public, only available through the FromPartsUnknown.net website and...*only costs $20*. That's like winning the lottery and scoring a half-and-half on the same damn day! Seriously, this is a gorgeous book and a worthwhile addition to any genre film fan's library. Hopefully we get a follow-up with more Lucha vs. Monster action!

AVAILABLE FROM *FROMPARTSUNKNOWN.NET* ~ *Review by Brian Harris*

THE PETER CUSHING SCRAPBOOK
by Wayne Kinsey, Tom Johnson with Joyce Broughton
Peveril Publishing
List Price £35 + S&H

I love Peter Cushing. He has been my favorite actor for as long as I can remember. Much has been written about the man and his films and the message is always the same: in addition to being a gifted actor, he was a gentleman, an artist, a collector and, above all, a loving husband. For years I have lined my library with books about the man and his films. But do I really need another?

In the case of *The Peter Cushing Scrapbook*, a new offering from Peveril Publishing, the answer is a resounding YES! Hammer Historians Wayne Kinsey (the man behind Peveril) and Tom Johnson—along with a lot of help from Cushing's long-time secretary Joyce Broughton—have put together a mouthwatering collection of Cushing treasures; a veritable eye-gasm of photos, artwork, notes, scripts and more...all of which offer an even greater appreciation for the man.

The scrapbook goes chronologically, with rare photos from Cushing's very early days, notes from his Hollywood days and his time with Olivier, right up through his television triumphs, his Hammer years and beyond, and into his twilight. Some of the highlights for me are samples of his artwork, be it on humorous cards he drew for his wife or handsome scenic watercolors. The doodles, paintings and notes on his script pages tell the story of a man giving his all to every project, even those that might not have deserved it! His attention to detail, with many costume designs and suggestions, provide more fuel for those of us who think he is the finest actor to ever grace the movie screen.

Everything is covered here—theater programs, TV magazines, sketches and notes, and the text is culled from many (credited) sources, making this a biography (and autobiography) as well as a collection of Cushing eye candy! A selection of film posters—usually a high point in a book of this type—seems almost unnecessary when viewed next to his original artwork, personal scribblings and the rare photos. One other treat is the selection of sketches from his impossible-to-find (or afford) book, *Tudor Tea Room Profiles*.

Kinsey, who has a staggering collection of his own, put the call out a couple of years ago to Cushing collectors willing to share what they had for this project, and the final product is an all-encompassing, very thorough and wildly entertaining collection of memorabilia from fans around the world. I'm proud to have shared my own **TOP SECRET!** (1984) script pages. This celebration of all things Cushing is a must for obsessed fans of the man (and I proudly call myself one). A bit pricey on American shores at £35 (plus postage) for a paperback, but it is 328 large pages of pure happiness.

Available only from the publisher at http://peverilpublishing.co.uk. Limited to 2000 units.

~ *Review by Mike Howlett*

FRIGHTFEAST COMIX #2
By Mark K.
frightfeast-comix.blogspot.com
Cover Price £5.00 UK, £7.50 Worldwide

When this little slab of brain-wrecking pen-and-ink terror slinks out of the sequential sarcophagus (also known as your mail box), *You* are *doomed*! Promising "Sights so horrible you might have frightmares for a week!", it sure as hell ain't kidding.

This tale, told in "goriffic picture-fiction" is one of the most blissfully bizarre hell rides through the gore-drenched imagination of an artist I can recall, so much so that when the hand of the creator's avatar actually appears in frame drawing a monkey with a nosebleed and beer, and promises that he'll try to follow his storyline, I had to smile and start all over again. Back to page one…right, let's follow along with the mayhem.

As a storyline goes, it's more about smashing the viewers head into the pages as they dodge flying eyeballs (*SNIFF*—Dick Ayers would be proud), dismembered tits and sharp objects in the hands of monstrous Nazis looking to demolish the next pound of flesh that crosses their path. There is a movie, an actress getting banged by her scummy director, womb-devouring mutants and exploding boobs aplenty. It's all a frightmare, of course, but can it be contained by the pages you are looking at? In a super cool color explosion/convulsion that carries straight to the back cover, you learn that it *can't*!

Read the opening page sideways and you get a message from Frightfeast GoreSlinger Mark K. that sums it up with "I like nonsense, it awakens the brain cells." And that it does; I found that I had a much stronger response to this book than I could have imagined. The artwork is inspired in it's pure dementia, page layouts don't just flow, they bleed out and drag your eyes over each nasty detail and run the reader in circles once you realize that you have *no* way of knowing what is going to be there when you flip the paper frames of this surreal cinematic sleazefest. It's straight up *art* in here for me…I'd love to rip the book apart and lay the pages out in one huge panorama of hell (hey there, Hideshi Hino fans, you'll love this). The inks and awesome slick paper really pop as sights I could never conjure pulse across the page.

It's disturbing, as it should be. It's as unique as the artist that forged it. You *will* have Frightmares when you can't resist the compulsion to shoot up some Frightfeast through your eyeball by going to *http://frightfeast-comix.blogspot.com* and ordering your own *doom*. Now, don't blame me when your brain vomits down your spine and makes you shit your pants with cerebellum fluids, though.

~ *Review by David Zuzelo*

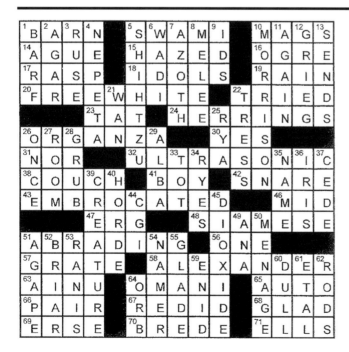

Key to the Weng's Chop
B-Movie Krisword Puzzle, #2
which can be
found on page 215.

A Pictorial History of HORROR MOVIES

DENIS GIFFORD

OOP = OUT OF PRINT
'Zines and Books from the Bygone Days of Yesteryear

Technically speaking, anything OOP is hard to find by any means other than searching high and low in book shops or on the Internet. But not all OOP books and magazines are horrendously expensive. While there are many out-of-print film books that go for a lot of money, Denis Gifford's A Pictorial History of Horror Movies can be found for a mere $5-10, and the original 1967 edition of Ivan Butler's The Horror Film (a.k.a. Horror In The Cinema, 1970 edition) for around $20 on a variety of online websites; suggested sites: half.com, abebooks.com, bibliopolis.com, and, of course, eBay. Unless you're a completist or collector, the true value is not what you pay for the book, but what's in it.

A PICTORIAL HISTORY OF HORROR MOVIES
by Denis Gifford
London: Hamlyn, 1973

I was informed by the mighty Tim P. that I should try and keep my OOP book reviews each at around 200 words; something I find difficult to do in this case, simply because this book is such a favorite of mine I could easily gush on at much greater length about it. But I shall honestly try to keep this as brief as possible.

The scholarly Mr. Gifford wrote a whole slew of movie reference books (including *Movie Monsters* and *Science Fiction Film*), most of which I must confess I've never owned. However, here's one I did own…and still do. It was not only the very first horror movie reference book I ever bought, but also my first-ever movie reference book in general, so it has extra-special significance for me. I gratefully credit it with profoundly influencing my still-ongoing love for movies in general, and horror movies in particular.

Profusely illustrated—including a good many stills which, to the best of my knowledge, have seldom if ever seen republication in other books—this quite hefty (over 200-page) hardcover tome covers the horror/fantasy movie genre right from its very inception in the late-19th century, all the way on up to the "present day" (i.e., circa the early '70s).

The author's prose style is engagingly readable, yet hugely informative too; dense in factual detail and generously sprinkled with wonderful witticisms, often with a distinct "Brit" flavor. Indeed, this book is so inherently British that it even includes some decent coverage of now seemingly forgotten post-Victorian English horror star Tod Slaughter, whose broad and hoary classic melodrama **MARIA MARTEN, OR MURDER IN THE RED BARN** (1935) was one of the first "scary" movies I ever saw (on Welsh telly back in the mid-'70s). While Slaughter's slam-the-hambone-into-overdrive mode of thesping makes Bela Lugosi's often histrionic style appear positively understated, he was/is an important figure in vintage Limey horror, and Gifford well knew it. Much like he really knows his stuff in other areas of the genre too, especially when it comes to the so-called Golden Age (circa the '30s to the '50s), which is well-covered here. In fact, Gifford also went on to contribute articles under the banner "The Golden Age of Horror" for early issues of the now long-defunct '70s UK mag *House of Hammer*.

What most stand out in my mind from his aptly-titled "Pictorial History" are a number of quite nicely-reproduced still photos, some of which were pretty shocking for the time, especially if you only happened to be in your early teens, as I was upon my initial purchase of the book. Two particularly gruesome images show the notorious axe-in-the-woman's-head shot from the obscure US version of **THE BLACK CAT** (1966) and a sprawled-on-the-seashore pose of the very mucked-up "Chlorophyll Man" from the Filipino schlocker **MAD DOCTOR OF BLOOD ISLAND** (1970).

Another sure indicator that this book originated in a time substantially different from the present is its invaluable appendix listing of some 165 horror movies which were then currently available in 8mm home movie versions (typically as greatly-truncated, roughly 8-minute prints on 200-foot reels). It was while scanning over this list back in about 1977 that got me started into ordering Super 8 movies through the Captain Company mail order department of *Famous Monsters of Filmland* mag.

Evidently, if the discussions I've had about this book online in more than one Facebook movie group counts as any sort of valid evidence, it is still fondly remembered by a goodly number of people, typically baby boomers. But perhaps it needs to be rediscovered by a whole new generation of film buffs. According to reports, copies are still not too difficult to come by, so those who are interested might want to check on eBay.

Even without the book's substantial contents, its impressive wraparound dust-jacket art by Tom Chantrell alone would be well worth the asking price! ~ *Steve Fenton*

THE FILM CLASSICS LIBRARY: FRANKENSTEIN and DR. JEKYLL & MR. HYDE
Edited by Richard J. Anobile
London: Pan Books/Darien House, 1974/1975

I bought both these books circa 1975, while still a resident of the UK. Although at that time I had never laid eyes on James Whale's 1931 filmization of *Frankenstein*—an experience which would have to wait till some years after I emigrated to Canada as a youth in 1976—the year before we left ol' Blighty for keeps I was lucky enough to catch the telly premiere of Rouben Mamoulian's up-till-then "lost" film, **DR. JEKYLL & MR. HYDE** (1932). Purchasing it in book form was a handy (if now antiquated) way of re-experiencing the film, albeit only in a static, silent medium. But my remembrances of the TV screening I had seen made it fairly easy for me to fill in the blanks.

Cover blurbs on both these volumes claim their contents to be "the most accurate and complete reconstruction of a film in book form." While they may have been the most intact known versions at the time of the books' publication, both these films later became available in more complete form than that seen here. Consisting of more than 1,000 photographic frame blowups, the 256-page *Frankenstein* volume presents a version of the film which has long since been made redundant by the more intact print discovered in the Universal vaults sometime in the 1980s. Hence, Colin Clive's "God" speech upon bringing his monster to unnatural life and the scene wherein Karloff dumps the little moppet into the lake to drown are nowhere to be seen here. Similarly, the over 1,500-image, 256-page *Dr. Jekyll & Mr. Hyde* volume doesn't include all the extra scenes seen in the currently extant version of the film, which likewise first came to light during the '80s, after long remaining unseen. That then newly-discovered, more intact print included a good deal more footage than is seen here, including a lengthy hallucinatory sequence involving Fredric March as J/H.

Reproduction quality—most noticeably apparent in the *Frankenstein* book—is often murky and blurred, with images frequently marred by such visual noise as dust motes and scratches on the emulsion of the original celluloid. But back in the mid-'70s when only a well-to-do minority of people possessed the luxury of home video cassette players, cable television was still very much in its infancy and we, the Great Unwashed, had to depend on few-and-far-between TV airings of movies to get our kicks, *The Film Classics Library* series (also including printed pictorial adaptations of Hitchcock's **PSYCHO**, 1960, plus a number other non-horror titles) was a real boon to movie buffs everywhere.

Now rendered virtually obsolescent by the passage of years and advance of technology, these books nonetheless are handy time capsules of what once was but shall never be again, for better or worse. ~ *Steve Fenton*

THE MOVIE TREASURY: HORROR MOVIES
by Alan G. Frank
London: Octopus Books, 1974

This was my second-ever horror movie reference book. While it is by no means as expansive or informatively in-depth as Denis Gifford's *The Pictorial History of Horror Movies* (first published the preceding year), Frank's book came as a welcome breath of foul air during my early teens in Wales, the UK; during the same formative period in which I not only discovered the escapist delights of the first *Flash Gordon* movie serial and Edgar Rice Burroughs' *Barsoom* novels with John Carter, but also such seminal British 'zines as *World of Horror* and *Monster Mag* (the latter of which was actually a glossy folded-up poster, usually of a very gory movie still blown-up to XL size. One can only wonder how many irate parents ordered their progeny to tear the gross things off their bedroom walls!).

Totaling 160 pages, Frank's *Horror Movies* makes for a fun read, and is generously illustrated with many nice stills, as well as some fairly decently presented poster reproductions printed in full-color on glossy paper. My original copy of the book—the same publisher also put out a fine volume I own entitled *Gangster Movies*, albeit not written by Frank—came enwrapped in a dust-jacket whose front cover bore a photographic portrait of the hooded skull-face from **DR. TERROR'S HOUSE OF HORRORS** (1965). After my original edition as good as fell apart due to overuse, years after the fact (circa 2009) I ran across a virtually pristine, barely-used copy in a Toronto remaindered bookstore's bargain bin—it set me back a measly $2 Canadian (original English cover price was £5). Talk about a steal of a deal! The dust-jacket to that edition (bearing the imprint of Cathay Books) depicted Christopher Lee as the Count in an action scene from the thorny climax to **THE SATANIC RITES OF DRACULA** (1973).

This is another '70s book which I had presumed was as good as forgotten by most, but—lo and behold!—when I just happened to mention it in passing during a recent Facebook discussion at a certain film appreciation group's wall, a surprising number of members there were more than familiar with the book, and we exchanged enthusiastic comments about it. Which goes a long way in proving that old books—if they're good enough—never die, they just fade away for a while…but might well return from the shadow realm of obscurity after they've long since been written off. So if you ever find one at a yard sale, flea market or used bookseller's, be sure to grab it while you can! ~ *Steve Fenton*

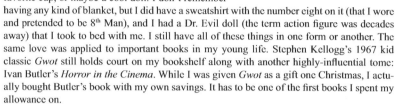

HORROR IN THE CINEMA
by Ivan Butler
Zwemmer, Second Revised Edition, 1970

When you're ten years old there are a lot of things in your life that you cherish; that security blanket, a favorite cup, or maybe a cool doll. I don't remember having any kind of blanket, but I did have a sweatshirt with the number eight on it (that I wore and pretended to be 8th Man), and I had a Dr. Evil doll (the term action figure was decades away) that I took to bed with me. I still have all of these things in one form or another. The same love was applied to important books in my young life. Stephen Kellogg's 1967 kid classic *Gwot* still holds court on my bookshelf along with another highly-influential tome: Ivan Butler's *Horror in the Cinema*. While I was given *Gwot* as a gift one Christmas, I actually bought Butler's book with my own savings. It has to be one of the first books I spent my allowance on.

The book is a small one, but its 4x5-inch format is packed with some of the most intelligently written film commentary outside of the few *Castle of Frankenstein* magazines and the early issues of *Famous Monsters of Filmland* (I would later buy at paper shows in the mid-'70s). *Horror in the Cinema* was published a few years before Gifford's *A Pictorial History of Horror Films*, which I got for Christmas in 1977. As with Gifford's book, Butler's is not some dumbed-down history, but a serious chow-down of research and information. Some of the chapters I digested with ease, while others, such as the final on Polanski and the film of the late '60s, I had some trouble comprehending until I got older, although I found what I read totally exciting, and light years ahead of the current incarnation of *Famous Monsters of Filmland* (at that time slowly devolving into idiocy). Horror didn't just mean monsters. That was a revelation for me. Horror meant films like **DEAD OF NIGHT** (1945), **PEEPING TOM** (1960), **LE CORBEAU** (1943), **LES DIABOLIQUES** (1955) and scores of others that never played on our Saturday afternoon monster movie host programs (and we had a lot growing up around Cleveland, Ohio back then).

As much as the text was a primer for my appreciation of film later in life, it was the 58-page "checklist" of horror films that caught my attention. So many movies to see! In the '70s I found some of the titles on 8mm film format from our local public library. Later came the video boom in the '80s and '90s, and now numerous websites and YouTube offer still more obscure titles. I was set for the next forty years, and I am still working on that list!

I went back later on that week and bought John Baxter's *Science Fiction in the Cinema* which is another incredible book to have read when I was eight years old. Both are well worth your time and effort to track down. ~ *Tim Paxton*

Own a copy of
MONSTER! INTERNATIONAL #3
for only $8 PPD (USA), $10 Canada,
or $20 for the rest of the world.
PayPal: orlof@oberlin.net

KRONOSCOPE ARCHIVAL REPRINT:
From the pages of MONSTER! INTERNATIONAL number three.

"Yes, there are sacred places and there are unholy places. God and his saints are present in the world as are Satan and his legions. It is a battle between light and darkness. As God chooses his own and not the contrary, so the Devil chooses his own. In the fight between good and evil, beware those who follow their own path . Holiness and depravity are two parallels that meet in infinity. Only the eagle can build his nest above the Abyss. You speak to me Satan; you challenge me. I fear you not because I know you; because I have looked upon your face."
- The exorcist mutters to himself prior to the exorcism in **UN URLO NELLE TENEBRE**.

THE EXORCIST MADE ME DO IT!

BY TIMOTHY PAXTON WITH DAVID TODARELLO

The belief that one's self or another's personality can be possessed, whether by supernatural entities (gods, demons, ghosts, etc.) or by corporeal means (hypnosis, brainwash, etc.), is a deep, hysterical and illogical fear. This idea that a human may be possessed by a supernatural personality, other than its own, happens in *all* religions. Throughout the centuries people have been slaughtered, tortured, and imprisoned because they were believed possessed by devils; their grotesque demeanor blamed on something society could neither understand or control. In our modern times 'civilized' communities worldwide have dealt with possession in a number of ways. The popular scientific approach of psychoanalysis easily explains cases of possession as mere hysteria, "diabolical possession is caused by belief in diabolical possession."[1] The metaphysical answer endorsed by the religiously inclined is an exorcism. "The time-honored custom of ordering demons away, by verbal charms and magical gestures, is still practiced by (1) primitive witch doctors and (2) the Catholic church. Protestant churches don't exorcise."[2] What constitutes a possession? Are the possessed monsters in the strictest definition? What of the exorcists and their roles in such a paranormal situation? These questions would be better answered if I were writing a dissertation on the socio-political/religious analysis of possession. But.... *Monster! International* is a movie magazine, so we had better stick to the cinematic treatment of the subject.

Cinematically, possession films have been a recent sub-category of the horror genre, their popularity building to a manic zenith within a four-year period after the release of William Friedkin's **THE EXORCIST** (1973). In these films the possessed take on the characteristics of monsters. Their physical appearance is unhealthy, and they have unusual powers not associated with their human counterparts. In almost every instance a human (most always a priest, but nuns and doctors qualify) faces the possessed creature and must oust the devil within him or her. While many of post-**EXORCIST** films betray their origin with the now popular motifs established in Friedkin's movie, there were productions prior to that landmark production. For the most part, these films were unique and, at times, misunderstood and/or disdained by the general film critic. Prior to Friedkin's feature, neither the Devil nor his minions were a popular element of this unusual sub-genre.

The characters in pre-**EXORCIST** productions were normally possessed by something other than a devil. Could this have been due to a taboo-induced nervousness Hollywood had placed on portraying the devil as real? Universal Studio's cold feet snipped Colin Clives' infamous line "Now I know what it feels like to be God!" from the James Wales 1931 classic **FRANKENSTEIN**. It wasn't until MCA re-released a "complete and uncut" edition of their videotape of the film that the controversial (but barely audible) utterance was restored. How would the early cinematic censors have reacted to the Devil's physical manifestation during possession scenes in many of the 70's **EXORCIST** clones? Satan's presentment would have broken the moral code of the time, and thus any appearance was forbidden or glossed over. (Few films from the 20's, 30's or 40's dared to be explicit in depicting the Devil or portraying his handiwork on the Earth. Edgar Ulmer's **THE BLACK CAT** [1934] approached Satanism with a rare zeal wherein Boris Karloff essays evil as Hjalmar Poelzig, the suave leader of a devil cult.) So, in that context, the Devil dabbled little with humankind. (Of course, Benjamin Christensen's **HÄXAN/WITCHCRAFT THROUGH THE AGES** [1922] is something altogether different, being a "documentary" on the subject of witches and the Devil.) For those directors who wished to circumvent this sticky topic, and were interested in the idea of a man possessed by "something" (other than women and fame), alternate means taken — with some unique results.

The spiritual possession of Leah (Lili Liliana) by the ghost of her beloved (Leon Liebgold) in the world's first exorcism film **THE DYBUK** *(1937).*

During the lean decades to follow, the Fiend rarely made a serious appearance in any film (outside of an odd "Passion Play" or Sunday School programmer commited to film) to challenge the will of God (that admission of moral and spiritual decay had to wait forty years). Devils were replaced by ghosts; and the reluctant recipient of their transcendental whims were usually abducted during seances or other means of spiritual contact. But, of course, any such occurrence would be explained later on in the picture as an act of charlatanism on behalf of the psychic. Despite the admission that "there are no such things as ghosts," there were few films which managed to wriggle around the inoffensive "it's just a farce" attitude. An uncustomary twist to the standard fake spiritualist motif is Victor Halperin's **SUPERNATURAL**. Made in 1933 by the man who directed the excellent **WHITE ZOMBIE** (1932), this is a tale of a malicious woman who,

---

1. Quote attributed to Dr. Henry Ansgard Kelley of the University of California, 1970. Pg 195. Ebon, Martin. *The Satan Trap*. Doubleday & Co., New York, 1976.
2. Pg 293. Walker, Barbara. *The Woman's Encyclodedia of Myths and Secrets*. Harper & Row, New York, 1983.

betrayed by her partner, a cheap clairvoyant, is sent to the electric chair for murder. Her restless spirit returns and possesses the body of the film's heroine (Carol Lombard) and kills the man who framed her. The pacified ghost then leaves Lombard's body to return to the afterlife. **SUPERNATURAL** is a film which whets a person's appetite for more, a potential dish which was never adequately realized and rightfully exploited.

With Hollywood awash in perpetual social censorship, afraid to give the paying customer more fright for their money, it was a Polish film which pioneered the *exorcism* movies. According to Gershom Scholem in his book *Kabbalah*, stories of these *dibbukim* (literally, abbreviated from *"dibbuk me-ru'ah ra'ah"*; translated: "a cleavage of an evil spirit" and *"dibbuk min ha-ḥizonim"*; translated: *"dibbuk* from the demonic side"[3]) were/are prevalent throughout Hasidic culture. A *dibbuk* is the troubled soul of a dead person which has not been laid to rest. This spirit becomes a demon and attaches —or cleaves— itself onto the healthy soul of a mortal and "it is thus the equivalent of possession." It is important to note that the film in which this demon/ghost-possession occurred was Michal Waszynski's **THE DYBUK/THE DYBBUK**, a rarely seen Yiddish-language production from 1937 based on a play by the famous Yiddish author S. Ansky. Waszynski's film had only been available, until recently, solely through Jewish film rental outlets and various specialty video stores. Though believed lost by many film scholars, several prints eventually turned up, although they were severely cut. Restored in 1989 by the noted National Center for Jewish Film Library, **THE DYBUK** now clocks in at a hefty 123 minutes; a good half an hour or more material was recovered. The film is intact and includes the crucial exorcism scene within the Temple which was, for reasons unknown, deleted from earlier prints.

The ancient Jewish idea of "cleaving" the soul was successfully incorporated in the 15th Century with a similar, more modern Catholic belief, closer to home and dutifully exploited by Friedkin. *Dibbukim* occur when the possessed commits "a secret sin" which opens "a door for the *dibbuk*."[4] There is only one way to get rid of a pesky *dibbuk* or demon, and that is to exorcise the creature. In **THE DYBUK** a rabbi must follow the proper protocols, which is true as well for the Catholic priests, who are duty-bound by a "solemn method of exorcising [which] is given in the Roman Ritual."[5]

The film takes place within a strict Jewish Hasidic community known as a *shtetlekh*, where two star-crossed lovers, Khonnon and Leah, are kept apart. When all fails and the impoverished young *yeshiva* student, Khonnon, turns to dark forces and appeals to Satan for aid in winning the hand of his betrothed, Leah. "If not through God, then how?" he cries desperately in the holy Temple, "Through Satan! Satan, I implore you! Help Me!" His plea is heard and a dark cloud envelopes the student, who then falls dead. The corpse of Khonnon is buried and the wedding of Leah to another man is set. Before she is to be wed, Leah's father asks her to visit her mother's grave and, as tradition requests, invite her mother's soul to the festivities. However, the distraught and heartbroken Leah breaks down next to Khonnon's grave and requests *his* spirit to attend. During the festivities Khonnon's wandering spirit "cleaves" to Leah's soul and possesses her in an unholy supernatural bond. "The bride has been possessed by a dybbuk," announced the mysterious Messenger, a solemn figure that walks throughout the picture intoning eternal Jewish wisdom spiced with doom and gloom (which usually goes unheeded and, by law in these sort of productions, there is a price to be paid).

The Reb Sender, the town leader and father of the bride, approaches Rabbe [Rabbi] Azriel, the Tsaddik of Miropole, and asks the learned and elderly man for help in exorcising the dybbuk from Leah. The first attempt to do so is met with contempt from Khonnon's spirit. The possessed Leah scoffs at the Rebbe's initial attempt, "Do not torment me, do not harass me," Khonnon's ghost warns, "I do not fear your oaths and excommunications. There is no more exalted height higher than my present refuge." Not to be undone, the Rebbe gathers together his students, and at the foot of the alter within the Temple and faces the possessed. Rabbe Azriel first warns the rebellious Khonnon that he will be excommunicated unless the spirit vacates Leah's body. Khonnon's ghost is spiteful and the old man blasts the spirit with holy knowledge. The ghost wails in ethereal agony and departs from Leah's body. However, the lovers are united in the end as Leah reaches out to Khonnon's departing soul, and upon touching it drops dead.

There were no instances of spitting, no foul mouthing, not even an attempt by the possessed to levitate objects or to strike the holy man. This was a civil exorcism, and the first depicted within cinema. This is not to say that the excommunication of Khonnon's spirit wasn't chilling. No doubt, to the devout Jews that watched the film in 1937 and thereafter, the scene where a possessed Leah talks back to the Tsaddik (a man who provides spiritual illumination to his community which he attains through a mystical union with God) is one impassioned with shock and emotion. What may seem tame by today's standards of horror was without a doubt as frightening to the religious who witnessed **THE DYBUK** in the 30's and 40's as where those shocked Catholics who shivered through **THE EXORCIST**.

Science fiction in the 40's had one way to skirt the issue in 1944 when Eric Von Stroheim played mad scientist to a couple of pounds of flesh in **THE LADY AND THE MONSTER**. The movie was the first version of the oft-filmed *Donovan's Brain* novel by noted SF author Curt Siodmak, and directed by George Sherman. In both the fiction work and film, millionaire tycoon Donovan is injured in an airplane accident and rushed to the abode of a slightly unorthodox scientist-doctor (Stroheim). There his brain is removed from his ruined body and kept alive in a jar bathed in nutrient-enriched fluids. The brain gains enormous telepathic powers once freed from the constraints of a body. Donovan's sinister gray matter uses these newly acquired energies to capture the will of a man. This psychic possession by a monstrous brain is without a doubt one of the most intriguing (and frequently copied) science fiction inventions. Science fiction would offer supplemental possessions by other means. Aliens enjoyed a brief period of ego-snatching in the 50's with **THE BEAST WITH A MILLION EYES** (1955, D: David Kramarsky), **QUATERMASS II/ENEMY FROM SPACE** (1957, D: Val Guest), **KRONOS** (1957, D: Kurt Neuman), **WAR OF THE SATELLITES** (1957, D: Roger Corman), **THE BRAIN EATERS** (1958, D: Bruno Ve Sota), **THE BRAIN FROM PLANET AROUS** (1958, D: Nathan Hertz), and **THE INVISIBLE INVADERS** (1959, D: Sam Newfield) and others, but none dealt with demonic possession and exorcism.

Devils and demons still lurked within the minds of screenwriters. Nevertheless, the ideas of demonic possession had to wait until the time came when our society (Hollywood, manager of America's collective consciousness) was unashamed to deal openly (i.e. cinematically, thus socially en masse) with such "sins" and their deadly, prophetic payback. The 60's opened with dead witches possessing the living as in Mario Bava's ground-breaking **LA MASCHERA DEL DEMONIO/BLACK SUNDAY** (1960), and two English ghosts were out to steal the souls of a little boy and girl in **THE INNOCENTS** (1960, D: Jack Clayton)[6]. Then the Devil began spreading his seed in Roman Polanski's oft-copied **ROSEMARY'S BABY** (1968), and a Satanist's powerful post-death ego enveloping a man in the cheap-shot **THE MEPHISTO WALTZ** (1971, D: Paul Wendkos). The occasional science fiction/horror production such as Eugene Martin's wonderful **PANICO EN EL TRANSIBERIANO/HORROR EXPRESS** (1972) was a relief as was Tom Moore's rarely seen **MARK OF THE WITCH** (1970, see page 60). Hardcore made a token stab at the horror genre when Gerard Damiano put **THE DEVIL IN MISS JONES** (1972).[7] But that wasn't going far enough. Documented cases of the Devil possessing men, women, children, and even animals were available, but not much was done to make them into true *horror* films. Since **THE DYBUK** there had yet to be an exorcist chasing these possessed souls and driving the devil from them.

Therefore, before this article fragments any further (as possession films are many, depending on your definition), I will now concentrate solely on the post-**EXORCIST** productions that plagued theatres worldwide primarily in the mid-70's emphasizing the marvelous mimicry of the Italian and Spanish movie industry, before the influence of **THE OMEN**, **HALLOWEEN**, and **CARRIE** took their toll. For the sake of space I will examine their handiwork, along with some American, Brazilian, British, German, Mexican, and Turkish productions. The super-kinetic hijinks of the powerful Hong Kong possession genre will have to wait until another installment is readied.

For those of you who haven't seen **THE EXORCIST**, I suggest seeing it for historic reasons, although the terror in it is subdued and at times lacking (especially when compared to later European productions). For additonal information on this film, read just about any good book on horror movies—

---

3. Pg 349. Scholem, Gershom, *Kabbalah* (1974), Keter Publishing House Jerusalem Ltd., Jerusalem, Israel.
4. Pg 349. Ibid.
5. Pg 139. Patai, Raphael. *Myth and Modern Man*. Prentice-Hall, Inc., Englewood Cliffs, N.J., 1972.
6. This is debatable. For some critics, **THE INNOCENTS** is not a ghost film at all, but a psycho-drama where the nanny of the two children is insane and imagines the whole thing. Unfortunately, by the end of the film, in this version of events, she kills the little boy and blames it on a ghost. But we know better....
7 In this Gerard Damiano film, Miss Jones (Georgina Spelvin) kills herself and lands in purgatory. There she is possessed by a sexually-overactive demon and sent earthbound to fuck anyone and everyone. This sad production is spiced by some neat plot twists and a great last five minutes where Miss Jones is back in her own personal hell where she cannot be sexually satisfied by her sole roommate, a man too concerned with fly shit to pay any attention to her squirming, aching genitalia.

L'ANTICRISTO: Although the Exorcist (Arthur Kennedy) has his bible destroyed, he continues the ritual by laying a crucifix on the possessed Carla (Carla Gravina). The Roman Catholic Church maintains the office of exorcist, whose rite of ordination states: "An Exorcist must cast out devils."[9]

there should be entire chapters dedicated to this influential film and its impact on modern day fright flicks.[8] It's odd, though, while **THE EXORCIST** changed the face of horror films for years to come (as did the before mentioned **LA MASCHERA DEL DEMONIO**), it seems tame when compared to the many imitations which followed in its wake. What Friedkin did with William Peter Blatty's book was to take the initial horror (leaving out all the parts dealing with temptation for some reason) and put substance to it. Subsequently, in productions like Alberto De Martino's notable **L'ANTICRISTO/THE TEMPTER** (1974) and Amando de Ossorio's morbid **EL PODER DE LAS TINIEBLAS/ DEMON WITCH CHILD/THE POSSESSED** (1974) that quality was beefed up and served as a full course meal. Few were novel in their conception, borrowing heavily from the original. Nevertheless, the films were entertaining in their execution, and some of them are excellent examples of horror. For some reason, no doubt an obsession with Catholic guilt and pent-up sexuality, the Italians produced more possession/exorcism-oriented monster productions than any other European country on the map (Hong Kong being the relative counterpart for the Asian end of the spectrum for different reasons).

If we are going to approach this chronologically rather than alphabetically by title beginning in 1974, then one should start with De Martino's **L'ANTICRISTO**. The **HOUSE OF EXORCISM** (available under the video title **DEVIL IN THE HOUSE OF EXORCISM**), originally known as **LISA E IL DIAVOLO/LISA AND THE DEVIL**, is Mario Bava's excessive tribute to Evil incarnate, and the film, originally made in 1972, has nothing whatsoever to do with *bodily* demonic possession. In it Elke Sommer is trapped in a spooky mansion in which the Devil plays with the souls he has captured. **LISA E IL DIAVOLO** is a beautiful mood piece and Bava's convoluted, nonsensical, but delightfully giddy masterpiece. What was done to it in 1975 to make it *profitable* for the US market is a true nightmare. The transformation of Bava's work into a possession vehicle took little or no effort on the part of director/producer Alfredo Leone, who acquired Robert Alda to act as a priest who must exorcise the devil from a possessed Sommer. In this *revised* edition, Sommer's soul was yanked by the Devil (Telly Savalas) during her stay at an angst-filled mansion. There are supplemental post-1972 sequences in which Sommer with chapped lips and red eyes vomits and screams curses at the ineffectual exorcist. It's a mess. Luckily, for those of you who have the money, Redemption Video, a British company, has recently released the uncut Italian version on VHS. God bless them!

1974: what a year! It was during this comparatively short period of time that the best imitations emerged. With Linda Blair's tortured image still fresh in the world's imagination, directors scrambled to set in motion their own variations on the theme. What country best to sponsor the sickest entries than Italy, home to the best Hollywood copy-cat directors the world over. Within months after **THE EXORCIST** was released, it was dissected, ingested, disgorged and excreted. Satan, his demons, and their devil-driven witches were to elope with souls of crippled women, naive virgins, and innocent children — and what a wild ride they would set us on!

Alberto De Martino's amazing **L'ANTICRISTO** was a favorite second and third billing in many a drive-in here in the States, even though the best scenes were snipped by sweaty-palmed censors. Always a man who was able to make a film look better than its budget would generally allow, De Martino fashioned one of the most original and best-looking of the **EXORCIST** clones. The film is quenched with dramatic cinematography, decent acting from all involved, guileful special effects, and a restrained though exhilarating score by Ennio Morriconne with Bruno Nicoloi.

Crippled when young, a wheelchair-bound Carla (Carla Gravina) is bitter and resentful at not having a fulfilled sex life. One night alone in her villa, she discovers an old playing card with the picture of the devil on it. An odd sensation surges through her lethargic loins and they burn as if on fire. That night at dinner she insults her family as she hurls obscenities at her recently re-married father (the late Mel Ferrer, an arch-duke in the kingdom of Italian Sleaze and star of multitude of gialo movies) and his new wife (Anita Strindberg, passive sleazette of Euro-cinema) as windows slam shut, pictures on the wall dance in mid air, and candles flair. The possession has begun.

However, at the point when you assume that the film is becoming nothing short of a brazen **EXORCIST** rip-off, De Martino pulls his trump card and delivers the sickest moment in this sub-genre's short history. When Carla retires to her bed she is metaphysically transported back to the middle ages and becomes involved in a Black Mass. She is initiated with her ancestor, a witch who was executed for deviltry. During the unholy mass the startled woman is fed the head of a toad and introduced to the Goat God. In a scene

---

8. Books to look out for: Kim Newman's highly entertaining and critical look at *Nightmare Movies*, Chapter "Devil Movies", 1989, Harmony Books; and Phil Hardy's flawed but essential *The Encyclopedia of Horror movies*, numerous entries by year of production, 1986, Harper & Row; for example. Issue 6 of Tim Lucas' *Video Watchdog* has monstrous coverage on the film as well.
9. The quote comes from Pg 208 of Montague Summer's book *The Discovery of Witches*, Cayme press, London, 1928.; and Pg 293. Walker, Barbara. Ibid. It has just come to light that in 1982 Pope John Paul II performed an exorcism on a possessed woman. The said woman fell before him "rolling on the floor and shouting." The pontiff didn't bat an eye and recited the trusty "Rite of Exorcism." The demons fled and the woman was cured.

which may leave many viewers choking, Carla is made to *tongue the puckering anus of a live goat* (this sequence was snipped for US release). She licks her chops and the Devil enters her by the way of spiritual rape. Her body trembles with each demonic thrust and her soul is soon secured by Satan. This dreamy though disgusting performance is punctuated by luscious cinematography by none other than Aristide Massaccesi aka Joe D'Amato, one of Italy's most prolific genre/sleazy directors to date.

The experience leaves Carla with new energies and she is able to walk, where upon she ambles into the countryside and spies a busload of Euro tourists. She lures away a young German and immediately fucks the lad and twists his head off. She becomes increasing rude to her family and they call the local herbalist, who tries to exorcise Carla. After the herbalist's humiliating defeat her family gets wise to the fact that Carla is "unwell" and her father sends for the provincial exorcist. The priest arrives and the fun begins. After a lengthy exorcism which fails miserably, Carla escapes from her house and runs into a rain-filled night. The determined cleric and Carla's step-father follow the woman and a fierce battle for her soul occurs in and around the Coliseum. Cornered by her parent, Carla is at last released from the grasp of the Devil by means of a large wooden crucifix thrust between her legs.

Few films from this year could measure up to **L'ANTICRISTO**'s intensity, although **CHI SEI?/BEYOND THE DOOR** has enough spookiness and plot twists to keep any die-hard monster fan entertained. What initially begins as dull and dry plot lumping **ROSEMARY'S BABY** with **THE EXORCIST**, directors Sonia Assonitis and Robert d'Ettore Piazzoli slowly — and painfully — take a potentially do-nothing possession film and suprise their audience. It takes almost an hour, but **CHI SEI?** evolves into a sick and cruel (and pretty damn clever) joke.

CHI SEI? stars the late, former Shakespearean stage actor-cum-exploitation king Richard Johnson, star of the 1961 Robert Wise classic ghost/possession flick **THE HAUNTING** and numerous odious Italian productions such as Lucio Fulci's dual shockers **ZOMBI 2/ZOMBIE** (1979) and **PAURA NELLA CITTÀ DEI MORTI VIVENTI/GATES OF HELL** (1980), Sergio Martino's **L'ISOLA DEGLI UOMINI PESCE/SCREAMERS** (1979), and Massimo Dallamano's possession film **IL MEDAGLIONE INSANGUINATO/THE NIGHT CHILD** (1974). Johnson is a mysterious stranger who complicates the life of a woman and her family. This is no ordinary family unit, though, as the pregnant mother is carrying a possessed child. The unborn creature's influence has its mother floating through the air, puking up blue glop, and cursing all who dare approach her. All of these horrors justifiably confuse her husband and their two children. Toss in the arrival of the ghost of her former lover Dimetri, who died in a car crash ten years earlier and recently resurrected by Satan, and you have another fine entry into this category of film.

The surprising climax comes from the ghost (Johnson) who is haunting his ex. Keeping the baby alive is the spirit's goal. If the child is born this side of the grave, the Devil promised Dimetri that his soul will be reincarnated into the newborn. However, just before the tot is to be brought into the world Satan gleefully informs the ghost that everything is all a farce. That is, our ever-vigilant shade will *not* be able to possess the child, even though the Prince of Lies pledged that he could. In fact, the child will not be possessed by anybody. The Devil was doing all of this just to be nasty! In a fit of rage Dimetri pounds away

L'ANTICRISTO (1974): In a failed attempt to drive the devil from Carla (Carla Gravina), the old priest (George Coulouris) and his assistant are mocked and spat upon.

at the swollen belly of the woman, crying in defiance until he collapses to the floor in a pile of clothing. The husband rushes into the room to discover his wife has given birth and a dead, deformed child (albino and without a mouth) in a sea water-soaked pile of rags on the floor. Cut away to the happy family on a boat. There they are celebrating the birthday of their youngest child, a boy who is in turn possessed by the devil.

CHI SEI? has its moments, in spite of the irritatingly dull segments. There is an unnerving scene in which an army of dolls come alive and terrorize the two kids, a creepy sequence where our expected mother eats a rotten banana peel off the sidewalk, and the crazed fury in which Dimetri pummels the pregnant woman. By the end of the film, when the deformed child is uncovered, there is a real sense of pity, for both the child *and* the ghost.

Whereas Assonitis and Piazzoli's film was a slow-starter which developed into an original brain-twister, the inverse can be said of director Mario Gariazzo's **L'OSSESSA/THE SEXORCIST/THE EERIE MIDNIGHT HORROR SHOW**. **L'OSSESSA** begins as an original film which after a half an hour degenerates into another mindlessly entertaining clone. The first half of the film is filled with respectably original ideas, while the last half, sadly, apes **THE EXORCIST**. Gariazzo introduces the evil force in the shape of a wooden Medieval statue, that alone sets it apart as being at least partially innovative. The artifact is of one of the two thieves who was tied to a cross and accompanied Jesus Christ on Calvary. In undoubtedly the film's best series of events leading up to the initial possession, a young woman painter (Stella Carnacina) accompanies some art restorationists to collect the large statue. It was uncovered in an old abandoned church where orgies had been going on for hundreds of years. They dislodge the life-sized statue and cart it back to their studio on a flatbed truck — with Stella practically drooling at its masculine beauty all the way there. Back at the studio they place the sculpture on a slab (unbound from the cross so they can work on restoring it). Alone, Stella is gripped by the thing's sheer demonic presence and when it creaks to life and rapes her she becomes possessed.

Enter the brief though destructive encounter with "Evil" and things start looking familiar: vomiting (here it looks as if she's regurgitating melted pistachio ice cream and candle wax), levitation, and so forth. In the final conflict between girl and super-priest, Stella attempts to seduce the man instead of grossing him out. It almost works. With renewed strength the exhausted priest faces his possessed adversary again, and the confrontation moves to an old church. There he is struck and killed the very instant that Stella is freed from her "sexual" possession.

Better known for his violent Westerns (**DIO PERDONA LA MIA PISTOLA/**

Carla Gravina is exorcisted by her step-father Mel Ferrer in Alberto De Martino's **L'ANTICRISTO** (1974).

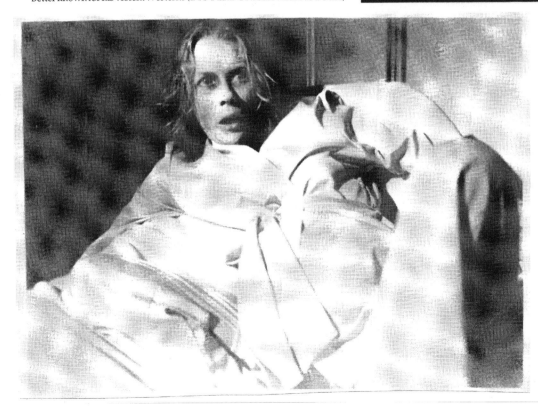

Juliet Mills is the woman terrorized by her unborn child -- which is possessed by the devil in the oddly chilling **CHI SEI?** (1974)

GOD WILL FORGIVE MY PISTOL, 1969; and **ACQUASANTA JOE/HOLY WATER JOE**, 1971) director Mario Gariazzo *almost* had something going right in the first twenty minutes of the film. The motif about the "living" statue could have been interesting to develop. Gariazzo would have had a bizarre Possession film crossed with **CURSE OF THE FACELESS MAN** (1958, D: Edward L. Cahn) if he played his cards right. However, the bets were weighted heavily in favor of **THE EXORCIST** and Gariazzo had to accommodate his paying audience. The folks who crammed into smoky Euro-theatres demanded the best imitations of US products their home-grown directors could supply. When the demand dictates the product, you gotta do what you gotta do.

Children fare pretty well in most horror films despite the fact that they are often the receptacles of evil. Their innocence and pre-pubescent acceptance of the world as Good makes them without a doubt easy prey for scriptwriters looking for chills. What is spookier than an ebullient young lass that suddenly switches gears and spits insults, levitates, and practices projectile vomiting? Most of these possessed children endure their ordeals and lead a blissful existence in an ideal cinematic afterlife. However, there are those few dark productions in which the youngster *doesn't* survive.

The few bits of **EXORCIST**-familiarity which creep into **IL MEDAGLIONE INSANGUINATO** are more than compensated for by other eerie elements the late director Massimo Dallamano (who died in a car crash in 1976) was able to conjure up. The possession stems from the ownership of an arcane artifact which emanates evil. Dallamano handles the film with a subtle flare, and despite the fact that he's working with a bad script manages to pull **IL MEDAGLIONE INSANGUINATO** through all the rough spots. Maybe it's due to his working under the creative wing of Sergio Leone on the Western epics **PER UN PUGNO DI DOLLARI/A FISTFUL OF DOLLARS** (1964) and **PER QUALCHE DOLLARO IN PIÙ/A FEW DOLLARS MORE** (1965) that saves this little picture from being something other than another exploitative blunder. Of course, it doesn't hurt that he also directed his own well-received Western **CREPA TU ... CHE VIVO IO/BANDIDOS** (1967), the superior Giallo-thriller **COSA AVETE FATTO A SOLANGE?/WHAT HAVE YOU DONE TO SOLANGE?** (1971) as well as the sleazy **IL DIO CHIAMATO DORIAN/ SECRET OF DORIAN GRAY** (1972).

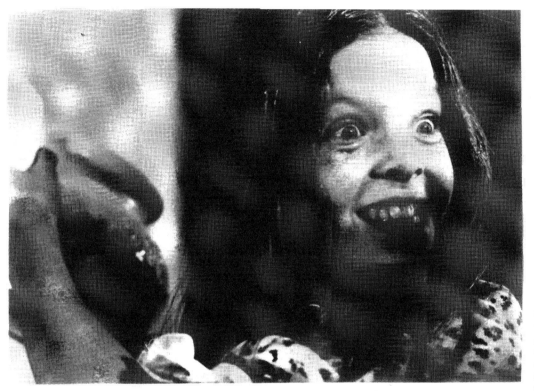

Possessed children are often the most lurid: a scene from Massimo Dallamano's manic masterpiece of EXORCIST-dirivative horror IL MEDAGLIONE INSANGUINATO (1974).

Richard Johnson (again) stars as a British TV documentary producer who is researching a program on Satanic paintings. In his pursuit of oddball material he comes across an Italian painting depicting Hell. What's unusual about this work is that it features a flaming woman in the upper left hand of the hellish scene. Upon closer inspection, he is shocked to see the figure resembles his recently deceased wife (who died mysteriously in a fire). The image is also wearing an amulet very similar to one he bought for his wife shortly before her death. His probing for the origins of the painting leads him, his daughter (to whom he gave the amulet), and his new secretary/lover to a mysterious castle in Italy. There the child becomes possessed by an evil spirit and panic erupts.

By the end of **IL MEDAGLIONE INSANGUINATO** it is uncovered that the child was *even* possessed when she burned her mother to death and tries to do the same to her father's new mistress! The terror builds and the little girl confronts the demonic painting in an abandoned chapel. In that sacred place she wields an uniquely double-bladed sword and sets to work destroying the piece of satanic art. We are unexpectedly jolted from our seats as Johnson rushes into the chapel and attempts to stop his daughter from her task. She turns to him as he gathers her in his arms for a loving hug. To our surprise *both* parent and child die, blood spraying everywhere, as the razor sharp blades pierce their bodies.

Another Possession Flick which sacrifices a young child in the triumph of Good over Evil is Amando De Ossorio's creepy **EL PODER DE LAS TINIEBLAS**. In the late 60's throughout the 70's, and even into the early 80's, Spain's chief producer of frightmare flicks was without a doubt Amando De Ossorio. While other Spaniards may have produced more films (Paul Naschy and Jesús Franco, for example), few were able to match De Ossorio when it came to atmosphere and chills (of course, that may not be saying much considering the rarity of Spanish horror films in total). His *Blind Dead* trilogy is still considered the pinnacle of Spanish horror, although other directors like Franco, Jorge Grau, Carlos Aured, and Leon Klimovsky each have produced their own masterpieces.

The film opens and we are introduced to the evil which will soon plunge everyone involved into a bloodbath. An old gnarled woman, caught kidnapping an infant for Satanic sacrifice, is taken to Madrid's main police station for questioning. Instead of telling the officials about the whereabouts of the child, the witch opts to kill herself by jumping out of the fourth floor window of the building. Her soul enters the body of the police inspector's ten-year-old daughter, Susan, who then becomes a foul-mouthed devil-kid.

The little monster floats in the air and has bad breath. She also hurls insults at her mother ("Aw, why don't you just fuck your boyfriend!"), kicks people, taunts a priest ("Does a priest have the same thing as a man? Are you queer or just impotent?"), gives her mid-section a spine-snapping 360 whirl, and all the remarkable insubordination associated with demon-possessed little girls. When Susan's maid cleans the little girl's room she is blitzed by plush animals, and her mother uncovers a phallic-shaped demonic icon in the toy box. The horror continues: a child is found sacrificed, the lover of Susan's mother has his penis cut off (and you-know-who gives it to her mother in a pretty little gift box), and a man is strangled. The monstrous child (now looking like the old witch, complete with balding head, wrinkles, white hair, and bad teeth) abducts another toddler and prepares the babe for sacrifice. A priest leads a joint

Spanish ad mat for **DEMON WITCH CHILD/THE POSSESSED**

investigation with the police and disrupts the Black Mass before the child is to be cut open for the Devil. The horribly disfigured Susan flees to the grave of the old witch with the cleric in hot pursuit. In a surprising conclusion the girl dies when she is impaled by a large metal cross in a churchyard.

De Ossario treads the unpleasant territory of pedicide when he sacrificed the child at the end of this grisly picture. Typically, a young girl would escape the clutches of the devil and live to tell the tale. In this film, and others like **IL MEDAGLIONE INSANGUINATO** and **THE CHILD** (available on video as **KILL AND GO HIDE**, 1977, D: Robert Voskanian), it would seem that the evil cannot be successfully abolished unless the poor child is herself exterminated.

Not far behind his fellow Spaniard, actor-screenwriter Jacinto Molina (aka Paul Naschy) struck on the idea of making a possession film. Now, his producing, directing, writing, and starring in monster films based on other popular critters is not new. Any monster fan worth his or her weight in salt should know this for a fact. Next to Lon Chaney, Jr., Paul Naschy is werewolf personified (he made numerous films featuring his hirsute alter-ego Waldimar Daninsky). Being a monster is his love in life. However, what makes his casting in Juan Bosch's **EXORCISMO/EXORCISM** so unique is that, like a few of Naschy's crime films, he *doesn't* play the part of a monster. In fact, in this Spanish production Naschy is a good guy — *he's the exorcist.*

After a night of erotic, dope-smoking, Satanic group-coupling, Richard Harrington and his lover, Lela Gibson, drive home in their Morris Minor. On their way to the girl's family chateau in Bristol (this Spanish-made film takes place in England), the drugged-fogged Lela, loses control of the car and sends it careening down a hillside, where in an unconscious state she becomes possessed. Her mother frets as Lela acts more and more demonic, and calls upon the local priest. Enter Naschy as Father Adrian Dunning, putting in an unobtrusive acting job and never showing much more emotion than a man on vallium. However, this soon changes and our burly priest manages to glare menacingly and bare his teeth when it becomes obvious that after Lela's near-fatal accident she has become possessed by her late father's jealous spirit. It seems that he went mad shortly before his death and was institutionalized. While dying at the asylum his wife had an affair with his doctor. Upon expiring he gained that knowledge, and when he has the chance entered into his daughter's body and "cleaves" to her soul. Now spewing rude comments, vomiting gobs of goo, attacking everyone in sight, and levitating in bed, Lela wreaks havoc with her mother. It's up to a heroic Dunning to save the day.

As **EXORCISMO** comes to the long anticipated showdown, the once physically delightful Lela is now a scarred, marbled-eyed, puke-spitting, boil and seeping wound-encrusted mess. In a last ditch effort to save the girl's soul Dunning forces the demon to transfer itself into the body of the family dog, Borg. The hound then viciously attacks Dunning, mauling the priest's arm while receiving a fatal blow from a fireplace poker. As the animal expires, the devil is exorcised and Lela returns to normal.

Probably more a blatant rip-off of **THE EXORCIST** than any other film to date, **EXORCISMO** does have its moments. The make-up job on Lela is impressive, especially considering the contacts the poor actress had to endure which made her eyes bulge out of their sockets with a pupilless, cataract look. Unlike other men Naschy worked with before striking out on his own directorial efforts (most notably Javier Aguirre and José Luis Merino), director Bosh lacks any whimsy when it comes to innovative camera work or character development (Naschy sleepwalks through his role as the priest), and not much has been heard of him since this film was made.

Taking a viewpoint that is more in line with his own cinematic sensibilities, another Spaniard, Jesús Franco, joined the fray and produced a unique deviation on the theme. The sexual possession of a woman by another female is not new in the cinema, although Franco's approach is, without a doubt, one of the illest. Bordering on his obsession with pornography, it's small wonder the film opens up and continues to have frequent semi-hardcore lesbian sex scenes (the majority of which star his actress-wife, Lina Romay). As is usual for a film of this breed, **LES POSSEDÉES DU DIABLE (LORNA L'EXORCISTE)/ "Women Possessed By The Devil (Lorna- The Exorcist)"** is a sex film with high horror overtones. Anyone familiar with the director's work would be interested in taking a look at this production, while it is not as brilliantly bizarre as his Horror Trilogy from 1972 (see the article *Monster! International* #2), **LES POSSEDÉES DU DIABLE** is blue enough to rank with most of his other films from the 70's, albeit as a possession movie it *just* barely makes it. There are relatively *few* references to **THE EXORCIST**, other than an exploitative title. However, since this is the closest one can come to a *strictly* sleazy Euro-approach to the theme (mixing sex and the devil) outside of the "lost" film **LOS RITOS SEXUALES DEL DIABLO**/"Sex Rituals Of The Devil" (1981, D: José

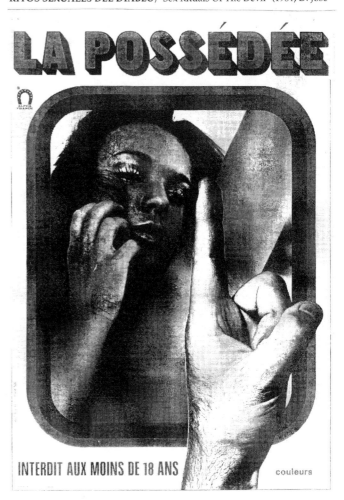

Italian video box cover art from Jesús Franco's **LES POSSEDÉES DU DIABLE** *(1974).*

A macabre Spanish poster for the "lost" sex & possession film LOS RITOS SEXUALES DEL DIABLO (1981).

enough to spook (if not confound) anyone.

German horror films aren't usually rated very well, although there have been exceptions (Michael Armstrong's **HEXEN BIS AUFS BLUT GEQUAELT/ MARK OF THE DEVIL**, 1969, for instance) even though it did manage to produce a minor **EXORCIST** clone when director Michael Walter made **MAGDALENA – VOM TEUFEL BESESSEN/BEYOND THE DARKNESS**. This morbid tale of a demon-possessed cocktease wasn't released in the States until 1976, and despite the title, there is little to recommend other than various choice bits of dialogue and deviantly provocative situations. A grisly opening sequence where a streetwalker discovers an old man crucified to a door is well worth the fright, although little else reaches that heightened sense of the ghastly.

Magdalena Winter is the beautiful "cloistered nun" of a teenager in an otherwise sexually over wrought boarding school for girls. While she is attending school, her doting grandfather is found nailed to a door on the night of Ash Wednesday. On his forehead is burned a strange icon, that of a raven's claw. Baffled, the police question various people and they come up empty — except that Magdalena is involved in some odd way. A gala is held at the school and Magdalena, unaware that her grandfather is dead and his corpse is stretched out in the morgue, sips at some wine and parties with her chums. Suddenly at the morgue the loud buzz-buzz of a fly appears and the mutilated corpse of Grandpa Winter bolts upright the very same instant that Magdalena is stuck down with what looks like an epileptic fit. As her peers shun her twitching body the careening buzz of a bothersome insect is heard, and it seems to settle on the girl. The possession of Magdalena has begun! After a few instances of manic violence where Magdalena threatens the lives of her loved ones, she is again taken by the demonic spirit of her lecherous grandfather. The demon attacks her again and violently rapes her in her bed, not unlike similar occurrences which happen in **L'ANTICRISTO**, **NURSE SHERRI** (1976, D: Al Adamson) and Sidney J. Furie's 1982 sex-possession production **THE ENTITY** where, of all people, Barbara Hershey is the focus of a fornication-famished phantasm. This time around, the monstrous possession takes a firm hold on the teenager's tender soul and turns her into a cock-crazed sex kitten.

Despite the first intriging twenty minutes, the remainder of the film fails to hold up under any sort of critical scrutiny. Director Walter never explores any interesting avenues, rather he focuses on Magdalena's apparent bout with Turret's Syndrome and her rampant sexuality. A few chuckles are chalked up whenever the spirit within the woman verbally attacks nearby individuals. Magdalena is brought to church the day after her ghost-rape where she is introduced to the parish's priest. She marches up to the man of the cloth and announces, "I want to take communion. But not in my mouth, but down here — *in my pussy!*" The startled priest is sprayed with additional insults: "You dirty nun-fucker! So, when are you going to screw your housekeeper again? Answer me, you motherfucker!" The Father reads from the New Testament and attempts to calm her heated and possessed soul. It does no good because Magdalena tears the bible in half and storms out of the chapel to find more poor horny men to tease! Before the inevitable exorcism she manages to taunt two drunken slobs into a brawl ("I want you inside me... Fuck me! ... The winner gets me. I'm worth it too. I need it badly! Ha Ha Ha!") and one of the men stabs the other to death. The possessed girl then sets fire to a doctor's country abode, axes the man who loves her, and then is forced to recite the Lord's Prayer. She manages to gurgle a few lines before coughing up a snake (the devil tormenting her) which is stomped on by her boyfriend. The pretty Magdalena is saved

Ramón Larraz), it is included in the overall article. The delicious perversion which arises with mixing these two volatile subjects simmers and comes to a laconic boil when small fiddler crabs emerge from the genitalia of the possessed female lead. The ordeal continues even after her boyfriend confronts the person responsible (a high-class blonde witch-bitch) and shoots her. Regardless, his girlfriend continues to spit out the crustaceans and eventually expires in his arms. Anyone else's exploitive direction would have hampered the precise build up of horror in this film, so when Franco's exceptional camera work and dilatory direction takes over, the instances with the crabs are eerie

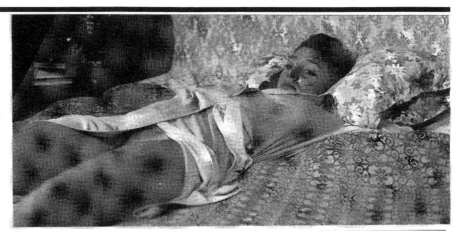

*Devils, demons, and ghosts delight in possessing the weak and unsuspecting -- especially voluptuous women who have the unfortunate happen: the monsters gain control of their souls by way of demonic rape. Not a pleasant manner to be violated as this scene from Al Adamson's **NURSE SHERRI** (1976) would have us believe. This sort of possession also occurred in Alberto De Martino's **L'ANTICRISTO** and Michael Walter's **MAGDALENA – VOM TEUFEL BESESSEN** (both 1974).*

Brazilian filmmaker José Mojica Marins plays himself in his only exploration into the 70's possession cycle: **EXORCISMO NEGRO** *(1974).*

during the quickest exorcism ever — and it's not even performed by a priest!

Brazil's José Mojica Marins explored the dynamics of a dualistic existences when he portrays himself in **EXORCISMO NEGRO**/"Black Exorcism" and comes face to face with his evil alter-ego Zé do Caixão. Marins is haunted by his own creation in this exorcist tale spiced with Catholic imagery and Macumba spells. Seeking a vacation from the hectic routine of filmmaking, Marins arrives home for the Christmas holiday to spend time with family and friends. He parties a little, then retires one evening to begin working on his next horror film. While puzzling over the new plot an evil force invades his home and possesses various loved ones. Each person possessed snarls and attacks Mojica, and he soon suspects witchcraft is afoot. It isn't until his friend's daughter is kidnapped by his cinematic alter-ego Zé that he must face the facts: his fictional demon has become a reality through the Black Arts. In a decent battle for the soul of his daughter, Marins comes face to with Zé and brandishes a hurriedly constructed cross. The symbol of good wards off the evil and saves the day.

EXORCISMO NEGRO isn't as powerful a film as you would imagine, coming from the man who made the creepy and sadistically violent Zé do Caixão trilogy **À MEIA-NOITE LEVAREI SU ALMA**/"At Midnight I'll Take Away Your Soul" (1965), **ESTA NOITE ENCARNAREI NO TEU CADÁVER**/ "Tonight I'll Be Incarnated Into Your Corpse" (1966), and **O ESTRANHO MUNDO DE ZÉ DO CAIXÃO**/"The Strange World Of Zé do Caixão" (1968). The weakness, no doubt, lies in the fact that Marins had little to do with the project other than star in it and work on the script. His direction is uninspired, and the principal photography (which was in color) was left to one of Brazil's top cinematographers. Still, despite these obvious handicaps, **EXORCISMO NEGRO** is able to produce ample chills for the viewer. One scene in particular has Marins stumbling into a room where the oldest daughter of this friend is trembling and squirming as if the spirit that dominates her is virtually squeezing her soul into a sexual pulp. His utter revulsion upon discovering her drives the point home that he must destroy his evil alter ego Zé. The final confrontation between the maker and his shade is filled with torture, bloodshed, and nudity one comes to expect from a Marins horror film — the problem is, we had to wait over an hour to see the carnage.

Turning stateside for the last Possession Film of this bountiful year, **ABBY** is William Girdler's plunge into the realm of demon disarray. The film is *still* banned by Warner Brothers from being released on legitimate video because of the supposed similarities between it and Friedkin's production. There are some affinities, but the dissimilarities are there as well. **ABBY** is *not* a Black version of **THE EXORCIST**. There are enough distinguishing points of originality which keeps it from becoming just another horror film in blackface. **ABBY** is *not* another **BLACKENSTEIN** (1973, D: William A. Levey) which was, despite some neat tricks, a tired re-telling of the rampaging patchwork creation of a misguided scientist bent on helping humanity. Whereas **BLACKENSTEIN** and the interesting but flawed **DR. BLACK, MR. HYDE** (1976, D: William Crain) fed off of blackploitational motifs (the bad white guys, etc.), and **BLACULA** (1972, D: William Crain) attempted a reasonably true to form Hammeresque approach (despite faults, **SCREAM, BLACULA, SCREAM** [1973, D: Bob Kelljan] was superior in many ways to the last few Hammer vampire outings), Girdler's **ABBY** relied heavily on the popular fusion of African religious beliefs with that of the rich US Black religious heritage. There is a distinct African-American feel to the production, something that a number of other low-budget blackploitational projects lacked. And besides that the film *is* scary.

Professor/Bishop Garnet Williams (genre actor William Marshall, star of **SCREAM, BLACULA, SCREAM**, STAR TREK episode "The Ultimate Computer", the defunct *PEEWEE'S PLAYHOUSE*'s "King of Cartoons", and the violent 1957 Rock Hudson/Sidney Poitier vehicle **SOMETHING OF VALUE**), on a trip to Nigeria comes across an ancient relic in a forbidden cave. The object is a small stone vessel with the carved image of a man possessing a huge erect penis. Puzzled at first on how to open the container, Williams, a religion professor of Louisville University on sabbatical in Nigeria to study the cult of Eshu, twists the image's erect member and the lid pops open. There is a rush of foul air, and the entire cave shakes with the force of a minor earthquake. Unwittingly, Professor Williams has unleashed a minor demon of the Eshu cult. This particular cult relishes disaster and death ... and the spirit unleashed is a really nasty one. Being especially shitty, this minor god of sexuality and mischief (known as "The Trickster" to the Yoruba religion) escapes the cave, killing everyone but Williams — the monster has plans to torment him further!

Back in the United States William's son Rev. Emmett (Terry Carter, star of Jack

Hill's **FOXY BROWN**, 1974) and his wife Abby (Carole Speed, who sang the production's theme song "My Soul is a Witness") move into their new home. Everything is perfect: Emmett is a nice guy who doesn't drink or smoke or cuss, and Abby is a pretty, faithful, and God-fearing woman — just ripe for demonic pickings! While taking a shower she is taken by the minion of Eshu and a chill wind blows through the house, knocking down dishes and lamps. Just to make sure Abby is in the monster's control, the devil violently possesses her for a second time in the basement while she is putting clothes in the washer.

During a church picnic Abby takes a large butcher knife and slashes her wrists. Emmett bites his lip and suspects something is dreadfully wrong with his once stable wife. He consults a doctor who prescribes a lot of rest and some sleeping pills. Things get worse as Abby vomits during church, and attacks one of the church-goers — urping goo upon the poor sod. Then while she is counseling a church couple who is having trouble with their marriage, Abby rips her shirt off and announces she's going to "fuck the shit" out of the startled husband. Emmett interrupts his wife's flagrantly blasphemous actions, only to have his masculinity insulted in front of friends. Abby then torments an elderly woman to the point that the oldster has a heart attack and dies. Fearing something more than common insanity is the cause of his wife's wild ways, Emmett calls his Father in Nigeria and begs for help. It sounds like demonic possession, Professor Williams concludes, and hops on the next flight to the USA.

Our heroes are joined by Abby's police detective brother Cass Porter (Austin Stoker, star of Carpenter's 1976 classic thriller **ASSAULT ON PRECINCT 13** and director Girdler's 1975 **SHEBA BABY** which co-starred Blackploitational queen Pam Grier) and the three of them comb the streets looking for the wayward demon. Meanwhile Abby picks up men and proceeds to fuck them then twist their heads in the traditional 180 degree technique for which demons are famous (**L'ANTICRISTO** has a similar scene). It isn't until Emmett spots her in a notably seedy bar that the exorcism comes into play. "Hold her down!" orders Williams, who then puts on an African dashiki and takes out various items of religious paraphernalia — both Christian and Pagan. Williams calls upon Jehovah *and* Loran to exorcise the demon from the poor woman's ran-

Canadian video box art from Jaun López Moctezuma's **ALUCARD**A (1975).

sacked body. In an explosion of spiritual energy the creature erupts from Abby and is imprisoned once again inside the aboriginal receptacle which Williams placed on the bar counter. Dazed but alive, Abby is happy to be back among her loved ones, and Williams returns to Nigeria to continue his studies.

The late director William Girdler was very active in the exploitation field for some time before his death in 1979 (he died in a helicopter accident). The concept of melding brooding Blackploitational epics with the new budding **EXORCIST** genre, and making a film as competent — and at times intelligent — as **ABBY** strikes me as both novel and audacious.

The following year was a lean twelve months for the Devil, when you consider that in the previous year there were ten possession/exorcism films. British director John Gilling lived in Spain for a while and made **LA CRUZ DEL DIABLO**/"The Cross of the Devil" wherein a man becomes obsessed with a woman and fears he has been possessed by a demon. The film is no longer available, and rumor has it that it was suppressed by Spanish unions in protest against Gilling working in Spain. The Brazilian film **SEDUZIDAS PELO DEMÔNIO**/"Women Seduced by the Devil" by Raffaelle Rossi is another instance of reworking an old project to make a new product. The movie is a remake of Rossi's own previous **O HOMEM-LOBO** (1968), about a young man who turns into a werewolf in a girl's boarding school. Rossi originally made this reputedly horrible picture for theatrical run, but it aired on Brazilian TV first. In the re-make the werewolf becomes a man possessed by the Devil, who attacks yet another reclusive boarding school. (So reclusive, in fact, that you have to take a 18th Century carriage to get there: Rossi lifted some footage from the 1967 Harald Reinl film **DIE SCHLANGENGRUBE UND DAS PENDEL/THE BLOOD DEMON** where a horse-drawn coach is drive through a forest decorated with severed human limbs.) **SEDUZIDAS PELO DEMÔNIO** was eventually released upon the unsuspecting movie house masses which expected

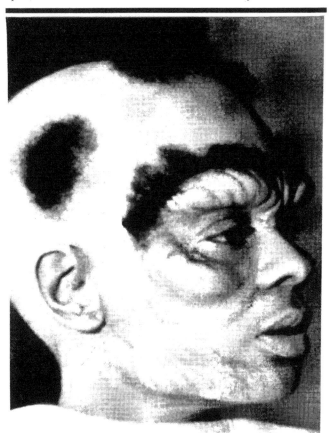

Carol Speed is possessed by an African demon in William Girlder's **ABBY** (1974).

a new **EXORCIST**-related flick. They were sorely disappointed. Today, Rossi is better known as the man responsible for introducing Brazil to hardcore porn films.

ALUCARDA is one of the rare instances in Mexican horror which doesn't feature a masked, wrestling do-gooder pinning monsters to the mats and fending off hoards of killer dwarves. On the contrary, what we are presented is an intelligently crafted story of two women seeking their individual sexuality. They must fight against society which is oddly structured within a devil-possession and crazy-nuns-on-the-loose film. Director Juan López Moctezuma may be better known to you as the producer of Alejandro Jodorowsky's classic psychodelic western **EL TOPO** (1972) as well as directing the equally bizarre **LA MANSIÓN DE LA LOCURA**/"The Mansion of Madness"/**DR. TARR'S TORTURE GARDEN** (1972) and the disappointing vampire film **MARY, MARY, BLOODY MARY** (1973) which starred an arthritic John Carradine as the bloodthirsty father of a half-human vampiress. This possession film is a production hip-deep in exotic locales (a dingy nunnery) and flaky characters (a six-foot tall hunchback with warts), and one wonders what happened to Moctezuma and what the man has been up to since making **ALUCARDA** (available on video as **INNOCENTS FROM HELL**).

When orphaned teenager Justine is sent to a convent she is warmly greeted by the sisters of that order. Things are not as they seem when the red-haired Justine rooms with the raven-haired Alucarda — the daughter of an unholy union between her deceased mother and the Devil. The two become fast friends and during one of their mischievous romps through the countryside Alucarda and her roommate encounter a giant hunchback who leeringly introduces them to his gypsy clan. After that odd encounter the two enter a mausoleum where both are possessed by a demon, possibly the same which impregnated Alucarda's mother. Later that day they disrupt a church gathering with chants of "Satan. Satan Our Lord and master. I promise thee I'll do as much evil as I can" and so forth. The nuns are horrified and call upon their local exorcist to remedy the problem.

Moctezuma carefully weaves the tale around the two girls in such a way that a person cannot help but get involved with the picture. The man's unique and quirky vision is amplified by beautiful, albeit disturbing, sequences. Soon after Alucarda and Justine are united as sexual sisters of the Devil, then run off to join the hunchback's Sabbath. There they strip down to the buff and begin the prance with the other naked witches in unholy rites. One of the nuns senses that Justine, her personal favorite among the orphans, is in spiritual distress and calls forth the wrath of God. While floating above the floor in her bare, cloistered compartment, our loving nun – blood oozing from her pores – transcendentally blasts apart the practicing witches while the two orphans flee back to the convent. This scene in particular is well executed and is an unnerving prelude to Alucarda's own deviltry. At the fiery climax of **ALUCARDA**, our dark-haired beauty psychically destroys the nunnery (beating Brian de Palma's **CARRIE** to the punch by one year) after clerics kill Justine during an unorthodox exorcism. A fantastic film which needs more attention than it has gotten.

Pre-dating **THE OMEN** by one year, yet borrowing heavily from **THE EXORCIST** and **ROSEMARY'S BABY**, Peter Sasdy's **I DON'T WANT TO BE BORN** isn't as absurd as it may sound. Released Stateside as **THE DEVIL WITHIN HER**, the film is not actually a "demon-possession" derivative in the sense that Satan himself is altercating for the immortal soul of a three-month old baby, but witchcraft is suggested — and thus, indirectly, the Devil is involved. The evil emanates from a bloated dwarf whose lustful attentions for a beautiful woman is spurned. An attractive, pre-super bitch Joan Collins is the recipient of the evil, and gives birth to a child which, according to her doctor, "didn't want to be born."

After recovering her strength our tentative mother sets about trying to care for her newborn. Things aren't what they seem as the child's rate of growth is out of control and within weeks the baby is almost the size of a one-year old. The infant has incredible strength and enjoys tearing up his room and spitting at his mother. Whenever the child's aunt (who is a nun, by the way) visits, he sets up a horrible howl. Small wonder since he is, of course, possessed. Told in flashback, former nightclub stripper Collins confesses to her sister (Caroline Monroe) that she rebuffed a lustful embrace by her dance partner, Hercules, a powerful and leering dwarf. After a bit of the old in and out with the nightclub's owner, Tommy, Collins is taunted by an angered Hercules who curses her: "You have within you a devil child. He will be as big as I am small!" Later on a trip to Italy she meets and marries her present husband (Ralph Bates) and they have the child. But whose kid is it? Does it belong to her husband, or Tommy, or, in some weird way, Hercules?

The child gets progressively violent, and at one point pulls a sitter's head under the water when she gives him a bath. Afterward, the same woman takes the little devil for a stroll around the park in a baby buggy. When she parks the carriage next to a pond, the dwarfish rogue pushes her into the water where she strikes her head on a rock and drowns. Later on he punches Tommy who comes over to look at the little tyke to see if it may be his. The situation deteriorates as the brat puts a mouse in another sitter's tea, murders his father (by hanging him from a tree!), decapitates a doctor (Donald Pleasence) with a shovel, and

Top: George Clayton as the possessive dwarf who menaces Joan Collins in Peter Sasdy's **I DON'T WANT TO BE BORN** *(1975). Above: U.S. ad mat from the same film. Curiously enough, when it was released onto U.S. video it bore the original British title.*

eventually hunts mom down throughout the flat and stabs her to death! It's up to Auntie Nun to exorcise the child. She attempts to hold down the hopping (!) infant while dodging flying toys and murderous blows from the tyke. Lastly she is able to pin the rascal down and administer the Rite of Exorcism. When the evil flees the baby (who then returns to normal), Hercules the dwarf stumbles, has a fit, and dies in the middle of a big musical number at Tommy's nightclub.

Sasdy's film is a far cry from his association with Hammer Studios (**TASTE THE BLOOD OF DRACULA**, 1972; **COUNTESS DRACULA**, 1973; and **HANDS OF THE RIPPER**, 1974), but light years head of his present-day TV material (most recently an episode of Thames' *SHERLOCK HOLMES*: "Sherlock Holmes and the Leading Lady") and sports several bizarre visuals and downright offbeat sequences. The scene where the child slips the noose around the neck of his father and lifts the man off the ground to garrote him is unusual and disturbing. At this point in the film you want to know if it is actually the kid doing all of this mischief or could it be the sexually deviant and diabolic Hercules tormenting Collins' life. This sick attitude towards the physically impaired isn't new, nor has it abated, since these wicked pygmies still inhabit "nightmare" sequences in movies, on TV, and notably reside within Heavy Metal rock videos. No matter how ancient our social stigma is towards the physically disabled, and even though in these modern times bias plays an ugly part in developing stereotypical type-casting for good and evil, it does gives these diminutive actors and actresses jobs.

1976 was the year of the Antichrist, and the introduction of Richard Donner's **THE OMEN** and its popular theme of the devil-child born to mortals and placed on the Earth to cause havoc. That film, together with **THE EXORCIST** and **ROSEMARY'S BABY**, along with liberal helpings from **CARRIE**, helped create more havoc. Not just was Satan stalking the earth to possess innocent women, but he was here to spread his seed and give rise to telepathically endowed bastard hybrids. The pure possession-cum-exorcism flick was soon to become a thing of the past; it's meteoric rise in popularity was to be eclipsed by its own stepchildren.

During 1976 there were a few films which touched on the possession subject without depending *too* much on what was popular for the day. Marcello Aliprandi's rarely seen ghost flick **UN SUSSURRO NEL BUIO/**"A Whisper In The Dark" borrowed more from **DON'T LOOK NOW** (1972, D: Nicolas Roeg) than **THE EXORCIST**, and **J.D.'S REVENGE** (D: Arthur Marks), a ghost/possession film set in an African-American urban setting. Quite the contrary can be said of the rest of that year's meager pickings. Eddy Matalon's **CAUCHEMARS/CATHY'S CURSE**, and Elo Pannaciò's **UN URLO NELLE TENEBRE/THE POSSESSOR**, are the two that clearly come to mind.

Eddy Matalon's Canadian/French production company added another motif to the already crowded arena of devil-spawned beings: the devil doll in **CAUCHEMARS**. This ghostly possession film asks the question: If your daughter found a strange doll which has its eyes sewn shut in an old dusty attic would you let her keep it? Matalon could have had a decent horror vehicle here if he had half a mind to do some directing. Everything is handled in a flat and emotionless style, keeping any suspense from developing and possibly cluing us in on why the doll wants to kill people. The plot winds hither and beyond as a young child, Cathy (proof positive that there are children uglier than Marian Salgado who starred as Susan in **EL PODER DE LAS TINIEBLAS**), discovers a bizarre rag doll in the attic of her new home. The creature is possessed by the mean-spirited ghost of a little girl who was killed in a fiery car crash with her abusive father. Once Cathy has the effigy in her arms she too becomes possessed by the ghost. The tyke terrorizes the community when she attempts to poke out the eyes of one little girl with a rusty nail, then sends her maid crashing through the second story window. The screaming woman impacts on the tarmac in front of Cathy's distraught and emotionally screwed-up mother. Making matters worse the child frightens the town psychic and tears the face off the family gardener. Cathy then corners her mother in the kitchen with a butcher knife and begins to make mincemeat out of her. Luckily for the both of them the girl's father grabs the possessed doll and tears the critter's eyelids off. For some reason the ghost of the dead girl is appeased and the haunting comes to an end.

*U.S. Video box art of the last true Italian **EXORCIST** rip-off, Elo Pannaciò's lyrical **UN URLO NELLE TENEBRE** (1976).*

Not exactly an **EXORCIST** rip-off plotwise, **CAUCHEMARS** does borrow heavily in the motif-thick field of "atmospheric" special effects. Cathy spits curses with her foul breath in the typical possessed child way ("You old bag," she addresses the psychic in the hollow voice possessed people acquire, "you'll burn in hell if you don't get out of here!"). The doll itself does a 180 degree head spin and floats around the house.

Sadly, despite all of **CAUCHEMARS**'s low-budget charms, this was the year when the last faithful **EXORCIST** rip-off was made, and as films of this ilk go, **UN URLO NELLE TENEBRE** is very appealing. Director Elo Pannaciò didn't have much to work with, considering he was utilizing dated material. Having the antagonist's sister being a nun is an added taboo. Placing nuns in demonic peril is a popular motif in horror films (see **I DON'T WANT TO BE BORN**, for example), as it added another dimension explored earlier in Brunello Rondi's critically acclaimed **IL DEMONIO** (1965, an intellectual's possession film) and Ken Russell's **THE DEVILS** (1971, a "false" possession film) and later in the infamous Italian nuns-amok film **IL ALTRO INFERNO/THE OTHER HELL** (1981, D: Bruno Mattei). Even making the sister a beautiful nun added just enough sexual frustration and guilt to keep the plot moving.

The film begins with a weird opening sequence wherein a crowd of on-lookers in St. Peter's Square listen to the Pope's plea for exorcising the devil from their souls, shots of a possessed Peter screaming, and flashes of some ambiguous Black Mass. These highly charged visual juxtapositions are effective, but not as punchy as the tasty dialogue between the possessed and those around him. Rivalling **MAGDALENA** with its roll of heretical utterances, the spicy banter in **UN URLO NELLE TENEBRE** is definitely the highlight, and sets the film up in a delirious and blasphemous timbre.

Peter is a pleasant young man (a welcome change from the innocent females) who is deeply religious and loves nature. While out on a field trip with friends he is possessed by a devil when he accidentally photographs an auburn-maned she-demon taking a bath at a waterfall. Despite his sanctimonious up-bringing, Peter is a hot-blooded Italian who, like anyone with a libido, drools at his unsuspecting model. After the woman mysteriously vanishes Peter finds a strange talisman in the stream. He pockets the charm not knowing that later when he drills a hole through it and puts it on a chain around his neck, the evil within it will soon burn a pentagram on his chest. At this point the audience is sufficiently clued in that Peter is in for a load of trouble; such evil icons have popped up for decades in films. From the time the priest discovers a devil fetish at a dig to when Regan began to make weird animals out of clay in **THE EXORCIST**, this motif was reinforced in almost every clone made thereafter: **O EXORCISMO NEGRO, CAUCHEMARS, IL MEDAGLIONE INSANGUINATO, L'OSSESSA, ABBY, EL PODER DE LAS TINIEBLAS,**

Spanish poster from another "lost" possession film, Giulio Petroni's L'OSCENO DESIDERIO (1977).

if these are direct translations from the Italian, or if the dubbers had a liberal voice in the matter.

At this point Elania takes it upon herself to approach her brother and declare her love for him. The devil within Peter strikes back: "Carrier of death, I am invincible! You know it, you know I am! Off with your mask and show yourself! Show what you really are!" The exorcist hesitates then continues the rite while the possessed spits insults for the final time: "There are no words to describe the crimes you commit on men! Stop appealing to fools and weaklings! You and I are the same!" Suddenly Peter coughs up at least a gallon of purplish-green vomit, and smoke pours from his mouth. The mark of Satan vanishes and the demoness vacates his body. Good has triumphed — or so we believe. Sister Elania takes a breather in her bedroom only to discover, painfully, that the brand of Satan has appeared, between her breasts. She takes it upon herself to purge the world of this evil and jumps off a cliff and plunges to her death into a shallow stream. However (one more twist, folks) a young boy (again) discovers the amulet in the creek and runs off with it.

UN URLO NELLE TENEBRE *occasionally* bristles with energy, and there are, unquestionably, very effective sequences throughout, but their sparsity only tends to frustrate the viewer. One particular item is the reoccurring "mondo" footage of an insane asylum which pops up every time Sister Elaina frets about her brother's condition. This scratchy, cinema verité footage depicts screaming female inmates beating each other, tearing their clothes off, and being "attended to" (whipped more like it) by their care-takers. Either Elo is equating spiritual possession with the mentally deranged, or he is making some weird statement that the mentally ill *are* souls possessed by actual demons and all they need is a good exorcism! One high note is the spacey, 70's Euro-rock soundtrack by composer Giuliano Sorgini. His use of spitting guitar, careening electric organ, and thumping bass reminds a person of a half-crocked *GOBLIN* (**SUSPIRIA, DAWN OF THE DEAD**, etc.) during a sloppy mic set.

1977: **STAR WARS** and **CLOSE ENCOUNTERS OF THE THIRD KIND** broke the box offices and a multitude of takeoffs followed suit (again, the Italians rose to the occasion and Luigi Cozzi [= Lewis Coates] and Alfonso Brescia [= Al Bradly] figure as two key names in this genre), and Hollywood coughed up its first "official" self-exploitive sequel to **THE EXORCIST**. **EXORCIST II: THE HERETIC** was made three years and at *least* fifteen imitations after

etc. As the diabolic possession unfolds, our victim's unflattering first act of deviltry occurs at a party. There he shakes a bottle of champagne, pops its cork, and sprays the foam all over his chaste girlfriend's new dress. He also curses at his mother and is spiteful to his sister, Elaina, the family nun. From then on in, it's Hell on Earth for his entire kin. He is repeatedly visited by the red-haired demoness, stares menacingly at his family, and spits as well. Adding insult to injury he kills his girlfriend at a disco, rapes his mother (in the form of the demon: "Don't resist it! You love it you lecherous sow!") and kills her by pushing her down the stairs. As he did with his mother Peter visits his sister in the shape of the she-demon. The creature crawls into Elaina's bed and ravishes the frightened nun ("Come! Come, you bitch in heat! Your virginity is mine!!"). Sensing that things are by no means normal, his surviving sibling calls in a priest.

A priest (Richard Conte, co-star of Richard Quine's **HOTEL**, 1967, and Coppola's **THE GODFATHER**, 1972, in one of his last roles) upon hearing of this horror from Elaina, bones up on all the information he can find about the demoness. The monster possessing the boy comes from 1723 when a witch at that time period is causing all sort of mischief. The red-haired beauty was running all over Italy seducing virginal men and women and exposing them to Satanism, and corrupting their souls. The exorcist is greeted by an obnoxious Peter as he approaches the house of the possessed ("Accursed interferer, go away! Go away!" screams Peter from his bed room window). The cleric and demon confront each other and Peter lets out a barrage of great one-liners. "I cannot stand the putrid stench of your garments! Go away!" To his whimpering sister he declares: "And you, you whore, don't ask that eunuch for help! You carrion bitch. Get out!" Soon after the exorcism is under way, our demon continues his slurs: "Stop! Stop! You fool. You enemy of life. Blind prophet of ignorance. I will never leave, you whoremonger! Traitor. Coward. You human excrement. Pox-tainted whore's son. Go away, lecherous swine!" One wonders

Seductive ad mat from Al Adamson's **NURSE SHERRI** (1977).

211

the fact. Although certainly a sloppy film, this John (**ZARDOZ**, 1971; **EXCALIBUR**, 1981) Boorman production did try to approach the subject differently. Calling in an African witch doctor (James Earl Jones) to squash an African-variation of the demon re-possessing Linda Blair (eleven years before her woeful appearance in Bob Logan's **REPOSSESSED**), the exotic locales and proceeding exorcism did, for the most part, keep your attention, no matter how often you giggled during the film. Curtis Harrington's ghost-possession effort **RUBY** is fun if not flawed (a drive-in favorite, this film is, sadly, only available on video in a seriously edited TV print). The silly US made-for-TV clone **THE POSSESSED** (D: Jerry Thorpe, who also directed television's **KUNG FU**, 1971, and **SMILE JENNY, YOU'RE DEAD**, 1974, the pilot for David Janssen's *HARRY O* series) popped up starring James Farentino as a priest investigating a fire at a boarding school. Then there's Giulio Petroni's obscure **L'OSCENO DESIDERIO**/"The Obscene Desire" which is a another in the series of "lost" films which has yet to turn up on video. The film is a sexual-demon-possession film from the man better known for his fantastic 1967 Western **DA UOMO A UOMO/ DEATH RIDES A HORSE**. A Spanish-Italian co-production, Petroni weaves a tale of a pregnant woman in Rome helped by a group of Satanists who believe that her baby was sired by the devil.

Aside from Robert Wise's artfully crafted ghost/reincarnation film **AUDREY ROSE**, and the Alberto De Martino's tale of the anti-Christ-cum-**THE OMEN** production **HOLOCAUST 2000/ THE CHOSEN**, little else resembled what was so popular just a few years past. However, whereas William Girdler was able to successfully coalesce the African-American experience with **ABBY** in 1974, **THE MANITOU** is a less-than-exciting, chock-full-of-stars approach which hardly says anything for the mythology of the Native-American. True, there are scant semi-truthful references to cosmic American demons in this flimsy tale, but the undeniable point of attack was Girdler's obsession for possessions. Here he attempts to fuse demonic possession with demonic impregnation. The result is an embarrassing mess which seldom rises above parody. Had he spent more time with the script and less with wooing big-name has-been stars, **THE MANITOU** (which wasn't that bad of a book) could have been original and entertaining.

Bogus clairvoyant (Tony Curtis, has-been actor #1) comes face to face with an authentic demonic situation when his girlfriend (Susan Strasberg, recognized name #2) has the fetus of a long dead Indian Medicine Man growing on her spinal cord. Terrified that the spontaneous growth will soon consume her, and suspecting the supernatural, he attempts to contact the spirit via a "kosher" spiritualist (Stella Stevens, noted low-rent actress #3). During a seance it is made known that the spirit possessing the woman is a four-hundred-year-old witch doctor. Curtis then contacts a crusty anthropologist (gruff old star #4, Burgess Meredith in his post-*BATMAN*/pre-**ROCKY** days) who informs him that it is *indeed* an Indian demon probably bent on reincarnating himself. When a doctor at the hospital attempts to remove the fetus via a laser the baby strikes out, wounding him in the hand. Curtis determines that there is just one thing to do: "fight fire with fire" and employ a modern-day Medicine Man to combat the ancient entity. After a lot of "authentic" Indian bravado on the part of actor Michael Ansara (vet #5) and "there isn't such a thing as magic" staunchness from a hospital administer, the witch doctor is reborn. Of course, all hell breaks loose and there are scenes of bloodshed and levitating objects, but what ruins the film, and keeps it from being anything but trite, is the time-worn ending that love conquerors all. Just when the deformed (stunted by x-ray exposure in the hospital) monster is about to conjure up the mother-of-all-demons, the creator of all, etc., etc. to blast the White man and his corrupt civilization, his surrogate mother/host bolts up in her hospital bed and blasts him with love. How's that for the corniest ending to any possession film ever made?

What Girdler had in mind was an end-all cosmic battle which pitted the modern white world against the ancient red one. It didn't work — and not just because of the racist attitude that white is right, but the effects were bad and most of the time the acting was an embarrassment.

Another American, Al Adamson is known for his hodge-podge projects: the poverty-row piece-meal horror production **BRAIN OF BLOOD** (1971), his western **THE GUN RIDERS** (1969), and **BLOOD OF DRACULA'S CASTLE** (1967). *Famous Monsters* war-babies may readily recall (and none too fondly) his work **DRACULA VS. FRANKENSTEIN** (1971), in which *FM's* editor Forrest J. Ackerman had a cameo. Adamson isn't a great director but he have a nose for exploitive material. Each idea, whether original or "borrowed," he would manipulate to its fullest, depending on how far he could stretch his budget — which never was very much to begin with. Even **THE EXORCIST** wasn't safe. **NURSE SHERRI** is his homage to the possession cycle, and, as with many of his other projects, this film is probably better known under other (mostly video) titles: **HOSPITAL OF TERROR, BEYOND THE LIVING, KILLER'S CURSE, HANDS OF DEATH,** and **TERROR HOSPITAL**.

YIKES! When **NURSE SHERRI** gets possessed be careful not to lose your head over it!

The evil spirit of a mad man possesses the amble body of Nurse Sherri and takes revenge on those whom he hated while living. Through various methods of extermination, Sherri and the ghost whittle down the cast until she comes at her boyfriend with cleavers in hand! If it isn't for the swift thinking of her two nurse-roommates who dig up and incinerate the corpse of the possessor, then Sherri would have minced her lover as well. **NURSE SHERRI** comes through with flying colors despite what you might think. Adamson's direction is tight and the script holds up well under the circumstances. It is not an instance of "so bad it's good", but rather "hey, it was better than I imagined." The final minutes top the film as Sherri snaps out of her possession. The town police inspector and the boyfriend both agree than the babbling young woman was taken over by the ghost and not responsible for the murders she committed under his spell. But, because no one else would believe their story Sherri will be committed to an institution for the criminally insane, although both men know that she isn't crazy. Nice twist there, and a real downer for the audience.

One final note: no doubt hard-pressed for cash Adamson acquired a canned soundtrack which included the title track from TV's *ONE STEP BEYOND* (Harry Lubin) and incidental themes from *THE OUTER LIMITS* (Dominic Frontiere). While readily recognizable to most SF fans, the most effective use of Frontiere's score is during the initial, sleazy possession. In what is possibly Adamson's most atmospherically-shot scene, Sherri is lying on her bed wearing nothing but a nightgown when the leering ghost invades her soul. As the music builds her negligee is supernaturally hitched higher and higher around her thighs and her legs are forced apart for the unearthly violation.

Before I close this exploration of 70's post-**EXORCIST** films, I would like to point out a movie which is, if you are as fascinated by the subject as I truly am, a wonder to behold. In searching for material, I was sent a video of Turkish origin. Maybe the correct way of describing it is that this movie is a *true* counterfeit of Friedkin's film. A doppleganger, if you care to take it further. Unlike **ABBY** or **UN URLO NELLE TENEBRE** which were heavily *inspired* by the '73 film, **SEYTAN**/"Satan" (D: Metin Erksan) steals *scene per scene* (and I am not making this up!) — and possibly word for word — almost every important and non-important aspect of **THE EXORCIST** right down to similar camera angles and, of course, Mike Oldfield's "Tubular Bells" score. The difference is, considering that Turkey is predominately an Islamic country, the demon and the clerics are Islamic. The will of Allah and the powerful words of the prophet Muhammad are summoned to dispel the demon from the Linda Blair look-a-like. And, you know what, this film is *much* more entertaining than Friedkin's project. It looks like an Italian clone, but takes the daring (and illegal) step toward total and complete absorption of the original's plot, taking **THE EXORCIST** and making it tolerable.

The 70'S wound down with **DAMIEN - OMEN II** (1978, D: Don Taylor), John Carpenter's masterful possession/stalker **HALLOWEEN** (1978), Norman J. Warren's witch's curse causing **TERROR** (1978), Ian Coughlan's equally wacky **ALISON'S BIRTHDAY** (1979), and pathetically popular **THE AMITYVILLE HORROR** (1979, D: Stuart Rosenberg). Each of those films had a little bit of **THE EXORCIST** in them, but none were specialized enough to be considered a clone. From here on out the idea of the Devil or a demon possessing an individual became commonplace, and already a dated cinematic cliché.

Stretching into the 80's and 90's filmmakers had little recourse but to look behind themselves for inspiration. Horror films of today are rare and at times often imitations of the Italian giallos from the 60's, 70's, and 80's, disguised as "psycho-thrillers". You can count the number of true-blue monster flicks released theatrically in the 90's on one hand. Oddball films like Sam Raimi's **ARMY OF DARKNESS** (1993) cannot be considered a real horror film, which, although jammed-packed with monsters, is nevertheless a slap-stick comedy. Making a monster film today is a shattered reality, where "originality" is taking the old and reworking it until it's truly dull. Few such re-workings have any merit. John Carpenter's **THE THING** (1982) it one of the last truly classic monster films of the 80's, borrowing more from the short story than the original 1954 film. Nothing very significant was produced which was as powerful a genre-jolt to the cinematic psyche as **THE EXORCIST**. One can argue that George Romero's **DAWN OF THE DEAD** (1979) sparked a mini-boom of walking-dead productions (which the Italians gleefully still exploit — see **DÈMONI 3** on page 60), and that **ALIEN** (1979, D: Ridley Scott), **ALIENS** (1986, D: James Cameron), and **TERMINATOR 2: JUDGMENT DAY** (1991, D: James Cameron) contributed heavily to the re-birth of mega-bucks Science Fiction monster fests (to be followed by, again, a delightful hoard of worldwide replicants), there are still remnants of the religious fear and frustration which made possession films rampant. **EXORCIST III** (1992, D: William Blantley, while not really following the sequel fad, is no less a very good film and actually has some traditional exorcism in it) and **REPOSSESSED** made it apparent that this trend is now dead if followed in its truest form. Exorcism and possession cannot be the central plot of a film anymore, it is too "old fashioned" nowadays to be able to pull in an audience — unless the priest packs an uzi and the possessed female is a body-building, ultra-feminist, tough-as-nails adversary. The chilling sanctimonious sacrilege is gone, replaced by the tired carnage of slash and burn action flicks and silly psycho-dramas. More's the pity.

THE DEVIL'S FILMOGRAPHY

SUPERNATURAL
USA, 1933. *p co-* Paramount Pictures Corp. *d-* Victor Halperin. *sc-* Harvey Thew & Brian Marlowe. *story-* Garnett Weston. *ph-* Arthur Martinelli. *art d-* Hans Dreier. *dial d-* Sidney Salkow. *p-* Victor & Edward Halperin. *cast-* Carole Lombard, Randolph Scott, Vivienne Osborne, Alan Dinehart, H.B. Warner, Beryl Mercer, William Farnum, Willard Robertson, George Burr McAnnan, Lyman Williams. *rt-* 60 min. *US dist-* Paramount.

THE DYBUK
US t - THE DYBBUK. Poland, 1937. *p co-* Feniks. *d-* Michael Waszynski. *sc-* Alter Kokynski, Anderej Marek. *based on the original play* The Dybuk *by* S. Ansky. *adaptation-* A. Stern. *ph-* A. Wywerka. *art d-* Anderej Marek. *set dec-* Rotmil & Norris. *historical advisor-* Majer Balaban. *m-* A. Kon. *cantorial m-* Gershon Sirota. *cam-* L. Zajaczkowski. *choreo-* Judith Berg. *cast-* Abraham Morewski, A. Samberg, M. Lipman, Lili Liniana, Diana Halpern, G. Lemberger, L. Liebgold, M. Bozyk, S. Landau, S. Bronecki, M. Messinger, Z. Katz, A. Kurtz, D. Lenderman. *restored rt-* 123 min. *US dist-* National Center for Jewish Film Library.

THE LADY AND THE MONSTER
re-release t- THE TIGER MAN. USA, 1944. *p co-* Republic Pictures. *d/assoc p-* George Sherman. *sc-* Frederick Kohner & Dane Lussier. *based on the novel* Donovan's Brain *by* Curt Siodmak. *ph-* John Alton. *art d-* Russell Kimball. *sp fx-* Theodore Lydecker. *ed-* Arthur Roberts. *m-* Walter Scharf. *cast-* Erich von Stroheim, Vera Hruba Ralston, Richard Arlen, Sidney Blackmer, Helen Vinson, Mary Nash, Lola Montez, Juanita Quigley. *rt-* 86 min.

L'ANTICRISTO
US t- THE TEMPTER. *exp t/GB t-* THE ANTICHRIST. Italy, 1974. *p co-* Capitolina Produzioni Cinematografiche. *d-* Alberto De Martino. *sc-* Alberto De Martino & Vincenzo Mannino. *story-* Gianfranco Clerici, Alberto De Martino & Vincenzo Mannino. *ph-* Aristide Massaccesi. *sp ph fx-* Biamonte Cinegroup. *art d-* Umberto Bertacca. *ed-* Vincenzo Tommassi *m-* Ennio Morricone. *p-* Edmondo Amati. *cast-* Carla Gravina, Mel Ferrer, Arthur Kennedy, George Couloris, Alida Valli, Anita Strindberg, Umberto Orsini, Mario Scaccia, Ernesto Colli, Remo Girone. Eastmancolor. *rt-* 112 min. *US dist-* Avco-Embassy (1976). *US video dist-* Embassy.

L'ANTICRISTO (1974)

CHI SEI?
US t- BEYOND THE DOOR. GB t- THE DEVIL WITHIN HER. trade t- WHO?. Italy, 1974. p co- A-Erre Cinematografica. d- Oliver Hellman [= Sonia Molteni Assonitis] & Richard Barrett [= Roberto d'Ettore Piazzoli]. sc- Sonia Molteni Assonitis, Antonio Troisio, Giorgio Marini, Aldo Crudo & Roberto D'Ettore Piazzoli. ph- Roberto D'Ettore Piazzoli. art d- Piero Filippone & Franco Pellechia Velchi. sp fx- Donn Davison & Wally Gentleman. ed- Angelo Curi. m- Franco Micalizzi. sd mix- Bruno Brunacci. sd fx- Roberto Arcangeli. as d/2nd unit d- Luciano Palermo. p- Ovidio Assonitis & Giorgio C. Rossi. cast- Juliet Mills, Richard Johnson, Gabriele Lavia, Nino Segurini, Elizabeth Turner, David Curtis, Barbara Fiorini, Carla Mancini, David Colin Jr. Widescreen, Eastmancolor. rt- 110 min. US dist- Film Ventures International.

L'OSSESSA
US t- THE EERIE MIDNIGHT HORROR SHOW. GB t- THE SEXORCIST. Italy, 1974. p co- Tiberia Film International. d/story- Mario Gariazzo. sc- Ambrogio Molteni. ph- Carlo Carlini. sp fx- Paolo Ricci. ed- Roberto Colangeli. m- Marcello Giombini. p- Riccardo Romano & Paolo Azzoni. cast- Stella Carnacina, Chris Avram, Lucretia Love, Gabriele Tinti, Luigi Pistilli, Gianrico Rondinelli, Umberto Raho, Giuseppe Addobbati, Piero Guerini, Ivan Rassimov, Elisa Mantellini. Widescreen, Eastmancolor. rt- 88 min.

IL MEDAGLIONE INSANGUINATO
alt t- PERCHÈ?! US t- NIGHT CHILD. US TV t- THE CURSED MEDALLION. Italy, 1974. p co- Magdalena Produzione/Italian International Films. d- Massimo Dallamano. sc- Franco Marotta, Massimo Dallamano & Laura Toscano. ph- Franco Delli Colli. ed- Antonio Siciliano. m- Stelvio Cipriani. p- William C. Reich & Fulvio Lucisano. cast- Richard Johnson, Joanna Cassidy, Evelyn Stewart [= Ida Galli], Nicoletta Elmi, Edmund Purdom, Riccardo Garrone, Dana Ghia, Eleonora Morana, Lila Kedrova. Widescreen, Eastmancolor. rt- 95 min. US dist- Avco Embassy. US video dist- Embassy.

EL PODER DE LAS TINIEBLAS
alt Spanish t- LA ENDEMONIADA. US t- DEMON WITCH CHILD. export t/US video t- THE POSSESSED. Spain, 1974. p co- Richard Films. d/sc- Amando de Ossorio. ph- Vicente Minaya. art d- Fernando González. sp fx- Pablo Pérez. sp makeup fx- Ramón de Diego. ed- Pedro del Rey. m- Victor & Diego. sd- Antonio Alonso. cost- Agustín Jiménez. as d- Francisco Rodríguez. p- Isaac Hernández. exec p- Julio Vallejo. cast- Julián Mateos, Marian Salgado, Fernando Sancho, Ángel del Pozo, Roberto Camardiel, Tota Alba, Maria Kosti, Kali Hansa, Daniel Martín, Fernando Hilbeck. Eastmancolor. rt- 87 min. US dist- Coliseum.

EXORCISMO
US video t- EXORCISM. Spain, 1974. p co- Profilmes. d- Juan Bosch. sc- Jacinto Molina & Juan Bosch. story- Jacinto Molina. ph- Francisco Sánchez. art d- Alfonso de Lucas. ed- Antonio Ramírez. m- Alberto Argudo. cast- Paul Naschy [= Jacinto Molina], Maria Perschy, Maria Kosti, Grace Mills, Roger Leveder, Juan Llaneras, Marta Avilé. Widescreen, Gevacolor. rt- 98 min.

MAGDALENA – VOM TEUFEL BESESSEN
US t- BEYOND THE DARKNESS. GB t- MAGDALENA - POSSESSED BY THE DEVIL. Germany, 1974. p co- TV 13. d- Michael Walter. sc- Jean Christian Aurive. makeup- Hedy Dolensky. ed- Karl Aulitzky. sd- Günther Stadelmann. a rt d- Peter Rothe. cost- Lilo Nobauer. cm- Ernst W. Kalinke. m- Hans M. Majewski. p- Josef Hadrawa. cast- Dagmar Hidrich, Werner Bruhns, Michael Hinz, Peter Martin Urtel, Rudolf Schundler, Karl Walter Diess, Günter Clemens, Elisabeth Volkmann, Eva Kinsky. rt- 84.

LES POSSEDÉES DU DIABLE
alt French t- LORNA L'EXORCISTE; LES POSSEDÉES DU DÉMON. France, 1974. p co- Comptoir Français du Film. d/sc- Clifford Brown [= Jesús Franco]. ph- Robert de Nesle. cast- Lina Romay, Pamela Stanford, Guy Delorme, Jacqueline Parent, Howard Vernon, Jesús Franco. Color. rt- 90 min.

EXORCISMO NEGRO
See page 28 in the M!I dossier on José Mojica Marins.

ABBY
USA, 1974. p co- Mid-America Pictures/AIP. d- William

CHI SEI? (1974)

Girdler. sc- Gordon Cornell Layne. story- William Girdler & Gordon Cornell Layne. ph- William Asman. p des- J. Patrick Kelly III. set dec- Barbara Peter. sp fx- Sam Price. ed- Corky Ehlers & Henry Asman. m- Robert O. Ragland. sd- John Asman & Chuck Hallam. makeup- Joe Kenney. as d- Hugh Smith. p- William Girdler, Mike Henry & Gordon Cornell Layne. cast- Carol Speed, William Marshall, Terry Carter, Austin Stoker, Juanita Moore, Charles Kissinger, Elliott Moffitt, Nathan Cook, Bob Holt (voice). Color. rt- 89 min.

ALUCARDA, LA HIJA DE LAS TINIEBLAS
US video t- SISTERS OF SATAN; INNOCENTS FROM HELL. Mexico, 1975. p co- Films 75/Yuma Films. d- Juan López Moctezuma. sc- Juan López Moctezuma, Yolanda Moctezuma & Alexis T. Arroyo. ph- Xavier Cruz. art d- Kleomenes Stematiades. sp fx- Abel Contreras. ed- Max Sánchez & Jorge Peña. sd- Francisco Guerrero. sd mix- Ricardo Saldívar. sd fx- Gonzalo Gavira. makeup- A. Ramírez del Río. p mgr- Antonio Rodríguez. as d- Rafael Villaseñor. p- Eduardo Moreno & Max Guefen. cast- Tina Romero, Susana Kamini, Claudio Brook, David Silva, Adriana Roel, Betty Catania, Lily Garza, Martín Lasalle. Eastmancolor. rt- 90 min.

I DON'T WANT TO BE BORN
GB re-release t- THE MONSTER. US t- THE DEVIL WITHIN HER. prod t- THE BABY. advertised(?) t- SHARON'S BABY. Great Britain, 1975. p co- Prizebourne/Unicapital. d- Peter Sasdy. sc- Stanley Price. story/exec p- Nato de Angelis. ph- Kenneth Talbot. art d- Roy Stannard. sp fx- Bert Luxford. makeup- Eddie Knight. ed- Keith Palmer. m- Ron Grainer. p- Norma Corney. cast- Joan Collins, Eileen Atkins, Donald Pleasence, Ralph Bates, Caroline Munro, Hilary Mason, John Steiner, Janet Key, George Claydon, Hilary Mag. Eastmancolor. rt- 94 min. US dist- AIP (1976).

CAUCHEMARS
GB/US video t- CATHY'S CURSE. France/Canada, 1976 p co- Makifilms/Les Productions Agora. d- Eddy Matalon. sc- Eddy Matalon, Alain Sens-Cazenave & Myra Clément. ph- Jean-Jacques Tarbes & Richard Cuipka. sp fx- Eurocitel. ed- Laurent Quaglio, Pierre Rose & Micheline Thouin. m- Didier Vasseur. makeup- Julia Grundy. p- Nicole Mathieu Boisvert. cast- Alan Scarfe, Randi Allen, Beverly Murray, Roy Witham, Linda Koot, Mary Porter, Dorothy Davis, Peter McNeil. Color. rt- 91 min. US dist- 21st Century (1980).

UN URLO NELLE TENEBRE
prod t- L'ESORCISTA 2. US t- NAKED EXORCISM. US Video t- THE POSSESSOR Italy, 1976. p co- Colosseum International/Manila Cinematografica. d- Elo Pannaciò. sc- Aldo Crudo, Franco Brocani & Elo Pannaciò. st- Giulio Albonico. ph- Franco Villa & Maurizio Centini. ed- Fernanda Papa. m- Giuliano Sorgini. p- Luigi Fedeli. cast- Richard Conte, Françoise Prévost, Elena Svevo, Patrizia Gori, Jean-Claude Varné, Mimma Monticelli. Widescreen, Technicolor. rt- 90 min.

L'OSCENO DESIDERIO
Spanish t- POSEÍDA. alt Italian t- LE PENE NEL VENTRE. Italian prod t- LA PROFEZIA. Italy/Spain, 1977. p co- Cineiniziative/Titán PCC-Altamira. d- Jeremy Scott [= Giulio Petroni]. sc- Giulio Petroni & Piero Regnoli. ph- Fausto Rossi & Leopoldo Villaseñor. ed- Marcella Benvenuti. m- Carlo Savina. cast- Marisa Mell, Lou Castel, Chris Avram, Victor Israel, Laura Trotter, Javier Escrivá, Jack Taylor, Paola Majolini. Panavision, Eastmancolor. rt- 97 min.

THE MANITOU
USA, 1977. p co- Avco Embassy/Enterprise. d/p- William Girdler. sc- William Girdler, Jon Cedar & Thomas Pope. based on the novel by Graham Masterton. ph- Michael Hugo. sp fx- Dale Tate & Frank Van Der Veer. p des- Walter Scott Herndon. conceptual design/2nd unit d- Nikita Knatz. sp fx- Gene Grigg & Tim Smythe. sp makeup fx- Tom Burman. ed- Gene Ruggiero & Bub Asman. m- Lalo Schifrin. makeup- Joe McKinney. sd fx- Fred Brown & Michelle Sharp-Brown. exec p- Melvin G. Gordy. cast- Tony Curtis, Susan Strasberg, Michael Ansara, Jon Cedar, Stella Stevens, Ann Sothern, Burgess Meredith, Paul Mantee, Jeanette Nolan, Lurene Tuttle, Felix Silla, Joe Gieb. Widescreen, color. rt- 105 min.

NURSE SHERRI
US, 1977. p co/dist- Independent-International. d- Al Adamson. sc- Michael Bockman, Gregg Tittinger. idea- Al Adamson. ph- Roger Michaels. sp fx- Optical Systems Unlimited. makeup- Tom Schwartz. art d- Ann McDonald. set dec- Joe Arrowsmith. ed- Michael Bockman, Gregg Tittinger. sd- Robert Dietz. as d- Adam Roberts. script sup- Michael Bockman. p- Mark Sherwood. cast- Jill Jacobson, Geoffrey Land, Marilyn Joi, Mary Kay Pass, Prentiss Moulden, Erwin Fuller, Clayton Foster, Caryl Briscoe, Jack Barnes, Bill Roy. Eastmancolor. rt- 88 min.

SEYTAN
Turkey, circa 1975. p co- Saner Video. d- Metin Erksan. sc- Yılmaz Tümürk. p- Hulki Saner. cast- Cihan Ünal, Canan Perver, Meral Taygun, Agah Hün. rt- 101 min.

Weng's Chop B-Movie Krisword Puzzle, #2 by Kris Gilpin.

Since I was a kid (& have always been a huge film buff) I've searched for film-based crossword puzzles and have never understood why there have been so relatively few of them ever made, with millions of film lovers all over the world—so a few years ago I simply started to construct my own at www.tinyurl.com/3seq3cc, on the great, huge crossword site, BestCrosswords.Com. I have 135+ puzzles on there so far; please try more of my old ones—do the film-trivia clues first & enjoy,

ACROSS

1. Alan Rudolph's 1974 **NIGHTMARE CIRCUS** was a.k.a. THE ____ OF THE NAKED DEAD.
5. In **ABBOTT AND COSTELLO MEET THE KILLER, BORIS KARLOFF**, Karloff played ____ Talpur.
10. 'Zines.
14. Chill, dude.
15. Pricks have ____ some people to death in certain organizations.
16. Brute, like Bill Thurman in Larry (L.) Buchanan's **CURSE OF THE SWAMP CREATURE**.
17. A B-movie bad guy's voice is often ____y.
18. Props from **FLESH GORDON** and **RAIDERS OF THE LOST ARK**.
19. L. Buchanan's Bergman knock-off (ha!): 1970's **STRAWBERRIES NEED** ____.
20. L. Buchanan's 1963 racial rape Drama was called ____, ____ AND 21.
22. L. Buchanan truly ____ to make good bio-social dramas, they were just too ineptly-made.
23. Sylvester, to Tweety.
24. Red _____ are misleading clues in mystery movies.
26. Dress material, from the Costuming Dept.
30. Great prog-rock band, who helped work on the TV episode, *The Freddy Krueger Special*.
31. Alas, L. Buchanan's films were neither Oscar ____ Golden Globes-worthy.
32. Having frequency beyond the audible range.
38. How many soft-core sex kittens got hired via the casting ____?
41. Pop singer Fabian starred in L. Buchanan's '70s gangster bio-drama, **A BULLET FOR PRETTY** ____.
42. Animal catcher.
43. Moistened and rubbed with a liniment or lotion (oh, baby).
46. Central (prefix).
47. A vast area covered with sand and shifting dunes, as a feature of the Sahara Desert.
48. Character(s) in **BASKET CASE** and **SISTERS**.
51. Wearing off or down by scraping or rubbing.
56. Great 2009 Aussie prom-girl revenge flick, **THE LOVED** ____ S.
57. We usually appreciate sick shit flicks that ____ on wussy critics' nerves.
58. Jeff, who overacted wonderfully in L. Buchanan's **CURSE OF THE SWAMP CREATURE** (also in **HORROR HIGH**).
63. Hokkaido native.
64. Mideasterner.
65. The "Bad Guy" in 1977's goofy **THE CAR**.
66. L. Buchanan made a droopy ____ of Marilyn Monroe movies.
67. L. Buchanan ____ **DAY THE WORLD ENDED** in 1967 as **IN THE YEAR 2889**.
68. Great instrumental from Traffic's "John Barleycorn Must Die" album.
69. Of or pertaining to Gaelic, especially in a Scottish film.
70. Braiding or embroidery (archaic).
71. Corner pieces, used in the Construction Dept.

DOWN

1. **THE EXORCIST** featured blood and ____.
2. This John was in L. Buchanan's so-boring-it's-almost-funny, **CURSE OF THE SWAMP CREATURE**.
3. Con, in a…con movie.
4. Catnip, in a Brit film.
5. Co-star in the great **SEVEN PSYCHOPATHS**.
6. Dry riverbed.
7. The alchemical name for mercury.
8. Like a massive battle against zombies in a horror flick.
9. Tags.
10. L. Buchanan made **DOWN ON US**, a conspiracy bio-drama about Hendrix, Janis & this rock singer.
11. L. Buchanan used Tommy (**OLD YELLER**) Kirk in **MARS** NEEDS WOMEN and ____ in 1969's **'IT'S ALIVE!'**.
12. His "In the Hall of the Mountain King" composition was heard in **NEEDFUL THINGS**.
13. They complete 1964's funny ____ **ME NO FLOWERS**, and the quote from **RETURN OF THE LIVING DEAD**: "____ more cops!"
21. James, director of **SAW**.
22. Long Rapunzel feature.
25. A shag rug, in a Swedish film.
26. 1985 Jim Carrey vampire comedy, ____ **BITTEN**.
27. "You're tearing me apart, Lisa!" is epically screamed in the funny, non-horror shit flick, **THE** ____.
28. Like popcorn and coke at the movies.
29. Ms. J., from the horror-comedy, **IDLE HANDS**.
33. One had glowing red eyes at the end of **ANGEL HEART**.
34. Three Stooges' 1950 short, "Three Hams on ____", and literary classic, *Catcher in the* ____.
35. Like Larry Buchanan…or Pippi Longstocking.
36. ____ Bahr played ____ Reisen in **THE LAST EXORCISM**.
37. Formally surrender, as in a Civil War movie.
39. L. Buchanan movie titles: _____ **OF DESTRUCTION** and **THE EYE** ____ S.
40. 2009 French battle flick between gangsters, cops and zombies, **THE** ____.
44. Fake visual FX, and when it's obvious, it sucks!
45. A compound containing two oxygen atoms per molecule.
49. Sarah Polley's name in 2004's **DAWN OF THE DEAD**.
50. Bertrand Blier's great **GOING PLACES** was bout a sleazy, funny ____ a trois.
51. Some L. Buchanan epics left our mouths ____ (mainly 'cause we fell asleep during them!).
52. Pipe type.
53. Queens or princesses, in an Indian film.
54. One who rats out someone, as in a cop/gangster flick.
55. Forest clearing.
59. Thora Birch's name in **GHOST WORLD**.
60. Some L. Buchanan films are so ____ (like **'IT'S ALIVE!'**), it's almost funny.
61. We really do love L. Buchanan's goofy flicks, like **ZONTAR: THE THING FROM VENUS, HUGHES & HARLOW: ANGELS IN HELL,** ____ (Latin).
62. Actors in **THE BIRDS** and **THE AMITYVILLE HORROR**.
64. 2005 horror flick about a meteorite crashing a party in Hawaii, **THE** ____.

Answer key on page 194 -- NO CHEATING!

215

ABOUT THE CONTRIBUTORS...

Mark K. Allen - used to publish the *Cerebral Fallout* 'zine, did some "shitty" artwork for many pointless bands and is currently trying to have fun with comic books.

Joachim Andersson - is a practicing rubbermonsterfetishist and worshiper of '70s exploitation (preferably Spanish horror smut). While not watching movies he dabbles in electronic music (music featured in a Danish torture porn flick and released a dark ambient album in 2007 that included a tribute piece to Jesus Franco's lovely **OASIS OF THE ZOMBIES**). Buys more movies than he watches and feels somewhat uncomfortable with writing about himself in third person. Visit his blog at *rubbermonsterfetishism.blogspot.com*.

Jared Auner – "I would like to thank Timo Raita for all the great research, insight and all-around hard work that he put into our article on **THE WITCH**. It was his enthusiasm for this film that made me want to see it in the first place, so I hope I did some justice to this oddball movie he likes so well. Look for our 2nd piece on Finnish cult films in the next issue, wherein we delve into the bizarre world of **SENSUELA!**"

David Barnes - has his own line of comics and also creates vintage "grindhouse" t-shirts. His work can be seen at *zid3ya@yahoo.com* and *myspace.com@paramere*.

James Bickert - Raised by finger banging alcoholic mosquitoes in the swamp-filled drive-ins of Southeastern Georgia. He is currently working on **FRANKENSTEIN CREATED BIKERS**, the follow-up to his 2012 exploitation feature **DEAR GOD NO!**

Stephen R. Bissette - a pioneer graduate of the Joe Kubert School, currently teaches at the Center for Cartoon Studies and is renowned for *Swamp Thing*, *Taboo* (launching *From Hell* and *Lost Girls*), "1963", *Tyrant*, co-creating John Constantine, and creating the world's second "24-Hour Comic" (invented by Scott McCloud for Bissette). He writes, illustrates, and has co-authored many books; his latest includes *Teen Angels & New Mutants* (2011), the short story "Copper" in *The New Dead* (2010), and he illustrated *The Vermont Monster Guide* (2009). His latest ebooks are *Bryan Talbot: Dreams & Dystopias* and the *Best of Blur* duo, *Wonders! Millennial Marvel Movies* and *Horrors! Cults, Crimes, & Creepers*.

Lawrence Conti - is an established graphic artist and ravenous cinephile based in NYC. He can be found scouring Chinatowns all over the East Coast slaking his thirst for rare Asian films. Follow his rants on weird, wild, foreign films and television at *extralarry.wordpress.com*.

Tim Doyle – Visit Tim at *NakatomiInc.com* and *MrDoyle.com*.

Danae Dunning - is a Goth/metal/hippie chick from Hobbs, New Mexico, USA. Her other interests besides movies are music (just about anything except rap, big band, and polka), writing poetry, and driving people insane. Her first experience in horror that she remembers was somewhere between the ages of two and four when she saw **FIEND WITHOUT A FACE** on TV. She was scarred for life, but in a good way. Her mainstay is horror, but she loves exploitation, some sci-fi and fantasy, even a few chick flicks. And she is the proud owner of **EMMETT OTTER'S JUG BAND CHRISTMAS** on DVD. She is also working on broadening her horizons by exploring the films of The French New Wave.

Steve Fenton - prefers to remain as much of a mystery to others as he is to himself.

Kris Gilpin - grew up in Florida (hated it), went to L.A. for 22 years, has an IMDb.com page, interviewed/wrote for many film 'zines during the '80s (he's in this year's great *Xerox Ferox* book) and is now still trying to find personal happiness, this time in the Midwest…

Travis Goheen - Made in Canada, writer for *Cinema Sewer* plus several other publications. Movie junkie looking for the next fix, not a cure. Greatest thrill in his life was sitting down and talking to HK Director Herman Yau following a double feature of **THE UNTOLD STORY** and **EBOLA SYNDROME**.

Jeff Goodhartz - Is a self-righteous and self-serving man of the people who has been watching and writing about Asian Cinema for far too long. His current 'blog is *Films from the Far Reaches* (as he's never above a shameless plug). He's quite shameless.

Greg Goodsell - recently had his interview with the fabulous character actress O-Lan Jones published in Steve Puchalski's indispensable *Shock Cinema* magazine. Read it today, and let Greg know what you think at *gregoodsell@hotmail.com*.

John Grace - is the co-host of the Damaged Viewing podcast, available on iTunes or at *damagedviewing.podomatic.com*. He also contributes to *Exploitation Retrospect*. Mr. Grace is determined to school his young son in the appreciation of all things that make living in this modern world a must. The ways of the Tarmangani.

Brian Harris – is a pathological midget-tosser, a professional church heckler and for some reason he's compelled to sniff old people as they walk past him. When he's not tossing, heckling or sniffing, he writes for many magazines including *Paint Huffing Times*, *Cooking With Allah*, *Popular Mugging* and *Your Colon & You*. His book series *Gimp: The Rapening* has been put on the "DO NOT PURCHASE" list by the National Association of Literary Taste Against Irresponsible Self-Publishing.

Mike Howlett - is the author *The Weird World of Eerie Publications* (Feral House) and recently made *The Weird Indexes of Eerie Publications* available as a made-to-order book on Lulu and Amazon. There is clearly no hope for him.

Karl Kaefer - "Worked" at a drive-in, where his mind was warped by watching too many Italian Eurotrash and HG Lewis films. He graduated to the grindhouse theaters of NYC, where he would spend afternoons watching kung fu & Blaxploitation flicks. He still finds the strange and bizarre much more comfortable than the bland and boring. Karl co-writes a blog with Ms. Vicki Love, and no matter what she says, the 1970s were the best decade in film.

Andrew Leavold – is the founder and co-owner of *Trash Video*, a writer and film critic, TV presenter, festival programmer, MC, agnostic evangelist and occasional guerrilla filmmaker.

Vicki Love – "From managing newspaper editor to teacher of the dreaded English, my one constant has been writing and the love of science fiction. Now you all can choose."

Nigel Maskell - began his journey into genre cinema four decades ago when he accompanied his father to see **ENTER THE DRAGON** at the tender age of four. He managed to gain admission to the adult-only feature when his father reassured the cinema owner that the film was unlikely to have any effect on one so young. This, as it turned out, was incorrect. For four obsessive decades Nigel has immersed himself in the world of genre film. In 2008 he founded the *Italian Film Review* 'blog.

CT McNeely - fervently enjoys all three types of movies: those about ninjas bent on revenge, robots intent on domination and aliens out for blood. He lives somewhere out in the country with his wife and his dog where he writes and is deeply suspicious of outsiders.

Tim Paxton - Has been publishing stuff about monsters since 1978, and currently lives to write about fantastic cinema from India. He is even considering publishing a book on the subject. What a knucklehead.

Graham Rae - Graham Rae started his writing career with the legendary *Deep Red* magazine at age 18. Over the last 25 years he has written for everybody from *Film Threat* to *Cinefantastique* to *American Cinematographer*. He still writes occasionally about exploitation movies, and is featured in the new John Szpunar book *Xerox Ferox*. A selection of his writings can be seen at *facebook.com/RaeWrites*.

Timo Raita - has been in love with **THE WITCH** since he first saw it on television in 1987. His earliest TV *fantastique* memories are from the late '70s when he saw the European miniseries *The Mysterious Island of Captain Nemo*. Since then, inventions like the VCR, LaserDisc, and later DVD have greatly aided in his seemingly never-ending hunger for cinematic exploration. He still lives in the small Finnish town where he was born.

Steven Ronquillo - is a pretentious know-it-all who looks down on his fellow film fans and refuses to reveal his faves to them unless it makes him look good.

Amber Skowronski - is a special effects artist and illustrator living in Los Angeles. She is available for commissions and you can find her portfolio at *amberskowronski.brushd.com*.

Tony Strauss - has been writing about cinema in print and online for nearly two decades. His existence as that rarest of most annoying of creatures—an artsy-fartsy movie snob who loves trash cinema (yes, it's possible)—often leaves him as the odd man out in both intellectual and low-brow film discussions. Most movies that people describe as "boring" or "confusing" enthrall him, while the kinds of movies that are described as "non-stop action" usually bore him to tears. He has a BFA in Film, but don't hold that against him.

Dan Taylor - has been writing about junk culture and fringe media since his 'zine *Exploitation Retrospect* debuted in 1986. 26 years later the publication is still going strong as a website, 'blog and, yes, a resurrected print edition. Check it all out at *Dantenet.com, EROnline.blogspot.com* or *Facebook.com/ExploitationRetrospect*.

Douglas Waltz - lives in the wilds of Kalamazoo, MI where he is experimenting with primitive pottery techniques. His 'zine, *Divine Exploitation*, has existed in print or online form since 1988 and can be found at *divineexploitation.blogspot.com*. His recent book, *A Democrazy of Braindrained Loons: The Films of Michael Legge* can be purchased at *https://tsw.createspace.com/title/3814218*. Douglas would like you to know that all Jess Franco films are good. ALL OF THEM!

Salvatore Tarantola - Artist born, raised, and currently living in Brooklyn NY. Influences include Wally Wood, Crumb, and Moebius. Loves Japanese sci-fi and Hammer films.

Jolyon Yates - is still drawing the NYT best seller *Ninjago*, has drawings for Stephen Bissette's new *Tales of the Uncanny* comic, and is the assistant inker on the comic *Wild Blue Yonder*, which is like **MAD MAX** in the air. He also did a little drawing and acting for **GODZILLA** (2014) in which he will play the major role of "Engineer Fleeing in Terror". *jolyonbyates.com*

Dave Zuzelo - is a full-time HorrorDad, a full-time Media Mangler and a full-time Trash Cinema Sponge. He is also a sometime blogger at Tomb It May Concern (*David-Z. blogspot.com*) and enjoys spewing words of sleazy musing across every publication that will have him. Check out his book *Tough To Kill- The Italian Action Explosion* and see just how many exploding huts he can endure, and he'll beg for more!

WENG'S CHOP WOULD LIKE TO GIVE A SHOUT-OUT TO A FEW HARD-WORKING WRITERS WHO DESERVE SOME LOVE, RESPECT…
AND ESPECIALLY, CREDIT:

John Berger at *eng.fju.edu.tw*

Heather Boerner at *commonsensemedia.org*

Arthur Borman at *allmovie.com*

Lisa Marie Bowman at *unobtanium13.com*

Matt Deapo at *grindhousedatabase.com*

Mary Ann Doane, professor at UC-Berkeley

M. Enois Duarte at *highdefdigest.com*

Brian Eggert at *deepfocusreview.com*

Melissa Garza at *scaredstiffreviews.com*

Robert Graysmith, author, *The Girl in Alfred Hitchcock's Shower* (Titan Publishing)

Bradley P. Guillory at *angelfire.com/movies/gore/stainedlens.html*

Ron Hogan at *subtlebluntness.wordpress.com*

jhailey@hotmail.com, an IMDb contributor

Jim at *eatmybrains.com*

MaryAnn Johanson at *flickfilosopher.com*

Alex K. at *ruthlessreviews.com*

Laura Kipnis at *slate.com*

Bill Landis, author, *Sleazoid Express: A Mind-twisting Tour through the Grindhouse Cinema of Times Square* (Simon and Schuster)

Shawn Levy at *oregonlive.com*

Mike Massie at *gonewiththetwins.com*

Patrick McGilligan, author, *Alfred Hitchcock: A Life in Darkness and Light* (It Books)

Monty Moonlight, an Amazon Vine™ reviewer

Steve Pattee at *horrortalk.com*

Jason Pitt at *critical-film.com*

Lawrence P. Raffel at *monstersatplay.com*

George R. Reis at *dvddrive-in.com*

Richard Scheib at *moria.co.nz*

Steven Jay Schneider at *scope.nottingham.ac.uk*

Christian Sellers at *retroslashers.com*

Adam Smith at *empireonline.com.au*

Matthew Toomey at *thefilmpie.com*

Joe Wawrzyniak, an IMDb reviewer

Karl Williams at *allmovie.com*

Robin Wood, author, *Hollywood from Vietnam to Reagan…and Beyond* (Columbia University Press)

Made in the USA
Charleston, SC
05 March 2014